TONY FLEMING

RIDING
THE
TIDE

ART, ENGINEERING AND A THIRST FOR ADVENTURE

A MEMOIR

Copyright © 2014 by Tony Fleming

"*There is a tide in the affairs of men.*
Which, taken at the flood, leads on to fortune;
Omitted, all the voyage of their life
Is bound in shallows and in miseries.
On such a full sea are we now afloat,
And we must take the current when it serves,
Or lose our ventures."

William Shakespeare
from "Julius Caesar"

Table of Contents

Introduction

I was born into a comfortable environment at a good period in history and at exactly the right time to avoid being co-opted into the various conflicts of the 20th century. It may also turn out to be the optimum time to have been able to enjoy the comforts and inventions of human development before our effect on the environment alters life as we know it. I have never been in any doubt that I was born lucky.

It is said that you make your own luck, and to a certain extent this is true, but you also need some of the genuine article. Luck may be responsible for throwing opportunities in our path but, whether we take advantage of them or let them float on by, it is our personal decisions that decide our fate. On looking back, I can recognize those times when, faced with clear choices, I chose a certain path. I sometimes wonder what might have been the outcome had I chosen differently. My life has undoubtedly been steered by grasping the opportunities that came my way—which explains the Shakespeare quote and the title of this book.

Tony Fleming
California. 2014

Book 1
UK

LAUNCHING
AND DEVELOPMENT

1935 – 1958

Chapter 1

August 1935 to September 1943

Birth to Boarding School

I recall memories of early childhood, World War II, and the many homes we lived in while following my father around England and Scotland.

I was born at a house called Lighthill in the hamlet of Great Bealings in the county of Suffolk, in England, on August 19th, 1935.

Both my father and mother were born in 1900, and they were married at Fountains Abbey in Yorkshire in 1932. My father had lied about his age and joined the Royal Flying Corps in 1917 and had been a career officer in the Royal Air Force ever since. In 1921 he had served in what was then called Mesopotamia—now Iraq. At the time I entered the world, he was stationed at Martlesham Heath, not far from Great Bealings. He was in a unit formed for the testing of new aircraft designs. In those days, aircraft companies were small private companies run by individuals, and most of the testing of the new designs was carried out by the Air Force.

In September 1936, when I was 11 months old, my father was posted to Abu Sueir, near Ismailia, Egypt. My mother, myself, and an English nanny accompanied him; and while there, I contracted whooping cough. Of course I was too young to remember anything about this, but, to hear about it from my mother years later, she absolutely hated her time in Egypt. She used the experience to define "abroad" and never left the shores of England again! The family returned from Egypt early in 1937, and my father was posted to a succession of fighter bases in southern England. Over the ensuing years, we followed him all over the country as he was posted from one Air Force base to another. By the time I was sixteen, we had lived in 26 different houses—many of them for only a few months at a time. I really don't remember the order in which we lived in all these places, and my memories consist of vignettes of incidents without any clear recollection of the order in which they occurred.

My very earliest memory is of visiting my mother in hospital in Edinburgh a few days after she gave birth to my sister on May 2nd, 1939, when I would have been about 3 years 9 months old. As part of the softening-up process to prepare me for my transition from being an only child, I had been told that I was going to have a sister to play with. I can clearly recall the layout of my mother's room, with the basinet on the right as you entered and my mother's bed placed so that she was facing the door. There was a bay window on the left. I took one look at this swaddled infant and decided that she would be pretty useless as a playmate. I quickly recovered from this setback by eating my mother's grapes, which I remember were green.

My next memory was my 4th birthday. We were living in a rented house in Abbotsford Crescent, in Edinburgh, and we had just returned from some kind of family holiday. The house was set back from the road and had tall iron railings in front of it with a matching gate. I can remember that there was some kind of problem getting the gate to open, and there were some Air Force personnel present. The gate was eventually opened, and we went up the steps into the house and through the front door into the entrance hall. On the left was a tall grandfather clock with its face smashed. There was chaos everywhere, and on the wooden-topped kitchen table someone had mixed up a kind of porridge of flour and all kinds of stuff from the kitchen cupboards. There were torn-up family photos scattered all over the floor, and my tricycle had been hurled into the back garden. I remember someone saying that whoever had broken in must have raided the booze and gone on a rampage after that. I don't remember anything being said about items of any value being stolen, and I don't recall being upset or traumatized in any way. I just thought it strange that people would behave like that.

This was just two weeks before the outbreak of World War II, and, although I can't be certain, the reason we were living in Edinburgh was most likely because my father was stationed at Turnhouse—then the home of 603 Squadron—and much later to become Edinburgh Airport. The very first German raid of WWII was on the Forth Bridge and surrounding docks on October 16th, 1939, just one month after war was declared. One of the German planes was shot down and was the first to be brought down over Britain during WWII.

For a number of months we stayed with my mother's elder sister, my aunt Sybil, who lived in a large house with extensive grounds in the town of Skipton, in Yorkshire. They had woods out the back of the house and also a fancy rockery with all kinds of exotic plants, each with its own white-painted wooden stake to identify the species. I amused myself and also my aunt—but I'm sure not the gardener—by switching all the labels around. I have no idea what prompted this piece of devilment.

I was born left handed and, because in those days that was considered to be a defect, my mother somehow forced me to convert to being right handed. Maybe because of that, I developed a severe stammer. I have only a very hazy memory about this, and fortunately the stammer went away round about age four. Historically, being left handed was looked upon in a bad light. The word "left" is *sinister* in Latin and *gauche* in French. It might have been good if they had stopped halfway and left me ambidextrous, but I continue to favour my left leg for kicking and such, which, when I reached school age, required some adjustments by the person holding the ball when converting field goals in rugby football.

By the time the war broke out in September 1939, my father was too old to be an active fighter pilot. Instead, he was one of the controllers in the Battle of Britain and commanding officer of various fighter stations. In 1940, at the time of the Battle of Britain, he was stationed at Hawkinge, on the south coast and the closest RAF station to Europe. We lived not far away at a place called Angmering-on-Sea. The English Channel was only a short walk down the road, but the beach was closed off with coils of barbed wire because there was significant risk of a German invasion. I don't remember exactly which months we were there, but my feeling was that it was in the summer. The Little Ships saga at Dunkirk took place in June 1940, not long before my fifth birthday.

I was supposed to have a nap every afternoon, presumably to give my mother some respite. I had a high-sided cot which I used to climb out of and go roaming around making a nuisance of myself instead of taking a nap. A coarse brown net, referred to as a pig net, was placed over the cot in an attempt to restrain me. I don't think this can have been very effective because the incident I remember best was that, having continually interrupted my mother, who was downstairs trying to chat with a friend, and having been threatened with dire consequences if I didn't keep quiet, I was rummaging through the log basket when I came across a large chunk of jagged metal, which was clearly shrapnel from some kind of projectile. Of course, despite her threats, there was no way I could keep quiet about this exceptional discovery, and I certainly got her attention when I appeared with my trophy, the origin of which was never determined.

The other incident I recall while living there was a fire just around the corner at a house with a thatched roof. I remember seeing the flames licking around the eaves. I visited Angmering about 50 years later and had no trouble finding the house we had lived in, the house with the thatched roof, and my way to the beach. I have often wondered at the process within our brains that allows us to recall directions and find the way to a place. I had remembered a long drive up to our house's front door, but in reality it was only a few yards.

At age 6, in 1941, we had moved to Gerrards Cross about 20 miles west of London. This was the time of the London blitz, when the Germans bombed the city for 76 consecutive nights. To put this in perspective, imagine a 9/11 every night for 76 nights! The blitz killed more than 43,000 civilians and destroyed or damaged more than one million buildings. We were not directly affected, but I clearly remember standing on a chair looking out of my bedroom window, when I was supposed to be asleep, and watching the glow in the sky of London burning. I also remember seeing searchlight beams probing the night sky and hearing bombers passing overhead. The German planes did not have synchronized engines, so they could be identified by the *wum-wum-wum* noise they made. I don't remember ever feeling any worries or concern. The windows of my room had one of those bars with holes in it to control how much they were open, and I used to entertain myself by spitting in the holes and watching the spit drip through while all this drama was going on around me.

Later the same year we moved back to Scotland, when my father was stationed at Drem, not far from the small town of Gullane. Over a period of years we lived in three different houses in this small town, which was located on the coast of the Firth of Forth about 24 miles east of Edinburgh. The first house, called Ravenswood, was in the Muirfield section of town. I remember air raid sirens in the middle of the night and being hustled out of bed to go to the air-raid shelter in the garden while white searchlight beams probed the sky. The garden had a lot of black currant bushes which I can remember plundering. I also remember our first day in this house because what sounded like the front door bell would ring, but there was never anyone at the door. The mystery was solved when we discovered there was a bell push under the carpet in the dining room—which was currently empty— and every time someone stepped on it as they crossed the room, it rang a bell in the kitchen.

I had three nannies in my early years. The first, whom I only recall from photos, was Nanny Hackett, who looked after me when I was a toddler, including our time in Egypt. My father later referred to her as "that dragon of a nanny". The second I just remember as Nanny Plumpkin, who was my nanny at the time we moved back to Scotland. She had a drawer full of nanny-style, grey felt hats, and it occurred to me that they would be greatly improved if they had feathers in them. So, after a visit to the beach, I came back armed with a fistful of giant seagull feathers and, when no one was looking, stuck one in the crown of every one of her hats, making a big hole in each.

In March 1941, after a few months in Scotland, we moved back to southern England, where we lived in a series of houses. One was called the Limes, at Chalford, just east of Stroud in Gloucestershire. The house had been picked by my father and it was so unappealing that my mother gave notice the day we moved in. I clearly remember that first night. I had a bath in one of those stand-alone tubs which are supported on four feet with plenty of room for monsters to hide underneath. The bathroom was gloomy and had a very high ceiling. It was very creepy. I played with the rough neighbourhood boys who pinched my toy pistol and refused to give it back. The boy who had it claimed that it had never been mine and was his. They were older and tougher than me, so I couldn't do anything about. It was my first experience of duplicity and injustice!

We visited my paternal grandmother at their farm called Hainey, just outside Cambridge in the county of Suffolk, in August 1941. I remember the huge working horses with feathery fetlocks, picking mushrooms from a fairy circle and searching the hedgerows for eggs laid by the free-range chickens. I also remember taking a bath in a tin tub in front of the kitchen range.

That same month we moved into yet another house. This one was called the Water Garden and had a series of ornamental ponds which gave their name to the property. In retrospect it really was a most unsuitable place to have small children. When we first arrived, we were shown around the property by the resident gardener, who was called Allcock. I remember being given a stern warning about staying away from the ponds. Later that same day my piping voice was heard to cry, "I'm in, Allcock" as I stood chest deep in one of the ponds, surrounded by water lilies and croaking frogs.

It was a great place to explore. I found a field completely covered with cowslips and a copse in which I discovered a very nice fishing rod concealed under the ground ivy—presumably belonging to a poacher. I also recall, disgracefully, throwing eggs at a wall because I wanted to see them smash. This was at a time when eggs were rationed—although we had our own chickens, so it was not quite so serious. At mealtimes I had to eat everything on my plate no matter how long it took. On one occasion I sat until 2 o'clock in the afternoon before being allowed to leave the table, only to get the same plate back at supper time in the exact same, congealed, condition in which I had left it.

In May 1942 we moved yet again, to a rather grand house called Througham (pronounced Thruffam) Manor, near the village of Bisley, just east of Stroud. This was way out in the country, and our electricity came from a generator that was started every evening. Our immediate neighbour was a well-known author called Michael Sadleir, who had written a book called *Fanny by Gaslight*. Petrol was rationed in those days, and the Sadleirs used a pony and trap to visit the nearby town of Stroud, and I remember on more than one occasion clip-clopping along the country road looking at the rear end of a horse. There was very little traffic to worry about at that time.

I had to walk quite a long way to school each day, dawdling along a country footpath. School was in somebody's house with a very few other children—probably with a governess. The Sadleirs had a pack of bloodhounds, and one day I went for a walk with Mrs Sadleir accompanied by the dogs. While they were off investigating some smells of interest to them, we ran off over the fields and hid up a tree. A few minutes later the hounds came streaming over the hill at a full run, noses to the ground following our scent. They made a beeline to the foot of the tree where, without hesitation, they looked up at us, tails wagging furiously.

My mother and any other adults present always listened to the latest war news at 6 pm every night, and we kids had to shut up. The announcer always seemed to be mentioning what sounded to me like "proper gander" and I wondered what a goose had to do with the war.

On one occasion, a big drystone retaining wall gave way in the garden. I was standing looking at the mess when the guy responsible for the garden came up and said to me, "Did you have anything to do with this?" I hadn't, but I remember feeling a bit affronted that he thought I might have done.

Around this time my mother hired a governess, because we were always moving around and school work was disrupted. The governess was referred to as Nan and was a lot of fun. She was always coming up with "famous last words" whenever I said anything to which she felt they could apply. Two examples I still remember are in response to my saying: "I wonder where that arrow went" (after shooting off my bow and arrow) and "Good, the level crossing gates are open", referring to the gates at the railway crossing. The other thing I remember about Nan was when I was about 6 years old, we were running down this road with my sister in a pram, when Nan suddenly skidded to a halt and picked a four leaf clover out of a clump of it growing at the edge of the road. Having personally spent hours searching for four leaf clovers when I was growing up, it remains a mystery to me how she could have spotted one while on the run.

In 1942, when I was around seven, we moved back to Scotland to another house in Gullane called The Cottage, which was located on the side of town closest to Edinburgh. We had a small garden in which we grew some vegetables and kept a few chickens. It backed onto the ruins of an old church, which I used to explore by climbing all over the crumbling stone walls. My mother made me wear a trendy cap that I greatly disliked. I very sensibly managed to lose it in the ruins, and it was never replaced. By this time, I had started more formal schooling and had to take the bus every day to a place called North Berwick. On the way, it passed through the village of Direlton where there was—and still is—a fine ruined castle complete with a proper dungeon.

North Berwick was also where I had to visit the dentist. The drill in those days was a scary device, driven by a belt that ran over a number of pulleys. On a couple of occasions I had to have some teeth extracted. The first time I elected to have "gas" which was supposed to knock me out. I know I was coming around while the last tooth was being extracted—I could hear the cracking, splintering sound. Both the dentist and my mother said that I imagined it, but I know that I did not. On the next occasion, I elected to have an injection rather than gas, and this time the dentist was talking to my mother when he suddenly whirled around and, with this enormous pair of silver pliers in his hand, started pulling my teeth.

It was also at North Berwick where we used to buy live lobsters from the fishermen down at the harbour, just offshore from which is the Bass Rock, white with the guano of the gannet colony. A good-sized lobster cost half a crown, or two shillings and sixpence, equivalent to 1/8th of a pound (today 12½p) although, of course, a pound was worth much more in those days. We would take the lobsters home and plunge them, still alive, into a huge pot of boiling water. I was never very comfortable about that, but they were delicious to eat dipped in butter, so that quickly overcame my scruples!

There is an isolated conical hill about 600 ft high at North Berwick called North Berwick Law, on which a German aircraft came to rest after it was shot down. I remember going with my mother to climb the tor and take a look at it.

There were at least three golf courses around Gullane, which were not much used because of the war. At this early age I developed a liking for golf and was the proud owner of three clubs. On one occasion, I was on the golf course, addressing the ball, when a lady showed up to watch with a young daughter. I can still feel the humiliation I suffered when I played my shot—the head of the club flew off, trailing behind it the string that was supposed to be holding it in place, like the wire behind a wire-guided missile. The head of the club went farther than the ball, and I have never felt the same about golf ever since. I don't remember whether it was before or after this incident, but at some kid's birthday party I was showing off how to swing a club. When I swung it back over my shoulder, another kid had moved in behind me and the club cracked him just above the eye. In seconds his face was a mask of blood, and of course all the parents got very excited. I felt not the slightest hint of remorse - thinking that it served him right when everybody knew that you should not walk behind a golfer swinging a club!

I learnt to ride a bike when we lived here, and once I had mastered it, I whizzed around everywhere with complete disregard for the rules of survival or common sense. On one occasion, when I was several miles from home and practicing riding with no hands, I fell off the bike on some gravel. A piece of gravel went into my knee (I still have the scar), and a kind local resident bound up the injury with a bandage. I was able to ride my bike home, and for some reason I don't understand to this day, I took off the bandage

17

and threw it onto a pile of rubble before going into our house. My mother was furious with me for being late for supper. I kept pointing to my wounded knee but my recollection is that my being late received more attention than my injury. Eventually my mother took me off to the local chemist shop for advice. I wasn't sure then, and am still not today, why she chose this course of action, but the chemist suggested she take me to a local hotel which had been taken over as a barracks for Polish soldiers. I remember going into this robust, noisy environment full of soldiers in uniform where we eventually met up with a military doctor, who treated my knee. I went on my own to see him in this barracks every day for a month, where he dressed the wound. He wouldn't take any payment, and on the last day my mother gave me a box of 100 cigarettes to give to him, which he also refused to accept. After I took them back home, my mother and I both marched back again and insisted he take them.

On another occasion, I came whizzing out of a side street straight into the main road without stopping, and seeing that I was about to be tee-boned by a jeep, pedalling like mad to get past the front of it and feeling rather pleased with myself when I did. I doubt the poor driver even had time to apply the brakes. "That Fleming boy will get himself killed" was apparently the word around town.

Somewhere I had read about how to make gunpowder and had made a list of the ingredients, which, as I recall, included sulphur, saltpetre and carbon. I went to the chemist and asked for them, and he asked what I wanted them for.

"To make gunpowder", I said truthfully.

"We don't have them", he said firmly.

Another incident I remember from this house was swinging a door back and forth from the handle side and being told by my grandmother to stop it before I caught my fingers in the door. I remember thinking: silly old bag—how can I get my fingers trapped on the edge of the door away from the hinge? About one minute later I had caught my fingers and was thinking bitterly how was it that grownups were always right?

The last incident that comes to mind from this time was when I went off by myself and found a rich plot of blackberries. I ate a lot of them and then decided I should take some home for my mother. So I thoughtfully filled the pockets of my new corduroy shorts with nice juicy blackberries. By the time I got home these had mysteriously become blackberry puree and my shorts decorated with fetching purple stains. My mother was livid, and I was deeply hurt that she was not appreciative of my thoughtfulness. She was so mad that she picked up a stick to beat me, but I wedged myself into the 6-inch gap behind the wardrobe and stuck there like a limpet until she had cooled off. When we discussed the incident many years later, her recollection was that she had given me a bag into which to put the blackberries and, as all clothes were rationed at that time, each piece of clothing was precious. I think it was this incident that finally sealed my fate and made her send me to boarding school.

However, before this happened, we moved to another house, also in Gullane, called Quillet, around the end of 1942. This was a two-story house, and it was from here that I went off to boarding school three weeks after my eighth birthday on August 19th, 1943. My father was posted to Peshawar, on the border of Afghanistan, around that time and later to Chittagong, so we stopped moving around so frequently. I know my father visited us at Quillet and he bought me an air gun. He was a hunting, shooting, and fishing man and was, rightly, very strict on safe handling of weapons. Before I was allowed to handle this very primitive and weak weapon, I had to read a book called *The Young Shot* and learn by heart the poem at the start of the book written by Mark Beaufoy in 1902:

> *A Father's Advice*
>
> *If a sportsman true you'd be*
> *Listen carefully to me. . . .*
>
> *Never, never let your gun*
> *Pointed be at any one.*
> *Though it may unloaded be*
> *Matters not the least to me.*

When a hedge or fence you cross
Though of time it cause a loss
From your gun the cartridge take
For the greater safety's sake.

If twixt you and neighbouring gun
Bird shall fly or beast may run
Let the maxim ere be thine
"Follow not across the line."

Stops and beaters oft unseen
Lurk behind some leafy screen
Calm and steady always be
"Never shoot where you can't see."

You may kill or you may miss
But at all times think of this:
"All the pheasants ever bred
Won't repay for one man dead."

The so-called friendly fire incident when Dick Cheney shot a fellow sportsman could never have happened if either—or, better still, both—of them had followed the rules in the verse that begins "If twixt you and neighbouring gun . . ."

There was a steep bank below the house, and I thought it would make a nice safe background to practice shooting into, even though it meant shooting in the direction of the house. My father didn't agree and was very upset with me and confiscated the gun for six months.

After my father went overseas, he left his shotgun and bag of cartridges in the cupboard under the stairs. I opened up the shells, removed the powder, and put it into a brown paper bag until I had a nice pile. I then took it out into the sand dunes and set light to it, expecting and hoping for a nice big bang. Fortunately for me it just flared up, which left me disappointed but still in one piece.

A couple of times a circus came to the town and set up the big tent on Goose Green. I found that very exciting, watching the tent being erected and seeing the animals and later the show itself.

My mother's mother was a permanent resident at Bisset's hotel in the middle of town, and we used to go and have lunch with her every Sunday, although I don't remember visiting her at any other time. I am sure she was very nice but we had a rather distant relationship. She came from Lancashire and still spoke with something of a Lancashire accent—pronouncing the word "one" similar to the first syllable of the word "wander" and "boots" more like "bots."

Quillet was only a short walk from a fine sandy beach lining the Firth of Forth, with lovely sand dunes between the house and the shore. The beach featured prominently in my memories of this time. There were other kids, and our families often used to meet on the beach and swim in the chilly water. One time there were the remains of a large, raggedy, red jellyfish, which stung many of the kids, because you only had to touch the tiniest fragment of it to suffer a painful sting. On another occasion there was a full-size ship high and dry on the sand at low tide, so we could walk all around it. When I asked what had happened I was told that it had "overrun its anchor". I still don't know what that means! The rock pools left behind when the tide retreated were full of sea anemones and other interesting creatures. I used to try my hand at fishing and, on one occasion I was successful, because my mother had seeded the pool with a can of sardines. I must have been really simple-minded because I triumphantly seized my "catch" and ate them for tea!

The beach had big wooden poles erected on it to discourage enemy landings. However, the enemy never showed any signs of showing up, and many of the poles had fallen over. Many years later, on January 31, 2013, I met an American at a boat show in Seattle who told me that that he had stayed in Gullane in recent years and he told me that the remains of many of the WWII beach obstacles were still present on the beaches.

Chapter 2

September 1943 to September 1947

Cargilfield

I leave home to attend ~~to~~ Cargilfield Boarding School, first in the highlands of Scotland and then back in Edinburgh. We move house from Scotland to England.

It was from Quillet that I went to Cargilfield boarding school, and I was anxious to go. On the morning of my departure in September 1943, just three weeks after my eighth birthday, I remember being all excited and sitting on the stairs with my little bag ready to leave. I wasn't quite so keen the second term, but of course that lay in the future.

The school, normally located in Cramond—a suburb of Edinburgh not too far from the Forth Bridge—had been evacuated to the highlands of Scotland because of the war, and it required a train journey from Edinburgh to reach the small village of Comrie, where it was now located, in a big country mansion called Lawers.

I don't remember the journey from Quillet to the railway station in Edinburgh but, because of petrol rationing, it was probably by bus through a succession of small towns with names like Aberlady, Longnidry, Prestonpans, and Musselborough. I clearly remember getting on the school train, at least part of which had been laid on especially for this load of kids heading for the school. Of course I didn't know a soul, and I found myself in a small compartment with a few other new boys all about my age. It was still the age of steam trains, and off we chuffed to our unknown destination in the highlands of Scotland. It must have been a terrible moment for my mother, but it was the start of a great adventure for me.

We had to change trains at a place called Gleneagles—now famous as a 5-star golfing resort. When we arrived there, we could not open the door of our compartment—the train had no corridor—and my companions and I imagined ourselves being carried off, trapped in our train, to some remote destination deep within the mountains. We couldn't even get the window down and banged away on the glass until a passing porter heard us and let us out.

Eventually we all arrived at the small hamlet in Perthshire and set out for the 2-mile walk from Comrie railway station to the big house of Lawers. The walk took us through woods edged with rhododendrons. It was early September, so these were just a sombre green and the leaves of the trees in the forest were beginning to turn. It must have been a strange sight to see this column of small boys making their way along this woodland track. I was asked my name and promptly gave it as Antony Fleming but was immediately shushed, and I learned that first names were never used! There were 109 boys in the school, and it was quite common for many to have the same surname. In this case, the most senior would be, for example, Fleming Major, the next Fleming Minor, and then, if there were more, the surname would be followed by the Latin suffixes Tertius, Quartus, Quintus (meaning 3rd, 4th, 5th, etc.). It seems odd now but not at all strange at the time.

I don't recall the exact scenario when we eventually arrived at our destination, but we were allocated a bed in a dormitory holding around 24 beds. As the building was not a purpose-built school but a big country house modified to suit, some of the arrangements were a bit rough and ready. Down the centre of the dormitory was a pair of long, white-painted washstands facing each other. There were holes cut in the top to hold circular china basins. On the floor beneath the basins were china jugs holding warm water known to us—I know not why and never questioned it—as fug water. On the counter tops were glass carafes containing drinking water for cleaning our teeth. I had only been there a few days when I and another boy, performing his ablutions at the row of basins opposite me, fumbled the handover of a full drinking water carafe. In a perfect example of Sod's Law (aka Murphy's Law,) the carafe dropped straight into a basin full of fug water, knocking out its bottom and crashed onto a full jug of water unhappily sitting right beneath it. There was a stupendous crash, and broken glass and china flew the whole length of the dormitory, riding on a tidal wave of fug water. This was followed by a horrified silence. I had already realized that discipline was pretty strict in this place, and I did not dare think what might lie in store for someone responsible for such mayhem. To my relief, it was accepted as a genuine accident and not the result of horseplay, so no punishment was meted out.

This was not the case when, a few days later, I and the boy in the next bed were caught using our beds as trampolines after lights out. There was normally a two-week amnesty on serious punishment for new boys, but this was waived in our case, and we each received two whacks with a cane on our behinds from the headmaster as a result of this breach of discipline. Such punishment was unpleasant from two aspects. One was the obvious one of physical pain, because it really hurt and left big bruises, but also from the psychological point of view. After committing some transgression, the ominous instruction was "come and see me in my study after lunch", so there were often many hours of anticipation to endure, especially if the offence had been committed on the afternoon of the previous day. There was usually a queue waiting outside the door at the appointed time, and the whacks being administered to a victim ahead of you were clearly audible through the closed door of the study. Of course this is unthinkable today and any teacher caught striking a child would be in serious trouble; but, I have to say, that in those days the rules were clearly laid down and the consequences of breaking them were clearly stated. If you broke them and got caught, the prescribed punishment was administered in accordance with the rules. The thing was not to get caught!

Discipline was strict but that was understood, and I don't recall myself or anyone else resenting it. The dormitory windows had to remain open regardless of the weather. We had to have a dip in a bath of cold water every morning. The water was run the night before, and during the Scottish winter there were occasions when there was a film of ice on the water in the morning. This was no excuse to avoid taking a dip, and, if necessary, you had to break the ice before immersing yourself. It was a beatable offence to skip the bath. I recall a time when some of us did and paid the price. At first we couldn't figure out how we got caught until we twigged that someone had been feeling the towels to see which were dry. After that we dampened the towels!

We must have been extremely fit because we played rugby football in the winter—in the snow, if necessary—and cricket in the summer. We went for runs and long walks through the surrounding mountains when we weren't playing games. On one occasion, we came across a cache of ammunition presumably for the use of resistance groups should the Nazis invade Britain. For outside recreation we explored the local forests and were allowed to build dams from rocks and turf along a mountain stream that ran down the hillside behind the house. In the spring we went looking for birds' nests—not to disturb them but simply to observe them. My record was 37 nests one spring. We used to keep tabs on the nests and watch the eggs hatch and the baby birds grow up. I remember there was a blue-tit's nest in a hole in a tree, and when the young birds were ready to fly, my friend and I inadvertently disturbed them, and they burst out of the nest into the nearby branches. The parent birds were frantic, and we tried desperately to put the babies back in the nest, but, of course, once the birds have flown they have flown forever.

On one occasion we were given a scavenger hunt in which we had to find a number of objects—one of which was a bluebell. I had been paired with a boy who was a lot less knowledgeable about nature than myself. We entered a clearing in the woods where there was a clump of yellow primroses. I still remember the dismay I felt when he rushed forwards with a cry of, "Bluebells"!

The cutlery we used had bone handles, many of which were in poor condition from rough use. Everyday things were in short supply, so one of the masters made replacement wooden handles on a primitive lathe, which must have impressed me because I still clearly remember it. He tied a homemade bow, made from a branch, to an overhead beam. A piece of line led down from the centre of the bow string down to a short hinged piece of wood on the floor. On its way down, the line wrapped a couple of times around a spindle so that—with the bow providing the spring-back energy—the spindle would rotate back and forth as you pressed and released the weight of your foot on the hinged plank. A piece of wood was inserted between the centres, and a chisel was used to shape the wood into a knife handle as it was spun back and forth by the spindle.

We had highland dancing lessons, so I learned to dance the Highland Fling as well as a couple of sword dances and the Eightsome and Foursome reels. We had occasional lectures from visiting lecturers. One was from a guy who dressed up in one of those old fashioned diving suits with a big round copper helmet with faceplates protected by metal grids. At the end of his talk, he clumped up and down the wood-floored temporary hut with leaden boots.

Most of our teachers were quite elderly because younger people had been called up to fight the war. My Latin teacher was Miss Stuart. To teach us the Latin verb for "to love", she would say *"Amo, amas, amat, amamus, amatus, amant"*—meaning "I love, you love, he or she loves, etc.," counting each one on her fingers until she came to *"amant"* when she would say that, as we only have five fingers, we have to point to the centre of our palm.

Our school uniform was a kilt. We had one for everyday and a second which we wore on Sunday. When the first got too tatty, the Sunday kilt took its place and we had a new one for Sunday.

Quite soon after we joined the school, we were segregated into those who were judged to be good at games and those who were not. I was in the latter group, which was almost certainly an accurate assessment, but I do remember thinking that I hadn't really had much of an opportunity or encouragement to be part of the good group. It didn't seriously bother me, but there was one occasion when I had my revenge. This took place during a practice session in what are called the "nets", where cricket balls are hurled at you by a succession of bowlers. There are odd occasions when, no matter how bad you are, you "get your eye in"

26

and for some reason cannot fail to hit every ball that is bowled at you. This was one of those occasions and I was having a fine time knocking every ball for six—as they say. Of course, these were not using approved classic shots with the bat, and the master who was coaching the good boys in the next net saw what was happening and remarked, in my hearing, that he was going to sort me out. He then delivered some special kind of googly ball which he was sure would outfox me. The ball connected very satisfactorily with my bat, flew past his ear at high speed and disappeared into a dense thicket of rhododendrons never to be seen again, despite a thorough search!

I don't know that I could honestly say that I enjoyed school, and it definitely did not constitute the best years of my life, but I certainly did not dislike it, either. I suppose we were lucky to have been evacuated up into the highlands of Scotland into such beautiful surroundings. During the war there was a shortage of people to work the land. Much of the work previously carried out by men was now done by women, and sometimes there were too few of them. One of these times was during the potato harvest, and on several occasions we were loaded into trucks to help go "tattie howking". For us this was just a grand day out: first, we had the novel experience of riding in the back of a truck, and second, we had an afternoon away from school. A tractor went around and around a field with a spinning device on the back uprooting the potatoes; we were paired off and each given a section of the field. We had to get all the tatties in our section collected and put into baskets before the next circulation of the tractor.

We complained about the food, but actually it was not bad, especially considering that it was war time and all food was rationed. Naturally, breakfast started with porridge. The Scots eat their national dish with salt rather than sugar, which did not suit my taste. We used to get cereal for a change on Sundays, and we did get sugar with that. So, every Sunday, I would fill a matchbox with sugar and use a small amount on my porridge during the week. Butter was also rationed to just 2 ounces per week. We had a kind of bun called a bap. These had been baked in quantity on a large tray, and where they touched there was a soft spot in the side of the bap. We used to stick our fingers through there and scoop out the soft bready interior and eat it dry. Then we would line the inside of the bap with the entire week's butter ration and fill any remaining space with marmalade. It was heavenly and well worth doing without butter for the remainder of the week!

We never had any tropical fruit such as oranges and bananas, as these would have had to be imported into Britain by sea, and with Germany sinking every ship they could, cargo space was needed for essential supplies. So we never saw those fruits, and we had long discussions about whether you peeled a banana by pulling down 3 strips or 4. Sweets (aka candies) were also rationed, and we were allowed just five per week.

We had to sit down and write a letter home every Sunday. My mother kept all of mine and I still have them. They make amusing reading. We were allowed a couple of weekend visits from our parents each term. We always looked forward to these visits, but actually I think we would have been happier without them. I remember counting down the days until the outing weekend and then, when it finally arrived, counting down how many hours were left before it was over, and then enduring the subsequent days getting resettled back into the routine.

I revisited Lawers 60 years later and looked at it from the outside. Nothing had visibly changed from the way I remembered it. There was the big Wellingtonia tree I used to climb, with its thick, spongy bark. Ironically, I recently discovered that this species is a native of California. The playing fields had reverted back to their original agricultural function, but the big stone we use to climb on was still there. A recent troll through the internet revealed that this stone is mysteriously old. What a thrill we would have had if we had thought we were sitting astride an ancient phallic symbol!

The school moved back to its normal home in 1945, at the end of the war. In the reverse of what happened at Lawers, the school's playing fields had been ploughed up for agriculture, which had turned up an immense number of small stones, which all us little boys were given the task of collecting before they could be used for games.

We played rugby, soccer and hockey in the winter, and cricket and occasionally rounders (called baseball in the U.S.) in the summer. We again practiced cricket in the nets as at Lawers. In cricket the ball is supposed to hit the ground in front of the batsman. On one occasion, when I was wielding the bat, a ball failed to do this and landed on my head. It didn't hurt too badly and I threw it back. The master supervising the net said "Fleming, where did that ball pitch?"

"On my head, sir," I replied.

Back in our proper school buildings, we had such facilities as an indoor swimming pool, which was in use during the summer term, and we were taught to swim. During the winter months the pool was covered, and the place was used as a gymnasium and lecture hall where school plays were put on. The biggest production in my memory was the production of the Gilbert and Sullivan comic opera *Iolanthe,* in which I participated. I knew the whole production by heart by the time it was over.

We had a school chapel when we were back in the proper school premises, and I sang in the choir—even getting down to one of a group of six boys—still singing with our unbroken soprano voices. Our biggest "production" was *The Pied Piper*, which started off with the words:

> *"Hamlin Town's in Brunswick,*
> *By famous Hanover city;*
> *The river Weser deep and wide*
> *Washes its wall on the southern side;*
> *A pleasanter spot you never spied;*
> *But, when begins my ditty,*
> *Almost five hundred years ago,*
> *To see the townsfolk suffer so*
> *From vermin, was a pity."*

The chapel was also used for assembly and the showing of films. One I clearly remember was the 1946 black-and-white version of *Great Expectations* with John Mills. We all jumped in our seats and gasped when the convict appeared during the graveyard scene. Many years later, when I first became interested in making films, I read in a book on editing how the director, David Lean, had achieved the shock effect by catching the audience on the rebound. I still have a copy of that version of the film in my collection.

Cargilfield was certainly a good school and still has a fine reputation today. It is now coeducational, which will certainly have changed its character. The main exam we studied for was the so-called Common Entrance to qualify for entry into the public school of one's choice. Public Schools are in fact private schools, and my name had been entered for Sherborne in the county of Dorset, in England. I was a lazy little tyke and only did the minimum amount of work to stay out of trouble. Just before I went into the room to take the all-important maths exam, my teacher saw me and commented that he didn't know why I was taking it as it was a complete waste of time. I thought then—and even more so now—that this was a totally irresponsible remark. For some reason I can't explain—and I don't suppose that he could either—I passed with 85 per cent. I certainly didn't deserve it!

We were still living at Quillet when the war ended. I can still identify the exact spot when, while out walking with my mother and my sister, a woman stopped us and told my mother that the war was over. This was on August 13th, 1945, just before my 10th birthday. All my childhood memories up to that point had been coloured by the war. The main personality outside my own family who was most familiar to me was of course Winston Churchill. Although there was no TV in those days, his picture appeared in all the papers, and his gravelly voice was always on the radio. I could not understand it when I heard that he had been kicked out of office after holding the country together during the war years. I later came to understand the reasons, but it seemed to be an extreme case of ingratitude to a nine-year-old.

For reasons that I don't think even she could explain, my mother decided to move from Scotland to the county of Suffolk, close to the East Coast of Southern England. She did this even before I left my school in Scotland so, instead of having just a few miles to travel home in the school holidays, I had to take a train all the way from Edinburgh to London and then change trains and head out in a northeasterly direction. The new house, called Marsh Acres, was out in the country near the town of Saxmundham. It was quite a large L-shaped place, lacking electricity and set in one acre of land, which had been left untended during the war years. Consequently, the garden was a complete jungle, which was great from my point of view. I reckon we made the move in the spring of 1947, when I was 10. My mother later remarked that she "must have been mad"!

She would come to London to meet me on the train from Edinburgh, and we would spend a couple of nights in the very nice Connaught Hotel. On one occasion, my father, who had recently returned from Chittagong, was also there. I hadn't seen him for years, so he was pretty much a stranger to me. My school tie was plain red in colour, and the only thing I can remember from that first meeting was that, after seeing my tie, he asked me whether I was "communist or something". I had not realized that my parents' marriage was on the brink of breaking up. When my mother finally told me, it did not make much of an impact. Even at that age I felt that it was none of my business, and it really didn't affect me either emotionally or in any practical way.

The first thing I remember about Marsh Acres were the millions of daffodils in the spring time. For those who are not aware of it, daffodils, like tulips, stem from bulbs which lie dormant beneath the ground for most of the year and then burst forth from their place of concealment in the spring. The other main memory is going upstairs to my bedroom holding a flickering oil lamp, the light from which threw grotesque, leaping shadows on the wall of the staircase.

The big country kitchen was located in the short arm of the L. In it was a big coal-heated range called an Aga. It was the only room in the house that was heated. Fortunately, I was away at school for the winter of 1947, which was exceptionally harsh. My mother told me that the mercury retreated into the bulb at the base of the thermometer and sulked there for 10 days. She said she had to wear gloves to make the bed because it was so cold.

Other vague memories I have of this house are getting a mild dose of some childhood disease and amusing myself in bed by reading encyclopaedias.   Strange child! Outside, there were interesting things to discover. The grass everywhere was around shoulder high for me, and I discovered some raspberry canes with delicious fruit in one area of the garden. Elsewhere, in what had at one time been a tennis court, I was experimenting with matches and inadvertently set the whole area ablaze.

Chapter 3

Sherborne

I attend Sherborne School and recall the royal visit celebrating the school's 400th anniversary. We move house yet again and I experiment with electricity, water and lead casting, with disconcerting results.

It was while we were living in Marsh Acres that I changed schools and moved on to Sherborne in the county of Dorset—not so far away as Scotland but still requiring a change of trains in London to reach it. I left Cargilfield in July 1947, one month before my 12th birthday, and started at Sherborne in September, when I was just 13.

As is always the case, going to a new school meant starting all over again at the very bottom. Sherborne had over 500 students and, like most schools of its type, roomed them in a number of different houses, each with its own housemaster, who was also a teacher. The students met at the central school buildings for classes each day. There was rivalry between the houses both on the playing fields and academically. Discipline was generally pretty tough, but to what degree depended very much on the current Headmaster and head boy of the school, plus the current housemaster and head boy of the house you were assigned to. At my time, every one of those posts was held by firm disciplinarians.

I was in Abbey House, which housed about 60 boys. The junior half of these were relegated to what was called the Day Room, which was itself divided by an imaginary line into the senior table and the junior table. Seniors could go to the junior side but not the reverse. Above this level, boys shared study rooms, with usually three boys to a study. There was a strong hierarchy, and it was very firmly discouraged to even talk to a boy more than one year junior or one year senior to you. You had to be neatly turned out and have all three buttons of your jacket fastened at all times when outside your house. We wore stiff removable collars. Each boy had his own "tuck box", which was a wooden box with a hinged lid, about 18 x 12 x12 inches in size, in which he kept goodies sent to him by his parents or bought in the town with pocket money.

On Sunday mornings, we had to sit at the big tables in the Day Room and write a weekly letter to our parents. Before we started, we were addressed by the four boys who administered the Day Room. After making routine announcements, they would sometimes continue that there was someone in the Day Room who was slacking, behaving inappropriately, or otherwise letting the side down. While they were saying this, everyone would be thinking, "Wow, that sounds like me"! Then they would say, "And it's so and so, and he's going in the bin!". This referred to a rubbish bin in the corner of the day room which was about 30 by 48 by 36 inches high. It had a door at the bottom of the long side, which was hinged along the top edge. The victim was grabbed by the gang of four and shoved head first into the bin, which was usually quite full of paper waste. The victim's tuck box was put in on top of him, and then a couple of the four seniors would jump up and down on top until the rubbish was sufficiently compressed to enable the victim to crawl out of the door at the bottom. I don't know how this barbaric custom started, but I was determined that it would never happen to me without a hell of a fight. Although I never had to put it into effect, I had a plan to run over the top of the table if they came for me and wedge myself into a narrow gap between two sets of lockers and fight like hell. I would most certainly have lost eventually, but I was not going to go quietly!

The most junior boys, which of course included all newcomers, were little more than slaves. They were referred to as "fags", which is unfortunate given the way that this word, along with several others in the English language, has been hijacked and given an entirely different and derogatory meaning by those who apparently lack the wit or imagination to create new words of their own.

These fags, of whom I was one, had to keep every place clean, including the prefects' study rooms. Also, they had to run errands for the prefects, who had only to stand at the top of the stairs and yell, "Fag" for someone to come running to do his bidding. When you ran an errand, the prefect concerned would sign a chit, and the sting in the system was that, each week, every fag had to have chits within two of the fag who had accumulated the most signatures. This ensured that there was no slacking on anyone's part. The most heinous crime, which brought down the worst punishment, was forging a prefect's signature.

The most prominent building in the town of Sherborne was the abbey, which was founded by St. Aldhelm in AD 705. There was a school on the premises at that time, and King Alfred the Great (believed by legend to have "burnt the cakes") was recorded as being one of the early pupils. The school was given a new charter by King Edward VI in 1550, so the school celebrated its 400th anniversary while I was there in 1950. The celebrations included a visit by the king and queen of England on June 1. Quite a number of the school buildings incorporated the original monks' cloisters. The library, chapel and some of the other school buildings were actually attached to the abbey. The abbey clock struck the time every 15 minutes, and an 8-bell peal rang out on Sundays and on other days when the town's bell ringers practiced their skills.

I was in the choir, which meant that I had to sit in the choir stalls at the inner end of the chapel, near the altar. As the entrance to the chapel was at the opposite end, it meant that I had to walk the whole length of the chapel, past the seated congregation, to reach my seat. We had to attend two services on Sunday—three, if you include Holy Communion for those boys who had been "confirmed". The second main service of the day was at 6 pm. Supper was served at 5 p.m., and as a very junior fag, I had to clean a prefect's study after supper and then get myself over to the chapel and into my seat in good time before the service started. The cleaning had to be to a high standard, with prefects running fingers along obscure ledges to check for dust. I was already a bit grubby from the cleaning, and I had to pretty much run to get to the chapel in time. All during this time the eight bells from the abbey were pealing nonstop as the bell ringers rang the changes. Ever since then, in a parody of one of Pavlov's dogs, I have associated church bells with this unpleasant and stressful experience.

The walls of the entry lobby to the chapel were carved with the names of Old Shirburnians killed in the two world wars, together with the dates of their deaths and the dates they attended the school. Especially in the case of the First World War, it was depressing to see how many boys went straight from school to their deaths in the trenches.

As in Scotland, the day began with a mandatory dip in a cold bath followed by breakfast that started with porridge. At the end of each day we went to our dormitories and had to report to the prefect in charge, wearing just our pyjama bottoms. We had to stand to attention in front of him and say, "Please, so-and-so may I wash, please". Of course he would say yes, but might well deliver a fist blow to the stomach to check your reflexes and the condition of your stomach muscles. Actually, they could not fail to be in good condition considering that, every night, we had to do 20 pushups, 20 leg ups, several up-and-overs on an overhead bar in the washroom, plus during the day we had PT every morning, gym once a week, and either going for a cross-country run or playing Rugby football or other games every day of the week except Sunday.

There were other sports, too, which were supposedly voluntary. However, this was accompanied by phrases like, "You know what everyone will think of you if you don't volunteer—don't you?". One of these was boxing. This was supposedly to teach us self-defence, but I could not see that this would be much use if a bad guy was coming at you with some kind of weapon. If they had been teaching some form of martial arts, I would have been all for it, but the thought of being punched on the nose did not appeal to me. This sport was an inter-house competition, with each bout being three rounds and three masters acting as judges. We wore either a blue or red sash. If there was a clear winner, the result was straightforward. If all three of the judges did not agree on the result, then it was announced, for example, "Win by red, good try by blue". My goal was to lose in the first bout so I would not have to fight again, but I could not make this obvious. I achieved my goal of losing, but it was a split decision, and I was horrified to think that I came so close to going through to the next round.

We played rugby football in the winter months and cricket in the summer. I was never much good at sports. On one occasion I was playing fullback, which was the last ditch defence position after the attacking side had broken through. The opposing forwards were kicking the ball ahead of them and I was the only person between them and our goal line. There was no escape. I had to do my duty and fall on the ball with my back to the opposition to give time for my team to rally round me. Naturally the opposing forwards set about kicking me out of the way with their studded boots, and when the fray had moved on, I was seen to be wandering around the field in a more aimless fashion than usual. Actually, I had been kicked on the head and was suffering from concussion. My recollection is that it was twilight and everything was dark. Another player was detailed to take me back to the house, but I kept wandering off, and he had to keep going after me and pulling me back. Gradually my sight returned, and when I got back to house, the house matron thought I was shamming and didn't take me seriously until I threw up all over her.

Each day after breakfast, it was off to the chapel for a short morning service, followed by dispersal to our classrooms. Each teacher had his own classroom, and we all had our schedule of which classrooms we had to attend at what time for which subject. Being let out late from one class was not considered a valid excuse for being late at the start of the next, so we often had to run from one to another between each class. We also had to do military training one afternoon per week, and learned to march up and down and drill to a high standard. We were taught to shoot rifles and went out on field exercises from time to time. On one of those, I learnt the value of staying perfectly still to avoid being detected. Myself and a couple of others were cut off from the rest of our troop in an open hazel wood and avoided detection by simply lying around the base of hazel bushes and almost got stepped on. We were wearing khaki but not camouflage.

Despite the draconian discipline, most of us quite enjoyed school, although I am sure that few would admit to doing so. The strict rules did not stifle creative devilment. For example, we had boys sneaking out to visit girls in the nearby girls' boarding school in the middle of the night, although I was too chicken to do anything so daring. They were caught out when there was a false alarm fire in the middle of the night and they were found to be missing, causing panic among the staff. The missing boys did get a hot reception when they returned from their escapade.

To those who scorn and mock the system, I have to say that most of us who "enjoyed" this type of schooling came from at least comfortable—if not privileged—family circumstances. It served to toughen us up when other kids might have had this instilled into them simply by everyday life. Although the discipline may sound harsh, it rode lightly on the shoulders of most who experienced it, and in no way stifled creativity in risk taking. In my opinion, life itself requires self-discipline, and any that I have come across since leaving school could be shrugged off as a joke by comparison, so I feel it has stood me in good stead and am grateful that I experienced it.

We had much more freedom than we had at Cargilfield and were free to go into town when we had no other duties or responsibilities. We had to be neatly turned out at all times and faced punishment if spotted by a prefect with buttons undone, etc. Certain shops were off limits, but they were few in number.

About one year after I changed schools, we moved from Marsh Acres to a more suitable house in 1949 and stayed there for several years. The new house, called Five Gables, was also in the county of Suffolk but was located in Witnesham, not far from the county seat of Ipswich. It did indeed have five gables, along with a one-acre garden with an ornamental pond, a productive vegetable garden, and a sizeable orchard. The house had been owned by serious gardeners, who had grafted trees in the orchard so that one tree bore more than one type of apple. The fruit trees produced far more fruit than we could possibly eat, and it was years before I could bring myself to actually pay for an apple. Our water came from a well in the garden, with a pump which started when the water level in the roof tank became low. The gables were accessible by climbing onto the porch roof, and there is a photo, taken in 1952, of me and my sister sitting astride one of the gables. I remember calling down to my mother from this lofty perch. I would have had a fit if I had been the parent, but I don't remember her getting too worked up about it.

I developed an interest in fantail pigeons, and we bought a pair. We soon discovered that they breed about every six weeks, so the numbers multiplied exponentially. Not only that, but resident pigeons attract the wild variety, and in no time we had 40+ sitting on the roof, pecking the mortar out of the roof tiles. The local farmers were also not too pleased when this flock descended on their fields of grain. With huge ingenuity and stealth, I managed to entice them down to the ground and captured them. We put them in a basket and drove them 40 miles away in the car. Of course by the time we returned home, they were back sitting on the roof. We also kept rabbits, and my sister and I used to walk the hedgerows every day during the school holidays, picking food for the rabbits, and so became very familiar with all the plants—and birds—of the countryside. It never occurred to us to wonder who did this chore while we were away at boarding school, but it must have been my poor mother.

We had a small Yorkshire terrier called Topsy, who was part of the family. While I was away at school I had a letter from my mother telling me that Topsy had died—having had her bowel punctured by a chicken bone left accidentally in her food. I think I cried for about three days after getting the news. I was further dismayed when my mother bought a poodle called Simon as a replacement, but he turned out to be a marvellous dog of great character and sense of humour. I have favoured poodles as a breed ever since.

We had a gardener called William, who was in his early twenties. He did good work but was slightly mentally challenged. I certainly did nothing to help because I was always playing tricks on him. The worst was taking one of my father's shotgun cartridges and putting it in a plant pot, and before lighting a small candle under it, placing it close to where William was working. I then hid nearby to await events. When it went off with a tremendous bang, poor William leapt a mile into the air. It was a miracle that he didn't suffer a heart attack.

The property was built on a slope, so that the upper part of the garden was much higher than the orchard at the bottom. The house was in the middle, with a pond just above it. I had read somewhere how water could be made to flow uphill by using the principle of a siphon. I thought this sounded rather neat, so I filled a hose with water, stuck one end in the pond, and took the other end down to the lower part of the garden. To my delight it worked, and water flowed merrily out of the pond until it was empty.

I did a lot of experimenting while living at Five Gables. I would read about stuff in books and then try to put what I had read into practice. I had a kind of Meccano set that allowed you to cut and bend metal and punch holes in it to make things. I also had a system of rubber Minibricks, which long preceded Lego. I read about how to make an electric motor and bought all the bits but never got that to work. I wired up electricity to a shed in the garden but somehow managed to connect the two live wires together. I had my sister, standing on a chair, turn on the power while I went to the shed to watch the lights come on. When she flipped the switch, it blew the door of the fuse box clean off! I had read about casting, and I melted an old piece of lead pipe in a tin lid heated over a primus stove. I had made a hollow in some soil I had taken from the garden, and I poured the molten lead into that, holding the tin lid with a pair of pliers. I hadn't reckoned on the soil being damp, and the steam from the moisture spat the molten metal back onto my hand. I still bear the scars from that incident!

I always had a number of projects on the go, and one of these got me into trouble when I filched a piece of wood from a lumber yard. It wasn't very big, and I had retrieved it by climbing through a hedge. My mother asked me where I had got it, and when I told her, she made me take it back and go and apologize to the manager of the lumber yard. I absolutely dreaded going to see him, but he was very understanding and allowed me to keep the piece of wood, but it taught me a lesson I never forgot.

I was given a powerful kite as a present. Supposedly it was ex-RAF and used for hoisting aerials into the sky. It made a distinctive noise, resembling that of a light aircraft. On one occasion a sudden gust snatched the reel holding the line out of my hands, and it went bounding off across the fields. I gave chase and almost caught up with it when it became hooked in a hedge, but as if to taunt me, when it was almost within my grasp, it broke free and took off again. It then headed for a church, and I had visions of it smashing the stained glass windows, but at the last minute it leapt over the steeple. Finally, it became entangled in the upper branches of an unclimbable tree. I was miles from home by this time, and it was getting dark, so I had to leave it purring in the gathering gloom. I returned the following morning when the wind had dropped, but there was no sign of my kite, and I never saw it again.

I was very keen on conjuring at the time and had a whole array of tricks. I don't remember where I got all the stuff, and I had several books on the subject. I used to give "shows" to anyone I could persuade to watch.

I also developed a kind of game where, using one of my mother's knitting needles in the fashion of a miniature billiard cue, I had to knock a ping pong ball into a maze built with minibricks. I had it set up so that, if the ball reached the inner sanctum, it pushed two metal plates together to close a circuit and light a bulb. The problem was that I really had little idea of what I was doing, and had no one to advise me, so I was using 240 volts AC. On one occasion, I forgot to turn off the power before I reset the plates and got a hell of a shock when I grabbed hold of the plate.

I had a permit for a .410 shotgun, and I used to go out shooting rabbits in the adjacent farmer's fields. I would gut and skin the rabbits and then dress the skins. The meat was used to make delicious rabbit stew. I'm afraid that on one occasion I discarded the lessons I had learnt about gun safety and amused myself by shooting the heads off flowers without paying attention to what lay beyond the flower heads. Actually, there was the whole orchard and a hedge, beyond which lay a busy road and, across that, a small village store. My mother was inside the shop one day while I was decapitating flowers, and she heard the pitter patter of spent shot hitting the windows. The lady serving her commented that it might be rain. My mother agreed with her, but knew what it was, and stayed chatting with the shopkeeper and until the fusillade had ceased. I soon found that, while I enjoyed stalking the rabbits, I really didn't want to kill them. It got to the point where the only reason I pulled the trigger was that, if I did not, all my careful stalking became meaningless. Guns are tools designed to kill or maim—with a secondary function of making holes in pieces of cardboard with rings on them. My only interest in guns is the precision engineering of the mechanism.

I started taking photos at this time, using a small box brownie camera. I had read somewhere about a kind of pinhole camera called a camera obscura, which was supposed to be able to project an image in a dark room. I remember trying to make one of these out of cardboard and shutting myself in the heated linen cupboard to try it out. This was another of my failed experiments, but I suppose these were the early seeds that later sprouted into an interest which has remained with me my entire life.

In rummaging through the attic, I came across an old banjolele (a cross between a banjo and a ukulele) that had belonged to my father, and I was interested in learning how to play it. We had a couple of elderly spinster ladies living nearby who played the violin, so I went and asked them if they could teach me. People who play classical violin are not likely to be familiar with a primitive instrument like a ukulele, but they knew of a sign writer in the village who played the accordion and thought he might know. So off I went to see Percy, who, it turned out, could play pretty well any instrument from a Jews harp right on up through Swanee whistle, recorder, guitar, saxophone and accordion. He showed me how to play my banjolele, and, as the chord fingering was the same as for the top four strings on the guitar, he encouraged me to move up to the guitar, which is of course a much more versatile instrument.

I think it was probably through Percy's influence that I

became interested in modernizing our gramophone. We had an old wind-up portable model with a scratchy needle from which the sound came out of a sound box. I had read about electric pickups, so I got hold of one of those and plugged the output into the back of our big wireless set. This pickup had fibre needles which you had to sharpen after playing a couple of records.

Lying in bed in the dark, I used to listen to a scary radio programme called *Appointment With Fear,* whose host was a man named Valentine Dyall, who called himself "The Man in Black". He used to sign off by saying, "This is your story teller, the Man in Black, wishing you pleasant dreams". I remember one story in particular, called "The Hands of Nikamen", which involved an archaeologist opening a tomb in Egypt with a curse on it and the mummified hands of the body inside came and attacked him. As I lay in the dark, I was sure I could hear the hands scrabbling on the doors of my bedroom!

We used to go boating in a rowing boat on an inland lake known as the Mere, at a place called Thorpeness, and I had sailing lessons on the river at Aldeburgh given to me by an old salt who told me to push this or pull that, but I never understood the reason, so I did not learn much.

In 1952 I had a go at building my first floating craft. Actually, this was just a raft that used drums as flotation. I christened it "Sea Horse". I assembled it in the garden and somehow we got it to the sea at Aldeburgh, which was at least 20 miles away. The maiden voyage was not a success, because *Sea Horse* capsized in the waves and broke up in the surf and the wreckage never made it back home.

The beach there was shingle and my sister, my mother, and I used to walk along it looking for semi-precious stones called Carnelian, and also pieces of amber which had found their way across the North Sea from the Baltic. I remember being on a bus one day and overhearing two women talking in the seat in front of me. One of them was commenting on what a lovely day it was. Her companion responded "We'll pay for it—you'll see!". I thought to myself, what a terrible attitude. Unfortunately, the pessimist turned out to be right. A couple of weeks later, on the night of January 31, 1953, there was a terrific North Sea storm which caused terrible flooding along the east coast of England and the Netherlands. We went to the seafront of Aldeburgh a few days later, and I remember seeing what looked like bullet holes right through the netting-reinforced glass, caused by beach pebbles driven by the gale-force winds.

On the road between Witnesham and Ipswich there was a railway crossing at the village of Westerham. On one occasion a spark from the steam locomotive set light to a field of stubble, and the fire engine was prevented from reaching the fire because the gates were closed due to the very same train which had started the blaze. The fire raced across the field to a couple of newly harvested stacks of corn, which burned well into the night. While the fire fighters were concentrating on those, the fire sneaked around and completely destroyed their fire engine, which had been parked in the field.

Back at school, we had a wide range of teachers, each with his own way of teaching. There was one whose classroom doubled as a museum, and the French teacher used to hurl anything handy from a stuffed owl to a chunk of natural rubber at inattentive students while, in a different classroom, another teacher had a water pistol he used for the same purpose. We had one eccentric chemistry teacher who threw large chunks of sodium into the swimming pool so we could see it race around before exploding. Another science teacher, using the same element in what he thought was a cautious manner, inadvertently caused an impressive explosion which had broken glass raining down from the ceiling— providing a wonderful opportunity, over his protests, for his students to rush around shouting "Fire! Fire!" when, in fact, there was no such thing. New teachers had the worst of it. One had his back to his desk while he was writing on the blackboard. Smelling something burning, he joked, "I hope you haven't set fire to my books" when that is exactly what his students had done! We were given a choice of studying history or geography and, even though I preferred the latter, I chose history simply because I was scared of the geography teacher.

As at my previous school, I did the bare minimum amount of

work to keep me out of trouble, but the teaching was so intense and focused that even I learnt more than I had a right to expect. The exams we were aiming for were O-Levels (with "O" meaning "ordinary"), A-Levels (with "A" meaning "Advanced"), and then University Entrance. I took my O levels and, over two attempts, got adequate—but not good—pass marks in math, physics, chemistry, Latin, English language, and French. This was thanks entirely to my teachers and very little to do with my own efforts. We did not have things like yearbooks, but I am sure that, if we had, I would certainly not have been picked as anyone likely to succeed. I found that if I was interested in something I could pick it up pretty quickly; but, if not, I just as quickly became bored and did not pay attention. To the despair of my mother, my school reports were full of such phrases as, "Could do better if he tried" or "Another term wasted"!

In those days, smoking was still considered "cool" and like most of the kids at that time, I would occasionally pinch one of my mother's cigarettes and light up. Actually I found it pretty disgusting, but on the school train at the end of term, almost everybody smoked. I had decided that a pipe was a step up from a mere cigarette, so I bought one and stuffed it with cigarette tobacco. Like most pipe smokers, I had a hard time getting the thing to light, and after several attempts, gave it up in favour of a game of "chase through the train" with the pipe still in my mouth. There must have been a dying spark lying dormant in the bowl, which, brought to life by all my puffing and blowing, without warning filled my lungs with tobacco smoke—leaving me gasping for breathable air. That was the end, and I never smoked again!

By this time, it had become obvious that my preference was in practical matters of a technical nature, but when it was time to start thinking about what to do for a career, I really had no idea what form this should take. A visit to the Ransome and Rapier factory in Ipswich, which manufactured heavy equipment, made me realize that this kind of engineering did not appeal. This was further confirmed when I visited another factory, owned by a friend of my mother, which specialized in heavy-duty springs. Then, another friend of my mother suggested an apprenticeship with De Havilland Aircraft. This immediately struck a chord, so I applied. I can still remember the thrill of receiving my acceptance letter with the DH logo of a small airplane depicted in plan view, with a letter D superimposed on the left wing and a letter H on the right.

I left Sherborne in July 1952, at the relatively early age of 16, and went to Hatfield in Hertfordshire to be an engineering apprentice at the De Havilland Aircraft Company in September, when I was just 17.

Chapter 4

De Havillands, Part 1

Apprenticeship

I leave formal school and embark on an engineering apprenticeship at De Havilland Aircraft, where I develop an interest in cars.

I don't recall feeling any tugging at the heartstrings when I left Sherborne. I was too keen to get on with the next, more adult, stage of my life.

Our family car had been a pre-war Rover for as long as I could remember, with the registration number DYU 14. When I was 16, my mother let me drive the car a bit on deserted airfields. As soon as I was 17, on August 19th, 1952, I obtained a provisional license and took eight driving lessons in Ipswich over a period of 10 days. I took my driving test on the same day as my last lesson and passed the test. The reason for the haste was that I had left Sherborne in July and was starting my apprenticeship at De Havillands at the beginning of September 1952.

Not long after this my mother sold the Rover, and bought a most unexpected car—an Austin A40 Sports model. I drove this whenever I could, and it was lucky that I didn't have any accidents in it, because I exhibited all the traits that cause newly qualified young drivers to be so accident prone. On one occasion, I was going flat out across Salisbury plain with my foot literally on the floorboards. A police car came up behind me and rang its bell to stop me. I was absolutely terrified, but I hadn't broken any laws, and they just gave me a stern talking to about the number of young drivers killed. They were quite right, and it had a salutary effect.

Being an apprentice raised me another level of freedom from boarding school, but there were still rules that had to be obeyed. I was an "indentured" apprentice, which meant that I had signed on with De Havillands for five years. The apprentice school was at a converted house called Astwick Manor, where I was still a boarder but had a small individual room rather than sharing a dormitory. There was a canteen attached, and we had to attend practical classes every day in a workshop attached to the residential building and also spend one day a week plus three evenings at Hatfield Technical College. My pay was just 30 shillings per week—1 pound 50p in today's money, but of course a pound bought a lot more back then.

The first big difference was that for the first time in my life I was surrounded by people who came from an entirely different social group. Although it was never overtly stated, when at public school, my fellow students and I had it somehow instilled in us that we were destined to be managers or officers, rather than workers. Almost all of us came from comfortable middle class backgrounds and lived in nice homes. We all spoke what was known as King's English, which had the unique quality among the many English accents of revealing your social background without giving any hint of which part of the country you came from. We tended to feel superior to people who spoke with a regional accent. My mother was especially snobbish in this respect.

I now found myself entirely surrounded by people of whom not a single one spoke with my accent. In fact, two years were to pass before I was to meet another public school boy. I quickly realized that any notions of superiority due to social background were utter nonsense and I had better give up any ideas I may have had in that respect. This was the first very valuable lesson I learnt and was a practical example of the old saying of not judging a book by its cover.

I soon had friends amongst all sorts of people I would never have met if I had not chosen to become an engineering apprentice. There were a few foreign students among the apprentices. These were usually exceptionally bright and hardworking. For us English blokes, this apprenticeship was something we took for granted as part of our birth right, so we really did not appreciate its value. For foreign students it was a marvellous opportunity, gained only by dint of hard work in being selected from probably hundreds of applicants in their homeland, so they represented not only themselves but also their families and even their countries. One of these I remember was called Rana Singh, who wore a turban. We thoughtlessly nicknamed him Ramjet Sinjee, which he seemed to accept remarkably well—although I suppose he really had no choice!

It was lights out in the hostel at 10 p.m., and I set up a communication system with a fellow apprentice in another room using Morse code transmitted through wires we ran through the cable trunking.

The school was set up with sections for fitting, sheet metal work, machine shop, woodworking, and a small drawing office. The first two and a half months were spent in Fitting, which entailed learning to use hand tools. This involved being given a piece of rough mild steel roughly 2 inches wide by 4 inches long by 1/4-inch thick, which had to be squared up and polished like a mirror. A rectangular hole, about 1½ inches by 1 inch, was cut in the centre, and a separate piece of metal had to be made to fit exactly into this hole, whether slid in from either side or either way up. Only files could be used, except for a drill to start the hole in the middle. I set out to prove that I was going to be the best filer ever, but my enthusiasm soon faded away, especially when, after days of laborious work, the final result was briefly evaluated by an instructor who then tossed it into the scrap bin before he gave you a similar but more intricate exercise. I think the authorities made a great mistake in doing this. It would have been much better to have given us genuine parts to make that could have been used to construct light aircraft. If they measured up and were good enough, they could be used; if not, they could be tossed. That would have given us real incentive to turn out components which had some practical value.

After two and a half months we moved to the sheet metal

section, where, using a variety of hammers, mallets and tucking pliers, we made parts like air scoops out of aluminium sheet. Here I learned that a strip of 1/16-inch aluminium could be made to support your weight by cutting large holes in it, swaging the edges, and then bending over the edges of the strip.

This was followed by four months in the machine shop, learning to use lathes, milling machines, shapers, grinders, etc., before rounding off with two months in the drawing office and one month in the wood shop, where we each had to make a tool box. I still have mine 60 years later, although it is a pretty rough job.

There are a few odd incidents that I remember from those days. One was a craze that developed for making flying objects in all sorts of weird and wonderful shapes, and launching them by hooking them onto a length of shock cord held at each end while the inventor and builder of the object pulled it back and released it as if from an oversized catapult. Some of these devices crashed immediately while other disappeared off into the distance. The authorities put a stop to the fun when one device looped back overhead and swooped in at low level from behind to fell an unsuspecting student by smacking him on the back of the head while he was looking the other way.

I had always been interested in archery, but many of my arrows had lost their points from firing them into trees. I machined replacement points out of brass, and these were wickedly sharp. I brought my bow to Astwick Manor and decided to see just how far I could shoot the refurbished arrows. There was an extensive lawn in the middle of which stood a tall Wellingtonia tree about 80 feet high. I stood one side of this tree and stationed a buddy on the other side to see where the arrow landed. What was I thinking! The arrow flew over the top of the tree and announced its arrival by the swoosh it made as it flew over his shoulder and buried itself six inches in the ground behind him. It would certainly have killed him had he been standing a few inches to one side.

I also used my newly acquired machining skills to make a small canon out of bronze stock. This was designed to fire 1/4-inch diameter ball bearings, using powder removed from shotgun cartridges. I tested this canon at home and used a piece of 1/2-inch plywood as a target, which I propped against a hedge with a footpath on the other side of it. The ball bearing passed right through the plywood as if it were cheese just moments before an unsuspecting pedestrian walked past.

While most of our instruction was of a practical nature, we also attended classes on safety and occasionally films illustrating what could go wrong. We were warned of the dangers of exploding grinding wheels, and I clearly remember a film on the collapse of the Tacoma Narrows bridge due to a design flaw. I have since driven over the replacement bridge many times, and each time I remember the cautionary tale about its construction. The film we watched can now be viewed on YouTube.

Given the fact that we were all rather irresponsible teenagers, it is surprising there were not more incidents in the workshops. A surface grinder is a machine designed to just skim a few thousandths of an inch off the surface of the work piece, which is attached to the moving bed of the machine by magnets. On this occasion the machine bed was set too high, so that when the fast spinning, grinding wheel encountered the work piece, the magnets could not hold it and it was sent zinging around the workshop, ricocheting off the brick walls. It was a miracle it never hit anybody.

For transportation I had a bicycle, which I used to visit the cinema three times per week. I quite often went home at the weekend and could leave my bike in a bike storage shed at Hatfield railway station. The journey involved taking a slow train into London which stopped at every station and went through many tunnels. It was still steam engines in those days, and if the window was open when entering a tunnel, the compartment filled with smoke. Then I had to cross London on the Underground and catch another train out to Ipswich. When awaiting the train on Hatfield station, the express train to Scotland, called the Flying Scotsman, used to come through the station at about 70 mph. It was an awe-inspiring sight as it approached the station on a downhill curve, coming straight at you, before it thundered through the station belching steam and smoke with the ground shaking underfoot. The reciprocating forces from the huge 8-foot diameter driving wheels imparted a rocking motion to the huge locomotive.

In December of that first year, London and the home counties were hit by a devastating smog. Visibility was down to 6 inches, and you could not, quite literally, see your hand in front of your face or even the loom of the light from a lit street lamp when standing directly beneath it. I had a beige duffel coat, and the moisture that condensed onto it looked exactly like black ink. It lasted for four days and killed 4,000 people—mostly the young, elderly, and those suffering from respiratory problems.

After one year at Astwick Manor, I moved into lodgings. My first digs were with a couple from Newcastle, where they have a very strange accent which is hard to understand. In fact, until this time, I had always assumed it was some kind of artificial funny speaking that comedians on the radio had made up as a joke. While there, I remember going into a nearby grocer's shop (it was before the days of supermarkets), where I overheard a newly married young woman asking the shop assistant for some bacon. "You know, enough for a man for his breakfast, like." *Wow*, I thought, *fancy being married and not knowing how to order bacon!*

After Astwick Manor, we were sent out into the main factory, according to our area of interest. Mine was electrical, so I was sent to the Propeller Company. De Havillands was a huge place, employing 4,000 people, with different factories set around a large airfield. On one side was the aircraft company, and on the other were the Propeller and Engine companies, as well as what was called Special Projects, which built air-to-air guided missiles.

Being an apprentice, I was given a lot of lowly jobs. In the Propeller company I sat at a work bench next to a guy who was an avowed Communist. He had a favourite song which he sang or hummed all the time.

She gets too hungry, for dinner at eight.
She loves the theatre, but doesn't come late.
She'd never bother, with people she'd hate
That's why the lady is a tramp.

His job was doing the wiring looms on pieces of aircraft equipment, and he did meticulous work, which took several days. The multi-coloured wires were tied together with hand tied lacing in those days. The chassis were made of aluminium sheet painted matte black. We used nuts in the department, some of which were steel and others were non-ferrous material, but both types were cadmium plated so they looked identical. There was some kind of feud going on between the foreman of the department and the QC inspector, who was hell-bent on finding problems with the finished work. On more than one occasion he used a magnet to identify steel nuts being wrongly used, which entailed cutting out all the wiring, replacing the offending nuts, and starting over. After this had happened a couple of times, I asked my companion whether it didn't drive him nuts (no pun intended) to have to do his work over again and he just said that he didn't care "so long as they pay me".

A lot of valuable time was wasted in playing tricks. One of the best was to drill a hole in the bottom corner of the thick white china mugs in which tea was served from the tea trolley that came around at break time. The hole was drilled using a special and expensive drill bit and located so it was facing the body of a right-handed person holding the mug by its handle. The hole was then plugged using white wax. A couple of minutes after nice hot tea was poured into the cup, the wax would melt, and a jet of scalding liquid would strike the holder of the mug around chest level.

Another good one of a more technical nature was to take a ball race around 4 inches in diameter, held by a rod through its centre, and get the outer part up to an impressive speed by shooting an air hose nozzle at it. We were able to measure 40,000 rpm using a stroboscope. The bearing was then released by removing the rod, and it would take off in a shower of sparks as it struggled to gain traction on the concrete floor. Finally, it would hurtle off down the length of the shop and smash into the brick wall, knocking off chips, and bounce back several feet for another go, and another and another, until it finally ran out of momentum.

My own efforts were on a more modest scale. On the wall of the workshop we had rolls of electrical cable and also rolls of sleeving in matching colours that looked identical except there was no conductor inside. Experimental electrical circuits were made up by the engineers by taking cardboard boxes with holes punched in them to support various components which were then wired together with a rat's nest of wires. One lunchtime, I substituted a couple of these wires selected at random with lengths of sleeving with a bit of wire sticking out of each end. I figured it would take my victim several hours to find the problem, as it was always the components that give trouble and seldom the interconnecting cable. I watched, full of anticipation, as the technician came back from lunch and turned all the equipment back on, followed by his puzzled look as nothing was behaving as it should. But I was very impressed that it only took him a couple of minutes to find the problem, followed immediately by the cry of "Tony!"

We had many different power supplies in the lab and thick rubber mats on the floor to discourage electrocution. On another occasion, I moved back the mat and connected one lead from a Mega to the metal cabinet in which a technician was working and the other to ground. A Mega was an instrument for testing insulation, and by turning a handle, it would generate up to 1,000 V but at a very low current so, although it could impart a considerable jolt, it was not dangerous. I waited until my victim had his hands inside the cabinet and his feet on the concrete floor and spun the handle. The reaction was immediate and quite satisfactory, although I was disappointed that I hadn't had time to get the handle up to speed.

Tricks were also played on apprentices by the seasoned work force. If not aware, you could be sent to the stockroom for a long weight (wait!) for emery sparks or even for a Goliath Washer— which turned out to be a circular piece of steel about 3/4 of an inch thick and 3 feet in diameter with a hole in the middle. It was quite a sight to see a skinny apprentice trying to roll this thing into the workshop without being overwhelmed and flattened. On the other hand, a "wavy flat bastard file" was a legitimate tool.

We shared the tea trolley with an adjacent machine shop. They had apprentices there, too, but of a different type from myself. They were vocational apprentices, training to be machinists, whereas I was supposed to be studying engineering. In the queue was a machinist I considered quite old—probably in his forties—smoking a pipe. One of the apprentices, around my age, said "Wotcha got in there, mate? Camel shit and bus tickets?". I was full of admiration for his imaginative mixture.

On the other side of us was a building where propeller blades were vibrated, sometimes to destruction. The noise was deafening, and it wasn't unknown for a blade to break off at the root and go scything through the building. We tested rubber shoes for de-icing propellers, and propeller assemblies were so finely balanced that the weight of a single cigarette paper—used to roll your own cigarettes—placed on a blade was sufficient to cause an entire four-blade assembly to rotate until the paper fell off.

At this time the De Havilland company was building a wide variety of aircraft, which included the Otter, Beaver, Heron, Dove, Venom fighter plane, and the experimental twin-boom DH 110 supersonic fighter which, on the month I joined the company, blew up and disintegrated in a very public way over the Farnborough air show, killing both its pilots as well as 29 spectators on the ground. The DH 108 had crashed six years earlier, killing the test pilot, Geoffrey De Havilland, Jr., son of the company's founder. The most important aircraft being built by the company was the Comet airliner, which was the first jet-engine airliner to enter service and which predated the Boeing 707 by several months. Tragically, the Comet contained a fatal flaw that resulted in a number of catastrophic accidents. The Comet was the first of its kind with a pressurized cabin, but no one knew the reason for the failures. As part of the investigation, the fuselage of an aircraft was enclosed in a water-filled test tank with the wings and tail sticking out. The fuselage was pressurized and depressurized to simulate take offs and landings while rams were used to raise the wings up and down. (When an aircraft is on the ground, the wings are a dead weight, hanging from the fuselage, while in flight the fuselage hangs from the wings.) In June 1954, the fuselage cracked because of metal fatigue that had started at the corners of the cabin windows due to the corner radius being insufficient. The windows were originally supposed to have been glued as well as riveted, but rivets only had been used, and the type of rivets may have contributed to the failure. This tank was right outside the building where I worked so

I had a close-up view of what was happening.

It was here that I met Collyn Rivers, who was to have a great influence on my life. Collyn was an engineer with an instinctive practical knowledge for electrical circuitry and the way things should be done, rather than having studied the theory in college. He also had a passionate interest in cars.

Having a driving license, I was obviously very keen on getting a car of my own. Anything new was out of the question for people in our situation, so all our interest was in elderly, pre-war vehicles. I knew nothing about cars and would probably have settled for more or less anything if I had not been re-educated by Collyn. Because of his influence, my first vehicle was a 1934 Frazernash BMW cabriolet. This sounds a lot more grand than it was, because at that time the BMW was still in the early stages of recovering from WWII and in 1955 was only building small, two-seater bubble cars, in which the passengers sat side by side and the front of the car opened, which was not too good if you were involved in even a minor front end crash! Although built in 1934, the design of my BMW was well ahead of its time, with a stiff tubular chassis, independent front suspension, rack and pinion steering, and other advanced features. Their 328 sports cars dominated road racing in the years before the war.

Collyn encouraged me to share his interest on motor vehicles and motor racing. We would sally forth to visit Silverstone and watch the stars of the era such as Stirling Moss, Fangio, Askari, Mike Hawthorn, and others. Leaving before dawn, we would take the BMW and build a mini grandstand over the car out of Dexian slotted angle and watch the racing, usually in the pouring rain. We also visited Silverstone (and Goodwood and Oulton Park) for amateur events, often organized by the Vintage Sports Car Club.

I experienced my first road accident in this car, while it was stationary. Collyn and I were waiting to turn right at a road junction on the Great West Road, on the outskirts of London. With absolutely no warning, we were struck from behind by a Ford Popular—surely one of the worst cars ever made. The passenger seat in the BMW could not have been latched securely because it shot backwards, depositing Collyn onto the back seat. He leapt out, berating the driver of the car which had run into us, while I was stunned into inaction by the whole incident. Actually, I felt a bit sorry for the guy who had so inexplicably run into us, as he was bringing one of his elderly parents home from a stay in hospital. He had to be towed away, but the BMW just had a few dents we were able to take care of ourselves.

I used this car for quite a while before getting the notion— almost certainly inspired by Collyn—of rebuilding it as a sports car. This was in late 1954 or very early 1955, because I remember having the car in its original form parked beside the Comet test tank mentioned earlier, and I have photos of the stripped-down chassis sitting in the snow. I reckoned it would take me about six months to rebuild the car, but of course it took at least two years to get the job done, including every minute of my spare time and every ounce of my tenacity. I was absolutely determined to get it finished, and it taught me a lot in that respect. I neglected my studies and forewent almost all social activities, but it proved to me that, if sufficiently determined, you could achieve things well beyond what you initially believed were within your ability. There was one particular piece of panel beating that I believed was beyond my skill level, and I arranged for a professional panel beater from a local garage to do it for me. He could only come at weekends, and when for the third weekend in a row he begged off, with the excuse that his dog had swallowed a needle, I decided to attempt it myself. It only took me a couple of hours to accomplish what I had believed was beyond me. It was a valuable lesson.

A few months after the BMW was finished, Collyn saw an advert in *Motorsport* magazine for the engine, gearbox, back axle, brakes, and wheels from a crashed 328 BMW. With his encouragement, I decided to buy these parts and upgrade my car to a high performance vehicle. The engine, with its three downdraft carburettors, would no longer fit under the bonnet, so I locked up the centre hinge and made an air scoop to accommodate the carburettors. The spring centres on my car did not match the pads on the back axle housing, so these were cut off and re-welded to suit. I had bought five wheels from the crashed car and one of them had attractive triangular slots. I decided that I would make the other four wheels the same, but this involved cutting 12

57

triangular slots in each wheel. My recollection is that each triangle required the drilling of twenty-seven 1/4-inch diameter holes, making a total of 324 holes per wheel, or 1,296 altogether. The rough triangles then had to be knocked out and each of the 48 triangular slots hand filed to shape. This is where my training in the Fitting shop of De Havillands came in handy.

With the car back on the road after the second rebuild, I was driving it home from St. Albans to Berkshire when it seemed that the car had jumped out of gear. I tried to stop, but neither the foot brake nor the hand brake had any effect. I looked over my shoulder and saw that the rear wheel on the driver's side, with brake drum and halfshaft still attached, was slowly coming out. Fortunately, the car stopped before it came all the way out, and I had to figure out what to do. I jacked up the car, dismantled all the bits and reassembled them, but I still had no idea what had caused them to come apart in the first place. The wheels were attached to the hub by knock-on wing nuts that had been mutilated when I obtained them, and I had spent hours filing them back to shape before having them re-chromed. It was unthinkable that I would do anything to damage them. I borrowed an axe from a nearby farm and, using a chunk of wood between the axe and the wing nut, managed to get the nut loose without damaging it. I re-assembled everything and was soon on my way. The same thing happened twice more before I reached home. On the last occasion, it was at the top of a small hill and I could see that the car was not going to come to rest before the halfshaft came right out, so I ran the car into the hedge to stop it. This was on a narrow country lane, and I had everything in bits when a bus came along that could not get past me. The driver just sat there with his arms folded across the steering wheel and the bus engine going *vrrrrm, vrrrrm, vrrrrm*. I was working as fast as I could, leaving out half the nuts to get the car moved, when a woman came out of the bus and started berating me for holding them up. I'm afraid she received a very rude response that sent her back to the bus.

The source of the problem was a real mystery until Collyn realized that the re-welding of the spring pads on the very thin back axle casing had slightly distorted the casing, so that the attachment at the outer end was no longer at right angles to the line

58

of the halfshaft.

Driving the BMW provided memorable experiences—some wonderful, and some not so good. The best was driving the open car in beautiful weather through the gorgeous English countryside, redolent with the smell of clover and new-mown hay, with the resonant boom of the exhaust in my ears and the wind in my hair. Less fun was having to drive at night in freezing fog with the windshield folded flat because it had iced up, and I could not see. Tears streamed from my eyes and my face was numb with cold. The top part of the steering wheel became coated with ice if the wheel was not turned for a quarter of a mile, and my passenger was wrapped in a thick coat in a bundle on the floor just forward of the passenger seat.

I remember being outraged when petrol hit 5 shillings per gallon. Today it is 25 times that figure!

I put my heart and soul into the building of that car. I was absolutely determined that I would finish it, and that it would be as detailed and as perfect as I could make it. It was all consuming, and it had a detrimental effect on my studies. I decided that I would stop all work on the car for three weeks before exams every year, but all I did was sit with my books open in front of me, looking out through the window of my digs, thinking of all the jobs I could be finishing if I wasn't sitting there! I was lucky because, even though my exam results suffered, the lessons learned in building that car stood me in good stead for the rest of my life. What I was later able to achieve in building the boats that bear my name was really only an extension of what I learned while building the BMW special 30 years earlier.

Chapter 5

De Havillands, Part 2

Lodgings and Personal Relationships.

I learn what is like to live in digs and go to work every day. I make friends with people from backgrounds very different from my own. I construct a car and attend Naval Reserve training. I experience the hazards of boating and tour Scotland, including climbing Britain's highest mountain.

Collyn and I started sharing lodgings, or digs. One of them was in a block of flats opposite the main gate of De Havillands. Here, I'm afraid, we rigged the electricity meter by removing one of the rivets securing the name plate and inserting a hooked wire through the hole to stop the plate from rotating. We used strawberry jam to secure the rivet when the wire was removed.

We also shared a caravan parked at the end of the drive of a house in the country. Amongst other lessons, it was here I learned the dangers and volatility of petrol. We were having trouble getting the heating stove to light, so I tipped petrol into it. The resultant *whoosh* removed my eyebrows. One day I came into the caravan to see a cat on the table, tucking into some meat we had left there. I made the mistake of grabbing the animal, which promptly turned into a spitting, snarling whirlwind of slashing claws and vicious teeth. Big mistake!

The caravan was well out in the country, and with my car in bits during the conversion, I had to walk quite a way through country lanes from the nearest railway station on my return from weekends at home. I clearly remember one such night walking up a sunken lane with woods on one side and a typical English hedgerow on the other. There was a moon which cast eerie shadows across the road. My footsteps created a metallic ringing from the asphalt surface, and I began to fancy I could hear other footsteps behind me. I stopped and the other footsteps stopped, as well. I looked behind me but could see nothing except the deep shadows which, in my imagination, could have concealed anything. The woods were deep and mysterious, with sinister noises. The words from the "Rhyme of The Ancient Mariner" seemed very appropriate:

> *Like one that on a lonesome road doth walk in fear and dread*
> *And, having once turned round walks on and turns no more his head*
> *Because he knows a fearful fiend doth close behind him tread.*

Of course it was all a figment of my imagination, but I was very relieved to reach the caravan and shut the door.

Collyn and I later shared other digs in nearby St. Albans. In one of them, our landlady was a Mrs. Bligh, who was in her 80s. She was remarkably forbearing and, looking back, I can't imagine why she—or her neighbours—put up with us. With her permission, we painted the walls of our room in all sorts of garish colours and, after installing enormous speakers, played rock and roll music and sound effects from racing cars at high volume.

All of my various digs were an experience in their own way. Central heating was unknown in most English houses at the time, and in one set of lodgings I remember being so cold that I would wear every bit of clothing I could get into and then pile what I had left over on the bed, while I pulled all the bedclothes over my head. I slept in the foetal position, and any extension of the feet towards the bottom of the bed was like an expedition into icy Siberia.

I had another set of digs with Mrs. Bland, an elderly widow

with an alarmist view of the world. This was hardly surprising, as she read only the *News of the World*—a sensationalist, gutter press publication that fabricated stories when they could not find any sufficiently lurid to suit their taste. I wasn't allowed to have any visitors because she and her late hubby had never had any, and "what would the neighbours think!". Her only companion was a budgie on which she doted and which was allowed to fly around the room. One day she was in a great distress because the budgie had disappeared. It became worse when she discovered its forlorn corpse in the cushions, crushed when she had accidentally sat on it.

Every morning, Mrs. Bland used to serve me a cooked breakfast of greasy undercooked bacon, which was quite inedible. As soon as she went out of the room, I used to roll it up in a paper napkin and, for some extraordinary reason I am quite unable to explain, I hid these napkins on top of the wardrobe in my room. One day when I was at work she found this cache of fossilized breakfasts, and had it out with me when I came home. Why, she asked, had I not told her that I didn't want the breakfasts instead of having her waste time and money on cooking them? I really have no idea unless it was because I didn't want to hurt her feelings, but I could certainly have made up some story and, at the very least, I could have taken them out of the house instead of leaving them where she could find them. I don't remember what I told her, but to this day I have no explanation for my stupid actions.

Collyn had a variety of elderly cars, many of which I was able to drive from time to time. One of the weirdest was a Stoneleigh, probably built in the 1920s, which made a sort of chuffing sound. It had very long springs, which meant it could ride over rough ground in great comfort. There was a bull-nosed Morris and an open, sporty AC. These were followed by a rather grand Chrysler that had hydraulic, external contracting brakes and wooden, spoked wheels, on which you changed just the rims instead of the whole wheel if you had a flat tyre. The grandest of all was a 4½-litre Bentley similar to that driven by James Bond in *Casino Royale*.

I'm afraid to say that I managed to dent two of Collyn's cars. The first was the Chrysler, which he had lent me to drive home to Berkshire. The car had two defects at the time and one relevant quirk, all of which contributed to the accident. The first defect was that the hydraulic brakes were not working, and the second was that the horn was disconnected and lying on the back seat. The quirk was that the handbrake operated on the transmission shaft, and if you did not keep hold of the release lever, the brake would seize onto the shaft and be almost impossible to release. I was approaching a crossroads on a beautiful summer evening, traveling at modest speed.

As I approached the blind junction at which I had right of way, I heard a car horn blow. My immediate thought was that no one blows a horn approaching a crossroads unless they are not going to stop. Under normal circumstances I would have applied the brakes and blown my horn, but neither of these options were open to me, and I did not want to use the handbrake because that would have tied up my left hand. So I just hoped for the best while expecting the worst. Sure enough, a vintage Rolls Royce came through the Halt sign without stopping. Because I had been anticipating him, I swerved to the right and we collided at an angle. The impact sent him diagonally across the road, through a closed five-barred gate, and into a ploughed field, while I finished up in the hedge with the rim of my left front wheel knocked over its retaining rim and looped around the front axle. Amazingly the wooden-spoked wheel was undamaged, and no one was hurt. It was fortunate that we were both in substantial vehicles of about the same size and weight.

On the other occasion, Collyn had lent me his Bentley, and while I was still within the De Havilland premises I collided with a cyclist. It was dark and raining and the cyclist had his head down and no lights. I did not see him and was just pulling away from an intersection when he crashed into the radiator, putting a sizeable dent in it with his ribs before being launched over the top of the bonnet complete with his bicycle. Fortunately, he wasn't seriously injured, but I had to tell Collyn that I had bent another of his cars.

It was through Collyn that I met Carole, who also worked at De Havillands and who was also very keen on cars. Having been to an all-boys boarding school, I was very shy and felt awkward around girls. I was 19 at the time, and Carole was 21 and understood boys a lot more than I understood girls. It was all relatively innocent compared to the scene a few years later. She laughed at me when, at 19, I told her that I was afraid I was being left behind everyone else when it came to having a girlfriend. I think I was pretty goofy. Although she was my first girlfriend and I was in love with her—and I know she felt a fondness for me—we were not really an item. I renewed contact again with Carole 44 years later in 1998 and she shared with me some poems she had written about me when we were young together.

> *"Listen, my little one, you are all hurry*
> *All restless energy, overspent*
> *Leaping ambition, needless worry*
> *And desperate, driving discontent*
>
> *Half-formed ideals are as real*
> *And surely fixed in you, as are*
> *Your shining faith, the honest zeal*
> *That drives you on to chase a star*
>
> *Yours is the way of urging haste*
> *To know all that there is to know*
> *The meaning of experience, and taste*
> *Of faith disturbed that trails it so*
>
> *Your dreams will go as all illusions go*
> *You will be shown the bitter, tarnished truth*
> *You will learn nothing from it though*
> *You are all high ideals. You are all youth."*

And

> *"You are all youth and all the word conveys*
> *The swift keen air of wintry days*
> *The sultry sweetness of a summer's night*
> *The lovely mystery of morning light*
> *All purity, all courage, all desire*
> *To scale the heights and feel the fire*
> *That sears the heart and blunts the mind*
> *When childhood's sheltering sleep is left behind."* 1955

We were part of a group of friends with a common interest in motoring. We used to talk in the usual way that young people do, but my recollection is that it was mostly about cars, and our discussions were in coffee shops rather than in bars. In a way I was rather outside the group, because I was obsessed with completing the car and I did not dare to allow myself any degree of social life, because I was afraid that it would seduce me away from spending hours in a cold, cheerless garage. This antisocial behaviour probably stopped me from being tempted into becoming a smoker. I spent every penny I had on my car and had little time to sit around setting the world to rights. A couple of people in the group were older than the rest of us. One was Jim, who worked in the Ballito stocking factory in St. Albans; and another, just a few years older than myself, was John Korving, who later became Carole's husband. Collyn left to join Vauxhall motors research department and Carole later left to join the BMC motor racing dept.

Back at De Havillands, I had been moved from the Propeller Company to Special Projects, where guided missiles were built, and I was issued a special security pass. Here I spent about six months in different departments, one of which being the vibration lab, where we had to test both missile parts and ship-borne test equipment, to see how well they would withstand tough conditions. Mainly this consisted of mounting equipment on vibrators, which were like huge multi-kilowatt loudspeakers, with platforms substituted for the usual paper cones. The idea was to reveal weaknesses in the equipment being tested in a range of frequencies at different rates of G forces. We were very efficient at shaking things to pieces, and it was quite amazing to watch stuff fly apart when it reached its resonant frequency. Using stroboscopes, we could see how components were moving, and we had to write detailed reports to accompany the wreckage we returned to the designers of the equipment we had destroyed. The noise level in the lab was horrendous, but there was no thought in those days to wearing ear protection, and I am sure that my hearing has suffered slightly as a direct result of the time I spent in that lab.

I don't remember how many departments I went through during the remainder of my apprenticeship, but it was quite a few. In one I remember a Welshman who spent much of his time quoting from *Under Milk Wood,* by the Welsh poet Dylan Thomas. I do not remember his name, but I do recall a clever solution he came up with to solve a tricky problem, which taught me that a simple decision is often the best. He had to create an intricate waveform for some project he was working on. We had a number of oscilloscopes in the labs. It was possible to set them up so that a vertical trace moved from left to right across the circular screen. He first made a mask out of cardboard so that the visible part of the screen was now rectangular instead of circular. Using the camera hood attached to the oscilloscope, he substituted a photoelectric cell in place of the camera. As the vertical trace moved across the rectangular opening in the mask, the light recorded by the cell was now constant, which provided a flat waveform. By inserting an additional mask cut to the shape of the required intricate waveform, the cell now gave an electrical output to match the new mask. Thus the shape of the waveform could be adjusted in seconds with the snip of a pair of scissors. All this took less than one hour, whereas going the electronic route could have taken days.

I also worked in the telemetry lab, which specialized in capturing and recording data being transmitted by the test missiles in their short lives before they blew themselves up. It always struck me what a waste it was of real talent and money to design stuff intended to destroy and be destroyed. I also began to question why I was doing all this studying when I discovered that the janitor was earning almost as much as the junior engineers, whose ambition and horizon seemed to be limited to becoming departmental section leaders. It didn't seem much to look forward to and I was hoping for something a lot more exciting in my future life.

There were also other things happening away from my life as a De Havilland apprentice. The military draft was still in effect in England during this time, and I would have been called up for a two-year stint in the armed forces if I had not signed up for an apprenticeship, which deferred my call up until the end of the apprentice period. At the time, you could be dispatched to any branch of the armed forces if you had not made any prior provision. I had an interest in the Navy and with aircraft, so I signed up as a reservist in the Fleet Air Arm. This involved going for training 11 weekends, plus one two-week stint every year. I was sent to *HMS Hornbill* which, despite its name of "Her Majesty's Ship," was actually an airfield at Culham, near Abingdon in Oxfordshire. I had to go there in naval uniform, which is quite complicated to wear. I remember being dismayed the first time I was addressed as "Jack" (from "Jack Tar") at a left luggage counter in Paddington Station.

I was designated "Electrician's Mate 2—Unclassified" which is about as low as you can get! Because of my level of education and my job at De Havillands I had taken—and passed—every exam open to me within the first six months, with no possibility of any advancement for the remaining four and a half years. I spent most of my time at the weekends either cleaning the lavatories or taking the officers' bike up the hill from the base to the officers' mess, only to be overtaken on my way back down the hill by another officer riding it back down, so it was waiting for me when I got to the bottom.

The regular ranks who attended weekend training did not consider they had had a proper night out on Saturday if they had not gotten blind drunk and been involved in a decent punch up. So they would lurch back in the early hours covered in blood and, in one case, climbed into the bunk above me and then barfed over the side so the vomit cascaded down and sprayed onto my pillow. Needless to say, I did not take much pleasure in this or gain a very high opinion of our fighting forces. Their vocabulary was also rather limited. I remember one sailor cursing that his "effing shoe effing laces were effing well effed!"

The bunks were two tier and in a long row either side of a wooden barracks. The clean-up procedure was that the guy farthest from the door would sweep around his bed space and pass the sweepings along to the next bed, and so on down the line. My bed was about halfway down, and when it got to me, the guy next to me refused to accept the accumulated sweepings, so we got into an argument. The Chief Petty Officer came in to see what was happening, and he ordered me to sweep up the accumulation, so I started to argue with him. He just said, "Sweep it up" and I refused. He repeated his instruction in a distinctly ominous tone, and I figured I had better do what he said. He told me afterwards that if I received an order I had to obey it and then argue about it afterwards. He was right, of course. A ship is a fighting machine and no place for people to dispute orders.

While under training, I had my first ever flight. This was in a De Havilland Dragon Rapide, which was a biplane made of plywood—a design which first flew in 1934. Flying was not an everyday event for the ordinary person in 1954, so it was an exciting experience seeing the land drop away beneath me for the first time.

The planes being flown by the weekend RNVR pilots were Sea Furies, with monster Bristol Centaurus radial engines. They were a marvel of intricate engineering, and I remember one reservist fitter struggling to install a component that he couldn't get to fit and working his way around the engine, removing adjacent components. This squadron was the last to fly these aircraft with the five-bladed props; being naval aircraft, they had folding wings. Engines were started by firing a cartridge into the cylinders to turn over the engine, which gradually spluttered into life, emitting clouds of smoke from the ear-splitting exhaust stubs.

We were moved to share the airfield at RAF Benson with the Queen's Flight. One weekend the base was to be visited by the group captain, which set off the usual run-around of, "If it moves salute it and, if it doesn't, paint it white". Seeing all the fuss and bother, I was struck by the thought that my father had been a group captain, and I had never realized the weight that pulled.

I came to know one of the test pilots at De Havillands, and he took me up in a Meteor jet, which was one of the company's test aircraft. He did a bunch of aerobatics, including loops, step rolls, and barrel rolls, and he flew me from the airfield at Hatfield over my home just outside Ipswich in less than five minutes. This was on a Friday, and it took me over two and a half hours to make the same journey by train later that day. I remember the dirt falling past me into the canopy when the aircraft was upside down and the dragging feeling of the G forces at the bottom of a dive as well as the feeling of weightlessness at the top of a loop with the earth above me and the sky below.

This pilot's main job was to fly fast jet aircraft a few feet above the runway, so that technicians crouched beside the runway could test the ability of the missile's infrared homing sensor to follow the heat from the jet exhaust. He told me that he had to hold the joystick forward as the aircraft bounced off its shockwaves from the ground. It was a most impressive sight with a layer of mist hovering above the wings as the aircraft screamed at head height along the runway at around 600 mph. He did this one time with me on board and, although the runway seemed to approach quite slowly, it flashed beneath us in a matter of seconds.

In June 1953, while I was serving my naval training, we had to prepare for inspection by the newly crowned Queen Elizabeth II in Horseguards' Parade, in London. This involved going down to Portsmouth and being drilled for four days prior to the event. Everyone bitched about how hard it was, but I felt very superior and thought the whole thing was a bit of a joke because neither the discipline nor the standard came remotely close to matching what I had experienced at school. Unfortunately, the event itself was a bit of a disaster, because torrential rain dissolved the white Blanco on our matelot hats and belts and bled white all over our dark blue uniforms. However, the young queen managed to look quite regal as she rode her horse side-saddle between the soggy ranks.

At some time during this period we went with my mother for a week's holiday on Lake Windermere, in England's Lake District. We were joining some long-term friends of my mother's. I chiefly remember it as a prime example of just how easy it is to get into trouble on a boat, as it seemed to be a litany of minor disasters that are quite humorous in retrospect but were quite alarming at the time. My mother's friends were quite well to do and had a motorboat—probably around 35 feet—and also a couple of sons a bit older than myself. The first episode was when the owner rashly allowed us to take the boat down the lake by ourselves. On the first evening we lowered the anchor to the bottom and retired for the night. I was awakened by thumping, shouting, and the flashing of lights. It appeared that we had drifted into another boat. The next night we went right down to Newby Bridge at the extreme southern end of the lake. When we got up in the morning, the battery was completely flat. We could see a service station on the shore, so we disconnected the battery, lowered it into the dinghy, and rowed ashore, to discover that the service station had no battery-charging equipment. Two of us then decided to hitchhike down the lake to the owner of the boat to get another battery or ask what to do. We instructed the other boy just to return to the boat and leave the battery in the dinghy.

We returned to the boat with a service guy and a replacement battery in another boat. We could not see the original battery in the dinghy, and when we asked where it was, the third boy pointed to the water. He had tried to lift it back aboard by himself, and as he leant forward, the dinghy shot away from under him and, if he hadn't let go, he would have accompanied the battery to the bottom of the lake. Although we looked, we never did find it!

The other events of that week involved a small sailing dinghy. We went with the owner of the power boat, and after they had dropped anchor some distance up the lake, my sister and I got into the dinghy to go sailing. The trouble arose because they thought I knew how to sail, and I thought they knew that I did not! There was a nice breeze, and we scooted off downwind. I had it figured out that I would tack back upwind and then bring the dinghy's head to the wind when we reached them out in the middle of the lake. The problem was that it took me quite a while to figure out how to make the boat move upwind, and they got fed up with waiting and went home.

So now I had to sail the boat much further downwind and then bring it alongside a jetty that stuck out into the water at right angles from a lee shore. This was quite a different situation, further complicated by the number of boats anchored all around the jetty. On our way to our rendezvous with the jetty, we were approaching a buoy while still well out in the lake. I had noticed a bunch of powerful keel boats obviously racing in close quarters, and to my horror I suddenly realized that they were heading for the same buoy and that we were going to get there at about the same time. I had no idea what to do—so I did nothing! We were right alongside the buoy as the first boats rounded it three abreast, with their crews yelling and a tremendous rattling of blocks and shriek of winches as they hardened up on the wind. We continued to drift across the course and by good fortune there was just sufficient space for the next group of boats to pass between our stern and the buoy.

We continued running before the wind at a good pace as we approached the jetty. As I swerved around each of the anchored boats, the wind caught the back side of the sail and slammed the boom across to the other side of the boat in a process known as gybing. In alarm, I thrust the tiller the other way and the boom came scything back, missing our heads by inches. This was repeated several times until we rammed the jetty at undiminished speed. Overlooking this was the hotel terrace where all the sailors, the owner of the boat, and my mother were taking their afternoon tea!

In the final episode, my sister and I were bobbing around in the same dinghy in the middle of the mirror-calm lake with not a breath of wind. It was all very peaceful, then I noticed that the ferry from Bowness was approaching us. This is quite a short crossing, and the ferry pulls itself across the lake on a chain that is submerged except where it is lifted by the ferry. The oars had been tucked away under the dinghy's seats, and I only had time to extricate one of them when the chain came up under the boat, pushed the bow under the ramp, and pulled the transom up onto the chain sprocket—unshipping the rudder as it did so. It was evident that the ferry had been left to find its own way across the lake. My sister and I climbed up onto the ferry ramp to look for someone in charge. A head popped out of a hatch, saw what had happened and said, "Stop the ferry, Bert". Bert duly halted the ferry, and we climbed back into the dinghy and were pushed back into water minus one oar and the rudder. The ferry continued on its way, and after it had passed, the wooden oar and rudder floated to the surface. We were able to retrieve them, using the remaining oar for propulsion. It is really amazing that I ever went aboard a boat again.

On the home front, my mother decided to move from Five Gables in East Anglia to a thatched cottage in Whitchurch Hill, up the hill from Pangbourne on the River Thames, after hearing my glowing description of the scenery seen from the train on my visits for naval training. The cottage, with its thick thatched roof and exposed beams, was charming, and I remember my first visit sitting in front of a blazing fire in the little parlour, eating beef stew.

One year, Collyn and I went on a camping trip to Scotland in his AC vintage touring car. The engine kept on stopping, because the SU electric fuel pump would conk out and required a thump to get it working again. Fortunately, it was mounted on the bulkhead under the bonnet, so we tied a piece of string to it and every time the engine faltered, we tugged on the string to get the pump going again.

We had the canvas hood down for our drive north. The Midlands were still pretty dirty in those days, and smuts rained down out of the skies. We stopped at a grocer's shop to buy some butter, and the shop assistant looked at us in astonishment, "Booter?" she said. "Booter? We dawn't sell booter 'ere!". It turned out we had to go to the dairy to buy "booter"!

Once we had crossed the Scottish border, we drove up the West Coast, where the road would loop around the head of the sea lochs and then climb over the next promontory to descend again around the head of the next loch. It gave us the feeling that we were passing a series of gates leading us ever deeper into the Scottish Highlands. We stopped at the top of one of the climbs and heard the strains of the bagpipes from an unseen piper. It was an eerie and appropriate sound in those rugged and remote surroundings, and it has stayed with me over the years.

We camped along the way, but I remember in particular camping amongst some of the fierce-looking Highland cattle in Glen Nevis at the base of Ben Nevis, which at 4,406 feet is the highest mountain in Britain. Looking at the mountains, whose tops were concealed in cloud, we noticed a stream of diminutive ant-like figures making their way diagonally across the adjacent mountain. We figured this must be Ben Nevis, so we thought that can't be hard, and set off to climb it, ill equipped and with all the rashness of youth. It turned out to be a really difficult climb, which went on for much longer than anticipated. Breasting each rise only revealed another—as is the way with all mountains. The path was steep, and when we got to the top everything was wrapped in a grey, clammy mist. As is also the way with all mountains, the descent was even harder, as tired muscles had to control our jelly legs down the steep rocks.

When we came to leave our campsite, the wheels of the AC lost traction and spun on the boggy ground. Collyn reduced the tyre pressures and was able to drive the car out. This was another valuable lesson learned, which I was able to use to advantage in later years.

The military draft was still just in force when I completed my apprenticeship in August 1957, but it was about to come to an end. I was now 22, and I certainly did not wish to spend the next two years in the military. To my way of thinking, a stint in the military can wean people away from the home environment and impart some discipline in their lives, but I had lived away from home since I was barely eight and had endured strict discipline at school plus had military training, including the use of guns, at school and during my apprenticeship for the last 10 years. I did not feel that I needed to learn anything that the military could teach me, and I wanted to get on with my life.

I had been sitting at a desk in front of a blackboard for 16 years—including my studies at Hatfield Technical College—and I was thoroughly sick of it. I didn't want any more lectures. I wanted to get out there and do something. Britain was different from the United States in that they did not come after you if you were not in the country, so the way I could avoid being conscripted was to go abroad. Once again, my mother played a part, because she had a friend who lived in what was then Southern Rhodesia. Britain still had most of her colonies in those days, although the winds of change were starting to blow. So it was decided that as soon as my apprenticeship finished at the end of August, I would leave for Southern Rhodesia, in Central Africa.

However, fate had another episode in store for me before this happened. My sister, Carolyn –known in the family as LuLu—had been studying at a secretarial college in Devon, and the course finished at much the same time as my apprenticeship. She had a couple of friends there, one called Jill and the other, Sandra or Sandy. Sandy's parents lived in Singapore and she was returning there at the end of August. Sandy came to stay with us for her last couple of weeks in England before returning to the Far East. During this time, we fell for one another and it was really a bittersweet situation. I knew that within a few days she was going to a place that seemed unimaginably far away, and I would be going to an unknown future in the middle of Africa. Well, there it was. One of those unfortunate bits of timing—a brief encounter but one which, as it turned out, would have far-reaching effects well into the future.

Much had happened during this five-year period. I had been an apprentice and learned technical and working skills at a major aircraft company. I had served in the Navy Reserve and had taken to the air for the first time in propeller and jet aircraft. I had learnt to drive and built a car with my own hands. I had fallen in love twice. I had climbed the highest mountain in Britain. And now I was about to leave the country to who knows what. My precious car was left in the hands of Collyn to sell and was advertised for 395 pounds. In a surprising development, which I will expound on much later in this memoir, my BMW Special resurfaced in Germany in 2009, in concourse condition, so the work I had put into it stood the test of time.

De Havillands was taken over by Hawker Siddeley just three years after I left, and 17 years after that, it became part of British Aerospace. That spelled the end of the facility in Hatfield. The airfield was redeveloped and was even used as one of the locations for the film *Saving Private Ryan*. Astwick Manor was converted to luxury apartments in 2004.

Book 2
AFRICA

TAKING THE PLUNGE

Nanyuki

Nairobi

Mombasa
Zanzibar
Dar es Salaam

Mbeya

Lusaka
Salisbury

1958 – 1959

Chapter 1

September 1957 to Early 1958

Arrive Rhodesia and Idol Mine.

I fly to Rhodesia and become a Learner Miner at the remote Idol Mine deep in the African bush.

The plane was a Britannia four-engine turbo-prop, which, despite its nickname—the Whispering Giant—still seemed to generate a lot of interior noise for the passengers. Strangely, I do not remember anything of the actual leave-taking at Heathrow, even though I was making my first solo departure for foreign parts, with no idea when I might be returning. It amazes me now that my mother could have been so self-sacrificing not only to let me go but even to encourage my departure. The route to Salisbury went via Rome, Benghazi, Khartoum, and Nairobi, where we had the good fortune to break down for six hours, so the airline arranged a bus trip for the passengers to the game park just outside the city. In the park, I was impressed by all the animals wandering free while we sat in our mobile cage; and, in the city, the novelty of the billboards advertising such familiar things as Cadbury's cocoa with happy black faces. There was a signpost at Nairobi Airport giving the distances to all sorts of remote places.

Looking down on the vast semi-desert areas of Africa, I remember thinking that the little blobs of vegetation reminded me of the way hair grows on the head of the countries' inhabitants.

After 25 hours of travel, we arrived in Salisbury. I was met by a long-time friend of my mother called Pat Hadden, whose brother had promised to help me look for a job. She drove me to her house not far from the centre of the city, in a wide street lined with jacaranda trees in full bloom. Against the cloudless sky they formed an enchanting avenue of bluebell blue, with each tree standing in its pool of fallen blossoms. The streets were tarmac, with wide verges of dry grass and red dust. The smell of dried grass and dust is the very scent of Africa—pungent and evocative to those who have experienced it. The house was a simple but pleasant bungalow, with its own small garden in front and, at the back, a small separate living quarters for the servant.

I knew South Africa practiced apartheid, but "federation" was the word used to describe the system in the Central African colonies of Northern and Southern Rhodesia and Nyasaland. The rest of the world understood this to mean equal rights for everyone—in fact, they used to ask if you wanted your coffee black or federated—but, in reality, it was just apartheid under a different name. Buses and park benches were segregated, and blacks were not even allowed to enter department stores but had to make their purchases through little windows down the side. How they knew what was available I have no idea, and at the time I never thought to ask, although it must have struck me for the question to have stuck in my mind for all these years. Living areas, too, were segregated, and a black person had to have a permit to be in a white area. This was similar to the hated pass-laws in South Africa, which were later to be the cause of so much unrest. Ostensibly these laws were to protect the blacks themselves, and there may have been some justification for it, because the traditional laws of hospitality required an African to provide a bed and sustenance for every stranger who showed up on his doorstep under the guise of being his brother. A brother was anyone from the same tribe, so a servant living in a tiny room on a minimal wage could find himself having to share his meagre possessions with an endless stream of his kin drawn to the city. As odious as the laws were, this aspect was never mentioned by those who opposed them.

Within a couple of days, I went to see Pat's brother, Mike, about a job. He asked me whether I wanted to work in the city or in the bush. Without knowing why, I said I preferred the city, and he arranged an interview for me at a place overhauling diesel engines. The man in charge was English and, pre-judging me by the way I spoke, he said, "You'll avter get yer 'ands dirty 'ere". No one could ever accuse me of being a person concerned with keeping my hands—or any part of me—clean, but I had no interest in fighting that kind of stupid prejudice. So I told Mike that I had changed my mind and was more interested after all in a job in the bush. In fact, a life the bush was so much more in tune with my nature, I cannot think why I did not choose that option in the first place. Before I left, Mike gave me a piece of advice which I have not always followed but which I completely endorse. He said, "Always settle into a place as if you intend to stay there for a long time. If you don't, you will spend your whole life camping. Everyone always stays in a place longer than they expect, and temporary arrangements have a habit of becoming permanent."

A few days later I was flown out to the location of a mica mine, in a remote area not far from the Mozambique border. There was Mike, a fellow called Ron Tatham, myself, and the pilot in a four-seater Cessna. The terrain was very dry and rugged, and we circled the location of the mine and living area before flying on to Fungwe airstrip, about 20 miles away. We buzzed the strip a couple of times to chase the cows off it before making a bumpy landing on the rough surface. At the edge of the field was a small shelter made from rough poles, and beside that stood an African holding a hand fire extinguisher. Also waiting were a battered American Army Jeep and Peter, a well-spoken Englishman in well-pressed khaki shirt and shorts. Introductions were made, and we climbed into the Jeep for the journey to the mine.

The road was just a rough track through the bush, which here was a mixture of grass and trees. After half an hour, we crossed the Mazoe River, reached the mine, and met Fred Schultz, the mine manager. Fred was a tall, white, rangy Rhodesian with a dry sense of humour. He had lived in the bush and been a miner all his life and talked of nothing but gold. It had a fascination for him, but despite a lifetime of looking, not much of it had stuck to his nicotine-stained fingers. He was married to a coloured woman—half black and half white—and their daughter Yvette was about four years old and always into mischief. Outraged cries of "Yvette!" regularly rang across the compound as her mother discovered the latest of her daughter's depredations. Fred used to amuse himself in the evenings by shooting the rats scuttling across the rafters of their hut. As I said at the time, "You could tell Fred's house because it was the one with bullets coming out of the roof."

And so, in October 1957, at age 22, I started work as a Learner Miner at the Idol Mine operated by Rhodesia Mica Mining. My pay was 50 pounds a month, and I saved every penny of it because food and lodging were provided by the company and the nearest shop was in Mt. Darwin, more than 100 miles away, over roads which were impassable in the wet season and which took the truck one week to negotiate for the round trip in the dry. This part of the country was set aside as a native reserve, and no whites were normally allowed to live there. But in Rhodesia mining made all things possible, and we were among the few exceptions to the rule.

The mine was primitive, with three working shafts, each about 80 feet deep. Not for us the mighty headgears with their huge rotating wheels. Instead, over each shaft were four-legged frames made from 4-inch diameter steel pipe with a steel pulley set in the top. The "cage" was simply a large metal bucket suspended at the end of a perilously thin cable. You descended by reaching out and pulling the cable towards you and putting one leg into the bucket. The other leg was used to fend off from the jagged walls as the bucket swung back and forth. One hand was used to hold the cable and, unless the other could grab the air pipe, there was a good chance the bucket would spin round and round, making you so giddy you could not stand up without support and would spill out of the bucket into the muddy mess at the bottom of the shaft. Each hoist was operated by an operator who sat on a seat made from an old packing case and manipulated a lever to control the electric winch.

The shafts were about 100 yards apart and followed the underground line of the quartz reef. Grouped around the main shaft were a number of sheds with corrugated iron roofs supported on rough tree trunks cut from the local bush. These sheds were used to cut and sort the mica, and one was a workshop with welding and other equipment. Nearby was the compound where the mine workers lived. This looked like any other African village with its circular huts, their walls made of sticks stuck into the ground side by side and then plastered over with red mud and thatched with grass.

The bush hereabouts was dry and dusty, and the rains only fell for about two months a year. Much of the vegetation was thorn bush, with here and there massive baobab trees, which stored water inside their bloated trunks. Their grey leathery bark resembled the hide of an elephant, and they were known locally as "devil trees" because it was said the devil became enraged and pulled them out by the roots, replanting them upside down. At certain times of the year, these strange trees would bear greenish pods with seeds inside surrounded by a hard white powder. This was the source of cream of tartar. The terrain was rugged and rock strewn, with isolated hills, or kopjes, sticking up from the bush.

We whites lived in another compound about three miles away, on the banks of the Mazoe River, which provided the only source of water for the villagers in the area. Our huts were also made of wattle and daub with grass roofs, but were rectangular rather than circular. Except for sleeping, I shared with Robin. His hut was divided into two sections. The larger part was living/dining, with the remainder for his sleeping quarters. We sat at a table for eating and always had table napkins. I was a little surprised by this elegance, but Robin said, "It's very easy to slip into slovenliness in this kind of environment, and you have to keep up standards, even in the smallest things."

There were chairs and small tables set all around the walls, and no matter which chair you sat in or which hand you reached out, there was always a pick handle within easy reach. The purpose of these became clear my first evening, when the kitten suddenly darted out and started batting a small brown scorpion back and forth. Robin casually looked up from his book, grabbed a pick handle, blatted the creature into oblivion, and continued reading.

Scorpions had to be taken seriously, and I was warned to shake out my boots every morning before putting them on. Although I never found one inside, I did this meticulously—feeling every time I did so like a character in some boy's adventure story. Scorpions also liked to gather around the generator, because of its warmth. This was switched off at 11 o'clock every night, and you had to step very carefully—especially after you had shut down the generator and all the lights went out.

Many other creatures shared our huts. Wood borers steadily munched their way through the beams supporting the roof, and streams of fine sawdust trickled down onto everything below, including the unprotected record rotating on Robin's record player. There was a kind of brush arrangement that rode on the record just ahead of the needle, like a mini road sweeper, to push the dust aside.

I slept in a separate structure made from a piece of heavy green canvas stretched over a centre ridge pole with two subsidiary ridges on either side to form a kind of tent with both ends open. Screens made from tall grass and sticks provided some privacy at each end. The floor was packed mud, but another piece of green canvas was laid on the ground with a bed sitting in the centre of it. The bed was enclosed by a mosquito net, which was supposed to be white but like everything was stained red by the all-pervading dust.

The cooking was done by a diminutive, plump African who went by the name of Tiki. A tiki was a small Rhodesian coin and was an allusion to the cook's size. He was married and had five children who all looked exactly like him. When Tiki went fishing with his children, they followed behind him in single file, in size order, with Tiki leading the way and the smallest bring up the rear, like a series of Russian *matrioshka* dolls. Tiki had one pair of shoes, which he wore only on Sundays. One Sunday he came rushing into the hut, bubbling over with excitement because a large scorpion had attacked his foot as he entered his kitchen, but, being Sunday, it had only succeeded in blunting its sting against Tiki's boot before being crushed for its impudence. On any other day of the week, the boot, so to speak, would have been on the other foot.

Tiki used to bring me tea at 5 o'clock every morning, and one day he woke me full of excitement as he pointed to a circle of footprints in the dust around my bed, just outside the floor canvas. I had been visited during the night by one or more hyenas, and I am glad I did not awake while they were prowling around my bed. The hyena is a cowardly creature that eats carrion or preys on the weak and helpless. If unsure of the strength of their quarry, they will sometimes run at it and take a swipe on their way past and then stop at a safe distance to evaluate the results of their action. I imagine they must have been discouraged by the white bulk of my mosquito net.

Although we lived in the middle of a native reserve, there were still many wild animals in the bush with which we occasionally came in contact. Our link with the outside world was a radio-telephone used on a regular schedule with the office in Salisbury. One night a herd of elephant came blundering through the compound and knocked down the aerials. Crocodiles lived in the river and occasionally went off with one of the women taking a bath. There were also a pair of hippo, until some cretin drove out from Salisbury and shot one at point-blank range from the bridge and left its body slowly circling feet up in the pool below. At night, a sound similar to the sawing of wood betrayed the presence of a prowling nocturnal leopard.

Work in the mine started every day at 2 a.m., when the men went down to start clearing away the debris from the previous day's blasting. These crews were called "lashers" from the local word meaning "to throw away". The waste rock and blocks of mica were loaded into little trolley cars and pushed to the base of the shafts along rail tracks laid in the tunnels. They were hoisted to the surface, and those containing waste rock were pushed along more tracks to the edge of the dump, where the contents were added to the growing pile of "tailings"—a distinctive and unsightly feature of any mine. The useful mica was sent to the shed, where the "books" were split and sorted. Mica is a strange material, looking more man-made than natural. Even though the books might be several feet thick, the mica could be split into papery thin leaves, and the term "book" was very appropriate. Mica was precisely graded according to size, colour, flatness, and freedom from the colourful impurities that would interfere with its effectiveness as an insulator.

We did not start work until 6 a.m., just as the big red ball of the sun was climbing over the horizon. We spent the first two hours organizing and preparing the work before returning to the compound for breakfast.

By the time we had finished eating, a line had formed outside the small building that served as a dispensary. For security, this building was the only one built of rough, locally made bricks, and it had a tin roof. Strictly speaking, there was no obligation to provide medical facilities to anyone who did not work for the mine, but it was hard to refuse them to local people whose only alternative was to go to a mission clinic 35 miles away over rough country. The most common problems were with eyes, coughs, and stomach complaints. There was stuff in bottles shaped and sized like those for red wine for each of these complaints, but our real ace in the hole was penicillin, which we used and abused for everything when the bulk medicine—or muti—failed to do the job. Penicillin in vials intended for injection had instant results when a couple of drops were applied to even the most festering of eyes, and several children were saved from certain death by injections of this miraculous drug. But, alas, we were not always successful, and I saw my first dead person while at the Idol Mine. She was a young woman, the wife of one of the miners. She died very suddenly, had complained of a headache just the night before. From what I have been told since, she probably suffered from a brain haemorrhage. As she lay there on the rude bed in the hut, she could have been asleep, but looking down on her body, I was struck with the very strong impression that the person who lived in that body had gone and all that was left was the empty husk. The husband was crying quietly nearby, and my heart went out to him.

On another occasion a pair of twins was born, and the midwife said that one was born without an anus and subsequently died. I do not know whether this was true, because it was still common practice only to allow one of a pair of twins to survive. According to superstition, twins were supposed to bring bad luck to the tribe, but the real reason was probably that it was too hard to rear two children simultaneously in marginal conditions, and it was better to kill one from the outset to give the other a better chance of survival. There were no cemeteries or graveyards in the bush, and bodies were buried in any convenient location and covered with rocks to prevent their them from being dug up by wild animals.

By the time the sick parade was over and we returned to the mine, the lashers had finished for the day and the drillers—or hammer-boys—had gone down to start preparing the rock face for blasting. They used rock drills driven by compressed air jack-hammers. These are a cruder but more rugged version of the tools used to break up road surfaces, and the noise in the confined underground chambers can be imagined. Water was injected down the centre of the drills-bit to lubricate the carbide tip, flush out the debris, and keep down the dust so, added to the percussive roar of the drills, were the combined discomforts of the shriek of escaping air, working in a fine mist of oily water and being shaken to bits by the jumping jack-hammers.

There was no electricity underground; the only light came from the flickering flames of carbide lamps. These were metal cylinders about three inches in diameter and six inches high, with a carrying handle on the top and a small spout sticking out of the side. The top part unscrewed from the bottom, and lumps of carbide were put in the bottom section and water in the top. The water dripped onto the carbide, creating acetylene gas, which came out of the spout and, when lit, burned with a weak yellow flame.

Meanwhile, on the surface, men and women would be splitting, cutting, and grading the mica into boxes, and down in the nearby creek, charges were being prepared for blasting. Both gelignite and dynamite were used and came in sticks about nine inches long and one inch in diameter. Aluminium detonators were crimped to the end of lengths of fat white fuse cord and pushed into holes made in the ends of the sticks of explosive. To be effective, the explosive had to be tamped tight in the holes and, for this purpose, cylinders of sand, made to the same size as the sticks of explosive, were formed by rolling river sand in cylinders of scrap paper.

Drilling was usually finished by around noon, and the rule of the mine was that blasting took place at two in the afternoon, when work finished for the day. I will never forget the first time I went down to watch the loading of the face and the lighting of the explosive charges. I shared the bucket with one of two foremen— or boss-boys—as we went down the shaft, carrying the explosives, already primed with detonators, in cardboard gelignite boxes with fuse wire threaded through the top to act as carrying handles.

On that particular day, two lots of charges were to be set off in the one tunnel — one at the face of the reef on its way through the adjoining ground, and the other closer to the main shaft in a "riser" being driven up from the bottom towards the surface. I accompanied the boss-boy loading the horizontal face. Working from the holes at the centre, he pushed the gelignite down each hole with the detonator innermost and the fuse folded back alongside the stick. On top of each stick of gelignite he put two sticks of dynamite, followed by two cylinders of sand. He pushed each of these down the holes with a long pointed stick which he then used to tamp the whole lot down tight, using what seemed to be an alarming amount of vigour. The centre holes had been drilled at converging angles with the rest drilled straight and in concentric rings. The centre charges were set to go off first, so as to blow out a cone-shaped wedge of rock, followed at intervals by the rings, innermost first, so each ring of rock was blown into an increasingly large space in the centre.

Soon the face sprouted all over with fuse cord, and the boss-boy looped these together in groups, according to the order in which they were to be fired. Only the interior of the fuse burned, so each fuse would burn individually and not jump across to its neighbour even when in intimate contact with it.

In the meantime, the second face between ourselves and the shaft to the surface was also being charged. Drilling a shaft up from the tunnel below was a difficult and dangerous undertaking, because the drillers, balanced on timbers wedged into the vertical walls, had to push the drills up into the ceiling, and all the water and debris rained down on top of them. The fellow loading the charges had to push all the explosives into the holes above him and, after lighting the fuses, climb down about twenty feet of timbers propped into the walls and beat a hasty retreat before tons of rock face and all the timbers came down on top of him. If he slipped and hurt himself on the way down, it was all over for him. The two loaders shouted to each other when they were ready to light up, and we started slightly in advance. The fuses were difficult to light with ordinary matches, so a special device called a chisa stick was used. Its name derived from *chisa*, the local word for fire. This hissed and burned rather like a smaller version of the flares used in the U.S. to warn of road accidents, but it was held in the hand and had a very hot flame. It was ideal for the job because there was no time for unreliability in the lighting of fuses, where timing was critical and any delay could quite literally be fatal.

Working from the centre, the boss-boy began lighting the fuses, which hissed and sparked. He worked methodically and, I increasingly thought, with excruciating slowness, pausing after lighting each ring before moving on to the next one. It took several minutes to light them all, and by the time he had finished the last in the outer ring, those in the centre were just disappearing down the holes in the rock face. I was getting increasingly nervous—especially with the thought of the other set of fuses already burning between us and the shaft—but my companion seemed in no hurry to leave, and I assumed he knew what he was doing and valued his own skin, and I did not want to look foolish in his eyes. After making sure that all fuses were burning, and he had not missed any, he said "OK, baas, let's go". It seemed ironic he should still call me "Boss" when I was so ignorant and he held my life in his hands!

We walked back to the second face and stood waiting at the bottom for the other man, while the fuses sparked and winked above our heads like fireflies. After what seemed an eternity, the man joined us and we set off towards the shaft at a leisurely pace, while all the time my mind was occupied with those spitting fuses as they hissed their way down towards the waiting explosives. Finally came a rapid succession of heavy thumps and with them, not the blast of air I had expected, but a pressure wave which was felt on the ears and which immediately extinguished the carbide lamps, leaving us in total darkness. The pressure in the tunnel had momentarily exceeded that in the lamps, interrupting the flow of gas and extinguishing the flame. My companions were completely unfazed as, to them, this was routine, and we continued to feel our way along the tunnel in the inky blackness, accompanied by more thumps and pressure waves as blasts followed in quick succession. Finally, a welcome glimmer of daylight from the shaft could be seen ahead, and soon we were back on the surface.

After blasting, work was finished for the day, because the

mine had only natural ventilation and it took several hours for the dangerous gases caused by the explosives to disperse. The 2 o'clock rule for blasting was for safety reasons, but I will never forget the day one of the men decided to break it. When the distance from the face to the shaft became too long, it was decided to add a new shaft. This was to be Shaft Number Four, and the work went quickly because there was no valuable mica to worry about and the distance from the rock face to the surface was short and direct. On this particular day, the new shaft had reached the required depth and had just started its horizontal drive to follow the reef. The work had finished early on this embryo shaft, and everything was ready for blasting by noon. The foreman had seen no reason to delay and, without consulting anyone, had gone down to charge and light up.

Unfortunately, in a classic example of Murphy's Law, Fred had chosen that particular day to stop the generator for routine maintenance — cutting the power to the electric winches when the foreman was in the bucket on his way to the surface, just twenty feet above the bottom of the shaft with fuses already hissing beneath him. When the winch stopped, an urgent cry came from the operator at the top of the shaft, and frantic efforts were made to restart the generator but, being hot, it refused to start.

In common with much of the equipment designed for use in the bush, the generator had to be started by hand, and sweat poured from the ebony bodies of the two men wrestling with the heavy handle like athletes working the coffee-grinder winches on a modern racing yacht. When they fell back, exhausted, two more sprang forward to take their place, their calloused feet scrabbling in the loose dust. A crowd quickly gathered as the word spread, and you could physically feel the tension in the air. Everyone's thoughts, including mine, were on the man marooned in the bucket, the spitting lines of fire hissing their way along the thick white fuse cables below him, and the blizzard of deadly shards that would erupt as soon as they reached the charges.

Fred had already been standing by the generator when it was stopped. "Stupid munt," he fumed, as he urged on the men working the handle and fiddled with the throttle. "Bloody stupid fucking kaffir." Then, remembering a trick, he sent a worker down to the Jeep to bring back a rag soaked in petrol. As he ran back with it, there came a dull rumble from under our feet and a cloud of dust erupted from the shaft. With the rag held near the air intake, the diesel instantly burst into life with violent pre-detonation, and everyone's eyes went to the headgear with its now slowly turning pulley. The bucket emerged from the ground containing, to everyone's relief, the enraged figure of the boss-boy whose terror, with the catalyst of relief, had turned to extreme rage. He leapt out of the bucket and came down the hill with murder in his eyes at such speed that his feet only touched the ground every six feet. When he reached the engine shed, he leaped upon the unfortunate engine boy and would have killed him had he not been stopped by the onlookers. The whole incident had been entirely his own fault, and with the relief of a happy conclusion, the crowd gave way to the uninhibited mirth only Africans can show— literally rolling on the ground in an orgy of hilarity.

Everyone tends to use the tools at hand to fix a problem, and at a mining camp, this tool is dynamite. Kill a snake? Put a stick down the hole. Move a tree or a boulder? Blow it up. Frighten off the crocs before you go swimming? Toss a stick into the water. One Sunday I went with Fred and his family to visit a fellow miner several miles away. The track was atrocious, but we went in Fred's battered American car, which managed to lurch its way to our destination, scraping its belly most of the way. There I was introduced to Fred's friend, who carried the most appalling scars on his face, arms, and upper torso. He had been mining in the bush with the mine on one side of the river and his living quarters on the other. He commuted from one to the other every day by swimming. He knew there were crocodiles in the river but threw a half stick of dynamite into the water before plunging in. Apparently the creatures became used to it and even came to regard it as some kind of dinner gong, because one day he plunged into the open jaws of a waiting crocodile.

"How did you escape?", I asked, amazed that, even though battered, he should still be here to tell the tale.

"I put my thumbs in its eyes and pressed as hard as I could

until it let me go."

Talk about presence of mind—I was impressed! A crocodile does not brush his teeth too often, and even if you survive the actual bite, you are lucky not to succumb to the septicaemia which inevitably follows.

Every evening just before sunset, Robin and I used to go down to the river to bathe. Because of the crocodiles, we chose a place where the water was shallow and there was good visibility all around, so they could not sneak up on us. And because of bilharzia we chose a place where the water ran fast. One of the hidden plagues of Africa, bilharzia is a parasitic disease of the liver, causing years of lethargy and premature death. It has been estimated that perhaps as many as 80 percent of rural Africans suffer from it. One of the links in the life-cycle of the parasite is a water-borne snail, and after passing through it, the larvae infects humans by actually penetrating the intact skin of a person entering the water. Once in the body, the parasite finds its way to the liver, where it takes up residence and breeds into adult worms. Their eggs are passed out of the body in the urine, which goes into the streams and the cycle repeats. The only cure — at least in those days — was a succession of increasingly large doses of antimony, administered by injection through a large needle, which had such unpleasant side-effects the cure was reckoned to be worse than the disease. It was generally believed you were safe if you stuck to fast flowing water –so that is what we did!

In the mornings we used to wash and shave, using an enamel basin on a metal stand just outside Robin's hut. Every day a steady parade of women, kids, and domestic animals passed the edge of our unfenced compound, on their way to the river to wash, drink, and collect water. The healthiest looking animals were always the goats, which were able to find nourishment in the most barren of environments. It seemed they would eat anything, and one morning a goat ate up our bar of soap with evident enjoyment.

Some of the women used to walk miles each day to and from the river, and on the return journey carried large metal "debbies" full of water on their heads, with only a ring made from woven grass to cushion the load. These held five gallons of water,

90

weighing 50 pounds plus the weight of the container. They placed small branches in the debbies to act as baffles to stop the water slopping and spilling. This was a heavy weight to carry on the head, especially up the steep bank from the river, but they walked with a fine upright carriage and seldom used their hands to support the load on their heads. Many also had children strapped to their backs, and among the women was one I noticed whose belly was grossly swollen in pregnancy. The next day I saw her again—no longer pregnant—with the same heavy load on her head and with a tiny baby on her back.

It was the obligation of the mine to provide rations to the workers. These came in the form of maize meal, salt, peanuts, and meat. We had kerosene-powered refrigerators, but there was no general refrigeration, so the meat had to be killed and eaten the same day. In fact, it was so fresh that it was eating grass when we went to collect it. We used to drive about 20 miles to a general store operated by one of the few other whites in the reserve. Each week he obtained a cow for the meat ration. For humane reasons it was shot in the middle of the forehead with a rifle and then, because we had a few Muslims in the crew, its throat was cut almost before it had hit the ground. The blood gushed out, and most was caught in an enamel basin. In its death throes, the wretched animal continued to moo through its ripped open throat. Flies buzzed and settled on the carcass, and mongrel dogs sidled up to lick the blood off the grass. Women and children stood around to watch as the animal was skinned and disembowelled. It was enough to turn the most rabid meat-eater into an instant vegetarian. Only us whites got to select "cuts" of meat. Everyone else just got "meat" which was dished out according to weight, without any regard to which part of the animal it came from. I really do not know whether this was actually as unfair as it sounds, as my impression was that, when they had it, Africans normally just hacked lumps off the carcass without being too worried about the niceties of butchering. After being cut up, the meat was put in the back of the Jeep and covered with hessian before we sped off back to the mine. On one such return journey Peter suddenly clamped on the brakes, and as we skidded to a standstill, he pointed to the left and cried, "Look"!

I looked. "What is it?" I said. "I can't see anything."

"There. Kudu."

Kudu are large antelope about the size of a cow but with long spiral horns. I continued to stare at the open bush but could see nothing. Then, suddenly, an ear flicked and they appeared as if by magic before my eyes. There were about ten of them, standing in the open in full view under the dappled shade of some trees. Now that I could see them, it was inconceivable I had not seen them before. They were beige in colour, but the line of their backs was broken up by faint vertical patterns. This and the fact they stood perfectly still had been their only camouflage.

Looking back, I am really not sure what we did for recreation. I only know I was never bored. We certainly did a lot of reading, and to get books I joined the library in Mount Darwin. The books used to come out ten at a time in a metal box with the truck, and were chosen by the librarian according to a pre-arranged list of preferred categories. After being read, the books were sent back on the truck in the same metal box. It was a system that worked very well and was a Godsend in a country like Rhodesia for the many people in situations similar to our own. I was at the Idol Mine for Christmas 1957, and I received a box of assorted goodies from Fortnum and Mason—a long-established purveyor of fine foods in London. Organized by my mother, it was an inspired gift to receive in this remote and far-flung corner of the British Empire.

It was very hot, with temperatures going as high as 106 $^{\circ}$F (41 $^{\circ}$C), but it was also very dry, and I did not find the heat a burden. One Sunday I decided to climb the most prominent kopje overlooking the river. I took my rifle, in case I should surprise a leopard in the rocks, and set out on my climb. It was all rocks and boulders and hard going, but when I reached the top, I was rewarded by fine views over the surrounding bush. As I sat there, I noticed a succession of dust devils making their way over the landscape. Some were robust and some so weak they faltered and disappeared after just a short distance, but I saw they all started from the same spot. I marked the place by carefully noting the landmarks and made my way to it. It turned out to be a simple saucer-shaped depression in the ground, but every few minutes a little gust of wind would come along, spin around inside the saucer picking up dust and dried leaves, then set off downwind through the bush as though it had a life of its own, which, in a way, it had. Dust devils are a feature of any hot dry environment and are well named. They are really just miniature whirlwinds, and you can stand quite close to even the biggest without being affected. One in particular stays in my mind.

It was a hot afternoon; the bush lay heavy and still. I do not know where everyone was—maybe they were sleeping—but I was on my own. Slowly I became aware of a rustling in the trees on the other side of the river. I peered through the trunks and saw a pillar of dust and leaves gyrating high above the mopani forest. It was the biggest dust devil I had ever seen, and it was coming directly towards me, although the river, which I could not see, was in its path. As it came closer, the noise increased to a roar, and it hit the river bank on my side with a resounding thump. Then I saw the powerful broom at its base sweeping the ground and hurling dust and leaves high into the air. It continued towards me, then turned toward a group of grass-roofed huts where a number of scraggly chickens were scratching in the dirt, blissfully unaware of the whirling threat heading their way. I watched in gleeful anticipation as the column of dust twirled its way towards them, but at the last minute it neatly side-stepped the huts and their inhabitants and disappeared into the distance.

Sometimes I used to walk in the bush to look for guinea fowl. These plump chicken-like birds have grey plumage covered with white polka dots. They move around in flocks, seldom fly far, and, if anything, are even more stupid than chickens. They were quite good to eat, although the meat was a little dry. They made an ideal quarry for me—the world's worst hunter, who could not hit a barn from the inside. The method of tracking was simple. I would walk a short distance away from the compound and fire a shot in the air. The flock would immediately set off a chorus of alarm calls to advertise their presence and tell me where they were. Once located, they stood there, waiting for me to shoot at them, and once I had done so, they would flutter into the air, glide about 50 yards, and then wait for me to take another shot. The only hazard was getting lost, because it was easy to lose your bearings as you followed this strange progression through the featureless bush, where it was literally impossible to see the wood for the trees.

On one occasion, I was standing under the mopani trees, loaded rifle in hand, when I heard a rustling of dried leaves. A young antelope delicately picked his way through the forest and stood, stock still, his black nose quivering as if he sensed danger. He was broadside on to me and only a few feet away. Even I could not have missed had I fired the weapon in my hand, but even though we would have enjoyed a change in diet, the idea of turning this beautiful creature into a bloody mess was unthinkable to me. I made a slight noise, and he bounded away through the trees.

Two days after my arrival, I was given the job of cutting claims through virgin bush. Whenever a prospector found a likely source of minerals, he had to "peg" the claim and register it with the bureau of mines. I forget the details now, but so far as I remember, a peg was a board with his name and date on it, and if it looked to be a valuable site, it was in the claimant's interest to get it registered as soon as possible. He was then allocated a certain number of squares of land on which to develop his claim, and each corner of every square had to be marked with a claim marker. He was then supposed to cut lines through the bush from one corner peg to another. These lines had to be straight, regardless of the terrain.

Clearing thorn bush of all vegetation in a swathe eight feet wide down ravines and up the side of rocky kopjes was a rugged task. I was put in charge off a group of about 15 men, with none of us speaking a word of each other's language. Somehow we managed, but I kept finding myself trying to use French—I suppose because subconsciously I knew English was no good, and the only other language I knew was French! The local *lingua franca* was Chelapalapa ("like this, like this"), otherwise known as Kitchen Kaffir, or Fanagalo, which was used all across Southern Africa for communication. Further north, it was replaced by Swahili. Like most African languages, it had long vowel sounds, which made it ideal for shouting over long distances. As we hacked our way across the country, we came across a huge black scorpion the size of a lobster, very different from the small brown variety that entered the huts or gathered around the generator.

It was very quiet in the bush away from the mine, and sounds carried a long way. Peter had lived most of his life in this type of area and, unlike me, had not been subjected to an industrial environment. Consequently, his hearing was more acute. Visiting vehicles were a rarity. We seldom had more than two per month, and when they came, Peter could hear them when they were still five minutes away. We might be reading in the heavy silence of a hot afternoon when he would look up and say, "There's someone coming".

I could hear nothing, then about two minutes later I would be able to hear the faint buzz of an engine. The lower-pitched rumble of a truck could always be heard before the higher pitch of a light vehicle. Visitors were usually officials doing their rounds—police, District Officer, and the like—or fellow miners or prospectors. A new face and a chance for conversation were always welcome.

Strangely enough, the longer I stayed in this remote environment, the more reluctant I became to leave it. I was almost afraid to face the rush and bustle of what we consider civilization, and when I did eventually make a trip to Salisbury, I was at first quite alarmed by the traffic and felt a real country bumpkin.

During all this time I continued my correspondence with Sandy, whose busy social life in Singapore was about as different from mine as could be imagined. I also kept up correspondence with my friends in England, and also, of course, with my mother and sister. I still thought of England as home, and as my money accumulated in the bank every month, I felt secure when the amount equalled the cost of the ticket back. But I was not at all homesick and really enjoyed being where I was. It was so different from my previous life, with its constraints of school and industry. I felt as if I had burst out into the wide world and was in reality living a life of adventure like those in the books I had avidly enjoyed as a child. It was a thrill to me to sit on the big rock overlooking the Mazoe as the sun went down, setting the sky ablaze, before the coming of dusk filled the heavens with a zillion unfamiliar constellations. I gazed at the Milky Way and watched cascades of falling stars. When the moon was full, it hung like a gigantic lantern in the sky—bright enough to read a book by its silver light. At such times, I felt the music of *Swan Lake* would have been a perfect complement; but, alas, I had no way to play it. The iPod would have been ideal, but that invention lay many years in the future.

Chapter 2

Early 1958 to October 1958

Grand Parade

I move to less remote Grand Parade mine and describe my life around the township of Karoi. I reject an invitation to become a tobacco farmer and decide to hitchhike to Singapore.

I seem to have a mental block about leave takings because, once again, I cannot remember actually leaving the Idol Mine—or even my initial arrival at Grand Parade.

Grand Parade was much more developed and located in the centre of a tobacco growing area, although there were no actual farms close to either the mine or to its associated depot. The nearest township of any size was Karoi, about 20 miles away and situated on the main road 160 miles north of Salisbury. Despite being the only town for a hundred miles, it only consisted of a strip of buildings lining both sides of the main road, but it did boast a hotel and a country club where the local whites, including myself, disported themselves, drank too much, and coveted each other's wives—there being a great shortage of women. Friday was the day that everyone went into "town" to stock up on supplies and then repair to the club. Our nearest settlement had the unlikely name of Miami and consisted of only a post office, store and police station. Rhodesia Railways ran a trucking service which took over where the rails stopped, and they brought the mail twice a week to the post office.

The roads from Salisbury to Karoi and north were strip type, while those from Karoi to Miami and to Grand Parade were dirt, but quite well maintained and graded. From Grand Parade to the mine, they were just rough tracks, deeply rutted where water had used the road as a shortcut. The mine itself was on a saddle halfway up the slope of a hill. It provided wonderful views over the surrounding bush, which hereabouts was undulating terrain covered by endless mopani trees, whose large shiny leaves covered the ground with a crackly brown carpet. The manager's house, where he lived with his family, was constructed of locally made brick with a corrugated iron roof, but the mine buildings were mostly made of poles from the forest with tin roofs, although the workshop did have rough walls of homemade brick. Power was supplied by a horizontal, single-cylinder Ruston engine, which even then was about 30 years old. It had a huge flywheel and was started by wrapping a rope around a big flat pulley and having a team of about six Africans jog off down the hill with the loose end. As it unwound from the pulley, it slowly rotated the shaft with its huge flywheel. The valve lifter was dropped, and the engine would fire and then take at least a minute to reach its full speed of around 100 rpm. It was marvellously reliable, and all the moving parts were exposed and simple to maintain.

The depot was much more fancy and must once have been the thriving hub of a group of productive mines. One of these was the "Last Hope", whose overgrown signboard could still just be seen, almost hidden in the long grass. The buildings at Grand Parade were not only brick, but were actually plastered and painted white—stained the familiar ochre from the dust. There were three quite nice houses. One lived in by the boss, Trevor Cherry and his wife, Mike, which had a well-kept garden. The other two were vacant when I arrived, and over a period of time I lived in them both, although I cannot now remember why I moved from one to the other.

Our water supply came from an abandoned mine on the premises, so water was never in short supply, as all mines attract water like iron filings to a magnet, even when the surface of the surrounding country is dry and dusty. Shortly after I arrived I suffered a stubborn bout of diarrhoea. The mine manager's wife recommended castor oil, which, being an emetic, seemed the last thing I needed. She explained that castor oil would clear out the system and I would be cured. I was sceptical, but after two weeks of suffering stabbing stomach pains that left me gasping, I was ready to try anything. The castor oil tasted just as foul as I had remembered from my childhood, but she was right—although I later learned that the water in the mine contained traces of arsenic and every newcomer suffered the same problem of mild poisoning until his system adjusted. If you went away for more than about six weeks, you had to go through the same unpleasant acclimatization when you returned.

My new job had less to do with the actual mine and more to do with the depot. The mica was brought up from the mine to the depot for cutting, sorting, and packing, and the waste was thrown onto huge glittering dumps which had been growing for decades from the residue of all the now-abandoned mines in the district. Previously, this detritus had no value, but a new use had been found for it in a number of industrial products, including Formica.

We also had a market for washers of various sizes, stamped out of mica, which could be spotty and cracked provided they did not actually fall apart. These were made on the premises by groups spending the mornings sorting through the dumps looking for suitable material and the afternoons turning their gleanings into washers, using dies and hand-operated fly-presses. I was put in charge of this group, and I thought the output—as well as the income of the workers—could be increased by changing to piece work, with one group collecting the raw material and another working the presses. I surreptitiously timed the output they were already achieving and set that as the base for the existing wages. If they made more than they were already turning out, they would get more than they were already getting, which should have been a foregone conclusion because all they had to do was to work the presses and not spend time on the dump first.

The first reaction to the introduction of my little scheme was that what I had asked of them was impossible. When I insisted, and they found I was correct in my contention that they could double their wages, they worked for half the time until they had

99

earned their previous wages and then took the rest of the month off to sit around their huts drinking beer and watching their women slaving away. I found this very annoying and went round muttering about ingratitude and how could the Africans ever expect to get ahead with this kind of attitude. Eventually it dawned on me that perhaps they were the smart ones because, unlike most of us, they had sense enough only to work until they had sufficient for their needs.

I had been brought up with the idea that everyone needed a job to survive, but in the traditional African village this was an alien concept. In the village everyone had their tasks. The women did most of the back-breaking labour, dug the fields, gathered the crops, pulverized the grain, did the cooking, washed the clothes, gathered the firewood, fetched the water, made the beer, bore the kids etc., etc., while the men did a bit of hunting when there was anything to hunt, fathered the kids, and drank the beer. There was no cash, and what little trade that existed was done by barter. It was only when cash was needed to buy things like bicycles, radios, batteries, mirror sunglasses, and other everyday items that the need for cash became more compelling. It took me a while to realize this basic fact of rural African life.

I cannot really remember the details now, but somehow the situation was resolved to everyone's satisfaction, and more sophisticated stamp presses were introduced. These were powered by electricity from our own generator, which was also of the antique horizontal variety, but being smaller than the engine at the mine, could be started with a handle. It now became imperative to keep the engine running all day, while during the same period there was less time for maintenance. This also came under my area of responsibility. We had some power tools on the place, and when something went wrong with the engine and some machining was required to fix it, I found myself in the Catch 22 situation in which the machines needed to fix the generator could not be used until the generator was fixed. On one occasion, I had planned for weeks to go away for a long weekend, and after months of trouble-free running, the engine started playing up on the very evening I intended to leave, and it took the whole of my planned weekend to trace the trouble, which turned out to be due to a frog wedged tight a couple of feet inside the intake pipe from the cooling water tank. The new presses were much faster but more dangerous. Fortunately, we never had anybody chop off any fingers, but the presses would have had no trouble doing so, and it was almost impossible to fit any practical guards around the dies because the mica was so irregular it had to be held by hand. On one occasion I went into the shed and found one man so drunk he could barely remain on his stool. My blood ran cold at the thought of the damage he could have done himself, and I sent him packing with curses suitable from a young, self-righteous white overseer.

Then the new presses developed the unfortunate habit of breaking in half. At first this had me puzzled, because they were quite massively built. The top part of the die chopped through the mica into the bottom, and the washer so formed was pushed out by washers made from rubber, which acted like a spring. I came to the conclusion the rubber was too solid, with the result that the press was being brought up short before it had quite reached the end of its stroke. I tried reducing the thickness of the rubber, but then the mica washers remained stuck in the bottom of the die. We did not have any softer rubber, so I tried to think of a way to soften the existing stuff without reducing its thickness. I came up with the idea of cutting notches all around the underside of the rubber washers so there would be less material to compress, although the thickness would remain the same. This worked like a charm, and this simple modification ended the expensive problem of broken presses. Although I never told anyone about it, I was secretly very proud of this solution, and I mention it here because it was the first time, at least in my working life, when I realized I had the type of mind that was able to pinpoint the root cause of a problem and then come up with a simple solution. I believe everyone is born with at least one natural talent, and the trick is to find out what it is, and some never do. I gradually came to the conclusion that this was mine, and over the years it became something I was able to rely on more and more. Sometimes it might take one or two days, but I could absolutely rely on a solution being presented to me provided I had spent sufficient time thinking about it before allowing my subconscious to take over and finish the job.

We received a large order for raw waste from a company

overseas, and the first time was a disaster. The mica on the dumps was quite wet and it was loaded into hessian sacks. For some reason there was a delay of about two months before the shipment could leave, and this brought us into the rainy season. A fleet of enormous trucks from Rhodesia Railways came to the depot, and when loading started, we found damp had rotted most of the sacks so that they spewed mica all over the place, so most of it had to be re-bagged. The rains had turned the small stream below the depot into a sizeable torrent, and although the ford—or "drift" to use the local term—was not deep enough to bother a big truck, they picked up sufficient water on their driving wheels to prevent traction on the steep slope on the other side of the stream. This situation was hopeless with an articulated truck on which, under these conditions, most of the weight comes off the driving wheels. The first two trucks just made it out, but then an articulated tried to rush it and slid inexorably back into the river with all eight of its driving wheels spinning impotently on the slippery surface. That was it! The truck was jack-knifed in the riverbed and could go neither backwards nor forwards. There was no other practical route out, and we had ten more trucks, each with an irate white driver, stuck on our side of the river. They remained there for three days, and the consignment of mica missed the ship in Beira, Mozambique!

The rainy season was the cause of many amusing mishaps with vehicles. In fact, now I come to think of it, I really had an amazing amount of adventures in the course of driving. Most of them occurred in a battered American Army Jeep, which landed me in a heap of trouble. There was the time it came to a standstill in the very middle of a flooded river, with the water just below the sides. The water jetted up through a hole in the floor like a miniature fountain until the level inside the vehicle was equal with that outside. I waded ashore and went to get help from a coloured man living nearby with a black woman and a tribe of coffee-coloured kids. He pushed me out of the river with his Land Rover, and as we went up the slope, I tried get the engine started. Suddenly the Jeep fired, and I roared ahead then stalled and, before I had the wit to stop it, the Jeep rushed backwards down the slope to crash into the front of my benefactor's vehicle with a bone-jarring impact that almost snapped my head off my shoulders.

Fortunately, both vehicles were built for that kind of treatment, so only my ego was bruised.

There was much to be learnt from the local people when it came to simple, but effective, ways to get things done. I remember the mine manager telling me that if you wanted a large boulder moved it was best to just give the instruction and leave them to it. He said that, often as not, when you came back the boulder had been moved. I saw an example of this one day when we had a truck stuck in the mud up to its axles. While I was contemplating pulling it out with another vehicle and wondering how to do that without also getting that one stuck, the local Africans simply got 40 people and pushed it out. You get a lot of traction from 80 legs and feet!

One evening I was driving along a bush track as the sun was setting and the sky was ablaze with colour. I was particularly struck by the way the orange glow reflected off the side of the bonnet, until I smelt a funny smell and realized the orange reflection was flickering in a suspicious manner. I stopped and opened the lid to the engine compartment to find a sea of flame. I was just wondering what to do when inexplicably the fire just went out by itself. The oil-filled air-cleaner had come loose and upended itself onto the starter motor. The resulting short-circuit had touched off the spilled oil but fortunately had not spread beyond it.

One night, when the river was flooded, I had taken a very roundabout back track, and as I slid and slithered through the mud, the lights got dimmer and dimmer and the engine began to lose power and splutter in an ominous manner. I diagnosed a dying battery with little or no charge from the dynamo, so I switched off all the lights—fortunately there was a brilliant African moon. There was a temporary improvement, but gradually the power lessened, and I changed down through all eight of the Jeep's gears to keep going until the engine gave a final cough and died. At first the silence was deafening, but gradually I became aware of the subtle sounds of the bush at night. The haunting flute-like call of a night bird and the unexplained crack of a twig or rustle in the undergrowth with the distant sound of native drums. The moon was almost full, and its harsh, silver light gave the landscape the look of an etching, with pools of deep shadow under the trees. I was not in the least apprehensive, but as I set out to walk the eight miles back home, I was struck by the strangeness of my situation and how improbable it would have seemed only a year earlier. Even while I was doing it, I found it hard to believe it was really me who was walking through the African bush entirely alone. I did not encounter another soul during the two hours it took me to get back.

I had another long walk one night after an incident I was lucky to survive. I had spent the day sailing on a miniscule dam just outside Karoi and was whizzing home in the Jeep after a couple of gin and tonics on an empty stomach. I was in a hurry because I had instructed my cook to go home if I was not back by 7 p.m., and it was getting on for that time. If I missed him, I knew the wood burning stove would be out, and it would require a major effort on my part to get some hot food and, not having eaten all day, I was hungry. The road undulated, and it was surprisingly chilly each time it dipped into a minor valley, or "vlei". The Jeep was a great vehicle for driving off-road but it was not intended for ripping along over twisty dirt roads. The trouble started where the graded road curved as it went over the brow of a hill, and the vehicle began to slide across the loose dirt as the weight came off the wheels. I was doing just over 50 mph and was not too concerned as I corrected the slide. Unfortunately, I over-corrected, and the vehicle snapped into a reverse slide. I cursed and over-corrected a second time. This time I knew I had lost it completely as the Jeep hurtled across the reverse camber and hit the bank at the edge of the road. I felt myself flying headfirst through the air and I clearly remember thinking, "This is it! You have really done it this time, Fleming!". Believe it or not, I landed on my head, but I must have been on my way over because I immediately afterwards found myself sitting on my bottom. I was amazed to find myself alive and apparently unhurt. The Jeep had re-crossed the road and was making impressive smashing noises before a particularly large and final crash accompanied by the tinkle of broken glass brought it all to a halt and silence reigned.

I checked myself all over and could discover nothing wrong.

Nothing at all! No pain, no blood. Not even a single bruise or scratch! I cautiously stood and found myself about fifteen feet from the road, surrounded by jagged rocks and fallen trees. I crossed the road and followed the path of destruction created by the Jeep as it had rampaged through the bush. It had knocked over maybe half a dozen medium-sized trees before locking itself around one of the biggest in the vicinity. One look at the front suspension was enough to tell me it was not going to get me home that night. It was not only me that had been thrown out. Everything else in the Jeep was strewn over the landscape—even the sails had come out of the sail bag and were draped over the ground. I collected everything I could find and stuffed it under one of the fallen trees and started the long walk home.

Soon after I set out, I looked at my watch to check the time and found it missing from my wrist. My sandals had been repaired by a local cobbler just the previous week and as I walked, the nails came through the soles into my feet. I thought about taking them off, but the road was covered with sharp stones so I kept them on. It took me two hours walking to reach home, and my only wounds were from the nails in my shoes! I did not see anybody on the way, and the Cherry's drove past the crash site later that night and did not notice anything unusual. It had been a miraculous escape considering I had been ejected from behind the steering wheel and over the top of the windshield before hitting the ground, which was strewn with rocks and trees, headfirst at 50 mph!

The next morning, I told Trevor what had happened, except that I blamed the accident on a broken steering rod. I am not sure he believed me, but since the rod in question was mangled by its conflict with the tree and I was the one who had to repair the damage, there was not a lot he could say. I took a bunch of Africans with me with the truck and offered a reward to anyone who found my watch, but I was the one who found it ticking happily away under the sails I had hidden under a tree. Only the pin attaching the strap to the watch was broken. I even had the Jeep fixed by the end of the day!

On another occasion I had a real steering failure, but once again I lived a charmed life. This time it was in the company

GMC truck, which was a powerful brute with a big V-8 engine. I had been up to Miami to collect the mail and then realized I had forgotten to bring something that was supposed to go on the outgoing truck. I tore back to Grand Parade with my foot on the boards, swerving around the bends at speeds up to 70 mph, then down the steep hill into the ford, my wheels emptying the river as I roared across. Up the hill on the other side and then into the Cherry's drive to swing around the neat circle of flowers outside their house. To my astonishment, the truck ploughed straight through the middle of the flower bed, mashing the dahlias and tearing up the neatly tended roses before coming to rest in the middle of the carnage. The wheel spun around in my hands, disconnected from the steering, and I was sobered by the thought of what could have been the outcome had this happened on one of the previous bends.

The track to the mine from the depot was very rough, as no grader ever passed that way. One day I was making my way up one of the hills when I unexpectedly met a truck full of Africans on a bend in the road. Instead of stopping, the truck left the track and carried on straight into the bush, bouncing over the uneven ground with all the passengers hanging on for dear life. As it disappeared into the shoulder-high grass, the voice of the unseen driver shouted in explanation "No brakes, boss!". I went to check that they were OK and found everyone screaming with laughter.

Sam had a big dog that was half German Shepherd and half Rhodesian Ridgeback. Like most dogs with white owners, it regarded anyone black with the greatest suspicion, even though I never personally came across a case where any white owner trained their dogs to be that way. The dog always used to ride around in the Jeep, and one day I happened to turn around when Sam was driving just in time to see the dog do a sideways backwards somersault over the tailboard when we were bouncing along at about 20 mph. He was completely unhurt and came racing up behind and leapt over the tailboard with a great grin on his face. Of course he could not stop on the metal surface and crashed into the back of the seats. "That dog's a clown", said Sam, "but the munts are terrified of him. He knows it, so he plays on it."

One day we took delivery of a small dump truck that was dropped off at the depot, and it was my job to get it to the mine. Like all these vehicles, it had no springs and the driving wheels were at the front with small steerable wheels at the back. Everyone knows what it is like to steer a car going backwards, but this was a thousand times worse with its short wheelbase and the seat right over the wheels. The steering was very high geared, and whenever you turned the wheel the slightest amount, you found yourself being hurled sideways. On a rough track, without springing, it was even worse, because there was only the steering wheel to hang on to, and you could not help but turn it every time you hit a bump—and the track was nothing but bumps. It was a case of positive feedback in its most negative form. It took me nearly two hours to make the three-mile trip as I swerved wildly from side to side with my body airborne for most of the way. This mine was more fully developed than the Idol, and I went down it quite a number of times. Many of the miners smoked, and they made their own cigarettes using home-grown tobacco and ordinary brown wrapping paper. They had the curious habit of keeping the lighted ends inside their mouths so the drips from the roof would not put the fire out!

Even though the mine was located on the shoulder of a hill, it was surprisingly prone to being struck by lightning, and some of the strikes were impressive in their ferocity. One day Sam's wife was struck. She had been lying on a rubber mattress on a steel-frame bed. The strike hit the power lines, set the bedside lamp on fire, jumped across to her shoulder and down her leg, before jumping down to the bed frame and into the ground. She had minor burns on her leg but, other than that and being thoroughly shaken up, was not seriously hurt.

All mines are prone to flooding, so one of the biggest dangers of lightning was blowing up the generator and putting the pumps out of action. This actually happened, but fortunately we were able to get everything working again before the situation became too desperate.

The company also used to buy mica and a few other minerals from other small producers. These usually consisted of one man, perhaps with his family, who worked small claims with a handful of helpers and who literally scratched a living from the ground. Sometimes they had almost no equipment, and holes for blasting were drilled by hand by "hammer boys" using drill bits and 5-pound clump hammers. The Africans who earned their living this way had shoulders on them like oxen. This group viewed Rhodesia Mica Mining as Big Business and, consequently, with the greatest suspicion that they would be cheated. Looking back on it, I can sympathize with them because after all their work they really had no choice but to bring the product of their toil to us and accept what we paid them, based on our grading. The grading of mica was very complex and took into account such factors as size, colour (brown, ruby, green, spotted, etc.), and flatness, which could best be checked by tipping the sample against the light and evaluating the reflection of a regular shaped object such as a window frame. This way, any ripples would show up immediately. In fact, we were scrupulously fair in our gradings, but we were always suspected of pushing the grade down so as to buy at a cheaper price and increase our profit. One day an aggressive young white Rhodesian accused me point blank of cheating him. I tried to show him the reason for the low grading was lack of flatness, and I held the sample against the light so he could see that the reflection was so distorted it resembled a fun-house mirror. He looked me straight in the eye, called me a liar, and said the piece was completely flat!

I was so angry I finished up white and trembling, and it was three days before all my feathers were back in place. I have sometimes been accused of being angry when I have just been excited about something. I have only been deeply angry three times in my life, and this was one of them. In the end, of course, they had to accept our evaluation and price because they had no choice. But in fact it was correct anyway.

Another mineral we used to buy was beryllium—beryl for short—which was often found in proximity to mica. In its purest form beryl was the gemstone emerald, but it was more usually crushed to make a metal of the same name, alloyed with copper and other metals to enhance their properties. Beryl grew in perfect hexagonal shaped crystals varying in size from miniscule to more than 12 inches across the flats and in lengths as long as 20 feet. The rock was green in colour with the clarity and hue varying according to its purity.

Life on the depot was varied and interesting. Trevor Cherry, my boss, was English from the same type of background as myself and was a qualified accountant. Mike, his wife, was Rhodesian and quite a few years younger than he. One day I saw Trevor cleaning an automatic pistol, and I asked him about it. He said he took it from an Italian officer he captured during World War II. He demonstrated it by shooting a row of tin cans off a wall without missing once. I was most impressed. He had fought in Burma and been captured by the Japanese. He showed me the scars on his wrists where he had been pegged down to the ground by pieces of split bamboo driven between the twin bones inside his arms. The bamboo had been lit so that it slowly smouldered its way through the flesh. Trevor said the prisoners were not very well guarded because, being in the middle of the jungle, the Japanese did not consider there was anywhere for them to escape to. But Trevor decided that anything that happened to him in the jungle could not possibly be worse than what would happen if he stayed where he was, so one night he strangled the guard and made his escape. He was lucky to encounter a friendly group of local people within three days, and they helped him get back to British lines. Now Trevor was a respectable English accountant, but just 12 years earlier he had been a jungle fugitive and had killed in cold blood.

Domestic life was typical of all such bush settlements. It was different but very comfortable. Water was pumped from the now defunct underground mine tunnels into overhead tanks, so we all had running water. Water was piped to an oil drum built up over a fireplace, so when the fire was lit, we had hot water. Sometimes it was so hot it came out of the pipes as steam. All waste water from baths and basins ran out through holes in the side of the houses and was channelled down to the kitchen gardens, where it was used to water the vegetables. This did not work too well with melons, which sucked up prodigious amounts of water along with whatever was in it, so if you used Lux soap, you got Lux-flavoured melons!

Of course we all had servants to carry out various tasks, and the Cherrys had several because they had a more elaborate establishment. Mine was called Black, according to the name he had been given by some earlier employer. He washed my clothes, cleaned the house, chopped the firewood, and cooked my food. Actually he had a pretty easy time, and there was not a lot for him to do. One day I received a message from him to say there was a snake in the house. I asked where it was and was told on the table.

I said *"On* the table?"—thinking perhaps he meant under the table.

"No" he said, "on the table—eating the sugar!"

I went to the house and there sure enough was a six-foot-long tree snake on the dining room table. I did not quite know how to deal with it, so I took the coward's way out and shot it with my .22 rifle. This exercise knocked a bit of plaster off the walls, but they were so rough already it did not make any difference.

Snakes were quite common, and you always knew when there was one in the trees because the birds set up such chatter of alarm calls. One time when the Cherrys were away, I had to look after their animals, including a turkey hen with a brood of young chicks. One morning I found her cold and stiff with all the young birds trapped under her rigid body. I am not sure what killed her but it is almost certain it was a snake.

There were a number of dangerous varieties of snakes, including black mambas, tiny kraits, spitting cobras—which could spit poison straight in your eyes from a range of several feet—and, perhaps worst of all, the puff adder. These are beautifully marked but incredibly ugly with their flat diamond-shaped heads and short fat bodies. They were lazy creatures and relied on the camouflage of their colouring and markings for protection. They liked to lie across paths in the sun and, being hard to see, were frequently stepped on by bare-footed Africans. Unlike the cobra, this snake struck backwards—over its shoulder, as it were—so when stepped on, it just struck back and injected a heavy dose of poison into the leg of the unfortunate trespasser through its long, wicked-looking fangs. The bite of the puff adder was frequently fatal.

The Cherrys' cook was called Sam. He just showed up at their door one day with an impressive list of references. It so happened that Mike was looking for a new cook, so she asked him "Can you cook?".

"Madam," he replied, "that is my job."

So she hired him, and he turned out to be a really excellent cook. I asked him one day how to make rice pudding and, before replying, he asked me whether I wanted to eat it that day or in two days' time, since the answer to that would decide the method of cooking. Because he could produce such tasty European food, I asked him if he preferred that or the traditional African diet. He told me that when he was at home his wife did all the cooking, and he preferred normal African fare. I found this hard to accept as the local food was so basic and consisted mostly of maize meal mixed with water, which seemed to me more suitable for blocking up holes in toilet pipes than eating.

We all wondered why a cook of Sam's calibre would have been knocking at doors looking for a job, and this question was answered one night when Mike had some guests for dinner. They were supposed to be having roast duck, and when the time for the meal to be served came and went, Mike went to investigate and found the duck with its feathers still on and Sam dead drunk on the floor under the table. She fired him after that, but if it had been me, I think I would have accepted his occasional lapse in view of his excellence the rest of the time. After all, none of us is perfect!

The toilet in Rhodesia was always referred to as the "PK". This is short for *picannin kaya,* meaning "small house". This was the traditional type of toilet even in quite well-developed houses and consisted of a deep pit with a seat built over the top of it and enclosed by a small hut. Usually they were surprisingly free of bad smells due to the cleansing the action of millions of disgusting looking white maggots that revelled in the living conditions at the bottom of the pit. It was best just to park your bum on the seat and get on with it and avoid feasting your eyes on the activity below. I heard one story in which the owner of a rare smelly toilet had tipped some kerosene down there to improve the situation shortly before the arrival of some guests. The next morning one of the guests had gone in for a leisurely crap and smoke. He had disposed of his fag by throwing it down the toilet and the resulting explosion blew him out through the door with, as my informant described it, "his bare arse glowing like a baboon's!"

The subject of maggots reminds me of the disgusting habits of the blow-fly. These creatures lay eggs inside your underwear while it is drying on the line, and if the iron is not hot enough, they somehow get into your skin. After a while you feel this kind of itchy spot, and if you squeeze it, out pops this little white wriggly maggot. It is not pleasant to remove living maggots from your own flesh, and I still bear the scars left by a couple of them.

The bulk of white people in the area were tobacco farmers. After World War II, the British government encouraged ex-soldiers to settle in Rhodesia. As an incentive, the government offered 40 acres of totally undeveloped bush except for an access road and a water supply. They also offered interest-free loans and if, after five years, you could show you had made a good go of the place, you were given the title deeds to the property. Most of the farmers in the area were from this scheme and were interesting people who had worked very hard. Before they could grow anything, they had to clear the land, which hereabouts was covered with trees. Once cleared, the land had to be ploughed and all the rocks removed. For living quarters, most people started with a rondavel, with a grass roof virtually the same as your standard African hut, except maybe bigger, and with the mud walls painted white. Later, a second hut might be built and then linked to the first, so in this way the house gradually grew in size.

When things were more established, you might get a local brick maker to come and make enough bricks on the premises to build a more permanent structure—although nothing was really permanent in Africa, as no sooner was something complete than the local termites would set about returning it to nature.

I have mentioned the township of Karoi as the centre for local social activities, and it was here that the farmers and ourselves would go every Friday for R and R—or perhaps I should say G and T. This of course is short for Gin and Tonic, of which I used to drink vast quantities in those days with very little effect. I remember sitting on a bar stool at the club one evening when a woman said to me, "Why don't you fall down?"

I said, "Why should I?"

She said, "You have drunk thirteen of those things, so by now you should be on the floor!"

I must have been reasonably sober—I certainly felt it at the time—or I would not remember the conversation so clearly after all these years. One night on the way home, I was jammed into the front of the GMC truck with a couple who were staying with the Cherrys. He was driving, so his dishy wife was squeezed up against me. I know I was not entirely sober, but I can remember her saying, "Christ, you are like a bloody octopus" and him saying what sounded to me like, "I'll give you a tip".

"A tip?" I said, thinking he was going to give me some precious gem of advice.

"No", he said, "a clip", then added, "of the type you get round the ear!"

After I had been there a few months, several of us formed the Karoi Sailing Club. We used to sail 14-foot dinghies on the puddle of a dam just outside town. The sailing was pretty hopeless, because the dam was so small and there was hardly any wind except for the occasional little dust devils that used to spiral their way across the water and create havoc amongst our little fleet of drifting boats. Of course on the water they were no longer dust devils because there was no dust, and they became invisible except for the pattern of ripples they left on the water. But it was a good way to relax and we all had a good time.

Compared to the Idol Mine, Grand Parade really seemed like the centre of civilization. We were visited one day by a man who had driven to the area from Salisbury, some 160 miles away, to sell insurance to people in the area. He probably thought he had travelled to the back of beyond and was very amused when I described Karoi as being the centre of things. At the time I could not understand what he found so funny.

I made several trips to Salisbury, and it always seemed to be quite an expedition, especially in the rainy season. For most of the way there were strip roads. These were roads which had a laterite surface except for two parallel strips of tarmac each about two feet wide. You drove with your wheels on these strips until you met a vehicle coming the other way, when you would both swerve to your left so that you each had your right-hand wheels on your left-hand strip. As soon as you were past, you went back onto both strips. Everyone drove at least at 70 mph due to the immense distances that had to be covered. The police used to hide behind bushes miles from anywhere to give out speeding tickets. I remember one Rhodesian telling me, "I was 100 miles from the nearest town when this guy came out of the bush and flagged me down with his hat. I thought the poor bugger was lost and dying of thirst. When I stopped, the bastard handed me a speeding ticket!"

In the dry season, the high plume of red dust towering behind every vehicle made them visible for miles. During the rains, the dust turned to slippery or glutinous mud, and it was easy to lose control as you manoeuvred on and off the strips at unabated speed. It was common at these times to see vehicles in the tops of trees and other places that defied the imagination to figure out how they got there. Many of the bridges were quite low, with guard rails only about 12 inches high. When the rivers rose, the bridges completely disappeared beneath the surface of the muddy water and their exact whereabouts had to be estimated from the disturbance to the water flow. Edging a vehicle across bridges under these conditions was a bit like blind man's bluff, especially when the view forward was restricted by a long, high, hood.

On the way back from one of my trips to town, I gave a ride to a young white hitchhiker. I was driving a GMC pickup truck, and he had to sit in the back because the passenger seat was piled high with stuff I had put inside the cab for security. The back was also quite full and loaded with provisions, including a big bag of grapes which had been bought by myself as a luxury. When I eventually arrived home, I found my passenger had shown his gratitude by eating all my grapes. Because of this and a couple of other unhappy experiences in other places, I only gave rides to hitchhikers under very exceptional circumstances, even though I had been a hitchhiker myself and a few months later I was to travel several thousand miles in that manner.

While in Salisbury I visited a tobacco auction, which to the uninitiated looks like black magic. Bales of tobacco with the tops opened and a handful of leaves pulled out are laid out in rows on the floor of huge warehouses. The auctioneers were mostly from America and would come to Rhodesia at the end of the tobacco season in the United States. They would walk at a fast clip down the rows, chanting what sounded like a non-stop religious mantra. One well-known auctioneer even used to chant to the tune of "Yankee Doodle Dandy". The auctioneer was surrounded by a group of buyers who, by signs invisible to me, indicated their bids as his unintelligible chant went up and down the price scale for a cost per pound. Following behind was a clerk, who by some miracle was able to identify the buyer and the price paid. This information was written on a ticket placed on top of each bale. The grower checked this information, and if he felt the price was too low, he could tear the ticket; but for every ticket he tore, the buyer was also entitled to tear one, and naturally he would choose the bale which went at the highest price. All these bales went up for re-auction, and there was always the chance they might not reach the previous price, so it was a good self-regulating system.

Once, Trevor and Mike went to South Africa for a three-week holiday and I was left in charge of the depot. Trevor told me not to bother with any correspondence, which could await his return. No sooner had he gone than I started receiving cables that demanded a response. They were signed "Brimetacor" which meant absolutely nothing to me. I went through the filing cabinet and came across a file headed "British Metal Corporation" which had a familiar ring. Sure enough, on their letterhead I saw their cable address was the same as the one on the cable I had received. Some of the information I had to supply was a priced invoice with the prices for many grades of mica, measured in pounds and ounces, the prices to be listed in pounds, shillings, pennies, and half-pennies. Arithmetic has never been my strong point, but I struggled with this thing and sent it off. Until Trevor returned, I continued to receive a succession of cables reading: "Dear Sir, we beg to point out what we believe to be an error in your invoice." They were always right!

There was always something new and interesting to see and do, and I learned a lot. I walked through the bush to "Garnet Hill" and learned how easy it was to walk in circles without a landmark or compass to guide you. I helped in the start-up of an exploratory adit mine, which is one with its entrance driven into the side of a hill rather than through a shaft coming down from the surface. In this case, of course, the initial blasting was above ground instead of below. Even in those days I liked to take photos, and I was keen to photograph the blasting. The rocks flew high in the air with a lazy slow-motion action, but they returned to earth a lot quicker and closer than I had anticipated, and I cowered behind a tree as they came crashing through the bushes all around me. This mine was to look for asbestos, and we did find small amounts packed like seams of cotton into the rock. Fortunately for our future health, it never came to anything, as we now know that asbestos often causes cancer.

But Rhodesia Mica Mining was losing money, and the company decided to shut up shop. Actually I was not at all upset by this. In fact, I was rather pleased, because after one year I was beginning to get itchy feet and wanted to move on. But, having been taken on as a sort of apprentice miner by an acquaintance of my mother, I did not know how to leave without seeming ungrateful. This way the problem was taken out of my hands. A very nice English couple immediately offered me a job as a Tobacco Assistant on their farm, and I seriously thought about it for a few days before turning it down. It was one of those decisive crossroads, and I often think how differently my life would have turned out if I had taken the job.

But I wanted to experience new places with different cultures. The African peoples may have cultures going back for centuries, but there was no visible evidence of it. There was nothing written down and, other than some ruins at Zimbabwe (which years later gave their name to the nation when it ceased to be a colony), there were no monuments. I was still exchanging letters with Sandy in Singapore, and this gave me a goal and a destination.

I decided to hitchhike to Dar-Es-Salaam on the coast of

Tanganyika, then take a ship from there to India and eventually on to Singapore. I thought I had better go armed, so I exchanged my rifle for a .25 Beretta automatic with a barrel so short there was a real danger of blowing away the end of your finger when you pulled the trigger. But it made a reassuringly loud bang, even if the chances of actually hitting the intended target were almost zero. I made a list of all the things I thought I would need, equipped myself with an 8 mm movie camera, and was ready to go. I wrote and told my mother about my plans and received a furious reply to the effect she would never have wasted all that money on my education if she had known I was going to fritter it away by such irresponsible actions. I replied that I was sorry if I was a disappointment, but my mind was made up.

Chapter 3

October 1958

Hitchhike to Mombasa

I hitchhike to Dar-es-Salaam and take an Indian ship to Zanzibar and Mombasa where I unexpectedly become a member of the Kenya police.

I cannot remember who picked me up on the first leg of the journey I hoped was going to lead me to Singapore, but I know that, on that first day, I managed to get as far as Kapiri Mposhi, just across the border between Northern and Southern Rhodesia. The border between the two territories —later to become Zambia and Zimbabwe—was formed by the mighty Zambesi River, and the road north crossed it at the Otto Beit Bridge.

Kapiri Mposhi was little more than a clearing in the bush, and the hotel a collection of small huts scattered among the trees. That evening, I made enquiries among my fellow guests and cadged a lift with a British civil servant working in Tanganyika. He had bought a Peugeot 403 while on leave in England and, instead of returning directly to Dar es Salaam by sea, he had decided to ship the car to Cape Town and drive it north over the 3,000 miles through South Africa, the Rhodesias and across Tanganyika. The road cut through undulating terrain clothed for thousands of square miles by an unbroken mantle of mopani forest. Only occasionally, when breasting a rise, was it possible to get a brief outlook, blinkered by the trees on either side, of the ochre road slashing through the purple hills, with each range succeeding another in two-dimensional silhouettes until they faded into infinity. "Miles and miles of bloody Africa" as the old hands called it with a weary

118

sigh of wonderment at its immensity.

Although this was the main route north, the road was either strip or plain dirt. Every vehicle trailed its plume of fine red dust, which found its way into every crack and crevice and penetrated into even the folds of clothing inside your suitcase, so that every garment came out stained in wild and unwelcome tie-dyed ochre patterns. Overtaking was hazardous. The closer you came to the vehicle in front, the thicker the dust and the worse the visibility. You had to feel your way right up to the rear of the vehicle you were trying to pass, then poke your nose out to see if the way was clear. Getting safely past required the co-operation of the vehicle in front. My driver told me a cautionary tale.

In Tanganyika, fuel was delivered around the vast territory by fleets of Fiat road tankers, and the drivers were paid according to the amount of deliveries completed. They fought to avoid anything that would slow them down, and getting caught in another vehicle's dust was one such hazard. Once in this position, you could find yourself eating his dust for miles. On a long cross-country journey, my friend came up behind a fuel truck. He battled his way through the dense cloud and blew his horn, but the driver refused to move over. "In fact," my friend said, "he did everything possible to prevent me getting past by swerving his vehicle across the road whenever there was a chance to overtake." Air conditioning was unheard of in those days, and in the heat the windows had to be open. So when stuck behind another vehicle— especially a truck –the choice lay between being suffocated by the heat or suffocated by the dust.

After eating the bastard's dirt for nearly an hour, I was driven to uncontrolled fury. Again and again I tried to get past, but he blocked me every time. Finally, I tricked him by edging out as if to overtake in the normal way and then switching to the blind side and blasting my way through by leaving the road and barging up an embankment. Once past, I was hell bent on revenge. I slowed down and fishtailed the rear end of the car, raising dense clouds of dust. I could hear the driver behind me blowing his horn, but I was out for blood. There was a long straight slope ahead of me, with a hairpin bend at the bottom before the road climbed sharply to the left. I gradually increased speed on the downslope, continuing to slide the car back and forth across the road to generate as much dust as possible. I whipped around the bend and up the hill, and then stopped and got out of the car. I could see the truck racing down through the thick trail of dust, with the continuous bleat of the horn rising above the noise of the engine. When he reached the corner, he missed the turn and left the road with a tremendous crash. As the dust drifted clear, I saw the truck lying on its side, its wheels slowly turning and the driver running away from the wreck as fast as his legs would carry him. I got back into the car well satisfied that justice had been served, and it was not until much later that my conscience began to bother me!"

Late in the day we came to the border at the small town of Tunduma. Officials checked the car and our papers. In those days there was a lot less sensitivity about the transport of firearms, but the paperwork had to be in order and was still a lot of hassle, so I tucked my small Beretta down the front of my underpants figuring that no one would look there unless they had good reasons for suspicion. But I first took the precaution of making sure the gun was unloaded. The consequences of having it go off did not bear thinking about!

After checking my papers, the immigration official insisted I pay him a cash deposit equal to the value of a ticket back to the UK. This amounted to about 120 pounds, which was a good proportion of all the money I had! I explained that I would be leaving the country hundreds of miles away at Dar-es-Salaam, but he said I could collect the money at the point of departure when I showed proof I was leaving. In any case, I had no choice but to pay it if I wanted to cross the border.

My companion had told me that almost all the cars in Tanganyika were Peugeots and almost all the trucks were Fiats. Sure enough, just as soon as we had crossed the border, this is the way it was. There was, too, an immediate change in the terrain. The hills became more rugged and rock-strewn, and the continuous tree cover began to break up and was soon left behind. After a few miles, we came to the small town of Mbeya with its buildings nestled among the hills, interspersed with large boulders and splashes of purple from the jacaranda trees now in full bloom.

The next day we headed northeast over a rough road with many diversions caused by construction. The next town, Iringa, was strikingly situated on top of a flat-topped hill rising abruptly out of the surrounding country. The road wound upwards around the precipitous sides of the hill, and we felt as if we were climbing some medieval fortification.

After Iringa, the road gradually descended from the high land which forms the central landmass of the African continent. As we lost altitude, the temperature began to rise and vegetation became more lush and tropical. Just outside Morogoro, where we spent the night, I was excited by the first coconut palms I had ever seen outside the pages of a book. We were now not far from the coast, and the people, too, began to look different. I had not known what to expect, but the Muslim influence was very evident. Many women were dressed from head to toe in black chadors, some of which left only their eyes showing. It is amazing just how much can be expressed by just a pair of eyes. Others protected themselves from the sun with umbrellas that came in only one colour—black. There were white-garbed Arabs, their chins fringed with curly beards, wearing white Muslim hats embroidered with gold thread. Nearly all the small stores, known as *dukas*, were run by Indians. The commonest form of dress was a shirt and a patterned sarong called a *kikoi*. As soon as we had crossed into Tanganyika, the *lingua franca* changed from Chalapalapa to Swahili. This is actually the language of the people who live on the coast, but a simplified form, known as "kitchen Swahili", had developed and was used by all the peoples of East Africa and the Belgian Congo to communicate with one another.

Morogoro was the last town before Dar es Salaam, and the next day we drove through fertile land and many small villages. Suddenly, without warning, a nanny goat ran across the road just ahead of us with a billy goat in hot pursuit. The nanny made it, but there was no hope of avoiding the billy. With a loud crash we sent him spinning off into the bushes, followed by bits of Peugeot. Another tragic case of an overwrought male being done to death by his libido. We did not stop, because to have done so would have

121

involved endless arguments over compensation, whereas the damage to the car was appreciable and the goat should not have been on the road in the first place. The car could be driven, but one wing, the lights, and the radiator grill were badly damaged.

On the outskirts of Dar-es-Salaam, the road led through spectacular plantations of lofty coconut palms. The fronds of their raffish mop-like heads shivered in the stiff breeze, and between their elephant-grey trunks, leaning in every direction, could be glimpsed an occasional white-domed mosque with castellated walls. The edges of the narrow road were lined by endless throngs of people decked out in every kind of garb and colour imaginable. Herds of bleating goats mingled with droves of bicycles and wooden handcarts stacked high with local produce. Drovers yelled at heavily loaded donkeys, which brayed their lunatic cry in protest, and children laughed and waved as we passed through this polyglot pageant. The warm air, redolent with the rich smells of unfamiliar spices, had that balmy feel found only in the humidity of a tropical breeze. I had reached the edge of the immense continent of Africa, and the vibrant scene assaulted my senses and thrilled me with excitement in anticipation of the adventures that lay ahead.

Dar-es-Salaam means "Place of Peace" in Arabic, and its focal point was the harbour, which was formed by a narrow spit of land dividing it from the sea. The harbour entrance was narrow, and ships had to make a sharp turn to starboard immediately after negotiating the gap. The spit was covered with mixed groves of coconut palms and casuarinas, through whose feathery fronds the trade winds sighed without ceasing.

Fish traps of mangrove poles driven into the sand lined the beach on the harbour side, and every morning people would come down to buy fish from the local fishermen. Especially fascinating to me was the sight of the Arab dhows tacking back and forth across the harbour with their great billowing lateen sails—often formed from a patchwork of old white flour sacks with the trademarks still visible in faded red. Tacking every few minutes and manhandling the heavy, skyward-slanting boom, with its voluminous sail, was a tricky task in the brisk wind. I spent many hours on this vantage point, observing passing life and staring out at the Indian Ocean. I drank in the brilliance of the tropical colours and revelled in the exotic blooms I had never seen before. Riotous cascades of bougainvillea tumbled in dazzling hues from every wall, regiments of flaming canna lilies lined the parks, and Flame of the Forest trees dripped bloody blossoms onto the sidewalks.

Tanganyika had been a German colony before the British grabbed it at the end of the First World War, so much of the architecture in the centre of Dar-es-Salaam had a Germanic flavour. This included the immigration office, where I went to retrieve my "deposit". First of all, I was told I would have to go back to Mbeya; and then, when I vehemently protested, the British official went into a back room and returned with a file about half an inch thick, bearing my name! After looking through it for a few moments, he conceded I could have my funds returned if I presented a ticket showing when and how I was leaving. Alarmed to find he had such an official looking file bearing my name, I could not imagine what they could have found to put in it. I looked around for a way to continue my trip East, and I found an Indian ship which took "Deck bunk class" passengers to Bombay via Zanzibar and Mombasa for three pounds if you brought your own food, and five pounds if they fed you. This seemed like a pretty good bargain, considering it included crossing 3,000 miles of Indian Ocean, so I booked my passage and splurged the extra two pounds to cover three meals a day for the next eight days. There were a great many Indians in East Africa, originally brought there by the British from India to serve as coolie labour. Of course they brought their religion with them, and many were Hindus, for whom it was customary to burn the body of the dead on a funeral pyre. There was a burning ghat on the outskirts of Dar-es-Salaam known irreverently amongst the local Europeans as the "Burma Grill!"

After spending about three weeks in Dar, and with my finances re-fortified by the return of my funds, I went on board the ship on the due date. I found my bunk on the lower tier of a double, in the middle of a sea of similar bunks which completely filled the hold. I was completely surrounded by Indians of both sexes and of every type and shade of colour. As the only

European, I was something of an oddity, and it was not long before one of the Indian ship's officers found me and insisted I shared his cabin. "It is not suitable for you to be sleeping with all those bloody Indians, is it?" he said. "You are having a drink, yes?" Without waiting for an answer, he took a bottle of whisky from a drawer and, before I could protest, filled a tumbler to the brim. He handed it to me and waited expectantly for me to knock it back. Actually I cannot stand the stuff; besides, it was only 10 o'clock on a hot morning. I thanked him for his generosity and took a small sip. Fortunately, the ship was about to sail, and when he slipped out shortly to attend his duties, I was able to pour most of the whisky down the sink.

We sailed shortly thereafter. I went out on deck to watch as we passed though the tricky harbour entrance and looked out over the narrow headland where I had passed so many hours watching ships like this one heading out into the dazzling blue ocean of the Indian Ocean.

Our first stop was Zanzibar, which, although it had been a British Protectorate since 1890, still belonged to the Sultan of Zanzibar, along with a 10-mile-wide strip along the entire Kenyan coastline. The principal export from the island was spices, and the prince amongst them was cloves. Everywhere you looked there were cloves spread out to dry in the sun, cloves heaped in pyramids, or sacks of cloves piled in ramparts. They were introduced to the island in 1818 from the Moluccas, but within only a few years, three-quarters of the world's supply were coming from Zanzibar, giving the island its other name of "Spice Island". Their scent was almost overpowering, and you could smell them on the breeze long before the ship reached the harbour. The ship was staying overnight, so I decided to disembark and put up in a small and very cheap hotel run by a French woman. The tiny rooms were divided by the flimsiest of partitions, so there was not much in the way of peace or privacy. When she heard I was going to Singapore, she said I must be sure to visit the "Worlds" which she said were full of all kinds of fascinating oriental wonders— inferring that most of them were sinful. Sadly, by the time I eventually reached there, they had either been closed down by the puritanical government or had been cleaned up and were a shadow of their former selves.

Zanzibar had an exotic past and had been ruled for many years from Oman, at the mouth of the Persian Gulf. In fact, it became so important as a source of slaves and spices that the Omani Sultan, Seyyid Said, transferred his court from Muscat to Zanzibar in 1832. For many years it was the most important town on the coast of East Africa. The old town of Zanzibar was a warren of narrow streets connected to labyrinthine alleys which twisted and turned between whitewashed houses with massive brass-studded doors and lintels intricately carved in the traditional Arab style. Many of the people wore Muslim dress, but there were also many Hindus, as evidenced by the necklace of mango leaves strung over the doorways.

I took a tour over the island in a taxi with the driver as my guide. He showed me the plantations of clove trees and a fascinating ground plant (*mimosa pudica*) that folded its feathery leaves and appeared to lie down and die if you touched it. Many years later, I found that the Chinese name for this plant translated with the charming name of "shy grass."

I visited the old slave market where, in the last century, slaves were brought from the interior of Africa by Arab traders for sale and then, in most cases, transported in dhows to the Arabian Peninsula as domestic servants. At least 50,000 slaves passed through the Zanzibar slave market every year, and it was really this trade in living human flesh that brought colonialism to East Africa. After missionaries, including Livingston, had alerted the practice of slaving to the attention of the Victorian British public, pressure was brought to bear on the government to put a stop to it. This was achieved in 1873, when the British Navy sailed into the harbour and threatened to blow holes in the Sultan's palace, which was conveniently located on the waterfront, unless he signed a decree outlawing the slave trade. The trade continued to flourish on the mainland, where slaves were also used to transport ivory from the interior down to the coast. The Brits soon realized the trade would start up again as soon as the troops climbed on their boats and sailed away, so they were pressured, not only into staying, but also into extending their mandate inland.

In August 1896, Britain and Zanzibar fought a 38-minute war—the shortest in recorded history—after Khalid bin Barghash had taken power following the death of the Sultan Hamid bin Thuwainis. The British had wanted Hamoud bin Mohammed to become Sultan because they thought he would be much easier to work with. The British gave Khalid one hour to vacate the Sultan's palace in Stone Town. Khalid failed to do so and assembled an army of 2,800 men to fight the British, who launched an attack on the palace and other locations around the city. Khalid retreated and later went into exile. The British placed Sultan Hamoud in power at the head of a puppet government. The war marked the end of Zanzibar as a sovereign state and the start of heavy British influence.

I went down to the docks to watch the loading of dhows and small coastal freighters by some of the most muscular men I had ever seen—including the well-built miners I had worked with in Rhodesia. All day long they laboured under the tropical sun, humping huge sacks up narrow wooden gangways which bounced and swayed dangerously under the load.

At the end of the day, I returned to the ship and we set sail for our next stop—Mombasa, the principal port for Kenya. I was surprised to find that Mombasa too was an island, and that the entrance to Kilindini Harbour on the South side required the negotiation of two right-angled bends as the narrow channel wound its way between the island and its protecting reef. After traversing the immensity of the Indian Ocean, the ocean swells rose up into spectacular rollers as the bottom shelved. Feathered plumes of spume hundreds of yards long streamed from the tops of the curling crests as they reared, toppled, and dissipated, backlit by the sun, in a welter of foam on the ramparts of the reef. We arrived late in the afternoon, and as the ship was scheduled to stay for two days, I had plenty of time to look for my friend Peter Monroe. Peter had lived with his mother in Honeysuckle Cottage—which looked as its name suggests—in the same English village as my mother's house. Although we had not been close friends, I was excited by the idea of meeting someone from a familiar spot in that faraway outpost of the Empire on which, although none of us had yet realized it, the sun had finally begun to set.

I knew the address of the place Peter was staying, and I set off to find it. I wandered around and, just as the sun was setting, finally had to admit I was lost in an area of neat bungalows festooned with bougainvillea and other flowering shrubs. I fancied I selected one at random, but it must have been fate that directed my footsteps to that particular house. The door was opened by an Englishman. I explained my situation.

"Come on in," he said, "and have a beer."

It turned out that he held a senior rank in the Kenya Police, and soon he was asking me all kinds of questions. "What address are you are looking for?" he asked. I told him. "That's the house of the vicar of Mombasa. What's the name of your friend?" He looked up the number and phoned the house. "This is Guthrie, Kenya Police. I am calling for Peter Monroe."

This business-like approach produced immediate results. Peter was not at home, but was at that very moment appearing in a production being put on by the amateur Little Theatre Club. "Come on," Guthrie said, "I'll run you over there. It's not far." On the way, he asked what I was doing and what my plans were. Then, to my astonishment, he offered me a job as an Inspector in the Kenya Police Reserve, in a detachment guarding the Naval Armaments depot run by the British Admiralty on the mainland. I demurred, saying that I was only stopping in Mombasa for a couple of days. "Well", he said, "if you change your mind, just come and see me. Here's my card."

I went round to the stage door and asked for Peter. I followed the directions and confronted him just as he was about to go on the stage in the middle of the show. I shall never forget the look on his face when he saw me, as he had no idea I was coming or that I had even left Rhodesia. "My God, what the hell are you doing here?" he said. There were frantic wavings from the stage manager. "I've got to go on. Just hang on and watch through the wings and I'll see you in a bit."

After the show, we went off on Peter's scooter for a drink at the yacht club and then to the vicar's house, where I slept on the settee. Peter worked in the unlikely profession of a flour miller and had to go off to work early, so I was left to my own devices. By midday, I had decided I really liked the look of Mombasa, and as I had no particular timetable, it would be stupid not to take up the job offer made to me so unexpectedly. It had, after all, been my intention to pay my way by working, and here was a wonderful job offer that had come my way without my even looking for it! I took out the card Mr. Guthrie had given me and went round to his office.

"If that offer is still open," I said, "I would like to take you up on it." Well, it was and I did! In an instant I found myself transformed from being an almost penniless vagrant into an inspector in the Kenya Police Reserve.

I still had my pistol with me, and one of the first things I had to do was to hand it into the police for safe keeping. This was still the time of the Mau Mau rebellion against colonialism, and the rebels had obtained most of their weapons by stealing them. If you allowed a weapon to be stolen, you were prosecuted by the police, so it was strongly recommended to hand weapons in to them for safe keeping.

Chapter 4

October 1958 to Summer 1959

Mombasa. Mtongwe and Heron Bruce.

I describe life in Mombasa and as Deputy Officer Commanding Police at the Mtongwe Naval Armaments Depot. I take part in the rescue of a local woman from a well and describe the visit of the Queen Mother.

I returned to the shipping office and told them I would not be continuing with the voyage. They gave me a refund of three pounds. I celebrated that night with Peter, and the next day went to the depot to meet my new boss. His name was Major Heron Bruce, and his appearance and personality suited his splendid name. He must have been in his late fifties and was a wiry man of medium height. His most prominent feature was the bushy white moustache which adorned his upper lip. He had the habit of stroking the outer ends upwards with the thumb and first finger so that the ends turned up, giving him a rakish air. He wore the white bush jacket, wide-legged white shorts and white stockings with blue tops that were the uniform of the Kenya Police. But he preferred white shoes to the regulation black and wore a dark blue forage cap in place of the peaked cap. He carried a brown leather swagger stick and was a very imposing figure. The African constables were terrified of him, but, as I gradually came to discover, his forbidding exterior concealed a warm-hearted man with a wild sense of humour—although he remained a strict but fair disciplinarian.

As a young man he had gone out to the sugar plantations at

Demerara, in British Guiana. He told me the young estate "assistants" used to get up to all kinds of wild activities to release their high spirits. Every assistant had his own room in a multi-story dormitory and each was allocated his own mule to get around the vast estates. One time they decided to take a mule up to the fourth floor.

"It was the funniest damn thing you ever saw" he told me. "It wasn't too hard getting it up there, but the fun really started when we tried to get it to go back down. Nothing would persuade the animal to go down the stairs—not even blind-folded or backwards. In the end, the authorities had to knock out the window, and the wretched beast had to be lowered to the ground by a crane erected on the roof."

Another popular amusement when well-oiled after a party was to leap fully clothed into the drainage ditch alongside the road and wrestle one of the numerous alligators out onto the grass. "The important thing was to get an arm lock around his jaws before he took your head off."

The sugar estates had raised ramps about six feet high for inspecting the underside of company vehicles. These were used for a variation on the game of chicken, with the winner being the one who drove his vehicle up the ramps the fastest without it shooting off the unprotected end.

"Good fun", he said, "but a bit hard on the vehicles!"

"Heron", as he was commonly called, later joined the Colonial Police and was involved in tracking down cattle rustlers. This was a high-risk occupation, because the offence carried the death penalty and the rustlers had nothing to lose if they gunned down their pursuers. "They may as well have been hung for a cop as a cow."

He told me too about some of the characters he met around that time. "There was an old bush pilot who used to fly with an Indian mechanic in a ropey old float plane with the engine mounted above their heads. They sat one behind the other in separate open cockpits. The engine was always conking out, but the mechanic could usually fix it by standing up and tweaking it while they were still in the air. One time he could not get it fixed in time, and they had to come down in a hurry. In heavy jungle, the only possible landing spots were lakes and rivers, but this time the only choice was a lake barely large enough to land on.

"The problem with the motor was soon fixed, but how to take off from a lake that was too short? That was the question. A float plane cannot be held against the brakes, so they hacked a liana from the forest and tied the tail plane to a tree. The pilot gave her the gun and when the plane was bouncing on top of the water, the Indian stretched out along the top of the fuselage and cut them loose with a blow from his machete. They got off OK, but it was touch and go for a bit. They still had leaves and bits of tree sticking in the floats when they landed."

Heron had later seen action in Palestine at the height of the blood-letting, just before the United Nations succumbed to political lobbying and agreed to the creation of the State of Israel on Palestinian lands. He then went to Aden in its last days as a colony. There he used to drive around in an open MG with a live cheetah sitting in the passenger seat. One day, he told me, he knocked himself unconscious when he jumped his horse over the rail surrounding the patio at the Aden Club. "Bloody animal jumped too high and I hit my head on the edge of the roof. Felt a bit of a fool, but a couple of pink gins soon put that right!"

He had a farm "up country" somewhere near Nakuru in the "white highlands". The farm was run by his wife, while Heron remained on the Coast. I never heard any explanation for this unusual arrangement. He certainly never spoke badly of his wife. He was an interesting man, but perhaps she found him impossible to live with. Apparently Heron found me acceptable material for his deputy—my official title was "Deputy Officer Commanding Police". I was allocated an African servant and a small two-bedroomed bungalow at the edge of the palm trees. I had to go to the Indian tailor in town to be measured for my uniform, which was the same as that of my boss except I wore a dark blue peaked cap and black shoes.

The day I collected my uniform I also went shopping for food, including a big chunk of stewing steak which I put into my *kikapu*—a capacious carry bag woven from the fronds of the coconut palm. When I unpacked my starched and gleaming white uniform, I saw to my dismay that its pristine appearance had been violated by blotches of blood from the steak. My new servant was unfazed. He knew how to take care of that, he said, and loped off to his quarters to return a few minutes later with a bottle of Dettol disinfectant. I looked at it doubtfully.

"Are you sure" I said.

"*Ndio, Bwana*" he replied, vigorously nodding his head, his cheerful black face split in a wide toothy grin.

"OK," I said doubtfully.

He liberally dosed the stains with neat Dettol, and the offending garment was left to think about it overnight. Sure enough, the next day the stains had gone. In their place were big ragged holes edged with brown as if someone had placed live coals on the cloth. Ndege looked crestfallen. "*Samahani,* "he said softly.

I ruefully accepted his apology. What could I say? The problem had been my fault and he had only tried to help. I went back to the tailor to order a new uniform, this time at my own expense.

The depot was in Mtongwe, on the other side of Kilindini harbour from Mombasa Island. There was an Admiralty ferry which ran from the docks across the harbour, where it landed at a fenced jetty area with an armed guard in a sentry box at the gate. The ferries were jaunty tug-like vessels with names like *Burundi-* Swahili for "gun". From the jetty, it was a 10-minute walk up the hill to our living quarters and the entrance to the depot. The road was public access and ran through plantations of coconuts, kapok, and cashew. The fruit of the cashew is bright yellow and bell-like, with the hook-shaped nut stuck on the bottom like a clapper. The nut has a poisonous covering and must be roasted to get rid of it. Dotted among the trees were small houses with roofs and walls woven from palm fronds. Palms provided many of the necessities of life including *pombe*. This potent alcoholic brew is made from the sap dripping into cans from the end of the amputated flower stalk. It is collected every day by agile men dashing up the trees using notches cut into the trunks. At the top, usually about 30 feet above the ground, the climber has to pull himself up into the crown of the tree using the overhanging fronds.

The Africans' craze for *pombe* was shared by bushbabies— small nocturnal primates that closely resembled the Australian koala bear. These small grey furry creatures would untie the cans and hurl them to the ground after swigging the contents. Naturally this did not endear them to the legitimate *pombe* collectors, and whenever a looter was detected, a furious chase took place as yelling men scampered up trees trying to catch the miscreant as it leaped from tree to tree. They were seldom successful unless the bushbaby had drunk sufficient to topple in an alcoholic daze into the arms of its pursuers.

On a bluff overlooking the jetty and the harbour were the living quarters of the European Admiralty staff responsible for the administration of the depot and maintenance of all the munitions it contained. These were considerable, because this was the main re-supply depot for all British naval ships east of Suez. The houses, with their red-tiled roofs, had a fine view over the harbour and were cooled by the constant trade winds blowing through them.

About 10 minutes' walk up the road was the actual depot where the munitions were stored in underground bunkers. Well separated from one another and covered by grass and other vegetation, the bunkers looked like a series of grassy mounds among the coconut palms and other fruit trees. The whole depot was surrounded by a tall chain-link fence with watch towers every hundred yards. These were not manned full-time, but each tower had a searchlight which was switched on at intervals by regular night patrols. Nocturnal creatures would often be caught in their powerful beams, and in particular the huge eyes of the tiny bushbabies would shine back at you out of the dark like great red lanterns, even when they were hundreds of yards away.

The police station was a small hut just outside the wire. The interior was divided into a general office and a smaller one for the Officer Commanding Police (OCP), Heron Bruce. As Deputy Officer Commanding Police (DOCP), I had a desk just outside his door in the general office, which was also occupied by a police sergeant and one or two clerks. The most important feature in the general office was the Incident Book. This was a large ledger in which every incident, no matter how trivial, was entered together with the time it was reported. Generally, things were very quiet and very little happened to break the routine.

Every morning, in an elaborate pantomime resembling a scene from a comic opera, defaulters were brought up before Heron Bruce, who sat behind his desk looking very fierce and imposing. His leather-bound swagger stick was placed on the blotter in front of him, and he was flanked by myself on one side and Police Inspector Omar Mohammed Omar on the other. Both of us standing rigidly at attention, wearing our peaked caps. The unfortunate African constable who had committed some misdemeanour was stripped of his beret and belt and sandwiched between two other constables, one in front and one behind. The trio stood waiting in line astern just outside the office.

In a voice powerful enough to rattle the windows, Omar Mohammed Omar gave the orders. "Prisoner and escort, forward march! Left! Right! Left! Right! Prisoner and escort, right face!"

The trio would now be facing Heron Bruce, with all three of them scared to death. It was not uncommon for the wretched miscreant to actually be shivering with fear. Although Heron spoke fluent Swahili, as part of the charade he would speak only in English, with the translation going through Omar. Particulars of the case, usually involving some trivial matter of discipline, would be brought up and, after a series of questions and answers—all faithfully translated by Omar - Heron would deliver his verdict and punishment for the offender. At the end of the proceedings, Omar would call out, "Prisoner and escort, right turn! Quick march! Left! Right! Left! Right!" and out they would go. On one occasion, one of the escorts was so nervous he turned left instead of right, finding himself facing away from the exit instead of towards it. It took all my will power not to burst out laughing, and once the door was shut, even Heron permitted himself a smile.

The two Arab Inspectors and myself worked shifts. The night shift started at midnight and ran till 8 a.m. I used to really hate this

134

because I found it so hard to stay awake until midnight and also very hard to sleep during the heat of the day. There was no air conditioning in those days, of course. We used to patrol the whole area in a Land Rover to make sure the constables were not asleep at their posts. Omar was worth two of me when it came to experience and generally knowing how to deal with any situation. The other Arab inspector was not so good, and one night, when it was his turn to be on duty, he called me up at 2 o'clock in the morning. I had come off duty at midnight and was fast asleep when the phone rang. He told me he was down on the jetty and there were two Europeans there who were drunk and who were refusing to leave. He asked me what he should do. I had no idea what to tell him and was dithering about trying to decide whether I should reluctantly put on my uniform and go down there when he said they were getting into a small boat and leaving of their own accord. With great relief I hung up, staggered back to bed, and instantly went back to sleep.

The next morning, Heron called my name from inside his office. "Fleming!"

"Sir!"

"Shut the door." I shut it and stood to attention in front of his desk.

"I understand you had a phone call from the inspector this morning concerning two Europeans on the jetty."

"Yes, sir."

"What action did you take?"

"Well, none, sir. He told me the men left of their own accord."

Heron exploded and gave me the most severe dressing down I have ever experienced. "That's no excuse! Don't you realize that one of your men was calling on you—his superior officer—for help. He needed assistance, and you failed him! How do you think that makes him feel about you? You should have gone down there and arrested the bastards at gunpoint and marched them off to the brig! You are supposed to be Deputy Officer Commanding

Police, responsible for the security of this establishment, and you utterly failed to live up to that responsibility! Is that clear!"

"Yes, sir," I said, severely chastened.

"Dismissed!"

I slunk back to my desk with all the Africans in the office looking at me. They undoubtedly overhead every word.

Five minutes later, the dread call came again.

"Fleming!"

"Yes, sir." *Now what!*

"I am driving into Mombasa at noon, can I give you a lift?"

Heron Bruce was a great boss. He never bore a grudge, but he was a stickler for discipline, and you always knew exactly where you stood with him. He was entirely right in what he said to me, and it taught me a lesson I never forgot.

One day, a few weeks later, when Heron was away, I sitting at my desk with the punka-wallah fan circling lazily overhead when I heard a commotion outside the office. A moment later, the sergeant came running into the office. "Sir, come quick."

Outside on the road were a group of people all talking at once, waving their arms and pointing down the road towards the village. "What's going on?" I asked.

"Sir, they say a woman has fallen down a well. They can hear her screaming. They need help."

The city fire brigade was on Mombasa Island and would take a minimum of an hour and a quarter to reach us via the Likoni ferry, followed by a tortuous drive through the bush. The only possible local facilities capable of dealing with any sort of emergency lay with the depot fire brigade, consisting of a couple of Land Rovers and about half a dozen men. Clearly there was no time to be lost. I ran to the fire station right behind our office and told the Indian fire chief what had happened.

"If it's off the base" he said, "I need the authority of the base commander."

"I'll call him."

I dialled the number to find that both he and his deputy were away. Heron was also away, so it was left to me to make the decision. That was easy. To me there was only one possible course of action. Acting on my authority, we jumped aboard the fire station Land Rover and sped through the gates.

With the crowd running ahead to guide the way, we wound our way through the palms for a few hundred yards before coming to a group of people gathered around a well with a low circular wall built from coral blocks. A crossbar made from a length of rail supported on two coral pillars spanned the opening. Peering down, I could just see a small circle of reflecting water broken by the huddled shape of the woman, who was crying out and moaning. At least she was alive and conscious.

We threw two ropes over the rail and tied a bowline in the ends, and the Indian fire chief and myself dangled over the void and were lowered to the bottom in a series of jerks that stretched the manila ropes and made them creak in protest. I hoped they were strong enough. The deeper we went, the more the slime-covered walls closed in on us in a series of steps, until at the bottom they were only three feet across. Moaning in pain, the woman lay huddled in water which reeked of rot and decay. She had obviously bounced off each ledge as she fell and had a number of broken bones. As we struggled in the knee-deep water, I am afraid we were not very gentle with our method of readying her for transport back to the surface. She was as floppy as a rag doll and kept slipping out of the loops, so we had to truss her up in a web of ropes like a fly caught by a spider.

Two more ropes were sent down, and then all three of us set out for the surface. To the rhythmic accompaniment of African chants, we progressed toward the surface in a series of wild rushes, each of which jerked to a stop so abruptly that we flew out of the loops in which we were precariously perched, only to bounce back into them with a force that set the knots creaking and groaning. All three of us had to go at the same speed so that the Indian and myself could hang onto the woman and prevent her from falling out of her cocoon or spinning like a top. When I looked up, I could see a disc of daylight fringed by a circle of black faces peering down at us. About 12 feet from the top, one of the three strands in my rope broke and started to unravel as it passed over the rail. *Uh-oh*, I thought, as I envisioned a fast, unplanned return trip to the bottom. I grabbed hold of the rope supporting the woman in case mine gave way completely—but it held. Willing hands helped us over the parapet, and the woman laid was out onto a stretcher and loaded into an ambulance. I looked down at the ruins of my uniform, now smeared with green slime and blotched with blood. At least this time the stains came from a source more honourable than seepage from a packet of steak.

Later, Heron asked me about the incident. "Did you go down the well yourself?"

"Yes" I said, and thought I detected approval in his nod.

"I discussed it with Moakes at a cocktail party last night." he went on. "He told me that if he had been in the office, he would have refused permission to go."

I was shocked.

"He said his primary responsibility was to the base, and he would have looked pretty foolish if it had blown up while the fire brigade was off fishing some local village woman out of a well."

Now, with 35 years of hindsight, I can see that maybe he had a point, but I am glad it never came to the test. The way I felt at the time, I would have given the order to the fire chief to go even if Moakes had refused permission over the phone. That would undoubtedly have gotten me fired.

On one occasion the base was visited by a Naval Officer, and I had to mount a guard of honour. Heron gave me some pithy words of advice beforehand. "Look the bugger straight in the eye" he said, "and if he asks you any questions, for Christ sake don't say you don't know. If you don't know the answer, just make it up. If he asks why the constables are all short, just tell him they are from the Bongawalla tribe and they are all small. He won't know any different."

On the appointed day, we were all ready and drawn up for

138

inspection. The Naval Officer and myself were brought face to face, and I stood to attention and gave him a snappy salute. Remembering Heron's advice, I looked him straight in the eye and, after the briefest of moments, they slid away from mine. *Gotcha*, I thought, gleeful that the ploy had worked so well.

Mombasa was visited by the Queen Mother, and we had to send a detachment of constables to help guard the route. Heron took me over in his MG for the rehearsal. On this day, the surrogate royal car left Government House and drove out to the airport. After a short pause, it turned around and drove back to Government House by another route, which would be the one taken by the royal visitor on her arrival. We had been designated that section of the road next to Government House, so there was more than one hour between the outward and return journeys. We duly stood at attention and saluted as the acting Queen Mother went by on her way to the airport. But as soon as the tail of the Rolls disappeared around the bend, we got into Heron's MG and roared off in the opposite direction.

"Just time for a couple of quick snorts at the Yacht Club" he said as we squealed round the curve.

Time passed quickly as we sat under the shade of the scarlet-blossomed flamboyant trees, with tankards of fresh lime to slake our thirst, and we barely made it back in time to take up our positions before the Rolls passed us on its return journey. At the subsequent debriefing, Heron was asked if there had been any problems.

"Everything went fine" he said with a straight face. "There was a dense crowd, but we managed to keep them under control. Had a couple of trouble makers, but we bopped them on the head and threw them in the brig."

A few chuckles came from around the room, but the senior police officer running the meeting was not amused.

On the actual day, our sector was very quiet. I stopped a car driven by a European just before the Queen Mother's car was due. He was very irate. "Your mate up the road just let me through, and he's got a lot more pips on his shoulder than you have" he snarled.

I waved him on. He did not look like a terrorist and I hoped the Queen Mother would understand.

Associated with the royal visit were a number of parties to which Heron was invited, and which, to judge by the size of his hangovers, he obviously enjoyed. One morning he told me, "I looked in the mirror and thought 'I don't know who the hell you are, but I'm going to shave you anyway!'"

Heron was very direct and had little patience with prevarication. On one occasion one of our police radios was broken, and he told me to give it to the European in charge of the relevant repair section, who had just come by the office. The man, a stocky little fellow from England's North Country with a belligerent manner, refused to take it and had started to give me a long tale about responsibilities and the signing of forms when Heron, overhearing what was going on, came out of his office. He took the radio out of my hands and thrust it into those of the other. "It's bust" said Heron, "Let's get it fixed!" And that was the end of the matter.

The African constables and non-coms stayed in communal barracks just outside the compound. We really had very little to do with them outside of work and, as I look back on it now, it seems to me that I should have taken more interest in their lives— although perhaps this would not have been appreciated at the time, and to have done so would certainly have been outside the tempo of the times. But one night I had a small inkling of the kind of difficulties they faced.

About eight in the evening, one of our best African sergeants came to my house and asked if I would come to see his child, who was sick. I walked with him over to his quarters and saw his daughter, aged around five, who had vomited an alarming amount of blood into an enamel basin. There was so much I was reminded of the basin of blood when we slaughtered the meat in Rhodesia. He said he had taken her to the local doctor, but the doctor had not been very helpful. The sergeant said he was worried because he had previously lost one child with similar symptoms under similar circumstances. I did not know what to do, but clearly the situation was serious. The nearest hospital was on the island, so it was there we would have to go. I phoned Peter to meet us at the ferry jetty on the island and arranged for the police Land Rover to take us down to the ferry. After we arrived at the African hospital, I accompanied the sergeant to see the duty doctor, who was an Indian. The doctor was obviously not pleased to see me and asked why I was there. I explained the situation and how I had come to bring the family to the hospital.

"We can be trusted to do our job, you know" he said in a somewhat belligerent manner, thus confirming my growing suspicion that he could not. I told him that I was sure he could, but that having already lost one child, this man, for whom I was responsible, had come to me for help and needed some reassurance. Perhaps Heron's dressing down had done some good.

In any event, the child was admitted, and a few days later returned to her family. I am sure that had I not been there, the sergeant would have been given short shrift; and I am sorry to say that, even so, I was not able to find out what had been the real cause of the child's vomiting so much blood nor of her long-term prognosis.

I had one brush with the medical authorities myself. One afternoon after lunch I found myself feeling very weak and with an obvious fever. I retired to bed and found myself alternating between running with torrents of sweat and shivering with such violence that my teeth were chattering. By about 7 p.m., I began to feel better; and by 8, I could get up. The next morning, I felt quite well and assumed the whole event was over, but the same cycle occurred that afternoon, and I sweated so much that the mattress on my bed was soaked. After three days of enduring this, I went to the hospital on the island and was examined by a doctor who said I did not have malaria, even though I had all the symptoms. Heron's advice was to retire to bed with a huge slug of whisky and lemon, which I did, and a couple of days later I was cured and the symptoms never recurred.

Chapter 5

Summer 1959

Mombasa Town and Social Life

I chronicle the history of Mombasa and join the Yacht Club and the Little Theatre Club.

Before coming to Kenya from Rhodesia, I had heard about the Mau Mau uprising and the white settlers, who were generally depicted as a bunch of tyrants with a whip in one hand and a glass of gin in the other. As usual, the popular picture was entirely wrong and I found that race relations in Kenya were much more relaxed than those in Rhodesia. Mombasa was a colourful coastal town in which Africans, Arabs, Indians and whites lived together in relative harmony.

The city has a colourful history dating from about AD 900. It was a prosperous trading town by the 12th century, with trade links reaching as far afield as India and China. The first known European to visit Mombasa was Vasco da Gama in 1498, and two years later the town was sacked by the Portuguese. Over the next 400 years the town was administered by Arabs, Portuguese, Omanis and, finally, the British when the Sultan of Oman formally presented the town to the British in 1898. It is the main port for Kenya, which gained its independence from Britain in 1963—five years after my visit.

The most prominent landmark left behind by the Portuguese was Fort Jesus, overlooking the entrance to the old port. Now a picturesque ruin, it had been the scene of numerous sieges and massacres. Much of it was constructed of coral, which was still the building material of choice in the form of coral blocks chopped from coral quarries. The buildings were not high, and tough mangrove poles, cut from the nearby estuaries, were used for scaffolding. Visitors always remember the arches in the shape of giant tusks which spanned the road to Kilindini docks. In those days it was called Kilindini Road, but it was renamed Moi Avenue after independence. The climate was generally hot and humid but was leavened by the almost constant blowing of the monsoon winds off the ocean. The wind caressed the skin, it sighed through the casuarinas along the seafront and rattled the fronds of the coconut palms. Buildings dripped with the riotous colours of bougainvillea and other tropical flowers, climbers and shrubs.

The language spoken on the coast was Swahili, which, in a simplified form, was used as the *lingua franca* in the whole of East Africa. *Jambo* was the term of greeting for any hour of the day, to which the reply was also *Jambo,* followed by *habari?* meaning "what news?" to which the response was invariably *msouri,* which means "good". If it was in fact not good then you could follow up with *lakini,* meaning "but" and you could then go on to explain how a thief had stolen your life's savings, your house had burnt to the ground, and your wife had run off with a sailor.

I was fortunate in knowing Peter, because through him I had an immediate entrée into the local social life instead of having to spend several weeks finding my own way, which is usually the case when you arrive in a new place. In small towns like Mombasa, there was very little in the form of ready-made entertainment, and this encouraged people to produce and participate in their own, which was much better than simply watching the efforts of others. The foreign community organized their own clubs, and as Peter and myself shared many of the same interests, he was able to introduce me to both the Yacht Club and the Little Theatre Club.

Despite the many sharks that cruised the harbour, Mombasa was a wonderful place to sail and a great improvement on the puddle I sailed on in Karoi. The sea was warm and blue, and the wind blew so reliably that you could sail somewhere secure in the knowledge that you would be able to get back. It was generally believed that if you did capsize, the sharks would not attack you if you stayed within the protection of the sails and I never heard of anyone sailing being attacked, although occasionally sailors were taken who made the mistake of swimming from their ships in the docks. Within the harbour it was quite common to see big fish jumping clear of the water as they chased their prey or sought to escape being eaten themselves. On one occasion, four of us were hanging over the side of a large dinghy called a jolly boat when, without warning, a large fish shot from the water and plunged back in just behind our backs. We hardly had time to say, "Aaah", when that fish was followed almost immediately by a huge kingfish, about 4 feet long, which rocketed out of the water right next to the boat, sped through the air over our heads and ripped right through the cotton mainsail splitting it from luff to leach 20 feet above the water. Few people believed our almost incredible fish story when we limped back to the Yacht Club. Perhaps if it had been a few years later, after the advent of dacron sails, we might have had the fish as evidence, although having an angry sailfish thrashing around in a small boat would have given us a different story to brag about.

The Yacht Club was a simple affair situated on the south side of the island and open to the breeze. It was surrounded by scarlet flamboyant trees, and the entrance was shaded by a cashew tree with its bell-shaped, canary-yellow fruit, each with its hook-shaped nut hanging beneath it like a green clapper.

The bar was presided over by Ali, who wore a white *kanzu* and whose smiling black face was topped by a red fez. A popular drink in the heat of the day was fresh lime. This was served in large dimpled beer tankards filled to the brim with the watered-down juice of fresh limes sweetened with sugar. On days when it was a bit sour, Ali would warn you that it was a bit *kali*. *Kali* was one of a number of useful Swahili words which had found its way into the local English. It could be used for "sharp" as in the case of a knife, "bitter" or "sour" for taste, or even for "angry" ("The boss is in a *kali* mood today."). Another useful word was *maradadi*. This meant to be smart or well turned out as with clothes, a boat, or even a vehicle. In addition to sailing, the Yacht Club was a centre

144

for other social activities, including eating. It is a curious fact that the hotter the place, the hotter—or more highly spiced—the food. Mombasa was home to many Goans, Indians from the old Portuguese territory of Goa, on the West coast of India. They had brought with them their own exceptionally potent form of curry, which was served every Sunday lunchtime at the Yacht Club. I remember one English guy eating a plateful of this curry with sweat running into his eyes and coursing down his body. "If this is hell," he gasped, "I love it!"

Despite the heat, Christmas and the New Year were celebrated in traditional style. On New Year's Eve everyone took part in the violently energetic Scottish eightsome reel—a dance more suited to the frigid Scottish Highlands than a tropical island just one degree north of the equator. After completing the sequence of intricate manoeuvres required by the dance, everyone enjoyed themselves so much they changed from their New Year's finery into their tatty sailing clothes and did it again and again, until they collapsed exhausted on the wooden boards

Sometimes we sailed into the quiet upper reaches of the estuary away from the sea, and it was here that I saw my first pelicans. With memories of bedraggled birds with dirty feathers flopping around on the ground at the zoo, I had always thought of the pelican as the rather comic ungainly bird "whose beak can hold just as much as its belly can". But in flight they were a miracle of grace, as they glided seemingly forever with their rose-pink breasts almost touching their reflections in the mirrored surface of the water.

On the Northern side of the island was the Old Harbour, the meeting place for the dhows from Arabia. For centuries, these traditional craft had been sailing to East Africa across the Indian Ocean on the northeast monsoon, returning a few months later when the winds swung to the southeast. They had no form of mechanical power and harnessed the wind with their triangular lateen sails. They were built entirely of wood, fastened with pegs instead of nails. The high poop provided the captain's quarters, leaving the ragtag crew to occupy whatever space they could find. In the centre of the ship was an open fireplace, which seemed a bit hazardous on a wooden vessel, but which worked okay in practice.

The Old Harbour was bordered by the Old Town, redolent with the smells and sounds of the coast. Narrow, winding streets were crowded with men wearing the *kansu* or women, the *buibui*. I used to go with Peter on his scooter to Arab coffee shops, to drink tiny cups of bitter coffee sometimes accompanied by a hunk of sweet, sticky halva. This Middle Eastern sweetmeat is known in the West in its more refined form as Turkish Delight, and we watched it being made in a small room behind our favourite shop. The ingredients were placed in a large copper pot set over an open-topped charcoal fire, which had to be stirred continuously for over an hour by a man perched beside it wielding a large wooden paddle. The man's skin glistened as he squatted beside the fire in the equatorial heat. He must have dripped a lot of sweat into the mixture!

The Arab dhow captains made a picturesque sight around the town with their curly black hair protruding under their untidy turbans. They wore colourful sarongs with white shirts and had right-angled daggers with ornate handles stuck into their waistbands. On their feet they wore Arabian Nights shoes with pointed, upturned toes. They carried an air of unmistakable authority as befitted the captains of ocean-going sailing vessels that crossed and re-crossed the Gulf of Arabia. On one small coaster being unloaded at the dock, I noticed that the captain was a suntanned young European with blond hair and—with what impressed me most of all—one gold earring.

There were three ways to get on and off Mombasa Island. To the north was a floating pontoon bridge; to the West, a causeway carried the road and rail links to Nairobi; and to the South, the Likoni ferry took passengers and vehicles across the narrow channel. One day while I was waiting for the ferry, amid a colourful throng of African men, women, and children, a heavily loaded two-wheeled cart pulled by one man started down the steep slope to the water's edge. Almost immediately the man was overpowered by the cart and found himself propelled down the slope towards the water at an ever-increasing speed, so that his feet barely touched the ground. With shrieks of "Aiiiiiyee!" the crowd turned to watch the inevitable sight of the cart and driver plunging into the harbour at high speed. But we reckoned without the skill of the puller. On the brief intervals when his feet were on the ground he managed to swerve the cart back and forth across the slope like a skier performing schuss, and he broadsided it to a standstill just inches away from the water. The crowd went mad with mirth and howled with uninhibited laughter. There are no people who can enjoy a joke with such abandon as the Africans, and they doubled up and staggered around with laughter and the tears streamed down their faces as they cheered and congratulated the hero of the hour.

Another major focal point for self-entertainment was amateur dramatics, which was exceptionally well provided for in Mombasa. Unlike any other group I have encountered since, the local club even had its own building, containing a small theatre with changing rooms, a practice room known, as tradition demands, as the Green Room, and even a bar. This was the Little Theatre Club, and it was the place I had met Peter the night I arrived. During my year in Mombasa I was involved in two major productions—a pantomime and an Old Tyme Music Hall.

When, through Peter, I went to help at the pantomime, I said very firmly that I would do anything to help but I would not, under any circumstances, appear on the stage. In 1957, the chosen theme was Robinson Crusoe—with variations—and I started off by painting scenery but, inevitably, one night there was a shortage of pirates, and I allowed myself to be persuaded to be a stand-in pirate as a temporary measure so that rehearsals would not be disrupted. Somehow there never seemed to be enough volunteer pirates, so I became a permanent member of the pirate crew. Then one night the chief assistant pirate failed to show up and somehow I found myself filling his place. Later still, the script was revised, and for a few moments I even had the stage to myself. Fortunately, I did not have to say very much, as I played a very dumb assistant. My most memorable line was:

Pirate Chief: "I'm going down the beach to reconnoitre."

Me: "Wreck a what?"

Much to my surprise, this remark brought roars of laughter from the audience every night.

The pantomime was in preparation and rehearsal for about eight weeks and ran for ten performances. It was one of the most enjoyable things in which I had ever participated, because there was such powerhouse of energy created from the coming together of so many people. I began to understand how it would be possible to become stage struck. The audience loved it—especially the children—and it was a great success.

A few months later came the Old Tyme Music Hall. This was a truly marvellous production for which all the seats were removed from the theatre and replaced with tables and chairs. The audience was served drinks throughout the performance by singing waiters who were dressed up with mutton-chop whiskers and long white aprons. From time to time, the waiters would go up on stage and harmonize traditional songs such as "Nelly Dean". As the evening progressed, the audience got steadily merrier and joined in with more and more ribald comments.

The show included a series of traditional music hall acts with performers singing such songs as "I'm One of the Ruins That Cromwell Knocked Abaht a Bit" or "Knocked 'Em in the Old Kent Road". There was a chorus line, and the *pièce de résistance* was an old-style melodrama containing every cliche it was possible to think of. There was of course a hero and a heroine (poor but honest), as well as a villain, who was the local squire. There was the demon drink (sarsaparilla) and a diabolical bomb, and the climax came when the heroine was tied to the railway lines in front of the approaching express. The villain was called Sir Murgatroyd Maltravers and his assistant (myself), Habbakuk Hook. Once again I played a rather dumb assistant, so the producers must have felt I was well suited to filling that kind of role.

The Master of Ceremonies, who kept the whole evening going introducing the acts and cracking awful jokes, was none other than my boss, Heron Bruce. He was perfectly suited for the job and was even able to produce his own top hat and tails.

The show ran for 13 performances and could have run much

longer but for the exhaustion of the cast, who had to work during the day. It was incredibly popular, and many people came back to see it night after night. Each show ran for three hours, and on some nights we had two performances, with the second starting only 20 minutes after the first had finished. Each night, each artist thought of ways to improve on their previous night's performance, so the show became funnier as time went on. Those of us watching from the wings laughed so much it was hard to breathe.

By the last night the whole performance was running as smoothly as a well-oiled clock, and everyone gave their absolute utmost. This was traditionally the time when the stage crew played tricks on the cast, especially in a farcical show like this one. My high point came when I was on stage with the villain and he was expounding on what the diabolical bomb was going to do to the heroine's father (so that the villain could have his way with the heroine). At one point the squire strode up to the bomb and struck it with his riding crop (naturally he had to have one of those), whereupon a bell went off, which the squire hastened to silence by apparently adjusting the package. On the last night, he had no sooner done this and turned away to face the audience when the bell went off again—and again—and again. The stage crew kept the harried squire dodging back and forth while the audience yelled insults and advice to him. It was several minutes before he could continue. It fell to me to carry the bomb off stage with the intention of placing it to do its deadly work, but, unbeknownst to me, the hero had popped out of the grandfather clock when I wasn't looking and had reset the timing mechanism. The bomb exploded just after I had exited stage left, and as I staggered back on with ripped clothes and blackened face, the chandelier crashed to the ground in a cloud of dust simulated by a small amount of flour provided by Peter. On the last night, the stagehands emptied about two pounds of the stuff right on top of the villain, who stood there looking like a white ghost with a small pyramid of flour heaped on the crown of his top hat. In the final scene, the heroine was strapped to the tracks in front of the approaching express, as I struggled with her father, the signalman. She screamed and sat up, complete with the section of line to which she was strapped as the train, in the form of a large profile of the engine from the UPU line, came to a halt inches away in a cloud of what was supposed to be steam but which was, once again, flour. This was blown across the stage using a small hand-operated blower, but on this last night the crew had found a monster, and the whole stage and everyone on it disappeared in a huge cloud of flour from which they emerged white and sneezing.

As I stood in the wings that last night with the riotous laughter ringing in my ears, I was saddened by the thought that the following night this place, now bursting with energy and laughter, would be as silent as a tomb and never again would this particular group of people come together to create this volcanic energy. There was a wild party after the show, at which almost everyone drank too much. After it was over, it was much too late and much too risky to return to our respective homes on Peter's scooter, so the pair of us crossed the street to the cemetery and stretched out on a couple of tombstones. My uncle Roy was reputed to be buried in this cemetery after he died of Blackwater fever in 1930, but, although I looked, I was unable to find his grave.

While I was in Mombasa, I used to go around with Dulcie, one of the nursing sisters from the European hospital. I cannot say she was my girlfriend in the normal sense of the expression. She was a theatre sister, which meant that she assisted in all operations and was on call 24 hours per day. Occasionally they might have to work all night on some emergency and still have to work the following day on the scheduled operations. Occasionally we would drive out to some beach venue only to find out on arrival that Dulcie had to return to the hospital for an emergency which quite commonly involved British soldiers on leave from Aden who dived into shallow water whose depth was difficult to judge due to its clarity. The common outcome was a broken neck, resulting in paralysis or death. A terrible penalty for a minor error of judgment.

Peter had always been a fanatic about knives and guns. He liked to make his own knives and, before coming to East Africa, he used to recondition antique guns at his home in England. Once, he was heating the barrel of a muzzle loader with a blowlamp to loosen the plug which closed the breech, when it exploded. "Blew a hole right through the wall of Mother's cottage," he said with a grin, "It must have had that charge in there for a couple of hundred years. Quite amazing!" Peter borrowed a car from a friend and we went out into the bush along the Nairobi Road to go hunting. The biggest animal he ever got was a very small deer called a dikdik, which was about the size of a medium-sized dog.

We used to drive out into the bush late at night and sleep in the car until the dawn came up "like thunder"—to quote Eartha Kitt. It was always so peaceful, with the silence only disturbed by the murmur of African drums from some distant village and the hooting call of the night birds. On one occasion we crossed into what was then still the colony of Tanganyika and were stopped at the border by African border guards. It was not really any problem, but it is an alarming experience having some person about whom you know nothing stick a rifle in through the window with the muzzle only an inch from your eye.

Outside the town, African women still used to go around naked from the waist up. There was nothing very erotic about it because it was commonplace, but the breasts of the young women were very pointed and stuck out so far in defiance of the laws of gravity. In the older women they hung, flat and shrivelled, down to their waists, flapping as they walked, like a couple of leather pouches.

Chapter 6

Summer 1959 to August 1959

Mombasa. Family Ties.

I locate and meet up with my father after 13 years. My sister arrives. We take the train to Nairobi and stay with my father up country in the shadow of Mount Kenya. I describe a Mau Mau incident and go on safari. I visit Treetops and fly around the peaks of Mount Kenya.

I'd had almost no contact with my father since the divorce, but I had some idea that he might be in Kenya, so I asked Heron how I might find out where he was.

"Your father's not Donald Fleming by any chance is he?" he replied.

"Yes," I said.

"Oh, I know him. We've propped up many a bar together!"

He made couple of phone calls, and within 15 minutes I had my father's address and phone number on an up-country farm.

The next question was what was I going to do now that I had found him? I had not thought that far ahead because Kenya is a very large country and, not even being sure my father was still there, I had not expected to get such a prompt answer. I did not feel up to telephoning him. To do that meant going through the complexities of making a long distance call and I was always uncomfortable using the phone. Besides, what on earth could I say to him? He had not heard from me since I was a small kid, and he had no idea I was in the country. On the other hand, a letter might take too long. Even though the country was large, I had not reckoned on the communication in the relatively small size of the expatriate population, and since Heron had already called some mutual acquaintances to find out my father's address, he would hear of me through the grapevine if I did not act quickly. I decided to send him a telegram. After pondering for a couple of hours, I sent something like, "Am in Mombasa and would like to meet you" and gave the address and telephone number.

I had an almost immediate reply asking how long I was going to be there. I had failed to mention that I was living in Mombasa and not just passing through on a ship. I answered this question and followed it up with a letter giving more details. Knowing that my father had retired from the Air Force many years earlier, I addressed the letter to Mr. D. M. Fleming, not realizing the importance that most retired military men give to maintaining their rank. This oversight earned me a rather pained reprimand in his reply. "Why have you not addressed me by my well-earned rank?"

It turned out that my father was living with a former Air Force buddy, Mongoose Soden, on a small farm in Timau, situated at about 8,000 feet on the slopes of Mt. Kenya. Among their near neighbours was a family called Llewelyn, who were planning to visit Mombasa within the next two weeks. So Mr. and Mrs. Llewelyn came as a sort of advance guard to check me out and report back to my father. They drove down in their Peugeot and picked me up outside the dock gates. They were very pleasant and easy to talk to and told me about my father's situation.

Mongoose Soden had married a wealthy socialite who had died slowly and painfully a few years earlier of multiple sclerosis. Mongoose had his own small plane—a Piper or Cessna—which was ideal for making day trips to Nairobi and for getting around this large country, in which flying conditions were ideal for most of the year. So, about three weeks later, Mongoose flew my father down to Mombasa to meet me. We arranged to meet for dinner at the Mombasa Club, which I had never before visited.

I had not seen my father since I was about 12, and I was quite nervous about the meeting. I had really never known him, and I remembered him as a rather aloof and brusque man. After so many years I wondered whether we would even recognize each other. I went up some wooden stairs to a small crowded dining room overlooking the water and spotted him immediately. We looked so alike there was absolutely no doubt it was him. He recognized me at the same time and he stood to shake my hand in a very British fashion. Mongoose had stayed out of the way, so there was just the two of us. Over dinner we talked of what we were doing, but there remained an atmosphere of restraint between us. We agreed I should come and stay on the farm when I had some leave from my job.

From my point of view, I do not remember feeling any strong emotions. I felt merely that he was my father, whom I hardly knew, and it was only right and proper that we should be in touch and know each other. I had never felt any need to take sides in the separation. In fact, I had always felt it was really none of my business. I had told my mother that I had located and planned to meet my father, and I think she had some worries that I might abandon her in favour of him and perhaps be adversely affected by what she viewed as his rather irresponsible attitude to life. Of course this was a quite unrealistic worry, but also quite understandable.

It was about this time that my sister decided to come out to stay with me. My father met her off the plane when she arrived in Nairobi, and they spent a couple of days together before she continued her journey to Mombasa—so she visited the farm before I did. She always felt more negatively about Father than I did. Mother said this stemmed from an incident when, as a little girl, she had tried to climb on his lap and been brusquely pushed aside. Lulu stayed with me in my bungalow and before long found herself a job as secretary to the town clerk. She got herself an old scooter for transportation, but it was not very reliable, and I remember her being reduced to tears on one occasion when it refused to start.

One day I was called at work to be told Lulu had been involved in a road accident and was in the hospital. I went rushing over there and asked the English nursing sister where my sister was. "Miss Fleming has had a minor accident and there is no need for all this fuss" the nurse snapped.

This was hardly the response I was expecting to my perfectly reasonable enquiry, since I had not known anything about Lulu's condition. "I am her brother and only relative for thousands of miles", I replied hotly, "and all I have been told is that she was involved in an accident." I was reluctantly allowed in to see her. She had suffered only a shaking up and a few scratches, so she was allowed home before the end of the day.

I had continued to keep in touch with my ex-colleagues at De Havillands, and one day I received a letter asking if I would like to join them on a trip they were getting together to "survey" the roads of Africa for the British motor industry. My friend Collyn, who was now working for the research department of Vauxhall Motors, was the moving force behind this idea. As I was entirely free of the constraints that usually make it impossible to take advantage of this sort of opportunity I accepted with alacrity. They planned to leave England the following September, so I resigned from the Kenya police in July, and in August, Lulu and I left Mombasa for the interior and a one-month stay with father in Timau.

We decided to go by bus. It took all day to cover the 300 miles and climb the 5,500 feet to Nairobi. We were the only whites on the bus and among the very few passengers going all the way to the capital. The bus made its way through the scrubby thorn bush, stopping to let local people get on or off along the way. All local buses had full-length roof racks piled high with bicycles, baskets of produce, bundles of firewood, and even live goats, which bleated in protest at the lurching and swaying.

The overhead racks were crammed with smaller belongings, and as we bounced over a pothole, a portable radio about the size of shoebox fell out of the rack and bounced onto Lulu's head before crashing to the floor and smashing into a million pieces. With a cry of dismay, the African owner dropped to his knees to scoop up the shattered remains of his prized possession. He was totally unconcerned about the fate of my sister, whose head had been the primary point of impact. Fortunately, her head was harder than his badly stowed radio and she was unhurt.

At one point we stopped to pick up a heavily pregnant lady who had one child strapped to her bosom and held another by the hand, while on her back she had a huge bundle of firewood supported, as was the local custom, from a band passed around her forehead. This brought exclamations of astonishment from the lady from the coast sitting in the seat behind us.

We ground our way into the chaotic Nairobi bus depot just as dusk was falling, to be met by Father, looking distinctly ill at ease and out of place. An African bus station was definitely not the sort of place in which he felt at home! He whisked us off in a Land Rover to more familiar territory in a better part of town. He took us to the Muthaiga Club, which was the home away from home for settlers visiting the city. The service was impeccable, and the food, prepared under the supervision of a Swiss chef, some of the best I have ever tasted. Accommodation was in individual cottages, or *bandas*, set amongst the trees. It was altogether a most civilized place to stay.

The following day we set off for the farm, which was about 160 miles due north of Nairobi. Along the way, the road climbed another 2,500 feet, skirting the flanks of Mt. Kenya. We bypassed the townships of Thika and Nyeri—famous for their tea and coffee plantations—and the landscape opened up into vast vistas as we continued to climb the flanks of Mount Kenya—a mountain so huge that it could really only be seen from a distance, its bulk disappearing into the clouds on our right.

The single-track railway ran alongside the road, along with a line of telegraph poles that stretched to the horizon with scarcely a curve. On many of them, sentinel fish-eagles perched motionless, awaiting their prey. Characteristic flat-topped thorns dotted the landscape many of them hung with the nests of weaver birds. We crossed the equator at a large roadside sign and entered the small town of Nanyuki. Its single main street was divided down the centre by a luxuriant tangle of brilliantly coloured bougainvillea. The shops on either side included banks, grocers, butchers, suppliers of agricultural equipment, and firms of accountants, providing all the services needed by a farming community. Here we stopped and bought meat and other provisions, which gave my father an opportunity to show off his children to his acquaintances.

We continued north over a road that began to twist and turn as it negotiated the creeks and valleys higher up the mountain. On the approach to one bend was an attention-getting sign which read: "You MUST slow down." At last we reached Timau, consisting only of an Indian *duka*, which doubled as a post office, a police post and a huddle of huts. The *dukas* in the old East Africa were a mainstay of the way of life. Almost always run by descendants from the Indians brought over by the British in the early days, they often provided the only source of provisions and commerce in remote areas. As well as providing such vital services as mail, they also ground maize into the staple corn flour and bartered one type of commodity for another. They also made loans and advanced cash against crops—a service of great importance to small farmers who often only got paid once or twice per year.

We turned off the main road and followed a rough track for another couple of miles before drawing up in front of a low wooden bungalow fronted with colourful flowers and surrounded by trees. A couple of young boxer dogs bounded out to meet the vehicle. What a delightful spot.

It was late in the afternoon when we arrived, and the sun was well down. The air was cool and dry, with the scent of pines. Backed by a stand of tall eucalyptus trees, the long, low bungalow was settled comfortably into the slope. It was clad with wood and roofed with wooden shingles. Blue wood smoke from the stone chimney spiralled lazily into the air. In front of the cottage were flowerbeds bright with roses, along with a lawn that sloped down to the bottom wall. Beyond the walled garden was the start of the forest that clothed the flanks of the mountain. In the distance were the snow-covered peaks of Mount Kenya. It was quiet but for the soft tones of Swahili from the unseen African huts behind the house and the distant rush of a stream.

Mongoose came out to meet us, and our bags were taken by two cheerful African servants, each wearing a white apron and red fez. We were shown to our bedrooms in the guest wing of the house. Using plenty of rusty, scalding water which erupted, geyser-like, from the taps accompanied by bursts of steam, we washed away the dust of the six-hour journey. A cheerful fire burned in the stone fireplace and imparted a homely atmosphere to the book-lined room. Over the mantelpiece hung a picture of Wanda Soden as a young girl. She wore a red dress, and her eyes seemed to follow you across the room and to be looking directly at you no matter from where you viewed the painting.

We had some drinks and then, when he felt it was time to eat, Mongoose pushed the bell beside his chair. The servant appeared. *"Ndio, Bwana."*

"Please serve the food."

"Ndio, Bwana" and almost immediately, a delicious three-course meal appeared.

Neither Mongoose nor my father ever told the servants what to prepare, and mealtimes could vary by as much as an hour. Yet whatever time it was called for, the food was always served immediately and was perfectly cooked. All this was achieved on a cast-iron, wood-burning stove with a 20-minute reaction time and a temperament as unpredictable as wounded buffalo.

We were awakened the following morning by a servant bringing a pot of tea on a tray. The air was cold and clear, and we had a wonderful view of snow-capped Mount Kenya through the picture window by the breakfast table. Over the following days, we had a chance to explore. Like all settler establishments, Mongoose Farm was very self-sufficient. There was a well-equipped workshop with all the tools needed to carry out repairs or simple construction. If you wanted to extend your house or build an aircraft hangar, you just went ahead and did it. If you needed bricks, you hired a local brick maker, who came and made them on the premises.

Water was obviously very important in this arid area, where rain only fell during the long and short rains in March and October. Timau was well favoured in this respect because, at 17,500 feet, Mount Kenya had its own climate, with frequent snow storms that fed the numerous streams flowing down the mountain, providing a continuous, year-round flow of water. One of these streams ran through Mongoose farm and had been stocked with trout by my father, who had also cleared fishing paths along its banks. Behind the house were two large water tanks, each holding 500 gallons. They overflowed almost continuously and the surplus water was directed through the garden as it sloped gently towards the stream. Intrigued to find out where it came from, I followed the steady thumping I could hear down by the stream. I traced it to a piece of rusty, cast-iron machinery with a domed head squatting beside the water. It sat there emitting a steady heartbeat, but there were no wires attached to it, nor had it any sign of a motor. Water ran down to it from a channel cut into the top of the bank which joined the main stream higher up. The energy from the falling water was used to compress air in the dome, which kicked back and pulsed a small percentage of the falling water into the pipe leading to the storage tanks. Maintenance was restricted to replacing two rubber flap-valves once per year, and for that you had an unlimited supply of water. It was called a ram, and it was the most ingenious device I had ever seen.

Tended by an aged gardener, the herbaceous borders were full of flowers; but roses, with blooms the size of cabbages and scents of matching proportions, predominated. The kitchen garden was a marvel, full of every kind of fruit and vegetable, both tropical and temperate. Pineapples and oranges grew alongside apples and blackberries. Passion fruit rambled next to raspberries, with every plant so confused by the climate that you could find blossom and ripe fruit together on the same tree. Local monkeys found this cornucopia irresistible and had to be discouraged by an electric fence and netting. Local leopards were attracted by the monkeys but found the domestic dogs even more tasty, and my father had lost several dogs to them.

Mongoose and my father had known each other in the Air Force in the years before the Second World War, and after his wife died, Mongoose asked my father if he would like to come and share his house. My father was delighted to do so. Since coming to Kenya, after his divorce and retirement from the service, he had tried a number of jobs and found none of them very satisfactory. He had spent some time in the Prisons Service and also with the Locust Control Service. This involved driving out into remote parts of the country looking for locust swarms when they were still in the formative, or hopper, stage. This was before they could fly and were relatively easy to exterminate. The ground crews would then call in air support, who would spray the hoppers with insecticide.

Locusts were an ever-present threat in countries like Kenya, and they inflicted a plague of biblical proportions when they darkened the sky and stripped the landscape of every bit of greenery within a few hours. Another menace was the kwelya bird. About the size of a sparrow, these tiny birds would swarm in their millions and could strip a field of wheat in a few hours. At night they would roost in trees in such numbers that their weight would break the branches. One drastic method of dealing with them was to place drums of petrol below the roosting birds and set them off with explosives. The resulting fireball incinerated the trees and everything in them.

Farmers also had to contend with other, more lethal, hazards. Marauding lions used to help themselves to livestock, and one farmer lost 30 head of cattle in one night to a lioness teaching her cubs how to kill. A lion kills by leaping on the neck of its prey and then using its weight to break the victim's neck. In this incident, the lioness had used the cattle for practice but had not eaten any of them. Cattle rustling, too, was prevalent among the Shifta tribesmen from Somalia, to the north. One farmer lost a prize breeding bull flown out at enormous expense from England. The bull was taken only as meat and was chosen just because of his size. The raiders came at night but by dawn were many miles away, lost in the vastness of the desert.

Until recently, there had been even more deadly threats, in the form of the Mau Mau rebellion. This had been over for only a couple of years by the time I arrived in Kenya, and memory of it was still fresh in everyone's mind. This was a guerrilla movement aimed at getting rid of British rule. The main victims of its brutal campaign were innocent Africans, who were often horribly mutilated if they failed to co-operate with the terrorists. The farm had not escaped their attention. On the day of the attack, Mongoose's wife, who had been bedridden for many months, was taken out for a visit to a neighbour. On their return in the Land

Rover, they saw Africans running out of the house, tripping over the ends of the blankets they were carrying away. Something whizzed overhead with a noise like an angry insect.

"What the hell was that?"

"It's a bullet, you bloody fool!"

With their ill-assorted collection of firearms, the ammunition often did not fit the weapon, and bullets would tumble as they whizzed through the air. Everyone blazed away, but no one on either side was hit. When the owners went into the house, they found everything soaked in kerosene and the servants vanished— never to return. If they had arrived just a few minutes later, the house would have been in flames. They reasoned that the servants had been threatened into helping the terrorists and had finally given the word when, for the first time for months, they knew that the crippled wife was safely out of the house.

It had been a time of great stress. A common time for attack was when the servant served the evening meal. At such times, it was customary to have a revolver in your hand until the food had been served and the door re-locked behind the servant. Not a very relaxed way to live. But although the Mau Mau campaign did ultimately help to pressure the British into leaving Kenya, it had been suppressed by the time I arrived in the country.

Mongoose had suggested to my father that perhaps he would like to breed chickens, to supplement his income and keep himself busy. My father replied that he hated the bloody things, but he would like to try his hand at growing pyrethrum. Pyrethrum is a member of the daisy family with many yellow-centred, white-petalling flowers sprouting from a single plant. They are hardy and drought resistant and, as the yellow centre contains a natural insecticide, they have a built-in resistance to predatory insects. By the time of our visit, my father had several acres under cultivation, and the fields full of yellow daisies were very picturesque as African women moved among the flowers, picking off the flower heads. These were then spread out on wooden trays to dry in the sun before being bagged and sent to the processing plant. As we drove up to the fields one day, I asked my father why he did not cultivate some of the apparently lush land closer to the house. "It's sour land" he replied brusquely, "any fool can see that!" I retired hurt. Not an easy man to make friends with.

The climate was almost ideal and a welcome contrast to the humidity of the coast. In fact, it was almost too dry, and until the body acclimatized, the skin cracked around fingernails and the inside of the nose dried out. Every day dawned with a clear sky, and the summit of Mount Kenya, which dominated the landscape, thrust its snow-capped summit into the blue. By nine o'clock, individual blobs of cloud would begin to appear and gradually link together until, within a few minutes, the entire summit would be wreathed in its grey mantle. By noon, this usually resulted in a storm which would affect only the top few thousand feet of the mountain, while the plains below continued to enjoy the sun streaming down from an otherwise cloudless sky.

White settlers in Kenya used to say that if you could see your neighbour's house it was getting too crowded and time to move on. While we stayed with my father, we visited a few of the closer settlers who lived within a few miles but comfortably out of sight. The most colourful of these was "Tiny" Gibbs—so named because he was well over six feet tall. He and his wife lived in a large Tudor-style, half-timbered house buried in the forest a little higher up the mountain. He and his wife spoke English with strong Cockney accents, in contrast to the BBC variety used by most English residents. Their garden looked as if it had been transplanted from an English country house, except that the strongly scented rose blossoms were the size of lettuces, peacocks strutted about, and there were ponds full of large trout. The sitting room was again very English, except for the leopard skins, unwillingly contributed by marauding predators, which adorned the backs of the overstuffed, chintz-covered armchairs. Tea was served in a solid silver teapot by a *kanzu*-clad servant wearing the usual red fez. When I revisited Kenya many years later, after independence had become a reality, I was sad to hear that this beautiful house had become a home for chickens.

In the 1920s, Tiny had been a District Officer in the colonial service. He had been the sole authority in the Northern Frontier

District, north of here, which bordered Somalia. Even in those days it was a lawless area, with cattle raiding by Shifta tribesmen from across the border and disputes over scarce water resources in the form of wells. It had taken Tiny nearly six weeks to reach his posting from Nairobi, using bullock carts until, reaching the escarpment at Isiolo and descending into the desert, his party switched to camels. His posting was for three years, so they had to take everything with them—including whisky! He acted as judge and jury to settle tribal disputes. Cattle rustling was a capital offence (and still is today). Cattle thieves had nothing to lose by shooting their pursuers, so it was a dangerous game.

Mongoose and my father organized several outings and mini-safaris for myself and my sister. One was to Treetops, just outside Nyeri on the road back towards Nairobi. This was a small lodge built on heavy wooden poles, in fact tree trunks, beside a forest pool and salt lick. It had originally been a natural lick, but now salt was added. The original Treetops had been in a tree and was where Princess Elizabeth and her husband, Prince Phillip, were staying when she got the news that her father had died and she was now Queen of England. The original Treetops had been burned down by Mau Mau terrorists, and this was a replacement. Just before sunset, we were driven part way from the hotel just outside Nyeri, and we walked the last few hundred yards accompanied by armed "hunters". We climbed steep stairs to the lodge and awaited events. After dark, the pool was floodlit, which the animals seemed to accept as some kind of moonlight.

Shortly after dark a few antelope appeared, but the first animal of any real interest was a female rhino with young. She fiercely objected whenever any other animal had the temerity to approach, even though the pool was at least a hundred yards across and there was ample room for hundreds of animals. A short time later a herd of elephants appeared, which drove the rhino nearly mad with rage. She made little rushing charges at elephants many times larger than herself, and I was surprised to see that the elephants gave ground. Eventually some sort of accommodation was reached, and peace began to reassert itself.

Among the elephants was one small enough to be able to stand

163

beneath its mother's belly, securely protected from the outside world by the stockade formed by four solid legs. This small elephant had watched the performance of the irate rhino from his secure location, and as soon as the rhino's back was turned, he trotted out and gave her a resounding whack across the behind with his trunk, before rushing back to the security of his lair under his mother. The rhino was outraged by this insolence. It was hilarious—as well as instructive—to see an animal exhibit a cheeky sense of humour and play a joke on another.

Mongoose also took us flying in his Cessna to the summit of Mt. Kenya, with its glaciers. We climbed steadily over the rain forest and over the boggy high ground before circling the jagged peaks of the mountain. On another occasion we made a trip by Land Rover up the flanks of Mt. Kenya along the Sirimon Track. A sign at the base of the track stated that elephants had right of way. We managed to climb above the rain forest and onto open moorland before getting bogged down in the notorious black cotton soil, from where we looked down over a vast landscape that seemingly stretched forever until lost in the blue horizon.

Mt. Kenya exercises a powerful influence over the whole area. I used to look up at it often, and on a later trip to the area I climbed to Point Lenana which, at 16,354 feet, is the third-highest summit on the mountain and the only one accessible to hikers. The main summits of Batian and Nelion require serious mountain climbing skills. During the Second World War, there was a prison camp in Nanyuki for Italian soldiers captured during the fighting. The mountain exercised such an influence on some of them that they broke out of camp just to attempt to climb to the summit. Two nearly died in the attempt, and when they got back to Nanyuki, they broke back into the camp!

Mongoose and my father also took us on a safari to the edge of the desert north of Mt. Kenya. The most memorable spot was Buffalo Springs, where pools of crystal clear water, surrounded by dom palms, unexpectedly appear in the otherwise barren surroundings. During our visit, a local lad with a mixed herd of sheep and goats gave the stark scene a biblical feel. The sheep and goats appeared almost identical, except that the tails of the goats go up while those on the sheep hang down. When I revisited the site a few years later, the pools were surrounded by a gaggle of minibuses and a horde of noisy Italians shouting at each other at the tops of their voices. I was glad I was able to see it in the days before it was included on the tourist route.

It was fascinating to drive through country almost empty of humans but alive with so many varieties of animals. We drove up to Archer's Post and the Uaso Nyero game reserve. Here, a large river of the same name flows through the arid country and attracts multitudes of game. The river never makes it to the sea, and eventually succumbs to the desert and is absorbed by the sand. East Africa enjoys the most beautiful and varied species of birds I have ever seen. Hoopoes, rollers, glossy starlings, and many others share your breakfast table. Driving through the thorny bush we saw elephants, baboons, reticulated and Masai giraffe, Thomson gazelle, Grant's gazelle, gerenuk, sable, bush buck, hartebeeste, wildebeeste, impala, oryx, dik-dik, wart hog, jackal, vulture and both Plains and Grevy's zebra.

All too soon, it was time to leave and return to my homeland to join the others on our great overland journey. It was said that once you drank from Africa's fountain, you would always return. It was not too hard to say *"Kwaheri"* because I was already planning my return.

Book 3
AFRICA

THIRST FOR
ADVENTURE

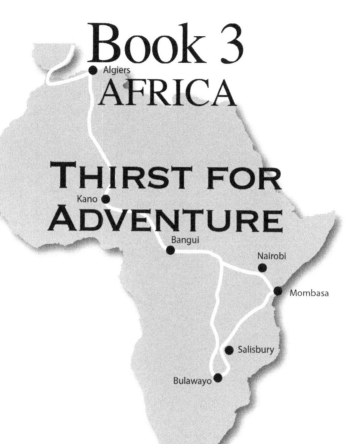

Algiers

Kano

Bangui

Nairobi

Mombasa

Salisbury

Bulawayo

1959 – 1960

Chapter 1

September 1959 to November 1959

UK to Kano

I arrive back in England and, after a short stay, join my friends in Paris on the first leg of a driving trip to southern Africa. I describe our journey through Europe, North Africa, and the crossing of the Sahara Desert to Kano, in Nigeria.

I had retrieved my Beretta pistol from the Kenya Police shortly before leaving the country and, although it sounds strange now, in those days it was not prohibited to carry weapons on board aircraft so I took it with me on the plane. When I arrived at Heathrow, I handed it in to Customs and told them that I would be leaving the country at Dover in about two weeks and they said that they would have it there ready for me to collect.

It was August and the countryside was a tangle of lush, rather tired, overblown vegetation. Even after only 18 months away, I found its miniature landscapes quaint and cosy after the sweeping vistas of Africa. In my bedroom that first night in the Cottage, I swatted 12 mosquitoes, thinking that this was the most I had seen since I had left England. Strange how things never turn out the way you expect!

I had been expecting that all my friends and acquaintances would be dying to hear about my adventures in Darkest Africa. In this, too, the reality was quite different from what I had expected.

The next day, on my way to the village shop, I passed one of the local residents leaning on his garden gate, puffing on his pipe.

The front door of his cottage was a few feet behind him and the mauve and pink hollyhocks framing the opening were taller than he was. He greeted me as I made to hurry past.

"I hear you'm been away" he said.

"Yes," I replied. "In Africa" expecting him to be greatly impressed.

"Aaaah" he said, as he puffed the smoke into the still air. "One of them foreign places. I'm happy enough right here. Got everything I need."

"Silly old fool," I thought as I went on my way. "No wonder this country is going to the dogs."

It was to be many years before I came to realize that maybe he had a point after all and that, being content with his lot, he was perhaps to be envied. In my own case I was always driven by wanting to know what lay around the next corner or over the next hill.

But his reaction was typical, and when I later drove to St Albans to visit my old haunts and lookup my old acquaintances, the conversation usually went something like this:

"Haven't seen you around for a few weeks."

"Actually, I've spent the last one and a half years in Africa."

"You don't look very brown" (This at the end of a rare, hot English summer when everybody except me carried a healthy tan). "Thought it was hot there."

"Well, it's winter now, and it's the rainy season."

"See any lions?"

"Well no—but lots of other animals. Tons of elephants."

"Don't need many of those to make a ton!" (guffaw) "Did you see the football on telly last night?"

And that would be the end of the conversation.

On the night before my departure for Paris and the start of my next adventure, I found it hard to sleep. All kinds of thoughts ran rampant through my head, chief among which was that I must be crazy. Here I was, about to leave the security of my home, buried in the secluded peace of rural England, to join a couple of friends on a 25,000-mile journey in a military surplus truck across the Sahara and into the heart of Africa.

The next morning, my undoubtedly worried but heroically calm mother drove me to the railway station for the first leg of my long journey. Remarkably, Customs had been as good as their word and, at Dover, I collected my gun. As I stood on the deck of the French cross-channel ferry *Arromanches* and watched the famous white cliffs sink below the horizon I wondered how soon it would be before I saw them again and what I would have experienced in the meantime. On arrival in Dieppe I took the boat train to the Gare du Nord in Paris, where I was met by Collyn and introduced to the vehicle that was to carry us so far and be our home for the next nine months. Collyn manoeuvred the clumsy vehicle through the chaotic Paris traffic to the camping site run by the Touring Club de France in the Bois de Boulogne, where I met up with Rex, who was growing an embryo orange beard.

We had some time to kill before we could get our visas, so we drove out of Paris and camped at a small town called Moret-sur-Loigne. I think the others expected me to have a fair amount of cash, but I had to disappoint them. When we pooled our resources, we found we only had about six hundred dollars between us. This was not quite as bad as it sounds because, if the trip went ahead as planned, the Mobil oil company was going to provide all the fuel and Collyn had persuaded a lot of other companies to provide preserved food of one sort or another. Principal among these was a vast number of packets of Irish Soda Bread. Given that our cooking facilities consisted of just two Primus stoves, we tried cooking this stuff in every way we could think of, but the result was always an indigestible doughy lump.

In fact, whether we were even going to be able to start our trip depended entirely on convincing a woman hidden behind a firmly closed door in the Prefecture de Police in Paris to grant us visas for

171

Algeria and the Sahara.

To see this person, one had to press a bell, and either the door sprang open or a red light came on. When you did eventually gain an audience, she would examine your documents and, if she did not like what she saw, she would merely hand them back with a decisive *"Non,"* and you were left to try to figure out what to do about it. No explanation was ever forthcoming. Eventually, with the help of a letter from Mobil Paris, we were successful, but during the three weeks it took to get our visas we were spending our precious money on food without moving a single mile in the direction of Africa. During that time, we lived as economically as we could by getting as many free samples as possible from the women running the stalls in the farmers' market and even, on one occasion, boiling up nettles from the hedgerows for soup.

Eventually we got underway on September 29th on a drive across France. It was tremendously exciting to be on the road at last, but I do not think that any of us believed that we would actually achieve our goal of driving down to South Africa and back. It all seemed too far-fetched. Certainly without Collyn it would never have happened. It was his idea, and it was his determination that had made it happen.

The drive that first day was marvellous! Everything looked so French that it just wasn't true. We passed several fairy-tale chateaux which still carried the opulence and grandeur from a past era.

We went through Nevers, which was all twisty streets with cobbles and quite fascinating. The view looking back over the bridge crossing a large river on the way out of town was exquisite, with the church and the rows of shuttered houses. Quite unreal.

The next point of special interest to me was a small village—name, St. Antoine! As we went south, we saw more and more vineyards with horses drawing carts containing big wooden barrels of grapes, and other carts in the vineyards which contained devices for crushing the grapes on the spot. I remember thinking of the contrast between all those man hours being used to produce something for pleasure instead of, as at De Havillands, being used to create something intended only for destruction. Horses were much more in evidence here than in England.

As we continued on our way the sun began to set to our right where some steep hills could be seen rising up. On the top of one was a spiky monument which stood out against the colouring sky. In the valley below we could just see the shapes of the houses in the mist which had begun to form. In their midst a church spire stood out sharp and pointed.

We ground our way slowly through the mountains of the Massif Central and in places came across signs that read "Here thirty people were murdered by the Germans. Passer-by do not forget." After all these years I have not forgotten.

Five days after leaving Moret we reached the Spanish border at Perpignan. In France we had little problem with language, but none of us could speak one word of Spanish so communication was much more difficult. It was illegal in Spain to camp anywhere except in officially designated places, and these were few and far between and they also charged money. Our attempts to find camp sites were often foiled by the Civil Guard, with their shiny black hats with the back flap turned up, who seemed to be everywhere and showed up in the most unlikely places.

Spain was not at all what I had expected. In fact, away from the cities, it was hard to believe we were still in Europe. Horse-drawn transportation was common, and we saw water being raised to higher level by blind-folded oxen walking round and round in a circle attached by a wooden pole to a horizontal wooden wheel. This wheel had pegs which, acting like a primitive gear, engaged with others on a vertical wheel to which were tied earthen pots. These scooped water from one level and, as they were overturned when their section of the wheel reached the top, emptied their contents into a wooden trough at a higher level. We saw several windmills on which the sails were literally that—suspended from spokes radiating out from the central hub. In Cartagena, Collyn was sent back to the truck to change into long pants; apparently shorts pants were not permitted!

As we went south, some of the roads were not even surfaced

and palm trees began to appear. On our last night in Spain, we found a place up on a hill and there below us we could see the unmistakable shape of the Rock of Gibraltar. Looking at it through binoculars, we could just discern the faint outlines of land on the far side of the Straits. "Well," we said, "at least we can say we saw Africa!"

The following morning, October 12th, we crossed the border at La Linea and were once more under the protection of the British flag. The policemen even wore pointy hats! We spent a couple of days spending some of our precious funds on re-provisioning and we climbed to the top of the Rock where we made the acquaintance of the famous apes. Supposedly, the story goes, if they ever disappear, the British will no longer control the rock. Two days later we crossed the Straits bound for Tangiers and the African continent on the ferry *Mons Calpe* and looked back at the cloud that streamed off from the top of the rock but which dissipated downwind as fast as it formed on the pinnacle.

Soon we landed in Tangiers where, whenever we stopped, we were immediately surrounded by all kinds of dodgy-looking characters. Small urchins came up to us in the street trying to persuade us to buy English-language newspapers. They not only tagged us immediately as English but even which of several newspapers to offer us! At one point we were hailed by some young French soldiers. "What the hell are you doing here?" one of them shouted. "How did you know we were English" we asked. They simply laughed in response— it was that obvious! One of them spoke English with an Asian Indian accent. He said that he had learnt English from a Sikh when he was in India.

Wherever we parked the truck, even after we left the city, we were immediately surrounded by crowds of curious onlookers standing in a silent ring around the truck. It meant that we had no privacy and it was quite unnerving.

I had expected Morocco to be desert stretching right down to the sea but, instead, we found great mountains which had us grinding up precipitous slopes in low gear for many miles. Down in the valleys, running streams were lined with pink and white oleanders in full bloom. After a few hours of ascending and descending the mountains, the brakes decided they had had enough. They would slow the truck to walking pace but not bring it to a halt and we had to leap out and find rocks to drop in front of the wheels.

At one spot we were flagged down by a tall distinguished-looking Arab with a grey beard and garbed in a brown burnouse. Walking a few steps behind him was his diminutive wife. We stopped to give them a lift to the next town of Berkane. The man climbed into the back of the truck and went inside to sit down leaving his wife standing in the road defeated by the vertical climb into the cabin. It was left to us to boost her up and, later, to help her down when, after 15 Kms, we stopped at his request. He just jumped down and set off down the road without a backward glance while his wife stood in the doorway wondering how she was going to get down.

The day before we were to cross into Algeria, we found a hidden spot in the mountains and we were spared the crowds of curious onlookers who always stood in a silent ring around the truck whenever we stopped. We decided to make it a day of maintenance and catching up chores. Collyn and Rex insisted we hide the Beretta away in the bowels of the truck and so we unscrewed the engine cover inside the cab, concealed the pistol inside and then smeared the screw heads with dirt to make them look as though they had never been disturbed.

In 1959, Algeria was in the throes of a full-blown war of independence with the local Arabs. France did not even view Algeria as a colony but as part of mainland France with the Mediterranean merely as an extra-wide river. A typically uncompromising example of graffiti painted on a wall translated as "France will remain in Algeria. It is her right and her duty to do so!"

We crossed the border into a compound stiff with heavily armed French troops and heavily fortified with coils of barbed wire. The truck was directed over a vehicle inspection pit while we were let to the office on the other side of the compound. Here we were required to complete questionnaires in which one of the questions was whether we had any firearms. Having said "no" we were then individually searched. It was fortunate indeed that we had had time the previous day to conceal the pistol because normally I would have stuffed it down the front of my trousers where it would certainly have been found. Given the tense circumstances, the French would not have been very understanding and our trip would undoubtedly have come to an abrupt halt right then. In the meantime, the truck was given a thorough going over by a variety of troops and gendarmes in different uniforms but they failed to find the pistol which was becoming ever more of a liability - as is usually the case with all firearms.

We left the compound by driving along a raised embankment bordered by barbed wire towards a tall guard tower with its door some 15 feet above the ground and the ladder drawn up inside. Truly an example of "pull up the ladder Jack". A black soldier kept a machine gun trained on us for the whole distance which was a distinctly uncomfortable feeling.

Once out in the country, we passed many toppled power pylons and other numerous signs of conflict. Everywhere were troops in Jeeps with wire-cutting pylons sticking up from their front bumpers. These were countermeasures against the guerrillas' nasty habit of stretching wires across the road at head height to decapitate anyone riding in an open vehicle.

The country was beautiful with groves of citrus trees and vineyards sprouting from the black earth. For these to be successful, French vines had to be grafted onto local roots. The French settlers, who were very single-minded about staying in Algeria, were called *Pieds Noirs*, or "Black Feet". Originally a derisive term but now one worn with pride in the form of lapel badges.

A curfew (from the French word *couvre-feu*, meaning "cover fire") was in effect every night and it was illegal—as well as foolhardy—to spend the night anywhere other than in a protected area. We spent every night in encampments and even shared the French troops' evening meal. The food was a big improvement over our own austere rations and, while there was no water on the tables, there were carafes of both red and white wine. I could imagine the reaction of the typical British Tommy to that! We stopped in Oran—a beautiful city where the entire French fleet had been sunk by the British in WWII to prevent it from falling into German hands. A move which caused outrage to the French who were supposed to be our allies!

Eventually we reached the capital Algiers where we were well taken care of by the local Mobil staff. It was fortunate for us that we had their backing because we would normally have had to lodge large sums of money with the Touring Club de France before being issued with permits to cross the Sahara. We took a look around the city and accidentally found ourselves in the old district with its markets or Kasbah. Here the streets became increasingly narrow with buildings crowding in on either side until they met overhead to form a dark tunnel. Strange Fagan-like characters scurried to and fro and a little girl came running towards us carrying a stick which she pointed in front of her and shouted "*Fusil* (gun)! Boom! Boom!"

The Mobil company were a tremendous help. In fact, without them, I doubt we could have continued through this war-torn country and into the Sahara. A Monsieur Du Barry, who was Swiss, was delegated to help us with paperwork etc. He was very helpful and polite to people who helped us, "*Je vous remercie mille fois*" (I thank you 1,000 times) was a phrase he used often. Algiers was a very French-looking city and the women very attractive and stylish. We noticed that at the entrances to the big stores, men were frisked and women had their bags searched presumably to search for bombs. A precursor of what lay in the future in other parts of the world. Also, if you went into a cinema you had to stay there until the end of the programme so, if you set off a bomb, you would go with it. Suicide bombings were apparently not so much in fashion at that time!

After two days we were cleared to head South and set off for the Atlas mountains, on the other side of which lay the vastness of the Sahara Desert—bigger in area than the entire United States of America. It seemed to be perfect guerrilla country and we felt quite vulnerable as we ground our way slowly up the steep grades through the heavily wooded hillsides past signs stating that it was forbidden to stop. The truck grew increasingly gutless and Arab

177

drivers behind the wheel of big Berliet trucks constantly overtook us, banging on their doors shouting *"Vite! Vite!"* Rex gloomily remarked, "Now I know what a sitting duck feels like"!

This area was reckoned to be one of the most dangerous in Algeria and it was not hard to see why. At every bridge was a guard post, flying the French Flag, with the entry door high above the ground - accessible only with a ladder which was pulled up inside after use. The concrete around every door was heavily pock-marked with bullet holes.

It was clear that something was seriously wrong with the Bedford. When we reached the town of Bhogari at the top of the mountains, 3,900 feet above sea level, we took a quick look but found nothing obviously wrong. The next day we continued on to Blida, but with the engine now starting to miss and backfire, it became doubtful at one stage whether we were even going to make it to town. We diagnosed the problem as burnt-out valves, which meant removing and dismantling the cylinder head. We found a desolate yard in which to work adjacent to the Mobil station owned by Madam Chicheportiche! It was now November, and the weather had turned cold and grey with frequent heavy showers which turned the ground into glutinous mud. Fortunately, we were equipped to do the work and set to grinding the valves for what turned out to be the first of several times. We shared these bleak surroundings with a crazy guy who lit a fire of burning tyres. He apparently made a habit of this because he and his clothes were black with soot. At one point he rolled around in the remains of his fire. It was a relief to get out of there and continue on our way.

We spent the next night at La Ghardaia, in a large open space where there were huge trucks with balloon tyres used to transport equipment to the oilfields deep in the desert. We decided to rotate the tyres, and a young local lad turned up and was very helpful. We felt sure that he would want to be paid—and he deserved it— but we had so little cash that it was a bit of a dilemma. However, he did not return the following morning and never asked for anything.

We were now entering the desert proper, and just south of La Ghardaia we finally felt it was safe to camp out in the open. After supper we climbed to the top of a small hill to watch the sunset. The horizon spread out in a great upturned bowl, the colours of which ranged from indigo in the east to red and amber in the west. There was absolutely no sound except for the faint whisper of the wind, and even this died as we descended into a hollow, and the silence became so tangible that we were afraid to break it. The only sound that became apparent was the ticking of my wristwatch. We returned, humbled, to the truck—our refuge in this immense desert—looking tiny and insignificant against the stark landscape.

The next stop was the large town of El Golea, where camel caravans congregated in a large open area bustling with people and noisy camels. The oasis town boasted 17 springs feeding water running through open channels into gardens to irrigate citrus trees and vegetables. These gardens were separated from each other by walls which, like all those in the town, were built of mud. We climbed to the top of the ruins of the 10th century ksar, built into a hill on the outskirts of town. From here we had a magnificent view over the town and the extensive plantations of date palms— believed to number between two to three hundred thousand. Beyond, stretching to the distant horizon, we saw the Grand Erg Occidental on one side and the Grand Erg Oriental on the other. These names mean the "Great Western Emptiness" and the "Great Eastern Emptiness" respectively, and are reputed to be the most feared places in the Sahara as they are huge areas of great billowy sand dunes.

The road south of the town was tarmac with signs that read "Danger Sable" and tendrils of sand slithered over the blacktop, driven by the wind. They reminded me of guilty snakes. "Just give us time," they seem to say "and your precious road will disappear."

The next major feature was the Tademait Plateau—an extensive, featureless, stony plateau. The track was heavily corrugated and we were unable to find any speed at which we could drive which would which lessen the vibrations transmitted to the vehicle. The truck dragged behind it huge plumes of fine red dust which found its way not only into the truck, but into everything inside it. This being November, it was not terribly hot during the day but the corrugations heated the tyres so pressures had to be constantly checked and air let out. During the night, temperatures dropped almost to freezing, so the tyres were deflated in the morning and had to be pumped up again. Fortunately, we had an engine-driven air compressor, so this was not too much of a chore. We saw few other vehicles, but if one came by when we were stationary, they always checked to see if we needed assistance. There was an unwritten rule that all travellers looked out for one another.

The sunsets were magnificent, 360-degree affairs. After dark, the skies blazed with unimaginable numbers of stars that added to our feeling of insignificance in our tiny mobile cabin stopped in the middle of a desert that extended for thousands of miles in every direction.

The plateau came to an abrupt end with an escarpment that was only visible from a short distance away, and here we stopped for the night. In the desert, I slept on a camp bed in the open with my head towards the truck so that, unless I turned around, I could see nothing but desert in every direction. At dawn the following morning, I awoke to see a series of nipple-shaped hills extending off into the lavender distance. These were obviously the remnants from where the plateau had extended eons ago.

A hundred miles south lay In Salah, a town of close-packed mud buildings which seemed huddled together against the encroaching sands. Here we met a French officer from the Foreign Legion. He said that he had served 30 years in the Sahara Desert and he hoped never to be posted anywhere else. The desert was a powerful and fascinating place.

South of In Salah we ran for many miles, parallel with a line of cliffs. At one point we stopped, and Rex said he was going to walk across to a squared-off boulder shaped like a cube of sugar. A few minutes later I looked for him but could not see him. Through binoculars I was finally able to spot his diminutive figure completely dwarfed by the immense boulder, now obviously very much farther away than we had thought. The scale of everything in the desert is deceptive, and it is not until you have the truck or a person for comparison that you realize the true size of your surroundings.

The track swung left and headed for a break in the cliffs. At the turn lay the burnt-out remains of a military Jeep, which we stopped and examined. We turned into the gorge and came across a small, square fort which looked very much like something out of a storybook. It was manned by a small group of French soldiers and, after we had checked in, they offered us beer kept cold in their kerosene-powered refrigerator. We were able to communicate using my fractured French. We asked about the burnt-out Jeep, and they told us that it had caught fire and that all the ammunition on board had been set off by the heat of the fire and there were bullets flying in every direction. This introduced the word "*mitraillette*" into the conversation. This translates as "machine gun" in English, which led to a proposal to have an international shooting competition between them and ourselves! Using their .303 rifles, we chose a cave high up on the surrounding cliffs as a target. We could see where the bullets hit by the puff of dust from the rock. We won the competition hands down—mainly because I put every shot right on target. Normally I cannot hit anything, so it must have been the beer that made the difference!

We had barely finished the competition and retired to celebrate with more beer when a mobile broadcast van showed up from Radio Diffusion Militaire. This was one of those outfits that visit troops serving in the field to interview them and then broadcast messages from the troops to their parents from a radio station in Algiers. This was a jolly party and they had me play my guitar, which I did atrociously because of being bombed.

The next morning, a bit hung over, we continued up the gorge, following a dried river bed. Sedimentary strata tilted almost to the vertical extended to the horizon, revealing the bare bones of the stark landscape. At the top of the gorge we found ourselves in an open area of fine white sand with numerous natural rock formations, each individually sculptured by the sand and the wind. They were fascinating shapes and appeared as if they had been set out for an exhibition of outside art.

We passed small camel caravans, with one person walking alongside the animals, picking their way through the stony landscape, and we encountered the occasional road crew. As a place to stop for the night, we picked an outcropping of purple lava which looked as though it had just boiled out of the ground and solidified. It turned out to be more than 50 miles away and 5 miles long—another example of how you can be fooled by scale and distance in these surroundings.

We arrived at the administrative centre of Tamanrasset, located at almost 4,500 feet above sea level with its backdrop of the weirdly shaped Hoggar Mountains. The town, with its mud buildings and unpaved streets lined with casuarina trees, had a pleasant atmosphere. We were able to refuel here, and while doing so, we were besieged by turbaned Arabs looking for a ride south. We agreed to take one called Akhmadou.

South of Tamanrasset, the track—or *piste*, as it is called locally—became increasingly sandy. We became stuck several times and had to dig ourselves out and make use of the sand mats we had carried with us all the way from England. We also experienced some overheating. We had a can attached by a hose to a spigot on the radiator cap. When the water boiled, it was caught in the can. The person riding in the passenger seat would periodically feel the weight of the can through the opening windshield, and when it became heavy, we would stop and pour the water back into the radiator. We came to the conclusion that we needed to pressurize the radiator, and we achieved this by making a valve, similar in principle to that found on a bicycle tyre, out of a piece of wood and a short length of hose.

We reached the tiny oasis of In Guezzam, semi-buried by encroaching sand, where we took showers from buckets of water drawn from the well. Just south of there we crossed the border into Niger, marked with a pole resting on oil drums. We began to see increasing scrub, followed by trees and dried grass. We had now reached the Sahel—a semi-desert region which extended over the whole width of the African continent just south of the Sahara.

We saw a few trees on the horizon and then a broken-down shack, a well, and lots of cattle (the first we had seen for ages) that had humps just like the cattle in Kenya. There were also some goats and camels, as well as a few Arabs. This was In Abbangarit, where our passenger was getting off. We stopped, and when he alighted he was joyously greeted by his friends. He collected his belongings and we took aboard another Arab, who was bound for a place called Tegguidda, 60 miles down the road. We bade a fond farewell to Aghachmadou and were soon on our way.

After about 5 miles we came across another group of Arabs who were standing at the side of the road. We stopped and gave them some matches and a little sugar and tea in exchange for some milk which was still warm from the goat, or possibly camel, and which we drank out of a big enamelled basin on the spot. We were unsure whether it would seem rude to drink it all or just part of it. We drank it all, but there was a lot and it was quite a challenge! The people we met in the desert would never take anything without offering something in exchange. There were several young girls amongst the gathering. They were quite attractive, being dark but having European features. They were unveiled—unlike the men.

After we had left them, the countryside changed abruptly, and the ground was carpeted with a yellowish sort of grass with quite a number of thorn trees. It was quite obvious that the only factor that had really changed was the annual rainfall, as the terrain appeared to be the exactly the same and just as flat as ever. We saw about 10 gazelle feeding in the grass.

Just as the sun was setting, I became aware of a crashing noise behind, and after Collyn had stopped, I went round to the back to have a look and found that we only had one sand mat left on the back and that the spare wheel was almost off. We had been over some vicious humps on the last stretch (little gullies across the road), and the jolts had unshipped everything. We turned the truck around and found the mats about 1/2 mile back down the road; we tied them back on with nylon cord. The Arab that we had with us now seemed very withdrawn, so we decided that the best thing would be to take him right to the village he wanted to go to, but after it got dark we reversed this decision and stopped for the night at the side of the road. We gave him a lighted stove but he just sat and looked at it for about an hour. We then found out that he hadn't any tea, so we made him a cup and decided that we would take him the rest of the way after supper. However, when the time came we found that he had gone to sleep, so we decided to stay where we were, after all. Compared to our previous passenger he seemed quite dim, as he was unable to comprehend sign language, which usually works surprisingly well.

We awoke the following morning to find that we were on a large area of dried mud with crazy-paving patterned cracks. We could also see the village our guest was bound for, only about 1½ miles down the road! The village was built of mud and singularly unattractive, but our passenger was surrounded by his friends as soon as we drew to a halt. We took off right away to avoid being pressured into picking up another passenger! Driving in this area required concentration because small rivers and streams had left small gullies across the road that could only be spotted at the last minute.

The main town of the area was Agadez, with its distinctive mud minaret spiked with wooden poles, which dates from 1515. Here we encountered several vehicles which were about to tackle the Sahara northbound. A couple of them were not only quite unsuitable but had nobody with them capable of fixing anything— or, indeed, any tools or parts with which to make repairs. We fixed up a few things for them before continuing our journey.

From here on, the road became extremely rough, diving without warning into dried riverbeds or immense potholes. We only managed a few miles a day, and we lost the hatch over the accommodation quarters so that, at the end of a tiring day, we found everything on the floor covered with a thick layer of dust. Collyn was very annoyed. "Don't they realize that this is the main road to Europe?" he fumed. I really didn't think that had much relevance to people in these parts.

We stopped near an ants' nest and spent time watching hundreds of ants carrying small pieces of grass down inside the nest. They had to bring each piece about 15 yards and when they got it to the hole, they had to turn around and take it down backwards!

We passed several water holes where the locals watered their animals, with the oxen drawing up the water in leather skins. There were large numbers of sheep, goats, cattle, donkeys and

184

camels at each place. We waved at the people as we went past and they waved back, but we didn't stop.

The trees became more numerous and the vegetation began to look more permanent. We saw three ostriches, some hornbills and one or two weaver bird nests. The road for the most part followed river beds and the going was really rough, with gullies and small ditches running across the road. It is definitely the worst road I had been on anywhere. We saw several road gangs using earth to patch the odd hole.

We stopped for lunch shortly after being trapped behind some stupid camels who just ran down the road in front of us. We followed them for about a mile, then decided that the best thing would be to stop for lunch and give them a chance to get off the road. After lunch it was my turn to drive. I found that it required much concentration and gear changing to cope with the surface. The scenery was the same—thorn scrub bush for mile after mile.

In the distance I saw what I took to be the smoke from a bush fire, and as we approached, we came across some locusts. At first, I thought, they were fugitives from the fire, then I realized that the "smoke" was actually insects. I estimated the swarm at about 20 miles long and a mile wide. As we reached its centre they thudded against the front of the truck. It was an incredible sight to see them silhouetted against the orange evening sky. Where they were resting on the vegetation, the normal green colour of the bushes was replaced with a mauve hue, turning them into trees of living creatures.

I stood looking out of the top of the vehicle, watching the thousands of insects hurtle towards and past me. I turned round and saw them streak away towards the rear of the truck. The sensation, which was like rushing through a living tunnel, was one that I shall never forget. Occasionally locusts would thud into me and drop onto the roof momentarily before re-joining the seething mass with a whirr of wings.

When we stopped for the night, which was as soon as we could after clearing the locust swarm, the back of the truck was a horrible mess, with everything thrown onto the floor because of the severe jolting that had taken place as we bounced over the rugged road surface. The rear skylight had shaken itself loose and was completely missing, so everything was thick with the dust that had come in through the hole.

The following day we arrived in Zinder, at the border with Nigeria. We drove around looking for the immigration office and picked a fort—with rows of sinister-looking vultures perched along the battlements—as a likely location. It turned out to be the wrong place, and after waiting around for an alternative office to open at midday, discovered that formalities were handled on the road to Kano.

Kano was a very large city with a population of over two million. The majority were Hausa people, who considered themselves greatly superior to the people of Bantu origin from the south. Nigeria gained its independence from Britain in October 1960.

We had successfully crossed the immensity of the Sahara Desert and were now ready to tackle Equatorial Africa.

Chapter 2

November 1959 to January 1960

Kano to Bulawayo

Our journey continues through the heartland of Africa to our most southerly point of Bulawayo in Southern Rhodesia.

We stayed a few days in Kano, catching up on maintenance, before continuing south through Nigeria to Cameroon and on through Chad to the Central African Republic—which, up until then, I had never even heard of. Many of the roads were little more than tracks through the bush. On one occasion, Rex and I were sitting up on the roof of the truck, with Collyn at the wheel, when ahead of us we saw the track drop abruptly into a dry river bed. As we continued on at undiminished speed, we realized that Collyn hadn't seen it! We yelled but it was too late, and we plunged into the dip, and the back end of the truck flipped up as we came up the other side. Rex and I hung onto the roof rack for dear life. We came to a halt on the other side amid furious recriminations. The interior of the truck was turned upside down, and we were lucky that no one was hurt. As we moved off, it occurred to me to question whether the spare wheel was still in place on the back of the truck. Rex crawled back along the roof to take a look and found it missing. We turned back to look for it, but although we searched for more than an hour, it had disappeared for good in the head-high grass.

The following day—in a classic case of Murphy's Law—we had our first flat tyre. Normally we would simply have changed the wheel and then fixed the flat at a town that had suitable equipment, but now we had to do it ourselves out in the bush, using only the tools we had. It required considerable force to break the tyre loose from the rim of the truck wheel. It took several hours of work—including the three of us, with arms linked, jumping up and down on the tyre with the wheel lying flat on the ground —before we managed to break it free. We had to go the rest of the trip without a spare.

The day after that, we became bogged axle-deep in mud when I suggested to Rex, who was driving, that it might be safer to drive closer to the muddy centre of the road. Even the four-wheel drive could not get us out, so we had to make use of the hand winch strapped to the front of the vehicle. We drove stakes into the track ahead of us to serve as a ground anchor and, as it was my suggestion which had gotten us into this mess, it fell to me to crawl on my belly through the glutinous mud to attach the end of the cable to the underside of the truck, serenaded all the while by squadrons of mosquitoes.

We had to go to Fort Archambault (now renamed Sahr) because Collyn had set up a Poste Restante mail pickup there. Our route took us to Bongor, just across the border in Chad, but when we arrived at the banks of the Logone river, which marked the border between Cameroon and Chad, we found that, apart from dugout canoes, there was no way to cross to the other side. There was no ford, no ferry, certainly no bridge. So there we were, surrounded by locals (who in this area were pretty well stark naked), looking across the wide river with no way to reach our destination. We finally found an alternative route down a road which barely existed, with grass growing between the tyre tracks to the height of the windshield.

The border between the three countries of Chad, Cameroon and the Central African Republic was extremely erratic in this area, and when we finally reached a tiny border post at Fianga, in the Central African Republic, we discovered that we had inadvertently exited Cameroon without officially leaving the country. We were sent further out of our way to Pala, where there was a more senior official. The post was closed at midday for siesta and reopened at 3.30. The French official said, "Well, you're here aren't you?" and stamped our vehicle carnet. We then had to visit immigration in another office. There we found that the official had gone hunting and wouldn't be back for three days! We returned to the customs office, where the helpful official stamped our passports with customs stamps!

We were now free to continue our circuitous route to Fort Archambault. Before reaching it, we encountered the first of the ferries typical in that part of the world. These consisted of two or three small boats tied together, side by side, with a platform straddling their width. In Fort Archambault we had to go through customs and immigration again to enter Chad.

After a couple of days here we continued south. Rex was again at the wheel when, after our experience with being stuck in the mud, he moved closer to the shoulder to avoid some deep pot holes. Unfortunately, the shoulder collapsed, and the truck lurched over at a perilous angle. Attempts to reverse out only made the situation worse. We set up the winch and took the cable over the roof and attached it to the chassis on the other side, to prevent the vehicle from capsizing while we figured out how to pull it back onto the road.

At this point, a couple of trucks full of Africans appeared. They were extremely helpful and starting cutting trees and digging with terrific energy. There was soon a good space around the wheels, and wood was packed in behind. We slackened off the winch cable and tried to reverse out, but the truck jumped off the sticks and went in worse than ever. Fortunately, the second truck turned out to have a rather thin and tired-looking tow cable, and a pull from this, combined with sand mats and Collyn driving, got us back on *terra firma*. We were delayed three and a half hours by this event, and would have been there considerably longer without the help of this cheerful group of Africans who wanted nothing in return for their assistance.

Over the next few days we encountered a number of odd incidents as we made our way along the rural roads of Africa. We had left the Sahel behind and the terrain was becoming much more jungle-like, with tall trees. In one spot, the road climbed a steep slope that was little more than a series of boulders. It was no real problem for our four-wheel-drive truck, and it was also a good photo opportunity. A smaller truck arrived from the opposite direction and stopped to see if we needed help. Inside were three American women missionaries who had been attending a conference at Fort Crampel (now called Kaga-Bandoro), just to the south.

Later that day we came across a Citroen truck with a chassis which had broken in half after the rivets holding it together had sheared off. Unfortunately, it wasn't just a matter of replacing these with bolts, as the two halves of the chassis had pulled apart and dropped on the ground. We jacked up the chassis, placed our truck against the front of the broken truck, and connected our winch to the rear half so that we could winch the two broken halves of the truck together. The holes still did not fully line up, so we drilled them out using a "gut-buster" hand drill, which was not an easy job. It was dark by the time we had finished. The guys with the truck were very grateful and presented us with a couple of live chickens while the village headman gave us some grapefruit. They also wanted to buy us some beer, but the local beer shop was shut.

The next day we came across a couple of guys with a dead cow at the edge of the road. They wanted to get the cow to their village about seven miles further down the road. We never did find out why they had this dead animal so far from home. We hoisted the carcass onto the back of the truck and took them where they wanted to go. In return, they offered us whichever piece of the cow we wanted. Meat was a rarity in our diet because of the cost, so we chose the fillet. We ate it the following day, and it was rather disgusting. It was then I realized that meat should be hung for a while before being eaten.

Later the same day we came across an African who was hitching himself across the road on his bottom. We thought at first that he was a cripple, but saw that he had been injured when he pointed to his back. He was unable to stand, so we had to lift him into the truck using one of the seat backs as a stretcher, and we sat him on the truck floor. He had a bad cut on his knee, which Rex bathed, while Collyn drove to the next village. Here a black soldier questioned our passenger and wrote out a note for the commandant in Fort Sibut, about 12 miles further down the road. We arrived there about 20 minutes later and went straight to the dispensary, where we met a very nice French doctor who took care of the patient and also took the note. From it we gathered that the man had been robbed of 3,500 francs, and it was a case of robbery with violence. From here we could have continued straight to Bangui, but we turned left to Bangassou, because we had been assured, in both London and Paris, that we could obtain visas there to enter the Belgian Congo.

We carried on through thickly forested terrain and came across yet another disabled Citroen truck. The driver told us that he had been stuck there for two days! The problem turned out to be a fuel line blocked by a leaf! We had just cured this and were adjusting the ignition timing, which was also wrong, when a black Peugeot arrived. Out of it stepped an East Asian who we believed was the owner of the truck, accompanied by a coloured guy and an African of lighter complexion than was the norm in this area. They produced a colossal thermos of ice, a bottle of soda, and a bottle of Scotch, so we all had a couple of whiskies apiece!

It was time to dispatch the first of our chickens. We were too ignorant and "chicken" to wring its neck, so we held it against a tree and decapitated it with a machete. Its headless neck flailed around, pumping out blood, so it was a gory procedure.

We passed through the small town of Bambari and continued on to Bangassou. Collyn had done everything he could to get all necessary visas before the start of the trip, but visas for the Belgian Congo could only be obtained no more than six weeks before the intended date of entry, and we had known it would take longer than that to get there. Collyn was told the same thing in Paris and had been assured that there would be no problem getting our visas in Bangassou. This turned out to be nonsense because this was only a small town, with few facilities. We thought we would try our luck entering without visas, so we went down to the ferry to cross the wide Ubangi River, which marked the border between the Central African Republic and the Belgian Congo.

We arrived at the shore of a large river—bigger than the

Thames at Tower Bridge—which looked like something you would expect from a scene in the movie *The African Queen*. We waited 10 minutes for the ferry and nothing happened so, on the advice of the African who had inspected our carnet, we blew the horn. Immediately figures could be seen in motion on the far banks. A drum started beating—more figures, and then the sound of an engine, and the ferry started coming across. It was made up of three boats with a platform slung across them, the ferry being turned sideways as it came alongside. The driver was very skilful at the job. As we made our way across, it made me think of "the great, grey-green, greasy Limpopo River set about with fever trees" in the *Just So* story, "The Elephant's Child" by Rudyard Kipling!

The customs and immigration post was situated a short distance from the ferry in the middle of dense jungle. We tried arguing for ages with a very nice but firm African official, but we were denied entry and had to return across the ferry to Bangassou. We now had to re-enter the Central African Republic, and the French official there suggested we send a telegram to the Belgian consulate in Bangui to see whether we could be permitted to enter the Congo at Bangassou. He did this for us at no charge, and when the reply came the following day, it said we had to present ourselves in Bangui. We had no alternative but to return the way we had come—a detour of some 1,000 miles over very rough roads!

We set off at 4 a.m. and, taking turns at the wheel, drove without any breaks all the way to Bangui, taking about 24 hours for the journey with only about 10 gallons of fuel left out of the 180 gallons' full capacity. It was Friday, so we needed to get everything done that day or we would have to wait until after the weekend. We had a frustrating time waiting around for people to show up, but in the end we got our visas and had the truck refuelled and serviced. Bangui is also on the Ubangui River, and we found out that the ferry charge here was 3,000 francs, whereas in Bangassou it was free. If we crossed at Bangui we would still have to drive east the same distance to reach our intended route, so we decided to backtrack—yet again—to Bangassou. Once there we re-crossed the Ubangui river and this time we had no problems with customs or immigration. We were finally in the Belgian Congo. The jungle was very lush, and the road muddy and rough, with large potholes where vehicles had obviously been stuck. We crossed a number of primitive and dangerous-looking bridges made with logs with the top surface flattened. Many of the logs showed signs of rot. Few of the bridges showed any weight limit, but one said 8 metric tons, which was close to our estimated weight. In one place the road and railway shared the same bridge, so we had to be sure that no train was coming before venturing onto the bridge.

We encountered an English guy driving a VW bus with "Round Africa Tour" painted on the side. He was a most unusual person who read verse in Latin for recreation. He spoke English with a foreign accent, having been speaking French for two years. He said he had been trying for two days to remember the English word for the arms that wipe the windshield—here, he made a reciprocating motion with his hand. We told him, "Windshield wipers!"

He told us that he had once been cursed by an African chief because "I touched his bloody drum". After this, all sorts of misfortunes happened, including in Dar-es-Salaam, when he was being given a lift to the docks. He was telling the driver about the curse and had just said "The trouble is that I don't know what will happen next" when their car was run into from behind by a truck, and they both finished up in hospital. The African truck driver told them that his vehicle had just leapt forward. The Englishman got the curse lifted by an Arab in Mombasa, and ever since then he had worn an amulet around his neck.

Shortly after the town of Buta, we came to a bridge posted with a weight limit of only 4 metric tons. We got out and inspected the bridge, and decided to take the risk even though we exceeded the posted limit by almost 100 percent. To go around meant a detour of several hundred miles. It was Rex's turn to drive, and Collyn directed him across the rickety bridge, while I stood by, camera in hand, ready to film the crash which fortunately did not take place.

The roads became extremely muddy and slippery as we

approached Stanleyville—since renamed Kisangani—which is located 1,300 miles upstream from the mouth of the mighty Congo river. We were brought to a halt in one place by a tree which had fallen across the road, and in another where the truck simply slid sideways down the camber into the bank. We refuelled here and had a look around the city, which was quite large and well developed. Unknown to us and its inhabitants, a savage future lay ahead. Eleven hundred foreign hostages were seized there in 1964, and the city was pillaged in 1966.

We only stayed a few hours before leaving town to search for a place to spend the night. We eventually found a clearing in the jungle used by road maintenance crews. It was pitch dark when, without warning, the background noises of the jungle were pierced by the most unnerving noise. It started with a series of extremely loud ratchet-like sounds which came progressively closer and closer together on a rising note and culminated in a blood-curdling shriek that ended as if choked off by strangulation. After a short pause, the series would start again. It made our hair stand on end, and we had no idea what it was. We later discovered the calls were made by a small rabbit-sized animal called a tree hyrax, which produces a volume of sound out of all proportion to its size.

On the subject of size, we now started to see diminutive people carrying diminutive bows. These were the pygmy people—I would guess under 5 feet tall. A small group came by while we were preparing to get under way. They all carried tiny bows—perhaps 2 feet in length—and arrows with the points wrapped. Spear tips were also wrapped—presumably because they had poison on them. They spoke Swahili, and we bought some rice from them. They also tried to sell us one of their bows for 30 francs. I would have liked it, but of course no money! I asked to see their bows in action and was surprised at their performance. The bows were about 2 feet long; the "string" was about 8 inches from the bow; and the arrows were only about 1-foot long. The "string" was a strip peeled from the skin of the bamboo, and the bow they showed us had fur above and below the handle. The arrows had obviously been carved from thicker sticks; the arrows for birds were plain sticks, and those for animals had spear-type points—usually poisoned, although they had none of these with

194

them. For flights, they used a leaf pushed through a slit in the arrow, thus forming a two-finned flight. They said that their arrows would kill a buck, and having seen the performance of these things, I can believe it. We asked them if there were a lot of snakes in the area and they said there were. I asked what would happen if they were bitten by a snake. They said, "You die" as if I had asked a silly question! I asked about the poison they used on their weapons, and they said they tested it by nicking a leg so the blood ran down. Then, pressing the blade of a knife against the trickle, below the nick, to act as a barrier, they applied the poison to the blood which should instantly coagulate!

We drove up the road to Epulu, where there was a government elephant training station and a small zoo where the principal attraction was the very rare Okapi, of which they had quite a large number. We signed a book and went in. There was not much to see except the Okapi, which really were strange-looking animals. They had long necks and their hindquarters were much lower than their shoulders. They had mouths similar to those of a giraffe, with immensely long tongues which allowed them to lick the top of their heads. They were chestnut in colour, with white stripes on their hindquarters. There were a couple of young animals, as well as several adults. These were the only Okapi in captivity in the world.

Soon the road began to climb above the jungle canopy, which stretched out below us like a green carpet all the way to the blue horizon. We were now in the land of agriculture and beautifully manicured coffee plantations. It was a relief to have escaped the jungle through which we had been driving for three weeks. On December the 19th we crossed the equator at 7,200 feet, and it was beginning to get quite chilly. We had views of the Ruwenzori Mountains, which top out at over 16,000 feet and carry snow on their peaks throughout the year.

We came across some children selling strawberries at the edge of the road. In exchange for one Mobil hat and two cans of food we were able to get quite a lot of strawberries and some Cape gooseberries. That evening, after crossing a pass at 7,750 feet, we found it quite cold as we dined on strawberries and cream.

The following morning the road began to lose altitude and, at the entrance to the Albert National Park, descended a steep escarpment. The view from here was absolutely breath-taking. Stretched out below us was a vast plain with mountains on the far side and beyond them, barely visible through the mist, the shapes of three volcanoes. To the left, the expanse of Lake Edward stretched to the blue horizon. The valley floor was full of game and, through binoculars, we could see elephant, buffalo, zebra, giraffe and many types of antelope grazing peacefully on the rich grass. It was truly the epitome of the promised land, flowing with milk and honey. We were entering the Western Arm of the East African Rift valley.

At the base of the escarpment, we came across a sign warning of elephant and, almost immediately, we came across the real thing. We stopped and, through our binoculars, we could see literally hundreds of them. We descended to the valley floor and passed through land well-watered by streams, rivers and huge lakes. Numerous antelope of many varieties, as well as some very solid-looking buffalo, browsed on the lush vegetation. Flowering shrubs lined the road and, all around, high mountains soared into blue skies each wearing a wig of towering white clouds.

We passed the Rwanda game camp and watched some baboons in the trees at the edge of the road. Some five miles further on we stopped at hot springs where the water was so hot that it was actually boiling and the air smelt of sulphur.

We headed towards the volcanoes, the tops of which were shrouded in cloud, and arrived at Rutshuru which was a very small place. From there we took a very rough road to Goma. The road was being worked on and appeared to be made of the clinker-like lava which lay beneath the surrounding forest. All the roads in this locality were made from this material and black in colour.

At Goma, situated on the shores of Lake Kivu, we turned off onto a very fine tarmac road. We tried but failed to find a way down to the edge of the lake. The road passed through fields of lava which flowed through the landscape in wide, solidified rivers. It was most extraordinary stuff—its surface crinkled like the skin on a milk pudding. A notice at the side of the road said that the lava was from the Nyiragongo volcano, which last erupted in 1938. Since our visit it has done so again, with catastrophic results.

Just after the tarmac ended, we rounded a corner and came across a heavily loaded truck and trailer which had jack-knifed and effectively blocked the road. The driver had extricated the truck but the trailer was still stuck and, with one wheel right at the edge of the steep drop into the lake, was perilously close to going over the edge. We tried for a while to get the trailer out for him using our winch, but although it started to move, our ground anchors would not hold.

The driver decided to press on to Bujumbura, his destination, and then come back with help to unload the trailer. He was an African driver and he regularly drove between Mombasa, on the Kenya coast, and Bujumbura—a distance of some 1,200 miles. He spoke good English and was very nice, in total contrast to some of the Belgians we had met.

One in particular peremptorily ordered us to get out of his way when he found the road blocked and we were working on trying to recover the trailer. Collyn and myself had a flaming row with this obnoxious individual, who eventually barged his way through, tearing up his tyres on the angle bars we had driven into the road as ground anchors and bouncing his bodywork off the rock face at the edge of the road. He threatened to call the police and we told him to get on with it. He was accompanied by his over-painted wife and was driving a gaudy American car.

We were beginning to think that their reputation for arrogance was well deserved, to judge from the behaviour of a number of the Belgians we encountered. Certainly, if you drive a truck, you are assumed to be African and expected to get out of the way of the good white folks— even if it means you finish up in the ditch, and we came across quite a number of trucks in that situation. Some had tried it with us also, but we refused to comply and they had to swerve out of our way at the last minute.

Their attitude may stem from the days of King Leopold of Belgium who fervently wanted a colony of his own. In 1876, to fulfil this ambition, he became the founder and sole owner of the

Congo Free State, a private project undertaken on his own behalf. He used Henry Morton Stanley to help him lay claim to the Congo. At the Berlin Conference of 1884-1885, the colonial nations of Europe committed the Congo Free State to improving the lives of the native inhabitants. However, from the beginning, Leopold did the exact opposite and ran the Congo for his personal gain, using a mercenary force to impose his will on the people. He extracted a fortune from the Congo, initially by the collection of ivory, and then, after a rise in the price of rubber in the 1890s, by forcing the population to collect sap from rubber trees. Villages were required to meet quotas on rubber collections, and individuals' hands were cut off if they didn't meet his quotas. His regime was responsible for the death of an estimated 2 to 15 million Congolese. This became one of the most infamous international scandals of the early 20th century and Leopold was ultimately forced to relinquish control of the Congo to the Belgian government.

Our observation was that very little had been done for the local people in the way of providing schools or medical facilities and that what there was had been supplied by dedicated missionaries and religious groups. Ironically it was these same groups who bore the brunt of the terrible violence that erupted when Belgium suddenly declared the Congo independent in August 1960—just a few months after our visit. Tragically the violence continues to this day in what is now known as the Democratic Republic of the Congo. We were fortunate to have travelled through here when we did. I often wonder about the fate of those people—both local and foreign—whom we met during our visit.

We said goodbye to the truck driver and set out in the dark and the rain over the slippery surface. We had great difficulty finding anywhere to stop along the twisty road which had been hacked out of the hillside with a drop straight down to the lake on the other side. Finally, we found a spot where the verge was just wide enough to accommodate us safely. Looking across the lake we could see a faint glow against the clouds from the crater of the still-active volcano.

I slept outside and awoke at dawn to see a magnificent sight.

There was the volcano, silhouetted against a flaming sky while its cloud mantle was filled with subtle colours of every shade. A plume of steam issued from the crater and this whole, marvellous scene was reflected in the still waters of Lake Kivu which lay at our feet. It was incredibly beautiful and I hurried to awake the others. I took some photographs, hoping to capture at least something of the scene which faded all too soon.

We continued on to the picturesque town of Bukavu, built on a series of peninsulas overlooking Lake Kivu. We visited Mobil and met the American manager and, later, his French wife. They were very hospitable and took us out to dinner at a nice restaurant which made a very pleasant change.

From Bukavu we continued on to Uvira, at the head of Lake Tanganyika. The road followed the shore of this enormous lake for a while before climbing back into weird mountains that looked more like folds in a piece of baize cloth—steep, smooth and vivid green with few trees. Over this section the single track road was only one way at a time. When we arrived at a barrier and an African beat on an oil drum with a stick—if this was responded to by an answering beat from somewhere out of sight, it meant that the section was clear and you could proceed. If there was no response, you stayed put, as it meant that another vehicle was in the section. This process was repeated every half-mile or so down the road, which had gradients steep enough to require first gear. The road was very twisty and often very narrow with a big drop on one side.

The next day was Christmas Eve 1959. We descended to the shores of Lake Tanganyika and the town of Albertville—since renamed Kalemie—which had coconut palms and one main street where we purchased a few provisions including a bottle of Dubonnet.

The road then left the lake and climbed once more into the mountains. We came across an African pickup truck with a puncture and no means of repairing it. We repaired it for him— our Christmas good deed—received his thanks, and continued on our way. Just as we were looking for somewhere to stop, we pulled over to let the pickup pass, and when he was in front he slowed down and waved at us to stop. We stopped and he got out with a bottle of whisky which he gave to me to open. We passed out three cups and gave him back the bottle. He had a swig, asked us where we were going, returned it to us, and then pushed off, wishing us good luck—most extraordinary.

We saw a village but found it completely deserted. We stopped to forage and found mealies, tomatoes and a great bunch of unripe bananas. We piled all these in the truck and shortly thereafter stopped at a place where we had a wonderful view over a great sweep of country. We had a bit of a job to get the truck level and even had to dig a hole for one of the rear wheels to do this.

Christmas Day 1959! We had a relaxed day. We listened to the BBC World Service, which came through loud and clear. Lunch was soup, bread rolls and Christmas pudding! Dinner was cabbage, peas, carrots, potatoes and stewed lamb chops, finished off with more Christmas pudding, coffee and canned fruit. We made hats out of poly roll and hung up some more inside. To sustain the spirit, we had some whisky from yesterday and a bottle of Dubonnet. A quiet Christmas, but quite pleasant. It poured with rain all day, which was a bit dismal as we were trapped inside and couldn't go out or savour the view.

We decided to make the next day a holiday, as well. We took our time getting up and then Rex and myself went down to the deserted African village to forage. It was a real mystery. It just looked as though the inhabitants had left at a moment's notice, leaving everything behind. In fact, the whole of this area seemed to be devoid of population which was almost sinister. We found lots more tomatoes and made it back to the truck just before it began to rain in earnest.

The following day we continued our journey. The road was wet and very slippery, some parts worse than others, and in those places we skidded all over the place - just missing a tree on one occasion. The country was undulating and the trees gradually became fewer. The cloud was very low and was only just above our heads. "Depressing" was the only word to describe the surroundings.

We came to a steep pull up out of a small valley and, even with four-wheel drive, could not make it up the slippery road. We fitted tyre chains and all was well. We took these off again at the top of the climb. In the morning we had gone near the edge of the road to avoid some mud, and the road had collapsed. The nearside rear wheel sank in to a depth of about 15 inches, and we had to dig it out. We crossed a lot of extremely dicey bridges and felt very apprehensive at each one we came to. They were just timber bridges, the timber being about 8 inches in diameter, with their soundness very much open to doubt.

We went down a steep descent with an almost sheer drop on one side into a tree-lined gorge from which we could hear the rush of water far below. The road was very slippery and we stopped and refitted tyre chains as a security measure. Even so we slipped around quite a lot. We came to one culvert which obviously wouldn't hold us, so Rex and myself did a bit of digging and modified it using the odd bits of timber available. It bent and creaked ominously—like the bridges—but we made it across.

The following day we had more of the same with many rickety wood bridges. We afterwards discovered that they had a 2.5-ton (metric) weight limit on them, so we were too heavy by over 3 times. Rex was driving and Collyn and myself got out to inspect each bridge before we crossed and then stood back to watch the fun while directing Rex. My heart was in my mouth at each crossing, and some of the bridges sagged in a frightening fashion.

The country gradually became flatter until we reached Lake Mweru, with Pweto at its head. The lake was very nice to look at and disappeared into the distance. We could see Rhodesia on the far shore. We had arranged to visit a couple who had been part of our group at De Havillands and who had moved to Rhodesia from England a few months ago. We decided to keep motoring during the night so that we could arrive on New Year's Eve.

I had just got to sleep—it seemed—when I was awoken by Collyn, who wanted some help to fit the tyre chains. We were driving on a piece of new road construction and, even with 4-wheel drive, we could make little progress. We battled with the wretched things and finally got them on, though we finished up well coated with mud. I went back to bed after sitting in the front for a while, and Collyn continued to drive. The vibration in the back with chains fitted was terrible.

We passed many colossal ant heaps rising up amongst the trees. I stopped and photographed one that was at least twice the height of the truck. Gradually the road dried out and conditions improved. We got to Elizabethville (since renamed Lubumbashi) at about 2 o'clock. We went to the Mobil station, where we took on fuel and were met by the manager who arrived later. He was American and was very nice.

The following day we left Elizabethville at about 8.30 and after 40 miles we got onto tarmac and before long found ourselves at the border with Northern Rhodesia (now Zambia) at a place called Kasumbalesa.

We got to Kitwe at about 4.30 and asked at the Post Office for the whereabouts of Grosvenor Crescent, where our friends, Bill and Anita, lived. We tried to follow their directions, without success, and we eventually wound up at a Mobil station where we met a very helpful type who phoned the police to find its location, but they too denied its existence. As Collyn had posted letters to that address and received replies, he obviously would not accept this. The guy at the Mobil garage then called the fire station, and here we were lucky. We went round there, saw it on the map and were then guided there by our helpful friend from the garage. We arrived at our destination to find Bill and Anita sitting outside their house.

The following day we all went out in the evening to celebrate the new year—1960. Bill was not very satisfied with his job. He had been pleased to have been selected from over 1,000 applicants, but when he arrived in Kitwe he found that he could have done the job by the second year of his De Havilland apprenticeship. When he asked why they had demanded such high qualifications, he was told that, even with those, they had more applicants for the job than they could reasonably handle.

Over the next 16 days we took a welcome break from daily driving. We relaxed with our friends and carried out overdue maintenance—including removing the cylinder head—again—swapping around the wheels and scrubbing the truck inside and out. One of Bill's colleagues arranged for us to tour the huge underground copper mine as well as a nearby open-cast operation.

We went to the lab where Bill worked, and when we saw various odd bits of electrical equipment, I decided that laboratory work was definitely not for me! We were then taken across to the mine itself, where we met the general manager's assistant, who took us to see the underground manager, who in turn took us to see the shift boss, who was taking us round.

We went to the changing room where we were given boots, overalls and hard hats. We collected lamps and batteries which fixed round the waist with a belt. We had our photographs taken for the mine magazine before being taken to the head of the shaft. When the cage came up, it was a crude metal affair with three compartments, about 9 feet square, stacked one above the other. This shaft went down to something like 2,700 feet, with a couple of stops on the way. Further descents were taken care of by a sub-shaft. The present depth of the mine was 3,700 feet deep, but it was proposed to take it down to around 9,000 feet. The sub-shaft was necessary because of the dip of the ore body. This mine had an estimated life of 40 years.

The maximum speed that the lift in this particular mine attained was 1,800 feet per minute, though on one other Copper belt area there was a cage which reached 3,000 feet per minute. This made me ask about the cable that supported the cage! This was replaced every two years and cost 6,000 pounds. One of the main troubles apparently was supporting the weight of the cable. When we reached the bottom level of the main shaft, we walked along a wide drive with a concrete floor fitted with railway tracks.

After about a quarter of a mile we turned off into a mine "section" through a small closed door. We saw several of these doors, whose function was to control the air that was pumped down for ventilation purposes. After going through the door, we could see the start of the reef quite distinctly. The junction with the "country" rock was on the footwall and pyrites sparkled in the reef like flecks of gold.

We climbed steep ladders, which were quite difficult and physically demanding to negotiate. These led to older workings where we negotiated a small tunnel which looked highly dangerous. The floor was littered with rock which had fallen from the ceiling. There were also pools of water, some of which were quite deep. We peered down a large hole, about 250 feet deep, where stoping had been carried out.

We retraced our steps and descended to a level below the one from which we had climbed. We walked until we came to a group drilling for more stoping. The holes were in the order of 90 feet deep and drilled with a diamond rotary drill. It was very hot and humid and the sweat poured off us, saturating our overalls.

We climbed down more substantial ladders until we came to a main drive, and here we got into another cage—the sub-shaft—and descended to 3,410 feet, where we visited the pumping station, which was clean and had a polished floor. It handled about 3,000,000 gallons of water a day. We were told that the Bancroft mine in the same area handled 8,000,000 gallons a day with additional flow when it rained! It was a bit disconcerting to think that there was nearly 3,500 feet of rock above your head!

It was quite cold in the main driver, especially as we were now soaking wet. We went back up to the 2,700-foot level and waited for the cage to return us to the surface. The cage was run by a winch man on the surface controlling the massive headgear. There was a system of bell signals which told the winch operator on which of many levels someone was waiting for the cage. By some miracle he was able, not only to keep track of this, but also to stop the cage at exactly the right level—bearing in mind that the cage was a three-story affair, and the winch cable itself stretched different amounts according to how much of the cable was suspended in the shaft. There was one special emergency signal which had priority over all others. The mine operators told us they are able to get an injured man from anywhere in the mine into hospital in less than 15 minutes. There was an emergency ring while we were waiting for the lift. There was just a whoosh and a blast of air, with the cage itself invisible, as it shot past the open grill doors guarding the entrance to the shaft.

Back on the surface we had hot showers and tea, which were very welcome.

The open cast pit at Chingola was very different. At the time it was 200 feet deep and made use of massive equipment such as mechanical shovels which lifted 9 tons at a bite and loaded them into trucks carrying 35 tons. We walked alongside—and were dwarfed by—a huge, walking, German-made bucket-wheel excavator.

Finally, it was time for us to continue our journey. We were quite sad to leave. We had a farewell party on Jan 18th and left the following day for Lusaka, where we spent one day before continuing on to Livingstone and the famous Victoria Falls. Here the mighty Zambezi River drops into a narrow canyon running at right angles to the river. The resulting spray reaches well over 1,000 feet, creating rainbows in the sunlight. The African name is *Mosi-oa-tunya*—which translates as "The Smoke that Thunders". These falls are twice the height of Niagara and well over twice the width of Horseshoe Falls. The first European to view this famous landmark was believed to be Dr. Livingstone on November 18th, 1855.

We crossed the border into Southern Rhodesia, passed through the coal mining town of Wankie—now called Hwange—and on to Bulawayo. This was our furthest point south—about 65 miles north of the border with South Africa.

We could have continued into South Africa and it would have been very satisfying to have been able to say that we had been all the way to Cape Town, but it would have been hard to justify continuing the survey of African roads into this more industrialized country. More to the point, perhaps, apartheid was being strictly enforced in South Africa at that time, and we wanted no part of that obnoxious regime. So, for the first time since leaving England we reversed direction and headed north.

Chapter 3

January 1960 to May 1960

Bulawayo to Europe

I describe our return journey north, visiting old haunts in Mombasa and also revisiting my father. We continue north across the Sahara Desert, where we have to remove the cylinder head in a sandstorm.

On January 23rd, 1960, we arrived in Salisbury (now renamed Harare), and I was back in familiar territory. We stayed with Pat Hadden, the friend of my mother I had stayed with when I had first arrived here two and a half years earlier. I visited other people I had known when I was living and working in the country. The local newspaper, the *Rhodesia Herald*, wanted to do a story on us and took our photo beside the truck.

We left five days later and drove to Karoi, where we stayed with one of the tobacco farmers I had known when I lived there. The following day we went on a tour of the farm and saw how the tobacco leaves were harvested and processed. We went next to Miami and the depot, where everything seemed under control. The next day we went for a sail on the tiny reservoir, which was quite a contrast to the wonderful sailing I had experienced in Mombasa.

After being loaded up with all kinds of goodies by our generous host, we left the following day up the main highway north and took the turn off to Kariba, site of the huge dam across the Zambezi, which had been under construction while I had been living in Karoi. The road was dirt but in good condition and had been built specifically to provide access to the site. The road builders had given evocative names to certain features such as Razor Ridge and Puff Adder Ridge.

Eventually we could see the lake in the distance. The scene was one of desolation, with the branches of dead and dying trees reaching skyward from the water. We climbed a steep hill next to the observatory building, and there below us lay the curved dam. It appeared smaller than I had expected, but this was an optical illusion because the face of the dam was 425 feet high. A jet of water from a hole 7 feet in diameter sprayed out in a curving arc to provide water downstream while the lake behind the dam was filling at a rate of about 1 inch per day. There was a smell of hydrogen sulphide in the air from the rotting of drowned vegetation.

We were given a tour of the unfinished underground machine hall and were able to stand between the generator rotating at 125 rpm above our heads and the water-driven turbine beneath our feet. The shaft connecting the two was 3 feet in diameter, and the total rotating weight was 600 tons with a diameter of 25 feet. Five additional machines were in various stages of assembly, with the last being little more than a hole in the ground. The machine hall and transformer halls were huge and carved out of solid rock. The latter contained massive transformers weighing 225 tons apiece which had been brought to this spot fully assembled from England.

Once across the dam, we were back in Northern Rhodesia (now Zambia) and had to pass through three fly gates where the vehicle was sprayed to discourage the migration of the tsetse fly, which causes sleeping sickness in humans and weakness, leading to death, in domestic animals.

Back on the main highway, I retraced my route from when I had hitchhiked up this same road in 1958. We stopped briefly at Lusaka and at Kapiri Mposhi, where I had obtained my main lift north, and took the fork in the road that led to Mbeya and Tanganyika (now called Tanzania). The country here was mopani forest, and it was only at the top of the occasional hill that you got any view and were able to see the red road running through the endless trees all the way to the blue horizon. We had no problems at the border with Tanganyika and it was amazing how the terrain changed immediately at the border, becoming much hillier. In the pleasant town of Mbeya there were Eucalyptus and even a few fir trees.

We passed by the hilltop town of Iringa and shortly thereafter descended a steep escarpment, resulting in an increase in temperature and the appearance of many baobab trees. We continued on to Morogoro, which has coconut palms and is backed by 9,000-foot-high mountains. This is a very fertile area and we saw sisal, bananas, coconuts, cassava, coffee, papayas, mangoes and kapok. It was now quite hot as we reached Tanga on the coast of the Indian Ocean. The last time we had seen the sea had been the Mediterranean at Algiers.

We crossed the border into Kenya, and on February 9th arrived in Mombasa and met up with my friend Peter at his delightful traditional house among the coconut palms. We spent the next few days meeting up with the friends I had made while I lived and worked here, including Heron Bruce. We did a lot of sailing on the beautiful harbour with Dulcie. We also contacted the local Mobil agency, and on February 21st, a guy from the organization came looking for Rex with the message that his mother was dangerously ill. We managed to get Rex on a plane to Nairobi the following morning. We heard later that he arrived back in Bolton on February 23rd to learn that, unfortunately, his mother had died two days previously.

When Collyn and I left Mombasa on March 1st, I had quite a lump in my throat. I had enjoyed my time in Mombasa and I was leaving a lot of friends behind. We took the road to Voi and as we climbed, we left behind the coastal region with its lush vegetation and coconut palms and were soon traveling through thorn bush. The local women were bare breasted.

We took a diversion back into Tanganyika, heading for the town of Arusha. This was mainly to see Kilimanjaro, the highest mountain in Africa at 19,341 feet and its nearby companion Mount Meru at 14,977 feet. Disappointingly, both mountains were hidden in the clouds, but the following day they shyly revealed themselves in all their snow-capped magnificence. The surrounding plains teemed with wild animals, including wildebeest, hartebeest, Thomson's gazelle, ostrich, zebra, gerenuk and giraffe. The landscape was dotted with flat-topped acacia trees, most with the nests of weaver birds hanging from the branches. The local people in this area were mostly Masai types, with men dressed only in a red blanket and carrying spears. The women were lavishly decorated with beads and anklets. We met a couple who had ridden a motorcycle out from England via Italy, Egypt, and the Sudan. The needle of the carburettor had broken off and disappeared into the engine but they had made—and soldered in place—a replacement fashioned from a key for opening a can of corned beef! We worked together, using a nail, to make an improved model.

We turned back into Kenya and headed to Nairobi, which somehow managed to combine modernity with the air of a frontier town. Its streets were ablaze with colourful bougainvillea. While we were there we took the opportunity to visit Nairobi National Park on the edge of town and drove down dirt roads, viewing a wide variety of animals, with Nairobi's high-rise buildings just visible on the horizon.

After a couple of days, we continued north, skirting the shoulder of Mount Kenya, to Nyeri and Nanyuki, before arriving at the tiny settlement of Timau. Along the way, Mount Kenya, at 17,057 feet, was completely clear and looked stunning against the blue sky following a snowfall the previous day. We arrived at Mongoose Farm in the afternoon of March 5, where my father and Mongoose himself were expecting us.

We spent 10 days with my father and Mongoose and visited with many of their settler friends. We did some maintenance on farm machinery, for which Mongoose paid us, which was very generous of him. I went fly fishing for trout almost every day and, when successful, we ate the catch for breakfast. Even though we were in semi-desert surroundings, the stream through the property flowed continuously, fed by the melting snow from Mt. Kenya, which dominated the skyline. The ram kept pumping water into the water tanks and the overflow irrigated the gardens producing a cornucopia of fruit and vegetables. There were apple trees in fruit and blossom at the same time, as well as oranges, lemons, pineapples, granadillas, blackberries, peaches and grapes. Vegetables included cabbage, leeks, carrots, onions, lettuce and tomatoes.

The settler era was coming to an end, with independence from Britain just around the corner. Most of my father's neighbours were in his age group. One was Dr. Rhino Jackson—so called because he "charged on sight!".

Later that same year, Mongoose made numerous flights into the Congo to rescue Europeans who were being attacked and murdered in the violence that erupted when the country was granted its independence from Belgium. The stress of the operation at his age undoubtedly contributed to his getting sick, which led to his death a few months later. He generously left the farm for my father to live in for as long as he wished to do so.

It was sad to leave but we had to continue our journey, so we said goodbye on March 16th. The farm was at 7,500 feet above sea level and now we headed towards the Aberdare Mountains, which climbed to over 9,000 feet. It was the rainy season and the road was very muddy and slippery, which caused the truck to slide down the camber and collide with the bank at the road's edge. The rain was extremely local; it could be raining on one side of the road but not on the other. We passed the towns of Nakuru and then Eldoret, crossing the line of the equator several times. We left Kenya and crossed into Uganda, spending one day in the capital, Kampala. The number of Asian Indians was very noticeable. They were mostly descendants of Indians brought here as labour in early colonial times, and they now ran most of the shops and commerce in East Africa. Ten years later, when the tyrant Idi Amin took over, he expelled most of the Asians and confiscated their property.

We skirted Lake Victoria, which is the size of England, and could see the Ruwenzori Mountains on the horizon. Also called the Mountains of the Moon, their highest peaks wore a mantle of snow.

Next came Lake Edward and the Queen Elizabeth game park. There was a sign saying "Beware of Hippos" as we pulled off the road for the night at the edge of the lake. We noticed some rounded grey rocks in the water and it was not until they moved that we realized they were hippos! I was keen to take photos of them, but they stayed in the water until the moment when the light meter on the camera said it was too dark to take photos. We heard them moving around the truck during the night and I got up before dawn to try again, but the last hippo disappeared into the lake just as the light meter began to register.

We crossed the border into the Belgian Congo and found ourselves back in thick jungle. We came across a European walking down the road carrying a briefcase. We picked him up, and he said he wanted a ride to the next town, where he had a friend. We took him to his friend's house. It did not appear to us that the so-called friend knew the man, but he was very hospitable all the same and, being an experienced traveller himself, offered us all showers and then provided us with an excellent meal. Our hitchhiker then said that he would like to go with us to Bangassou, so we agreed to take him. Before reaching the border with the Central African Republic at Bangassou, there is a main immigration station at Bondo, where we had stopped on our way south. Our hitchhiker got out of the truck before we reached Bondo and said he would meet us on the other side of town, which was suspicious. However, there he was, waiting for us, after we had visited the authorities.

When we arrived at Bangassou there was no escaping the border post and the hitch hiker was detained for having no papers. We surmised that he might be a deserter from the Belgian forces, but we never knew. The same African, who had denied us entry for having no visas on our way south, was at the post. I think he was understandably a bit annoyed with us for giving him aggravation on the way down and then dumping a dubious character on him on the return journey.

We crossed the Ubangui river again on the same ferry to the town of Bangassou and drove straight to Bangui. This was the fourth time we had traversed this piece of road! By this time, we were running very low on fuel and had to buy some in Bambari. It was quite a coincidence that the only other time we had come close to running out of fuel was along this same stretch of road.

We reached Bangui on March 29th, and this time spent three days in the town, during which we refuelled and carried out some maintenance on the truck. It was here that I saw my first dry storm. On the opposite bank of the Ubangi River, menacing black clouds built up, emitting thunder and lightning. The wind drew a dark line on the water as it sped across the river with thick mist beneath it that looked like rain. But when it arrived it had all the elements of a thunderstorm—minus any rain. Very strange!

We met a Frenchman who took us for a run up the river on his boat, and who also introduced us to water skiing. I had never done this before, but after a few failed attempts, managed to get up on the skis. So I learned to water ski on the Ubangi River, with the Congo on one bank and the Central African Republic on the other!

We left Bangui on April 2nd and reached Kano, in Nigeria, on April 8th, having passed through Cameroon on the way. We took a more westerly route than we had on the way south. On entering Kano, we took a wrong turn and accidentally discovered the old town, with its huge, green-domed mosque. We couldn't imagine how we had missed it—and been in ignorance of its existence—on our previous visit. However, apart from this find, our return visit was one of frustration. We were supposed to pick up permits and visas there, which had been arranged by Mobil for us to cross the Sahara by way of Timbuctoo. They should have been left for us at Poste Restante in the main Kano Post Office. We were quite sure they were there, but the Nigerian Post Office officials maintained they were not. We looked over the official's shoulder while he was checking the mail under the appropriate alphabetical letters and could see that they were all mixed up. Under "T", for example there would be letters addressed to names starting with all letters of the alphabet. He got quite mad with us and asked if we did not trust him. Of course the answer to this was "no" but we could not say so or he would simply kick us out and there was no one we could appeal to.

In the end we never did get our visas for Timbuctoo, so that was a lost opportunity of a lifetime simply because someone could not be bothered to do his job properly. What made it worse was that our visas for the original route had expired and had not been renewed because we had been expected to take the alternative route. As if that were not enough, access to the Sahara was due to close on May 1st, less than three weeks away—and we still had to get there!

While we were parked in the Mobil fuel depot, alongside tanker trucks and fuel storage tanks, Collyn and I were working on the recalcitrant electric fuel pump, located in the truck's cab not far from our own capacious fuel tanks. Suddenly a spark from the contacts ignited some spilt gasoline and we had a potentially disastrous fire on our hands. The closest extinguisher was engulfed in the flames, but fortunately Collyn grabbed another, which worked extremely efficiently. It could so easily have led to total disaster. That would have been no way to repay Mobil's hospitality! They even took matches and lighters from you when you entered the depot.

We tried in vain to solve the visa problem with Mobil's help, but in the end had to leave on April 23rd and head for Zinder in Niger, with little time to spare.

While in Kano we met some other trans-Sahara travellers, including some Americans who were driving a Jeep truck around the world. They were sponsored by Jeep and also by Coca Cola, so they had bottles and bottles of the stuff. They had lost the use of their 4-wheel drive, so we agreed to travel across the Sahara together, and to help them out, we took on board a number of crates of Coke. We were still in the Sahel and hadn't even reached the Sahara itself when we went over a significant bump and there was a tremendous crash from the back. We stopped and I jumped out to take a look. I opened the door to be met by a tidal wave of Coke and Fanta from 14 family-sized bottles, which left broken glass and a sticky residue to be cleaned up.

It was along this stretch that we saw water being drawn from a well using a leather bucket. Surrounded by people and animals, the bucket was attached to a line pulled by a black and white ox being ridden by a small boy. In another spot there was a small group with their camels. The men wore conical furry hats and they were very cooperative when I asked to take their photos. They spotted some mud on the truck and asked when and where it had come from. The rains were expected and they were anticipating their arrival.

On April 25th the truck was pretty gutless, and when we checked the cylinder compression we found it to be very poor, so we thought we had better remove the cylinder head and grind the valves before embarking on the Sahara crossing. Our American friends continued on, and we arranged to meet in Agadez. While we were doing this, an Arab showed up who was walking to Agadez! He asked us for a lift and, by pointing at the sun, we indicated we could take him tomorrow. We ground the valves and reinstalled the cylinder head with a used gasket because we had run out of new ones. We fed our Arab passenger with bread and jam that night. He was exceptionally nice and very polite. We got going again the following day and reached Agadez, where we encountered a number of people preparing to cross the Sahara.

After crossing the border into Algeria, we spent the night in the tiny oasis of In Guezzam, just 15 days before it closed for the summer. The southern section is the toughest part of this route, as there is much soft sand, limited sign posting, and a steady climb in altitude towards the Hoggar Mountains. We got stuck and had to dig out and use sand mats several times. The truck began to give more trouble with engine water leaking from somewhere, then erupting under the filler cap, and finally locking the engine so it would not turn over on the starter motor. We diagnosed a leaking head gasket and obviously could not continue until we had dealt with it.

We removed the cylinder head again and refitted it with another used gasket well smothered in gasket cement. The wind had risen and there was sand blowing everywhere, so we had quite a job to keep it out of the engine. After we had everything together, we found we had stopped the leak into the cylinders but not the pressurization of the radiator. We caught the overflow water in a can which, when full, emptied back into the radiator. However, some water was still lost, and we were down to just 4 miles per gallon of water at one stage. The wind continued to increase until we almost had a sandstorm. It was a worrying time and an illustration of how quickly things can get out of control.

With great relief we finally made it to Tamanrasset and Collyn had a go at checking the cooling system. He couldn't find anything wrong other than a leaking water pump gland, which he replaced. Fortunately, this seemed to solve the problem, although we couldn't figure out why.

The following day, May 2nd, together with the Americans, we took a diversion into the Hoggar Mountains to visit the hermitage at Assekrem. Almost immediately we came across several pools of clear green water, which was not something I had expected to see in the Sahara. We camped for the night nearby.

I was awakened the next morning by flies, but I pulled my shirt over my face and went to sleep again. We eventually got up sometime after nine after taking some photos of the pool. The sky was overcast but it cleared up for a while later after a few drops of rain. There was a very strong wind blowing, and when it was from behind the truck, our dust blew up and overtook us.

The road first wound its way over generally fairly open areas of land with a surface very similar to that of the Tademait Plateau—rising all round were weirdly shaped hills with columns of basalt resembling organ pipes.

We saw a Tuareg woman at the edge of the road, which was quite a surprise as we were miles from any habitation. Then we spotted another figure way up on the hills with a large herd of goats. From time to time we saw donkeys and goats feeding on the scrub in the river beds.

The road began to climb steeply and we had to use low gear in low range several times. At one place a huge vertical cliff of basalt towered above the road. The wind was pretty fierce by this time and made a strange roaring noise as it blew round the huge buttress of rock.

We reached the turn off—left up to the hermitage at Asekrem and right to Hirafok and thence to the new road to Arak. We were some way ahead of the Americans at the turn off, so we left a Coke bottle at the edge of the road and drew an arrow on the ground pointing up the left turn.

We had some steep climbing after this turn and had to use ultra-low several times. We had quite a lot of gradients 1:3. We eventually made our way, after negotiating several hairpins, up to the top of the climb. The road reached a sort of col and continued beyond and actually returned to Tamanrasset. We left the truck at this spot. It started to rain and was extremely cold as the wind screamed and shrieked over the top of the col. The temperature in the back of the truck was 55 degrees C (131°F). There were one or two Arabs to be seen around, and their clothes were torn and flapped around by the gale. Collyn put on his anorak and I got out my jersey.

The road was at 8,724 feet, and we had an extremely steep climb on foot up to the hermitage itself, which was at 9,118 feet. We struggled up to the top—and a struggle it was, at that altitude. At the top there were various little rock houses tucked away and also a lot of meteorological instruments. There was a wonderful view from the top of the strange mountains of the Hoggar. The outlook was grey with the overcast and the rain squalls.

We were looking at one of the topographic charts they had up there when a bearded, bespectacled chap wearing a woolly monk's habit came up and started talking to us. The rain started coming down again, and he invited us into his little stone hut which stood nearby. There he told us that he had been up at the hermitage for a year; he carried out theological studies and also took meteorological readings three times a day. This station was part of a group of five in the Hoggar, and it was being enlarged even to the extent of having radar cloud scanners fitted. He told us that the word *Hoggar* means "the place of Mountains" in Arabic and *Tanezrouft* means "the place of thirst".

We went down to the bottom and returned to the truck. When Collyn moved the truck, the dust blew up, reducing visibility to zero. I was standing outside to guide him and got the benefit of most of it. It really stung when it whipped against my legs. The rain was driving nearly horizontal and the inside of the truck seemed a heaven after the blitz outside. We had double helpings of mushroom soup and then continued on our way over a road which lost altitude in a series of hairpins. Although the road twisted and climbed, its surface was very good, and all the way we noticed numerous roofless stone shelters and walls built to protect the road workers from the wind, which blew constantly up here.

We went down the turning where we had arranged to meet Dean. After a few hundred yards we came to a little river bed full of green vegetation and pools of water. We walked down it and found it to be most attractive with some quite deep pools—I saw fish in one of them, but they were not very big. There was also a small waterfall.

The stream went up a deep canyon whose sides were made up of those weird columns of basalt. In one place the weight of the rock higher up the hill had pushed the lower columns over on their side, and they stuck out of the side of the hill like the end of a wood pile. We saw lots of migratory birds, mostly swallows and house martins. We saw some even bigger and deeper pools than we had yesterday and walked as far as a place where another canyon joined the first one.

It was indeed a surprise to see all the vivid green, flowers, birds and fish in the middle of the barren waste of rock. We passed some lava hills and came across one place where we had a splendid view over a big valley with a surprising amount of vegetation in it. We descended on a rough road and after a few miles came across the vivid green vegetation, trees and reed and mud huts of Hirafok. Here we turned left and followed a road which crossed several riverbeds and passed through rocky terrain. It was appallingly rough in places, and we crossed one step so high that Collyn was able to sit on it with his legs almost vertical to the piece below. We followed the Jeep and it was amazing to see it bouncing up and down and flipping sideways as it crossed the rough terrain. The Jeep became stuck in one riverbed where it was not possible to take a run at the sand because of an extremely rough and steep descent. We used the standard procedure of winching to get them out.

After about 15 miles, the road followed wide flat river beds and improved immensely. Eventually we reached the main road, where there was a large concrete sign marking the mileage to Algiers—1,938 kilometres (1,204 miles). We took some photos and pressed on to In Amguel, where we picked up an Arab looking for a lift. This village also produced a splash of green in the grey wilderness.

The road was extremely good and we saw the big lava mountains coming up that we remembered from last time. This time we were passing it for six miles. One can easily imagine the lava bubbling up through a fissure in the ground and producing the great mountain. The mountains all round looked lovely this evening and the pastel colours looked beautiful. It was a clear day and quite cool.

We stopped for the night not far from the road. The dynamo stopped charging just before we stopped for the night. Collyn decided to leave it until we got to Arak. The truck was beginning to show increasing signs of wear after its long journey over rough roads.

We reached Arak to find that the crew we had met on our way south had been redeployed. We removed the dynamo from the engine and replaced the worn bushes. The following day we continued north up the familiar road. We stopped briefly at In Salah and then climbed up onto the monotonous Tademait Plateau. The corrugations were, if anything, even worse than last time and the truck took a terrible battering. In fact, the vibration was so bad that the roof of the cab became detached from the top of the windshield!

We continued north through El Golea and Ghardaia. Near Djelfa, on May 10th, we were back on smooth tarmac for the first time in many miles and immediately noticed wheel shimmy. The roads had been too rough up to now to notice such subtle defects. When we got out to check, I noticed a bulge in one of the tyres. As they were stamped "SG"—for Smooth Going—this was hardly surprising, considering the punishment they had taken.

We saw a series of road signs in French. The first one said: "Excessive speed will send you..." the second one continued: "to prison certainly..." the next: "to hospital perhaps..." and finally:

"to St. Peter too soon!". Shortly thereafter we reached the top of the Atlas Mountains and descended the Chiffa Gorge down to the coast.

At Maison Carree we met up with Mobil, who said they had sent the paperwork for both Sahara routes to Kano, which confirmed that the post office in Kano had been responsible for us not getting them.

We drove westwards through the lush, beautiful coastal countryside. There were many storks building nests on top of chimneys. We crossed into Morocco and took the road to Fez. As before, the road signs were massive concrete affairs taller than the truck. We barely stopped in Fez because we were accosted by some touts as soon as we entered the town, which did not look too exciting anyway. We drove north until we reached Ceuta, on the Mediterranean coast.

Chapter 4

May 1960 to November 1960

Europe to England

We drive across Europe through Spain and Andorra, taking in the Monaco Grand Prix before crossing the Alps and returning to England. I work as a farm labourer and pick cherries. I interview for a job with a British trading company for a job in Hong Kong and briefly experience life as a traveling salesman in the UK.

Ceuta is one of the Pillars of Hercules: Gibraltar, across the strait, is the other. Ceuta in Morocco is Spanish territory, just as Gibraltar in Spain is British territory. This being the case, I think it is a bit hypocritical of Spain to be demanding the return of Gibraltar to Spanish sovereignty when they are doing the exact same thing in Morocco a few miles away across the Strait.

The next day, May 18th, we went to embark on the ferry that was to take us across the straits to Algeciras, Spain. The truck would not start and it was not until Collyn changed the ignition coil that he got the engine started, just 15 minutes before the ferry was due to leave. We barely made it and were the last vehicle to board. We arrived in Algeciras and drove into Gibraltar for a couple of days and did some sightseeing on this impressive rock fortress. We then re-entered Spain and took the road to Granada, where we visited the amazing Moorish Alhambra palace. We also bought a number of bottles of Sherry (Jerez) and liqueur.

From here we headed for Madrid, where we stopped briefly. The main post office looked like a palace. Parts of rural Spain were still very rural and I saw water being raised by a donkey harnessed to a horizontal wooden wheel.

Once on the road we noticed more and more civil guards. We thought there were a few more than usual but, after seeing them on the tops of all the hills—silhouetted against the skyline with their rifles and ancient profiled hats, standing in the middle of fields of corn, alongside the road, and in all sorts of unlikely places in their hundreds, we realized that something must be up. Eventually the mystery was solved when we came across a decorated arch with "Franco, Franco, Franco" written on it. Every village had small groups of expectant people and, in one place, there were rows of chairs set out. Eventually a car with red lights on the front appeared and signalled us to the side of the road. It was followed almost immediately by a string of cars travelling at high speed. It wasn't possible to pick anyone out but, for sure, one of them contained *Generalissimo* Franco.

We saw the Pyrenees in the distance and took the road to Andorra. The road twisted and turned and ran most of the way through steep sided gorges with a fast flowing river at the bottom. We saw a small hydroelectric dam tucked away. Shortly thereafter we heard a funny noise. Stopping to investigate, we discovered a puncture in one of the tyres with air coming out through the sidewall. With just the two of us, we anticipated an awful job getting the tyre off, but having seen how it was done at Djelfa, it was surprisingly easy. The only snag was that the bolts which should have been holding the two halves of the wheel together had nearly all broken off, and there were only three left! We robbed bolts from the chains and the exhaust system to replace them. They weren't the right size but better than nothing.

On our way once more, we passed through the border from Spain into the tiny principality of Andorra, tucked away in the middle of the Pyrenees. The road followed a narrow valley carpeted with wildflowers. At its base, a fast-flowing river leapt and tumbled among almond trees just coming into blossom.

After passing through a couple of tiny hamlets we arrived at the main town of Andorra la Vella, which dates from 1278, and were able to park in the centre. We walked down to the end of the

221

shops and decided to eat out for a change. We chose a medium quality restaurant where, for only ten shillings per head, we had soup, rice done up with odds and ends including mussels, roast chicken with lettuce, and ice cream. A bottle of red wine was placed on the table where you might expect to see water in other parts of the world.

The following day, the road continued to climb through the mountains. The scenery was breath-taking, with rich green grass studded with beautiful wildflowers. Fast running streams, lined with silver birch, came bounding down in a welter of foam, and higher up—right up to the snow —there were pines. We continued to climb, gradually getting nearer the snow line until, rounding a corner, we saw a spectacular group of peaks still almost completely white. We climbed towards these and saw quite a large group of horses and colts, the adults with large, soft-toned bells round their necks. One lay down in the road right in front of the truck but didn't stay long! The climb terminated in a sort of ladder-type ascent where the road zigzagged back and forth up a very steep mountain side. Eventually we reached the summit at 8,000 feet. At the top we found a Mobil and also an Esso station! There was a magnificent view of huge, snow-covered mountains. As we started our descent, cloud covered the peaks and then floated down to the pass itself. The snow was about six feet deep on one side of the road where it had drifted.

We came to the French border, where the customs official was initially a bit difficult about the amount of petrol we were carrying (fuel is much more expensive in France than in Spain). He was more amenable when we told him that it had been supplied gratis by Mobil. He had a look inside the truck and poked around a bit. Collyn commented that the guy didn't know whether to be awkward or not! Finally, he allowed us to pass and we climbed again to 5,200 feet at the Col de Perche. The snow wasn't too far away and the yellow broom was beautiful—brilliant yellow and profuse. We saw the railway—an amazing feat, building it through this sort of country. We saw some old-fashioned railway carriages painted bright yellow, but I don't know if they were still in use or not; these were parked on sidings in the stations.

The road continued with alternate ascents and descents and we saw many wooden snow fences, some of which had collapsed under the weight of snow. We went through an amazing boulder-strewn area aptly named *Chaos de Targasonne*. The names in this area were often very odd—Ur, Via, Llo and Lus, to name but a few—presumably these are Catalan names. We were still at 5,000 feet while only 50 miles from Perpignan, which was at sea level! The road then went down an amazing descent. Below us we saw the twists and turns of the road appearing at all sorts of odd places and levels in such a bewildering variety that we could not imagine how they could all join up into one coherent and useful road. Mixed up with the road was the railway, which passed through many tunnels, ran along the edge of cliffs, and over a fine suspension bridge.

At the base of the mountains the valleys opened up, and we passed one village which was almost entirely inside a castle-like structure. I also saw a horse drawing a huge load of hay, the horse wearing a fetching pair of black-and-yellow-check ear covers!

In Perpignan, we gave a ride to an Australian couple and the next evening stopped for the night about 8 miles from Montpellier, within sight of the Mediterranean.

At Aix-en-Provence the countryside became slightly hilly and more scenic. We saw "Nice" on the signposts and at Frejus we came alongside the azure sea. We followed the coast until we reached Monte Carlo, to which we had come to watch the Grand Prix.

We walked around the circuit and saw the famous casino, but didn't go inside as we decided that we looked a bit scruffy. All the corners along the race circuit had protective straw bales and there was plenty of rubber on the road from the practice that had already taken place. There were many exotic cars being driven by people who obviously had the Grand Prix spirit. We passed garages where racing cars were being worked on and saw the beautiful Team Ferrari trucks, as well as a Lotus and Cooper *equipe* set up.

If we wanted to have a decent view, we would have to pay at least 3,000 francs for the privilege. We finally picked a place along the front. We located a good spot to put the truck and brought it into town from the outskirts where we had initially parked it.

After breakfast we went round to the Touring Club de Monaco to see about some seats. They had some, but we hadn't the correct money so we couldn't pay for them until the banks opened. We had the seats kept for us, however. We went off to find a bank, but they didn't open until nine, so we spent the intervening time walking down by the yacht basin, which again was full of lovely boats including a smaller one from Australia.

The time moved on. The Prince and Princess of Monaco arrived and did a tour of the circuit before going to their box. The race started with the full 16 cars. All in all, it was a terrific race, very exciting in its own right, and of course the venue and the closeness of the cars made it all the better. On a regular race track it is hard to have any real idea how fast the cars are moving, but here, as they rip through regular streets with their throaty exhausts echoing off the buildings, you feel the full impression of speed. It would have been nicer if the weather had been better, but then, of course, it would not have been so exciting.

After the excitement of the Grand Prix, we decided to go into Italy to Turin—or Torino, to give it its correct Italian name—and then, if the pass over the Alps was open, continue on to Geneva. We backtracked to Nice and turned inland away from the coast. Almost immediately the road started to climb so that, after only 18 miles, we had reached the Col de Braus at 3,400 feet. En route we had negotiated 21 steep hairpins with another 16 on the descent from there to Sospel, where we were back down at 1,150 feet.

After Sospel we started to climb again, and reached 2,840 feet before another descent. We stopped on the way up to pick some cherries we saw growing on the roadside. From the top of the Col we had a marvellous view of huge mountains laden with snow. The road had 13 hairpins on the climb up to the Col and six on the way down, in addition to plenty of less severe bends.

We reached a small town which had a very full river running through it and we stopped between it and the road about five miles out of town. The truck was doing odd things, with water blowing out of the exhaust pipe after a long descent. We were also losing water out of the radiator and occasionally the water would burst forth, steaming and under pressure, from the top of the radiator. We were about 20 miles from the Italian border with more climbing ahead of us. We were a bit concerned about whether the vehicle would hold together and whether this diversion had been such a good idea!

We had a wash in the river before moving off the next morning and the water was freezing. We continued the climb and noticed several little shelters by the road, presumably in case people got caught out in a blizzard. We went up a narrow gorge and saw a fine little village which appeared to be wedged in a crevice up a steep piece of hill. The railway came up the pass with us—or rather, it used to—because we saw that quite a number of bridges were down. Presumably they were blown up during the war. Almost every house not actually in a village was deserted, and even some of those in the villages were in ruins. We saw several shattered blockhouses on the hillsides. It was a shame to see the railway in its present condition, as its construction had obviously taken a tremendous effort and so much of it still survived.

Way above us we saw fair quantities of snow on the peaks. Then the road really started to climb and negotiated a series of 17 hairpins, one right after the other—making a total of 24 hairpins for the ascent. At the top of this final set of hairpins was the French border post, and the road immediately entered a tunnel which was at least a mile long, lit by sodium lamps, and in places braced with wood. At the other end we came out into Italian sunshine and went through customs and immigration. Everyone was extremely pleasant, especially the vehicle inspector, who spoke good English. He also said that he spoke Swahili as he had spent some time in East Africa—presumably as a prisoner of war. No one expressed any wish to look inside the vehicle.

In Italy I noticed people using cows for such unusual tasks as pulling ploughs and carts. The main road was lined with stones, painted black and white. At frequent intervals there were advertising signs on either side of the road. We drove into Turin, which was big and industrial. We continued on and stopped for the night at the edge of a big river about 10 miles from a place called Aosta. We had climbed up a fair way but still had a long ascent ahead of us, as the St. Bernard Pass topped out at 8,000 feet.

24,000 miles came up on the odometer that day. It would be the last 1,000-mile turnover we would see on the trip.

June 1st was misty and chilly. We reached Aosta and saw two signs—one to the Gran San Bernardo, and one to the Picolino San Bernardo. We took the turning up to the Great St. Bernard, but hadn't got far out of the town when a lorry came past and the driver pointed up the road and shook his finger. We suspected he meant that the pass was closed. We rounded the next bend and found that the driver had stopped. We stopped, as well, and he told us, in French, that there was snow up on the pass and it was closed on the French side. It was extremely nice of him to stop. We turned around and sought information on the state of Little St. Bernard. We found out from a garage that the pass was open.

We started to climb and saw houses with the roofing tiles made out of large pieces of flat stones. The top story of the house often seemed to be left open under the gables and the ground story used for the animals. The inhabitants lived on the middle floor. We saw cattle on the roads with huge bells round their necks fixed on with wide leather belts, usually with a bit of brass fancy work. We saw a sign: *"Vista del Mt. Blanc"* but the mist concealed everything from our view. We climbed up amongst pine trees and the smell was wonderful. Streams hurtled down the steep hillsides, in some places forming wonderful waterfalls. With 15 miles to go, we were still 4,178 feet lower than the summit, and the road renewed its rate of climb with nine hairpins followed by a short tunnel.

We came to a place where an avalanche had crossed the road, leaving uprooted trees and piles of loose earth. The river was full of dirty snow and the water flowed beneath it. We negotiated another 15 hairpins, and the snow became ever deeper until we were driving through a narrow trench, barely wider than the truck, with walls of snow reaching as high as 12 feet on either hand. We stopped at the Italian border and were questioned by a cheery crowd who again weren't a bit interested in looking inside the vehicle. One of them spoke French and he asked quite a few questions about the trip. I asked him how long the pass had been open, and he said that it had only been open since the previous afternoon! He said that about 15 vehicles so far had passed through the checkpoint.

We continued on to the French Post, about 150 yards away. We had hoped that the mist and cloud would clear so that we would see Mont Blanc, but no luck. The road zigzagged backwards and forwards down a steep mountainside. We lost a tremendous amount of altitude very quickly and made our way to Annecy, where the truck had spent some time before I joined the trip. Annecy was an attractive little place situated on the shore of a lovely green lake and overlooked by snow-capped mountains. We walked round the medieval old town, which had a river running through it. We crossed flower-bedecked bridges and watched the swans. We bought some cherries and camped near the lake.

The truck was leaking water out of the silencer and there was a slight hydraulic lock when we came to start the engine that morning, so the situation was continuing to deteriorate. We drained the water from the cylinder head when we stopped for the night. The cylinder head gasket had obviously broken down, but we had no spares, and we were becoming increasingly concerned whether it would stay together for the rest of the trip.

The following morning, we headed for Geneva. We crossed from France into Switzerland a few miles before we reached the city. Lake Geneva looked lovely with sailing boats of various sizes in the foreground and the city beyond with a backdrop of snow-capped mountains. We only stayed for a short while before crossing back into France, en route for Paris. We shortly had to stop again at French Customs, who wanted to charge us an exorbitant amount of duty for the fuel in our tanks. We told them that we had bought the fuel in Nice and had only passed briefly through Switzerland because that was the way the road ran, but they insisted on duty being paid until Collyn took down some jerry cans and started pouring petrol down the gutter. After that they became very excited and could not wait to get rid of us!

We had one more serious climb to 5,000 feet and picked up a Dutch hitchhiker who asked whether we would be home for Whitsun. We asked when it was, and when he said it was the coming weekend, we decided we would try to get to Paris that night and cross the English Channel on the coming Sunday.

The truck was consuming alarming amounts of both water and lube oil, so we had to keep stopping to put water into the radiator and oil into the sump. Even after a short stop of just 15 minutes there was a slight hydraulic lock, so the trouble was getting progressively worse.

We reached Paris at 11:30 that night. After some tricky navigation through a system of one-way streets, we parked near the Mobil offices. We drained the water out of the cylinder head into a bucket before going to bed. We had driven 348 miles that day.

The truck was in need of major work, but we were nearly home! It now only remained for us to drive to Boulogne, where we embarked on the cross-channel ferry *The Maid of Kent*, which had only been launched the previous October. The ferry was equipped with a turntable, which made it easy to turn around. We showed our passports and paid 26 pounds for our tickets. By 3:15 we were underway, and France soon faded from sight in the hazy conditions. Our dust-stained truck, with its map painted on the door showing our route, stood out amongst the more mundane vehicles. One man said to us that we were courageous young men, but that was certainly not the way we saw ourselves. "We only drove where other people lived" I told him. Another, who turned out to be the owner of a new maroon Rolls Royce, questioned Collyn about our trip. He told us that he had only recently come into money and had always wanted to do an African trip. Now he had his chance.

After one and a half hours underway, the white cliffs appeared through the haze and we were back. We drove off into the customs hall mindful of the bottles of booze we had stowed in our spare tyre mounted on the roof. I hoped that the engine would not conk out or one of our threadbare, smooth-going tires would not expire

228

before we cleared the customs hall. The young Scots customs official was pleasant enough and asked us to list everything we had on board.

"You really mean everything?" I asked.

"Yes" he said. But he soon gave up after I started off with each piece of cutlery, etc.

We drove out onto the streets of Dover and found that England now seemed like another foreign country. We were back to driving on the left after so many months of the other side. When we tooted our air horns we received such a barrage of hostile glares from people on the streets that we never used them again. We stopped en route and unpacked the bottles from the cab. I climbed into the back to change my clothes and pack my gear while we were motoring into London.

Collyn dropped me at King's Cross railway station, and it was at this mundane spot that our incredible odyssey effectively ended on Friday, June 3rd, 1960. I took the London Underground to Paddington, and at 9:05 telephoned my rather surprised mother. At 9:30 I left Paddington, and 45 minutes later arrived at Reading railway station where she was waiting for me. Twenty minutes more and we were back at Thatched Cottage after 25,000 miles of travel. It felt good to be home after so many miles of roughing it.

I was now nearly 26, and it was time to start thinking about what I wanted to do with the rest of my life. I had found that I enjoyed the solitude of the deserts and remote places, and with my engineering background I thought that perhaps I might be able to find a career in oil exploration or similar. I wrote off several letters to prospective employers but, not surprisingly, the responses—if they came at all—were rejection notes.

I was living at home and wasn't too bothered about it, but my mother was becoming more and more anxious about what would become of her wayward son on whose education she felt she had wasted a lot of money.

While trying to figure out what to do, I took casual jobs such as working on farms. The first of these was shovelling grain inside a grain silo, which resulted in my getting a raw and extremely painful sore throat due to some infection from the grain. There are unexpected hazards in the most mundane of places, but in those days no one gave any thought to wearing a mask. My next job was picking cherries, and I learned such safety tips as making sure you place your ladder so that if the branch gives way the ladder falls into the tree rather than away from it. One of my fellow pickers was a comely lass from one of the local villages, with whom I developed a close relationship. As my mother would have severely disapproved of such a liaison, it was best to keep it quiet in the interests of avoiding confrontation.

In the meantime, my mother—quite unnoticed by me—continued to worry about her unemployed son living at home. I no longer remember the exact train of contact, but one of her acquaintances from the past knew someone in a British trading company called William Jacks, which had offices in the city of London. The position open was for a young assistant to join the company in its Hong Kong office. The company handled every imaginable product from sandpaper to hospital sterilizers, and from glue to quarry equipment. I had already reached the conclusion that staying in the conventional technical field did not pay very well and that something involving technical sales was likely to be much more rewarding. I went for an interview to the firm's offices in London and was accepted. At the last interview I remember the director saying rather wistfully, I wish I was a young fellow of your age going out to Hong Kong. So the next step was decided much by chance; but, once again, it was my self-sacrificing mother who had pointed me in the next direction my life would take.

Before leaving for HK, I had some minimal training. The first concerned quarry equipment. I met the sales rep on a bleak November day on a railway station just outside London. He took me around to several worksites which, in this part of the country, were mostly gravel pits. At each spot, my guide put on a different coat, hat, boots, and accent to establish rapport with the client. I am not sure I learnt anything about the equipment but I was impressed by his chameleon-like adaptability.

On another occasion, I went to Sheffield to a plant making autoclaves for medical sterilization. The pressure inside was raised with steam, and then the pressure dropped to a vacuum so that all the moisture boiled off. The main thing I remember was staying in a small boarding house in which all the guests except me were traveling salesmen. We had dinner sitting around a big table and one of those present was being coy about what product he represented. He told me that life would be impossible without it as it held everything together and he asked me to guess. Of course I couldn't, and he told me it was thread. I remember thinking how lucky I was not to have a job trailing around dreary industrial towns trying to sell stuff to people who, more often than not, had no interest in buying it.

Hong Kong was an exciting prospect. When I had visited the William Jacks office in London, I was shown messages to and from people with names like Wong or Lee and district names like Wanchai, Kowloon and Taikoo. It was the mysterious East, with its ancient culture, which had originally beckoned me from the primitive   mud   huts   of   Africa.

Book 4
HONG KONG

CHANGE OF COURSE

1960 – 1969

Chapter 1

November 1960 to June 1962

Life in HK. William Jacks

I travel to Hong Kong and start work in a downtown office. I join the Yacht Club and experience my first typhoon. I join the HK Auxiliary Air Force and learn to fly. I meet Mary, who will become my wife, and switch jobs to start my career in boatbuilding.

Eventually the day of departure came, and my mother and sister came to see me off at Heathrow. The flight was again BOAC and when the flight was called, the stopping points—Athens, Bombay, Bangkok, Hong Kong and Tokyo—sounded incredibly exotic. It was a 25-hour flight to Hong Kong and, under the terms of my contract, I would be in HK for three years before being eligible for six months leave, so that would be the minimum time before I would see my family again. In fact, because of the way things turned out, it would be five years before I returned to the land of my birth.

We arrived in HK at twilight, and as we began to descend, I was entranced by the scattering of rugged, outlying islands, their craggy peaks glowing lavender in the setting sun. Although I did not realize it at the time, all these islands were communist. Not only was Hong Kong a capitalistic sore on the body of mainland China, but it was ringed on the seaward side by communist territory.

Slowly, the amazing sight of HK unfolded, with the famous peak dominating a harbour sparkling with a million lights reflected in the now-black waters. We banked perilously low over the roofs of the buildings, and I looked down into the bustling streets neon-lit by Chinese characters.

I was met by my boss, Nobby Clarke, and his wife and taken in their chauffeur-driven car through bustling, exotic streets to the Hong Kong Club, located in the central district of HK island. As the airport was in Kowloon, on the mainland, this meant crossing the harbour on one of the dozens of ferries which plied the waters day and night. The name Hong Kong comes from the Chinese words meaning "Fragrant Harbour", which was not the adjective most people would use to describe that rather smelly piece of water! They dropped me off at the Hong Kong Club, and I was shown to my comfortable room by a Chinese staff member wearing a white, oriental-style uniform and traditional black Chinese slippers. I was weary from the long journey but entranced and somewhat disbelieving to find myself in this exciting and unfamiliar environment. I almost had to pinch myself that I was really here. I felt like a character from Joseph Conrad or Somerset Maugham as I stood on the balcony looking down at grounds of the HK Cricket Club under the shadow of the Bank of China.

The next morning, I walked to the William Jacks office in Princess Building, just across the HK cricket ground from the HK club, in the very heart of downtown Hong Kong. The building, and its companion, Queens Building, were old colonial style and, in common with most of the buildings of the time, lacked air conditioning. Ventilation came from overhead fans whose downdraft created blizzards of paper from anything not firmly anchored with a paperweight. Pick up the wrong one and your papers would fly across the office like a flock of skittish birds.

Nobby Clark introduced me to the staff, who were all Chinese with the exception of Norman Senior, who was probably in his fifties and responsible for the building department, selling door locks and similar hardware. As I have mentioned, the company represented a huge range of products. Most of the business was brought in by the Chinese staff, who conducted their negotiations in the dimsum tea houses around the city. On my first morning I was taken to one of these by Herman Chen. Today, when there is hardly a town on the planet which does not have at least one Chinese restaurant, it may be hard to believe, but I had never tasted or been exposed to Chinese food until I arrived in HK.

The restaurant where Herman took me was a packed seven stories. Chinese tea was served in small cups, and myriad dishes brought around by pretty Chinese girls carrying large trays in front of them supported by a strap extending from their shoulders. They would cry out their "wares" and, if you wanted what they had on offer, you would beckon them over and they would place them on your table. There were all kinds of small dishes, some of which were steamed and served in circular bamboo containers through which the steam could circulate. When you were finished at the end of your meal, a staff member would total up all the dishes and containers on your table and charge you accordingly. Cantonese is one of the noisiest of Chinese dialects, and the sound level in the restaurant was loud with the waitresses calling out, the clatter of dishes, and the hum of conversation. It was a fascinating scene, and I took to Chinese food like Peking duck to water.

We visited work sites where William Jacks had customers to whom they sold construction equipment. Many of the labourers were petite but tough Hakka women dressed in black smocks and loose black trousers. They wore white gloves and white socks made with a divided big toe. On their feet were sandals similar to flip flops, with a thong between the big and adjacent toes. They wore flat circular hats, woven from fine bamboo, with a black pelmet around the perimeter. They worked in pairs, moving large rocks slung from a bamboo pole supported on their shoulders, managing all the while to look very feminine with their clean white socks and gloves. HK was one huge construction site, with older buildings being demolished to make way for high-rise structures. Scaffolding, even on buildings 15 stories high, was assembled from bamboo poles laced together with strips split from the outer skin of the same material.

I had always imagined Hong Kong to consist of just the city with its famous and much-photographed skyline. Instead, I soon discovered, the city was named Victoria and situated on Hong Kong Island. On the other side of the famous harbour lay Kowloon, and beyond that, the New Territories, which extended about 20 miles to the border with China. The name Kowloon was

236

a corruption of the words meaning "Nine Dragons" named for the peaks forming the backdrop to the city.

It seemed surprising that Maoist China would permit this relic of colonial imperialism to exist on its soil, but there were advantages to both sides to continue the status quo. Most obviously, China did not have to administer the city, and they were paid in foreign currency for all the food and water they supplied. HK was the entrepôt for trade between the mainland and the outside world and provided a listening post for the west as to what was happening across the border.

The tallest mountain in Hong Kong was Tai Mo Shan, and its top, from which there was a fabulous view, bristled with antennas of all shapes and sizes. It was a very sensitive security area and, a few years later, when I climbed to the top with a friend, we were accosted by a couple of Royal Air Force personnel in a Land Rover. We were a considerable distance from the fence surrounding the antennas when they demanded to know what we were doing there. We replied that we were simply admiring the view and they said it was forbidden to "be close to a closed area!". We said we thought the whole point of having a closed area was that it was closed to areas which surrounded it. My companion was carrying a binocular case and they told him that it was "illegal" to carry binoculars. He opened the case to reveal an apple, an orange and a packet of sandwiches. That pretty well finished the conversation and off they lurched in their Land Rover, leaving us bemused over the absurdity of the situation.

Trade was the business of HK and the very lubricant that greased the wheels of commerce. It was not unusual to see a ship flying the hammer and sickle next to a ship flagged in the U.S., while large numbers of junks, sporting the communist flag, crisscrossed the harbour, and the British flag flew from government buildings on shore. Since the 1860s, a canon has been fired at noon each day from the typhoon shelter near the Yacht Club.

After a few days at the HK Club, I moved to the Melbourne Hotel, in the downtown Tsin Sha Tsui district of Kowloon. I commuted across the harbour every day on the Star Ferry, which had been running since the 1870s. There were four ferry piers on each side of the harbour, and during rush hours, there was a ferry every 30 seconds. There were first and second class, with the latter at a lower level where you could peer down into the engine room and be closer to the water and the action. The ferries were double-enders, with a helm station and propeller at each end, so they shuttled back and forth across the harbour without having to turn around.

The first thing that caught my eye were the flocks of petite Chinese girls, each dressed in a traditional, tight-fitting, Cheongsam, split to mid-thigh. In those days almost all the women wore them and they had to be made to measure. The Chinese girls made Western women look almost ox-like by comparison.

By way of contrast, there were also a number of babushka-style women who looked as though they had stepped out of the pages of a book by Tolstoy. These were the last survivors of White Russians who had fled the revolution across the breadth of the Soviet Union to arrive in Shanghai, and who had since been displaced from there by the communist revolution. There were many Chinese from Shanghai in the city, and much of Hong Kong's success has been attributed to their business acumen operating within a legal framework provided by the British.

The Melbourne Hotel was situated in Mody Road, on the site now occupied by a massive Holiday Inn. It looked like the setting for a novel by Somerset Maugham. There were palm trees outside, and I had a room with a deep balcony on the first floor overlooking the street. There was no air-conditioning, but the room had what was known as a swamp cooler, in which air, driven by a powerful fan through water-soaked pads, was cooled by evaporation.

Within a couple of weeks of my arrival, I had a strong desire to see what Communist China looked like, so I took a train from the railway station, which at that time terminated at the Star Ferry. The train stopped at Sheung Shi, more than a mile from the border, and took passengers no further unless they had a special permit. This was a bit of a disappointment, but I was fascinated by the beauty of the landscape and how traditional everything looked, with buffalo in the fields and people with conical hats working the fields. On a later occasion I was able to drive to a spot on a hillside overlooking the border and take in the view. Of course it looked much the same, but it fascinated me to think that this short distance away was a place with a totalitarian way of life so different from anything I had ever encountered.

Six months earlier I had been in the middle of the Sahara Desert, and now here I was in HK with a population (in 1960) of three million crammed into an area of 425 square miles. The general perception of HK is that it consists of one seething mass of people, but this is far from the truth. It was a couple of years later but, to illustrate the contrasts, I arranged to meet a friend on the top of a certain mountain during Chinese New Year in the eastern part of the New Territories. I confused the route and climbed other mountains before finding the right one. Measured on a map, with no account taken of the ups and downs, I covered 25 miles during the course of that expedition during which I met only six people. I was able to stand on top of mountains and look around 360 degrees without seeing any evidence of mankind—no dwellings, boats, structures, not even any disturbance in the landscape—while only a few miles distant from the greatest population density in the world. In fact, three-quarters of HK territory is countryside, of which 440 square kilometres (170 square miles) has been set aside for country parks and protected areas.

As I write this, the population of Hong Kong has exceeded seven million, with a maximum density of 53,110 people per square kilometre (130,000 per square mile, or one person every 24 square yards). But despite the overcrowding, and its corresponding pollution, life expectancy in Hong Kong is the 2nd highest in the world, at 79 years for men and 84 years for women; and infant mortality is the 4th lowest.

Within one month of my arrival I was sent to visit a reservoir site at Shek Pik, on the Western end of Lantau Island. This involved a 40-minute ferry ride from Central District to Silvermine Bay, at the Eastern end of Lantau, followed by a 30-minute drive in a Land Rover along a single-track road. Lantau, now the site of HK's magnificent new Chek Lap Kok airport, was sparsely inhabited in 1960, but a big earthen dam was being built in a collaboration between the French company Soletanche and British Soil Mechanics. When I arrived, I was introduced as the "man from Consolidate Mechanics"—the brand of air compressor William Jacks represented. I had not been given any reason for my visit, nor had I been primed in any way. I was introduced to Ray Mann, a bearded British engineer who had been up most of the night trying to deal with a problem with one of the air compressors. He immediately launched into a detailed description of the problem, obviously looking to me for answers. I realized that there was no possibility of fudging this guy, so I simply told him that I hadn't the faintest idea what he was talking about, but if he went over the problem with me I promised to get him an answer as soon as possible from the manufacturer. Fortunately, he went along with that, and I was able to get him the answers. He told me long afterwards that I had gained his respect by admitting my ignorance. It was a good lesson learned. We subsequently became friends, and it was through him that I eventually met the lady who was to become my wife.

I even visited an iron ore mine at Ma On Shan (Horse Saddle Mountain), which was certainly something I never expected to find in crowded Hong Kong.

I was very naive in business matters, and my boss never took the time to explain things to me. He probably had no idea how naïve I really was. For, example, the concept of "overhead" and the cost of actually running a business never occurred to me. I considered a profit margin of 20 percent to be outrageous, even when that percentage was a gross margin (what the hell was that?!) from which the cost of doing business had to be deducted. One day, my boss sent me off to the HK Aircraft Engineering Company to visit their purchase manager, a hard-headed Dutchman. My mission was to find out why they had stopped buying abrasive papers from William Jacks and, if necessary, offer him a 50-percent discount. I had great misgivings about this, because even I realized that, if it was still worthwhile for us to do business with him after offering him such a huge discount, we must have been ripping him off in the first place. When I met the buyer he told me they had found another supplier with better prices, and when I dutifully offered him the 50-percent discount, he came back with exactly the same reaction that I had anticipated. Although I didn't say so, I privately agreed with him, so we lost that business through greed. In those days, airlines would fly their aircraft to HK for major overhaul because it was cheaper than doing the work in their home countries. An early example of outsourcing!

I used to go around to various companies and visit their purchasing and engineering managers, to make their acquaintance and see if they needed anything. It must have been annoying for them. I found they fitted into two groups. The first had desks littered with piles of files and paper and had phones ringing all the time. The others had immaculately clean desks with maybe five perfectly sharpened pencils exactly lined up. I fit into the first category and was rather contemptuous of the second group, who I felt were collecting fat salaries for doing nothing. I eventually came to realize that actually they were the better managers because they knew how to delegate and so had time to actually manage.

One day I visited the Green Island Cement Company, located right on the harbour in downtown Kowloon. The plant manager's office was built at the base of a tall chimney stack. On this particular day there had been a thunderstorm just prior to my visit. The manager was standing outside his office, looking a bit shaken. He said "If they ever tell you that lightening never strikes twice in the same place, don't bloody well believe them". It seems that the lightning conductor ran through his office, passing right under his chair, where he had been sitting when the chimney was struck. The resulting flash passed right by his feet and filled the office with smoke and the stink of ozone. He fled the scene but after a few minutes decided to return to his office—just in time for a repeat performance!

I had arrived in HK in November, and with so little time to get established, I spent Christmas Day hiking through the New Territories. I was used to being on my own and was pretty self-sufficient after my years in Africa, so this did not bother me. In fact, I took almost a perverse delight in it. On New Year's Eve I went with Norman Senior and a few of his friends on a tour of the bars in Wanchai—made famous by the book and subsequent film

Suzie Wong. I tried to keep up with the seasoned drinkers but failed dismally. I remember sitting on a bar stool with one of the local bar girls saying to me in effect, "What's a nice boy like you doing in a place like this?". I went back across the harbour on the Star Ferry, and as I walked off the ramp on the Kowloon side I remember, to my undying shame, how the whole ramp seemed to rear up and I fell over, trying to keep my drunken balance. By some miracle I made it back to the hotel and didn't wake up until midday on New Year's Day. I realized to my horror that I was supposed to be at my boss's house for drinks at the Peak mid-levels on Hong Kong island. I dragged myself out of bed and back across the Star Ferry. Of course I was late, and everybody was already there when I arrived, looking and feeling like death. The last thing in the world I wanted was another drink. I apologized profusely, and everyone except me thought it pretty funny. By this time, I had been in HK only about eight weeks. It was not an auspicious start to 1961.

One of the best ways to get settled into any new place is to join a club in which you share the same interests as those represented by the club and its members. With this in mind I joined the Royal HK Yacht Club, whose premises were on Kellet Island. Founded in 1890, it received its royal charter in 1894. It was located on a small island that had been connected by a causeway to the Wanchai area of HK island in 1959. The causeway and an adjacent sea wall formed a typhoon shelter crammed with boats, many of which were small sampans providing live-aboard homes.

Sailboat races for many different classes were held at weekends, and of course the Yacht Club had a bar and a restaurant. The club provided the focal point for my social life, and although I didn't know it at the time, it was through it that my future career was decided. People with boats were always looking for crew, and it was by volunteering to fill this need that you became integrated into the group. As with most sports, much of the pleasure lay in knocking back drinks at the bar, reliving the cut and thrust of the latest contest.

One day I walked into the bar and saw the guy with whom I

242

had shared a study at Sherborne. This was a classic example of "small world", for not only had there been more than 500 boys at any one time at Sherborne, but we lived in eight different houses scattered round the town, and in senior years we shared a study room with just two others. He was in the Royal Navy and was just passing through HK. Another person I met through the Yacht Club was Anton Emmerton, who was in Hong Kong doing his military service in the army. Our future paths were to become closely linked, and he will feature prominently later in this story. For a while we shared crewing duties on another member's L-Class yacht. These were ponderous boats with no engine, so had to be brought to their moorings in the congested typhoon shelter under sail alone. Anton was standing on the foredeck, directing the helmsman, while I stood ready to drop the sails at the instant they were no longer needed for propulsion. The boat was brought to a sudden stop by running into a line under the water, which catapulted Anton head first over the bow into the fetid water. In the ensuing confusion to avoid running him over, the boat collided with the back of a sampan, unhitching a cage of chickens which fell into the water, driving the occupants into a clucking frenzy as they tried to avoid imminent drowning. The Chinese owners of the sampan were leaping about yelling in Cantonese as they frantically tried to rescue their livestock and fend off our boat, the sails of which had now come down, smothering everything. Eventually order was restored and Anton and the chickens fished out of the stinking water with no lasting harm to either, except for a few ruffled feathers. Anton disappeared into the showers to ward off being devoured by lethal bacteria or contracting some hideous disease.

Typhoons were a fact of life in Hong Kong, and having read all about them as a boy, I was quite anxious to see one. So I was quite pleased when a typhoon warning was issued by the Royal Observatory, especially as I did not own any vulnerable property to be concerned about. I went to work as usual, taking, as it turned out, one of the last Star Ferries to cross the harbour before the service was suspended. The ferry helmsmen were skilled at handling the ferries under all kinds of conditions. When I reached the office I found that it was closed, but by now it was too late to re-cross the harbour. Wondering where to go, I decided on the Yacht Club, where I had a grandstand view of this relatively minor typhoon with wind speeds reaching 90 mph. The centre of the storm passed right over Hong Kong, and the hurricane-force winds coming from one direction dropped, within 10 minutes, to absolutely zero for nearly two hours as the eye passed over the colony before returning, again within a few minutes, to full velocity, this time from the opposite direction. The club had a recording barometer, and as the eye of the storm approached, the pen on the recorder dropped so rapidly you could see it moving on the paper drum.

I moved from the Melbourne Hotel, first to a single room in Tsim Sha Tsui, and later to a mid-levels apartment on Hong Kong Island. The latter was in a brand-new, modern 12-storey building, built in 1961, with 12 apartments per floor. Being a new building meant that other residents were making noisy alterations which reverberated throughout the entire structure. Initially I had a wonderful view over HK harbour, with Kowloon and the hills beyond, but I had no sooner moved in when crews armed with bulldozers and a wrecking ball began demolishing the building across the street. They were followed by pile drivers that hammered away from morning to night every day, Sundays included. My wonderful view was then slowly but surely eliminated as the replacement building crept steadily skywards. Prince Philip, when asked what he thought about Hong Kong, replied that it "would be nice when it was finished". It's still not finished, and I doubt it ever will be. Queen Victoria described it as "this worthless piece of barren rock", when she heard it had become part of her realm under the treaty of Nanking in 1842!

I purchased a second-hand VW Beetle, which widened my field of exploration and allowed me to roam around the colony. Actually, this turned out to be the first of two Beetles because this one was demolished at the VW dealership, where I had sent it for service, when someone broke in during the night and whizzed around the workshop in one of the cars, eventually smashing into mine! They offered me a replacement a year younger than my original, so I was quite happy.

Through a friend of Ray Mann, the engineer I had met on Lantau Island, I was invited to a party at which I met a girl I rather fancied. Her name was Mary Thomas. She was a nursing sister at Queen Mary hospital, appointed from England on a three-year contract. She was not immediately taken with me, because after a long dry spell with no boyfriends, she had recently found herself spoilt for choice, and the last thing she wanted was another contender. However, I persevered, and after about six weeks of feeling sorry for myself, I thought it would do no harm to send her a note to say how much I missed her. Unknown to me, Mary had worked her way through the field and reached the conclusion that I might not be so bad, after all, so she had written me a note and put it in the mail box at my apartment block. She placed it in the wrong box, so I did not get her note until after I had posted mine, so our respective notes arrived simultaneously.

I had always been interested in learning to fly, and I found that it was possible to do this for free by joining the HK Auxiliary Air Force. I started flying lessons at Kai Tak International Airport, which had been built out into the harbour on land reclaimed from Kowloon Bay. It was acknowledged to be one of the trickiest airports in the world, and flying out of it as a learner pilot was pretty scary because its main purpose was, of course, to handle jets flying from the other side of the world. A slow Auster with a learner pilot must have been of extreme annoyance to the controllers. Almost every student pilot faces the challenge of trying to understand airport controllers, but this was made even harder in HK due to continual radio interference in the form of Chinese gongs and cymbals. With a constant stream of big jets on the approach, the pressure was on to decipher an almost incomprehensible message advising whether it was safe to proceed. It was dangerous to land within a couple of minutes behind a big jet because of wingtip turbulence, which can last as long as three minutes. A De Havilland Chipmunk aircraft was flipped upside down coming in to land too soon after a big jet.

The Auxiliary Air Force held an annual two-week camp at Sek Kong airfield in the New Territories, and here it was possible to fly in less fraught conditions. My instructor was seconded from the Royal Air Force, and he was very good. My problem was that I couldn't keep the aircraft straight on the ground after landing. Being a tail dragger, steering was accomplished by just the rudder, and being seated right at the front, you had to steer almost by instinct because if you waited until lateral movement was obvious, it was too late. So I never got to fly solo. However, I did get in quite a lot of flying around HK territory, including in a Westland helicopter at 7,000 feet over the harbour, piloted by Danny Cheung, who later went on to receive a medal for a night rescue of a climber who had fallen from Tai Mo Shan. I was present when this occurred. There were no night flying facilities at the Sek Kong airstrip, so the landing spot was marked by a cross created by the headlights of cars parked at each corner of a square. With no place to put down on the steep mountain, Danny had to hover with one wheel on the ground while the injured climber, who was an army doctor practicing for an expedition to Everest, was loaded aboard in gusty winds.

Meanwhile, back at the Yacht Club, a group of us signed up for ordering kits from England to assemble Enterprise sailing dinghies. These were 13-foot, double-chine plywood boats that were quite easy to build. A group of us worked on these in the sheds underneath the Yacht Club, which promoted camaraderie and provided us with our own boats at a reasonable cost.

My mother had always been of the opinion that if you trained as an engineer and diligently engineered things then one day you would finish up as Managing Director. I had long since reached the conclusion that nothing could be further from the truth, and if you started life tightening nuts then you were likely to finish it doing the same job. You only have to look at adverts for engineering and financial jobs to realize that technical people do not get paid very well compared to people who count beans or shuffle numbers around. That is why I had figured that working in sales as a technical representative would likely lead to a more rewarding result. This is probably still true, but it wasn't until I tried it that I realized that it didn't suit me. Not only was I not cut out to be a salesman, but I found that I much preferred doing stuff rather than supplying parts and equipment to people who did. Also, like most trading companies, William Jacks represented so many and such a wide range of products that it was impossible to have more than the most superficial knowledge of any of them, which meant that you, as an individual, could not do a decent job for either the manufacturer you represented or for your customers.

One of the companies I had visited in my job was Bireley's California Orange, which bottled and sold soft drinks. They were looking for a fork lift truck, and William Jacks represented Coventry Climax, whose plant I had visited before coming to Hong Kong. I knew there was a nine-month delivery from the factory in England, to which had to be added an additional two months for shipping to Hong Kong. On the other hand, Japanese forklifts were in stock in the colony, and they were better and considerably cheaper. I didn't see any point in wasting everybody's time when the outcome was obvious, so I told all this to John Newton, the manager of Bireley's. Such were my talents as a salesman!

Several weeks later I had a call from John to visit him at his factory, and I duly went there, expecting to be asked about another piece of equipment. Instead, he told me that his family had a boatbuilding yard in Junk Bay, out in the New Territories, and they were looking for someone with an engineering background to work for them. He suggested, if I was interested, that he could take me out to the yard and show me around. Was I interested?! To me this was like being offered the keys to the Kingdom of Heaven! A visit was duly arranged and we went out to the yard, which was only accessible by a small sampan taken from a small traditional Chinese village to which you had to walk from the nearest road.

At the yard, I found myself surrounded by many different types of wooden boats in various stages of construction. Carpenters, using mostly traditional tools such as bow drills, wooden planes and adzes, were working away, and there was a wonderful smell of fresh-cut timber. I was hooked! Much later I asked John Newton why he had offered me the job and he said that he had never met anyone who was so ill suited for the job I was doing! This did not sound like much of a recommendation to me, but I guess, in this case, it had paid to be frank. In fact, the recommendation came from an Australian Cathay Pacific Airline flight engineer named Don Brown, who I had come to know at the Yacht Club—which explains why joining the club had been a key factor in my career.

This was another crossroads moment where I faced two clear and distinct choices. The safe route with William Jacks, or the dodgy one that looked more immediately interesting. I chose the latter. For me, this was a once-in-a-lifetime opportunity, but I had the unenviable job of telling my boss that I wanted to leave William Jacks and change jobs. This was not a very pleasant task. American Marine repaid William Jacks the cost of my fare, and I had to go back to the start of a new three-year contract before I was due any leave. My boss wrote a letter to London saying that he thought I had been working on this move for some time, which was quite untrue. What was true was that I had let them down, and of course my mother was angry with me that I had left a job with a respected British company with head offices in London and branches all over the Far East for some unknown boat company in HK. Nevertheless, during my 18 months at William Jacks, I had sold UK 80,000 pounds worth of construction equipment, which I don't think was too bad for a naïve neophyte!

Chapter 2

June 1962 to August 1963

Life in HK. American Marine—Early Days

I start work as a boat-builder and experience the most violent typhoon in decades. I get married and experience a memorable honeymoon in the Philippines, which includes an unplanned cruise through the islands.

I started work at American Marine in June 1962. For my daily commute I had to drive out into the New Territories along winding Clear Water Bay Road and park at the top of the hill above Hang Hau village. From there, there was a walk down the hillside to the traditional village with its single, narrow street and houses with Chinese-style upturned eaves. From the jetty I took a small sampan across Junk Bay—usually sculled by a small girl using a single oar over the stern. A five-minute ride brought me to the yard, which was a collection of simple wood frame buildings roofed with corrugated iron.

The Newton family had decided to branch out into building boats, with the idea of exporting them to the United States. The first boats were small runabouts initially built at the bottling plant under the supervision of Joseph Kong. They soon realized that there was no money to be made in these small craft, but they were fortunate to get orders from a handful of expatriate yachtsmen in Hong Kong to build more sophisticated yachts. Two were cruising sailboats—*Morisum*, designed by Sparkman Stevens and owned by an American, and *Reverie* owned by a Swede, Chris Von Sydow. Another was a fast gasoline-powered planing boat called *Fantasia*. Through this the company came to realize that the way ahead lay with larger, more sophisticated, boats. They arranged to be represented in the U.S. by a company called Products of Asia in the person of Bill Shaw, who, many years later, became the chief designer and president of Pearson Yachts.

In those days if you wanted to build a yacht you would go to a naval architect and have him design the boat of your dreams. This design would then be put out to bid to various builders, and you would make your choice. Through the offices of Products of Asia, American Marine was able participate in the bidding process. Estimating the costs for a custom boat is a very complicated and tricky business because every boat is a new project. Whit Newton, with no previous experience, was responsible for estimating the cost, which involved such details as calculating the number of screws and board feet of wood required. Not surprisingly, he didn't always get it right. When the order was obtained, it was secured with a deposit from the buyer followed by a schedule of progress payments—e.g., 10 percent when planking was complete, another payment when the engine was in, more when the boat was shipped, and the final 10 percent when the boat was delivered to the buyer's satisfaction. The problem was that, as the company was losing money on almost every project, they had to keep getting deposits for new orders in order to have enough money to complete earlier ones.

I shared a small office with Bob and Whit Newton. Bob was the father and Whit was his youngest son. I had been hired by John Newton, who was the elder brother running the Bireley's bottling plant. Whit was working like a crazy man trying to do everything, but no one gave me any instructions, so I felt very awkward not knowing what to do while my boss was clearly overworked. Actually, I didn't have a clue anyway, as I had never even been aboard a boat you could stand up on without serious risk of being tipped overboard, and although I had an engineering background, I knew absolutely nothing about the mysteries of boatbuilding. But gradually I began to pick things up and created a job for myself.

After completion, the boats were hauled out into the slipway and put into a wood-frame cradle. They were then re-launched and towed into HK harbour to be loaded aboard the freighter that was to take them to their destination. Because of the cradle's drag, they could only be towed by the company's work boat at about 3 knots, and as it was quite a few miles from the yard to the harbour, the towing took several hours.

A few days after I joined the company, a sailboat had to be shipped. The boat was nowhere near being ready, but it had to go because it was already well overdue and the letter of credit needed for payment was about to expire. The interior was still being painted when the boat left the yard with Whit on board. On the way to the ship the painters all got seasick from the paint fumes, so Whit finished up painting the boat himself. When he got back he told me that this was not a good example of the way things were supposed to be, but as I was to find out, this was in fact very typical of the way things always were for each and every shipment!

During this time, we built many custom boats. One of the best was a large, beautiful Herreshoff sailboat called *Windsong*, similar to a smaller version of *Ticonderoga*. She was built in the traditional manner—right way up, with the hull supported by props secured at the base to stakes driven vertically into holes in the concrete. I was up at deck level, about 17 feet above the floor, when a side prop I was using to steady myself gave way and I lost my balance. I desperately tried to stay on the narrow staging around the deck, but I toppled off and fell to the concrete—landing on my feet surrounded by all kinds of hazards, including the vertical stakes and piles of wood. I was completely unhurt and no one even witnessed my miraculous escape!

Sailboats like *Windsong* had lead keels for which wood patterns were prepared and sand moulds made from those patterns. Lead was melted down from old pipes and other scrap and then poured into the sand mould, with bronze keel bolts cast into it. These keels could be very heavy in the case of a big sailboat, and sometimes it was simpler to cast the keel first and build the boat on top of it!

It was normal for boats to be literally months behind schedule, which was bad enough in itself, but the situation was made worse because the boat buyers were never kept informed. We had one situation in which a couple from San Francisco arrived at the yard expecting to be sailing their 53-foot Mason centre cockpit motorsailer back across the Pacific. What they saw when they arrived was the skeletal frame of a hull that had not yet been planked. The couple stayed on in a hotel in town and came to the yard every day for weeks. Naturally, as work proceeded they would see things they would like changed, and we complied with their wishes as much as possible because we felt obligated to them. What none of us realized was that each of these changes, no matter how small, caused more delays, which further aggravated the situation.

One piece of equipment new to all of us was a water maker that worked on the principle of pulling a vacuum inside a housing so that sea water inside boiled at the engine temperature of 180 degrees. With the boat stationary it would not produce any fresh water unless the engine was running almost flat out. Working on it meant crouching down in a tight engine space, beside a screaming, red-hot engine in an ambient temperature of over 90 degrees, with a very displeased owner glaring down at you with hands on hips. He was hardly to blame, but he made himself so unpopular with the yard workers that they all clapped and cheered when, while carrying cushions onto his boat, a gust of wind caught him and he sailed off the gangplank into the water.

We serviced the few local boats we had built, and I had a lucky escape when the owner of the powerboat *Fantasia* wanted to check whether the CO_2 fire extinguishing system was working. The only way to find out was to activate the release and see what happened, so I pulled the handle at the helm station and it came away in my hand! There was a second release in the small, congested engine space and, without considering the consequences, I crawled down there and pulled it. This time it went off with a loud whoosh and filled the whole space with a thick fog of carbon dioxide. Fortunately, I hung on to what few brains I had left to realize that if I breathed this in I was done for, so I held my breath while I groped my way out of the opaque engine space.

In a less dramatic but more entertaining event, I jumped down onto the sampan to go out to one of the boats on a mooring, crashed through the floorboards and did a back flip over the side into the water complete with clipboard. It's hard to maintain your dignity after an episode like that.

It made no sense for me to continue living on HK island while working in the New Territories, so I moved to an apartment on the top floor of a three-story building in a residential area of Kowloon Tong. On the morning of September 1st, Super Typhoon Wanda arrived as the 59th tropical weather system of the 1962 season. The wind was shrieking and the rain lashing sideways when I noticed water coming under the front door. I opened the door to find water cascading down the stairs like a waterfall. Dressed only in shorts, I went upstairs and thoughtlessly opened the door onto the flat roof. As soon as the door was slightly ajar, the wind took hold of it and flung it wide open, taking me with it as I hung onto the door handle and hurling me across the roof. The rain stung my bare skin like showers of needles. I immediately dropped to my knees and crawled back to the door, pulling it shut after me. During my brief excursion I had seen that the flat roof was flooded, most likely due to blocked drains, so I put on more clothes and went back to the roof. This time I was much more cautious when opening the door, and I crawled across the roof looking for the drains. Sure enough, they were blocked with leaves torn from the trees. Using my hands, I cleared them away, and as the water disappeared down the drain, it sucked my hand down over the opening, bending my fingers backwards. The only way I could remove my hand was to drag it sideways with my other hand. I realized afterwards that, when the down-pipe was full, my hand was holding up a column of water three stories high. From my vantage point on the roof, I saw flames rising through the rain and heard emergency sirens. It was an apocalyptic scene.

I retreated to my apartment. Around midday, the wind and rain ceased as the eye of the storm passed over HK. Probably very foolishly I got into my VW and drove out to the boatyard, looking down at it from the top of the hill above Hang Hau village. The storm surge, which reached as high as 17 feet in some areas, meant that the yard was now actually in the sea and breakers were sweeping through the buildings. Much of the roof had gone. I then drove down to HK harbour and saw waves breaking over the seawall, then I returned home to sit out the second part of the storm when the winds returned with equal ferocity from the opposite direction. The following day, Hong Kong looked a real mess. Fifty years later, this storm has still not been matched for size and strength. Maximum wind gusts recorded over Kowloon had been 161 mph and 12 inches of rain had fallen during the day. One hundred and thirty people had died, with another 53 missing. Twenty-four ocean-going ships were beached, with 12 more involved in collisions. One ship finished up on the airport runway and another, which fetched up on the wrong side of a railway embankment, had to be cut up and removed in pieces. The storm was 1,000 miles in diameter.

At the yard, the buildings had collapsed wherever there had been no boat to support them. Surprisingly few boats had serious damage, although several were full of water. The wind had hurled stones like cannon balls at the sides of the office building, breaching the wooden walls. Inside, it had torn the place apart, soaking blueprints in water and spreading them all over the place. Fortunately, we had no computers in those days. Most of the corrugated roof was gone from over the building sheds, and for the next three days, teams of workers scoured the surrounding hillsides to retrieve as much of it as possible. It is hard to conceive of nature's fury until you have seen it in action. I was going to see plenty more from uncomfortably close up over the next few years. Amazingly, Hong Kong was almost back to normal within three days—a testament to the resilience of its people and the efficiency of its government.

Away from the yard, I continued to sail at the Yacht Club and to develop my relationship with Mary. Like all nurses she did not work very social hours, so she did not often accompany me to the Yacht Club. In December 1961, after we had got to know each other a bit better, we decided to take a trip to the nearby Portuguese colony of Macau, which had been in existence since 1557—long before Britain set up shop in HK in 1842. Macau was known for its gambling casinos and also for the Macau Grand Prix, which was held through the streets of the town similar to the race in Monte Carlo. We took the Fat Shan ferry from central district HK across the Pearl River Delta to arrive in Macau just as the sun was setting. The ship coasted into the harbour, gliding across the still water with a total absence of vibration. The harbour was full of traditional Chinese junks, some ghosting under sail with others at anchor silhouetted against a blazing sky, with the setting sun a red ball sinking towards the horizon. It was as though we were on a magic carpet watching a tableau from the past. It was one of life's unforgettable moments. Tragically the Fat Shan ferry was to be sunk 10 years later during typhoon Rose on August 17th, 1971, with the loss of 88 lives. Macau was like old Hong Kong, of which only small segments remained in 1961. There were few high rises and most of the buildings were colonial style shaded with big trees. It was a restful place, totally lacking the frenetic bustle of Hong Kong.

Mary and I became engaged, but we delayed our marriage because she did not want to give up the bonus she would receive if she remained unmarried until the end of her contract. We were married on April 15, 1963, at a church in Prince Edward Road, Kowloon. The reception was held at Bob Newton's house overlooking Junk Bay, and we spent our wedding night at the Park Hotel in Kowloon before we left the next day for our honeymoon in the Philippines.

I guess that most honeymoons do not turn out as anticipated, and ours was no exception. We were supposed to have been flying to Manila, but Philippine airlines went on strike the day before and Cathay Pacific flights were all full. We decided instead to go to Manila on an American President Lines freighter. In those days, some freighters would accommodate a few passengers and it was a good way to travel. When we came to ordering breakfast on the first morning aboard, Mary was trying to decide whether to add oatcakes to the list when the black waiter politely commented, "I think that madam will find she has ordered sufficient!". He was right. We had thought that oatcakes would be those slim, crispy things you find in Scotland. These, it turns out, would have provided excellent service as doormats.

We spent a couple of days in the steamy heat of Manila with all the noise, bustle and flamboyant decoration of colourful Jeepneys, which owed their origins to American Army Jeeps left over from WWII. Our intended destination was the mountain resort of Baguio and, with Philippine Airlines still on strike, we had to take a bus. This was a ramshackle affair with hard seats and, of course, no air-conditioning. By the time we climbed aboard, the only remaining seats were right at the rear behind the back axle. The journey took most of the day, and we were bounced up and down as the bus negotiated the potholed road. At one point the bus stopped and a couple of guys climbed aboard, selling soft drinks. One stayed at the front of the bus and the other made his way towards the back, delivering bottled drinks and taking the money. When he got to us, I did not have small change and gave him a 5-peso note. He gave me the drinks and then went to the front of the bus ostensibly to get my change. Instead, the bus stopped and he and his buddy got off, leaving me feeling a fool with two over-priced drinks!

The Filipino sitting in the row in front of me turned around and said, "You were gypped, sir."

I said "I know." But what could I do?

The bus stopped at intervals along the way for people to visit a rest room and buy refreshments. At the next stop, the man who had spoken to me came back with an ice cream each for myself and my wife. I have never forgotten that kind gesture and, for me, it was well worth the small price of being "gypped".

Finally, we arrived, dusty and exhausted, at the hotel, only to find that our reservation had been given to someone else because we were late! After perusing the reservation book, the clerk said doubtfully, "Well, there is room Number XX."

I don't remember the actual room number, but "Double X" will serve very well. Comments like that are not a good sign and usually precede some awful event in a horror movie. In our case we were escorted to a barely furnished room with a naked light bulb hanging from the ceiling. When I turned the tap on the washbasin, it gave a cough and ejected a bedraggled cockroach followed by a dribble of rust-coloured water which drained into a chipped enamel bowl on the floor below. The following morning at breakfast, as I poured the tea out of a teapot, a large cockroach shot out through the spout and circulated slowly around in the cup. I did not mind too much, but this fell far short of the honeymoon of my new bride's dreams!

I read in the paper of a cruise through the Southern Islands of the Archipelago, and this sounded much more appealing. The strike was now over, so we were able to fly back to Manila. We booked a cabin on a small ship and headed for Iloilo, Zamboanga, Cagayan de Oro and Davao. The ship was an inter-island ferry, so its decks were crowded with local people traveling with all their belongings, amongst which were live chickens in open-weave containers and baskets of fruit, including evil-smelling durians. On the first evening, as the ship forged through the Sulu Sea towards the setting sun, I again felt as though I was playing a part in a story by Somerset Maugham. I remarked to Mary how romantic this was and she replied, "How can I feel romantic surrounded by all these Filipinos?". I guess we had different definitions of "romance" and this again had not featured in her expectations for a romantic honeymoon!

We went ashore when the ship docked at Iloilo on Panay Island. It was suffocatingly hot and the town looked very down at heel. Someone had told me about a super nice hotel at one of the places we were to visit, but I could not remember the name of the town. Mary said she wanted to return to the air-conditioned cabin on the ship while I went ashore. I accosted a couple of reasonably respectable-looking men coming out of a bank and asked them if they could tell me about a really nice hotel in Iloilo. One of them said he would take me and led me to a local bus which had wooden benches and completely open sides so you could get on and off from anywhere along its length.

The bus lurched out of town into the countryside, and I began to get worried how far we were going and how long it would take to get there. Finally, after about 30 minutes, we arrived at the place which was supposed to be this great hotel. Of course it was nothing of the sort, but we got off, took our seats at a rickety table and ordered Coca Cola. My companion was wearing a traditional barong tagalog shirt, which is a loose affair worn outside the trousers. He had a very strong accent which was not easy to understand. As we sipped our warm Cokes, he confided in me how he was an important security man working for the government, and to prove his point, he pulled up his barong to reveal a bloody great revolver stuck into his waistband. I now began to get really nervous. The minutes were ticking away towards the ship's departure time, and I kept saying that we ought to be returning to the docks. He didn't seem to be in any hurry and I imagined the ship sailing away into another tropical sunset with my new wife on board.

Finally, we boarded another bus and arrived at the ship about 20 minutes before sailing time. My new friend insisted on coming aboard and meeting my wife. We went to the cabin and ordered ham sandwiches and something to drink. As he talked, his mouth stuffed with food, he waved his arms around so pieces of ham and bread flew around the cabin and he became even more difficult to understand. I was terrified of upsetting him because of misunderstanding some incomprehensible remark. He made no move to disembark and I was afraid that we would be stuck with him for the rest of the voyage. Finally, after the ship started blowing its siren and announcing over the PA that visitors should disembark immediately, he left the cabin. Right after he had gone, I noticed he had left his pen on the table, so I rushed out into the corridor to return it to him. There was no sign of him either on the ship or on the dock alongside, so I was sure that he was hiding somewhere and would reappear as soon as we put to sea. Fortunately, my fears were not realized. He had left me his card and I posted his pen back to him when I got to HK.

The final stop was Davao and it was here that we found the hotel we were looking for. It was very nice, but by now we were almost out of money. All we could manage for an evening meal was to nurse a gin and tonic at the bar and eat all the chips and nuts within reach.

With the strike now over, we were able to fly back to Manila for our Cathay Pacific flight to Hong Kong. While we were waiting to board, there seemed to be some altercation going on between two groups dressed in white overalls huddled around the underside of the plane. One group were beckoning us to board the plane while the other group were shooing us away. Finally, the first group gained the upper hand, and we all duly trooped on board. Being somewhat technically minded and with some knowledge of aviation, I did wonder what it was that the two groups could not agree about.

After we arrived back in Hong Kong, we settled into married life. This was an especially big adjustment for Mary, which I did not fully appreciate at the time. For many years she had been an independent woman, earning her own money in a job with a lot of responsibility. For example, she had been a qualified midwife who had personally delivered over 300 babies in the poorer districts in England, at a time when most kids were still born in the home. Now she had lost her independence and had to rely on money provided by me.

Hong Kong's population was growing all the time and the territory was chronically short of water. This got so bad during the summer of 1963 that the water supply was rationed to just four hours every fourth day, meaning that taps were dry for three days and only ran for four hours on the fourth day. The demand was such during those four hours that if you lived on an upper floor you might get no water at all. Actually this shortage started before we got married, and I had the galling experience in my third floor apartment in Kun Tong of having no water and looking over my balcony to see the amahs from the ground floor apartment allowing water to run down the drain.

After we returned from our honeymoon, we moved closer to downtown Kowloon and acquired a puppy we called Pooch. He was a local, non-pedigree dog of the chow variety, with a black tongue and a tightly curled tail. These dogs are very clean and never seem to require house training. In this apartment, too, we had to collect water in basins and bathtubs during the four hours. This water was then used for washing, etc., before being tipped into the toilet tank which, when full, could be flushed. The so-called fresh water was sourced in the Pearl River Delta and brought into HK in tankers diverted from carrying oil. The delta water was brackish and contained a fair amount of salt—quite undrinkable and not very nice. The experience taught us to appreciate piped water and not to waste it. The HK authorities eventually built a parallel water system using sea water for flushing toilets.

During the summer my sister, Lulu, came out to HK to visit me, having travelled overland from England to India by bus. She ran out of money in India, so I arranged for her to fly directly from there to Hong Kong. She soon managed to find herself a job on HK Island.

Mary's contract at the hospital included her return fare to the UK, so we took advantage of this and she flew back to England UK for one month to see her family in August 1963. I did not accompany her because I was not eligible for overseas leave for another couple of years.

Royal Navy ships were regular visitors to the naval base at *HMS Tamar,* located downtown on HK island, conveniently close to the bars in Wanchai. Through my cousin's husband, who was also in the Royal Navy, we were contacted by a visiting naval officer named Michael Shard. One weekend we took him out along with my sister on a motorsailer boat that American Marine had available. While cruising around the Port Shelter area, the boat developed engine trouble, putting us in imminent danger of drifting onto the rocks. Michael nobly volunteered for the unpleasant task of squatting in the engine room, bleeding the diesel fuel system, while the rest of us scrambled to find some sails and install them on the mast. There was no winch handle to hoist the mainsail, so we used a screwdriver, which promptly bent. This unpromising start led to unexpected consequences because Michael was attracted to my sister—setting off a chain of events which will be revealed in due course.

The financial situation continued to deteriorate at American Marine. Events finally came to a head when the manager at the bank handling the company's account suffered a heart attack and another manager took over. He found the flood of red ink and realized that the company owed the bank over four million dollars, with no end in sight. He immediately introduced some very tight financial controls, including countersigning every cheque and the requirement that American Marine employ an auditor from a big accounting firm to be present to keep an eye on expenditure. The person appointed was Dave Wilson, an efficient and blunt-speaking accountant from the north of England. He eventually left the accounting firm to join American Marine and became a big asset to the company.

At this time, American Marine continued to build any kind of boat for which they could get orders. These included small plywood sailboats right up to 68-foot heavy-displacement powerboats. Included in this mix were a few semi-production powerboats such as *Wanderer,* designed by Bill Garden, and especially *Chanteyman*, designed by Angelman and Davis. Both of these designs fitted into the category of what later came to be known as "trawler-style" boats.

After their experience in building a number of *Chanteyman* boats, the Newtons had come to the realization that the only way forward lay in building production boats—although *Chanteyman*, with a round bilge, was not ideal for this purpose. A round bilge required frames that needed to be bent by heating them in a home-made steam box fed by steam from a home-made boiler fired by scrap wood. I clearly recall carpenters dashing through the yard with steaming frames and chucking them up to others waiting inside the hull under construction to clamp the frames in place before they cooled off. This was not very efficient from the production point of view!

The *Chanteyman* hulls were also very limber. One day I carefully lined up a shaft coupling to within three-thousandths of an inch while the boat was in the water. The coupling bolts were left disconnected, and I took another look at it after we had hauled the same boat up the primitive railway a few minutes later. To my astonishment, the two halves of the coupling were a clear two *inches* apart. I was very inexperienced in those days and did not know what to make of this. Not knowing what to do, I did nothing and hoped they might go back together when the boat went back into the water—which, to my great relief, they did!

261

One day, a workman dropped a wood block which had a nail protruding from it. Unfortunately, it ripped his pants and damaged his penis on the way down. I took him to a clinic in Kowloon to have his wound seen to by a western nursing sister. "He caught it on a nail", I said by way of conversation.

"Ugh" she said and swept off with a starched swish of bust and bustle.

"Well," I thought, "that wasn't very friendly."

Chapter 3

August 1963 to September 1964

Life in HK, American Marine—Learning Production

I figure out how to build production boats with the introduction of the Grand Banks. We design, build, and move aboard a houseboat, where I learn to survive multiple typhoons at close quarters. My sister visits and later becomes engaged during a cruise to Greece aboard a barquentine. The yard faces a serious financial crisis, and my daughter Jackie is born.

Bob Newton had identified a boat called *Spray*, based on the design of a New England fishing boat, which he felt could form the basis of a new production boat. Unlike *Chanteyman*, this boat had a hard-chine hull, which made it possible to make up the frames on the loft floor. These could then be set up on a jig and assembled, together with pre-cut planks, chines and keels, into a hull built upside down.

I can remember John Newton with an open atlas on the desk, trying to figure out what to call the boat. He finally settled on the fishing area off the coast of Newfoundland. Thus was the Grand Banks born. It was the turning point in the company's history— and my own.

The first of the new line was the 36, and when the prototype was being built in 1963, It just seemed to keep going up for ever; so much so that the roof of the building had to be raised and a small structure, resembling a Chinese temple, built on the top to accommodate the flying bridge. The initial reaction of everyone who saw it was, "What on earth is that?" But, once people became accustomed to the different look, the Grand Banks proved to be very popular. Up to that time, the choice had been either a narrow, gutted sailboat with the galley down below and limited deck space, or a plywood "gin-palace" which did not appeal to people who had sailed. Almost all engines were gas (petrol), which were both temperamental and potentially dangerous. The Grand Banks brought the galley up on deck, which greatly appealed to the women, and the engines started reliably when you turned the key and didn't explode, which appealed to everyone. The Grand Banks coined the phrase "The Dependable Diesel Cruiser" which was right on the money. If my memory serves me correctly, in those days, the GB 36 sold for around $23,000!

The orders started to come in, but we found ourselves in the ridiculous situation that the three boats we had to build every month were all finished in a frantic rush during the final few days. The painters, who had had nothing to paint all month now had to work overtime, while the carpenters had nothing to do. The end of every month was a crisis where we never seemed to be able to meet the deadline imposed by the bank. Theoretically we could not start work on any boat for which we did not have a firm order. But we knew that we had to start making components before we got the order to be able to build enough boats to meet our obligations to the bank, so a certain amount of subterfuge was necessary!

Up to this time, all our sales had been to the United States, but Whit had received a letter from Jack Taylor in England, who expressed interest in handling the GB over there. If the Grand Banks had looked a bit odd in the U.S., it appeared even more bizarre in the UK, where they had not yet heard of a flying bridge. Whit went off to England, putting me nominally in charge of production with strict instructions not to change anything.

I had been thinking all along that there must be a better way of running production than finishing the three monthly boats in a panic in the final days of the month. With 30 days in a month, it would seem much more logical to finish one every 10 days. The problem I had was how to figure out how much progress had to be made in the previous month on the first and second boats that were to be completed the next month. Then it came to me that if one boat had to be completed every 10 days, the labour required over 10 days for the entire 36 production line must equal all the labour required to build one boat. My first reaction was that the solution could not possibly be that simple. We had very accurate labour records, broken down into different accounts representing different trades and categories of work. I took these records and checked my theory against them and found out that it really was that simple, and that the key figure was not the number of boats per month, but the interval, in days, between each boat.

So all I had to do was to take the total average hours it took to build a boat and divide it by the interval to ascertain the number of man-hours we needed to invest every day on the entire 36 production line. Because of Sundays and rest days, an eight-day interval proved to be more realistic for three boats per month. There were eight working hours in every day, so by dividing the daily man-hour figure by eight, it was possible to calculate not only the number of men needed every day but, by using the breakdown of the accounts, what trades these men had to be. Following this basic calculation, it was immediately apparent that the reason we could not meet the schedule was because we did not have sufficient men to provide the necessary number of man-hours to make it possible.

I ran this idea past Dave Wilson, who could not fault my reasoning. At this point, Whit returned from England. He took some convincing that I was on the right track; but eventually— since Whit had other aspects of the business to attend to—by default I gradually took over the running of production. Combined with the knowledge of how many days it took to assemble a boat, the interval figure could also be used for many other things, such as the number of building stations and, therefore, the building space needed to accommodate them.

Whit's visit to England had been successful, and Jack Taylor ordered a boat for display in the London boat show in Earls Court, in the middle of London. Predictably, the boat was behind schedule and arrived in the London docks just before Christmas, only to find that it was too high to pass under the arch at the entrance to the old Victorian-era dock. It had to be offloaded onto a barge and towed around to another location, where it was put onto a truck. It was now Christmas Eve, and the route to Earls Court was along Oxford Street, festooned with Christmas decorations strung across the road. The police refused to give a permit to take the load down the road at this time, and the driver refused to drive the truck without a permit. The problem was that the show opened right after the New Year and, being one of the inside exhibits, the Grand Banks had to be inside the building six days before the deadline, or it would miss the show. Jack Taylor sat down with the driver and they shared a bottle of Scotch. Suitably lubricated, the driver agreed to drive without a permit, and they set off down Oxford Street, using a broom from the flying bridge to raise the decorations out of the way. They successfully reached their destination without becoming entangled with the decorations or being stopped by the police, and the boat made it into the show just hours before the deadline.

I was officially put in charge of production in June 1964, and after my method was refined, the construction time for a GB 36 was cut from four months to just six weeks. The jig cycle time for a 36 hull was one week, and the fastest we planked a 36 hull was one day. The GB 36 was followed by the GB 32, then by the GB 42. The GB 32 was marketed for $16,000, and the GB 42 for $34,000. Bill Russell, also from England, was taken on to handle the increasingly demanding job of purchasing supplies. This was often very challenging. I remember one occasion when we had boats which could not ship because we were awaiting the arrival of stainless steel tube from Japan. The ship carrying the tubing arrived in Hong Kong, but there was no delivery of tube. When we enquired we were told, "Oh, the ship had a record turn-around, so there wasn't time to unload all the cargo!"

The system for expatriates in Hong Kong was that your employer provided you with accommodation. Partly because of this, and also because of supply and demand, accommodation was extremely expensive. I thought it would be much better if I could live on a boat and pay for it with the rent money. That way I would be building up equity rather than just watching the money go down the drain every month—even though it wasn't really my money. I suggested this to the Newtons, and Bob Newton, the father, said that rather than just a regular boat it would be better to build a proper houseboat. He undertook to have two large steel pontoons constructed by someone he knew in the Kun Tong area of Kowloon, near the airport. These would be joined with steel trusses, and American Marine would build a plywood platform on top of those and a house on top of that. Actually the construction of the house would be very similar to the way houses are built in the United States, although I did not realize that at the time. Fortunately, this was all underway before the bank lowered the boom, or I am sure they would have put a stop to it.

The pontoons were really like a large catamaran. The tubes were mostly sealed for flotation but they also contained four cement-lined water tanks for fresh water collected off the almost-flat roof. Construction was completed around September 1963, and I christened the houseboat *Mbali*—meaning "Far" in Swahili. The houseboat was towed around to a protected bay called Hebe Haven on the other side of the Clearwater Bay Peninsula from Junk Bay. The sea was not rough during the passage, but both Mary and Pooch suffered from seasickness on the journey.

The Newtons had developed a small marina at Hebe Haven, so there was an access road and power to what a few months before had been an inaccessible spot. It was an idyllic location at this time of year, although rather remote for Mary's taste. We had power inboard, but no phone service. There was a footpath from the marina to a floating walkway leading out to the houseboat. The path went through thickets of bamboo and, on one occasion while cutting it back, I came perilously close to being bitten by a snake. I had reached out with my left hand to grasp a clump of bamboo and was moving my eyes down to the place where I was going to strike with my machete, when something made me reverse my glance to see a vivid green bamboo snake ready to strike only inches away from my approaching hand. I must have leapt about three feet into the air!

Around June 1963, a 120-foot staysail schooner sailed into HK, and the owner, Drayton Cochran, placed her in the care of American Marine for six months during the typhoon season. She was called *Westward*—so named because she had always sailed west since her construction at the Abeking and Rasmussen yard in Lemwerder, Germany, in 1961. This ship was to play an important role in the lives of several people mentioned in this tale.

Westward was anchored in Junk Bay, just off the boatyard, but during typhoons we took her to HK harbour and tied up to one of the giant mooring buoys intended for ocean-going ships while I remained on board. The only typhoon of any significance to hit HK this summer was Category 3 Faye, with winds of 125 mph. I was a bit apprehensive and the harbour a bit choppy, but we survived the storm without damage. *Westward* had an interesting engine arrangement. Starting was by compressed air, and you always had to ensure that you used the compressor on the engine to keep the air cylinders topped up. If you ran out of air, you would be in serious trouble. The engine had no reverse gear, so to go astern, you had to stop the engine, turn a wheel to reset the valve gear and restart the engine, which then ran backwards.

Anton Emmerton, who I had met at the Yacht Club, was now married to Anna, who had come to Hong Kong to stay with a friend. Anna was also a dinghy sailor and she and Anton had met at the Yacht Club. They had become engaged at about the same time as Mary and myself, but they had tied the knot earlier. In fact, they had moved into my mid-levels apartment when I moved to Kowloon after joining American Marine. They soon had a baby and, being adventurous types, had moved aboard *Westward* for a time while she was anchored in Junk Bay. Not the most convenient arrangement, having to row back and forth to the Chinese village miles out of town! Anton's military service came to an end towards the end of 1963, and the family returned to the UK.

My friend Rex who had been a fellow apprentice at De Havillands and who had been with me on the Trans-Africa Expedition, had also travelled out to HK, having taken a freighter from Liverpool up the Amazon to Manaus, proceeding from there by barge to the upper reaches of the river. From there, he made his way to San Francisco and from there to HK. When *Westward* came to leave HK for Europe in December, Rex was on board, as were my sister and Michael Shard, whose service with the Royal Navy had come to an end just in time for him to fly out to HK and join the vessel as navigator. He was motivated of course by his romantic interest in my sister!

A brief diversion here while we follow *Westward*'s voyage. She left HK around Christmas of 1963. By the time she had reached Penang, in Malaysia, Michael and my sister were engaged, and they were married when the ship reached Athens, where they left her to return to England. *Westward* continued on to southern Europe, where Rex stayed aboard to carry out maintenance. Jill, who had been friends with my sister at secretarial college in Devon, also had an adventurous turn of mind and had her eye on *Westward*. She caught up with the ship and came aboard. As a result of this meeting, she and Rex became partners and were subsequently married—of which more later! When they met, Rex did not know that Jill knew my sister, and Jill did not know that Rex knew me. They only realized that they knew brother and sister because they both knew someone who had a basenji—a breed of dog unusual because they do not bark. It turned out to be the same dog!

Back in HK, Mary and I were becoming accustomed to living on the houseboat. Our large glass sliding doors looked out over Hebe Haven, and the winter weather was extremely pleasant. At weekends numerous pleasure boats plied the calm waters of Hebe Haven. On one of them was a couple who water skied past the houseboat every weekend. They were Geoff and Francie, and they stopped and asked about the name of the houseboat. Geoff had lived in East Africa and recognized the Swahili word. They became our friends and taught us to water ski.

The houseboat made an excellent party boat and we held a very successful house warming/Halloween party. We had a big bowl of fruit punch and *Mbali* looked very festive, hung about with strings of colourful Chinese lanterns.

We decided that we should start a family, as Mary had just

celebrated her 30th birthday and I was 29. We had no problems in the fertility department, and we had no sooner made the decision than Mary became pregnant.

The timing was less than ideal. Within a month, the bank instituted even more draconian measures against American Marine, including an immediate reduction in our salaries— "to ensure we realized the seriousness of the situation!". This was really a stupid move because, in my case, I was only earning $100 per month and living from pay check to pay check. Groceries were ordered by phone from grocery shops in Kowloon, called compradors, and delivered by them on a daily basis, with the bill being settled at the end of each month. Having your salary cut without warning meant that you had no chance to cut back expenditure in advance of reduced income, and so you had to spend time worrying about how to pay the bills instead of concentrating on your job.

Although starting a family at this moment imposed additional hardship, in retrospect it was probably just as well, because it was quite a while before the situation improved. We had a very tight budget, and I think it must have been at this time that we sold Mary's car to get more money. This was a shame because it greatly restricted her movements and she loved that car. I decided to get a motorcycle and bought a Honda 125cc to get me back and forth to the yard every day.

All our fresh water on *Mbali* came from water falling on the roof, which was piped to cement-lined tanks inside the twin hulls, holding some 2,500 gallons. After a dry spell of several weeks, the tanks were getting very low and I began to become concerned. But we had some rain of low intensity for 24 hours and the tanks had filled to overflowing in that time. I was amazed that so much water could be collected from a 50- by 25-foot roof in such a short period of time. Unfortunately, when we awoke in the morning with the tanks almost full, the houseboat was leaning over to one side. This was because it had started with a slight list, so the water on the roof went to one side and from there into the tank on the same side, which increased the list, which increased the flow, etc.! I fixed the problem by re-routing the scuppers on one side to the tanks on the other—making the boat self-levelling.

When the warm weather returned in early spring, so did the mosquitoes. They weren't too much of a problem except at night, when trying to sleep. We put a net over the bed but, even with a fan blowing straight at it, you couldn't feel a breath of wind inside. We found the solution was to dispense with the net altogether and have the fan oscillating back and forth just a few inches above our bodies. The fan kept the air moving and blew the mozzies away as they came in for a landing. It was important not to allow the fan to blow directly on your body or you would awake in the morning feeling like Quasimodo—the hunchback of Notre Dame!

The negative aspects of living on the houseboat became all too apparent in May 1964, with the arrival of typhoon Viola. I had taken these storms into consideration before making the decision to live on the houseboat, but I did not know then what I know today, and a little knowledge can be a dangerous thing. Personal accounts from people who have experienced typhoons close up seem to be rather rare, so I think it is worthwhile to describe, in some detail, how it feels to go through them.

First, some general facts. In the northern hemisphere, cyclonic storms rotate counter clockwise due to the Coriolis Effect caused by the earth's rotation. Typhoons which affect HK usually approach from the south and travel in a north-to-north-westerly direction, so the speed of the storm over the ground must be added to the rotating wind speeds on its east side and subtracted on its west. Rotating wind speeds, which increase the closer one gets to the eye of the storm, consist of sustained winds (defined as lasting 10 minutes or more) augmented by violent and destructive gusts which strike any object in their path like the hammers of hell.

Many people think that a typhoon is a relatively contained affair—similar, perhaps, to a large tornado—which comes upon you suddenly. This has not been my experience. The storms have been huge and long lasting, and they descend upon you with increasing ferocity extending for many terrifying hours.

Typhoon Wanda, mentioned earlier in these pages, is well documented, and the figures for that storm provide an example of the magnitude and power of these monsters. At its height, Wanda was 1,000 miles in diameter—encompassing the full width of the

271

South China Sea, from the Philippines to the coast of China. The 953 mB low pressure in the eye of the storm created a dome in the sea 100 miles across, which increased in height as it reached the shallow coastal waters. The combined effect of this dome, together with the waters pushed ahead of it by the wind, caused the level of the high tide in Hong Kong to increase from the forecast 7 feet to nearly 18 feet, with the tops of the windblown waves an additional 6 feet above that. Twelve inches of rain fell during a 12-hour period. The human toll was 130 killed, with another 53 missing. 27,000 people lost their homes. 725 small craft were wrecked, and 24 ocean-going ships were beached, with an additional 12 involved in collisions. In this day and age, the one good thing about a typhoon is that you know they are coming and can make preparations. In 1937, before this was the case, the death toll in tiny HK from a similar storm was 11,000 when the total population was only 450,000.

Moving now to events close to home, the houseboat was moored near the eastern shore of a small bay named Hebe Haven. To provide a better idea of the events that follow, I will attempt to describe its layout. To the north and west, from which the initial winds normally came, the bay was protected by the bulk of Tai Mo Shan, a mountain 957 metres (3,140 feet) high, making it the highest peak in HK. To the south, the bay was separated from the open waters of Port Shelter by a line of hills about 100 feet high. The entrance to the bay, in the southwest corner, was angled in such a way as to deny the sea a straight shot into the inner reaches, where the houseboat and marina were located. To all appearances, Hebe Haven was as protected and secure an anchorage as you would find anywhere.

The houseboat was anchored with a ship's anchor and anchor chain, plus a pair of nylon lines tied to trees on the shore, with two additional lines running to anchors either side. I had designed the house with the bedroom end being very strong, with hinged wooden shutters to cover the windows. At the opposite end, the sitting room, with sliding glass doors, spanned the full 25-foot width of the house. The game plan was that, when a typhoon approached, all lines except the main anchor chain would be released, allowing the houseboat freedom to swing free with the bedroom end of the house facing the storm. During the storm-free winter months it had been much nicer to have the sitting room end facing the bay. With each link in the anchor chain being about 8 inches long, it was a major task to turn the houseboat around, and I had decided not to bother—thus exposing the weaker sitting-room end to the brunt of the first storms.

In the hours prior to the arrival of a typhoon there is often an uneasy calm. The humidity is uncomfortably high, the air still and, strangely, often abuzz with dragon flies. The mirror calm surface of the bay moves in a sinister way up and down the beach with a trickling sound. But there are no waves. There is an electric air of anticipation; you are fully aware that this is indeed the calm before the storm and within a few hours all hell will break loose.

This is not a time to relax. It is the time to check and recheck and tie down or put away anything that could be grabbed by the wind. Once the storm strikes, there is little opportunity to do anything but hang on and ride it out. The radio issues progress reports on the approach of the tempest. Fast moving clouds cover the sky and, as outriders from the wind, the first cat's paws ruffle and fan out across the water to be followed, almost immediately, by vicious gusts. Far from providing protection, Tai Mo Shan turned out to hook the winds down from the sky, hurling each gust like a thunderbolt into the bay, whipping its surface into a violent froth and carrying the water clear over the line of 100-foot-high hills to the south.

My next mistake, after failing to turn the house, was in waiting too long before disconnecting the floating walkway and undoing the secondary anchor lines. When wind strikes, we are accustomed to feeling it as an escalating force, but even the initial blasts of this storm were of such velocity that it was like being struck by an 18-wheeler. With each gust, the wide span of the roof initially depressed a couple of inches in the centre and then immediately snapped upwards to maybe three inches above normal. With gusts coming every few seconds and increasing in intensity as the storm approached, I began to fear that we would lose the roof entirely. I found some fittings and nailed them into the floor and roof beams in two places, and then tied rope between the roof and floor fittings to restrict the upward movement. I tried to buffer the impact by standing between the two vertical ropes and grasping one in each hand, acting like a sort of shock absorber. The plywood I had erected over the sliding doors deformed under the pressure of the wind pushing on the door handles and bending the glass doors. To relieve the situation, I partially opened the doors and used a hacksaw to cut off the door handles.

Typhoons are accompanied by driving rain that can easily exceed one inch per hour. The three or four feet immediately above the surface of the sea cannot be described as either air or water but a frenzied mixture of both that can be hard to breath. This water sprayed in through the openings, soaking everything inside the room, including me. I had a battery-operated radio so I could listen to updates on the storm's position, but they would often be an hour or two behind, and I did not want to know where the storm was two hours ago but where it was *NOW!* Of course power had to be disconnected, but it usually fails anyway during a typhoon. With no generator on board, as darkness fell, I had to rely on flashlights, and the screaming of the wind and violence of the storm was much more frightening in the black night, which seemed endless as I stood there doing my shock absorber act.

Finally, a grey dawn appeared, but with it a new hazard presented itself. As the storm centre passed over Hong Kong, the wind swung around to the southwest, coming from the direction of the entrance to the bay. Even though the fetch was only three-quarters of a mile, it was enough to generate waves three feet high. At first this was not too much of a problem as the ferocity of the wind flattened the waves, but as the wind speed began to subside, the size of the waves increased, and we were now on a lee shore. Apart from increased noise from the waves thrumming through the trusses supporting the houseboat floor, this did not affect me too much, but the waves ploughed through the nearby marina.

Fortunately, despite the above description, Viola was a relatively mild storm, with maximum winds of just 80 mph, and we survived a bit wiser and more or less unscathed. 1964 was an exceptional year, with five major storms to hit Hong Kong, and Viola was merely an introduction to what was to be a tumultuous typhoon season.

If typhoons seem to figure rather predominantly in these pages, it is because they are a fact of life in the Western Pacific. Their only predictable aspect is their unpredictability, and while we are on the subject I may as well describe the rest of the season. We had respite during June and July and perhaps got lulled into a false sense of security, because I still had not turned the houseboat around when typhoon Ida visited Hong Kong early in August. The houseboat had a deck 5 feet deep at the sitting-room end, 3 feet deep at the bedroom end, and 2 feet wide down both sides. I was on the sitting-room end of the deck when I saw one of the first serious gusts of the storm racing towards me over the water. I braced myself, but it knocked me over like a ninepin and blew me across the wet deck until I finished up against the front of the house. This time I had stainless steel rigging wires, instead of rope, to connect the roof to the floor, but Ida sported winds of 100 mph, and, early on, the wires snapped like cotton, with a noise like pistol shots. So I spent the next few hours in this storm in much the same way as I had the previous one.

This experience finally pushed me into turning the houseboat around, which was a major task considering the size and weight of the chain and the fact that it had to be done by hand without any outside assistance. But, in fact, it turned out that it was better in the summer having the sitting room facing the land, because it was more soothing looking out at green trees than squinting at the glare from the water.

Just one month later we were assaulted by Typhoon Ruby, which developed rapidly while in the South China Sea. The eye passed right over Hong Kong, with maximum gusts over 122 mph. This was a serious storm, responsible for 38 deaths, with 6 missing and 300 injured. Twenty ocean-going ships were in trouble, and over 300 small craft were damaged or sunk. It was fortunate that I had the experience of less powerful storms to get my act together. By this time, I had replaced the ropes and cable with solid poles capable of resisting compression as well as tension, and these, together with the stronger end of the house facing the storm, were a big improvement. But again I was late in releasing the secondary

275

anchor lines, which allowed the house to swing around to face the wind. I had a piece of wood tied to the end of each line so I would be able to find it again after the storm had passed. I had waited so long that the line had pulled through the cleat and the wood was jammed up hard against it. The nylon line was quivering and humming like a violin string under the strain. I hardly dared get near it, but I was finally able to kick the float free, and the wood struck the water with a fizzing sound about 20 feet from the boat.

Large ocean-going junks used Hebe Haven as a hurricane hole. I was a bit concerned because if one of them dragged its anchor and hit us, it would demolish the houseboat. But I ceased to worry when I watched one such junk, with five anchors already down, motor up into the teeth of the wind and drop a sixth anchor before dropping back to its previous position. I counted fifteen crew members on deck during this manoeuvre. It was during this storm that I first dived into the water to check the shackles connecting to the main anchor. This may sound a bit extreme, but you are actually much better off in the water because you are out of the wind.

I had our dog Pooch with me on-board and we were marooned out there for many hours. Pooch was showing increasing signs of anxiety about wanting to pee. I have mentioned how these dogs instinctively are house trained, so he was not about to go inside the house. As soon as I thought it safe to do so, I put him outside to go on the deck, which was already wet with rain and spray, but he ran round and around the house without going despite the added incentive of all that water sloshing about! Although the bay was still quite choppy, the storm had passed inland and was beginning to dissipate, so I threw Pooch into the water and he manfully swam the 100 yards to shore. As soon as he reached the beach he lifted his leg and peed and peed and peed. Finally, he couldn't hold his leg up any longer and just went on peeing.

Bill Russell also very nobly stayed with me on the houseboat. He was living in a small cottage out in the same general area on the Sai Kung peninsula. As soon as it was safe to leave the houseboat and go ashore, we drove to his cottage. It appeared OK from the outside, but what a mess faced us when we went inside! A brand new spring had erupted under the kitchen floor, and a torrent of water had flowed through the house, bringing with it an avalanche of rocks that were scattered throughout the house. The water level had subsided but there was a high water mark on the walls and on the remains of the furniture. Bill's wife and daughter had gone into town before the storm, but their poor dog was perched on top of the back of their settee trembling uncontrollably and very pleased to see us!

This storm absolutely devastated the marina. Not only had the three-foot waves ploughed through it as with earlier storms, but the tidal surge had been sufficiently high to lift the loops holding the floats in place over the top of the pilings, so that the pontoons, concrete floats, and boats had all finished up in a gigantic pile of wreckage on the shore.

Mary was pregnant during this time and had moved ashore for all of these storms. She stayed with the Hambleys, who lived on the tenth floor of a block of apartments in Kowloon. In this storm, Mary and Francie very unwisely decided to visit the hair salon before the storm had really got going. By the time they came out two hours later, large street signs, for which Hong Kong is famous, were being torn loose and sent bowling down the street. Not surprisingly, they had great trouble finding a taxi, but eventually one stopped and took them back to the apartment. When they got there and opened the taxi door, the wind took hold of it and tore it right off, no doubt leaving the taxi driver bitterly regretful of picking up these two idiots! They spent that night cowering in a closet in the centre of the apartment while the wind shrieked and howled and the building swayed. During the night the wind pushed a large, old-style air-conditioning unit out of its mounting hole and into the room. Having gained access, the wind then smashed the windows, sucked out the furnishings, tore up the parquet floor, and stripped the paint and light fittings off the wall, leaving the room a bare concrete shell.

Just two days later, before there had been time to fully clear the rubble, Typhoon Sally arrived with winds that had been as high as 195 mph but which had fortunately reduced somewhat by the time the storm reached HK. This storm was responsible for nine deaths.

The last storm of the season to affect HK that year was Typhoon Dot, whose arrival, four weeks later on October 11th, coincided with the birth of my daughter Jackie. Mary was in hospital on that day and I had been visiting her in the morning, awaiting the birth, when the doctors said that I might as well go home because nothing was going to happen that day—but Mary should stay in. I returned to the houseboat to continue my preparations for the storm when I got a message from the marina that I had a daughter! This storm also caused considerable damage and 26 deaths, so it had been quite a season. According to Wikipedia, 1964 was the most active typhoon season in the recorded history of Hong Kong.

Moving the houseboat back into position after a storm was a huge problem. I had a 16-foot sailing dinghy, and I would take a line down from the transom and another from the bow and tie them to links on the chain 16 feet apart. I would then stand on the sea bottom, holding my breath, and heave on the lines to get the chain off the bottom, using the buoyancy of the dinghy to support it. Each link in the oversized chain must have weighed at least 4 pounds, so 16 feet would weigh around 100 pounds. Standing on the bottom with my feet in the mud, I would then drag chain over in the direction I wanted it. As can be imagined, this was a tough and tedious business.

After our violent summer, much of the water entering the tanks during the storms had contained a fair amount of salt, which attacked the cement lining, causing the tanks to rust. Dealing with the problem involved grinding away and replacing the cement lining. To do this, I moved the bow of the houseboat in, so that it grounded on the shore. We did not want our house to be sitting at the angle of the beach when the tide went out, so I made a stack of wood blocks to slip under the outer end of the hulls to keep them level. High tide was at three o'clock in the morning, so that was when I had to pull the houseboat as far ashore as it would go and then get into the water and slide the blocks under the outer ends of the two hulls as the tide went out. This proved to be much more difficult than I had expected, because they wanted to float. I would

278

push them under one side and they would pop out the other, all the while the tide was going out and the underside of the hulls were approaching the sea bottom. It would have been a lot easier and less perilous if I had had someone to help me with the second hull.

When I look back, I shudder at the risks I took using the disc grinder. The voltage in HK was 240 volts, and I was using this machine standing waist deep in the sea, although I did take the precaution of connecting a ground wire from the body of the machine directly into the rod hammered into the sea bed.

With the drama and learning experience of the 1964 typhoon season behind us, things settled down; but, as any young married couple know, everything changes as soon as you have a baby. In our case it was particularly difficult because, living where we did, there was no way to get a baby sitter. One evening we desperately wanted to go out for a meal and decided to go to the Yacht Club. We had always been able to count on Jackie going to sleep in her basket whenever we went out in the car. We drove across to Wanchai, and she was fascinated by all the lights in the streets and showed no sign of going to sleep. We drove around and around, but eventually had to give up and took her in her basket into the Yacht Club and shoved her under the table in the dining room, where she finally went to sleep.

When the summer of 1965 arrived, I had learnt my lesson and turned the boat around early in the season. After the typhoon damage of the previous year, the marina had been rebuilt, and I was put in charge of its operation in addition to my responsibilities at the yard. A policy was established that when a typhoon was expected, the smaller boats were to be pulled out of the water and larger ones moved to moorings.

Fortunately, this year turned out to be very different from last and only Super Typhoon Freda was a serious threat to HK, and that went to Hainan and did not affect HK too badly from the point of view of wind. But we still had several warnings, which required us to take precautions at the marina and elsewhere. On one occasion, we were working to get boats out of the water with quite primitive equipment. The boats were put onto small trolleys with steel wheels so they could be moved when on land. The only way to turn the wheels was to bash them with a chunk of wood. I was engaged in this, putting my full weight behind the wood, when the middle finger on my left hand slipped unnoticed over the leading edge of the wood so that it came between the end of the wood and the steel rim of the wheel when the two crashed together. This resulted in a smashed finger, a fair amount of blood, and agonizing pain. I went across to the houseboat, nursing my injury, to see my ex-casualty-sister wife. When I showed her what I had done she said, "Don't make such a fuss. I've see much worse than that. You're getting blood on the carpet!"

The moral is: if you expect tea and sympathy for anything less than amputation—don't marry a nurse!

On another occasion, myself and my small crew had been working all day doing the strenuous work of moving boats without stopping to have anything to eat. It was already dark when I went into the nearby village of Sai Kung to try to buy some rice. At that time Sai Kung was still a typical rural Chinese village with twisting, narrow streets and traditional houses with turned-up roofs. It was raining and the village was absolutely deserted, with wooden shutters covering every door and window. Apart from the noise of the wind rattling the shutters, the only sound I heard was the click of mahjong tiles from behind the shuttered doors. I started yelling "*Fan!*" at the top of my voice thinking that was the word for "rice". Actually it is the word for cooked rice—which was not what I wanted. Eventually someone peered out to see what all the noise was about, and they helped this crazy foreign devil buy what he was looking for.

Even without typhoons there were other issues to deal with living on *Mbali*. One morning a strong side wind blew up, and one of the lines leading to the shore uprooted the tree to which it was tied. Immediately the houseboat started to drift sideways parallel to the shore, and the bolts attaching the floating walkway snapped like carrots. Fortunately, this happened just before I had left for work, so I went dashing along the shoreline to grab the offending rope, disconnect it from the downed tree, and try to attach it to a replacement. It was low tide and half the rocks on the beach were covered with slime and the remainder with razor-edged barnacles.

280

The outcome was inevitable—I slipped on one and landed spread-eagled on the other, slicing open my arms and hands, but I had to ignore the blood until I had dealt with the ongoing problem. I carry the scars to this day!

When the Grand Banks line was up and running, we were using considerable amounts of wood, especially the Philippine mahogany used to plank the hull. Initially we had plenty of wood stacked around the yard, and when this was used up, more was purchased and immediately went into the boats under construction. We were so ignorant that we never gave a thought to the moisture content in the wood. The first sign of trouble was when a boat was off-loaded from a ship in New York and immediately started to fill up with water. It turned out that the planking had dried and shrunk on the voyage from Hong Kong. Boatbuilding is littered with traps lying in wait for the unwary, and another sin we had unknowingly committed was that the edges of each plank had been cut at right angles to its surface instead of being at a slight angle. Without an angle, the gap between the planks is parallel all the way through, so outside water pressure can push the caulking right through the gap and inside the hull. The angle creates a wedge-shaped slot, so the caulking is pushed further into the gap by the water.

Fortunately, the dealer, Bill Higgs, was an experienced boater. He closed the engine intake seacocks and cut the intake hoses with a knife, so that the engines were sucking water from the bilge. He then ran hell for leather to the nearest shore, and the boat grounded just as it sank! This combination of errors was a major problem because we had other boats already on their way to their destinations, plus many others in the production line. In short order I had to bone up on moisture content, wood kilns, and associated subjects. We constructed our own kilns and heated them by burning scrap wood.

Chapter 4

August 1965 to August 1966

Life in Hong Kong. First Overseas Leave.

We take my first overseas leave in almost five years and visit Australia, Mauritius, Kenya and England. My infant daughter survives a near-death medical emergency in Kenya. We spend time in England and return to more crises in Hong Kong.

By now I had worked at American Marine for three years, and I was eligible for my first overseas leave since I had come to HK in November 1960. As you do when you don't know any better, I had planned an elaborate trip which, far from relaxing, turned out to be a bit of a disaster. We had built a fast, Raymond Hunt-designed boat called *Outsider* for a guy in Perth in Australia, and he had invited me to visit him. From there we were going to Cocos Island and on to Mauritius to stay with some friends we had made in HK, before going to Kenya to visit my father and then on to England to stay with my mother.

To fly to Perth, we were routed through Singapore, and things began to go wrong when our flight from Hong Kong was delayed so that we arrived in Singapore just in time to see our Perth flight leaving without us. Flights to Perth were very infrequent back then, so the next day we were routed through Sydney, from where we had fly to Adelaide and change for a flight to Perth.

Jackie was just 10 months old and was suffering diarrhoea, which was not ideal when traveling. We put this down to upset caused by a change in routine. When we got to Sydney and were told the time of our flight, there was yet another delay and we had to hang about for an extra hour or so. By the time we got to Adelaide, Jackie needed changing and we were told there was ten minutes until the next flight. Given all the delays we had been subjected to, I did not believe this, and I told Mary to go ahead and change the baby. Of course, this time they really did mean it, and they were calling us on the PA and chastised us for holding up the plane.

Eventually we arrived in Perth in an exhausted state and checked into a very basic motel. I found that the TV did not work, and when I went to the desk to ask about it I was told that I had to put money into it. I had never before heard of a TV which had to be fed money before it would deliver. When we awoke the following morning, it was just after noon on a Saturday. I went across the street to the supermarket to buy something to eat, only to find it closed at noon until Monday morning. Welcome to egalitarian Australia! It was a nasty shock after freewheeling Hong Kong, where for five years we had been able to buy pretty much anything at any time.

During our time in Perth I drove to Shark Bay, up the West Coast. I had been lent an American Ford Fairlane for the journey. After I left the suburbs of Perth, there were no warnings how far it was to the next fuel station, and there was basically nothing to look at, so I passed the time counting the seconds between mileposts. Finally, I realized that the fuel gauge was dropping at an alarming rate and there was no sign of any fuel station—in fact there was no sign of anything much at all. So I slowed down to about 20 mph and wondered whether I was going to make it anywhere before running out of fuel. To my relief, I saw a sign saying five miles to the next fuel, and I speeded up again. When I got there, I opened the window and the flies swarmed in. I was reminded of the words from the song "Life Gits Teejus":

> *"Open the door and the flies swarm in,*
> *Shut the door and sweatin' agin.*
> *Move too fast and I crack my shin.*
> *Life gits teejus, don't it?"*

283

I filled up and went on to Geraldton, where I spent the night. The dark-skinned aborigines spoke with the strongest Aussie accent I had ever heard. I went to a nice restaurant that evening and decided to treat myself to a glass of wine, only to find that they did not serve alcohol, but they said I could go to a nearby shop to buy a bottle and they would charge me to remove the cork. That was another new arrangement for me. I thought that they certainly liked to make things difficult for themselves in Australia. I don't remember anything very special about Shark Bay, but I probably wasn't seeing it under the best conditions and it was 47 years ago.

A few days later we drove to Albany, on the southwest tip of Australia. What struck me during this trip was how ordinary the farm dwellings looked with their corrugated iron roofs. They all looked like they had been transported from suburbia, even though they were standing by themselves in a rural setting. It was that egalitarian lifestyle again. The couple we had come to visit, who were quite well off, told us that if you had money, you had to keep it hidden and not show off with a fancy house or you risked being ostracized.

After 12 days in Western Australia, we flew on to Mauritius stopping to refuel on Cocos Island. Actually there are two Cocos Islands—one administered by Australia and the other, further north, by Equador, and I have briefly visited both of them.

My chief memory of Mauritius, a small island just east of Madagascar, was of the large piles of stones at the edge of the sugar cane fields. I t had been the only known habitat of the dodo, which went extinct in 1681. We met our friends here and then flew on to Nairobi in Kenya.

My father met us at the airport and drove us to the Muthaiga Club—a long-established "settlers" club in Nairobi. The problem, we now discovered, was that children were not allowed. I don't know what age qualified as children, but it would certainly include a 10-month old toddler. Accommodation was in small individual huts called *bandas,* so it was quite easy to smuggle Jackie in without alerting any busybodies. We pushed two armchairs together to form a crib. The next day we drove the 150 miles in the Land Rover up to my father's farm in Timau, 7,500 feet up the slopes of Mount Kenya.

Jackie was still suffering from diarrhoea and was clearly losing weight. We took her into the hospital in nearby Nanyuki and they decided to admit her—along with Mary—for observation. The following day they said that she needed to go immediately into the Gertrude's Garden Children's Hospital in Muthaiga, Nairobi. They contacted Kenya's Flying Doctor Service, and Jackie and Mary left immediately for Wilson Airport in Nairobi, while I followed in the Land Rover. The flying doctor service was free but they asked you, if you had the money, to make a contribution—preferably at least equal to the cost of the flight—so that others who had no money would also have access to the service. Naturally we made such a contribution.

Then followed seven harrowing days. The hospital was small and devoted entirely to caring for sick children. Nursing was of the highest standards as Mary, an ex-nursing sister, could attest. Jackie was placed in an isolation ward, and nurses changed their gowns when going from room to room. Jackie was attached to numerous tubes and tied to the bed to prevent her rolling around and pulling them out. We went to see her every day but were not allowed to touch her. When she saw us she would try to reach out to be picked up, but we could do nothing. She was very sick with some kind of gastro-enteritis. We were very lucky to find such an excellent hospital in Nairobi, and I am pleased to say that it is still going strong 50 years later. By the time she was released back into our care, it was time for us to leave Kenya and continue to England with all our money gone—but for a good cause.

We spent the next two months staying with my mother in her three-storey town house in Henley-on-Thames. When I had left England five years earlier I had been single, but I was now married with a young child. Mary had also not been feeling all that great on this trip, which was hardly surprising with all the stress and worry with a sick child. She went to see the doctor and came back with the unexpected news that she was pregnant, so we had another child on the way. I have to say that it was not very relaxing staying with my mother. She was used to living alone, and having your house invaded by three people, including a baby, for several weeks was not easy.

With the amount of work picking up at the yard, we had been discussing hiring someone else to help on the technical side. By this time, I was doing quite a lot of design work as well as running the production. The Newtons had decided to hire another Brit because they came cheaper than Americans and generally seemed to be more adaptable to living and working in less-structured environments. The question was where to find someone. We thought we would look in the UK while I was there on leave. John Newton came over from California, and we interviewed a number of candidates who had responded to advertisements. I had never before interviewed anybody, and I could see the shock on the faces of some of them when they saw this young guy (me) behind the desk. We did not find anyone who was suitable. They either did not have enough experience, or if they had, they were married with a couple of kids at school age and were nervous about re-locating the family to a place like Hong Kong. It is expensive to move a family all that way; and if, after a few months, they failed to work out, it was not only a waste of money but, more importantly, a waste of time and effort. This had really been the situation with regard to myself and William Jacks.

John and I then consulted a head-hunter who said that, if we knew someone reliable and reasonably smart, it was better to go with the person you knew, even if he was not exactly qualified for the job you had in mind, because he would be able to pick up the necessary skills. I immediately thought of Anton, who had been trained as an agricultural auctioneer before doing his military service. While in HK he had developed an interest in sailing and boats, and after completing his military service and returning to England, he had seen an advert in a yachting magazine for a boat auction. He contacted the sales company and said that he was a trained auctioneer interested in boats and asked whether they had any job openings. They did—and that was how he got into the boat business. John and I went to speak with him, and it finished up with John offering Anton a job working for him in sales in California. In view of what was to happen 20 years later, it should here be noted that it was through me that Anton joined American Marine and found himself living and working in California. We still did not have another person to share the load in Hong Kong, but ultimately that turned out not to be a problem.

When we arrived back in Hong Kong, the 1965 typhoon season was over and we found we had just missed Typhoon Agnes, which had dumped 21 inches of rain in six days, creating widespread flooding and numerous landslides. But we soon had another crisis to deal with. Initially we just had a rope guarding the edge of the walkways around the house, with the plan to add nylon netting as soon as Jackie was mobile. As is always the way, this was left until the last minute, and while Jackie was still just a few months old, we were visited one day by Geoff and Francie Hambly with their daughter aged about two. We adults were chatting when Francie said, "Where is Zena?"

She could only have been gone less than a minute. We all rushed out and there she was, floating spread-eagled and face down. I can see it as clearly as if it had happened yesterday. Geoff dived in and fished her out and laid her, limp and unresponsive, on the dining room table. Mary had been a casualty sister and started CPR and, thank God, within a couple of tortured minutes, Zena began to cough, throw up, and come back to life. Francie said, "Mary, you are a saint." They took Zena to a hospital for a check-up and made sure that there was no incipient infection from water in her lungs, but she was well enough to travel to Italy with her parents two days later. You may be sure that a nylon net was installed around the houseboat forthwith. Jackie started to get mobile only a few weeks following this near-tragedy, and she spent quite a lot of time on a leash like a small dog! Nicky was born the following spring, in March of 1966.

Things were now going well at the yard, and the GB programme went from strength to strength. We actually began to know what we were doing and these two factors turned around the company's fortunes. Changes were also taking place to the environment around the yard. A road was built from where we normally had to leave our vehicles, down to Hang Hau village, and thence through a cut in the hill behind the yard and on around the corner to where HK Oxygen built a facility. We no longer had to rely on a boat to bring supplies, workers and ourselves to the yard, which greatly simplified things.

The summer of 1966 did not bring any typhoons—just one tropical storm called Lola. However, you do not need a tropical storm to bring catastrophic weather problems—a line of thunderstorms will do very nicely. I awoke on the morning of Sunday, June 12th, 1966, to the sound of torrential rain drumming on the houseboat roof. I looked across at the marina to see numerous boats on the point of sinking. I threw on some clothes and ran across to the marina.

We had a watchman who was supposed to keep an eye on things during the night. Seeing no sign of him, I ran up to the office and found him fast asleep on a trestle bed. I was so angry that I just tipped him off onto the floor. We dashed down to the marina floats with buckets and started bailing boats. So many were on the point of sinking that all we could do was to take a couple of buckets out of each one and then run to the next boat. Despite our best efforts, boats were sinking all around us one after another. One boat, that I had noticed on a mooring, looked just a little heavy and had completely disappeared when I next looked up a couple of minutes later. Subsequent investigation showed that once the faulty toilet discharge fitting had gone under water, it leaked so badly that it took the boat down in a couple of minutes. The rain fell with such intensity that it was like standing under a waterfall. 382 millimetres (15 inches) fell that day, with 157 millimetres (6 inches) coming down in one hour—that is 1 inch in just 10 minutes. The damage on HK Island was incredible. The steep streets turned into rivers as water poured off the Peak. The raging torrents picked up parked cars, dumping them as piles of wreckage at the foot of each street. Water as deep as two feet poured into the harbour for hours over the entire length of the unencumbered north side of the island.

During another rain storm I was driving to work and came to a spot where the water was running down the road like a river. The water was peeling off the top layer of the road surface so that slabs of tarmac 3inches thick were being torn up and swept down the road. I got out of my VW with my traditional paper umbrella and the force of the downpour beat it to death, leaving me holding a few slivers of bamboo and tatters of oiled paper.

There were other accidents and tragedies at the marina. Once, a group of small children were leaning against the wooden picket fence that lined the edge of the upper level of the marina where the office and small café were located. It suddenly gave way under their combined weight and one little girl fell about 10 feet to the concrete below. She had been holding a Coke bottle, which broke, and she lost an eye. The following day I was down at the marina, replacing the fence with a steel railing and not feeling too good about what had happened. Somebody said caustically, "Closing the stable door?" I just replied that there were still plenty of horses around.

On another occasion when the marina was very busy, a small child was missed by his mother. A search was initiated and, when the child couldn't be found, the police sent out a search crew. An hour later one of the divers emerged from the water with a small limp body—another scene that haunts me to this day. He had been playing by the slipway where the boats were launched and probably went off the end at low tide and drowned unnoticed. It only takes a second, and every parent needs to be vigilant. It must be dreadfully hard to recover from an incident like that.

Chapter 5

Summer 1966 to November 1969

Life in Hong Kong. Riots!

Serious riots strike Hong Kong and affect the boatyard. I take up movie making as a hobby. I visit America for the first time and spend time at the new facility in Singapore. My daughter Nicky is born.

Meanwhile, momentous political events taking place in China were about to have a major effect on life in Hong Kong and for us at the boat yard. We were very busy and had been hiring workers—mainly carpenters—at a prodigious rate. Mao Tse Tung had started the madness of the proletarian cultural revolution in the spring of 1966, and the mayhem spilled over into Hong Kong one year later in the form of riots and protests in the streets. Communist-supporting trades unions were political organizations which cared nothing for the welfare of their members. The Carpenters Union was one of these, and they targeted American Marine for action—partly because we employed very large numbers of carpenters and partly because of the name of the company.

One morning I came to work and was told by some of the workers that some kind of confrontation was planned for three o'clock that afternoon. When three o'clock came around I made sure that I was out in the yard, and sure enough—bang on three o'clock, drawers and lockers were opened and out came hundreds of what later came to be known as "inflammatory posters". These were mostly written in Chinese and had messages like "Blood debts will be repaid in blood" and "Yellow-skinned Running Dogs"—referring to Chinese who cooperated with the authorities.

I grabbed one end of a roll of posters from one young guy in the metal shop, but he hung onto the other end, and we had this tug of war until I realized that this was completely ridiculous. So I let go and returned to my desk in the Production Office to await events.

In due course a deputation showed up with their five "demands". This was standard operating procedure. A translator was needed but my Number 1 Chinese had disappeared because he feared for the safety of himself and his family. Fortunately, my Number 2 was made of sterner stuff,

The first demand was that we were not to inform the police. I told them that it was too late for that, as their security had been so bad that we knew in advance of their actions and I had already informed the police that morning. The second demand was that the posters, which were now up on the walls all over the yard, were not to be removed and if we did remove one then we would have to put up two in its place. I told them that it was our factory and we would take them down as and when we felt so inclined. I don't remember what the other demands were, but they were some kind of similar nonsense.

The following day we were short about 80 people from the work force of several hundred. These had been the trouble makers from previous day. Work proceeded normally in the yard and we were under great pressure to get boats out by the June 30th deadline, especially a 50-footer that had to go to St. Croix in the American Virgin Islands. This was an expensive boat for the time, and if it finished up on the wrong side of the balance sheet at the end of the month it would have a seriously detrimental effect on the company's financial figures, which would get us into trouble with the bank. For this reason, we left up all the posters, much to the disgust of the security guards who were staunch nationalists—supporters of the anti-communist Kuomintang led by Chiang Kai Shek in Taiwan.

A few days later, I came to work and here were all these 80 guys sitting in a group each with a copy of Mao's little red book, chanting his sayings in unison. It was quite bizarre because other workers ignored them entirely and went on working right alongside them as if they did not exist. We informed the police but told them that we didn't want any kind of a confrontation within the yard because of the damage that might be caused.

At lunchtime, this group all got up and marched down the road into Hang Hau village. We were delighted to see this, and they made it even easier for us when they returned to the yard after the lunch break was over and we had the gates closed with a police Land Rover parked within the gates. The group, I shall call them the Maoists, then sat on the hillside in the hot sun and continued their chanting. They had glass bottles of soft drinks with them.

Fifteen minutes before quitting time at 5 p.m., the Maoists got up en masse and stood across the closed gates. The police anticipated that they were about to block the exit, but the Maoists just had another chant before marching up the hill to the open area around the corner where the trucks were parked. They all had their empty bottles with them, which surprised me, as littering was very common in HK and this didn't seem a likely bunch to be good citizens.

I jumped on my motorcycle and followed them at a distance to see what they were up to. Dave said he would come with me, and we rode up the slope and around the corner to see the group boarding two specific trucks among all the others that were waiting to take our workers back into Kowloon. I wanted to get the registration numbers for the police to radio into their HQ, so I parked the motorcycle and very rashly walked towards the trucks and started to write down the numbers. It was only now I realized the real reason why the bottles had been retained by the Maoists. They were intended as missiles, along with the stones they had collected and were now passing into the trucks. Some of them saw what I was doing and started running towards me. One of them tried to prise open the hand in which I had the piece of paper. Strangely, I did not feel the slightest hint of fear. In fact, I felt more annoyed than anything else (the Churchillian phrase came to mind: "What kind of people do they think we are?"), but it belatedly came to me that I was doing a Very Stupid Thing and, discretion being the better part of valour, the right course of action was to Run Away.

Dave said, "I'll hold them off while you get the motorcycle."

I said "Bugger the bike!"

We started to run, followed by a hail of rocks and bottles. By this time, the rest of the workers had left work and were coming towards us on their way to their transport. When they saw what was happening, they picked up the spent missiles from our attackers and threw them back so now we found ourselves in the middle of the crossfire! Fortunately, no one was hit, and the Maoists were summoned back to their vehicles so they could get underway.

I had hung onto the registration numbers of the trucks and gave them to the police, who radioed them into their HQ in Kowloon. Within minutes a couple of truckloads of riot police left their barracks and were headed in our direction.

The road between the yard and Kowloon was about 6 miles and wound through steep hills with no turnoffs. I envisaged a splendid pitched battle on the road when these two groups met, and this was something that could not be missed. So I jumped back on my bike and headed after the Maoists. Sadly, from my point of view, they reached the end of the road, where it disappeared into a maze of streets, just seconds ahead of the police, so there was no battle. Of course we had the names, addresses and photographs of all these people on file, and we handed these over to the police. They staked out their homes, but none of them returned home that night.

A few days after the incident at the yard, the police raided the headquarters of the carpenters' union in Kowloon, which was situated in a three-story building in the middle of a row of similar buildings. When the police tried to make entry, they were faced with steel doors and a barrage of missiles, including bottles of acid. They finally got in through holes they bashed through the dividing walls from the adjacent buildings, but it took them nearly seven hours to make entry!

There probably wasn't any real personal danger, especially out in the New Territories, but after the incident at the yard I was an easily identified individual and you are pretty vulnerable on a motorcycle, so for the next few weeks I armed myself with a water pistol filled with ammonia.

Back at the yard we worked frantically to finish work on the big boat. Pulling many overnight sessions, we put an incredible 36,000 man-hours into it in just one month. Finally, it was done, and the boat departed close to midnight on June 30th. As soon as it left, I went around the yard and started ripping down posters. When they saw what I was up to, the security guards enthusiastically joined in with delighted cries of, *"Ho! Ho! Ho!"* ("Good! Good! Good!") We had another three months to go before the next deadline, so we had some breathing space and could afford a bit of disruption.

But we were not yet out of the woods financially because the Letter of Credit for the boat expired at the end of the month, and we had already passed that date. The Nedlloyd ship carrying the boat was called *Neder Eems,* and she was anchored at the western end of HK harbour. The document that triggers the Letter of Credit is the Mate's Receipt, which is given to the shipper by the ship's first mate as proof that the boat has been safely loaded on board. For some reason I have never been able to understand, the first mate had agreed to give us the receipt before he had even seen our boat! This vital document was already in the hands of the bank. We had met the deadline on paper—now we had to make it a reality!

It was a long tow to the ship, and I was on board *Neder Eems* when our boat was being hoisted on board using the ship's derricks. The closer the boat came up to the rail, the more I was sure there was no way it was going to fit! The crew brought it inboard and started to lower it onto the deck. It began to lo ok as though the boat itself might just squeeze in, but a couple of frames and brackets on the ship obstructed the cradle. After looking at the situation, the mate summoned a welder and, in a shower of sparks, the obstructions were cut away. Against all odds, we had made the deadline! Ironically, we had the next boat of this size completed three months later when *Neder Eems* returned to HK. This time we knew it would fit because the brackets had never been replaced!

Riots continued in Hong Kong for the whole of the summer of 1967. The rioters planted bombs in the streets—some real and some fakes, but they all had to be treated as if they were the real thing, which caused enormous disruption. The rioters taunted the police and stuck fingers in their eyes. They would wrap themselves up with bandages red with fake blood, take photos, then accuse the police of atrocities. For a long time, the police held off taking action, until it was demanded by the public who were fed up with having their lives turned upside down. Through this tactic, the police got the public on their side and had their full support when they did act. There were some humorous incidents when huge loudspeakers erected on the Bank of China building in the central district blasted revolutionary music and communist slogans, which were countered by even larger speakers, installed on the adjacent Hong Kong Shanghai Bank building, blasting Western classical music.

For a while there were serious concerns that China was going to invade HK and take the territory back thirty years before the treaty expired. Matters came to a head on September 8th at a place called Sha Tau Kok, where the border ran down the middle of the main street. The police station was put under siege and came under fire from local Chinese militia, killing five HK policemen. An armoured column of Gurkhas, the tough Nepalese troops in the British Army, was moved up to the border, and the situation began to look quite ominous. Then the local Chinese militia were withdrawn and replaced by national troops, which showed that the central Chinese government under Zhou En Lai had no intention of invading Hong Kong. The riots finally came to an end in October 1967, when Zhou En Lai told the leftists in Hong Kong to cease their activities and China stopped funding their operations.

Despite all these problems, things were progressing at the yard. Some new designs were introduced, including the Magellan centre-cockpit motorsailer, starting in 1965. The GB was becoming very successful but no one really knew how long it would last, so an alternative design named the Alaskan was introduced in 1967. The first boat was a 46, designed by De Fever in San Diego. Unlike the Grand Banks, this boat had no aft cabin or flying bridge, but a pilothouse and a salon that opened onto a small aft deck. The boat was quite popular but not very good looking.

You would think that all these activities both at home and at work would have been enough to keep me more than fully occupied, but I wanted to find a new hobby and I remember my thought process in choosing it. I had been interested in photography ever since I was about 12 years old, but I was looking for something beyond that. This was well before the days of amateur video, so I thought about film. This would still involve photography, but would extend into being able tell a story, manipulate time, create titles, and introduce music and other aspects of audio. In fact, it offered enormous scope for taking it as far as I wanted to go. I joined the HK Cine Club and read a few books, so I was able to avoid the worst excesses of amateur film making—such as excessive zooming and waving the camera around in a manner known as "hose-piping". I also made the decision to film in the more expensive 16mm format rather than 8mm, even if the extra cost meant shooting less film. I realized that to get any watchable result would require hours of editing and working on audio, etc., and I did not want to invest all that effort into a small, amateur format that would result in a technically inferior standard that did not justify the amount of work that went in to it. I bought a used 16mm Bolex camera from one of the club members and subsequently acquired all the gear, lenses and tripods to allow me to film and edit the result. I did, however, shoot at 18 frames per second instead of the professional 24 fps in order to make the film run a bit longer. Each roll of film was 100 feet, and each foot had 40 frames. At 18 fps it ran for 3¾ minutes, and at 24 fps for 2¾ minutes. After that you had to open the camera, remove the film, and thread a new one. The camera was clockwork and there was no audio.

I continued to race dinghies at the Yacht Club, and the same group of us who had introduced the Enterprise dinghies hankered over higher performance boats. We selected the 505 class and imported from the UK a bunch of fibreglass hulls nested together to be assembled into completed racing dinghies. Mine was the bottom hull in the nest, and the small keelson had been crushed during transit. I was not too concerned as I had the facilities of a boatyard at my disposal, so it was less of a problem for me that it would have been for any of the others.

I did everything I could think of to save every ounce of weight on the boat to make it as fast as possible. I installed a locking arrangement at the top of the mast to hold up the mainsail to reduce the compression forces in the mast. Unfortunately, this also made the sail much more difficult to lower in an emergency. Alas, all these modifications did not overcome my mediocre skill, which kept me out of the top tier. Bill Russell was my crew and a bit on the clumsy side, so between us we did not do very well. The foredeck of the 505 had a sensuous double curve sloped down toward the bow and was finished like a grand piano. Bill was stretched out full length on it, trying to free the spinnaker from the forestay, when the boat hit a small chop and he slid slowly but inevitably headfirst over the bow. The boat ran right over the top of him and I grabbed him by the collar and hauled him aboard as he surfaced by the rudder.

Bill wore a wedding ring, which can be quite hazardous for an active man. I have heard of several cases where fingers have been lost by, for example, the ring causing a short circuit when coming into contact with electricity. In Bill's case the ring got caught on the boom end of the main sheet while I was hauling it in. The main sheet on the 505 has a purchase of 6:1, meaning that the force being applied by the helmsman is magnified six times at the other end of the line, thus 60 pounds of pull becomes 360 pounds. Bill's yelling alerted me in time before his finger parted from his hand.

I was always hesitant to use the spinnaker, which is the lightweight colourful sail you see ballooning out in front of a sailboat. There is nothing like a spinnaker for getting you into real trouble in short order. There was a major race in Hong Kong called the RNVR Trophy, which was a round trip from the HK Yacht Club to Lantau Island, a distance of about 28 miles. It was held in the winter so it could be quite cold. The race is open to all sizes of boats on a handicap basis. Bill and I were manoeuvring before the start, and seeing other boats flying their spinnakers, I decided we had better have a go at hoisting our own. I guess it took no more than 30 seconds before we capsized. A huge, unwieldy sailing junk gallantly tried to come to our rescue, but we were OK and I waved him away, afraid that he was going to smash us into the fibreglass equivalent of matchwood. We were soon upright and sailing again, but we were soaking wet and had lost all our victuals for the whole day before we had even crossed the starting line.

We carried on but I had firmly decided no more spinnakers. However, all the other boats pulled away from us with such alacrity that I relented and we tried again—this time successfully. We were almost at our farthest point from home when we capsized a second time. As I ran downwind to drain the water from the boat, a guy came over in a rubber dinghy and shouted that the finish line was in the opposite direction. At this point—cold, hungry and freshly soaked—that was the last thing of interest and we went home!

The Newtons had a small sloop called *Puhio,* which is Hawaiian for "fart". I crewed for them a few times and, on one occasion, we had a moment of drama also triggered by a misbehaving spinnaker. The sail had wrapped its centre around the forestay so that sections of the sail both above and below the wrap were filled by the wind. This hour-glass situation is a not uncommon event and one which makes it almost impossible to drop the sail. Whit elected to go to the top of the mast to release the halyard. Once up there, his weight at the top of the mast caused the boat to roll back and forth uncontrollably through at least 90 degrees, with Whit clinging on for dear life like a monkey on a stick.

In March 1968, the well-known American yachtsman Carleton Mitchell bought a GB 42, and he came to Hong Kong to see it built. This was his first powerboat after many years of sail, during which he had taken part in and won many high-profile sailboat races in yachts such as *Finisterre.* I worked with him on the construction of his boat, and he wrote about his experience in his book *The Winds Call:*

"She changed so fast during the early stages that more than once I suspected hulls had been switched while my back was turned. Many items were prefabricated. When assembled at the boat, an astonishing number of jobs could be going forward at once, because an unbelievable number of Chinese could work in a small space at the same time. One day, when the lunch gong sounded, I counted 36 coming down the ladders, and felt I had missed a few: certainly when I was aboard earlier there had been a man for every foot of length! Modifications discussed one morning were usually completed the next, and I was as satisfied with the craftsmanship as with the progress. Now as Sans Terre *responded to my touch on the helm, I felt the same kinship and trust I had enjoyed with my previous boats."*

Carleton Mitchell's 42 was shipped to southern California, and he later took it to the U.S. East Coast by way of the Galapagos Islands and the Panama Canal—a trip I was to make in a Fleming 65 some 38 years later.

Daughter Jackie spent her early years growing up on the houseboat. One day I came home and there was a long line of stuffed toys stretching out on the water away from the houseboat. "Teddy swimming" she said, pointing to the nearest one. On another occasion she threw the car keys over the side. Fortunately, I was right there when she did it, and I grabbed a nearby bamboo pole and plunged it into the centre of the rings, expanding out from the spot where the keys had hit the water. I dived in, followed the pole down, and found the keys right at the bottom.

In May 1968, we took a second long leave in England with two little girls now aged two and four. This time we did not descend on my mother but stayed nearby in an old coaching inn called the White Hart, which had been a hostelry for 500 continuous years. It was spring, with beautiful cherry blossoms, and it was a much more relaxed leave than on the previous occasion.

One morning we had been listening on the radio to the account of Robert Kennedy's nomination at the Ambassador Hotel in Los Angeles, and I took the kids down to breakfast. When Mary came down five minutes later she said, "They shot him!". It was scarcely believable. First President Kennedy, then Martin Luther King, and now Robert Kennedy. In America, it seemed, if you disagreed with someone, you simply shot him.

Coincidentally, it was just two weeks later that I paid my maiden visit to the U.S. John Newton met me in Baltimore, and I remember my first experience of ordering breakfast in America. The initial surprise was that we went to the drugstore. A drugstore for breakfast? Well, that's the way it was back then. Then came the long list of questions that even today leaves foreigners bemused. Just take the matter of eggs: poached, scrambled, or fried? If fried: well done, over easy, or sunny side? Hash browns? Bread? Brown, white, or English muffin (which they have never heard of in England). Tea or coffee? Cream and sugar? Gasp!

John took me to see the Egg Harbor boat plant, and then we drove up to Atlantic City and on to New York, where we visited Higgs, our boat dealer. I remember how hot and humid it was and how conversation was interrupted every couple of minutes by aircraft flying into La Guardia. From there we drove north to Hartford, Connecticut, and I saw one of our boats from which most of the paint had fallen off the hull to reveal bare wood. This was because, on the earlier boats, the painters had applied a thick coat of white filler to the hull prior to painting, a bit like icing a cake. The filler was later penetrated by water, which froze in the winter time, causing the filler to break away from the hull. We still had a lot to learn.

I was in California for the 4th of July 1968 and then back to Hong Kong one week later, having completed my first circumnavigation of the world.

The riots caused a loss of confidence in the stability of Hong Kong and brought about major changes for American Marine. The Hong Kong yard was situated at the base of a steep hill, and we were running out of space needed for increased production. At the same time Singapore was offering generous incentives for companies to invest. Whit went to visit the Economic

Development Board in Singapore, and the Newtons decided to build a second yard there. Funding for the Singapore plant was provided by the HK yard where, apart from three different sizes of Grand Banks, the company was now also building the Alaskan 49, 53, and 55, the Admiralty 50 motorsailer, the Magellan centre-cockpit motorsailer, and Calkin 50 sailboats in various configurations. The last two were built using a construction method known as strip planking, in which thin strips of mahogany were glued and edge-nailed together with bronze nails.

Also in Hong Kong, Rolly Tasker, the Australian sailmaker, had approached the Newtons about building a sail loft on the premises and one was duly constructed above one of the boatbuilding bays. The manager was a Kiwi named Neil Pryde, who later took over the business and became the world-famous maker of Neil Pryde Sails.

For superstitious reasons we never built any boat with hull number 13, which meant that any hull designated no. 14 was in reality no. 13. Maybe there *is* something in this, because during the construction of Magellan no. 13 (labelled no. 14), someone knocked over a can of thinners in the cockpit, which started a fire right under the sail loft. Fortunately, this was contained, but not before it did considerable damage to the boat. This was repaired, the boat completed and shipped to California. The very first weekend she was taken out by her new owner, the fog came down and she missed the entrance to Newport Beach harbour, went aground on the beach, and was declared a total loss.

John Newton, who by this time had moved with his family to California, told me that his goal was for American Marine to have a range of boats which would meet the boating needs of anyone and to have a service centre within one day's sailing of all the major boating areas in the world. With this in mind, the company had taken on an in-house naval architect in California named Bob Dorris. The Newtons wanted to expand the number of models in the Alaskan range, and they commissioned Bob to design a 49 and then a 53 and finally, a 55. Bob had an artistic eye, and these boats were much better looking than the original Alaskan 46. He also designed an Alaskan 45, which was basically a GB 42 hull with an extended and flared bow. John also wanted to add a fast powerboat with a deep "V" hull to the range of boats offered by American Marine, and Bob was tasked with designing this boat, which was very different from those we had been building.

This project had been on John's wish list for some time, and he and I had visited a designer in the English midlands a couple of years earlier. My first domestic flight in England was when we flew from London to Birmingham to meet him. Very early one morning we were sitting in this turbo-prop aircraft, waiting to take off from Heathrow, when it became apparent that the engines did not want to start. An electrician came aboard, followed a few minutes later by another who looked a bit more senior. In due course he was followed by someone even further up the ladder, and they all disappeared into the cockpit. Suddenly the prop blades started to rotate, and the technicians hustled back down the aisle to disembark. As they passed my seat, one said to another "What did you do?"

"I dunno, mate," came the reply, "It just started!"

With that they got off the plane, the door was closed and away we went!

Nothing came of that visit, but now the design had been handed over to Bob Dorris. This boat was also to be the first to be built in fibreglass by American Marine. For those not familiar with the process of building in fibreglass, it starts with building a wooden hull called a "plug". Over this is made a fibreglass mould which is used to produce "parts". It is from these parts that the actual boat is constructed. For this project it was decided that the plug would be built upside down in Hong Kong, and the production boat would be built in the new factory in Singapore. It was also decided to launch the hull in Hong Kong with engines installed, so that the design could be tested. This all went ahead with the hull being built under the new sail loft. This caused a problem because the hull could not be launched upside down, and there was insufficient space above it for any kind of lifting device to turn it over. It was left to me to come up with a solution. I had the metal shop come up with two large steel hoops which encircled the hull and were attached to it in a few places. We then arranged some simple rollers on brackets which were fixed to the ground. As the hoops rotated in the rollers, the hull was turned on its axis in a few minutes—although the preparation had taken some time.

The engines, running gear and steering were then installed, and the boat was launched. She ran around 30 knots, which seemed pretty good to me, but then Bob Conn, an engine specialist from the U.S., took one look at the pyrometers and boost gauges and commented that the engines were not doing a lick of work! Since I didn't know how to interpret the gauge readings, this was a surprise to me! The boat was then hauled, and Bob attacked the trailing edges of the prop blades with a hammer, curling them over slightly in a process known as "cupping", which only took him a couple of hours. The boat was re-launched and, much to my amazement, had picked up almost seven knots in speed.

The hull remained in the water, without any form of anti-fouling paint, for about one week while other adjustments were made. We ran it again, and I was shocked to see that she had lost five knots while the load on the engines remained the same. Bob had already returned home, and the loss of speed was a complete mystery to me. We hauled the boat and all seemed well, but I noticed that the bottom was looking a little grubby. I ran my hand over it and it felt just the slightest bit rough. I thought that this probably had nothing to do with the problem but we might as well clean the bottom. This was done, the boat launched, and she was back up to speed. Through this I learned that the smallest amount of growth not only increases drag but enlarges the area of the wetted surface by a phenomenal amount.

We also built a full-size mock up for the boat's interior that was complete right down to the upholstery. This enabled us to refine the design before construction started on the actual boat. Ultimately this wood plug was shipped to Singapore where, later in these pages, we will pick up the story.

We moved off the houseboat in 1968. The kids were getting older and Jackie was starting at kindergarten. We moved to Taoloo Villas, a small, two-storey apartment block along Clearwater Bay Road, on the hill overlooking Junk Bay. There were only six apartments in the block. I was able to buy my first-ever new car—a Toyota Corolla, just 18 months after that model first came on the market. One week later, when the Corolla was parked in a carport outside our ground-floor apartment, typhoon Shirley paid us a direct hit on the day after my birthday. The folks upstairs had recently had the glass re-puttied in all their windows. The storm sucked the glass out of all the upstairs windows, blew the shards around the car park, and scarred every single panel on my nice new car! That typhoon also demonstrated how an errant sheet of newspaper can blow up against a sturdy chain link fence and bring it down with the force of the wind.

During the summer months the prevailing weather came from the direction of the Philippines, across the South China Sea, making the climate hot and sticky. During the winter months it frequently reversed direction and came in, sometimes with considerable force, as the Northeast monsoon. One such event had been forecast during November, and I remember sitting outside one evening, gently perspiring, when I felt the first tentative gusts of the monsoon. Within one hour the temperature had dropped 20 degrees and I was looking for a jacket. I remember thinking how much energy this change represented. Here were hundreds of thousands of square miles being air conditioned in a few minutes, compared with how much power it took to cool down even one room with an air-conditioner.

I came home from work one day and Mary told me that Pooch had been struck by a car and killed when he ran across the road after a bitch in heat. He had been such a good dog and it was very sad. Another case of a male being done in by following his dick. I sorrowfully buried him in the garden.

Shipbreakers had moved in along the shoreline between the boat yard and Hang Hau village. Large freighters were brought in past the yard and grounded on the shore, where they were dismantled and picked apart. The steel plates were chopped up and turned into reinforcing bars in a rolling mill on the premises. It was a dirty, noisy, and, as it turned out, a dangerous operation. One morning there was a tremendous explosion that shook down the false ceiling and light fittings in the office. Within a few moments, the ship on which demolition work had just started was aflame from one end to the other. Workers at the seaward end of the ship were jumping into the water and swimming for their lives. These people were fished out by sampans from the village and by our own staff, although we did not have many small craft really suitable for this purpose. The worst tragedy to witness was a couple of workers trapped on top of the mast who had no means of escape and who were slowly roasted to death. The fire was so intense that its radiant heat began to heat up the dark varnish on the boats at our jetty, several hundred yards from the blaze, and we had to tow the boats further away.

Book 5
SINGAPORE

Malaysia

TURBULENT TIMES

Singapore

1969 – 1985

Chapter 1

June 1969 to November 1969

Introduction to Singapore and Malaysia

I describe life in Singapore after we move there from Hong Kong. We visit Bombay and Kenya, where I climb Mount Kenya. The boatyard is introduced to fibreglass. I take up flying lessons and we visit Malaysia.

Aside from our brief stop en route to Perth in 1965, our first real visit to Singapore was in June of 1969. As we stepped off the plane, the heat hit me like a wall, and I thought I must have walked into the jet blast from another aircraft.

Away from the airport, the overwhelming impression was of lush tropical vegetation and exotic flowering shrubs. The skies were filled with towering cumulous clouds which, on most afternoons, exploded in dramatic thunderstorms releasing sheets of torrential rain. Before you knew better, you welcomed these in anticipation of relief from the sweltering temperatures, but they soon passed and then steam arose from glistening streets, lifting the humidity off the scale. We were now only one degree from the Equator and in the very heart of the tropics.

Singapore Island is about the size and shape of the Isle of Wight. It even has similar geography but turned upside down, so that the River Medina in the north of the Isle of Wight is matched in Singapore by the Singapore River in the south. The population of the Isle of Wight is around 125,000 while that of Singapore in 1980 was about 2.5 million, although it has doubled in the 30 years since then. Singapore island is held like a gemstone in the claw-like tip of the Malay Peninsula, from which it is separated by the Johore Strait.

This was the first ex-colony I had visited, and I was mildly apprehensive as to how the inhabitants would treat someone from the ex-colonial power. But I need not have been concerned; I was received with great friendliness. Britain seems to have departed most of its colonies leaving surprising amounts of goodwill among the majority of their citizens.

As this part of my story covers living and working in Singapore for 17 years, I will include a short account of Singapore's history to provide context for the events which follow.

Singapore was little more than a muddy island at the foot of the Malay Peninsula when Stamford Raffles, employed by the British East India Company, recognized its potential. In 1819, he signed an agreement with the Sultan of Johore to set up a trading station to compete with the Dutch, who at the time enjoyed a monopoly on trade in the region. Within a few years, Singapore had become a hugely successful trading hub and home to a mix of Europeans, Malays and Tamils, as well as many Chinese immigrants who soon made up the majority of the population. It was designated a Crown Colony of Britain in 1867 and continued to grow in peace and prosperity.

This all changed in February 1942 when fortress Singapore, with its huge naval base, fell with minimal fighting to the Japanese, who invaded the island from the Malay peninsula, supposedly riding through the jungle on British-made bicycles, while the massive guns defending Singapore were all pointing out to sea, from whence an invasion had been expected to come. After the war was over Singapore reverted to Britain, but colonial powers had lost credibility with local people, who started agitating for more control of their affairs. Singapore became part of the Federation of Malaya in 1948, at which time the Communist Party of Malaya attempted a forceful takeover of Malaya and Singapore. A state of emergency was declared which lasted for 12 years. In a unique outcome, the insurgents were defeated by British special forces, who adopted similar guerrilla techniques to their adversaries, rather than by attacking them with massive conventional force as was later done in Vietnam.

The country of Malaya, which included Singapore, obtained

full independence from Britain in September 1963 under the leadership of the Malay prime minister, Tunku Abdul Rahman, who introduced a set of Bumiputra ("sons of the soil") laws which favoured indigenous Malays. Chinese made up around 45 percent of the population on the Malay peninsula, but in Singapore it was 96 percent, and the new regulations did not go down well. The resulting friction caused Singapore to be kicked out of Malaysia in August 1965, with the confident expectation on the Malay side that, lacking any natural resources, it would have to come crawling back. They had reckoned without the determination and leadership of Lee Kuan Yew, who set out to forge a viable nation from a disparate group of immigrants of mixed racial origin, each of whom had emotional ties to their mother countries.

His challenge was to create a sense of national identity and provide jobs for this diverse population, of which 50 percent were below the age of 16. To add to his problem, the British government chose this moment to conclude that it made no sense to spend nine million pounds per year to cut the grass and sweep up leaves at its now redundant army and navy bases. Accordingly, they decided to close them down -- releasing hundreds more people into the labour market, as well as depriving the local economy of tons of money which had been used to pay for food and services.

One of the strategies adopted by the Singapore government to solve these problems was the introduction of a massive industrialization programme, using tax and other incentives, to encourage investment in the fledgling country. It worked, and it was the reason why the Newtons built the yard and why I now found myself in Singapore.

On this initial visit we stayed at the Goodwood Park Hotel, which was very nice and had a swimming pool. Nicky was now three years old and one guest told us that she was very chatty and had told him all about our family history. Meanwhile, I went to the yard every day. It was certainly very different from the cramped location we had in HK. The Singapore government may have been generous with incentives, but they mandated strictly enforced codes on the quality of construction and the facilities to be provided to the work force.

The new yard was on a 13-acre site in the newly developed Jurong Industrial Estate. A Singaporean Eurasian manager had been appointed and workers employed, so that, as soon as the roof of the first building was up and the power switched on, work started on the building the first boats. The factory had its official opening on November 23, 1969.

The yard was built on the shores of the Jurong River. In the early days, huge sailing craft from Indonesia would enter the river from Indonesia. These boats had no engines or any sort of mechanical power, and the heavy sails had to be raised by the crew stripped to the waist and turning a windlass—pulling on its spokes with both hands, then using feet to hold it while they transferred their grip to the next spoke -- all the while chanting a shanty. Over the years it became polluted to the extent that hydrogen sulphide bubbling up from its murky depths would turn bronze fittings pitch black within three days.

Starting a new manufacturing facility from scratch anywhere is a tremendous undertaking. A factory is basically just a bunch of buildings and equipment which produce absolutely nothing until there are people present to turn them to good use. Initially, everybody is new, and nobody knows one another or how things are done. At quitting time, when everybody goes home, everything stops until the people return the following morning.

By the time of my visit, the new yard was already producing boats. On the face of it things were going well, but they kept running short of wood, screws, and other materials. I was sent down to take a look. It took me less than five minutes to spot the problem. There were far too many boats under construction to justify the number of boats being turned out. If you are completing a boat every six days and it takes 24 days to assemble a boat, then you should have four boats in the line, and you should be able to say that in six days' time this particular boat should be at the stage of the next boat in the line ahead of it. Instead, they had about 10 boats under build, with far too many in the early stages of construction. In other words, the beginning of the line—being relatively simple—was running faster than the latter stages, using up materials ahead of time and tying up money in work in progress.

After this initial short visit, we returned briefly to HK and left for our next family holiday before I settled in for serious work in Singapore. We flew to Bombay, where we spent a few days before flying on to Kenya. After a couple of days, we flew across the Indian Ocean to Nairobi and then Mombasa, where, at Silverstrand Beach, we stayed in a *banda* (a small palm-roofed cottage) right on the beach near Bamburi, just up the coast north of Mombasa. We enjoyed a relaxed time with Jackie now almost 5 and Nicky now 3½. We swam every day and admired the beautiful coral and tropical fish on the reef. We rented a VW Beetle and, after about one week, we drove up to Nairobi. On the way we passed through Tsavo National Park and stayed at Voi. We saw a very large elephant at the edge of the road and I stopped and got out of the car to film it. It clearly wasn't too pleased about this and started across the road toward us, making threatening gestures, so I threw the camera to Mary in the car and beat a hasty retreat. There had been stories about people in an open sports car who had blown the horn at an elephant that was obstructing the road and had had their car stomped on and their vehicle torn apart. As I recall, they had not survived the confrontation, although if that were the case, I don't know how anyone knew about the horn unless it was witnessed by others.

After a stop in Nairobi and a visit to Nairobi National Park, situated just 7 kilometres from the centre of the city. There was much wildlife to be seen, including a baboon that rode with us for some way, sitting on the bonnet of the car just forward of the windshield. We then drove up to stay with my father at Timau on the slopes of Mount Kenya.

I had always been fascinated with this great mountain, which was the dominant feature overlooking the farm. There had been a prisoner of war camp in nearby Nanyuki during WWII which housed Italians rounded up in Ethiopia. Three of them had escaped from the camp with the sole intention of climbing the mountain. They had a rough time of it and almost died in their attempt to climb the highest peak. After their ordeal they broke back into the camp! Their leader wrote a book called *No Picnic on Mt. Kenya*, still available on Amazon!

I decided I should have a go at climbing the mountain, which is a defunct volcano with three peaks. The two highest, Nelion (17,021 feet) and Batian (17,057 feet) require serious alpine climbing skills, but the third-highest, Point Lenana (16,355 feet), simply required stamina to get to the top. While my family stayed with my father, I joined a group with about 10 others and set off from Naro Moru River Lodge situated 6,500 feet above sea level. We were a mixed bunch, varying in age from teenagers to men in their forties. I was 34 and had come straight from living at sea level in Singapore. I gave myself an additional handicap by lugging a 16mm movie camera with three lenses, a monopod, and rolls of film.

The first part of the climb up the Naro Moru route was through rain forest along a muddy track which was slippery with plenty of roots to trip you up. You also had to keep an eye open for elephant and buffalo, and you could smell the dung from these large and potentially dangerous animals. After about 1,000 vertical feet, we left the trees, passed through a zone of bamboo and came out onto steep, soggy ground known as the vertical bog. Putting pressure on one leg to extract the other would cause the first to sink even deeper into the glutinous mud.

This gave way to more even, open ground in the Teleki Valley, where walking became much easier. Here we were surrounded by alien-looking plants called giant groundsel and giant lobelia. These plants grow only at high altitude in the mountains of East Africa. The main peaks of the mountain now came into view and we arrived at Mackinders Camp, consisting in those days of a group of tents where there was a small tarn. At this point it started to snow, and we had a snowball fight just 12 miles from the equator. There were magnificent views over the surrounding countryside stretching into infinity far below us.

During this first day, the teenagers were leaping around like gazelles while the rest of us plodded along, gasping for breath. I had several offers to carry my camera and gear, but I turned them down because I wanted to retain easy and immediate access to them.

When evening fell, the shadows of the surrounding peaks sped like dark wings over the land, and the temperature dropped to well below freezing. You could watch the ice actually forming over the running streams. We had some kind of meal, although I cannot recall the details. With the cold and lack of oxygen at nearly 14,000 feet, I found it impossible to sleep, and I have never looked forward with such eagerness to 4 a.m., when we were scheduled to get going. Small animals called rock hyrax lived up there. They raided the tents during the night and seemed to have a special liking for chocolate!

We set off in the pre-dawn darkness and trudged to the base of the scree— a 1,500-foot steep slope consisting of loose stones, on which you slipped back two paces for every three paces you took forward. This was exhausting at the altitude of 15,000 feet and we stopped to rest, gasping for breath, after every hundred paces. The only way I could shoot any film was to keep going when the others stopped, pull the camera out of my backpack, set it up on the monopod, and film people coming towards me after their rest period and then going away from me after they passed. By the time I had put the camera away and caught up with them, they had finished their next rest stop, so I had to keep going if I did not want to fall behind. This meant that each individual sequence cost me two rest stops! It was only after I arrived back in Singapore and had the film processed, that I realized a screw had come loose from the camera, allowing light to enter the body and fog a few frames whenever the film was stationary. This meant that I lost slightly more than one second at the start of every shot, but it could have been much worse. I could have lost everything!

On the second day, old plodders like me just kept going at the same pace as the previous day, but the teenagers now suffered from altitude sickness, with headaches and vomiting. It seems that what you lose in fitness as you age is compensated to some degree by an increase in stamina.

At the top of the scree we came to the foot of the Lewis Glacier, and here we were roped up. This glacier has since receded, but when I made the climb we had mostly loose snow, with slippery areas you needed to watch out for if you were not to go tobogganing back the way you had come—hence the need for ropes. Eventually, as the clouds closed in around us, we arrived at the summit. It was marked by an ornate cross which had been given to the Consolata Mission in Nyeri by the Pope and left on the mountain on January 31, 1933, by Italian fathers from the mission.

After a brief interlude at the summit, it was downhill all the way—picking up oxygen and energy with every foot descended. I found the descent very easy, but my eyes were giving me trouble because I had picked out a relatively light pair of sunglasses at the lodge before leaving. I paid for this mistake by suffering from a mild attack of snow blindness from the sun shining on the glacier at high altitude. We made it all the way back to the lodge—a descent of 16,355 to 6,500 feet—on that last day.

I re-joined my family and, after a couple more days at the farm, we set off in the VW across the tawny plains of Kenya to the Aberdare Mountains. Along the way we encountered troops of colobus monkeys leaping from tree to tree with their flowing black and white "cloaks". We arrived at the Outspan Hotel and the famous Treetops wildlife lookout where, in February 1952, Princess Elizabeth received the news that her father had died and she learned that she was now Queen of England.

We flew back to Hong Kong on September 2nd, 1969, where I remained for one week before going back to Singapore while the family remained in Hong Kong. It was a holiday to remember, and our first to be captured on film.

I was given strict instructions not to interfere in the production side of the Singapore company. My brief was to work with Bob Dorris, who had relocated from California to Singapore to teach us how to build fibreglass boats, specifically the new Laguna 33-foot design. I spent the next six months moving back and forth between HK and Singapore while my family remained in HK.

A small admin building had been erected in which Bob and myself shared an office. The whole area where the factory had been built was on reclaimed land and fronted onto the Jurong River. On the adjacent lot was a plywood factory, which relied for its raw materials on a stream of huge logs brought in by truck from Malaysia. This was before Malaysia wised up and realized that all the profit from their trees was being made in Singapore, where the value added was in converting those trees into useful wood products. The reclaimed ground was so jelly like that whenever heavy logs were pushed off the trucks several hundred yards away, the vibrations affected our building to the extent that it would put a jiggle in a pencil line being drawn on a piece of paper!

The plug we had built and tested in Hong Kong had now arrived in the Singapore yard. It was placed, upside down, in a brand-new building that had just been erected and was not yet used for any other purpose. Under Bob's supervision, this hull plug was prepared for the making of the hull mould. This process required the surface of the plug to be brought to a high level of finish, because each and every blemish in the plug would be faithfully reproduced in the mould, and thence into every production hull. The surface of the plug was coated with filler, which was sanded using long, two-man, sanding boards to ensure that the surface was fair without any hollows in it. This was hard, laborious work, especially in the heat and humidity of Singapore.

After several weeks of work, the day came when we were ready to spray on the special red gelcoat resin which was to become the working surface of the plug. Bob stressed the importance for this next step of having an entirely clean atmosphere. The floor was wet down with water to lay the dust, and the red gelcoat was sprayed over the whole surface. It was a Sunday, and it was almost like a religious experience with a group of us watching while the priest—a.k.a. the painter—turned the grey surface red with the back and forth sweeping motion of his hand holding the spray gun. When he had finished, the tools were flushed and we reverently slid shut the doors of the building, like closing the doors on a church.

The following morning, the doors were opened and we entered expecting to see the plug with a hard scarlet finish gleaming in the morning light. Instead we saw a dull, sticky, maroon mess, indicating that the gelcoat had failed to harden. We all stood there, looking back and forth between the sorry sight and Bob, waiting

316

for his reaction. Bob was a tall, rangy guy who you could easily imagine astride a western horse wearing a cowboy hat. He smoked evil-smelling *cigarillos* similar to those Clint Eastwood favoured in spaghetti westerns.

After some moments, he gave his verdict. "We'll shoot it hot" he drawled.

This translated as spraying more gelcoat on top of the existing mess, but this second layer would contain extra catalyst with the intent of causing the first layer to kick off. The re-spray was done later that day and the following morning the doors were again slid open.

This time, both layers of gelcoat had slid down the sides of the hull, leaving pools of scarlet resin puddled onto the floor all around the perimeter of the plug. All us acolytes stood in a group looking at this latest disaster, then turned toward the master for his reaction and words of wisdom. Bob stood for a moment. Slightly stooped, he removed the *cigarillo* from his mouth.

"Fucking thing's bleeding to death", he said.

To this day I don't know what caused the problem, and I don't think that Bob was entirely sure, either. The whole mess had to be washed off with acetone and the process started over. The next time it worked OK, and the plug was brought up to a mirror finish and carefully waxed to prevent the mould from sticking to the plug. It was now time to spray the plug with black gelcoat which was going to be the all-important surface of the mould. As before, the floor was wet down and the painter went to work. He covered the whole surface and we stood admiring the result. Then I noticed a small blemish—rather like a fly entrapped in the surface. I started to point it out to ask what it was when, right before our eyes, it spread like a cancer, and in a few moments, the entire surface of the hull was crinkled so that it resembled the skin of an alligator. This all had to be blown off with compressed air and done over again with gelcoat that had not been thinned.

Three weeks later the hull mould, now glassed and reinforced with steel, was ready to be separated from the plug. We banged and heaved, bashed wedges all around the flange, and blew compressed air in between the two but it seemed that the plug and mould were permanently attached. It was beginning to look as though we would have to chop up the plug inside the mould and remove it in bits. I remembered reading somewhere that a hull would float in just a film of water and the resulting buoyancy would exert enormous force. I suggested this to Bob and so, with nothing to lose, we turned over the mould with the plug still inside it and connected water hoses to holes through which we had previously pumped air. The plug instantly broke free with a tremendous bang, leaving a couple of spots stuck to the mould, which had been the cause of the hang up. These were easily removed and at last we had a working mould from which we could make the first hull and start work on constructing the first actual boat. The hull was only the first of many moulds required for the Laguna. Other major moulds were the deck, cockpit, salon roof and the flying bridge. There was also a host of minor moulds, such as shower pans and drip pans under the engines and many more.

While all this was going on, I had made a couple of trips back to Hong Kong, including 10 days over Christmas 1969 and the New Year which followed. It had been decided that the whole family would permanently re-locate to Singapore, and arrangements were made to this effect. The actual move was made in March 1970. In the meantime, the houseboat had been sold to the Shell company and also shipped to Singapore for onward movement to Indonesia. I'd had a hard time selling it and had reduced the price. When a buyer like Shell came along, with infinitely deep pockets, I was too naive to realize that I could have asked practically anything as they wanted the accommodation right away. It was only when I told their representatives the price and saw the looks of disbelief that passed between them that I realized my mistake, but by then it was too late. They wanted some changes made, including the installation of a generator, and I was able to make up a bit on those.

During our years in Singapore we made a number of excursions up the Malay peninsula by car, boat and plane. The first of these was a drive up the east coast. If you don't like trees, don't go to Malaysia, because that is all you will see. The indigenous forest is dense tropical jungle that it is hard to penetrate and survive in without specialized knowledge. Much of this had been cleared for vast plantations of rubber and oil palm trees. Originally rubber trees came from Brazil, where they were to be found scattered individually throughout the Amazon rain forest. In 1875 a handful of seeds was smuggled to London and propagated in the Botanical Gardens at Kew. Twenty years later, rubber trees were introduced into what was then the British colony of Malaya and grown in plantations. Latex is collected from the outer bark of the trees by rubber tappers, and the rubber industry was born just in time to meet the growing needs of the industrial revolution. The oil palm was introduced into Malaya in 1910. The oil extracted from the nuts is used for soap, cooking and, more recently, bio-fuel feed stock.

Our first stop was at the small town of Mersing, where a local boat chugged us out to a small offshore island. We landed on a white sand beach, paddled in pellucid water, and sat under the shade of coconut palms. It was a delightful spot although, like every apparent paradise, it had its snag—in this case the presence of biting sand flies!

The east coast of Malaysia was quite undeveloped compared to the west. The ferries across the rivers were small and similar to those I had seen in the Congo. The sunlight had a luminous quality which I was unable to figure out, until I realized that it was caused by an absence of pollution and that the atmosphere everywhere was supposed to be this way!

We stopped at a beach where female leatherneck turtles came ashore to lay their eggs. We followed a guide onto the beach and watched while a large turtle heaved her way slowly up the soft sand and dug a hole with her flippers. It was a long, laborious task before she laid about 50 soft-shelled eggs the size and shape of ping pong balls. Once done, she had to refill the hole before making her way back to the sea, leaving caterpillar-like tracks in the sand. The authorities later dug up the eggs and moved them to a protected area. We watched newly hatched turtles paddling around in a concrete tank like little mechanical toys.

Just north of Kuantan we visited the Charah caves, located within an isolated limestone outcrop which sprouted from the

319

jungle. We were led down some steps by a monk in a saffron gown into the cave, where there was a huge reclining Buddha. Beams of sunlight penetrated the gloom through a natural opening and allowed us to look out at the green mantle of the jungle stretching as far as the eye could see.

Farther north up this coast, the local people trained a type of monkey called a short-tailed macaque to pick coconuts at the rate of 50 nuts per hour.

We also drove up the west coast to the village of Kikup, built almost entirely on stilts over the water—or mud when the tide was out. Long before we reached the village, our nostrils were assailed by the overpowering stench of shrimp paste made from fermented ground shrimp spread out to dry on the narrow plank catwalks linking the atap roofed huts which constituted the village. At first the stink was barely tolerable, but it was ultimately strong enough to overwhelm and short circuit the smelling sensors. Nicky lost a flip flop over the side onto the mud, and had a screaming match when we would not go down to get it.

On another occasion we flew in a couple of small Cessna aircraft up to the resort island of Lankawi Island, located off the west coast of Malaysia, north of Kuala Lumpur. I was making another attempt at learning to fly at the time, and my instructor was an Australian lady named Mary O'Brien. I was known as 7:30 Fleming because my flying lessons were all at 0730, before I went to work. I remember the first lesson because we had no sooner got seated in the plane when Mary told me to call the control tower. For some reason, a microphone scares the bejesus out of most people, and I was no exception.

"What, me?" I said.

"Who else?" Mary replied, "You're the pilot."

We would take off from Singapore's international airport— shades of Hong Kong—and then fly to a smaller airfield at Seletar. I had the usual problem of trying to understand the controller and, as in HK, it was especially vital when returning to the main airport, where big jets were flying in from all around the world. On one occasion the controller said something that sounded like "Blee-ach" and I asked Mary what he had said.

"Sounded like 'blee-ach' to me," she replied.

One day we were doing touch and go—also known as hit and run—take offs and landings at Seletar during a strong crosswind. I was attempting to fly the downwind leg in which you fly parallel to the runway in the opposite direction to which you will be landing. The downwind leg is quite busy because you have to call the tower, and the controller might not respond right away because he could be occupied with other traffic. You have to go through the pre-landing checks, which become automatic as you gain experience, but for a novice each and every one has to be remembered and executed. They follow the mnemonic "Bumpffh" (which sounds the same as the English slang word "bumph" for toilet paper or official paperwork). In this case it stands for "Brakes, Undercarriage, Mixture, Pitch, Fuel, Flaps and Harness" —all items which need to be checked prior to a safe landing. I was so preoccupied with all this that I failed to look out of the window, and when I did, the runway, which should have been slightly to my right, had completely vanished and all I could see ahead of me was endless Malaysian jungle. Where had it gone? Panic! I had drifted sideways in the crosswind and the runway was directly beneath me.

Once this was sorted, coming in on the final approach, the aircraft was being tossed around and I had trouble controlling it. To my relief, Mary took the controls. When we were about 50 feet up, a gust of wind came through a gap between two buildings and the aircraft reared upwards. Mary pushed the control yoke forward and her seat, which had not been securely latched, shot backwards, leaving her leaning forward at full stretch trying to keep the yoke from coming back.

"Take control! Take control!" she cried.

I took back control while she returned her seat forward. No harm done, but it was a timely reminder that even something as minor as a seat latch can kill you.

I never did reach the level of competence where I could be trusted to take the aircraft up on my own. I do best when I am shown what to do and then left to get on with it, but flying is not one of those activities where this approach is practical. Having a flight simulator on a computer would have been of immense help in my case, but this was way too early for that.

In the 1920s, to escape the humid heat, British colonialists developed an area called the Cameron Highlands, which rise to an altitude of 3,900 feet. This mountainous area lies in middle Malaysia, just south of the capital, Kuala Lumpur. It is now a resort area with casinos and golf courses. We drove to Ringlet Hill Station for a few days.

The area had hit the international headlines in 1967, when an American named Bill Thomson disappeared without trace while out on a walk one afternoon. He was a well-known figure credited with revitalizing the Thai silk industry. The search for him involved hundreds of people over many days but failed to produce a single clue to his disappearance. The mystery remains unsolved to this day.

We also visited the historic town of Malacca, on the West coast of Malaysia. The town had been involved in international trade since its founding in 1400 by the last Raja of Singapura (present-day Singapore). It was captured by the Portuguese in 1511, and by the Dutch in 1641, before being acquired by the British in 1842. It is a very pleasant place and evidence of its past history can still be found.

Chapter 2

November 1969 to February 1971

Life in Singapore

I set up the Engineering and Development department and battle problems with the new, high-speed fibreglass Laguna. I experience a hair-raising delivery trip down the English Channel with the first boat. We enjoy a family Christmas in England after a flight via Tashkent and Copenhagen.

Back at the yard, another major element in the building of the Laguna involved the engines. The problem with this boat was that everything was a very tight fit and the hull had a 23-degree deep V, which required a lot of horsepower to drive it through the water. At that time, there were no engines of sufficient power that would physically fit into the hull. Never being one to give up when faced with a challenge, John Newton hired a seat-of-your-pants engineer named Bob Conn from Florida to come to Singapore to marinize and build special engines based on the Caterpillar 3208. The fact that Caterpillar did not agree to this did not faze John. He simply said that we would do such a good job that Caterpillar would have no choice but to agree! Bob Conn had been involved in high-speed boats and power boat racing for many years, so was a specialist in this field. He was the guy who had come to HK and spotted that the engines were under loaded and added pitch into the props with a hammer.

Marinizing engines is not a simple job, especially when you

plan to make most of the parts yourself. For example, the casting of the exhaust manifold requires wood patterns for the outside, the inside, and for all the intricate water passages in between. These patterns are then used to make sand moulds, which have to be assembled and set up in such a way that molten metal poured into them flows into every nook and cranny without leaving pockets of air. The castings then have to be accurately machined, and American Marine built and staffed an elaborate machine shop. Every engine had to be tested, and dynamometers were set up in a test room in which the noise levels exceeded 120 decibels!

Before we had our own dynamometers, we took the first assembled engine down to a test facility run by the British Army. The engine was removed from the truck and was hanging by a strop about six feet in the air. It occurred to me that maybe I was a bit close and should step back. I had no sooner done so when the strop let go and the engine crashed onto the concrete a couple of feet in front of me! We scooped up the remains and went back to the yard, rather wiser than we had been when we had arrived a few minutes earlier!

The space available in the boat did not allow room for any reduction ratio on the transmissions, so the shafts, at an exceptionally steep angle of 10 degrees, rotated at engine speed and the props had to be specially designed and custom made.

Bob Conn worked on his own, but I worked alongside Bob Dorris and I soon discovered that he had a very volatile and explosive side to his normal laid-back personality. He had told me how, when in the merchant marine, he had thrown the captain of the ship down the bridge stairs. He also recounted how, following a disagreement with his French wife at a party in California, he had done what he described as a "slow burn" and come home to toss his wife on the floor before throwing the bed out through the closed French windows.

"We were tip-toeing around on broken glass for days" he told me with his slow chuckle.

Apart from these very rare blow-ups, Bob was a talented and most amusing guy. One evening we went for dinner to the

Goodwood Park Hotel and ordered steaks at the Gordon Grill restaurant. Our main dish seemed a bit slow in coming, and we began to notice some unusual activity coming from the kitchen area. Then we heard sirens of approaching fire engines and saw red flashing lights through the translucent stained-glass windows. Smoke began to hover above our heads and helmeted figures appeared. All the other diners left while we continued to finish our wine. We finally concluded that we were not likely to get our steaks, so we paid the bill and left. Bob told me he dined out for months on the story of the Englishman who sat there demanding his steak while the flames flickered all around. Grossly exaggerated, but a good story!

Bob quite naturally wanted to work on the Laguna until every detail of its design was complete. However, the Newtons wanted him to return to California and move on to designing a larger, 38-foot Laguna, leaving me to complete the design details on the smaller boat, which I knew was well within my capabilities. Whit Newton was working out of Hong Kong and he flew down to Singapore to convey this decision to Bob. I was present in the room when he did so, and I cringed at the way he was expressing this idea—even though I agreed with it. I thought to myself, "You can't say things like that to Bob". But, much to my surprise, there was no strong reaction from Bob and we all went home for the weekend.

On the following Monday morning, I wished Bob "Good morning" in the normal way and he exploded like a volcano. He had done one of his slow burns over the weekend and was primed and ready to blow on Monday morning. It was absolutely impossible even to speak to him until Thursday, after which he was perfectly fine and even joked about it. I took over the detailing for the Laguna 10 from that time on and, not long afterwards, Bob returned to California to start design work on the larger boat.

Eventually, we completed the boat to the point when we could launch it and start running trials. The first major obstacle we encountered was that the boat would not steer! You could turn the wheel and the boat would bank as if it was going to turn, but it just went straight on. If you applied more rudder, it would bank even more but turn in the opposite direction.

Land was being reclaimed on the other side of the river on which the yard was situated, and a crude lift bridge with restricted opening times had been installed across it between the yard and the open water. Most of our trials had to be done in the highly polluted river, which was only about 50 yards wide, so it was quite alarming when the boat turned the wrong way. The plug had performed fine in HK and I couldn't figure out what was wrong. Bob Conn suggested different-shaped rudders and Bob Dorris, larger rudders; but both of these just made the situation worse. We tried everything we could think of, and I even became adept at swapping out rudders with the boat anchored off a beach on one of the small islands in Singapore waters. We did this by dropping a rudder, putting a short length of shaft in the hole to stop the boat from sinking, and then sliding a replacement rudder up from beneath the boat!

One morning at home, when sitting on the throne, the phrase "cavitation plate" popped into my head without my having the slightest idea where it had come from or even what it meant. We had a book in the office about high-speed craft and it mentioned cavitation plates over the props to prevent air being drawn down from the surface. I made a couple of brackets from strips of mild steel and used them to support bits of plywood placed over the rudders. I took the boat out and it steered like a bicycle! I progressively cut back the size of the plywood until each side was 2 inches fore and aft, and 8 inches wide. Smaller than this, the boat ceased to steer. With the solution in hand, the cause of the problem became obvious. The trailing edge of the rudders extended beyond the transom so, with the boat planing, the suction on the back side of the rudders was greater than the head of water above them. This allowed air to be sucked down to the rudders, which then stalled. Initially I planned to make bronze brackets to replace the plywood, but in the end we cut off the top of the aft end of the rudders, which worked just as well. I sent Bob Dorris a sketch of the modified rudders and he said that there was no way in the world that the boat would steer with rudders like that. The truth was just the opposite!

The next problem was that of performance. The boat ran nowhere near the speed it had in Hong Kong. The Singapore press got hold of the story that we were building a sexy, high-speed boat, and of course wanted to know how fast it would go. I refused to tell them until after we had run successful trials. They badgered me and said that I must have some idea. I annoyed them by refusing to speculate and said that I was not prepared to release any figures until after they had been ascertained by sea trials. Bob Conn used his hammer on the props but this time his magic did not work, and we only achieved a miserable 13 knots after his most recent attempt.

The problem turned out to be insufficient blade area for the now-heavier hull. Fortunately, there was an excellent, British-based propeller company in Singapore called Stone Marine, and they designed and made custom propellers which eventually produced the desired results. These had large, overlapping blades but they suffered from a problem known as root cavitation. Without going into technical details, this causes the metal to be eaten away at the root of the blades, which in extreme cases can result in a blade flying off and penetrating the hull. The anti-intuitive cure is to drill holes right through the blades in the affected area to relieve pressure differences between the front and back sides of the blades. This reminded me of the aeronautical joke in which a janitor solved the problem of an aircraft whose wings kept breaking off by drilling a series of holes across them on the premise that toilet paper never tears along the perforations!

We were under continual pressure to complete the first boat, but there were so many details that it took longer than anyone anticipated. For example, John wanted the sliding doors at the aft end of the salon to slide all to one side. This meant one fixed door and triple sliding doors. Normal sliding door locks do not latch. They simply close and then they can be locked. This is because they are designed for houses, which do not rock around except during earthquakes. On a boat it is necessary to be able to latch the door without actually locking it. There were no latching locks available which would fit our triple aluminium doors. I solved the problem by installing a conventional hinging door lock on the door jamb and installing a looped striker on the opening door. This is the reverse of the normal procedure, in which the lock is installed on the door and the striker on the jamb. This did the job, but it took time to figure out solutions to multiple problems such as this and to design and fabricate components to make them work.

At long last we were ready to ship the first boat, which left Singapore en route to England at the beginning of October 1970. I watched the boat loaded aboard the Ben Line ship in Singapore and then flew to London to see it offloaded in London docks on a grey November day.

Anton was there, as was Jack Taylor and his son Alan from our UK dealer, Solent Yachts, and a young American whose name I don't exactly recall, but I think it was Franklin, so that is what I will call him. He had come over from the U.S. to help the Italian dealer unload his first GBs and was killing time while the boats were held hostage by a dock strike in Genoa.

It took a while to get the boat ready for the offload and I discovered, by waggling the steering wheel, that the steering had become deranged while on the ship. Fortunately, because I had been the designer, it did not take long to fix, but by the time we got underway down the Thames it was beginning to get dark, which occurs quite early in November at that latitude.

We pulled into a place with the ominous name of Gravesend and tied up alongside a tug moored to a towering Victorian stone wall. Gravesend—what a name, but quite appropriate for this grim-looking place. It was low tide and we had a long climb up a steel ladder to be faced with a desolate prospect when we reached the top. It was like a scene from Dickens' *Great Expectations,* set in the same area. We trudged off across the featureless landscape in light rain to a second-rate pub for some second-rate food before returning to the dock and back down the ladder to the boat. It had been a tiring day that had started at 0600, so we had no trouble falling asleep.

The following morning, we were underway at daylight and headed out into the wide waters of the Thames Estuary and around the North Foreland into the English Channel, staying inshore of the treacherous Goodwin Sands. The weather was rough, grey, and nasty, with a strong westerly wind. The alternator on one of the engines showed an ever-increasing charge rate, and we thought it prudent to pull into Dover to check it out.

Dover's outer harbour is formed by a breakwater with a couple of narrow entrances. Once inside, we tied up to a mooring buoy and tried to examine the regulator in the tight confines of the hot engine room. The boat was rolling uncomfortably in the ground swell, and seeing nothing obviously amiss, we decided to press on.

I was sharing the tiny flying bridge with Jack Taylor, who was driving. I told him that the normal cruising rpm was 2500 and, without any regard to the prevailing conditions, Jack instantly pushed the throttles up to this speed, and we catapulted out through the harbour entrance, where the rough seas of the English Channel were striking the breakwater and reflecting back to collide with the incoming waves. We flew off the top of an almost vertical wave with a deep chasm beyond it. I braced myself for the inevitable impact but the deep V hull did a magnificent job of hurling the spray aside. However, the G forces were still considerable and the boat immediately lost power. Looking aft, I saw black smoke pouring from the starboard exhaust, leaving the boat wallowing in the confused and tumultuous seas.

I slid down the steep ladder to the cockpit and into the salon, where the others already had the engine hatches open and had armed themselves with fire extinguishers. The engine space was filled with smoke but there was no sign of any flames. Considerable amounts of water were sloshing around in the shallow bilge, and it looked as though the port engine exhaust had become detached from the turbocharger.

With some difficulty, we were able to turn the boat around on one engine and re-enter the harbour. As luck would have it, the tide was high and the lock gates could be opened to allow us through to the calm waters of the inner harbour. Safely tied alongside the dock, with both engines stopped, we reviewed our situation. We could see that the whole exhaust system, complete with its riser, had fallen off the port turbocharger and was lying in the bilge. This had allowed water from the transom exhaust to sluice into the engine room through the large-diameter rubber hose. The red-hot gases from the turbo had melted the line from the port transmission to the mechanical oil pressure gauge, allowing all the oil in the transmission, at 350 psi, to spray into the hot exhaust gas, to be ingested by the starboard engine. Why this engine had not run away and blown up I shall never understand, but it did explain the black smoke I saw coming from the exhaust. Water was still slopping around in the bilge, but no more was coming in. Everything in the engine room was coated in oil. To make matters worse, we were downwind of a small coaster from which loose coal was being unloaded with a crane. The strong wind was blowing coal dust from the crane bucket all over the Laguna. I was wearing a pair of Bata boots with some kind of synthetic rubber soles which dissolved in the oil. The sticky rubber picked up the coal dust, so everywhere I walked, I left black footprints. It started to rain. All we could do under the circumstances was laugh!

The first task was to clean up the mess and figure out why the exhaust had come adrift. Well, that was easy—there had been nothing to hold it in place! The heavy riser had simply been pushed into the turbo opening and sealed with a piston ring. Bob Conn had been a very clever and ingenious engine man, but detailing had not been his forte. Pushing it back in place was simple, but we had to prevent the same thing happening again, and for this brackets had to be made. This was tricky because the only place to attach the brackets on the engine was around the gearbox flange, which was a complicated shape. I walked the dock until I found a piece of wire which I could bend around the contours of the gearbox flange. I transferred this shape to a piece of cardboard, and we set off through the rain to look for a workshop in town. We found one about a half-mile away, and over the next two days, we walked back and forth, each time taking the bracket to the next stage. For example, although we had three bolt holes to drill, we drilled just one first so we could bolt the bracket it in place to ensure the other holes would be located correctly—a practical application of the adage "measure twice, drill once."

We had to make brackets for the starboard engine, as the same situation existed on that side. We carried spare oil on board and refilled the port transmission. With repairs complete, we were now ready to leave, but we had to wait for the weather and we could only leave at high tide when the lock gates could be opened. Finally, at 0200 on the morning of the third day, we headed back out to sea under marginal weather conditions.

Of course this was long before the days of GPS and chart plotters, so navigation was done the old-fashioned way by dead reckoning, confirmed by visual observation. We were looking for a particular lightship, and it was spotted on the horizon when Franklin was at the helm. A few moments later, he said that he could not hold a course on it. The lightship revealed itself to be a freighter underway up the Channel. After this happened a second time, it was apparent that we really did not know where we were and visibility was poor.

When Anton went out outside for a better look, one of the triple sliding doors came adrift, leaving him staggering around the small cockpit clutching the door—doing a kind of dance with the door as his partner! We managed to grab him before they both pitched over the side.

Then one of the engine alarms went off, showing low oil pressure on the port engine. We opened the hatch to find that the copper line carrying oil to the turbo had fractured due to vibration—spraying the entire lube oil contents from the port engine all over the engine room. We had no flaring tools on board to repair the line, and all our spare oil had been used to replace that lost from the transmission.

We were now down to one engine, and the speed of the boat dropped from 15 knots to about seven. Waves, which had previously been hurled aside by the flared bow, now broke over the boat. This caused the cabin side windows to leak prodigious amounts of water. There were u-shaped settees below these windows on both port and starboard sides of boat. We had removed the cushions, but water poured onto the flat areas outboard of the seatbacks. These had lee rails which, as the boat rolled, channelled the water around to the inboard edge, where it poured onto the sole. We put buckets at these points and collected five gallons of water every couple of minutes from each side.

At this point, all the joking ceased. We figured that, at the very least, we had another eight hours of this to endure, and there was a strong possibility that the oil line could also fracture on the starboard engine. We donned life jackets and moved the life raft into the cockpit.

In the event, we suffered no more emergencies, and with great relief we pulled into the first marina we came to in the Solent, which was probably Portsmouth. We re-flared the oil line, refilled the starboard engine, mopped up the water, and cleaned up the mess. We then roared triumphantly up the Solent at 30 knots, having taken five days for a trip that should have taken a few hours in our high performance boat.

When we arrived, completely exhausted, Franklin phoned the Italians to learn that the strike was over and he was required in Italy right away. We had to take the poor guy to Southampton railway station to catch a train to London, tube to Heathrow, and then a flight to Rome. When he arrived, he was arrested, due to some foul up over paperwork! The perfect end to a trying day! For our part, Anton and I went to a hotel, where we stuffed ourselves on tea and hot buttered toast. Let no one tell you that the boat business is dull!

With the first Laguna 33-foot safely (?) delivered, I returned to Singapore to continue work on the upcoming Laguna 38 and to set up the engineering and development department.

I made several visits back to HK over the next few months. One of them was to assist with solving some problems with a big Grand Banks 62 that was being built for Carleton Mitchell. One of these concerned ventilation of the engine room, which was getting too hot. It was decided to install large coaxial blowers to force air into the engine room, rather than relying on natural ventilation and air drawn in by the engines. We paid a visit to the row of small Chinese workshops in Canton Road, in the Shum Shui Po district of Kowloon, and ordered a pair of 12-inch diameter blowers. After we had them installed, we were standing in the engine room and I switched them on. They were so powerful that all the surplus screws and other debris that had accumulated in the ventilator trunking during construction ricocheted around the engine room and went zinging past our heads!

It had been Carleton Mitchell's intention to drive the boat on its bottom to the U.S. from Hong Kong, and he had even reached the point of filling the large freezer with frozen meat. But, at the last minute, concerns about fuel supplies and the range of the vessel across the vast expanse of the Pacific Ocean caused him to cancel his plans.

I also paid a visit to Honolulu for a meeting which had been arranged to bring all the disparate parts of the company together. We flew on different planes to ensure that a single accident did not wipe out the entire company—which, in my opinion, is always a wise decision. I don't recall everybody who was present but it included all the key personnel from California, Hong Kong, and Singapore. We each had to make a presentation of our areas of responsibility. We spent all of every day, over the course of several days, shut away in a smoke-filled room on what was really a self-congratulatory exercise. We saw almost nothing of Hawaii. On the evening before I had to give my presentation I had a couple of mai tais—a local, rum-based cocktail of the type decorated with fruit and one of those little umbrellas. They contain a fair amount of sugar, and when I awoke on the morning of my presentation I had the worst hangover I have ever had in my entire life.

For our family holiday over Christmas 1970, we flew from Singapore to Copenhagen via Tashkent on SAS. We landed in Tashkent in the early hours of the morning, and the aircraft rumbled its way over a very bumpy surface following a Jeep with a placard saying "Follow Me". As we deplaned, we handed our passports to an unsmiling Russian official who, in return, gave us one half of a card. The other half was placed in our passport, which he put in a box. We walked through a picket gate in a hedge and up the wide stairs of a building that resembled an official 1930s residence. At each turn of the stairs a grim Russian sentry stood motionless. In a room at the top of the stairs were tables laden with little red books of Mao's thoughts in many different languages, along with other communist literature.

When it came time to re-board, we handed our card to the guard, who fished out our passport, examined us and the picture carefully to make sure they matched, and handed our passport back to us.

Rex, with his luxuriant beard, later made the same journey and told me that when he came to collect his passport the guard had at first looked at his picture upside down and the faintest glimmer of a smile crossed his features when he realized his mistake and turned it right side up.

From Tashkent we flew to Copenhagen, where we stopped for a couple of days. We hadn't brought any heavy coats with us—first, because we didn't have any, and, second, because we thought we could manage without for a couple of days in Denmark. Wrong! It was so cold that we simply had to buy warm clothing. The irony was that Mary's very nice warm coat was made in—you guessed it—Hong Kong!

When we arrived in England, we again stayed in the White Hart Inn in Nettlebed. We had a room right up under the eaves, and when we awoke on Christmas morning the light coming through the curtains had that special brightness. When we drew back the curtains we saw that it had snowed during the night and virgin snow, still pristine, covered the ground and coated every branch.

"It's a REAL Christmas!" cried the kids.

They had never seen snow before, and it was a wonderful family Christmas with my mother, my sister and her husband, their adopted kids, and their dog, Rupert, bounding through the snow.

Every day we walked with the children along the banks of the River Thames and fed the swans and the ducks. It was all very English and could not have been more of a contrast from our life back in Singapore, to where we returned in February 1971.

Chapter 3

February 1971 to Early 1973

Life in Singapore

I go to Japan to solve Laguna 33 problems. We design and build the Laguna 38, which has to be completed in California due to a shipping strike. Rex joins the company and the Grand Banks line is converted to fibreglass. We make a trip to Bangkok, Delhi, Agra and Kashmir. I become president of the Singapore Cine Club. I go to Kenya to move my sick father to England.

Caterpillar never did permit the unauthorized turbocharging of their engines and refused to sell them any longer to American Marine. An alternative was found with the GM Toroflow engines, but the work of marinizing had to be done all over again. These engines produced 275hp and gave endless trouble, including being very smoky. Part of the problem was caused by faulty injectors, and it was exacerbated by the shape of the boat, which created what is referred to as the "station-wagon effect" in which the suction created behind the vehicle causes the exhaust to be sucked backed into it. Even though we had brought the Laguna's exhaust out below the water, the problem was severe and difficult to solve. We managed a partial solution by mounting a pair of aluminium deflectors at the aft end of the deckhouse.

Anton, who had been appointed European Sales Manager, bore much of the brunt of the complaints in Europe. He told me of one such confrontation when he visited a German buyer with Bob

Conn. He said they could see the customer waiting for them on the dock with arms akimbo and hands on plump hips—not an encouraging sign. This particular boat had an all-white interior—including a white carpet (never a very practical idea). He launched into an immediate tirade:

"My boat is black; my dog is black (hint: it had been white), my vife is black! I am black! All is black!"

It was left to Anton to try to pacify him while Bob got on with changing the injectors. Bob was a taciturn sort of guy. When I asked his impression of Greece after a similar trip over there, he said he couldn't see what all the fuss was about. "It's just a bunch of rocks" was his opinion of the cradle of Western civilization!

Fortunately, I had little to do with having to deal with the problems at the customer end, but I was sent to Japan to deal with a problem on a Laguna 33. I had never been to Japan before, and I was met by our dealer when I arrived in Tokyo. He put me on a train to the place where the Laguna was moored. I am not sure exactly where this was, but I believe it was somewhere on the Miuri Peninsula, south of Yokohama. All the PA announcements were in Japanese, and all the station signs written only in the same language. There were many stops, and I was terrified I was going to be carried off to God knows where. I don't remember how it was that I got off at the correct stop or how I found my way to where I had to go. I do clearly remember the yacht club, which was a very formal affair like the most prestigious clubs in the West. The owner of the boat spoke English and took me down to the boat. A couple of mechanics were there and, after questioning them, they seemed to have already checked the most obvious things. I apologized to them and said that, as I had been sent there, I had to check everything from the beginning, even though they had already done it. They were very gracious at accepting this. At one stage I asked if they had a torque wrench and they asked me what size, as they had several!

It took a couple of days to go through everything, and I stayed at night in a traditional Japanese Inn. It was quite delightful but I had a hard time accepting that I was really there in that environment. The "bed" was on the floor, which was quite comfortable. A meal was brought to me which was set out like a work of art, with attention paid to each individual porcelain dish and to the colours and textures of the food. I had a dressing gown to wear and the sash had been folded into a perfect pentagon. Outside the window were fields of rice, with bangers that went off at regular intervals to scare away the birds. In the mornings I walked down to the little marina, passing housewives on their knees, scrubbing the front steps of their houses.

I know it sounds ridiculous because this could not possibly be anywhere other than Japan, but I felt the whole atmosphere to be reminiscent of England. I could not put my finger on it, but it was definitely there. The British and the Japanese are both island peoples who have had a much greater effect on the world, commensurate for the size of their countries, than could have been expected. Empires rise and fall, and there was a time when Britain was a powerful, innovative, and adventurous nation quite out of keeping with its tiny size on the world stage.

The Laguna 38 was not quite as hard to build as the 33 because we now had some experience of building fibreglass boats, and it was larger, with more room to work. However, it had the same engines, with the same smoke problem. This time we even built a scale model of the boat and had it tested in the wind tunnel at Singapore University. Ultimately, the solution turned out to be wing-like extensions to the hull below the waterline which had a fixed down angle and which incorporated adjustable trim tabs. These allowed the boat to run at the optimum angle and kept the underwater exhaust from surfacing right behind the boat. The gap between the extensions created a rooster tail which dumped water on the exhaust when it did surface. This solution was only reached after many hours of testing, using all kinds of Rube Goldberg (a.k.a. Heath Robinson) lash-ups to test out new ideas.

The first of the new, larger Lagunas was required for the LA boat show in 1972. It was already going to be a close-run thing, but a threatened longshoremen's strike in Long Beach looked like it could sabotage the whole effort. It was decided to ship the boat, still unfinished, to San Francisco and then truck it down from there to Newport Beach for final completion. I was to go over there to

337

work on the boat. I flew to Seattle in January 1972, then to Newport Beach, and spent about one month working on the Laguna. We were just able to get it into a fit condition for the show, although we had to install outdoor carpeting on the flying bridge to hide the defects in the non-skid! I also learned never to leave masking tape on window glass. After a few weeks in the sun it becomes welded to the surface and can only be removed one millimetre at a time, with infinite care to avoid scratching the glass! This was a great time for me and allowed me to appreciate the climate and relaxed—yet efficient—California lifestyle.

Later in 1972, I was joined by Rex Yates, who had been a fellow apprentice with me at De Havillands, been with me on the Trans-Africa Expedition and who had sailed to England from Hong Kong on *Westward*. Since that time, he and Jill—who had been at secretarial college with my sister—had worked as partners taking care of charter vessels in the Caribbean. Rex was a qualified thermodynamic engineer, which was a great help with the continuing work on the engines now that Bob Conn had returned to the U.S. I had spent time at De Havillands in the vibration lab, where our job basically had been to test equipment to destruction. A very useful tool was the stroboscope, which, by adjusting the rate at which a powerful bulb flashes, makes it possible to observe high-speed events in slow motion. We thought that having one of these would be handy, so I called various supply companies in Singapore. When the reaction was, "What's a stroboscope?" I just thanked them politely and hung up the phone. Eventually we were able to order one through the U.S. office. It proved its value right away with a problem we had with throttle brackets fracturing in a few hours due to fatigue. Intuitively you would think they should be reinforced in a certain way, but the stroboscope revealed that the brackets were twisting rather than vibrating back and forth, and should therefore be reinforced differently.

Now that we were building Lagunas in fibreglass, it seemed only logical to think about converting the Grand Banks to fibreglass also. This concept was fraught with risk. The first concern was tampering with the Grand Banks formula. Nobody really knew why it had been so successful and therefore what it would take to destroy it. The second was that if word got out that

338

the boats were going to be produced in fibreglass, there was every likelihood that sales for wood boats would dry up instantly— leaving us nothing to build and no money to pay for the tooling, which could easily take two years to accomplish.

Howard Abbey was hired from Hatteras to make the tooling and initiate production of the first fibreglass GBs, while the whole project was kept secret. Howard set to work in 1972 and made two sets of moulds each for the 32, 36 and 42. While this was in progress, we had a visit by Jack Taylor from our UK dealership. He was on his way back from visiting his son in Australia and wanted to stop in Singapore to visit the yard. I knew that he would be sure to want to visit the fibreglass shop, where tooling for the fibreglass GBs was in full swing. So we hung up a bunch of lightweight, striped, plastic tarpaulins, and I walked him right past them, saying that we had to contain the overspray from the work going on behind them. Jack was of craggy countenance now made even more craggy because, while in Australia, he had walked straight through a glass door leading out to his son's patio.

In this memoir I seem to spend a lot of time describing family holidays, but the fact is that we did have generous leave arrangements. The normal expatriate allocation was leave every year with fares for the whole family paid to one's country of origin. Being a small company, we were able to adjust this so that the company would pay the same amount of travel but we could go wherever we wanted and we would personally make up any additional costs. This was indeed generous, but I was routinely working over 70 hours per week, with Saturday being a normal working day. That alone meant that you worked an extra 50 days per year over someone who got Saturdays off.

The company made several unsuccessful attempts to hire a production manager to handle the daily challenges of the building process. In any factory this is a challenging job, involving the scheduling and management of thousands of components and hundreds of people to produce quality product on time.

One of these was a personable Danish guy who was doing OK on the job but who found it frustrating to have to answer to the local plant manager, about whom we will learn much more later in this story. One day, my wife, Mary, overheard a remark from this guy's wife that he was about to leave the company for another job. Mary told me about it, and I confronted him. He admitted it was true and I told him that, as a director of the company, I was duty bound to act on the information which had come into my possession, but I would not do so for one week to give him the opportunity to do what he should have already done—i.e., give his notice of resignation—which he subsequently did.

In March 1972 we went to Bangkok, then to India and Kashmir. It is always blazingly hot in Thailand, even when compared to Singapore. We were only there a few days and visited a number of temples, some of these containing very large statues of Buddha, some decorated with gold leaf. The most memorable experience was a visit to the floating market. Bangkok is sometimes called the "Venice of the East" because it is built on the Chao Phraya River with a surrounding network of canals or *khlongs*. Long-tailed boats are unique to Thailand. They consist of a long, relatively narrow hull at the aft end of which an automotive engine is mounted on a swivel. Extending aft from the engine is a long shaft with the propeller on the end, and the boat is steered by swivelling the engine. These boats run very fast, and I remember the bizarre sight of a beautiful Thai girl, wearing a traditional straw hat, bombing down a *khlong* at high speed at the helm of one of these boats.

The market itself was fascinating with fruit, vegetables and every item you would find in a regular market on sale in small boats jostling for space. Along the edge of the *khlongs* people were bathing, cleaning their teeth and washing clothes. On shore, an elephant was being fed bananas.

From Bangkok we flew to Delhi—also extraordinarily hot. We would be going on to Agra the following morning by train, so we chose a hotel near the railway station. On the bus from the airport we stopped at a succession of grand hotels until everyone had gotten off except us. Finally, the bus stopped in the street beside a tall wall with a long staircase going up it. This staircase led to our hotel. I don't recall the name, but it was certainly a lot more modest than all the palaces we had seen. The air conditioning was of the swamp-cooler type I first seen at the Melbourne hotel in Hong Kong.

The following morning, we boarded the train for Agra. We ordered fried eggs for our breakfast. These were served with a dash of curry and brought to us from the kitchen car by a steward clinging onto the outside of the train. We passed through a landscape of parched, exhausted fields. When we reached Agra, the platform was a seething mass of porters eager to carry our luggage. We faced the impossible task of picking one from the throng. Somehow we selected one, and he insisted on carrying everything, of which we had a great deal. Not only did we have enough clothes for two adults and two little girls for two months, but I had all my camera gear, which included a heavy tripod. With the help of others, our porter loaded two large and very heavy suitcases on his head, tripod and camera bags slung on his shoulders, and smaller cases in each hand.

Once out of the station we faced a similar throng of taxi drivers from which to choose. It was not just a question of picking one for a ride to the hotel—the taxi driver would stay with you for the duration of your stay and be your tour guide. Our reasons for visiting Agra had been twofold. First to see the famous Taj Mahal and, equally important, Mary had lived here as a small child. Her family had lived in Agra, while her father worked for the Indian Railways, until they moved to England just before the outbreak of WWII. She had the address of their home, and our taxi driver was able to find the house, and Mary was able to speak to the lady who now owned it and have a look inside.

As is frequently the case, our taxi driver took us to a small jeweller's shop. The patriarch was partially blind and his sons served the customers. The old man said that he remembered Mary's family, and I think this was true because he knew the names. He said that he had a unique ring with some special history that he would like Mary to have. The ring was an emerald set around with small diamonds, and the price was around $100. When he announced the price, his son said, "Father!" in a shocked voice. It was either genuine or a very well-rehearsed act. I said that we were on our way to Kashmir and did not have any extra

341

cash to spend on jewellery. He said that he would take a cheque. I said that I did not have any cheques with me. He replied that he had one and produced a generic cheque form printed on extremely poor quality paper. He then asked which bank it would be on, and I said it would be my bank in the UK.

"But," I said, "there is insufficient money in that account right now."

"When would there be sufficient funds?" he asked.

"In about six weeks," I told him.

"Well then", he said, "postdate the cheque, and in the meantime you can have the ring valued, and if it is worth less than I am asking, you need not honour it!"

On that basis, I signed his cheque and we departed with the ring. I never did have it valued, but it is a lovely ring of great sentimental value and my daughter Nicky wears it today, 40 years later. A memorable and heart-warming example of trust.

India was the only place I have ever been where I really experienced culture shock. It was just so different from everywhere else. Walking the streets, we were constantly pestered by young kids asking for money or wanting to clean our shoes. The fact that we were all wearing sandals or flip flops did not deter them in the slightest. You would look down to see that they had somehow put something on one of your shoes which needed to be removed. Then there was the turbaned Sikh who wanted to tell my fortune. I declined his offer but then he said, "Well, if I tell you something and it's true, will you give me one rupee?"

I agreed, and he told me that I had one sister living in England! I gave him one rupee and then he told something else he could not possibly have known! I don't know how he did it. I know he had an accomplice working up the street—but so what? In the end I parted with about 5 rupees (equal to about 70 cents, U.S.), but it was well worth it for the entertainment value.

The streets of Agra were crammed with carts drawn by horses, oxen or people. The wheels were made from planks of wood nailed together and cut into a circular shape. Artisans sat cross legged in the street carving millstones out of blocks of stone, using hammers and chisels. We ordered a marble table top from a shop in which small boys were fashioning and inlaying, by hand, semi-precious stones such as malachite, cornelian, and lapus lazuli. The table top was duly sent to us in Singapore several weeks later. I titled the film I made of our trip, "Escape into Yesterday", and that accurately summed it up.

The Taj Mahal was a wonderful sight. It was located in rather a scruffy part of town and I had fully expected to be disappointed after all the hype about it. But it was a marvel to behold. There are other marvellous sights to visit including the ghost city of Fatephur Sikri, built in 1570 but abandoned only 14 years later due to shortage of water.

We returned by train to New Delhi and flew from there to Srinagar, in the disputed province of Kashmir. During the flight we flew over huge, snow-capped mountains. After landing, we took a taxi to Dahl Lake and a small boat called a *shikara* out to our palatial houseboat moored to an artificial island. From here we made expeditions to various outlying areas. As in India, we had the same taxi driver for the duration of our stay.

Among the places we visited was Gulmarg, where we all rode ponies. Jackie was in her element, and Nicky was initially all excited but changed her tune when we had to descend a very steep, narrow track in a forest with an almost vertical drop on one side down to a rushing torrent. Another place was Sonamarg, at nearly 9,000 feet, where the snow was quite deep and we were towed around on sledges. This was on the road to a very remote area called Ladakh. At the time of our visit the road had been closed to all but the military for 25 years because it was a disputed area contested by India, Pakistan and China. The road was opened a few years later, and Ladakh is now a tourist destination for the more adventurous. The road climbs as high as 11,320 feet and is only open between May and November.

When returning from one of these trips, our taxi had to pass a local bus that had stopped at the edge of the road to let down passengers. Our taxi driver was extremely careful; he slowed down to barely walking pace and sounded his horn continuously.

Nonetheless, a silly woman ran out from behind the bus and hit the side of the taxi. She really wasn't hurt, but fell on the ground and made a great fuss. Immediately everyone poured out of the bus, and of course they were all witnesses, although this was quite impossible as the incident had happened at the rear of the bus when everyone on it was facing forward. The "injured" woman was packed into our taxi together with a relative, and we went to a local village where there was some primitive clinic. There was endless argument, and the unfortunate taxi driver had to pay some money although he was entirely blameless, and if he had not been such a careful driver, the woman would have been severely injured. When we finally left Kashmir and said goodbye to our driver, I gave him a generous tip plus I repaid what he had to pay to the woman. Otherwise all his driving for us would have brought him nothing, and the case could be made that if he had not been driving us at that place at that time, he would not have been placed in that situation!

Severe winter weather restricts outside activities in Kashmir, with the result that there are many interesting handicrafts to buy including carpets, wood carvings and attractive small boxes in various shapes, made of papier-mâché. We wanted to buy a few of these souvenirs to take home but did not have any money to spare from what we still owed for our stay on the houseboat. I went to the proprietor of the houseboat and asked whether I could send him the balance after we returned to Singapore and he agreed. This was another example of heart-warming trust, as there was little he could have done had I failed to honour my pledge to pay.

On another occasion we were walking in the street in Srinagar when a Kashmiri gentleman came up to us. "Excuse me, sir," he said, "but are you English?"

"Er, yes," I replied, not knowing what to expect.

"Oh, let me shake your hand," he said.

It was really heartening to encounter this reaction from local people who had once been illogical subjects of Britain.

At Srinagar airport, we endured the most searching security I had up to then experienced and we returned home to Singapore.

When I had first moved to Singapore I had joined the local Cine Club. This was before the days of video, so we still used film. Like many clubs in the country, it had been started by members of the British armed forces, who made up the bulk of the membership. Around this time the British government decided to pull its troops out of the country, and so most of the club membership left. Being one of the few who remained, I was elected president. I was absolutely terrified at being expected to run the meeting, which was completely ridiculous because we all knew each other and we all had a common interest in making films. I soon got over it and having to stand up in front of a bunch of people did me a lot of good. On the basis of "if you can't beat them, join them", Mary also became a member and was elected club secretary. She wrote a number of humorous poems for the club's excellent monthly magazine, of which I still have bound copies. One was titled "Thoughts of a Cine Suffragette."

Some years ago, I'll have it known
(for fear of staying all alone)
I took to me a faithful spouse
To have a lover round the house.

The years they came and quickly passed,
His hobbies, many, didn't last,
Our home was neat, our evenings spent
In happy talk, I was content.

Then came a day I'll n'er forget
He brought him home a new-found pet,
All black and knobbly full of dials
Together with - 0h piles and piles
Of long black film, and tapes and screen
And every lens that's ever been.
Projector too, and books galore.
Dear God! There surely can't be more!

From then on in, my peace was shattered;
We never talked of things that mattered,
"Long shots, short shots, close-ups, zoom"
Would send me scurrying from the room.

And when on trips away we flew
That camera came—and tripod too –
And on my back this gear he'd force
What does he think I am - a horse?

With miles and miles of film he'd play
Then sit and cut and throw away.
"Oh what a waste" I'd cry with pain
"No good", he'd say, "must start again!"

This state of things just could not last
I'd go around the bend - but fast!
So though his talk passed o'er my head
I now no longer go to bed.
An eager interest now I fake
From time to time suggestions make
For should he now from film refrain
Ye gods what money down the drain!

To those like me, who find they're spliced
To cine addicts, here's advice:
From all that litter don't just run
Come on, join in—it's lots of fun!

I had another unplanned trip to make in the fall of 1972. I had been in contact with my father, and I had heard that he was in poor health and suffering from depression. Most of his old friends had died and he wanted to return to England. I had some doubts about the wisdom of that because he had not been there for 25 years, and the England he remembered was certainly not the one that existed today. However, the current situation was also far from satisfactory. I obtained permission to take another leave of absence from the company and flew to Nairobi. There I hired a car and drove up to Timau. He was now a lonely old man, living on his own, aside from two loyal servants, in an isolated house on the slopes of Mount Kenya. He was drinking too much and getting his booze from the local Indian-run *duka*, who were very kindly extending him credit with not very high hopes of getting it back.

Kenya was granted its independence from Britain in

December 1963, and to ensure that no long-term residents left the country owing taxes, the new government introduced a rule that anyone seeking to buy a ticket to leave the country had first to produce a certificate from a bona fide accountant certifying that no taxes were owing. When I questioned my father about this, I found out that not only had the farm accounts been allowed to lapse, but he had misplaced his cheque book. He claimed that it had been stolen by his servants, which did not seem very likely to me. To cut a very long story short, I took him into Nairobi to stay at the Muthaiga Club, while I ran around Nairobi and went back up to Nanyuki to get his affairs in order. I had an interview with a Kenyan official in Nairobi, and I had to be very deferential and careful with my words. I needed him to give permission for my father to leave, but, understandably, he was very sensitive about a young white guy being demanding—having had to put up with it for years. I had to make a final trip back to Nanyuki, 150 miles away. We had some money from somewhere but I am not sure where it came from, as the farm was not my father's to sell. Maybe it came from me but I used it to pay off his debts at the Indian *duka* and also gave quite a bit to his servants, without whom he would really have been in trouble. When the moment finally came for me to leave Nanyuki for Nairobi, I found I had locked the keys inside the car. It was just too exasperating, and I picked up a rock and broke one of the windows to get in. When I got back to the Muthaiga Club, I found that my father had signed over 90 chits for drinks during the three days I had been working on his behalf. I was absolutely furious and told him that if he had wanted to drink himself to death he should have told me from the outset, so that I could have avoided wasting time and money coming to Kenya!

The following day I took him to see the doctor, who, in front of me, gave him a real dressing down about drinking. "I hope you didn't give any money to those black buggers" he said—referring to the servants who had looked after him for many years.

"No" I replied.

Finally, it was time to go to the airport. I was on tenterhooks when we passed through immigration, in case the officials would find some reason to detain him. But there were no problems. The plane was an East African Airways VC10 that stopped in Entebbe before continuing on non-stop to London. My father had never been on a modern jet airliner before.

When we got airborne after the short hop to Entebbe, my father wanted a drink. I thought that a drink or two couldn't do any harm at this stage and might settle him down for the long flight. After that, he lit a succession of cigarettes and used the drink recess on his folding table as an ashtray. He asked the guy next to him if he was going to London; he babbled on that the "Gypos" were sure to get us as we flew over Egypt; and, most mortifying of all, he placed his cigarettes and matches just over the slope of the seat in front so that, when he reached for them, his fingers scrabbled around in the hair of the woman occupying that seat. When I grabbed his hand he told me not to be so "bloody irritable". It was not a restful journey.

When we finally arrived at Heathrow, I had arranged for a wheelchair. That is certainly a fast way through the system, as we were wheeled though a succession of doors marked "No Entry". The next question was where to take him. Being a retired officer from the Royal Air Force entitled him to stay at the Royal Air Force Club in Piccadilly, so I checked him in there. I then went to stay with my sister and her husband in North London, where they lived with three small children in a tiny house.

The following day I went to visit a gentleman from the Royal Air Force Benevolent Society, with whom I had previously been in touch. He was very nice but said they would discuss my father's case at their next meeting in about one month's time. Well, this was not something I had anticipated and was certainly a blow. I returned to my sister's place and we discussed what we could do, as I had to get back to work in Singapore and they were certainly not in a position to be able to put him up or take care of him. We had no solution to what to do with my father, who had not contributed financially or taken much part in raising us.

At about 8 p.m., the phone rang. It was the gentleman from the Benevolent Society I had seen earlier in the day. He said that he had been so impressed that I had flown from Singapore and thence to Kenya to rescue my father that he had contacted the other members of the committee and they had made a special exception in this case, and that I should take my father down to a Royal Air Force hospital in Swindon the following day. Whew! What a relief! I thanked him profusely.

I called my father to give him the news and told him that I would pick him up at 11 o'clock the following day. When I went there, I found that not only was he not dressed, but that he had messed the bed as well. I was pretty exasperated, but the poor old man was really very confused and not with it. I bundled him up and I'm afraid we just got out of there.

We drove down to Swindon, which is about 1½ hours west of central London. I found the hospital and checked him in. The sergeant orderly said "He doesn't look very well, does he?" I agreed. When I spoke to the doctor, I told him that we had just arrived from Kenya and that my father had spent the last 25 years living at around 7,500 feet above sea level. He told me that that had probably saved his life.

I returned to Singapore almost immediately. After the hospital had restored my father's health, he was moved to a residential facility on the South Coast of England. He was later moved to a residential home for retired Royal Air Force officers in south Devon. We went to visit him a couple of times over the next couple of years and found it very depressing. There were all these old men who had once had vital and exciting lives sitting around essentially waiting to die. My father passed away from lung cancer in May 1974.

The first fibreglass GB 36 was completed in 1973 and, accompanied by John Newton, Chuck Hovey was flown out from Newport Beach, California, as a guinea pig to test customer reaction. Chuck had been a valuable dealer right from the introduction of the Grand Banks. He had been a salesman for a company called Stewart and Ullman and was credited with selling up to six of the nine wooden GBs we had been building every month in Hong Kong. Chuck had no advance knowledge we were changing to fibreglass, and we took him aboard the first glass GB 36 at a jetty away from the boatyard. After a short cruise, John asked Chuck what he thought of the boat. Chuck seemed a bit

349

surprised by the question.

"Well, it's a GB," he said.

"It's fibreglass, Chuck" John replied.

I still remember Chuck's face. If his chin could have dropped, it would have bounced off his shoe laces!

"You're putting me on," he said.

We showed him the details which revealed the differences. The boat had passed the test when the most experienced salesman in the business could not readily spot them. Actually there was one hidden factor which made the fibreglass boats better and more comfortable. The keel on the fibreglass boat was filled with foam rather than being made of yacal—a timber so heavy that it did not float. On the other hand, the flybridge, being fibreglass reinforced with plywood, was heavier than plywood on its own. So, although the overall weight of the two boats was the same, the centre of gravity on the fibreglass boat was higher, which made it less "stiff" and therefore more comfortable.

Howard Abbey had not only supervised the tooling but also set up the modular form of construction for the GBs. He also had an opportunity to demonstrate that the old traditional methods of dealing with practical problems were still often the best. A GB 50 which had been built in HK was on its way to the UK and was being transhipped in Singapore, which meant being unloaded from one ship and reloaded onto another. While being moved from one dock to another, the driver of the transporter had taken a roundabout in the dock area too fast, and the boat had fallen off the transporter and landed on its side. We got the call, and Howard made a large number of wooden wedges and loaded them onto a pickup along with a pile of wood blocks and a bunch of carpenters armed with hammers. I watched with amazement as, in less than one hour, this substantial boat was back upright with minimal damage just by hammering a series of wedges between the wood blocks and the hull. There had been all kinds of talk about using a crane, but with the boat on its side, this would have been very difficult without serious risk of crushing the hull. We had some spillage of lube oil and battery acid to deal with, but this was soon accomplished.

Chapter 4

Early 1973 to Spring 1975

Life in Singapore

I take over running of the yard after I discover the local manager is stealing from the company. We make a trip to Sri Lanka and the Seychelles' Islands before going to Kenya and traveling to the remote north of the country. The Singapore yard has serious financial problems and faces bankruptcy. The owners depart, Bob Livingston arrives, and I purchase a house in England.

When I had set up a separate Engineering and Development section within the Singapore yard, I had been given strict instructions not to interfere with the running of the yard itself, and I did my best to comply with this. As I mentioned earlier, the yard was run by a Eurasian manager, but, in view of the events I am about to describe, I am not going to reveal his name. We had a Pakistani security guard, a devout Muslim, who, following these events, could never bring himself to mention this person by name but who would always refer to him as "that dishonest man, sir," so, in this account, I will simply refer to him as "TDM."

I had some pretty smart Singaporeans working for me in the engineering department and one of them would, from time to time, try to tell me about incidents of dubious—if not outright dishonest—behaviour that TDM was involved in. I told him that I didn't want to listen to gossip and tittle-tattle about things that did not concern me. I had already noticed, however, that TDM would pull me aside and tell me, (he said he thought I ought to know), that so-and-so was saying such-and-such about me and generally spreading poisonous gossip.

One day, my informant came to me and said that TDM was building a smaller version of one of the Lagunas for his own account on a property he owned on the other side of the island and, to this end, he had the plans of the existing hull lines being drawn up on the upper level loft floor. I felt that, on this occasion, there might be some tangible evidence, so Rex and myself arranged to work late one night. We went up to the loft floor and, without turning on any lights, took flash photographs. Sure enough, when the film was developed there was the evidence as had been reported. This changed my stance from disbelieving all that I had been told to accepting it as fact unless proved otherwise. The scales fell from my eyes and I could scarcely believe what was revealed.

This man was working every scam imaginable. He had set up shell companies which would buy materials needed to build the boats from regular suppliers and then resell them to American Marine, his employer, at a mark-up. The materials themselves, of course, went direct from the original supplier to American Marine. This applied to plywood, timber, electrical cable, marine hardware and castings. He took kickbacks from shipping companies and even took a 50 cent per head fee from the canteen at lunch time—having closed the factory gates to prevent employees eating outside—telling them that it was necessary to support the factory canteen. That doesn't sound much, but considering we had 1800 employees, it added up to $900 per day, tax free—six days per week. Not bad!

My boss, Whit Newton, would never hear a bad word about anybody, so I knew that I would have to gather absolute proof of TDM's malfeasance if I wanted him to believe what I had found out. I also had to protect my sources because I knew that TDM would do anything to maintain his lucrative activities. At this time, I had been allocated a company Mercedes to drive. It was air-conditioned and I really didn't need it simply to drive to work in the early morning and back in the evening when I was hot and sweaty anyway. So I gave it to Mary to drive, taking the kids to school and attending social events during the day. I drove a VW Beetle, which was very conspicuous because the kids had acquired stickers of Disney characters somewhere and wanted somewhere to stick them, so I applied them to the VW.

Using materials stolen from the company, TDM was building the illegal boats that Rex and I had spotted being lofted on a property he owned on the other side of the island. I started following trucks taking stolen materials out of the yard, but I couldn't use the VW, so I kept a rented car parked around the corner outside the yard and then followed the truck to its destination, taking photos. I also invited various informants to my house in the evening and would interview them. One day, someone told me that TDM had a Lamborghini on order—this was almost too much to believe! But Rex and myself went to the dealership one lunchtime and walked around the showroom. We admired the cars and talked with the salesman. One of us said to the other that hadn't we heard that a local man—something to do with some boat company—had a car on order. The salesman came back right on cue with the name of TDM, the model of the car and when it was due (in about six weeks)! He even told us its value when we asked.

By the time of Whit's next visit, I had prepared a thick dossier which left no room for the slightest doubt. With his letter of dismissal in his brief case, Whit gave TDM the opportunity to resign or be fired. He chose to resign immediately and asked to use his large company Mercedes to leave the yard. A couple of hours after it was collected, all the main bearings in the engine failed, so that was his parting shot. He really should have been prosecuted for theft, but most companies usually just settle for getting rid of the thief and don't want to spend time and energy on prosecuting the individual and having their own name smeared.

TDM could not have done what he did without the cooperation of a lot of other people in the yard. He obtained this by paying them salaries much higher than the going rate and then asking them to do things they knew to be questionable. Initially these were minor, but he gradually upped the ante. By this time, they were making payments on things like TVs, and they were trapped. These were mostly young guys, and they all expected to be fired. After TDM's departure, Whit put me in charge and I interviewed each of them individually. One guy sat in a chair across from my desk with tears pouring down his face.

"What's the matter?" I asked him.

"I'm so ashamed," he replied.

"It's OK," I said, "you were deliberately led into a trap. You have learned a valuable lesson,"

I did not fire any of them and they all became great assets to the company.

The lesson for me was the immense amount of damage that can be done to a company by one individual who is working for himself. The great majority of people come to work with the basic idea of just doing their job, with no ulterior motives. These people are easy prey to the person who comes to work with the single-minded objective of promoting his own interests over those of his employer or colleagues. He achieves this by poisoning relationships between others and setting out to get rid of people who stand in his way. He is playing the game of politics, working for his own benefit at the expense of the common good—just like a real politician.

On our next leave, in July 1973, we flew to Ceylon, renamed Sri Lanka in 1972, and from there to the Seychelles' Islands, in the Indian Ocean. This beautiful archipelago is the epitome of tropical islands. It is famous for Coco de Mer, a kind of double coconut which is said to resemble a woman's buttocks! We stayed in these beautiful islands for a few days before flying on to Nairobi in Kenya.

This was our first visit to the country since I had removed my father in 1972. We rented a car and drove up to Timau to stay with some of my father's friends. While there, we went on a short pony trek around the area, staying in one of the farm houses that had been abandoned by English settlers who had returned to England. It wasn't altogether a success and very nearly ended in disaster. The person renting the ponies was an elderly European lady who had been in Kenya for many years and all the tack—horse equipment—was in a badly run down condition. Jackie was the only real horsey person in the group, and she had a horse called Nguvu—Swahili for "Strong" -- to whom she grew very attached. She was riding on her own while we were leading Nicky's horse called Maradadi—meaning "Smartly Turned Out". Nicky objected to being led and, after much pestering, I let her go, upon which her horse took off into the bush. I went after her but I had to be very careful, because the more I chased, the faster her horse went.

Horses in general tend to go much faster when on the way home than on the way out. At the end of our short trek, for safety reasons, I was the only family member who rode back, while the other four horses either went rider less or were ridden by the local men who had accompanied us. As we began to approach home, all the horses took off at full gallop and went through the gate onto the property five abreast. The lawn in front of the house was as hard as concrete and we took it on a curve, which threw me off balance. I was standing up in the stirrups, pulling as hard as I could to slow the animal down, but there was no bit and the nose band was so high up as to be useless. The hitching post was beside the house and I couldn't see how we could possibly stop in time. The next thing I knew, I was lying on my back with the wind knocked out of me. Right beside me was a brick. If I had hit the ground just a few inches further on, I would almost certainly have broken my back.

After this little adventure, we rented a Toyota four-wheel drive vehicle and set off for Marsabit in the Northern Frontier District, known as the NFD. This desert area borders Somalia and has been lawless since colonial times. In fact, for much of that period the area was closed off from the rest of Kenya unless you had a special permit. My father had a neighbour called "Tiny Gibbs" who, needless to say, had this name because he was well over six feet tall. When I was introduced to him he was in his 70s, but as a young man he had been a District Officer in the NFD. He represented the law over hundreds of square miles for three years at a stretch. He told me that it took six weeks of travel to get from Nairobi to Marsabit, using oxen for the first part of the journey; then, after they had descended the escarpment into the desert, they used camels. Most of the population are ethnic Somalis, and cattle are an important part in the economy. Cattle rustling has been endemic for years and is punishable by death in Kenya, so rustlers shoot to kill in order to escape. These people are usually referred to as *shifta,* which is the Somali word for "bandit". The situation was quite stable when we made the trip, but 40 years on, it would be too dangerous to make that same trip because of the spill over from the fighting along the border with Somalia.

We headed north from Nanyuki to Isiolo, Buffalo Springs and Archers Post. At Isiolo we descended the escarpment from the highlands of Mount Kenya. At Buffalo Springs we came to pools of clear, clean water in the middle of arid desert. The water in the pools was replaced every 45 minutes by underground springs. The pools were surrounded by doum palms and, in a biblical scene, a herd boy was watering his goats—or maybe they were sheep. They look so similar in this part of the world. My method of telling them apart was that the goats' tails went up and sheep's tails hung down. At Archers Post we turned off to the Uaso Nyiro Game Park (now called the Samburu Lodge). Here we stayed in a small *banda* and ate breakfast out in the open under the acacia trees. There were the most beautiful birds, including colourful hornbills and superb starlings, anxious to share your breakfast. We drove out along the tracks and saw much wildlife, including herds of elephant.

We continued on to Marsabit, located on Marsabit Mountain which rises 3,281 feet above the surrounding desert. Our main reason for coming here—other than its remoteness—was to see Ahmed the elephant. He carried the most enormous curving tusks and had presidential protection in the form of armed askaris to protect him from poachers who were after his ivory. We went out with a guide and found Ahmed. We all got out of the vehicle and I set up the camera on a tripod to take film. I selected the telephoto lens on the camera turret and had the shock of my life when I looked through the viewfinder. With the magnification of the lens he was looking right at me and appeared to be just a few feet away. I looked up quickly and was relieved to find he was still some way off.

We also visited geological craters called gofs. One of the

357

most dramatic was Gof Bongole, where the land dropped away beneath our feet. Another contained beautiful Lake Paradise, surrounded by forest. A pair of elephant browsed along its shore while, far below, the surrounding desert stretched to the limit of visibility.

I was anxious to take film of our Jeep negotiating the rough, rock-strewn roads, and I had just found such a place when four young Samburu tribesmen showed up, each carrying a spear. They were clad only in a simple red piece of reddish cloth knotted over one shoulder, Masai style. They saw me with my fancy 16 mm camera and indicated that they wished to have their photos taken. When shooting film or video, there is no point in taking people standing still, so I declined to take their pictures. Then I remembered someone had told me that it was a good idea to take Polaroid instant photos of people and give them away, and then they would be more cooperative when taking the pictures you really wanted. I had brought a Polaroid camera with me for just that purpose, so I took a group photo of them. When I showed it to them, they were not remotely interested in the photo. They simply wanted money because I had taken it. There were three of them in the picture but you could just see the tip of the spear of the fourth, and this, they forcefully pointed out was grounds for money, for all four. They became quite threatening and demanded Mary's necklace and scarf in addition to the money. By some sleight of hand, I managed to show that I had no money in my pockets, and we managed to get out of there after giving up a couple of cheap ball point pens. There was no chance of jumping in the Jeep and driving away because it was pointing in the wrong direction and, at my choosing, was stopped in the middle of a track that more resembled a staircase than a road. At one point I made a move to go toward the vehicle when two of them barred my way by thumping the butt ends of their spears into the ground in front of me so they were vertical with the blades facing up.

I think these were probably just young men having a bit of robust fun with some stupid, white tourists but you can never be quite sure, and I had my wife and two young kids with me. As regards the matter of paying local people for photographs, I have rather changed my tune over the years. The mere fact that you are there driving a vehicle and have a camera means to these people that you must be immensely rich—which by their standards you are, even if you have saved for years to go on your trip. You stop your vehicle and take their photo usually without their permission and then go on your way with their picture as one of your souvenirs. They, on the other hand, are left with nothing and, to add insult to injury, you probably coated them in a few extra pounds of red dust as you drove away. I think they are entitled to some benefit. The tricky part is how to give it without adding additional insult.

We were relieved to get back to the tented camp. We recounted our adventure in the bar that night with the girls in tow. When we got to the bit that they were wearing nothing under their blankets, Nicky chirped up, "Not hairy. Not like Daddy!", which brought much laughter.

There was a tropical rainstorm on one of the nights we were in the camp. Torrents of water came into the tent, so when we stepped out of bed in the dark we found ourselves paddling in four inches of freezing water. Mary rinsed the kids down with water to remove the mud, and they picked up an infestation of ticks—presumably swimming for their lives in the flood water.

Water is the key to life in desert areas, and one of the most fascinating sights was to see local Boran people bringing their animals to the Tula Wells—now also referred to as the "Singing Wells" —to water their animals. Cattle had to be watered every three days while camels could last for five or six. I had not even heard of these wells before our visit, but they remain one of the most fascinating sights I have ever seen. These wells are about 100 feet deep, and many have been in use for 500 years. The water is drawn by a chain of men and women passing leather buckets full of water hand to hand up the chain, with empty buckets coming back down at bewildering speed, while the rhythm is maintained by chanting. The top bucket is tipped into a trough. Groups of cattle wait patiently on the deep red earth of the surrounding slopes for their turn to drink. When they are given the go ahead by the herdsman, they run down to take their place at their respective trough. They not only know which is their trough, but also which is their place in the line drinking from that trough. Women wait nearby to fill clay pots strapped to donkeys with fibre bindings. Spears are stacked vertically beneath the trees.

I was able to take some beautiful film of the activity at the wells, and I also recorded the chanting. Sadly, the tape was mislaid in subsequent years before I had the opportunity and technology to merge the sound with the film.

While in the area, I made a trip to the Chalbi Desert without the family. This 38,600-square-mile desert lies to the east of Lake Rudolf, where the oldest human remains on the planet have been found. The Chalbi was once part of that lake, but is now a flat expanse of clay and salt in the hottest and most arid region of Kenya. Here the horizon dissolved into shimmering mirages, and columns of mischievous dust devils danced across the landscape. I counted 26 at one time. I went with a local guide in our Toyota. I had several water bags hung on the outside of the vehicle, from which my guide liberally helped himself. We came to a small settlement in a dried-up riverbed where there were some huts with corrugated iron roofs. They must have been like ovens inside, as the very atmosphere danced and shimmered in the suffocating heat. Local women were drawing water from pools dug in the river bed. The pools were different colours. One was pink, another green, and a third a sulphurous yellow. All had streams of small bubbles rising to the surface. In addition to watering the animals, the water was used to wash clothes and people, and for drinking. My guide nonchalantly drank from one of the pools and offered some to me. I declined and said that I didn't think it would work too well for me.

"Why not?" he said in Swahili. "We are both men, aren't we?"

Needless to say, I didn't have the antibodies that would have allowed me to survive drinking that water, and as he had already drunk most of what I had brought in the bags, I had to go thirsty. We went to a place where there were herds of camels splashing around in a pool and came to an area where a white crust of salt covered the ground. At one time salt in the desert was more valuable than gold. Camel caravans would cross thousands of miles of the desert to trade in the stuff. As it says in the bible: "If the salt has lost its savour, wherewith shall it be salted?" My guide collected some to take back with us.

Since the time of my visit severe drought has affected this area, which, together with an increase in general banditry, has made a tough life even harder for the local people.

Driving south after our visit to Marsabit, it was dusk when I saw the long neck of a giraffe preparing to cross the road ahead of us. I slowed down, and more and more of the animals appeared, until there were more than 30. It is a very bad thing to run into a giraffe—and not only for the giraffe. You hit the long legs and the large body comes through the windshield.

We stayed for couple of days at the Mount Kenya Safari Lodge. As the name suggests, it was located on the slopes of the mountain just outside the town of Nanyuki. It is a wonderful spot, still in business forty years later. The lush grounds are full of the most beautiful birds including peacocks and the stunning crowned crane, which look completely out of place if you should happen across them in their natural scrubby African bush habitat.

Finally, on August 18th, 1973, it was time for us to leave the highlands of Kenya and return once more to the steamy heat of Singapore.

At this time, in the early 70s, amazing changes were underway at American Marine. The company was expanding into all kinds of activities. In fact, as events were to show, the expansion was over-enthusiastic. The company had acquired, or had part ownership of, 33 dealerships worldwide, including eight waterfront facilities in the U.S. In addition to the GM Toroflow engines, we were now marinizing John Deere engines in Singapore. A plant had been acquired to produce consolidated marine electronics in Singapore, and another to produce marine sealants in Los Angeles. A factory to build office furniture had been set up in Malaysia. The company owned an advertising agency which did work for other companies in addition to American Marine.

It was around this time that the company went public, and being one of the original group, I was given significant share options. They didn't mean a great deal in practical terms because you couldn't actually exercise the options. The share offering brought in quite a lot of outside money, but it was used up very quickly in paying down the bank loan and covering the expenses associated with the rapid expansion and new ventures. Many of these were great ideas, but they came along too fast and relied on continued boat sales. We now had more than 1,800 employees in Singapore and 1,200 in Hong Kong, with the two yards producing, between them, one boat per day. In addition, there were more than 350 employees in the U.S., where, incredibly, labour costs exceeded those at the two boatbuilding plants.

More money was needed, and this came from investment by a British-based trading company in Singapore called Inchcape Berhad. They invested around five million dollars, and I thought our financial troubles were over. However, the bank hijacked nearly all the money, and I found myself having to buy supplies for the drawing office out of my own pocket.

Inchcape was a trading company operating rather like William Jacks—the company that had brought me out to HK. With so much money invested, Inchcape wanted to have some say in the running of the company. They owned a car assembly plant in Shah Alam, just outside Kuala Lumpur in Malaysia, and they suggested that it might be productive for me to visit the plant to see how they controlled production. I was keen to go, and it was certainly an interesting and unusual place. Countries like Malaysia put a high tariff on fully assembled vehicles coming into their country, so vehicle manufacturers often set up assembly plants within the country using CKD kits—the letters standing for "Completely Knocked Down". Even so, very often the cost of setting up such a plant is not justified by the sales in that country. The answer was a contract assembly plant, which assembles many different makes of vehicles within one plant.

The plant I visited assembled VW, Mercedes, Renault, Land Rover and Bedford. There might have been others, but those are the ones I remember. I won't take the time to go into the details, but it was an interesting concept and one that made sense. The manager was an Australian and he told me that the quality of the

CKD kits varied from company to company. Some, like Mercedes, were thoroughly worked out in detail, whereas other looked as though they had "just thrown the parts into a box!" But even with Mercedes they had problems, such as when the windshields had been packed so tight that the pattern from the corrugated paper separating the glass had imprinted itself into windshields, and they could not be used. This meant that, not only could they not complete the cars, but they could not even move them outside. I guess everyone has bizarre problems to deal with!

One of the consultants who had visited American Marine was a German-Australian who spoke English with an accent which was an interesting mix of German and Australian. His take on my boss was: "Here's this fellah, Whit, going round and round in circles getting absolutely nowhere!" Certainly Whit was always rushing from one place to another, making endless notes and calling people on the phone at every opportunity. This was long before the advent of cell phones, so that was not an easy thing to do.

It was into this already precarious situation that the winds of change arrived, without warning, in the form of the oil embargo and soaring fuel prices, which resulted in long lines at fuel pumps in the U.S. Boat sales dropped to virtually zero, but the yards, with their large payrolls to satisfy, continued to ship boats to the company-owned dealerships to convert the latter's bank facilities into cash back at the factories. Finally, when these funds were utilized, the smoke blew away, the mirrors cracked and, for second time in ten years, bankruptcy loomed.

At this time, Bob Livingston came out to Singapore with his family from American Marine in California to take charge of the financial affairs of the company. The company's bankers in Singapore were the First National City Bank, and it was a stroke of good fortune that they had recently replaced the Singaporean manager with an American who was not only a boater but who recognized the value of the Grand Banks brand. The situation was dire. Not only was the company in debt to the bank to the tune of 15 million dollars, but they owed money to the employees, the vendors, the unions, the tax authorities, and the Central Provident Fund, which was the social security instrument in Singapore for the workforce.

Finally, in 1974, at the bank's insistence through the actions of the receiver, operations in the U.S. and Hong Kong were closed down, as were the various peripheral operations. The Newtons lost their company, and the work force in Singapore was reduced from 1,800 to 350. A handful of us—including myself and Anton—retained our jobs, but the future appeared grim.

For the past few years we had been living the good life. I was spending the money as it came in without giving any serious thought to the future. All of a sudden that future looked very uncertain, and I had no idea what I would do should American Marine close its doors. I had a contract that said that the company would pay the cost to repatriate myself and my family back to England, but that was meaningless if the company didn't have any money. In any case, what would I do if I went back to England? I was almost 40 and, in England, that was old enough to consign you to the scrap heap.

I decided the first thing to do would be to get the family back to England and find a place to live before the money ran out. My sister had moved down to North Devon, in the West of England, and my mother had moved there, also, to be closer to her. It seemed, therefore, that this would be the area to look, even though it was very rural and Mary was not really a country girl. Prices in that area would also be much cheaper than those closer to London.

So in the summer of 1974, we went to England and set out on a house-hunting exercise. North Devon is bleaker and poorer than the south, and the houses are generally less attractive. In the northern parts of the northern hemisphere, people usually prefer houses with a southerly aspect, so that they face the sun. If you live near the coast, people like a view of the sea; but on a north coast, facing the sea means facing north, so most of the houses actually faced inland and had a hill between them and the coast. This was very sensible, as the trees and bushes were permanently slanted towards the south—a clear indication that the prevailing winds were from the north.

The west country of England was laced with a network of

narrow sunken lanes. These were just wide enough for one vehicle and had intermittent passing places, so if you met another vehicle head on, one of you had to reverse to a passing place. The system worked well but was nerve racking if you were not used to it. Being sunken, you could see little of the surrounding countryside, and it was very easy to get lost in this maze. The situation was further aggravated by the capricious system of signposting. At each intersection a signpost would point the way to nearby villages, including the one you were looking for. But at the next intersection, that name would be nowhere to be seen, and you would have to guess which way to turn. A large scale Ordinance Survey map was essential, but the network of lanes was so intricate that it was still easy to go astray. On one occasion it was only by recognizing a particular tree stump that we realized we had been driving in circles.

Eventually we found a farmhouse called Treedown that fitted what we were looking for. The farmer who was selling was moving to a smaller bungalow on the farm. He showed us into one outbuilding attached to the house, where there was a hinged door attached to a single post in the middle of the room. Explaining its function, he said in his broad Devon accent:

"'Ee goes this way, and 'ee goes that way, and 'ee goes nowhere really!"

He wanted 25,000 pounds for the house, with four acres of land and a stream. This seemed a lot to us at the time, but we took out a mortgage and went ahead with the purchase.

We returned to Singapore and mentally began to prepare for the task of moving the family to England the following spring. But before making this major change in our lives, we took advantage of being in the boat business and cruised in a borrowed GB 42 to the Tioman Islands in the South China Sea. We went with Rex and Jill, who were both vastly more experienced than myself. The island archipelago is very beautiful. In fact, *Time* Magazine selected Tioman as one of the world's most beautiful islands and its beaches were featured as Bali Hai in the 1958 movie *South Pacific*. The islands are sparsely inhabited and surrounded by numerous coral reefs. We had a wonderful, adventurous time during which we hardly saw another boat. In the open sea were tugs towing barges to the oil fields further north off the coast of Thailand. The barges were often a half-mile separated from their tug and, I came to realize how, with visibility reduced in a tropical rainstorm and without radar, it would be easy to inadvertently pass between the two vessels, with potentially disastrous results.

We went ashore and found a mango tree in the jungle with much fruit dropped on the ground. We filled a bucket and gorged on mangoes back on the boat. They can be messy to eat, but we jumped in the sea to wash off the sticky juice, which had smeared our faces and run down our arms.

Chapter 5

Spring 1975 to October 1975

Life in Singapore

My family moves to England. The company fights for survival. I re-organize production control and there is disagreement over company ownership. I become involved in a new company to build coffins for export.

When the family moved to England, we knew we could not keep our lovely little family dog, Penny. Like Pooch had been in Hong Kong, she was also a local chow variety. She was very pretty and very much looked like a female version of Pooch. She had been born as one of a litter of puppies in the factory from whom American Marine bought propellers. She had been adopted by the manager of the factory. When his wife became pregnant, she no longer wanted a dog in the house and they were considering having her put down. We were horrified and said we would take her. She was a sweet dog and soon became part of the family. When still only six months old she was got at by a neighbour's dog and became pregnant. She gave birth to six beautiful puppies— three with fluffy hair and three with smooth. She was the perfect mother and cleaned up after them in the area they had on the patio, but as soon as the puppies could walk they would stagger over to the far side of the garden to do their business. These are a breed of dog who do not need to be housetrained.

We gave Penny to another English family whose father was a welding specialist on the oil rigs being constructed in Singapore—

some of which were towed, at 3 knots, by way the Cape of Good Hope, all the way to the North Sea! A few years later, this family moved back to the UK. They could not bear to part with the dog so they took her with them, and she went through the six months' mandatory quarantine when she arrived in England. She continued to live with the family in England for several years until they were relocated to Houston, in the U.S. By this time, she was getting on in age, so they gave her to an elderly relative who had more or less given up on life. Penny brought to this person a whole new reason for living, and they both lived out the remainder of their lives together. A truly remarkable story for a stray mongrel puppy born in a factory in Singapore.

When we moved into the house in Devon, in spring 1975, we had absolutely no furniture. We bought beds and a TV set. We sat on cushions on the floor and used the box the TV had come in as a table. There was an Aga range in the living room to cook on. The recess for this cooker had a wallpaper pattern that resembled a stone wall. I drew up a bunch of plans to change the layout of the house, including converting some of the barns and outhouses and moving the location of the front door. We employed a builder to carry out the work, and when he pulled down a dividing wall in the living room we discovered there was a real stone fireplace hidden behind the stone-patterned wallpaper!

From the days of their earliest memories our kids had been flying around the world visiting strange places and attending schools with students from a wide variety of countries. Now they would be attending a village school where all subjects were taught in a single room and many of the students had never been much further than the local town. I really wondered how well they would fit in, but there was never the slightest problem.

I reluctantly left Mary and the kids to settle into rural life in England, while I returned to Singapore to American Marine and to live on my own. It was really hard to leave and return to an unpleasant work environment. It was made even worse because I had to stop off in Brussels to meet the dealer there. I arrived at the hotel feeling glum and sorry for myself and went to find a coffee shop or similar to have a light supper. The only restaurant in the hotel was a formal dining room, and I rather grumpily settled for that. At the entrance they were handing out a free glass of champagne. I drank mine down and immediately began to feel a lot better, which led to me ordering a great dinner, including desert and wine. That glass of free champagne was probably the most cost-effective marketing tool ever!

The following day I had arranged to meet the dealer at a certain metro station. I had to go by train, and he told me where to get off. I looked out for the station at every stop. Finally, I identified it, but not until too late as the train was already leaving the station. I got off at the next stop to backtrack, but found myself in an almost deserted station. In my halting French I asked a rail official who was not at all helpful and just barked at me one word which sound like "*Vonze*" before he turned his back and walked away. I had no idea what he had said but finally figured it must have been "*Va onze,*" which I translated as "Go eleven". I went in search of platform 11 and found that I had to be careful as not all trains which stopped at that platform went to where I was trying to get back to. Eventually I made it, only to find that the concourse had multiple entrances, so I had to keep visiting them all until I finally encountered the person I was to meet.

Life back in Singapore was not much fun. I was missing the family, and we had to reduce the labour force from 1,800 to 350. This was done in three stages. Letting the first lot go was not too bad, as most of the first group had been lazy people who did very little work and wanted to cause trouble. However, beyond that it became harder and harder as really good people had to be let go through no fault of their own, and it was tough to be the executioner and decide who would go. I remember one pay day when the bank had still not reached a decision as to whether to provide the cash until after lunch. The money then all had to be brought out to the yard and sorted into individual pay packets. This took until well after five o'clock and all the employees were sitting around waiting for the process to be completed. They were remarkably good humoured about it. Bob Livingston said that he would throw himself out of the window but he was afraid he would only break his arm!

The other problem was that, as the company owed money to nearly all the suppliers, we could not buy any new supplies from them unless some of the money owing on previous deliveries was paid down at the same time. Also, all materials of any value that we did have on hand—for example shafting—were guarded by a watchman in the employ of one of the vendors. In effect these materials belonged to the vendor and were his security against payment for what we owed, so even though we had bought them, we had to pay down the debt owing to the vendor to be able to use them. In fact, we had very little to build anyway, because no new sales would come in until after all the inventory had been sold from the dealerships.

I was favourably impressed by the attitude of the local vendors. I mentioned this to the man who supplied the company with timber, whom we knew as "Timber Tan". In response he told me that when everything was working well, his business with the company had allowed him to make money. Now that the company was in trouble, it was his responsibility to do what he could to help it in recognition of the advantages he had gained from the relationship in the past. I thought that the world would be a much better place if more people took this attitude.

Money was extremely tight and every penny had to be saved. This was well before the days of emails, and even before fax. Fast communication was by telex, in which each individual word was charged for. Telexes were exchanged almost every day between the yard and places overseas, and discussions were held on how short the messages could be while still conveying their meaning.

Anton, who had also survived the cut, was living in California and we were in constant communication, mostly associated with our work, but the future of the company looked so uncertain that we thought we ought to be looking into alternatives. Anton came up with the idea of making coffins!

"Just think," he said, "no warranty!"

I put the idea to Cheong Wing Lee, the Singaporean who had alerted me to the behaviour of TDM, and he agreed to come in on the scheme. In general, Chinese are quite superstitious about anything concerned with death, but he was OK with this.

The three of us formed a small company called Trident Tradelinks, rented a small workshop, and Wing Lee co-opted some open-minded carpenters who had been laid off from American Marine. The coffins had to be knocked-down design to cut down on shipping. The first samples were traditional-shaped coffins and sent to an undertaker Anton had met in England. Later designs were much more elaborate rectangular caskets of the type used in the U.S. These had curved sides, and I devised a method of building them using a boatbuilding technique called "strip planking" for which I still hold the patent (Coffin and method of making the same. Nos. 805, 824; D-1107)! The problem with these was holding the veneer in place over the curved surfaces while the glue went off. To solve this, I devised rubber airbags which we made by gluing rubber sheets together using Super Glue. These did the job, but tended to come apart. Today I would have used vacuum bagging. It turned out that the warranty problem did not entirely go away because the caskets were on display in heated showrooms, and having come from the high humidity in Singapore, they were prone to cracking. Anton suggested naming the different models after the moons of Jupiter, which I thought were very appropriate—e.g., Europa, Ganymede, Callisto and Amalthea. The business was ultimately not successful because it required a lot more money and dedication than we could devote to it and American Marine began to claw its way back from the brink. But I think the idea could have succeeded if we had concentrated on it.

With the company pretty well dismembered, the task was to try to put the pieces back together. No one is going to spend a lot of money on a boat built by a company which might completely vanish tomorrow, so one of the first tasks was to convince dealers and potential customers that this was not going to happen.

In October 1975, Bob Livingston and myself flew to Europe on one of those 7-countries-in-10-days kind of trips. We started in Rome with one of those lengthy Mediterranean lunches that went on for hours and included wine. Business was only discussed during the final 10 minutes. We were due to fly out of Rome the following morning, but a strike by employees at the airport put paid to that plan. As this was our first stop, our entire itinerary was in jeopardy. We were able to save the situation by renting a car from a company that had a French BMW they wanted returned to France.

As is so often the case in life, this setback turned out to have advantages because of the interest of the drive—especially in the northern part of Italy, where the road passed through the Apennines. The high-speed road passed through an endless series of curved tunnels and viaducts which went on for hours, leaving you literally speechless, having expended your entire vocabulary of superlatives in the first hour. We arrived in Nice after a spectacular drive and were back on schedule.

We visited Italy, France, Germany, Holland, Belgium, Spain and the UK before flying back to Singapore. When in France I found that I could remember enough French from my school days to get by, but it was very rusty, so when I returned to Singapore, I signed up at the Alliance Française for French lessons.

Just one month later, we held a dealer meeting at the yard in Singapore to demonstrate that we were really in business. There were many different personalities involved and, as might be imagined, they did not always see eye to eye. Especially in Europe, they were always trying to undercut one another and sell into another dealer's territory. Among the colourful personalities was Carlos Kuntze, a blond, blue-eyed German who had lived in Venezuela for many years. He had very strong opinions, and when making a point, he would often stick his finger in your chest and address you as "Mister". Coming from Venezuela, he should have been inoculated against Yellow Fever. He had failed to do this so the Singapore authorities at the airport locked him up in quarantine for three days, and after flying all the way from Venezuela, he missed the meeting. However, he took it all in good humour.

Another character was our dealer in France, Jean-Jacques Bouillant-Linet. He was a large, tall man who had a French father and American mother. He had once been one of Charles de Gaulle's bodyguards. He was very French and spoke English with a delightful French accent. He had originally been appointed as

372

our dealer in France by Anton, who had many stories about Jean-Jacques, including their first meeting. Jean-Jacques could put away prodigious amounts of alcohol and was from that era where a man was judged by how well he could hold his liquor. Having survived a perilous, high-speed drive south from Paris in a car totally lacking brakes, the two of them were in a bar in Antibes where JJ, as I shall call him, was trying to out-drink Anton, who was equally determined to survive the challenge. JJ excused himself to go to the toilet, and when he failed to return, Anton went looking for him and found him asleep on the toilet with his pants around his ankles. He woke him up and together they staggered off to JJ's car, where his dog, Coco, was waiting for them.

JJ put Coco—an Old English Sheepdog—in the driver's seat and Anton, who was of course well oiled, giggled and said, "Is the dog going to drive?"

To which JJ replied, "It's our only hope!" and got into the front passenger seat.

They took off, with JJ steering and pushing the pedals. Down the road they were stopped by the gendarmes, who knew JJ well.

"Has the dog got a driving license?" they wanted to know.

JJ had to admit that he did not.

"Then he cannot drive," said the police. "Who is this person in the back?"

"That is my father," said JJ.

"Well, who is least drunk?" they asked.

It was decided that Anton qualified for this dubious honour, and he took over the driver's seat from Coco.

Coco and JJ had met each other in a bar somewhere and had somehow developed an informal relationship. They went everywhere together, with Coco riding pillion in a wooden box in the back of JJ's moped. On another occasion, JJ left a bar and, with Coco in his box, took off down the steep streets of Antibes toward the harbour. He lost control and started bouncing off the stone walls lining edge of the street. Anticipating what lay ahead,

Coco started barking and, when the inevitable happened, broke into a prolonged howl as he, the moped, and JJ sailed through the air into the harbour.

A few years later, Mary, my two kids, and myself went on a one-week cruise along the French Riviera with JJ in a Grand Banks 42. Coco came along, too, as he was a first-class boat dog. He was always first ashore and would go off and explore the town on his own. On one occasion the sea was unpleasantly rough, and JJ and myself were on the flying bridge, with the boat bouncing around and spray flying everywhere. Coco appeared on the flying bridge and immediately threw up. JJ was unsympathetic and said, "What are you doing up here you stupid dog? You know you always get seasick on the flying bridge!" Coco slunk back down again—which is quite treacherous on a GB 42 in rough seas. He went around the aft deck to seek some shelter just in time to get doused by a large wave. There are few sights more miserable than a soaking-wet, hairy dog!

JJ was an experienced boat person and had to deal with an unusual problem on the early GBs. On the first boats, the fuel tanks were in the lazarette, and while the vents were looped high up, they terminated below the quarter guard, just above the waterline. JJ was taking a bunch of journalists out for a sea trial when the engines kept stopping. He finally figured out that, with the boat rolling, the fuel sloshing back and forth in the tanks was acting as a pump. The timing was such that the fuel was moving away from the vent opening in the tank at the same time that the other end was under water with the result that water was being sucked into the tanks through the vents. This is a fine example of one of those traps I mentioned earlier, and why experience is all important to be a builder of safe and successful boats.

It took a long time but we gradually brought American Marine back from the brink. The oil crisis passed and the inventory at the dealerships—many of which had passed to the banks when the company-owned dealerships folded—was absorbed. This allowed us to start production again in a limited way. The gradual start was beneficial because it allowed us to reorganize production properly, without the pressure of having to turn out large numbers of boats.

I have always likened a production line to being like a locomotive. It takes a long time to build it up to speed, and when it has momentum, you cannot just stop it or make instantaneous changes in direction without the risk of a major wreck.

A good analogy for describing production planning is called "Dinner at Eight", which uses the scenario that a housewife has to go through every day. First she has to decide what to make for the family dinner at eight. She then has to purchase, or have on hand, the raw materials within her budget. She has to know at what time to start making the meal, in what order to cook the ingredients and what equipment to use so as to have the finished product on the table at eight o'clock. These steps accurately reflect those that any production manager has to go through.

This was still before the days of computers, but we did have a large and complex accounting machine. I suppose it was the beginning of a sort of computerized system, but it was still subject to the GIGO rule— "Garbage In = Garbage Out!" In those days, workers used to go to the stores with a requisition for the parts they needed for the task at hand. Each and every requisition was entered into the account for that boat. This took hours—if not days—and trips to the store were a good excuse to go and chat with your friends. If materials were lost or stolen, a worker simply went back and got more. By the time all the costs were in, it might be weeks after the boat had shipped, and if the costs were higher than they should be, no one had any idea why, and the accounting department just added a fudge factor into the amount to bring it into line with what was expected. In other words, all this elaborate charade of recording costs was a total waste of time!

To me, it was obvious that every standard boat in the production line had to contain exactly the same materials in order to finish it. So, if we checked that the boat was complete—which, of course, we always did—and we knew everything required to build it—which we had to know in order to buy it—then the list was always the same.

Based on this simple premise, I did away with the thousands of normal requisitions and replaced them with a single entry for each boat. We made up all the parts into kits issued to the right build stations at the right time so workers no longer needed to go in person to the stores. If a worker needed more materials to finish his job, he raised a special requisition. He was given the materials, but every special requisition was investigated. Maybe the boat had a special option, or the materials were faulty or mislaid, or maybe the list was wrong—in which case it was amended.

We made templates for each and every piece of plywood on the boat, laid it out for the most efficient cutting with the least wastage and centralized the cutting. This reduced plywood usage by a whopping 51 per cent!

There had always been a worrying amount of wastage when cutting wood—especially the valuable and expensive teak. Teak arrived in the form of logs which had first to be sawn into planks. When you totalled up the length of the cuts and the width of the blade, the volume of wood reduced to sawdust was alarming. By the time the timber had been further reduced to the sizes and shapes used in the boat, we had piles of odd-shaped off-cuts which were added to an ever-growing mountain. I had bought a table and noticed that the top was made of short pieces of wood joined in a process known as finger-jointing. I looked into this and learnt that the joint, created on special machines, was actually stronger than the original wood. We used a number of woodworking machines, but none of us were specialists in the subject and we had no time to learn. On one of my trips to England I recruited Colin Holmes, a woodworking specialist who had worked for the United Nations in various countries. With his help and that of a local Singaporean whom Colin hired as his assistant, we set up a finger-jointing machine and four-sided cutters, together with a system and crew to maintain them and keep the cutters sharp. We were able to convert the mountain of off-cuts into useful timber, as well as run the whole wood-shop much more efficiently.

I also felt that we did not adequately understand the advances in fibreglass technology. We had relied on what we had learned from Howard Abbey and it continued to be successful, but technology had moved on and we neither had the time nor the technical background to take advantage of the advances in materials and techniques. I brought in Colin Ayres from Perth in

Western Australia and put him in charge of the fibreglass shop. For reasons I am still not able to identify, this was not a success. When people decide that they are not going to make something work, they can find a thousand reasons to make that happen. The foreman of the shop decided that he did not like the changes and managed to sabotage the program so that the fibreglass shop began to produce less and less parts, which obviously jeopardized the entire production process. I could have gone to war over it but, in the short term, that would only have aggravated the situation. The Oriental way is to bend like the bamboo and then come back upright when the tempest has passed, rather than standing solid and uncompromising like the oak and then go over with a crash and finish up as firewood. I moved Colin from the fibreglass shop into the development department, where he contributed many excellent ideas. We continued to make changes in the fibreglass department but introduced them in more gradual and subtle ways.

When it came to labour, we already had the different areas of the boat broken down into about 40 categories, with a standard labour estimate for each. I had large sheets of paper made up in the drawing office for each boat, with the account categories down the side, showing the standard man hours and dates across the top. Each day the labour for the previous day was entered, together with the accumulative total. When the accumulative amount exceeded the standard, the next entry was made in red and an investigation made as to the reason. This allowed us to know instantly when the hours exceeded the standard, so it was easy to find out why. In fact, by keeping an eye on the physical progress of the work, along with the man hours, it was possible to see when the standard was going to be exceeded even before it actually did so.

Now we knew the cost of each boat the day after its completion and there was no more fudging. The principle being followed here was Management by Exception, in which you do not attempt to look at everything but only those things which fall outside the norm.

Unions in Singapore were closely controlled by the government. Any problems that the management and workers could not resolve themselves were required, by law, to go to arbitration; and the parties, were required, by law, to abide by the decision. It was essentially illegal to go on strike. But the workers had to pay dues every month to the union, and they grumbled about how little they got for their money. I used to attend meetings with the union committee every month, and I came to realize that a union is like any other organization, in that it wants to succeed. To be a member of the union committee meant that a worker had some status above just being another worker, but he had to able to justify it to his fellow workers. We really did not have any points of conflict with the union, but, on several occasions, when I came up with an idea which would benefit the workforce, I suggested it to the union members, and it was then presented to the workforce as an idea coming from the union and agreed to by me rather than the other way around. That way it took the monkey off the union's back when they were asked to explain what they did to justify the union dues.

The Lagunas were no longer in production, but problems with existing boats in service kept us busy. We had a test Laguna 33 sitting on the hard standing, and for some reason it was necessary to launch it and run the engines. The starboard engine took off and screamed up to unheard of rpm. Pulling back the throttle had no effect, neither did the governor that was supposed to control it. There was a violent bang, and the engine stopped with a big hole in the side of the block! I had been standing between the two engines at the time, and it was a bit scary. It was also a complete mystery as to what had happened.

We removed the engine and replaced it with another, assuming there had been something awry with the original. We started it up and, unbelievably, the same thing happened. This time, with shrapnel flying, a piston took out both sides of the block as well as the oil pan.

We installed a third engine and this time stood by with rags to stuff into the turbocharger intake to suffocate combustion. This engine ran away, also, but we were just able to get it stopped before it flew apart.

We sent the fuel injection pumps to Bosch to be inspected, and they found out that the pistons had rusted solid inside their cylinders. They were stuck so tight that the pin connecting the governor to the control mechanism had sheared right off—which also disconnected the throttle.

It was eventually ascertained that, in the tropical climate, water had collected in the fuel filters over the weeks when the boat sat idle. The filters are designed to separate the water from the fuel and they do this very efficiently until the filter is full of water, at which time, we learned, it will allow water to pass. Of course an engine will not run on water, but if there is enough fuel already in the pump to allow the engine to start, the water can reach the fuel injection pump. As soon as it does, it causes an instantaneous rusting of the pistons in their chambers. If you are lucky, they will rust in the shut position. If not—and we were not—they will rust in the full open position. An expensive lesson!

Actually the Lagunas were an especially fruitful field for providing hard lessons. In another example we had a boat which was not performing up to scratch, and the exhaust from one of the engines was putting out black smoke. We spent the best part of the week checking everything on that engine, including the propeller, but could find nothing wrong. Eventually the problem was traced to a partially blocked fuel line on the *other* engine. That one was not pulling its weight because of fuel starvation, so its companion was trying to compensate and became overloaded.

As I said earlier, boat building is full of traps, and experience is what counts.

One of the people who survived the savage cutbacks and the closing of the corporate offices in the U.S. was Dick Loh, who had been one of the sales personnel on the East Coast. Dick was a gruff individual who seemed to have an especial dislike of Brits, but myself in particular. He lived in Greenwich, Connecticut and there is no doubt that he did a good job in setting up dealers along that coast. Seventy percent of our sales emanated from that area, although this was partly because it was the seat of much "old" money—meaning it was in the hands of people whose fortunes were not so subject to the volatility in the economy. One of my responsibilities was in making the boats cheaper to build without cheapening their quality. But Dick viewed the slightest change negatively and, if he had had his way, we would never have changed a single thing in the boats because, in his opinion, every item was sacrosanct and vital to the continued sale of the boats. It was true that, after near bankruptcy, the bank insisted that cost be taken out of the boats by downgrading the specification, and since savings could not be taken from the boat's structure without reducing its integrity, they had to come from small, visible items. For example, removing the door from the hanging locker. This saved very little money but had a very obvious deleterious effect on perceived quality, so was counterproductive. It is typical of what happens when people start meddling in subjects about which they have no experience. I think that Dick blamed me for these changes.

After the situation had begun to stabilize, Bob Livingstone wanted to rationalize the ownership of the company. He proposed that he take 75 per cent of the shares and the remaining 25 per cent be distributed among the five of us who still had our jobs. This meant that each of us would only get 5 per cent against his 75 percent, which, unsurprisingly, did not go down very well. A company teetering on the edge of bankruptcy could be likened to a patient in intensive care. The first priority is of course to keep the patient alive. Once that was achieved, the patient had to be rehabilitated so that he could regain his ability to function normally. Bob could certainly claim the credit for working with the bank and the creditors to achieve the first step, but rehabilitation required the experience of people like myself and many others. Bob knew absolutely nothing about boats or how to build them. In a fit of irritation, I once told him that without people with technical skills, we would all still be living in caves and we wouldn't even have pencils to write with!

We had a stormy meeting in Bob's office, at which Dick Loh was present. Dick was the only person present, other than Bob of course, who believed that Bob should get 75 per cent of the shares. He said that every ship needed a captain. Ron Filbert, the chief accountant, whom Bob had brought into the company, responded that the captain did not need to own the ship! Being a minority shareholder means absolutely nothing. If you disagree with the policy of the company you can jump up and down and scream and shout all you want, but you are just a voice crying in the wind.

With all the animosity generated by this situation, the decision was referred to a lawyer in the U.S. who had worked with the company in the past and was familiar with its history. Ultimately, Bob finished up with just under 50 per cent and I was awarded more than 20 per cent, based on my long service with the company and the fact that I had been promised shares before the financial problems. I wound up with more than Dick Loh, which did not sit well with him. Actually, while the company remained seriously in debt, all each of us had was a share of less than nothing!

So now we were all shareholders, as well as directors and employees. I had never given any thought to these relationships before, but each of these positions had very different perspectives and responsibilities which did not necessarily coincide and which, as we shall see later, contributed to dramatic events.

Despite these disagreements, the fortunes of the company were steadily improving, and we were able to begin thinking about introducing new models. There had been a Europa version of the wooden GB 42, and we duplicated this model in fibreglass. Another new model was the GB 49, which was really 51 feet. The reason for this was that the hull was a stretched version of the old GB 48, which had never been built in glass. We did not want to call it the GB 50 because that would confuse it with the old flush-deck boat, which had only been built in wood. I did all the design work on the boat, and it turned out very well. The first boat was shipped in time for the 1980 Miami Boat Show.

Chapter 6

July 1976 to September 1980

Life in Singapore

I am co-opted into amateur stage production. I make boat trips to the Malacca Strait and the Virgin Islands and travel to England, Sumatra, California, Mexico, Penang, Bahamas, Sri Lanka and India. My sister's husband dies of cancer.

One day, Bob Livingston came into my office and said that a person he had met through the American Club was looking for someone to help her with making the scenery for a one-act play she was producing at the Stage Club—one of the amateur dramatic clubs in Singapore. I told him that I would be prepared to help provided that I didn't have to make any decisions or organize anything, because I was exhausted at the end of a day from doing exactly that. I said if she gave me a paint brush and a pot of yellow paint and told me to paint a flat surface yellow, I could manage that. He asked if it would be OK if he told her to call me, and I agreed.

A couple of days later I received the call, and she opened by saying that she understood that I was the guy who was going to be the Stage Manager for her play. I said "No, no, no," and I gave her my spiel about painting a flat surface yellow. She asked would it be OK if we met at the club, and I agreed.

So I went to the club, which I had never visited before and where I knew no one. It was located in a big old colonial-style house. I walked in and introduced myself and immediately they said, "Oh you're the chap who's going to be the Stage Manager for the *three* one act plays!"

And that's the way it turned out! I had never been a Stage Manager before—I did not even know what the responsibilities were! Actually having three separate plays—each of one act—on one night was much more difficult than having one multi-act play, because three individual plays meant three directors, three casts, and three sets. Because I did not know anyone, I more or less had to make and paint the sets myself. I also had to design and get made some of the props. For example, in one of the plays, there was one of those overhead candelabras which you can raise or lower, balanced by a counterweight. In this case, the counterweight was a bowl of fruit, to which the actors helped themselves—making the light fixture go up and down (humorous, huh?). This had to be controlled from off stage, and I had to fabricate a rig using Grand Banks steering components.

I also discovered that, while the director has sole charge of their production until opening night, it is at that point that the show becomes the sole responsibility of the Stage Manager, including dealing with last minute nerves on the part of the cast! It was quite a learning experience. So much for simply painting a flat surface yellow!

After we moved into Treedown, all my energies at work were taken up with the problems associated with the bankruptcy and in trying to bring the company back from the brink. Any overseas leave I had was spent in visiting the family back in England. Even after all the savage cutbacks, we had a lot of surplus capacity at the yard and I used—and paid for—some of it making components for Treedown, such as a really nice teak front door. I designed some knocked-down teak panelling for the study room in the house. We also had a huge surplus of power tools, and I bought a selection of these and sent them back to England.

After the girls had outgrown the village school, we decided to send them to Edgehill College—a school for girls in the town of Bideford. Although the school accepted both boarders and day girls, we lived a bit too far away for them to travel to school every day. I also hoped that, at some point, Mary would be able to re-join me in Singapore. Jackie started in September 1976, and I remember taking her there and dropping her off in the dormitory. There was one other little girl there, also called Nicola. I really felt like a tyrant leaving her there. The school had a very sensible rule that a child could not go home for the weekend for three weeks. We duly came and collected Jackie at that time and took her back on Sunday evening. She refused to get out of the car and stuck out her arms and legs like a Harley rider. I had to physically drag her out of the car, and then she refused to walk, and I had to drag her with her two heels leaving furrows in the gravel driveway. I pushed her inside the house, feeling like a tyrant. When we got home 45 minutes later we called the school, and the housemistress said that Jackie was fine and was chatting away to her friends. I could have killed her! Nicky followed her sister one year later.

Instead of taking my overseas leave in one chunk, I divided it into two shorter breaks and paid the extra airfare. I went back to England usually during school summer holidays and also at Christmas. The area was very rural and surrounded by the beautiful countryside of Exmoor and Dartmoor, where we were able to hike. I really enjoyed being in England. As it was at the time of the first oil crisis, there were all sorts of scenarios floating around about oil supplies running out, and self-sufficiency was a popular subject. I converted the AGA range from coal to oil and installed extra-large fuel tanks. The house was very private up a long drive and enjoyed a wonderful view over very English countryside. Right after we moved in, they (whoever "they" are) started erecting a line of gigantic power pylons which marched across the landscape like aliens from *War of the Worlds*. These monstrosities were totally out of scale with their surroundings and destroyed the vista. We strategically planted trees to conceal the worst of them from our view. The cooler weather and the beautiful English countryside were a welcome contrast from the unbroken heat and urban bustle of Singapore.

When the most critical stage of the financial crisis was finally overcome, we settled down into a pattern where either I spent my leaves at Treedown, in England, or the family visited me back in Singapore. While I was at Treedown in August 1977, my brother-in-law, Michael, and I decided to sail his Tornado catamaran out to Lundy Island, which lies 12 miles off the coast of North Devon. The Tornado was 20 feet long and 10 feet wide and consisted of two hulls and a canvas trampoline. Michael had been a navigation officer in the Royal Navy, but all we had in the way of instruments was a kid's plastic ruler with a cheap compass in the middle of it. We had to share one wet suit, with one of us wearing the trousers and the other the jacket. We set off from tiny Instow Yacht Club one morning, but by the time we reached the harbour entrance, the fog had come down and we lost sight of the land. There was not much wind and Michael set a course for the island, allowing an offset for the tidal stream. The tidal range at Appledore is 25 feet, so the tidal flow was considerable. We ghosted along when suddenly two enormous black fins surfaced right alongside the boat. They seemed exceptionally big because our backsides were only about 12 inches above the water. They could only have been killer whales and we had snuck up on them and caught them unawares. With a swirl of water, they disappeared.

A short while later we heard the unmistakable *thumpa-thumpa* of a heavy, slow-turning diesel engine. A small freighter materialized out of the gloom and passed at right angles to our course, about 50 yards in front of us. We could see through the bridge windows that there was no one on watch. Before it disappeared back into fog, we saw that the port of registry was Bremen.

After a couple of hours ghosting through the gloom, Michael reckoned we should adjust our course, as the tide had turned. After nearly four hours we began to strain our ears for the sounds of waves braking on the shore and our eyes for the shadowy hint of something more substantial than fog. Suddenly the island appeared, and we were bang on course. Before we left we had been under the impression that if we missed the island we would eventually land in Wales, across the other side of the Bristol Channel. In fact, when I later checked the chart, I realized that our course took us just past the southern coast of Ireland, and the next piece of land was Nova Scotia!

Lundy is ringed by cliffs and has a population of less than 30.

385

It does have a pub, and after dragging the catamaran up the beach, we climbed the steep path and had a couple of pints before setting out on our return journey. The fog was still thick, but midway through the return journey it suddenly lifted as if a curtain had been raised. The sky was blue and the North Devon coast was spread out before us. We decided to maintain the course we had set just to see where we would have finished up, and, if we hadn't altered course to avoid it, we would have hit the buoy marking the entrance to Instow harbour. Once again, Michael's navigation had been spot on, but looking back on it, we had really been quite foolish and were very lucky not to have got into serious trouble.

At Christmas that same year, the family came out to Singapore, and we made a cruise in a Grand Banks 42 up the Straits of Malacca on the West Coast. We were accompanied by a delightfully accurate stuffed representation of the Pink Panther we had christened *Merah Jambu,* which is Malay for the colour pink. The Straits are bordered by Malaysia, Indonesia and Singapore, and are one of the busiest waterways in the world. Every year as much as 40 percent of the world's trade passes through them in more than 50,000 ships. That works out to a ship every 10 minutes, day and night, 365 days per year. Apart from traffic density, hazards include poor visibility from forest clearance fires in Indonesia, piracy and wide variations in depth, including moving underwater sand waves. The route narrows to 1.5 miles in the Phillips channel, just off Singapore.

We stayed well inshore off the coast of Malaysia, so we were well away from most of the shipping. Piracy could not be entirely discounted. One of our Laguna 33-foot boats had been sold to the Shell Company which ran a huge oil refinery on Pulau Bukom, where the boat was moored. One night, pirates came aboard and forced the crew of two at gunpoint to drive the boat away. They managed to run the boat onto a reef, which tore a hole in the bottom. One of the crew dived overboard and escaped in a hail of bullets. The unfortunate coxswain, an older man, was not so lucky and was murdered by the pirates. The boat was salvaged and brought back to the yard for repair.

In March 1978, Mary and I were invited by Carleton Mitchell

to join him on a cruise through the Virgin Islands in the Caribbean aboard his Hatteras 48 Long Range Cruiser. It may be recalled that I had worked closely with Carleton on building his Grand Banks 42 and 65. I think I was quite an inept crew but the experience did widen my cruising horizons. We visited both the British and American Virgin Islands, and it was on St. Thomas in the latter that I experienced the only example of hostility by a local person in all of the hundreds of thousands of miles of travel I have done. In this case a black guy crossed the street with the sole purpose of banging into me on the sidewalk. Poor fellow. It must be horrible going through life carrying that kind of chip on your shoulder!

We then went to Southern California, which was Mary's first visit to the area. Bob Phillips from American Marine was our host, and we did the usual sightseeing things like a visit to Disneyland. We went to the attractive coastal town of Laguna Beach, built on steep hills overlooking the Pacific Ocean. Bob also drove us over the border into Mexico, first to the border town of Tijuana, and then further south to Ensenada. It was a stark contrast to California, just a few miles away.

A few months later, we were back in Treedown and made a visit down the coast to Boscastle and Tintagel, in Cornwall. The village and nearby Tintagel Castle are associated with the legends surrounding King Arthur and the knights of the Round Table.

Christmas 1978 was also spent at Treedown, where we had a real white Christmas. Devon was not used to snow, and the sunken lanes were filled to the brim with the stuff. It came so seldom that there was no proper equipment to shift it, so it had to be removed by a tractor one bucket at a time. We had a long drive which had to be cleared, but fortunately that led to a main road, so we were not cut off for too long. It certainly made a dramatic contrast to Singapore, where Santa Claus arrived on water skis!

Spring 1979 saw us all back in Singapore, from where we made a short trip to Sumatra, in Indonesia. We arrived in Medan, from where we took a bus to Parapat, situated on the shores of Lake Toba. This is the site of one of the world's super volcanoes. The lake is 62 miles long and almost 19 miles wide. Samosir

Island, in the middle of the lake, is large enough to require a bus service! It was a fun trip and all the staff worked very hard to please. It didn't matter what you ordered from the restaurant menu, you always got something different. But we never said anything because we were afraid that the waiter would probably commit suicide if we complained and everyone was so nice. There was a small group who used to entertain every evening. The singer was a small, skinny guy who had the most amazing voice that just seemed to flow out of his slender frame with no effort on his part, without the aid of a microphone.

August that year was again spent at Treedown, and it was while working in the garden that we heard about the Fastnet Race disaster on the radio. The fleet had been overwhelmed in the Irish Sea by a weather system which, after originating in the Gulf of Alaska, had whipped itself up into a tightly knit frenzy in the Irish Sea. 306 yachts took part in the 605-mile race from Cowes to Fastnet Rock and back, but only 86 finished the race. 125 crew members were rescued and 15 died. As the crow flies we were only about 100 miles from the scene of the carnage, and we drove down to the lighthouse on Hartland Point to view the raging sea.

A couple of weeks later, the British Queen's uncle, Lord Louis Mountbatten, who had been the last Viceroy of India at its time of independence from Britain, was murdered by the Irish Republican Army, who placed a bomb on his boat anchored off his holiday home in Ireland.

In between these two events we went out one evening to celebrate my birthday. We drove to the restaurant, situated in what had clearly been a country house on the cliffs overlooking the sea. When we went into the dining room, there were a bunch of dejected-looking people sitting at various tables with no food in front of them. No one was talking, and there was one woman with tears running silently down her cheeks. There was no sign of any staff and no smells of any food. The atmosphere was like something from an Agatha Christie murder mystery. We waited for about ten minutes and then left.

We backtracked down the coast, looking for an alternative restaurant. It was a Saturday evening in the height of the holiday season, so every restaurant was fully booked. Finally, we arrived at an isolated farmhouse called Poyer's Farm. By this time it was about nine p.m., beginning to get dark and it had started to rain. We knocked on the door and stood in a bedraggled group on the step. I think they took pity on us and invited us in.

The waitress who served us looked vaguely familiar to Mary, and the waitress seemed to look at Mary as though she had seen her before. Finally, they both realized that they had shared a cabin on the ship taking them to Hong Kong in 1960, where they were both nursing sisters. What an amazing coincidence—especially when you consider the unlikely chain of events which had brought us to this restaurant.

We met again a few days later. Mary's ex-colleague had married a Hong Kong policeman at a time when most of the force's officers were British. There had been much coverage in the press about corruption in the police force, and I asked him about it. He did not say whether he was personally involved, but he told me that, as an officer in the Marine Police, all he would have to do for a sum equal to his monthly salary to be paid into the bank account of his choice was to leave the duty roster lying on his desk while he left the office for 10 minutes. That would allow the corrupt cops to see who was on duty at what time, so they could safely smuggle goods into HK.

Christmas 1979 was again spent in Devon, and Christmas dinner was served in my sister's cottage. Her husband, Michael, had been diagnosed with cancer a few weeks earlier and he had been released from hospital for the holidays and was feeling very weak. The poor guy was only 42, and in the New Year he returned to Exeter hospital in South Devon. We would drive down to visit him. One time I asked how it felt to be in his situation and he just said that he felt he had failed in his responsibility to his family. One day in early February, we drove down to visit as usual. Visiting hours were not until 2 p.m., so we killed time walking around and visiting the Maritime Museum. Finally, we went to the hospital and I said we had come to visit Michael Shard. There was this kind of bleak atmosphere and the nurses all had frozen faces. Michael had passed away just a few minutes previously. My sister was there, looking numb. One of the nurses handed her a brown envelope containing Michael's personal possessions, including his watch. There was nothing to do but leave. My sister was going to drive back home on her own to face her five kids. Of course this was unthinkable and Mary drove her in my sister's car and I followed in ours. We arrived back at her cottage, and all the kids were sitting around. I knew I was the one who should take charge but I simply did not know what to do or to say. I have never felt so utterly helpless, and I have never forgiven myself for being so useless.

We took care of the legal formalities and attended Michael's cremation. Everybody told my sister that she would have to leave the cottage for somewhere less isolated and more practical, but she said that she had no intention of moving. The house was quite a mess, with electrical wires hanging from the ceiling. It was in the middle of a remodel, with Michael doing all the work himself. Even when he was fit, he was hard pressed to find the time because he worked most of the week in the family's furniture business in London, but when he became ill, he simply did not have the energy. I asked my sister how much money she had. She said that she had no idea. I said what do you mean you have no idea—you must have some idea. She said that when there was no money in the bank, the manager would phone up and she would tell Michael, and he would put more in!

Fortunately, Michael was well insured, and the UK social welfare system takes care of widows and provides child allowances for each child, so my sister was OK from a financial point of view, although she was devastated by the loss of her husband and found it hard to provide emotional support for the children.

I had to get back to Singapore to continue my work. The family came out in April 1980, and we went to the island of Penang, in Northern Malaysia, for a week. It was one of the best holidays we had ever had, basically because we didn't go anywhere or do anything except play on the beach and in the water and eat outside under the casuarina trees through which the winds sighed continuously. Their only drawback is that they drop prickly little fruit seed pods which bite your bare feet. Cheeky mynah birds would hop onto the table and share your meal. The food included such British overseas specialties as rum omelettes, which are absolutely delicious. The only sightseeing we did was to stop at the Sanke Temple en route to the airport at the end of our trip. This is also known as Snake Temple, as it is home to large numbers of pit vipers, which are draped in the bushes. You can also drape them over your shoulders if you feel so inclined.

One of the early customers for the new GB 49 were Tom and Jane Wright. They were both experienced boaters and had worked their way up from a GB 32. Tom had run his own company, and they were also keen scuba divers who cruised every year in the Bahamas with their three sons. As a reward for my work on the 49, in August 1980, I was given the chance to cruise with them for one week in the Bahamas.

I was very keen to go, although being trapped on board a boat with the owners, with no means of escape, could have been terrible with the wrong people. But we all got along extremely well and developed a friendship that lasted for many years—and one which had far-reaching results a few years down the road.

I had never previously visited the Bahamas and I was staggered by the colours of the ocean as I flew south from Miami to Nassau. The arrival forms for Nassau were not handed out until after we had disembarked, so they had to be completed in the Arrivals Hall, where there were no desks or tables. All the passengers were on their knees on the floor, like a Muslim prayer meeting.

The Wrights met me and I spent a delightful and instructive week with them on the boat, cruising through the island chain. I learned it was better to cruise with a slight popple on the water and to wear polarized sunglasses to better see coral heads hidden beneath the surface. I learned why it was necessary to use the "Bahamian moor" in a narrow channel where the tide ran back and forth and there was no room to swing. I also learned the good points about my design, as well as others which could be improved.

My cruise terminated in Georgetown, and we went ashore for me to catch my flight to Nassau, and from there to Miami and on to London. The Bahamas were so sleepy that London seemed as unimaginably far away as the dark side of the moon. I was picked up by a taxi driver with a deep black, wrinkled face. Tom asked him what time the plane to Nassau arrived.

The man thought for a moment and then he said in a slow, Bahamian accent, "Sumtaim he com early. Sumtaim he com lait. And sumtaim he dawn't com ataawl."

With that, we set of to the nearby airstrip, and I sat with other waiting passengers under the tree that served as the departure lounge. When the departure time came and went, one of the passengers asked the ground staff when the plane was coming.

"You see it when it arraive" was the answer.

When it did show up, we were in for a surprise. It was an old tail-dragger Dakota with a paint scheme that looked as though it had been executed by a deranged Peruvian artist with a collection of surplus paint at his disposal. The plane was covered in wild Aztec designs in a multitude of bright colours.

The pilot was a grizzled American who helped to load the baggage. When we were seated and he started the engines, his pipe came rattling down the sloping aisle. The air conditioning was a pair of Manhattan Marine fans bolted to the bulkhead. The blades were going *ting-ting-ting* on the guard. I was sitting next to a black Bahamian lad on his way back to college in the U.S. "Man, Ah shore hope de blaides don' flai off" he said.

We made the journey to Nassau without incident. We arrived late, but so was my flight to Miami. I began to be concerned about catching my plane to London. A couple of porters at the airport shared a joke so successful it had left one of them rocking back and forth on his chair, hugging one of his knees. Tears were streaming down his face. "Oh, mai Lor" he cried, "Oh, mai Lor!"

I arrived in Miami and ran across the airport just in time to claim my seat before it was given away to a standby passenger.

Bob Livingston was always on the lookout for the possibility of having other, cheaper yards to build the simpler boats like the GB 32. He would send me off to visit small yards in remote places. One of these was in Sri Lanka, where I went in September 1980. I don't remember too much about the yard except that it was very small and rural, but I went down with dengue fever shortly after I returned to Singapore. My first symptoms were a slight headache, slight rash, slightly aching bones, and a very high fever. Predictably, these came on one evening over a weekend. I knew I was burning up so I took some aspirin, wrapped myself in a wet towel and sat under the fan, all of which lowered my temperature. I went to see the doctor the next morning. I could feel that my temperature was down, but it was still over 100 degrees. They diagnosed dengue fever and sent me straight to the hospital because dengue fever is a reportable, mosquito-borne disease in Singapore, and is spread by mosquitoes biting someone who is infected and then going off and biting someone else. It is also known as "break-bone fever" because of the extreme pain that can be experienced in the joints. It can progress to dengue haemorrhagic fever where you bleed internally and from every orifice. Fortunately, I only had a mild dose. There is no actual treatment for the disease—just rest and taking plenty of liquids. I was in hospital and off work for five days, which is the only time in my entire life when I have been off work due to illness. I was very impressed with the actions taken by the Singapore health authorities. They sent someone to interview me to figure out where I could have been infected, then they made two visits to my house—10 days apart - and sprayed the entire area, including fogging the tall rubber trees which surrounded the property.

Bob also sent me to Cochin, Kerala State, in Southern India. This was to a yard which had previously built Bristol Trawlers for export to the East Coast of the U.S. I flew into Bombay and, on my first trip, was accompanied to the yard by an Indian gentleman from that city. The scene at the airport for our flight to Cochin was chaotic. Kerala State has the highest literacy rate in India, at an amazing 99 percent (equal to the U.S. and the UK), and their people were in demand for jobs in the Middle East. The airport was packed shoulder to shoulder with people returning home, loaded up with rolled-up mattresses and boom boxes. The Indian I was with called for the supervisor, and somehow we eventually got onto the plane.

The yard was situated on the water, outside Cochin city. It was a ramshackle affair but no more so than the old American Marine yard in Hong Kong. I am not sure how long they had been building trawlers for the parent company in Rhode Island, but the relationship had come to a halt. The Indians told me that the American who had been at the yard for two years would not eat any food sourced in India and kept his watch on New England time for the whole time he was in Cochin! I thought that the yard could possibly build some of our boats, but we would need to have a presence there to control production and quality. The red tape in India was simply incredible. They would jokingly say that the British left them with enough red tape to strangle themselves and, after independence, the Indians trebled it.

Practically all the materials had to be imported under bond because they were going to be re-exported in the boats. One example was bronze screws. These were imported in huge numbers, and when packed from the exporting manufacturer, the quantities in each box were measured by weight, so it was commonly accepted for the number count to be off by a few screws, plus or minus. Some government authority said that they wanted to physically count the actual number of screws in a shipment, so the yard had to unpack the shipment and tip tens of thousands of screws onto the floor so they could be counted. They found that there were a few more screws than had been declared, so they wanted to fine the company for fraud!

On another occasion a shipment of Ford engines from England was offloaded by mistake in Bombay instead of Cochin. The engines were imported under bond and would normally have gone straight into a bonded warehouse in Cochin. There was no established method to keep the engines under bonded control during transport from Bombay to Cochin, so they languished in a warehouse in Bombay for more than a year. I believe in the end they were shipped back to England. In the meantime, the yard had no engines to complete the boats and had to purchase more engines from Ford.

It was probably things like this that killed the deal. My hotel room had a candle beside the bed, which gave me a heads-up that the electricity supply was not all that reliable, and this was confirmed at the yard. The air-conditioner in my room groaned and rumbled and dispensed air at room temperature.

The problem with all these casual exploratory visits was that it raised the hopes of the companies I visited that we were seriously interested, and we always finished up by disappointing them. On a second visit to Cochin, I flew by Swissair from Singapore to Bombay and landed in the middle of the night. When I deplaned, the ground hostess handed me a note to say that my reservation on the Cochin flight later that morning was confirmed, which was a relief.

When I went to check in the following morning, I was told that, even though I had the note, I was on the waiting list. As before, the airport was packed with people carrying bed rolls and boom boxes. Well, I thought, last time my companion asked for the supervisor so perhaps I should do the same. I did so and when he looked at my ticket he said, "No problem. Number 57 on the waiting list. No Problem!"

Being number 57 on the waiting list sure sounded like a problem to me, but what could I do? Eventually they started calling names, and my name came up. It was quite impossible to make my way through the mass of tightly packed bodies to the check-in counter, so I followed the standard technique of handing my passport to the person standing next to me, who passed it to the person standing next to him and so on until it reached the counter. It was returned to me by the same method with the boarding pass inside. On my second visit I was there a little longer and was able to do a little sight-seeing.

Since my visit, the name Cochin has reverted back to its original name of Kochi. The town was occupied by the Portuguese in 1503 and St. Francis church, the oldest European church in India, dates from the same time. The Portuguese were followed by the Dutch and ultimately by the British. At the time of my visit, the congregation was still cooled by stiff lengths of cloth moving back and forth over their heads, propelled by ropes led over pulleys through holes in the wall where a punka-wallah would alternately pull and release the rope, often by tying it to his foot.

Cochin was also home to the oldest group of Jews in India, and when I was there, they lived on a special street, although I understand that most have now moved to Israel. Their immigration to this spot started as early as 70 AD, at the fall of Jerusalem. The oldest known Jewish grave in Hebrew dates from 1269 AD.

The entrance to the harbour was relatively narrow, and on one bank were located the so-called Chinese fishing nets. These were huge contrivances made of wooden poles which supported nets, 60 feet or more across, cantilevered out over the water. These heavy structures were counterbalanced by a series of stones tied along a length of rope. My initial thought was to wonder why they had not put all the stones into one simple net, but then I realized that, as the net moved from horizontal to vertical, progressively less weight was needed for a counterweight, and this was achieved as each stone came to rest on the ground. The system is so finely balanced that the weight of a man walking along the main beam is sufficient to cause the net to descend into the sea.

During my visit I had a meal at the home of the manager, who was a very nice man. He was married to a lady he had met at university. It was a love match and not an arranged marriage. It was also distinguished by the fact that his wife had suffered from polio as a child, which had left her with a limp. Most Indian men will not consider marriage to a "damaged" woman, so this made him a noble exception. The front room of his humble abode was given over to the worship of a multi-armed goddess whose picture hung on the wall framed with marigolds. Cooking was done over a wood stove in the back room.

On another occasion I was invited to the home of the company's chief clerk. On the way to his house, we stopped at a small shop and he bought *one* banana—for me. We would never consider buying just one banana, and this was a person who held an important position in the company. It was a sobering thought.

When it was time to leave for the airport it was after 9 p.m.

when the authorities switched off the traffic lights to save electricity. We came to a crossroads where the traffic was hopelessly interlocked, with vehicles pointing in every direction. Everyone was blowing their horn continuously. There was one lone individual standing in the middle of this vehicular maelstrom trying to sort things out at great risk to his life.

For some reason, now forgotten, my flight went to Madras, on the east coast. I landed there to meet someone for some reason. It was blisteringly hot. He took me to see a crocodile farm south of the city. I had never realized that there were so many different types of crocodiles, including the endangered Gharial, which have very long, narrow snouts. The other thing I remember about Madras is the continuous, non-stop, blowing of car horns. However, the main memory is my experience at the airport when it came time to leave.

I initially went to the airport sometime in the morning at the published time to catch my flight. Silly me! I was told to come back at 7.30 in the evening, as the flight had been delayed. I did so and stood in a long line to check in. When I got to the counter, I was told that I needed some document from the bank to do with turning in my surplus rupees. There was a counter for the bank but it was not yet open, so we all had to queue up again until it was. Having got this piece of paper, we then had to queue up again at the check-in counter. I checked my bags, believing that would be the last I would see of them until I arrived in Singapore. Wrong! After having my passport checked by immigration, I moved on only to be confronted by my bags and a person who asked me to confirm they were mine. I did so, and the porter looked at me expectantly and I looked back at him until I realized that the bags were likely to stay where they were unless I lubricated their path. I handed over a couple of rupees, and on they went. By this time, I was dying for a pee because there had been no facilities I had been able to find on the city side of the process. I eagerly sought out a toilet, only to find the door blocked by a large pile of sand. There was an arrow pointing upstairs to the WC. I climbed the stairs and found the place, where there was an attendant eager to help. Each basin had one of those gimbaled soap dispensers you have to turn upside down to dispense the soap. These did not actually contain any soap, so the attendant filled one with water and helpfully turned it upside down for me so the water ran over my hands. He turned on the taps and cold water ran out. He then held out a paper towel for me. It was like some sort of comedy routine. Of course he expected a tip, which naturally I gave him. Poor fellow. He was doing his best with very little, and the tip was well worth the entertainment value.

I went back downstairs to enter the departure area. There was the usual frame you have to walk through, and the carry-on bags went through the scanning device on a belt. There was a cat curled up on top of the scanner. After I passed through and sat waiting, I realized that the frame was not switched on and no one was paying the slightest attention to the scanner. Nothing seemed to be happening, and I peered through the window at the tarmac. I saw an Air India official and I asked him if there was a plane out there.

"No, sir," he replied.

"Where is it?" I said.

"Bombay, sir," he said. He looked at me sadly. "Never fly Air India, sir. Aaalways late, sir, aalways late!"

I remarked to one of my fellow passengers that maybe the plane had originated in the UK and was delayed because of snow. "That is good reason" he said, "snow in Bombay." And he laughed. The Indian public are so used to being messed about that they expect it and deal with all the frustrations with great patience and good humour.

Ultimately the aircraft never did arrive, and we were switched to a Singapore Airlines flight. It was a 747 and when it arrived it had a defective tyre that had to be changed. The aircraft was parked right outside the window, so we could see what was going on. After quite a delay, a group of people arrived. I counted 26. One of them got a jack similar to those on small wheels you see at a garage. He then proceeded to jack up this huge aircraft while the others stood around and watched. It took them well over an hour to change the wheel. It must have driven Singapore Airlines crazy, as efficiency was their mantra. In their maintenance workshop in Singapore they had one of those computerized systems where the storekeeper entered a part number, and an automated device picked the component off an inaccessible shelf and delivered it to the counter.

Chapter 7

September 1980 to January 1983

Life in Singapore

We take a family cruise on the Canal du Midi in France and decide to sell Treedown. The family moves back to Singapore. I describe renewed family life in Singapore and make my first visit to Taiwan.

By 1980, the work on Treedown was finished and the girls were both at boarding school. Having had to live in the disruption and turmoil of reconstruction Mary now spent a lot of time on her own, where it was so quiet that, in her words, the only sound was the sheep eating grass in the adjacent fields. Despite this, the cheapest lamb in the local town of Barnstaple was from faraway New Zealand. Mary was not at heart a country girl. She felt much more at home in a social environment in a city. She was, in effect, living my dream and not hers. Over the years of our marriage Mary and I had gradually grown apart. With life mainly centred around the needs of our children, our growing differences had been somewhat masked, and of course the six years when I had been working in Singapore while Mary and the family had been in England had certainly not helped. When Bob Livingston agreed that, in line with normal expatriate conditions, the company would pay the school fees provided the education was in Singapore, it seemed logical to bring everybody back together now that the company was once again reasonably stable. When I discussed this with Mary, she said that she would come back to live with me in Singapore because that was her duty. My reaction to this was one of dismay, and I said that it was better that she did not come if the only reason was because she felt it was her duty to do so.

Given all these factors, it made no sense to keep Treedown and leave it vacant. Jackie said she would chain herself to the fence rather than leave, but in the end she accepted the situation. We had a last Christmas there in 1980 before moving to Spring Cottage in the attractive town of Bath. I left it up to Mary to make the choice. I said that I had made the last one, and it had not worked out so well.

In April 1981, we made a family trip on the Canal du Midi, which connects the Atlantic to the Mediterranean, just north of the Pyrenees. We rented a canal boat and spent two weeks gently making our way through the countryside of southern France. It was a bit early in the season, and so was quite chilly, but the advantage was lack of other traffic at the locks. There was a speed limit of 4 mph, and you could stop and tie up anywhere alongside the banks, many of which were lined with plane trees. Canals tend to follow the contours as much as possible, so passed through rural surroundings. The locks were mostly manual and operated by beefy women who expected you to help operate the sluice gates. They spoke a flavour of French quite different from what I had learned at school, but we managed to communicate OK.

We usually ate in local restaurants, the only problem being that some were only open at lunchtime and others only in the evening, with all the shops being closed from around noon until 4pm. We were always being caught out and imagined newspaper headlines that read: "English family found starved to death on Canal." I had learned by this time the inadvisability of over-ambitious plans, so had limited our destination to the fortified city of Carcassonne, which had first been identified by the Romans as a hilltop fort in 100 BC. It was only 70 miles from our starting point, so that made the round trip 140 miles with many locks. It was a delightful, interesting, yet restful holiday. At one basin I had initially decided to dock on one side, then changed my mind to the other. I heard a plaintive cry of "D-a-a-a-d!" and there was Nicky ashore holding the extreme end of one of the mooring lines, which was tightening ominously. Unknown to me, she had jumped ashore. I told her to drop the line, which we pulled aboard and went round to pick her up. I recommend this as an interesting and restful holiday and further recommend you rent the optional bicycles as a way to extend your range.

We returned to Spring Cottage, where on one day I photographed spring flowers and apple blossom. The following day, they were buried in snow. Bath is a very attractive English town famous for the Roman Baths, which, after being "lost" for 1,200 years, were rediscovered accidentally in the 1800s by someone digging a well. All buildings in Bath have to be faced with honey-coloured Bath Stone, and older buildings which had turned black due to pollution from smoking chimneys have been cleaned and restored to their original colour. Spring Cottage was a nice enough house, also built with Bath Stone, but it did not sit well with me. You could not park in the street outside your own house because of other cars already parked there, and the street lights shone in through the windows at night. It brought home to me the different preferences between Mary and myself which six years of living separate lives had not helped.

We moved back to Singapore as a family in August 1981, and the kids both went to school at the United World College—or UWC as it was called. UWC (United World Colleges) is an education movement comprising 13 international schools and colleges, with national committees in over 130 countries. There were kids from 55 different nationalities, although teaching was in English. It is hard to conceive of a better environment for children able to attend this type of school when, in their formative teenage years, they share classes with kids their own age of every colour and creed and from every kind of family background. Not only that, but it was considered cool to study, and students looked down on those among them who did not.

One day a Dutch guy called Gil Hensen stopped by in the hope that we might have available jobs. Normally we would not, but his timing was fortuitous because once again we were searching for someone to look after the production. Gil had worked for a number of years in the yacht business in Taiwan, and he had a Taiwanese wife who had married him very much against her parent's wishes. When I offered him a job I don't think that he could believe his luck, because he had been unemployed for a while when he just showed up at the main gate on the off-chance.

Gil was an unusual character with a somewhat checkered career. As a very young man he had left Holland and gone to Eilat in Israel, at the head of the Gulf of Aqaba. There he had lived in a hippie community operated under anarchy. Anarchy actually means the absolute freedom of the individual, which Gil told me was in reality the ultimate tyranny, because it meant that anyone could do anything they wanted and there were no rules to abide by. So if someone wanted to play their radio at full volume all night long, they were fully entitled to do so and there was nothing to constrain them. It was an interesting observation and not one you would think of without personal experience of this supposed political ideal.

In November 1981, Bob, Dick Loh and myself made a visit to Kaohsiung in Taiwan. I do not remember the reason that prompted our visit, but I do remember visiting a shop in Wufu Road and buying a big bronze clock that I thought was the genuine article taken from one of the ships broken up in Taiwan. I don't think that the shopkeeper ever represented it as genuine and it turned out to be a replica with a simple electrical movement. Actually, it turned out to be an excellent buy. It looks great and I still have it. It keeps good time, chimes every half-hour, and the single battery lasts for more than two years. I don't think we came away with anything more valuable than my clock, but little did I know how large a part Taiwan was to play in my life just a few years down the road.

We had Christmas in Singapore, and in January 1982 we paid a short family visit to Hong Kong. This was the first time the family had been there since we left in 1970. We were able to visit the places where we had lived, the church where we married, and the kids could see the hospital where they came into this world.

Life in Singapore, which the foreign press has always portrayed as being the ultimate nanny state, was very pleasant. The government ran the country like a corporation and strictly enforced the laws. It was clean and efficiently run with the absolute minimum of corruption, plus everyone was very friendly and helpful.

Singapore is a food lover's paradise. With so many different cultures sharing the island, there was a great variety. Singapore is famous for places which are car parks during the day but which turn into food courts during the evening. All cars need to be out of these areas by 5 p.m. or they are towed. Then the food vendors move in. There are Indians whirling the paper-thin dough to make a meat-filled, multi-layered pancake called murtabak. There is every type of noodle, both in broth and fried. Mee goring, Nasi goring. Satay, usually cooked on a charcoal brazier and served with peanut sauce. Malay and Indonesian food tends to be very spicy, and fiery curries are a specialty of the region. Gula Malacca—a dish made from tapioca, served with brown sugar syrup and coconut milk to remove the heat. Chinese food from many different regions of China. Fresh fruit and refreshing juices squeezed to order.

There was one Indian restaurant we used to frequent which served blisteringly hot food. I never did discover its real name. It was above a Chinese restaurant and the sign in the stairs simply read: "Indian Food Upstairs" —so that is what we called it.

During one of Anton's visits to Singapore he was staying with me, and as a last-minute decision, we decided to go for a curry at one of the big hotels. We had no sooner walked through the door when the PA announced that there was a phone call for Mr. Emmerton. This is a very uncommon name, and we wondered who on earth could be calling him at this hotel when we had not even known that we would be here ourselves until twenty minutes earlier. Anton went to take the call and found out that it had been for his cousin whom he hadn't seen for 20 years and who was in Singapore on business! Another example of the small world we live in.

We also used to visit restaurants out of town built on rickety wooden structures hanging out over the water. The surroundings were rough and ready, but the atmosphere was authentic and the food delicious. One of these was at Pongol, where we liked to order deep-fried miniature squid. On visits to England, the kids used to enjoy regaling their grandmother about how nice and crunchy these were. Another similar restaurant was at Tuas, where the toilets were little more than cracks in the wooden floor hanging out over the water.

Singapore was home to many wonderful and hitherto unseen tropical fruits. There were hairy, scarlet rambutans, which had two seasons during the year. There were smelly jackfruit and even smellier durian—so offensive it was banned from public buildings and aircraft. There was soursop, pineapple and many varieties of bananas and plantains. Small bananas not much bigger than your fingers with thin skins and deliciously sweet. Mangoes and mangosteen. Pawpaw or papaya. Longan, lychee. Passion fruit and coconuts.

When going to a new place or country, it is very helpful to join a social club. We joined the Tanglin Club, which had been founded in 1865 and which was, until Singapore gained its independence, reserved for expatriates—especially Brits. This changed following independence, and at the time we were there, membership was opened to all nationalities, but the constitution of the club was changed so that no one nationality was to exceed 51 per cent of the membership. This controversial change was introduced with the intent of allowing the club to maintain its international flavour, and at the time of writing, the membership has reached 7,500, with 77 different nationalities. The club had a library and swimming pool, as well as excellent restaurants. Every Sunday they served a curry "tiffin"—huge bowls of delicious curry accompanied by a huge range of side dishes called sideboys. This was similar to the Dutch Rijsttafel, which originated in Indonesia.

There were also sophisticated night clubs and discos, as well as bars of all levels, from the famous one at Raffles Hotel, serving a Singapore Sling, to smaller places like the Halfway House on Bukit Timah Road, so called because it was halfway from Singapore city to the causeway and the border with Malaysia.

Singapore also had many interesting and colourful festivals representing the many different cultures. There was the Indian festival of Thaipusam, during which devotees pierced their skin and their tongues with spikes and carried elaborate kavadis on their

405

shoulders almost 2 miles to Sri Thendayuthapani temple through the tropical heat.

Another Indian festival involved fire walking over a bed of searing logs. I can personally attest to the heat of the fire which from 10 feet away would sear your eyeballs and blister the paint on the nearby temple walls.

The festival of Navathiri involved dragging a huge juggernaut through the streets, while Deepavali was a gentler affair also known as the Festival of Lights.

Chingay Parade was a colourful and noisy street procession as part of the Chinese New Year celebrations with big headed dolls, stilt walkers, acrobats and writhing dragons.

There were many activities to enjoy. One of them was a weekly outing with the Hash House Harriers, which was an informal international group described as a non-competitive running, social and drinking club. It was started in 1938 in Kuala Lumpur, fashioned after a traditional British paper chase or hare and hounds. A chapter was formed in Singapore in 1962 and since then it has spread around the world. Today there are reported to be around 2,000 chapters.

The starting point would be announced a few days before each run, and at the appointed time all kinds of fancy cars would arrive at the designated spot and well-dressed executives changed into scruffy running gear. Trails might pass through any sort of terrain and hashers might run through back alleyways, residential areas, city streets, forests, swamps, or shopping malls and might climb fences, ford streams, explore storm drains or scale cliffs in their pursuit of the hare. Local kids tagged along, dogs barked, and chickens squawked as they scurried out of the way of these savages slithering down muddy slopes and through native kampongs with cries of "On! On!" There were checks and false trails which allowed the stragglers, like me, to catch up with the serious runners. These days the trail is marked with chalk, sawdust, or coloured flour and finishes at the beer truck, where all the good achieved by the exercise is swept away by quantities of ice-cold beer. The Hash is often described as a "drinking club with a running problem".

Living on a hot, tropical island surrounded by water and being in the boat business, it was inevitable that weekend activities often involved boats and the water. At various times I had an inflatable rubber dinghy, a water-jet speed boat designed by Bob Conn, and a 16-foot Hobie Cat. We took the rubber boat up to Malaysia with us but it did not get much use before the rubber perished in the tropical sun. The jet boat had an unreliable engine and the bottom was so flat that it was incredibly uncomfortable. Also the water intake under the boat was prone to sucking up plastic bags and other debris when all progress stopped and the intake was cleared. Being jet drive, it would run in very shallow water. I remember skiing behind that boat with Mary at the helm when I looked down and realized that we were speeding along in just a few inches of water, well away from land. I didn't know what to do. If we hit bottom, we were in for a bad time, not only for the boat but for me. I would finish up on the jagged coral and injuries resulting from that would probably go septic. On the other hand, if I shouted for her to stop both the boat and myself would come off the plane and immediately go aground in the water we were in. In the end I did nothing and by good luck made it back into deep water.

The Hobie Cat was also not a total success. Since it was on the equator, Singapore did not have much in the way of wind, so conditions were seldom very good for sailing. The kids were still quite small and usually screamed when the boat did get up any speed, so its success as a family boat was limited. The result was that I usually took it out by myself. When there was any wind it went extremely fast with one hull out of the water. I learned the hard way that with a catamaran it is fatal to allow the leeward hull to submerge, as doing so invariably leads to capsizing and possibly even pitch-poling, where the boat goes end over end. It was while still learning this that I capsized while on my own. I got the boat upright OK, but it delayed my return to the Yacht Club, which was located on a river estuary. The tide was well out by the time I got back, and there was about 100 yards of black glutinous mud separating me from the slipway. I would either have to sit out on the river for a minimum of six hours until the water returned, or I would have to deal with the mud. I chose the latter. The mud was bottomless and too soft to stand on, so I had to "swim" through it on my belly, dragging the boat behind me. I was literally the Creature from the Black Lagoon by the time I made it to shore!

The main saga with the Hobie occurred when participating in the annual Round the Island Race. This was open to every size of boat, as the race was organized on a handicap basis. The route was from the western edge of the causeway and all around the island to finish at its eastern edge. The total distance was about 70 miles, so it was a long race in a small boat. The start was just after midnight in flat calm conditions under a full moon. The start was timed so that the fleet would have favourable tides in the narrow Johore Strait dividing Singapore from Malaysia. The starting times were staggered according to the size of the boats. We did not have a very good start because I knew that if we drifted over the line early, it would be impossible to get back over it with no wind and the tide against us. Once we got going, we overtook boats with every slight puff of wind. In the distance, off to the west, I noticed some lightning on the horizon. "That's what we need" I said to my crew. I knew there would be plenty of wind in the storm and the boat would take off like a racehorse. I figured we would be just out of the narrow strait by that time and turning south, so the wind should be on our beam—our fastest point of sail. I gleefully watched the storm's approach.

When it came, it struck with extreme violence while we were still in the strait, so we were heading into the wind. This meant we had to tack back and forth across the narrow channel, traveling at high speed through choppy waves about 3 feet high. The tropical rain was sheeting down and there was spray flying everywhere. Visibility dropped to zero and the black night was rent with jagged lightning accompanied by instantaneous thunder. It was apocalyptic but very exciting. The shores of the strait were fringed with bamboo fish traps which protruded well out from the shore. Definitely not things you wanted to run into in a small catamaran at high speed. If you missed the traps you would finish up in a web of mangroves with their tangle of roots, so we did short tacks to stay away from the invisible shore. Occasionally another boat would suddenly appear out of the darkness, traveling at right angles to our course and visible only by a flashlight being shone on its sails. I was trying to slow the boat down by spilling the wind from the sails, but this was made especially difficult by the fully battened mainsail. There was no possibility of dropping the sail because it was secured by a lock at the top of the mast. Finally, the inevitable happened and the boat capsized. The mast was hollow and supposed to be sealed, which prevents the boat from turning right over, but evidently the seal leaked, and the boat turned completely upside down.

If you must be in a boat which has turned turtle, a catamaran is an excellent choice because you can sit on the underside of the trampoline between the two hulls. These storms are short lived in Singapore, so there was no point in doing anything until things calmed down. At least the water was warm. We waved the flashlight around and hoped that no one would run into us while we awaited the coming of dawn.

With daylight we saw that we were entirely alone, with no other boats in sight. The shoreline on both sides of the strait was jungle. It looked like it was going to be up to us to rescue ourselves. The Hobie's mast was 26 feet long and the water was less than 26 feet deep, so the end of the mast was stuck in the mud. The tide was still running out, but with the mast dragging on the bottom, the boat was drifting slower than the speed of the water, allowing the current to fill the sails. With the pressure on them there was no possibility of taking the sails down—which was actually "up" as we were upside down! I decided to remove the mast from the boat by releasing the three stays which normally hold it in position. We did this successfully and managed to drag the mast with sails onto our capsized boat.

At this point good luck intervened, and a local fisherman appeared. With his help, we put the mast and boom onto his boat, and by turning the boat so we had some assistance from the dying wind, we together managed to turn the boat right side up. It is very difficult to right a catamaran which is lying flat on the water upside down, as it is even happier upside down than right side up. We loaded the mast back on board, and after thanking the fisherman, we paddled the wreckage to a rocky beach. As we stumbled ashore, we disturbed a venomous sea snake. It was here that we realized that the mast was full of water and extremely heavy. The water, having found its way in under 28 feet of pressure, would not come back out, so we could write the mast off as being nothing but a burden. We erected the boom vertically to serve as a short mast, raised the jib upside down and sailed slowly back to civilization, which took us six hours. There had been both a rescue aircraft and an escort boat—ironically, a Laguna 38 organized by me—but by the time they were in the air and out on the water, the surviving fleet had moved on, and they never thought to back check on the area where the storm had struck.

Actually the weather in Singapore was very consistent and free from extremes, except for the occasional short-lived *Sumatra,* which could bring winds of up to 70 mph. But Singapore has one of the highest rates of lightning activity in the world. I remember flying into Singapore one night with the aircraft manoeuvring between towering pillars of cloud intermittently lit from within by flashes of lightning.

One hot, sunny Sunday afternoon I was relaxing outside my house, disturbed only by the crack of the seed pods exploding from the surrounding rubber trees, followed by the consequent sound of the large seeds rattling down the roof. Suddenly, out of nowhere, came a tremendous flash followed instantly by an explosion of thunder. I nearly jumped out of my skin—talk about a bolt from the blue! I leapt out of my chair and looked back over the roof of the house, where a black cloud was approaching. Overhead the sky was a cloudless blue.

One night I was awakened by a crash of thunder and violent lightning flashes coming every few seconds. I wanted to turn off the main switch, but the flashes were so frequent that I dare not go near the switch. That storm blew out light bulbs that were not even turned on and wrecked the refrigerator. One evening, Rex's home was struck while he was out. All vertical wiring in the house was destroyed and the electricity meter was completely vaporized, with not even components remaining.

One evening as I was about to leave work to go home, I decided to wait a few minutes for the rain to stop. Suddenly there was a tremendous bang and one of the steel flagpoles was struck.

The lightning left the pole undamaged but blew a hole in the ground close to its base, throwing clumps of earth clear across the car park. Had I left when I originally planned, I would have been right beside the flagpole when it was struck! Thunderstorms are usually accompanied by a torrential downpour. The heaviest I have ever seen was during a sea trial on a Laguna 38, when the rain was so heavy that we could not see the bow of the boat, about 15 feet away.

Lightning could cause enormous damage. One morning in October 1975 I was at my ablutions in the bathroom when there was a low rumble and the bathroom curtains floated up to horizontal. An oil tanker called *Kriti Sun* had been struck and sunk by lightning while unloading at a single-point mooring off Jurong, 3 miles away.

During my years in the Republic, Singapore suffered a number of disasters, the worst of which involved another tanker. Singapore had huge shipyards involved in repairing tankers and building oil rigs. Tankers were potential floating bombs because of the vapours which remained lurking in their empty tanks. There had been a number of incidents, and the government had introduced increasingly strict measures to try to prevent them. This included the requirement of having a gas-free certificate for each ship before any "hot work" could be carried out. This usually referred to the type of arc welding carried out by workers you see in protective clothing surrounded by showers of sparks and silhouetted in a halo of purple light.

In October 1978, the 64,000-ton Greek tanker *Spyros* came into the yard for general repairs. Large numbers of workers—many of them women—were engaged in the filthy job of cleaning the bilges, while many decks above them, a worker tried to remove an access plate. As is commonly the case on ships, the nuts had been painted over many times and were hard to remove. The worker decided to use a gas torch to burn off the paint. His work area was adjacent to a vent leading from the ship's bunker tanks containing the fuel supplied to the propulsion engine. This fuel is generally quite stable but, as the subsequent court of enquiry showed, the ship's crew—no doubt on the instructions of one of the companies involved in chartering or operating the vessel—had installed a pipe linking the bunker tanks to the cargo tanks and were, in effect, stealing the cargo to run the ship. Most of us think of crude oil as just being a gloppy mess, but it contains all those fractions which will eventually be distilled into products like gasoline. The vapour in the vent from the now contaminated and volatile bunker fuel was set off by the gas torch and flashed back to the bunker tanks, which blew up like a gigantic bomb, resulting in a death toll of 78, with many more severely injured. The subsequent court of enquiry was closely reported in the *Straits Times* newspaper and provided an object lesson in how human error and greed can combine to result in tragedy.

An even more telling example occurred in January 1983—this time involving the cable cars which straddled the channel dividing Singapore from Sentosa Island. The drill rig *Eniwetok* was tied up at nearby Keppel Wharf for repair. The work had taken longer than expected and pressure was on to release the rig. The person in charge had finally issued an edict that, come what may, the rig had to leave the yard by 5 p.m. that evening, even though, contrary to standard company procedure, the tide was at that time flowing in the direction of the channel, with its overhead cable cars.

The pilot in charge of the ship movement had asked for the height of the rig and had consulted the chart for the height of the cables above the water. Satisfied that there was adequate clearance, he turned his mind to other considerations associated with the movement of this ungainly rig. The problem was that while the height of the cables above the ground was fixed, their height above the water varied according to the state of the tide; and the height of the rig varied not only for the same reason, but, it later transpired, there had been miscommunication about whether the height given for the derrick had been above the deck or above the water.

When the rig left the dock, it was accompanied by three tugs, one of which acted as a brake to prevent the rig drifting down current. The pilot could not see this tug from his position on the rig, so a man was stationed to keep an eye on it, as well as to report on the relative position of the rig as it left the dock. Once the rig had cleared the dolphins, the lookout considered that part of his job finished and decided to relocate to another part of the rig to take photographs. He had no sooner done so than the remote control hook on the tug malfunctioned and released the towline. The lookout was no longer in position to report this to the pilot, and there was some kind of communication problem between the tug and the rig, so the pilot was unaware of this critical event.

The result of this convergence of events was that the top of the derrick tangled with the overhead cables, releasing two of the cabins, which fell into the sea, killing their occupants, and leaving 13 others stranded in cars which were no longer secured to the cables but merely hooked over them.

Their rescue was problematic, as the nearest crane tall enough to reach the stranded cars was hundreds of miles away. The only solution was helicopter, but this was fraught with risk of the downdraft blowing the cabins off the cables. In the event, this was the method used successfully by a couple of skilled pilots flying at night.

You might be wondering why I would include these tales of disaster in a personal story. It is because they occurred within the orbit of my personal experience, and I believe they contain valuable lessons for us all. I know they did for me. They illustrate how the smallest action can have cataclysmic consequences— providing real-life examples of the butterfly effect. Who could have imagined that the decision to move to a better vantage point to take photos could have contributed to the deaths of seven people, and of those seven people what minor decisions did they make that caused them to be in those particular cabins at that moment in time on that fateful day? It is a reminder that, when designing products in which people trust their lives, the potential consequences of every decision must be carefully weighed.

We had a minor catastrophe of our own at the yard when the resin store caught fire one night a few hours after a new shipment arrived. Fortunately, as required by Singapore regulations, the storehouse was in a separate building made of brick, so although the fire took several hours to extinguish, it did not spread. It was a close-run thing because you could see the raging flames through the cracks in the wall. Fibreglass itself requires quite a lot to start it burning, but as Howard said, "Once it starts just run like hell, jump the fence, and don't stop to pick up your hat!"

Chapter 8

October 1982 to August 1983

Life in Singapore

Sandy reappears from the distant past. Repercussions of latent sparks from an old flame. I build a GB 42 to live aboard. I describe a boat trip to the Tioman Islands in the South China Sea. I visit Venezuela and the Dutch Antilles to deal with warranty problems. I relate a snowmobile trip with my daughters at Yellowstone and the Tetons between Christmas and the New Year. We visit Disney World in Florida and, later, undertake a camping trip in Scotland, during which we climb Ben Nevis.

As it had been in Hong Kong, it seemed to be a great waste of money to be paying large sums in rent every month, and I was again tempted into the idea of using the money to build and pay off a boat. An additional Grand Banks model I dreamed up was based on the flush aft deck GB 48, which had been built in Hong Kong in wood. It occurred to me that we could develop this new model by simply making a different aft deck mould for the existing 43 Europa model. Colin Ayres suggested that actually the Sports Cruiser model would be more suitable—and he was right.

This new model was named the Grand Banks Motoryacht, and I was going to keep the first boat, which we had used to make the plug for the new aft deck mould, but Bob Livingston sold it instead to the dealer in Copenhagen. This turned out to my advantage because there were a number of leak problems from the aft deck due to all the extra holes that had been drilled during the tooling process. These were virtually impossible to trace, but a very ingenious Danish shipwright solved the problem by first dripping kerosene into the holes to trace the flow and then following up with thinned paint which took the same path and sealed it off. I don't think I would have been smart enough to think of this.

Dick Loh told Livingston that if we sold that model, it would kill the company; but, in fact, we had sold 19 of them before the first one got out the door! In the end I finished up with boat No. 3, which I christened *Lion's Den*. I wasn't too impressed by the name, which came from the fact that I am a Leo and Singapore is also known as Lion City.

I made the boat single screw and installed a 30-year-old Gardner engine. These legendary British engines are famous for their quietness and fuel efficiency. They were installed in London buses and ran 2,000,000 miles before they were replaced. The old engines were then offered for sale either "as is" or rebuilt. I bought mine locally and it had already been in another boat. They were very popular with fishermen in the Far East because they were so simple, reliable, and fuel efficient. Spares were also readily available. I remember going into a traditional Chinese shop in Aberdeen in Hong Kong and buying injectors from a young Chinese girl. The floor of the shop was wall-to-wall Gardner engines and the shelves stocked with parts.

I discovered that the engine had originally been installed in a Foden truck in the UK (by coincidence, my mother's maiden name was Foden), and I did the marinization of the engine myself. I also installed a hydraulic emergency drive, using power from the generator. When I took the boat on its maiden trip, I was alone and the engine overheated. I checked the problem and found that the raw water pump shaft had sheared off. While pondering what to do, I heard the deep, visceral siren from a big ship. I looked up to see this gigantic supertanker coming towards me—maybe three-quarters of a mile away. I was stopped tight in the middle of the channel, which was not very wide. There was no room for the

416

tanker to go around me. What to do?

I had this conversation with myself:

Self 1: "You could use the emergency drive."

Self 2: "But I wasn't planning to try that today."

Self 1: "Well, maybe this would be a good time to try it."

Self 2: "But I don't know whether it will work."

Self 1: "Don't you think this would be a good time to find out?"

This conversation only took a few seconds, and that terrifying siren sounded again. I could just imagine the pilot demanding why that bloody fool in his toy boat didn't get out of the way. I didn't have a radio, of course!

I got the generator started and engaged the emergency drive, and I slowly—oh, so slowly—moved out of the path of the tanker as it continued to blow the siren. It was huge, with its enormous beam almost filling the horizon. Suitably chastened, I made my way slowly back to the yard on my emergency drive. I never had cause to use it again, but it certainly saved my bacon on the one time I did!

The relationship between Mary and myself had become more like brother and sister than husband and wife. We did not fight but we no longer had much in common. When we were in company, Mary talked about little else than the marvels of England, especially the royal family. When I tried to change the subject into something of more interest to others, she quickly brought it back and segued into discussing my perceived faults. Her idea of a perfect getaway was to be waited on hand and foot in luxury, whereas mine was striking out into some remote and rugged environment. There is nothing wrong with either of these preferences, but they were incompatible. I suppose in retrospect that we could each have taken the holiday in our preferred environment, but somehow this did not arise. We were both approaching 50 and probably both of us—but certainly myself— were evaluating whether what we had was a satisfactory basis for the remainder of our lives.

417

It was into this fertile ground of simmering mid-life watershed that an unlikely player from the past appeared on the scene. One fateful morning at work I answered the phone at my desk. It was Sandy—the girl I had fallen for just before she returned to Singapore, 26 years earlier. She now lived in Perth, Australia, was married with three children and was visiting Singapore with her mother. I was delighted to hear from her and invited her and her mother to visit the house. At some point I took her to the boatyard and showed her through the boats. Her life, living in a small town in Western Australia, had reached much the same point as my own, and the bittersweet memory of that time long ago when we did little more than hold hands reached forward from the past like a lingering fragrance. She told me much later that being in the cabin of the boat with its funny-shaped bunks, she had to restrain herself from pouncing on me, ready to give her all. When she admitted this, I was very regretful that she hadn't given way to her impulse. I would certainly have been surprised but have no doubt I would have risen to the occasion. How exciting that would have been!

But we behaved in a very English way and did nothing of the sort, but the spark had been struck, and over the next few days of their visit we met alone and in secret a few times and gradually bared our souls.

In due course this led to arranging a meeting in Sydney, where I borrowed a GB 36 from our dealer, and Sandy and I spent one week on board cruising the Hawkesbury River Estuary, just north of Sydney. It was of course a very romantic interlude, which only fuelled the fires of passion for both of us.

Over the next few months we corresponded and I made several trips to Perth, in Western Australia. Her husband, from whom she was already somewhat estranged, found out, and soon the jig was up. I had felt very uncomfortable deceiving Mary. We may have had our differences, but she deserved better than that. When I came clean and told her, she said "It's all my fault. Everyone needs love."

This reaction surprised me very much, but I moved into the spare room in the house. The following day, it was very different. She had obviously spoken to her friends, who must have told her that I was a total cad and should be kicked out of the house. So when I came home after work she had the fury of a woman scorned and I had to pack my things and go, which was not unreasonable under the circumstances.

Jackie and Nicky were both living with us at the time, so it was difficult for them. They had already figured out that something was going on, and they told me later that I had rather lost their respect by not coming clean earlier. They were more relieved than anything when I told them and were not judgmental.

I moved out of the house and went to stay with Gil Hensen and his wife, while continuing to do my work at the yard. In September 1982, Mary went back to England, shortly to be followed by Nicky, who was going to study hotel management at Bath Technical College. I moved back into our house on Hume Heights, and Jackie continued to study at United World College. This division had nothing to do with sharing the kids but simply because that is what worked out better for them for their continued education. Nicky did well at Bath and worked in restaurants as part of her training. She later went on to spend six months in the Cordon Bleu school in London.

Sandy moved to Singapore with her son and younger daughter, who were both teenagers. Her elder daughter remained in Perth. Sandy found the realities of her situation very difficult and very different from how glamorous it must have appeared on her initial visit. I was at work every day and Sandy did not know anyone in Singapore and was now isolated from her friends and family. It was tough on her kids, also, as they too had been moved to a totally different environment and away from their friends.

So often in life, the ship of dreams founders on the rocks of reality and, sadly, this is what happened with the relationship between Sandy and myself. So it was with sorrow - as well as disappointment on both sides - that Sandy ultimately returned to Perth and the life she knew in Western Australia.

Lion's Den was launched in July 1982, and in October 1982, on one of her first real outings, we celebrated Jackie's 18th birthday. We cruised the channel dividing Singapore from

Malaysia with all flags flying, and I remember we cooked spaghetti Bolognese!

We went out on the boat quite a few times, during which I learned some painful lessons. Singapore is surrounded by coral reefs and the water can be very shallow even when barely in sight of land. One weekend I attempted to take the boat through a narrow channel on a falling tide. The channel was not apparent from the appearance of the water; it did have some marks but it was not very clearly delineated. This was before the days of universal GPS and electronic charts. I allowed the boat to stray out of the twisting channel and before I knew it we were aground. On a falling tide, you have about one minute to get off or you become increasingly stuck as the water dwindles away. We were there for nearly eight hours and were so high and dry that we could get off the boat and walk all around it on the reef. The boat tipped over to 35 degrees, which feels a lot more than it sounds. Fortunately, because *Lion's Den* was single screw, there was no damage to the rudder and propeller. Fuel started to drip out of the tank vents as the boat leaned over. I tried to stop it by stuffing rags into the vents, but they simply acted as wicks. I had read enough to know to deploy an anchor while we were still stranded, so as to stop us being pushed further onto the reef when the tide came back in and we re-floated.

The tide started to come back and lapped around the boat. The level came over the bulwarks and onto the side deck on the low side of the boat, and there was still no sign of her wanting to lift. I began to worry that the water would find a way inside the boat before she floated, and then we would be in serious trouble. Finally, and almost instantaneously, she righted and began to float and drift but, thanks to the anchor, did not go further onto the reef. I started the engine, retrieved the anchor, and we went home with the only lasting damage being to my pride.

The Malay boatmen at the yard told me that they would never attempt that passage except at low tide, when you could see where it was. If you must go anywhere tricky you should do so on a rising tide when, if you do go aground, the rising water will get you off. They say there are two kinds of boaters: those who have run aground, and those who have yet to do so!

A much longer trip was up the east coast of Malaysia to the Tioman Islands, which we had visited nine years earlier with Rex and Jill. There are two chains of islands running parallel to the coast and to each other. My original plan was to pass between the two chains and spend the first night anchored in a small bay on one of the islands in the inner chain. However, we were delayed due to being held up while dealing with Customs when we entered Malaysian waters, and it was getting dark long before we reached our destination.

At the southern end, both island chains tapered away into small, unmarked rocky islets. I checked the chart and realized that, with only 3 miles separating the two lines of rocks, I would only have to be 1½ miles off course to hit them—and that distance was within my margin of navigational error. I had to come up with Plan B pretty fast, keeping in mind that I was the only person on board who had the remotest idea how to navigate or run the boat. I decided that it would be better to run between the land and the innermost line of islands. The land was a continuous line and the sea bottom shelved gently towards it. I could set the alarm on the depth finder to 10 metres, so all I had to do was to keep outside that. Also, there was a beacon shown on the chart, which should have been visible 18 miles away, and that would confirm my position and indicate where to turn towards the island where I planned to anchor.

I put this plan into effect but, although I strained my eyes to see it, there was no sign of the beacon. It was a really black night with no moon and hardly any stars—just the red and green navigation lights reflecting off the waves. Finally, I sensed, rather than saw, an even deeper black shape off our starboard side, which was the island where we planned to anchor. I located the bay, and it was with great relief when the chain rattled over the rollers and the anchor gripped the bottom! The following morning, I could see that the looked-for beacon was derelict and was one of many along this and the Indonesian coast that were out of order.

We spent one week exploring this chain of beautiful islands but not all was unalloyed pleasure. One day we had winds which blew from the south up this north/south island chain. You would naturally think that shelter would be found on the northern side of the islands, but we searched in vain and spent a most horrible night rolling around in the waves with such violence that the window blind retainers broke, leaving the blinds thrashing back and forth. I was at a loss to understand how this could happen on the leeward side of an island, but months later, a magazine article explained the phenomenon of refraction, whereby waves are deflected around a small island and come together from opposing directions at the leeward end to create confused seas.

From the very start at American Marine, the water tanks in all the boats had been made the traditional way, with double-turned seams along all the edges, which were secured externally with lead solder. One of our customers in Hawaii had come down with lead poisoning, and it was claimed by his lawyer that this was due to the lead solder used in the construction of the water tanks on his boat. This was utterly absurd because the water never came into contact with the solder, but he sued anyway. I don't remember the outcome, but we decided we would have to change the construction of the tanks to avoid the problem in the future.

One of the advantages of building a tank by the traditional method was that it formed a very strong tank with straight edges. Welding, on the other hand, caused the edge to buckle. To get around this problem, I decided that we would first bend one edge at right angles to hold it straight and then sit the joining edge on top of the bend and weld the two together. This method worked well but it contained a fatal flaw. Like most people, I held the mistaken belief that stainless steel was a bullet-proof material— stainless through and through. In fact, it is only the few microns on the surface which are stainless. Once they dissipate in the absence of oxygen, stainless steel will cheerfully corrode away. This phenomenon comes under the title of "crevice corrosion" and it manifests itself again and again under different disguises. Unaware of this trap, the turned-over edge in the revised tank construction had created a perfect crevice along every seam, and within one year of their installation the water tanks started to rust and leak. All the faulty tanks had to be removed and replaced— initially with tanks made of marine aluminium in Florida. The affected boats were scattered all around the globe, and replacing tanks in a boat is never straightforward, as the boat is usually built around them. The cost averaged $10,000 per boat, which was a lot more money then than it is today.

In January 1983 I was sent to Venezuela to check on some window leaks on a GB 42, as well as the water tank and some other problems on a GB 49. It was a very long trip from Singapore, which involved flying to San Francisco, waiting there for several hours for the five-hour flight to Miami, and then another flight lasting several hours to Caracas. Carlos was mad at me for only spending five days, so he picked me up at the airport right after I arrived and took me straight to the GB 42, which had terrible rust all over the engines. It really brought home to me the fact that whenever we shipped a boat to a new geographical area, we ran into problems we had never encountered before. You have to solve the problems like a detective, by collecting every scrap of information, no matter how irrelevant they seem. It was always hard to get this info—especially via Dick Loh, who always interpreted the request for information as excuses or a way to avoid responsibility. It took a lot of figuring out why the windows leaked, and ultimately it turned out to be because the engine-room air intake vents were not large enough. Engines are, in effect, positive displacement pumps, and they are going to get the air they need from wherever they can get it. If the intake vents are not large enough, air will be drawn from inside the boat, and if the windows are all closed and there is wind blowing, the suction will draw water up the 2-inch vertical drain height and cause the windows to leak.

Then Carlos took me straight to a dinner with a lot of GB owners. Right after dinner we went to a couple of owners' boats and discussed their various problems until about 2 a.m. Then Carlos took me to my hotel and picked me up at 0630 to drive for miles to look at the GB 49 which had problems with rusting water tanks.

The following day we flew to Curacao, one of the Netherlands Antilles islands—also known as the ABC islands (Aruba, Bonaire and Curacao)—to visit another boat. I was absolutely exhausted

423

by the time I flew back to Singapore. Carlos said it was all my fault for not allowing more time—and people think that being in the boat business is such a glamorous occupation!

After her extra year at school in Singapore, during which she made some lifelong friends and, as she put it, finally came to love school, Jackie returned to England in August 1983 and worked in number of odd jobs around Bath, including in a cashmere sweater shop, which was a very bad fit!

I spent Christmas of 1983 at my sister's house, and I flew with Jackie and Nicky to Yellowstone National Park immediately afterward. I had wanted to go somewhere snowy and wintry which did not involve skiing. None of us had ever skied, and I didn't want to spend our week falling down and aching all over. The Singapore travel agent came up with a package snowmobile holiday through Yellowstone, which seemed to fit the bill.

We flew from London and landed in Boston, where the wind was so strong that it was rocking the aircraft on the ground, while the unfortunate ground crew were out there in driving snow spraying de-icing fluid. We next landed in Minnesota, where we deplaned and spent the night. We were told that the temperature was -5, and it seemed incredibly cold. I thought that I must have become more sensitive to the cold after all those years spent in the tropics. I eventually realized that they were referring to -5 °F which is 37 degrees F below freezing (-20.5 °C).

The following day we flew to Billings, Montana where the temperature was -36 °F (-38 °C) and rented a car to drive to Bozeman. They told us that we had to start the car engine every two hours to stop the oil turning to glue and the battery dying. Somehow we got from Bozeman to West Yellowstone, where our tour guide met us and took us into Yellowstone Park on snowmobiles. Jackie was 19 and Nicky was 18. It was the most memorable experience. We had a wonderful guide, and being the interval between Christmas and New Year, we had him to ourselves.

Yellowstone is an amazing place at any time of the year, but in deep winter when the snow cover can be 40 feet, it is a wonderland. Although it was bitterly cold, we were well protected, and we had days with sunshine and blue skies. As we sped along, the sun reflected off the snowflakes and sparkled like diamonds. There was steam from the geysers in the frigid air, and this condensed and froze on the nearby trees, making them look like wax candles. From Yellowstone we went through to the Grand Tetons, a jagged range of rugged peaks which pierced the sky. Our guide had spent winters in Alaska and described the joys of owning a car in that environment. The first challenge, he said, was getting into the vehicle without having the key break off in the lock. Once past that hurdle, when you sat on the seats the vinyl cover could splinter into fragments, or the plastic rim of the steering wheel could break off so you were left with just the steel core. If you had taken precautions to keep the engine plugged in and had a heating pad under the battery, you had a better chance of starting the engine, but you had to take extreme care when putting the car in gear.

When you at last stopped, the tyres would have been warm, so they melted the snow and ice under them. As the tyres cooled down, the air inside them contracted, so they went flat at the bottom and froze to the ground. If you tried to take off too fast, the wheels spun inside the tyre, tearing loose the valve assembly. So, using the transmission, you had to rock the vehicle back and forth to break it loose from the ground. When you got moving, the tyres were no longer round but had a flat spot where they been in contact with the ground. So, until they warmed up, you drove down the road *ker-clump, ker-clump* until you came to the first bend, where they got out of phase with each other and *went ker-clumpity-klump!*

From Yellowstone we flew to Florida to stay with the Wrights. On the way we landed at Denver, which is right at the point where the Rocky Mountains rise sheer from the Great Plains. At the moment that the aircraft was right over the divide, to port I could see nothing but flat country spreading to the horizon while to starboard there was nothing to be seen but an endless vista of snow-capped peaks. Florida was of course a total contrast to Yellowstone, and we visited the artificial worlds of Disneyland and Epcot Center in warm weather surrounded by palm trees.

425

Later, in September of that year, we went on a camping trip to Scotland, during which we were camped in Glen Nevis, at the base of the mountain. The weather was beautiful and the mountain clear, so somehow we got around to the idea of climbing it. Thirty years had passed since I last made that decision, and I had forgotten just how hard it was. We made it to the top and back, but as before, the clouds had clouded the summit by the time we reached it.

When Jackie moved back to England in August 1983, there was no point in my continuing to live in a fancy house on my own, so I moved onto *Lion's Den*. It was my first experience of actually living on a boat, and it took a few days to become accustomed to it. Initially I kept the boat at the yard and anchored it off one of the islands at night. But the river was so stinky that this wasn't very satisfactory, so I moved the boat to Changi, on the other side of the island.

I moved the boat on my own, and the trip proved to be an object lesson in not taking things for granted and how small problems can quickly escalate into major events. Getting from Jurong, on the west coast of Singapore, to Changi, on the east, on a nice, calm, sunny day would not seem like much of a challenge. The first thing to go wrong was that the catch securing a locker door on the flying bridge broke, so the door started slamming back and forth in the undulating sea. The door had a glass panel which had to be secured before the glass broke. The autopilot wasn't working, so it was a bit of a challenge to leave the helm to look for some tape to restrain the door.

At the eastern tip of Singapore Island, I had to turn into the strait dividing the island from mainland Malaysia. The entrance was bordered on both sides by sandbanks. As I approached the turn, one of the afternoon thunderstorms dropped torrential rain, reducing visibility to virtually zero. Just before this happened I saw an oil rig ahead of me being towed at very slow speed by a couple of tugs. I also knew that this was a regular shipping channel, with ships coming in from the open sea and proceeding up to Sembawang. I did not have radar so I could not tell how fast I was catching up the tugs and I could not see any ships coming up behind me. The compass I normally had on board had been taken off for repair, as I did not think I would need one for such a simple trip, so I did not know exactly where I was in this restricted environment. I figured that I could rely on the depth finder to tell me if I was getting too close to shore, but that suddenly stopped working! I subsequently came to the conclusion that the enormous amount of water being dumped by the cloudburst had resulted in a layer of fresh water on top of the salt. I slowed right down to virtually a stop, but I was still subject to being shoved in any direction by the tide, and I remained worried about being in the way of big ships in this relatively narrow channel. After about half an hour the rain stopped and limited visibility returned. I had escaped once again—wiser but unscathed.

I tied *Lion's Den* to a mooring just off the coast of Changi and I commuted by car every day to American Marine. The environment was certainly a lot nicer than that of the Jurong River, but I could not pretend it was convenient. I had to row a small dinghy back and forth to the shore every day. When I got there I had to drag the tender out of the water and hope that no one would steal it or the oars. I had 400 U.S. gallons of water on the boat, which I managed to make last more than two months, but then I had to run a very long hose out to the boat from the shore to refill the tanks.

After I had been on board about two weeks, I decided to go for a short cruise one evening. I found that the boat would hardly move, yet the engine was working really hard. I had no idea what was wrong, but I dived in to check the propeller. It had so much growth on it that it resembled a cauliflower. I thought I would soon scrape this off, only to find that it was as tough as concrete and practically welded to the propeller blades. It was enormously hard work to remove and was so sharp that it ripped you up. It turned out that there were massive pig farms upstream, and the organic waste in the water was the reason for the prolific marine growth.

While living aboard the boat, I met an American who was living not far away aboard a sailboat made in Taiwan. He invited me on board and I was impressed by the quality. American Marine had been facing increasing competition from trawler-style boats being built in Taiwan for much cheaper prices. We referred to them as "Taiwan Turkeys" and were very derisory about their quality. Up to that time I had never actually stepped aboard a boat built in Taiwan, so I was surprised by what I saw.

One weekend I decided to move *Lion's Den* to a quiet spot for a change of scene. It was a beautiful, calm evening, and I anchored in a small bay in the lee of an island with a rocky shoreline. I awoke in the middle of the night in a raging thunderstorm, with torrential rain accompanied by a strong wind that was blowing me towards the rocks. I was still OK, but if the anchor dragged, I would be on the rocks almost immediately.

I started the engine and began to move the boat forward, hauling in the anchor chain using the remote control at the lower helm. After my earlier experience I now had radar installed, so I was able to judge my position relative to the shore. With the anchor up, I was able to relocate to a safer position and re-anchor, all without going outside and getting wet. I was rather pleased with myself, but it was another lesson about not being too complacent when anchoring for the night and expecting the weather conditions to remain unchanged.

Chapter 9

Early 1984 to February 1985

Life in Singapore

I construct the set for *Fiddler on the Roof* and act as assistant stage manager. I meet Angie. I chronicle the appointment of Tom Wright as an outside director and relate how this leads to a palace revolution, resulting in my departure from American Marine after 23 years. I visit Australia, the U.S., the UK, Canada and India.

Early in 1984, Bob Livingston told me that he had offered the facilities of American Marine to help with building the sets for a production of *Fiddler on the Roof* being produced by the Singapore Theatre's American Repertory Showcase–or STARS–and he asked whether I could handle this. Of course I said that I would be delighted. The next couple of months were spent in using the facilities and talents of the company's development department to build the set designed by Justin Hill. It proved to be a very interesting project, figuring out and making everything from a rotating stage, about 12 feet in diameter with three sets on it, to a self-contained water-trough with an old-fashioned pump which dispensed real water –using a boat bilge pump!

When set construction was finished, I went on to work as one of two assistant Stage Managers. The show ran for nine performances, including one day when there was a matinee in addition to the usual performance at 8 p.m. It was a huge production with a total cast, including singers and dancers, of over 80, plus at least the same number of backroom people and musicians. *Fiddler* has 60 scene changes—most achieved during a dimming of the lights lasting only a few seconds. We communicated backstage with walkie-talkies.

Fiddler is a wonderful show. In rare moments when we were not busy backstage, I would watch the audience through cracks in the scenery and follow the play of emotions on their faces—from dismay, followed a minute later by laughter, and then alarm.

I especially recall that electric moment just before the raising of the opening curtain. The show started at 8 p.m., but if there were still large numbers of people entering the theatre, "front of house" would call on the radio to delay the opening. Finally, the OK would be given and the chorus waiting in the wings would be given a three-minute warning. The orchestra in the pit would start the overture, and the tension was palpable as the magic moment approached. Three–two–one. The Stage Manager pressed the button. The curtain lifted, and we were off!

The most dramatic moment during the production was the return of the butcher's wife from the grave. Hidden from the view of the audience by slowly circulating, silent dancers, a trap door opened in the centre of the stage and the actress playing the part of the resurrected wife, seated on the shoulders of a gymnast to give her extra height, slowly rose above the circulating throng. Lit from below by a green floodlight, her hair was a matted tangle. Her fingers were extended by finger stalls of polished brass, like those worn by Thai dancers, and her face had skull-like make up. The children in the audience screamed in fright. It was wonderful!

The most poignant moment came at the end of the last performance. We had just two hours to clear the stage and the "villagers" were quite literally in tears as they saw their village of Anatevka being torn down. Some of the most memorable experiences of my life have been with amateur theatre.

It had been sometime in 1982 that Dick Loh suggested that we should have an outside director. Initially I could not see any point in this. After all, we all worked within the company, each with our own areas of responsibility, so why did we need an outsider in our group? The person Dick proposed for this job was Tom Wright, with whom I had cruised in the Bahamas. Tom was an experienced boater and had run his own technical company. We had got along well, and I realized that with him on board I would have a technical ally. At present, I was the only person with a technical background amongst a group of people who were all in accounting or sales. There is also the point that, working every day within the company, you sometimes cannot see the wood for the trees, and an outsider can bring a more objective view to the party. So, along with the others, I agreed with the proposal and Tom was appointed to the Board. GB by this time had restored its slightly battered reputation, and Tom was very flattered to be asked to join this unpaid position. But he made it clear that if he joined the board of directors he would take the position seriously.

A Directors' Meeting was held every year, and in 1984 it was held in Singapore. In early September, Tom and Jane Wright arrived a couple of weeks prior to this date, while Bob Livingston was away on his annual holiday. I picked up the Wrights at the airport, and during the drive into town Tom told me that, after being a director for two years, he had reached the conclusion that Bob Livingston had being doing a poor job as president, the company was lacking any direction, and that I should replace him –and what did I think? Wow! This had come out of a clear blue sky without any warning.

What did I think? In addition to running production, my title was Engineering and Development Manager. Most of the ideas I proposed were not adopted because Bob did not want to run up against Dick Loh, who was very opinionated and hard to get along with. If Bob pushed too hard, Dick would threaten to resign, which he did on a regular basis. Dick placed numerous obstacles in the way of Bob's visiting the dealers, on the pretext that he did not know enough about the boats. As Dick was responsible for the dealers producing the majority of the sales, Bob took the resignation threat seriously and backed down each time. In effect he took Dick's side over mine for the wrong reasons. I found this very frustrating because we were not doing any real development.

So, from the point of view of a director and a shareholder, I shared Tom's view, but he was asking me to vote to kick out my boss and take his job, which was not something I had ever aspired to or thought to be very ethical.

I told him this and also said that, in any case, Dick Loh would never in a thousand years agree to have me for his boss. Tom replied that he had spoken to Dick in the U.S. before he had come to Singapore, and Dick had said he agreed with his evaluation of Bob and would have no problem working for me.

"You absolutely amaze me" I said.

The following day, Tom spoke to Ron Filbert in my presence about his proposal. Bob had brought Ron into the company in California many years earlier, and they had worked together previously at a big international accounting company. Ron looked as though he had been kicked in the stomach when he heard what Tom had to say and said that he would need to discuss it with his wife and think about it overnight. The next morning, Ron said that he agreed with the proposal and would have no trouble working for me.

Dick Loh then arrived from the U.S. and confirmed to Ron and myself what he had already told Tom. So now all the conspirators were in agreement, and together we had shares to add up to more than 50 per cent. Bob Livingston returned all cheerful from his holidays a few days later, and knowing what I did, I felt like a real traitor and a hypocrite.

The directors meeting was not for at least one week, when the subject would be raised and Bob voted out of office. About two days after Bob's return I had a call to go to his office. When I arrived, Tom, Ron and Dick were already there, and Ron was confirming to a shocked Bob that we were all in agreement that he should be fired from his position as president of the company. When Ron had finished, Bob turned to me and I told him the same thing, after which we all left his office.

It transpired that Bob and Tom Wright had got into an argument during which Bob had told Tom that he should resign from the board. Tom had not been able to resist telling Bob that, on the contrary, his fellow shareholders had decided that it was he, Bob, who had to go. Bob told Tom that he didn't believe him and called us all into his office to hear from each of us.

432

The following morning Bob came into my office at 0730, questioned why we had reached this decision, and asked if there was not some other way. I told him my reasons and said that it was nothing personal and the problem with being at the very top was that there was nowhere else to go except out or down. He asked who was to replace him, and I said that my name had been put forward. I told him that I had neither proposed nor sought to take over the position, but that I wasn't afraid of it.

The atmosphere was very tense and not very pleasant over the next few days, but the day before the scheduled meeting, I had a call to go to Ron Filbert's office. When I arrived, Ron was there with Tom, looking very sombre. They told me that Dick Loh had switched sides. His shares combined with Bob's constituted more than 50 per cent, so the revolution was over–leaving Dick in a very powerful position because Bob was now beholden to Dick for retaining his job. Dick and Bob voted Tom off the Board of Directors. The ultimate result was really a foregone conclusion because you cannot expect to foment a palace revolution and then, if it fails, keep your head!

The following month, I went on an interesting to journey which took me first to Australia to see Bill Barry Cotter, who was building his own version of a GB 36. From there I flew to California, where I met up with Bob Phillips. I was in his office when the phone rang and he handed it to me. It was Anton, with whom I had lost contact since he had left the company a couple of years earlier. He and his family had returned to England, where he worked with Fairways Marine on the Hamble, just outside Southampton, where they built the Fisher motorsailer boats.

Anton had decided on the spur of the moment to get in touch with me and had called Bob Phillips to ask for my address. We arranged to meet that evening at a local restaurant called the Pleasant Pheasant, where he introduced me to his girlfriend, Leslie. I told Anton all that had been going on, and he told me that Fairways Marine had been through two bankruptcies and that he had moved back to California and was now writing books. Although he had become a published author, he was finding the writing life a bit tedious and had been thinking about getting back into the boat business. He asked me what I was doing over Christmas, and I told him that I would have my daughters with me. He suggested that I come to Newport Beach, where we could spend more time mulling over the situation. This was another of those strange coincidences in life.

The following day I left for Canada where I visited Bill Garden –the well-known naval architect. I called Bill and he arranged to pick me up in his Ford Thunderbird at 0730 on a certain street outside Victoria, on Vancouver Island. He duly arrived and I expected to be driven to his office in the city. Instead, we drove for some distance up the road past Sidney towards the main ferry terminals at Schwartz Bay. Here we turned down a narrow road to Canoe Cove Marina with floating, garage-style buildings on either side of the gangway. We came to a small open boat, where a couple of guys wearing black balaclavas were waiting for us.

The boat had a small, fully exposed, single-cylinder engine sitting out in the open. The engine was started by inserting a screwdriver into one of a series of holes around the perimeter of the flywheel. With the engine tonking away, we left the dock and headed out into open water. I had absolutely no idea where we were going and felt like we were on some kind of commando mission with the guys in the balaclavas. The shore was thick with conifers, and a seal popped its head out of the water while seagulls circled overhead. After about 10 minutes, we pulled into a tiny bay with a couple of floating docks to which were tied a pair of vintage boats. A rough sign nailed to a tree said: "Toad's Landing". There was a house in the trees on this tiny island, which was only about 100 yards across. Some chickens were picking among the undergrowth. We went inside the house, where a cheerful fire burned in the grate. The walls were lined with bookshelves and half models. Several large drawing boards occupied the centre of the room. It was a wonderful atmosphere and so completely unexpected.

I was there to discuss the possibility of having Bill design a larger GB. Ultimately this did not lead anywhere, but I appreciated meeting a naval architect I had admired for years because of his imaginative designs.

From here I returned to Singapore. It was interesting to have visited Australia, California, and Western Canada, one after the other, in a relatively brief period of time. The citizens of Australia exhibited a negative approach to life–similar to those in England, but not as extreme. In California the mood was positive and upbeat, and Canada was a watered-down version of Australia on the gloom index.

I made arrangements to meet my daughters in San Francisco just before Christmas. From there we drove down the coast to Newport Beach, where we had the use of Anton's apartment while he moved in with Leslie.

Leslie introduced us to her parents, who were very hospitable and with whom we celebrated a delightful family Christmas. The extended time in Newport Beach allowed Anton and myself to discuss the situation with our respective lives. Anton had sold a book and was writing another, but he was getting a bit fed up with sitting alone at home every day, bashing away on a typewriter. Word processing was just getting started, but neither of us had any knowledge or experience with computers. I told him about the Indian boatbuilding company in Cochin and said that they needed someone to market their boats. I was scheduled to go to England from California, and from there to Singapore. I offered to break my journey in Bombay and talk with the Indians to see whether they would be interested in working with Anton.

After Christmas I flew back to the UK and met up with my mother and visited the London Boat Show. I had been in touch with the Indians and arranged for them to meet me at Bombay airport on Jan 26th. I arrived there at about 8 p.m., but when I tried to go through immigration, they wouldn't let me through because I didn't have a visa. I said that I had never previously required a visa to land in India, and the official told me that since the UK had recently introduced a visa requirement for Indians, India had reciprocated. I told him that there was an Indian gentleman waiting for me at the airport and we had some potential business to discuss. The official said that if I left my passport with him and he gave me a receipt, he would agree to let me through.

So I traded passport for the receipt and met up with the guy who had come to meet me.

As soon as we were in the car, the guy told me we were going to a party. As we negotiated the crowded streets, the already chaotic traffic grew even more confused when we encountered a noisy procession proceeding in the opposite direction. Throngs of people in colourful dress, along with elaborately decorated elephants, competed for space with cars, rickshaws, buses and horse-drawn carts. The rhythmic drumming of the tabla and the wail of the shehnai filled the air along with the continual honking of car horns. Already fatigued and disoriented by the journey from staid and conventional England, I found it hard to accept that this was real and not some bizarre hallucination. When we eventually arrived at an apartment block, I found myself at a normal type of cocktail party with sophisticated people at which I was the only non-Indian and attractive doe-eyed women were dressed in colourful saris. It was all very bewildering. But contrast is the very spice of life, and this was the epitome of that. The following day I sounded them out about Anton and we agreed to keep in touch. I boarded my plane and continued on to Singapore.

When I got back into my office, my chief draftsman, Ong–who was almost Victorian in his strict adherence as to what was right and wrong–came into my office and told me that, while I had been away, Dick Loh had come over from the U.S. and that he and Mr. Livingston had made a lot of changes to the design of the tooling for the GB 36 Europa design, which were underway by the Development carpenters. I had learnt over the years that it was a mistake to get into any adversarial situations for at least three days after making a substantial East/West journey. You tend to say things that, in retrospect, would have been better left unsaid! I think that political leaders should take this into account! I thanked Ong but decided that I would not even go to take a look right away because I might get mad.

Bob Livingston came into my office the following day and said that while I had been absent, he and Dick Loh had made some changes. I said that was quite OK and that both of them were entitled to make changes as they thought fit. He then asked me what I was going to do to work better with Dick Loh. I replied that I felt I had done everything possible, but no matter what I did he simply did not like me; nor I, him. I told him that I did not see that it really mattered anyway. Dick lived in Connecticut; I lived in Singapore; and we each had our own areas of responsibility. I said that it was probably even healthy that his vice-presidents did not always agree and that it was his function and responsibility as president to listen to what each of his vice-presidents had to say and then make final decisions based on their input. He said that that was not good enough. I responded that in that case maybe I was wasting my time and the company was wasting its money and that I should leave. Bob said that that was a major decision and we should meet in one hour to further discuss it.

I was so fed up that I really did not want to discuss it further, and I went out into the yard to get on with my work. Bob came to find me and said that he wanted to consider it overnight and we would meet again the following morning. I interpreted this to mean that he wanted to discuss it with Dick Loh–who, of course, was in very different time zone–and also with his wife. At this point I really no longer cared about the outcome. It was as though the cards had been tossed in the air and I could not be bothered even to see which way up they landed.

The following morning, at 0730, Bob came into my office and said that he had decided it was best that I should leave. After 23 years in the job, he gave me two weeks. I reminded him that he had asked me to stay over Chinese New Year to meet with some prospective clients from overseas while he was away, so he amended the two weeks to four. He said they would have a farewell party. I said that was the last thing I wanted and, please, no party.

The news of my impending departure spread through the yard like wildfire. I had become more or less a fixture at the yard and a mainstay of running the production, QC and design. The word was, that if I could go, no one's job was safe. They said about me that I might be a bastard but at least I was a fair bastard, and I was happy with that description. The Chinese are very perceptive with their nicknames. Bob's nickname was "Moneyface".

Every group in the yard wanted to give me a going-away party. There was the office, various groups of carpenters, mechanics and more groups than I could possibly mention here. Even the apprentices (with little money), the security guards and the labour union. I was sorry to say goodbye to people I had worked with for so long, but it was worth it for the heart-warming send-off I got from everyone—except the colleagues at my level. Mind you, it is not very smart, at age 50, to leap out of a boat you have been in for 23 years without having another to step into and with no idea what you are going to do!

It was at this time that Angie came into my life, and the timing could not have been better. We had met during the production of *Fiddler on the Roof.* I have never understood what she found in me, because she was quite a few years younger and was one of those women who, when she entered a room, stopped all conversation. Her day job was executive secretary in a downtown company. Her night job was being with me! She really boosted my ego at a time when I was having some doubts over my sanity. She was delightfully wicked and wanted me to have my way with her on Bob Livingston's desk after hours as a kind of symbolic act. Sadly, I was too chicken to go along with it because I was afraid that the security guards would come along in the middle, but the idea was certainly appealing!

In the end, at her suggestion, she dressed fit to kill and came to the office at 4 p.m. one afternoon with a cake to share out amongst all the staff. In my senior position I had always been referred to as a respectful "Mr. Fleming" so it was a riot to see the reaction to this little affair. I knew that Bob had always had an eye for the local talent, but had been held in check by consideration for his wife. His eyes fairly popped out when he saw the lady on my arm.

And so it was that I departed from the company I had been with for 23 years, over which time I had absorbed everything I now knew about building boats. The pertinent question was where did I go from here? I was at one of those major crossroads in my life.

Book 6
INTERLUDE

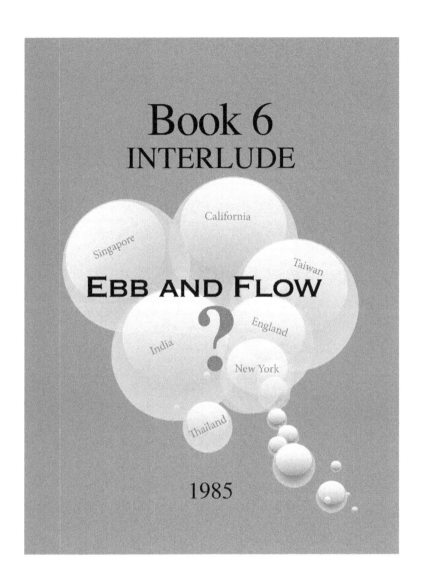

Ebb and Flow

Singapore

California

Taiwan

England

India

?

New York

Thailand

1985

February 1985 to October 1985

Life Between Singapore and Taiwan

I describe nine months of uncertainty and drastic change, during which I visit Taiwan, California, Thailand, Singapore and New York. I form a partnership with Anton and we decide to build the Fleming. We visit Taiwan to select a boatyard. My mother dies. I celebrate my 50th birthday shortly before moving to Taiwan.

My contract with American Marine closed at the end of February 1985. The Singapore government cancelled my work permit and gave me two weeks to get out of town, which I thought was a bit steep considering I had worked in the country for 17 years and contributed significantly to its economy. With no job and no income, my credit cards were cancelled, so my situation had changed dramatically! It's not super smart to abandon a job you have had for more than 20 years when you are almost 50 years old without having another one to go to. It's not an action I would recommend, but having done so, it is important to get your priorities right, so the first thing I did was to spend a week in Thailand with Angie in the small resort town of Phuket!

We had a wonderful, relaxed time after all the recent turmoil, and I learned another lesson from her. When we came to leave I had a small bag I could effortlessly carry on my own. A small boy wanted to carry it but I resisted, because I didn't feel inclined to pay for a service that I really did not need or want. Angie chastised me for being so stingy, and I realized that she was right. Here was this kid who obviously had very little and who was looking for a way to earn a little money—probably to give to his family. I gave him the bag and I have kept that incident in mind to this day. If you are lucky enough to have it—spread it around a bit.

We returned to Singapore and the following day I flew to Hong Kong and then on to Taipei. In those days, Taiwan was the boatbuilding capital of the world with around 70 boat-builders. I felt this would be a good opportunity to visit with Tim Ellis, whom I had met in Singapore a few years earlier. He had his office in Taipei. I visited several yards with him and stayed at his house in Tamsui. Taiwan was certainly very different from both Hong Kong and Singapore, both of which were, or had been, British colonies.

Tim was one of a number of foreign boat inspectors who, for a fee, would keep an eye on a buyer's boat while it was under construction and make sure it was complete and up to snuff before shipment. In the early days, using an inspector was a wise investment. There were many horror stories about some of the boats being shipped from Taiwan, and these left a bad smell that tainted the country's reputation for many years. Tim had branched out into representing products—e.g., autopilots and electronics— from overseas vendors but, from what I observed during my visit, this representation was more commercial than technical.

After a few days in Taiwan, I moved on to Southern California and stayed with Anton in his apartment in Newport Beach. We spent much time discussing our various options. Up to this time, I had only worked within the security of someone else's company and, despite all my experience, I had never considered striking out on my own, and I am not sure if it would even have occurred to me if it had not been for Anton. The obvious choice was for us to work together with the yard I had visited in Cochin. From my visit, it had been pretty clear that trying to sell the boats would be unlikely to work without having someone at the yard to interpret the instructions and make sure they were followed. We made contact with the Indians to see if we could work out some form of co-operation. There was no e-mail, of course, and not much fax, so communication was not easy or swift. Eventually we made arrangements to meet them in New York to discuss the matter.

Anton and I stayed in a small hotel on 44th Street in Manhattan. New York had a reputation for being famously rude, as illustrated by the oft-quoted story of the New York cop who, when asked for directions, responded, "Buy a map, buddy!" We were expecting universal rudeness but encountered only good humour. We met with the Indian representative, who was telling us about the parent company and its chairman "who", he said, "had a finger in every tart."

I allowed my imagination to run with that for a moment before murmuring, "In every pie."

He looked at me quizzically.

"It's a finger in every pie," I replied.

"Pie, tart—same thing isn't it?" he said.

I kind of wobbled my head, Indian style and smiled. "Tart" sounded a lot more amusing.

After endless discussion, nothing definite was decided. They were in no hurry, but for Anton and myself there was a degree of urgency to get things moving. We did some sightseeing including going up the Empire State Building and were impressed by how, in New York, you could pass from China into Italy simply by crossing the street. We also wanted to go up the Twin Towers, but the queue for the elevators was too long. Coming from California, New York struck us as a gritty but authentic city. It was springtime and the perfect time of year, when it was neither too hot nor too cold. Southern California was new and well groomed, with the best weather in the world, but somehow almost unreal—like a giant Disneyland.

We returned home and visited the Newport Beach Boat Show in April. Among the many boats on display was a Hinckley sailboat which, by reputation, was top of the line; but there were also some Taiwan-built sailboats which looked every bit as good— and in some respects better. These boats were being offered by Dan Streech from PRI, who later went on to build the Nordhavns. We spent some time going through the Mason and talking to him about building in Taiwan. We came away from these discussions realizing that the reputation for lousy quality did not necessarily apply across the board to all boats built in Taiwan. This was an important revelation.

444

Another boat we studied was a Bayliner 45 Pilothouse. While not known for rugged build quality, we found the layout ingenious and interesting. I made the comment that it differed from the boats we had been considering in that it was a pilothouse design. This prompted Anton to cry "Alaskan!"—rather in the manner of Archimedes shouting "Eureka!" from his bath more than 2,000 years ago. And it was indeed a Eureka moment because it set us on the path that ultimately led to the creation of the Fleming.

The Alaskan had been built by American Marine in wood in Hong Kong. The design had been introduced to provide an alternative to the Grand Banks, and it had sold well until the yard's closure in 1974. I had an old brochure I had brought with me from papers I had cleared from my office. I dug it out and we realized that there was nothing really comparable currently on the market. Bob Dorris had been the designer of all the Alaskans except for the Alaskan 46, and he lived in Newport Beach, so we approached him. He had now been retired for a number of years and was reluctant to get back into boat design. However, he said he would look at some of his old drawings. We waited a couple of weeks but nothing was forthcoming. Anton and I were in a fever of impatience, but Bob's nature was such that the more you pressured him the more he dug in his heels, so we dared not get too pushy. I heard that Bob's schooner *Faith* was in a slip being varnished by volunteers, so I went down and offered my services. This produced the drawings almost immediately. I think that Bob was worried about the mess I might make of his varnish!

We never had any intention of copying the Alaskan design, but it provided a paradigm for us to follow. We just wanted the drawings to remind us of its general features. It was, after all, 11 years since it had been in production, and when the subject of its possible resurrection had been raised at the reconstituted American Marine, Dick Loh had been vehemently opposed to it. Bob Dorris was our first choice for a naval architect, but after he had made it clear that he did not want to get involved with a new design, we approached Ed Monk in Seattle. Not unreasonably, they asked for $25,000 up front, which we did not have. Anton then suggested Larry Drake in San Diego, who had, in past years, been on American Marine's payroll. We went to see Larry, and he

445

generously agreed to do the initial design for a very reasonable figure, with an initial payment up front and a second instalment after the first boat was shipped. We would then make a royalty payment on each subsequent boat. This is usually a dodgy arrangement for the naval architect because it is common practice for builders to cease paying. Nearly 30 years later we are still honouring that royalty payment to Larry's wife, even though Larry himself has passed away.

Having ideas is all very fine, but they don't mean much unless followed by action. We had to decide the general parameters of the boat such as size, speed, range, and general layout; and we passed these on to Larry. Anton and myself used to go for breakfast every day to Coco's restaurant at Fashion Island, and the first sketches were roughed out on paper napkins. Yes, really—that old cliché!

We formed a company to build the boats, and we had to come up with a name for both the boat and the company. We gave serious thought to *Aleutian* but decided it was too close to *Alaskan,* and we didn't want people to think we had simply copied that boat. Our next choice was *Falmouth,* which is the name of seafaring towns both in the UK and Massachusetts. This was also dropped after we found that the majority of Americans pronounce it "foul mouth". We also discovered that there was an existing brand of boat with that name. Then a mutual friend suggested *Fleming* as a name for both the boat and the company. My initial reaction was one of horror, and I was dead against it. But they prevailed and said that if I had my name on the boat, I would have an extra incentive to make sure it was good! I cringed at the idea but I was outnumbered, and so that name was adopted. I am pleased now, of course, but I wasn't at the time.

There had always been a general belief that my area of expertise was on the technical side but that I had no clue about how to run a business. With this in mind, Anton insisted that he handle the business side. I had no problem with this, and in any case, without a Green Card I could not work in the U.S.

Around this time, I was alerted by my various friends in the industry that my old boss had sent out telexes to all and sundry that they should be cautious about doing business with me—inferring that I was not to be trusted! I know this to be true because one of my contacts sent me a copy of the telex.

I was still hankering after Angie, and I flew back to Singapore at the end of April for three weeks. Angie took me to a temple to have my fortune told. The attendant handed me a cylindrical container made from bamboo about 2 inches in diameter and 8 inches long in which were a number of slim bamboo spills, or sticks, each of which had a number. On his instruction, I shook the cylinder until one of the spills came out ahead of the others. The interpreter noted the number and referred to a book written in Chinese characters. He started to read but what he said had no relevance to my situation; I said nothing but he realized that he was reading from the wrong page and started over. This time he said, in essence, that the current project we had been pursuing, which involved dark-skinned people, would not succeed, but the project which followed would be successful.

The following day I accompanied Angie to a party which had the usual multi-racial mix of people you tend to find at parties in Singapore. One of the guests was a young woman I had never seen before who used cards to tell fortunes. Carefully laying out the cards, one by one, she told me that the current project involving dark-skinned people would not be successful but the one which followed would be! Amazing and hard to believe, but that is what happened and—best of all—it came true!

I returned to California, and Angie came over for a visit a couple of weeks later. We went on a road trip that took us through the magnificent scenery of northern California. Angie surprised me by asking how we were going to find our way when we had never been there before. It seemed to me to be a very strange question, and when I asked her about it she said that she was a Singapore girl and a "product of her environment". It made me realize how much we take for granted. If you have lived all your life in a small city state, you really do not need to know how to navigate!

We drove through the magnificent redwood forests, with their immense Sequoia trees, and into Yosemite Valley, overlooked by

447

the granite monoliths of Half Dome and El Capitan. We tried to observe any climbers on the latter, but they were invisible to the naked eye. It was only when we were offered a chance to peer through a borrowed telescope that we spotted miniscule climbers clinging to the sheer, 3,000-foot rock face, which typically takes four to five days to scale.

From there, we crossed the still snow-clad Sierra to reach Mono Lake on the eastern side of the mountains. Mono Lake is famous for its strange tufa towers and the brine shrimp that live in its saline waters. A ranger told us that, from the geological record, it was deduced that the seemingly permanent Sierra Mountains had been levelled by erosion and rebuilt to their present height of 13,000 feet at least three times.

We continued north to the ghost town of Bodie, which was founded in 1876 following the discovery of gold in 1859. The town had 65 saloons on Main Street during its heyday, but it gradually declined as gold miners moved on to more lucrative sites. It is considered California's premium ghost town and is held in a state of "arrested decay". Wandering through the surviving buildings of this remote, dilapidated town with views of the distant snow-capped Sierras is another reminder of the impermanence of human activity.

Angie and I returned to Singapore for one week at the beginning of July before I joined Anton in Taipei. We had previously contacted Tim Ellis, who had provided us with the names of five yards he thought might be suitable to build the boat we had in mind. Most of these were near Kaohsiung in the south of the country and we decided to take the train. We went to the railway station and found ourselves bewildered by crowds of people queuing at ticket counters with everything written only in Chinese characters. A young man came up to us and asked where we wanted to go. He stood in line for us and obtained our tickets and made sure we got on the right train and even helped us find our seats. Earlier, when we had been standing in the streets of Taipei consulting our map, a lady had stopped her taxi to help us before continuing her ride in the same vehicle. You certainly knew what it was like to be an illiterate foreigner in Taiwan but people were unfailingly nice and helpful.

Tim followed us to Kaohsiung but took the plane. Over the next few days we visited four yards. These visits usually involved sitting on hard seats, drinking Chinese tea, while we produced our primitive, hand-drawn sketches showing what we had in mind. It was July and extremely hot, and we were walking around with our feet in the very centre of our shadows.

The yards were widely dispersed, with none located on the water. One, in the congested tax-free zone, was close to the commercial harbour, which at that time was the third-busiest in the world. Here you could hardly squeeze between the boats parked higgledy-piggledy inside the building, while some of the work had spilled outside onto the sidewalk. The Tung Hwa Industrial Company, Ltd., on the other hand, was located 20 kilometres from town and was surrounded by rice paddies. Here we were met by the yard manager, John Sun, who was very personable and who spoke good English. I can still clearly remember arriving at the yard for that first visit. Little did I know how much that place was to become part of my life.

After about three days we went back up to Taipei to consider our findings. Of all the yards we had visited, only Tung Hwa demonstrated any real interest in wanting our business, to the extent that John Sun pursued us to Taipei. Much later I discovered the reason for this was the result of one of those bizarre chains of circumstance which occur in life and which illustrate that everything you do has consequences.

When I ran the Development Department of American Marine in Singapore, one of my designers was a Singaporean Indian of Tamil origin, named Kannaiya. He had very dark skin and the Chinese carpenters used to tease him mercilessly with remarks like, "Good job you smiled—I didn't see you standing there"! He took this hazing remarkably well—maybe because he was a staunch Seventh Day Adventist. This caused him a lot of grief because their Sabbath is Saturday, which was a normal working day for the rest of us. Kannaiya spoke English, Tamil and Malay, but not any Chinese dialect. Despite this apparent drawback, he left Singapore and went to Taiwan. He took a job at

Ocean Alexander, a boatbuilding company owned and operated by the unforgettable Alexander Chu. While Kannaiya was working for Alex, he met a Taiwanese named John Sun. Apparently Kannaiya had often spoken favourably about me to John, so John knew who I was when I showed up at Tung Hwa.

Anton and I met Alexander Chu during our visit to Taiwan. In his office he had a huge bar, and he started drinking early in the morning, so when you visited him you were offered not tea but Scotch. When we told him our reason for being in Taiwan, Alex opened the drawer of his desk and pulled out a brochure for the Alaskan. He told us that he had been so impressed by the boat that, a few years back, he had gone to Ed Monk and asked him to design a similar boat. That boat became the Ocean 50 Mark 1, and it would have been our major competition. Fortunately for us, Alex had decided he wanted to shift to the more European style of boats. He told us that he had literally just cut up the mould for the Mark 1 and was now building the very different Mark II. This was really a stroke of luck for us.

While John Sun was still at Ocean Alexander, Tung Hwa had been an unsuccessful boatbuilding company owned and operated by a Taiwanese known as the "Admiral", because he had been in the navy. He lived in Taipei and flew down to Kaohsiung once per week to visit the boat yard and dump more money into it. Seeking more investors, he approached various acquaintances including a Mr. Ling, who, with others, had provided funds in exchange for shares in the company. On August 22nd 1981, the Boeing 737 in which the Admiral was flying to Kaohsiung suffered structural failure in flight because of crevice corrosion. This was a similar incident to the 737 that lost the top part of its fuselage in Hawaii in April 1988. The difference being that, in Hawaii, the pilot managed to land; while the plane in Taiwan crashed, killing everyone aboard.

As a result of the tragedy, all the shareholders found themselves owning a company they neither wanted nor knew anything about. Of these, Mr. Ling was the main shareholder, and all the others looked to him for leadership. He, very wisely as it turned out, bought out all the other shareholders to give himself freedom of action. His business was manufacturing stuffed toys, and he knew nothing about boats, so he turned to a friend who had a son in the boat business. Personal relationships play an important role in Chinese culture, and the son was prevailed upon to take on the running of the Tung Hwa yard. This person was none other than John Sun. John was aware of both my position at American Marine and the reputation for good quality enjoyed by American Marine, and he saw this as an opportunity to bring some of that expertise to Tung Hwa.

In Taipei, John Sun introduced us to the Ling family, who, through the airplane accident, had become unwitting owners of Tung Hwa. The patriarch of the family was especially welcoming. He had built up the toy business from scratch when a visiting American had asked if he could make a stuffed toy of which he had a sample. Mr. Ling said, "Yes", even though he had never made such a toy before. He and his wife worked all night to make a sample, which they presented to the American the following morning—and so a successful business was born!

We participated in a meeting at which we told them that I would stay in Taiwan to supervise the making of the tooling and the building of the first boat. We retained rights to market the boat, and they offered to pay for the tooling with the proviso that we would give them orders for three boats by the time the tooling was complete. If we failed to do so, they would then have the option to take over the rights to sell the boats. This was a fair arrangement, as there had been no shortage of foreign buyers visiting Taiwan who had promised to sell lots of boats and then just gone off with the one they wanted for themselves. Their offer to pay for the tooling was a very big deal for us because we had virtually no money. There was always the risk that they could kick us out once we had provided the technical input—and there was a history of this happening to others in Taiwan. On the other hand, I was extremely reluctant to borrow money to fund the tooling. In the past, I had seen many instances where the person with the money—and therefore the muscle—had either destroyed the business or screwed the people doing the work by insisting on having his own way when he did not understand the business. We said that I would come to Taiwan to start work as soon as we had

451

drawings, which we expected to be within a couple of months. After the meeting we were hosted by the family to a fabulous dinner at a French-style restaurant.

Just before we had left California to fly to Taiwan, I heard that my mother in England had been admitted to hospital. I knew that she was suffering from lung cancer, but this had not manifested itself with any significant symptoms until, without warning, she suddenly found that she was unable to swallow her coffee. My sister had called to say that the hospital had said she might be able to go home in the near future. Feeling relieved, I prepared to fly back to California as planned.

Then, prompted by Mary, my ex-wife, I had a phone call from Nicky to say that she thought I should get back to England as soon as possible, because if something happened to my mother I would never forgive myself. I immediately changed my plans and arranged to fly back to England via Singapore. At Singapore airport, I bought a bunch of orchids which somehow managed to survive the flight back to England.

On arrival, I drove down to Devon and visited my mother in hospital with my sister. She was delighted with the orchids and proudly showed them to the others in the ward, along with the fact that I had personally carried them from Singapore. At the end of visiting time I said goodbye and, before leaving, visited the bathroom. On my way out of the building, I glanced across the corridor into the ward, where my mother was sitting on a chair beside the bed. She did not look in my direction and I did not speak to her. That was the last view I had of my mother, and I have always regretted that she did not look in my direction. She died that night, July 7th, 1985. The nursing sister told me she was sure my mother had just been waiting for my return. Three weeks later, I flew back to California to work with Anton and Larry to prepare drawings for the Fleming.

Anton and I had a good relationship with Chuck Hovey, of Chuck Hovey Yachts, and had known and worked with him for many years when he was a dealer for Grand Banks. Chuck now had his own brokerage company, and he agreed to be our dealer despite his personal rule never to sell a Taiwan-built boat.

Fortunately, he made an exception in our case. We were planning to build a 53-foot boat, but Chuck said that 50 feet would be better suited for local requirements. Chuck was very important to us, so we listened to what he had to say and reduced the length to 50 feet. However, during my recent years at American Marine, I had been asked to lengthen boats and this was hard to do, especially when planking lines were involved, so I suggested that we make the hull mould 55 feet and then block it off at 50 feet. After checking with Larry that stretching out the lines to 55 feet would not cause the chines to come out of the water at the transom, we made the decision to build the hull mould to the longer length.

Larry Drake had an excellent reputation for designing seaworthy hulls, but he was the first to admit that he did not necessarily design the best-looking boats. Also, he was not used to building in fibreglass, so his designs were more geared to wood construction. When building a boat, the first drawings required are the Lines Plan—delineating the shape of the hull—and the Deck Construction drawing. Neither of these plans provide a good idea of what the boat looks like. For that you need the Outboard Profile drawing, and the first version Larry drew for us was for a very clunky looking boat. We gave him a list of the changes we wanted in the outboard profile, but first we needed the Lines Plan and the Deck Construction plan which incorporated those desired changes. With those two plans, I could leave for Taiwan and get the work under way. The revised Outboard Profile could be mailed to me later.

In August 1985 I celebrated my 50th birthday. Anton lived in an apartment block on a bluff overlooking Back Bay, in Newport Beach. We used to go for walks every day, and on my birthday Anton came back with a pile of mushrooms which we cooked up. I went for a walk that afternoon but felt so ill along the way that I barely made it back to the apartment. I reckoned it was the mushrooms which made me sick, either because they weren't what they seemed or they had been sprayed with some kind of evil chemical. I told him that if he planned to poison his partner it was better to wait until after he had completed the work that was required of him!

453

The revised drawings were finally ready and on October 22nd, 1985 I left for Taiwan for the start of the next phase of my life. The tooling would probably be completed about six months after we started work, so in order to comply with the terms of our agreement with Tung Hwa, we only had about eight months in which to sell three boats. This was a tough sell with no track record and nothing to show anyone.

Book 7
TAIWAN

RIDING THE TIDE

1985 – 2007

Chapter 1

October 1985 to January 1986

Arrival in Taiwan

I describe the difficulties of my life in Taiwan and becoming established at the boatyard. I meet my first computer and experience my first earthquake.

Before describing my own experiences, I think it would be helpful if I were first to describe how the boatbuilding industry got started in Taiwan.

Taiwan had long built its own breed of fishing boats, but the country had its start building yachts with a few boat enthusiasts among the GIs serving first in the Korean and, later, the Vietnam wars. By taking advantage of the very low labour rate, these Americans figured that they could have a boat built very economically, using skills that already existed. From these pioneering efforts, and with the advent of fibreglass construction, it wasn't long before local entrepreneurs sensed the opportunity to build and export boats for the Western markets—primarily the United States.

Fibreglass was a perfect material because of the mould-making process. While its use required care and attention to detail, the mould-making process was essentially quite simple, and it had great versatility in creating interesting shapes, such as those found in almost any boat. The Taiwanese took to it like ducks to water, and soon yards sprang up all over the island. Of course very few understood the nuances or even the implications of what a yacht should be or look like, and the quality of most of the results left much to be desired.

In this they were aided by many of the so-called experts from the West, whose knowledge of the industry was driven by sales and who neither knew nor cared about the difficulties involved in the actual boatbuilding process. Although the Taiwan builders earned a reputation for unscrupulous dealings and bad construction, as often as not it was as a result of bad advice and equally unscrupulous behaviour on the part of foreign buyers, who should have known better and most probably did.

Numerous stories abound of newspaper being substituted for chopped strand mat when the latter ran short, and when one buyer went back to the yard and complained that his boat leaked, the proprietor supposedly led the complainant out onto the balcony overlooking the boats and, with a sweep of his arm, pointing to all those under construction, said, "Show me the boat which doesn't leak". In other words, the buyer got what he paid for—leaks and all.

The unfortunate result of all this was that Taiwan developed a reputation for building poor quality. One style of power boats the Taiwanese built in large numbers was what came to be known as the trawler. One of the reasons for this was that the success of the Grand Banks had not gone unnoticed, and so an almost endless procession of look-alikes flooded the market at much cheaper prices. Fortunately for American Marine, the copiers, like most people who copy, did not understand the fundamentals of what they were copying, and the results were markedly inferior. They did not look or run quite right, were not too reliable, and they worked on the theory that if teak was good then more teak was better, so large chunks of the stuff were used all over the boats. The generic name among the critics for these boats was Taiwan Turkeys.

It was generally believed that the average yard was very reluctant ever to say no. If a potential buyer went to a yard with a design he would ask them to quote a price, and when they had done so, the buyer would go to other yards and they would undercut the original quote. He would then go back to the first yard and tell them that he could get a better deal elsewhere. Eventually a low point was reached, and the buyer, well satisfied with his superior Western bargaining skills, would await his boat. What he failed to realize was that the yards lowered their prices simply by leaving stuff out—like maybe a lamination or two—or by installing cheaper equipment, so he finished up with an inferior product. As is almost always the case, he got what he paid for. These days, no self-respecting yard would do this. The price quoted provides the builder with the reasonable expectation of a fair commercial profit. If the buyer does not accept that price, the builder will not accept the order. Moral issues aside, the builder is not going to risk his hard-won reputation by building a poor boat for the sake of one sale. I have never understood why someone who intends to take himself and his family out onto the perilous ocean would risk their lives by trying to save a few dollars on the boat.

At American Marine we were very scathing and used to mutter that if you wanted cheap rubbish you bought Taiwanese, but if you wanted a well-crafted, dependable, diesel cruiser you had better buy a Grand Banks. Many people predicted our demise but 30 years on, American Marine are still building the Grand Banks and the Taiwan trawler has all but disappeared. Over the years, contenders come and go, but I maintain that if you stay abreast of the latest technology and techniques and continue to strive always to produce the very best product you can, you will continue to attract the discerning buyer. You obviously cannot afford to ignore or dismiss your competition—in fact I consider that it keeps everyone on their toes—but if you have an excellent product, priced fairly, you will attract those who are knowledgeable enough to see the difference.

At the time that we began to think about building our boat in Taiwan, quality had improved dramatically, but bad smells have a habit of hanging around for a long time, and all Taiwan boat building, regardless of actual quality, was tainted with the reputation of being inferior. When we said that we were planning to build our dream boat in Taiwan, most people thought we were mad, but I had always believed that Taiwan was capable of producing boats as good as anyone else, and it was simply a matter of applying oneself to that end and in finding a suitable yard.

People thought we were doubly mad for deciding to build a pilothouse design with classic lines rather than joining the trend of Euro look. Why would you try to turn the clock back, they said, instead of joining the wave of the future? Our feeling was that there was very little new in the way of building, and there was no future in joining the current fashion. All fashions have a limited life, and the latest fashion soon becomes out of date. There are plenty of people who simply like their boats to look like a boat, one which has been designed by people experienced in the practical issues of taking a boat to sea and docking it afterwards.

I arrived in Taiwan in October 1985. I don't remember who met me, but it was John Sun who decided I should stay in the Gwa Choon Hotel. This is the closest I can come to the way the Chinese name sounded. The English name was Gold Chain. The people in the hotel were nice enough, but they had an attendant on every alternate floor, and the one responsible for my mine found any excuse to accost me and, with a leer on his face, cry, "Massagy! Massagy!". If I took the lift down from my room on the 9th floor, he would stop it on the 8th so he could see who was in the lift. My laundry was never returned to my room, but he would wait until he knew I was in my room and then knock on the door and hand deliver it to me with cries of "Massagy! Massagy!"

Breakfast was served in a room overlooking the street, and I was picked up every morning at around 7 a.m. I ate my breakfast— usually consisting of an under-fried egg on under-toasted toast— and watched the world go by outside the window. Martial law was still in effect, and the school boys on their bikes were dressed in quasi-military uniform. The cars were all locally produced Yue Long brand, and the whole scene was drab. The hotel, though newly opened, was also drab, and the bathroom in my room had purple tiles and fittings, so the whole thing closed in on you and was utterly depressing. I am not ashamed to say that there were times when I was literally reduced to tears. Had I been much younger and less experienced, I am not sure that I would have been able to cope with the situation and overcome the seemingly insurmountable obstacles.

No one seemed to speak a word of English and all the street

signs were in Chinese, so it was very easy to get lost and very hard to get un-lost. I had a map of sorts and every evening I would walk a simple route, and every time I came to an intersection I would match the characters on the street sign with those on the map. This was laborious because to me the characters were just shapes with no meaning, and I had to interpret them stroke by stroke. Most were relatively simple, but some Chinese characters are made up by as many as 22 individual strokes.

After a couple of weeks, I was supplied with a huge, black, American Buick Le Sabre with flag poles at each front corner. I was terrified of getting lost along the one-hour route we took each day to and from the yard; and, each day, before I went solo, I tried to memorize the landmarks at each intersection because I knew that if took a wrong one it was going to be next to impossible to find my way back.

I also had to learn how to deal with the anarchic Taiwan traffic. Some visiting students from mainland China, when asked their opinion of the island's driving, replied that traffic rules appeared to be suggestions only. This was an accurate assessment that included which side of the road to drive on and at which red lights to stop. Some of the avenues in Kaohsiung were five lanes in each direction with, beyond those, an additional lane for scooters. I remember one occasion when all five lanes were stopped in both directions at a major intersection, with engines revving like the start of a Grand Prix. I was in the front row and was beginning to surge forward when, out of the corner of my eye, I caught a glimpse of a scooter undertaking a sweeping U-turn from the scooter lane on one side to the scooter lane on the other, across 10 lanes of accelerating traffic, with each driver hell-bent on taking off as fast as he could. By some miracle this lunatic escaped unscathed, but it was typical and you needed eyes in the back of your head.

At that time Taiwan had a human population of 20 million, and there were 10 million scooters, often driven with suicidal verve by a young male while his female passenger rode pillion, sitting side-saddle and reading a book. It was not uncommon to see a husband and wife with four children on a single scooter.

Despite the chaotic traffic, there was very little horn blowing and almost no animosity shown for behaviour which would have given rise to road rage in the U.S.—unless you actually brushed another vehicle, in which case a violent argument would ensue! I soon came to realize that if I did not aggressively turn in front of other vehicles at an intersection, I would screw up the system because they expected me to do it. This became the norm, and after I had taken one visitor back to his hotel he said shakily when he got out of the vehicle, "I hope you don't drive like this at home". I didn't understand what he was talking about!

Those early days were very tough. I knew no one. I had no one to ask questions of or use as a sounding board for ideas. There were only three stations on TV and not surprisingly they all broadcast Chinese programmes. There was an English-language radio station but I only found that out later, and in any case I did not possess a radio.

I could have made it a lot easier on myself had I known about and frequented some of the pubs where foreigners tended to congregate. But they were in a different part of town, and apart from not being much of a pub person, I had no income, so I could not afford to spend money for anything but necessities. We worked six days per week and my big day out was Sunday, when I used to go to the Kingdom Hotel, order a plate of spaghetti Bolognese, and read the latest issue of *Time* magazine. The music on the PA system was always Richard Clayderman playing the piano, and when I hear his music today, it takes me right back to those early days in Taiwan. There was a bookshop just up the street which sold pirated copies of English language books, including novels by Stephen King. These books were the only ones available in English, and as I would get through three books per week, this source was a godsend.

After about three weeks, I moved to a small apartment on the sixth floor of an apartment block in the Cheng Ching Lake area of the city. This was much nicer and also a few miles closer to Tung Hwa, which was in Wan Tan, in Ping Tung county, about 12 miles out of town. I used to get to work about 0630, just as the sun was coming up, to give me time to make the sketches and prepare the work for that day.

At the yard I was allocated a small office, which was a tiny, windowless room made of plywood and located under the ramshackle company office. Although it was mid-October, it was still uncomfortably hot, so I requested an air-conditioner, which was promptly supplied. It usually cools down in Kaohsiung in mid-November so, after the first month, I seldom used the air-conditioner until the following March.

I took with me to Taiwan the hull lines plan and offsets and also the deck construction plan that was supposed to reflect the revised deck. There had not been time to correct it before I left, so it was to be mailed on to me. The first job was to draw out the lines plan full size on the loft floor, and this was undertaken under the guidance of Lau Gau, described as a master carpenter. He had been involved in the tooling of most of the successful boats built in Taiwan.

When the revised outboard profile drawing arrived by mail three weeks, later I pinned it on the plywood wall and stood back to look at it. I was dismayed to see that it had the same clunky look as the old one, which meant that the deck construction plan I had brought with me was going to produce a boat with an equally dated look. We had no fax or e-mail in those days—just telex or expensive phones. I contacted Anton and told him that Larry had not followed our instructions and had raised everything up too high. Being unfamiliar with the tricks you can play using fibreglass construction, he had produced plans for a boat about 18 inches higher than I felt it needed to be.

I asked Anton to go back to Larry to produce plans reflecting what we wanted. Anton replied that this would lead nowhere, and I would have to make the changes. I protested that I could not just eyeball the shape of something 50 feet long and 16 feet wide, stuffed into the corner of a gloomily-lit building. It was one thing to do this with small components, but for something as large as the deck of a 50-foot boat I had to tell people exactly what to build in the first place, and you needed to be able to stand back far enough to judge the result.

463

Ultimately I lost the argument, and it was up to me to come up with the critical shape of the boat that would determine whether we continued to eat. I blotted out the existing lines on the drawing with white-out and redrew them according to my ideas. I then measured them as best I could and transferred the dimensions to the deck construction plan. It has to be remembered that at a scale of ½inch to the foot, 1 inch in real life is equal to just 1/12th of ½inch on the drawing, which is 0.04 inches, and 1 inch makes a surprisingly big difference, even on a 50-foot boat. One factor making this especially difficult was that the overnight change in humidity inside my cubicle caused the paper to alter its dimension by as much as 3/8 of an inch, so that the boat effectively grew by 9 inches! Despite these difficulties, I was able to come up with an extremely messy but workable drawing, and a set of dimensions to allow the building of the deck to go ahead.

For those not familiar with the process of building a fibreglass boat, it is necessary to briefly explain what is involved. First the boat is broken down into major elements which can be fitted together to form the completed vessel. These normally consist of the hull, the main deck and the upper deck, comprising the flying bridge and boat deck. In those days at least, each of these components had to be created in wood, the surface of which, through the use of putties and resins and many hours of back-breaking labour was brought to a mirror finish. These parts are referred to as plugs. Fibreglass is laid up over these plugs to create the reverse shape in what are referred to as moulds, and the plugs—over which so much care has been lavished and money invested—are discarded. Moulds that are hollow in shape—for example, the hull—are, appropriately enough, referred to as female moulds. Consideration always has to be given as to how the finished parts can be removed from the moulds. In practice, this means that surfaces you would judge to be vertical actually have to slope inwards at least 1/8 inch per foot to ensure that they will release from the mould.

Once you have the moulds, the actual boatbuilding process can begin. Successive layers of fibreglass, infused with resin, are laid inside or over the moulds, depending on whether they are male or female. The results are referred to as "parts" and it is from these that the boat is assembled.

The Fleming's hull had a series of dummy planking grooves running along the sides, which simulated the look of wooden planks. They gave the boat a distinctive appearance, but each groove in the hull appeared as a ridge in the hull mould, which would lock the finished hull part into the mould. To avoid this, the hull mould had to be split down the middle and the two halves moved sideways to release the hull part. As the moulds were extremely heavy and had to be kept perfectly aligned without any twisting, they were mounted on wheels running on accurately aligned steel tracks let into the floor.

In order to save time during the tooling process, both the hull and the deck plugs and moulds were constructed simultaneously. This was risky because you do not find out whether the first deck will fit the first hull until the parts are mated together—long after it is too late to do anything about it if they do not fit!

The most critical dimension in a pilothouse boat is, in fact, the pilothouse, because it is the only place in the boat where there are two full head-rooms, one above the other. I was determined to keep the overall height of the boat to an absolute minimum, so I pushed the accommodation sole as low in the hull as possible, kept the thickness of the pilothouse sole to a minimum by building it as a box section, and wanted to keep the pilothouse roof as low as possible. When it came time to add the roof beams over the pilothouse plug, I had a difference of opinion with Lau Gau which took place on Christmas day 1985.

Christmas is not generally celebrated in Taiwan, but I had gone to work because, frankly, I had nothing better to do. We differed in opinion over the height of the pilothouse roof by 2 inches, and I won the argument simply because I was the customer and the boat was being built for me. But Lau Gau went away shaking his head, leaving me full of doubts because I knew he was very good at what he did and had an excellent reputation for knowing what he was doing. Also, as the hull did not yet exist, all the measurements had to be taken from a reference line on the structure of the deck plug, and we would not be sure who was correct until we had both the real hull and deck and we could fit one on top of the other. Lau Gau spoke no English, and I spoke no Chinese, so there was plenty of scope for miscommunication.

The work progressed on the hull and deck plugs. The hull was built upside down, and as the frames were assembled on the jig it became possible for the first time to see the shape of the boat. At this point Tung Hwa held a ceremony which was the equivalent of laying the keel in the construction of a wooden boat. I hammered a token nail into the keel while the smoke and explosion of firecrackers filled the air. A table, laden with offerings—including beer—had been set up in front of the bow. The major participants, including myself, bowed our heads with smouldering joss sticks in our clasped hands—after which we toasted each other and drank the beer!

At the same time, the deck took shape and I was able to walk around on it to develop refinements and details to the basic design. Almost every sailboat had myriad details for such items as winch bases and genoa tracks, but most powerboats were very bland and lacked refinement. I wanted to build sailboat-level details into our boat, but this all had to be done at the tooling stage. If anything was overlooked on the plug, it remained overlooked until it came time to replace the tooling, which could be many years into the future. Tooling was too expensive and time-consuming to be replaced without very good reasons.

When the hull was faired and the structure of the main deck complete, Anton came to Taiwan. We were taken out to dinner, where large quantities of Shau Shing wine were drunk, and we felt it was important to earn respect by downing every *Kampai* ("bottoms up") to which we were challenged. Consequently, we were seriously under the weather at the end of the dinner, and the following day I had the worst hangover I have ever experienced. It was on this day that Lau Gau asked me where to locate the dummy planking lines on the hull. My mind was a complete blank as I stared at this featureless hulk, which looked like a giant stranded whale and lacked any reference marks such as the waterline. I could no more have told them where to mark the lines than I could have predicted the time of the next earthquake. I told them that I would let them have the answer the following day without having the faintest idea how to go about it. Ultimately, it was only because of my past experience in building wooden boats that I was able to figure it out.

Tung Hwa was already building another boat, called the Offshore 48, which also had planking grooves, but these were little more than scratches in the surface of the hull. After the grooves had been marked on our hull, Lau Gau came to me and asked for their dimensions. I had carefully measured those in existing wood Alaskans before I left California. I had also measured those in my own Grand Banks. The grooves on those boats were considerably larger than those in the Offshore. When I gave the dimensions to Lau Gau, he looked at me as if I were mad and left the office shaking his head. This was not very encouraging and sowed doubt in my mind so, as soon as he left the room, I dug out my notebook to verify that I had given him the correct figure.

The next day he came back to my office with a router bit of the dimensions I had given him. He thrust it into my face in a challenging manner. I took it from him and measured it. "It's OK" I said. Again he went out shaking his head.

He returned a few minutes later with a groove, cut with this router bit, in about the smallest piece of wood he could find—in this case an offcut from a strip of teak planking about 1½ inches wide. Of course the groove looked like the Grand Canal, but I measured it and pronounced it correct. It was a bit unnerving, to say the least, but the dimensions proved to be correct and looked just right on a hull 55 feet long rather than on an itty-bitty piece of wood.

I needed to write letters, and after one disastrous attempt at using Tung Hwa's office typist, it became obvious that I needed to do it myself. I considered a typewriter but realized right away that this was outmoded and ridiculous and I needed to learn how to use a computer. At that time, I had never even touched one and had no idea how they worked. I found a computer shop in Kaohsiung where the guy spoke a certain amount of English. The problem was that there was another language to be learned as well—computer-speak. This was in the days before Windows and computers used MS-DOS. To get the computer to do anything, you had to type in a series of coded, arcane instructions. I bought a desktop computer from the shop but initially did not bother with a printer. I figured I would first learn how to use the word processing programme Wordstar. This was anything but simple, with multiple menus and sub-menus. I struggled with the included tutorial, which used Mark Twain's description of his relationship with his father:

"When I was a boy of 14, my father was so ignorant I could hardly stand to have the old man around. But when I got to be 21, I was astonished at how much the old man had learned in seven years."

I would get one step into the tutorial and the computer would display some incomprehensible message and refuse to go any further. The next day after work I would drive all the way into the city and tell the guy who sold me the computer what had happened, and he would tell me what to do next. It took about two weeks of doing this every day before I made any significant progress.

When I had progressed to the point where I could actually type a message, I visited a computer show in Taipei and bought a printer. Most printers at that time were dot matrix, which made a high-pitch scream while printing out characters using a series of dots. The print quality was quite inferior and unsuitable for correspondence concerning an expensive product like a yacht. So I invested in a daisy wheel printer, which had a roller and worked more like a typewriter. It was slower and clacked like a typewriter, but produced better quality. I connected the thing to my computer, inserted the paper and pressed Print. The roller whizzed around and tossed the paper across the room and started typing furiously directly onto the roller. I pressed Stop, but it ignored me and carried on for at least a minute before finally coming to rest. I tried again with exactly the same result, so I had to make another trip to the computer store.

One morning I was shaving, completely naked, in the bathroom of my apartment when I heard a kind of rattling noise coming from the window blinds in the adjacent bedroom. This was immediately followed by the building swaying with a kind of rolling motion. There are few things more unnerving than earthquakes, which strike without warning and there is very little you can do! I was not reassured by the standard of construction I had observed in Taiwan. They never used vibrators to settle the concrete, and when the shuttering was removed, you could see large voids in the structure. I had read that you should stand in a doorway during an earthquake, so that is what I did. But as the shaking continued, I thought "this is ridiculous", so I went back to the basin—followed by the further thought "no, *this* is ridiculous", so I returned to the doorway. Then the water, sloshing back and forth in the basin, began slopping onto the floor. Finally, after what seemed like eternity—but was probably less than one minute—the shaking stopped. I threw on my clothes and got the hell out of there. There was an aftershock about one hour later which I did not feel as I was at the yard, but it caused a weakened building in Taipei to collapse, killing 13 people.

I continued to correspond with Angie for the first few months that I was in Taiwan but I knew that our relationship could not continue. She had always told me quite frankly that she was a girl who "needed to be kept warm". I obviously could not do that in my present circumstances, and Taiwan was no place for a girl like her. I am eternally grateful that she came along at the time she did. She gave my morale a tremendous boost and I always knew that I could never have handled a bombshell like her had I been much younger.

On the morning of January 29th, 1986, I was listening to the news and getting ready to leave for work. The announcer said that the *Challenger* shuttle had taken off from Kennedy Space Centre, and I expected him to continue reporting on another routine launch when he went on to say that it had exploded 73 seconds into its flight. That was so unexpected that the moment remains crystallized in my memory.

Chapter 2

January 1986 to November 1986

Taiwan

I recount some of the many obstacles encountered in building the first Fleming.

When they first come aboard a completed boat, people often ask me how on earth it is possible to conjure up something so complicated effectively out of fresh air. I always tell them that I make it up as I go along, and they think I am joking. Of course you need to have a broad idea of what the finished product will be, but I find that the details are best worked out on the job as you go. When I ran up against a problem for which I could see no immediate solution I never used to worry, because of a wonderful facility which I know is not unique to myself. I could absolutely count on the fact that I would be presented with the solution provided I first gave the problem a serious amount of thought. I could completely rely on my subconscious mind providing the answer within, at most, a couple of days, but it could come at any time—such as the middle of the night, when driving my car or cleaning my teeth.

With an object as strangely shaped as a boat, the two main reference points from which everything is measured are the waterline and the centreline—both of which are invisible. The long-awaited drawings included some hidden surprises. I discovered that Larry's drawing equipment was so worn out that his horizontal lines sagged down toward the end of their length. This meant that the centreline, instead of being straight, was a long, lazy curve which strayed as far as 9 inches off the true line over the 55-foot length of the boat. In another case he had not allowed headroom for anyone more than 4 feet high to get from the salon to the pilothouse! Another little trap that had me foxed for a while is that, while metric measurements are generally used in Taiwan, they also have tape measures marked in inches, but they are Taiwan inches—with each inch being equal to approximately 1¼ inches elsewhere! Using a tape measure purchased in Taiwan, it took me a while to figure out why I kept coming up with less room than the drawings said we should have! Coming from the U.S., the dimensions on all our drawings were in feet and inches.

There are many complexities in a modern powerboat and, aside from getting the lines plan from Larry Drake, I took care of every detail myself. There are significant decisions to be made every few minutes and for each and every one, factors such as cost, practicality, aesthetics, available skill level and many others had to be taken into account. There is one boatbuilding conundrum which appears in many different guises. This is hard to describe but if, for example, the ladder from the cockpit meets a roof with a camber, the inboard side of the ladder is longer than the outboard side because it has further to go to reach the higher part of the roof. As the ladder is at a constant slope, this extra length means that the inboard side of the ladder would terminate further forward than the outboard side. But both sides of the top of the ladder rest against the back of the house, which is at right angles to the centreline of the boat, so if you don't cheat the angles, the ladder will have a twist in it. Another strange effect is that in order to make that same ladder appear to have a constant width for its entire length, it is necessary to make it slightly wider halfway up. The entire vessel is full of tricks like this and it is this knowledge—together with understanding the importance of scale—which is essential to producing a result pleasing to the eye.

John Sun was the only person in the yard who spoke English, which meant that all instructions went through him. Actually this was fine because it meant that communication followed the chain of command. The problem, I later found out, was that when I thought he was translating what I had said, he was actually issuing his own, quite different, instructions. Naturally this gave rise to considerable misunderstanding and caused many problems.

471

He also gave me troubles in many other ways. On one occasion I saw the carpenters marking out a piece of teak for use on the very prominent teak rail cap. I could see a large defect in the centre of the piece of wood, so I rushed up to the office to tell John to instruct the carpenters not to use that piece for that purpose. He said he would. When I next went to the job site, I saw that they had cut the wood and were starting to recess the underside to fit to the fibreglass. I went back to John and told him, and again he said he would take care of it. This happened yet again with another step and finally they had it screwed in position on the boat. When I told John about this, he responded that it was too late to change! Well, there was no way I could allow it to stay on the boat, so he had forced us into a situation of confrontation. There were numerous times I felt I had walked through the looking glass to find myself in a world where everything was backwards and nothing made any sense. I just had to grit my teeth and develop enormous patience.

John had a very effective method of dealing with problems, which took me a while to figure out. We would sit across a table, and I would say something and he would not respond. He would stay silent. We are used to situations in which we make a point and the other person responds and we go back and forth. If the other person says nothing, the natural tendency is for you to say something, if only to break the silence. If you do this, you inevitably say more than you really intend. Once I had figured this out, I also stayed silent, and I found that I could outlast him!

On one occasion he simply got up from the table, turned his back on me, and sat at his desk, which was in the general office with several girls doing clerical work. In any culture, turning your back on someone in mid-conversation is considered extremely rude, so I got up and left the office, slamming the door behind me. I went to my office and had just sat behind my desk when John came in and accused me of being rude and upsetting the girls by slamming the door. I told him that I had spent 25 years working with Chinese people in Hong Kong and Singapore and had always found them to be very polite, but, I said, "I have to tell you that you are the rudest person I have ever met."

He kind of stiffened and said, "So you think I'm rude?"

I replied, "You are, without doubt, the rudest person I have ever met."

With that he got up, left my office, and slammed the door!

I learned that whatever you do, you must never lose your cool. The other person may rage and shout and bang the desk and then, as soon as they run out of steam, you simply return in a calm voice to the issue that originally caused the outburst, as though it had never happened. No matter the provocation, you must never lose your cool, because if you do, you lose face (i.e., respect) that you will never recover. To my way of thinking, the poem "If," by Rudyard Kipling, sets down in a wonderful way the standard to follow in living your life. The stanza in that poem relevant to this situation is:

> *"If you can keep your head when all about you are losing theirs and blaming it on you; if you can trust yourself when all men doubt you . . . etc."*

For many years the exchange rate between the Taiwan dollar (generally known as the NT) and the U.S. dollar was stable at around 36 NT to U.S. $1. Almost immediately we started work in October 1985, the NT began to strengthen against the U.S. dollar, which meant that for each U.S. dollar you got less NT. A few weeks after we had started work on the Fleming project, John came into my office and said, "We are going to have to stop the project. We cannot continue unless we raise the price."

There was absolutely no possible way we could raise our price when we were brand new and were trying to persuade buyers to purchase an unproven boat from an unknown company. I bargained with John and eventually came up with a formula by which the price for the initial three boats would not change but would gradually increase after that, so that the average for each boat over the first 10 would be what they were asking. One problem was that John had not done his homework when he quoted us the initial price and had based his estimate on the Ocean 50, which had a displacement of 46,500 lbs. By comparison, the Fleming 55 was 42 percent larger with a displacement of 66,000 lbs.

The Taiwan dollar continued to strengthen against the U.S. dollar, and every evening as I drove home from work I would listen on the radio with dread to the latest exchange rate, which inched up every day. Having re-negotiated a new "firm" price, about every six weeks John would come into my office and threaten to stop the work unless we paid more. It was an absolute nightmare, and every day when I went to work at 0630, I would wonder what new obstacle I would face that would have nothing to do with the relatively simple and straightforward process of building a boat from scratch.

The other side of the coin was that Tung Hwa was investing a large amount of money in constructing a huge new building which would house both the Offshore 48 and our Fleming 55. This showed a confidence on their part in the future of Taiwan boatbuilding.

On the personal side, I was living the life of a monk—minus the prayers. Not only did I not have any money, but I had to commit myself totally to the project, with no time or mental resources available for anything else. I had been asked on a few occasions whether I would undertake boat inspections on behalf of the Offshore 48s being built in Tung Hwa. Even though I could have used the money, I was reluctant to do this because I knew that it would surely bring me into conflict with the yard as I handed out a long list of defects before I would sign off on the boat, which would allow them to cash the LC. The boats were always behind schedule, so inevitably the defect list was compromised in order for the boat to be shipped before the LC expired. On the one occasion that I did weaken and agreed to do the inspection, I was stiffed by Tung Hwa's dealer in San Francisco, who never paid me. I am sorry to say that the boat business attracts more than its share of unprincipled charlatans, and it is one of the reasons why it makes a lot of sense for a yard and a dealer to work through an organization like Fleming Yachts, which has a foot in both camps and a reputation to protect. The yard does not have to attempt to sort out the crooks from the good guys from the multiplicity of dealers in a foreign country, and the dealers do not have to be concerned about the integrity of a yard on the other side of the world and worry whether they are going to get the boat they ordered with no recourse if the deal goes bad.

My visa for Taiwan lasted for six months. At the end of that time, I had to leave the country, after which the visa would be renewed for another six months. The obvious place to go to was HK, which was only about one hour away by plane. Theoretically, I could have gone to HK and returned one hour later, and that would have been sufficient absence to meet the visa requirement. In fact, the trip provided a welcome break from the ugliness, foreignness, and austerity of life in Kaohsiung.

It is certainly very different today, but at that time I would have described Taiwan as a "hardship" posting. One of the reasons for this was that martial law was in place until 1987. All foreigners resident in Kaohsiung had to register their presence at the police station in Fong Shan district. My first flight out of Kaohsiung to Hong Kong was in April 1986. At that time there were only about three overseas flights per day out of that airport and I was waiting for my China Airlines flight to be called. It was considerably overdue, but no announcements had been made. I was chatting to a Taiwanese guy who spoke English and he was telling me about martial law and how everyone hated it.

There was also a group of Westerners waiting for the same plane, and they must have been visiting entertainers because one of them started doing some funny tricks with a hat. Slowly, one by one, they started playing musical instruments and entertained the waiting passengers, who lost their dour expressions and began to smile and clap. Then, without warning, a guy in a uniform strode into the middle of the group, waving his arms and loudly berating them, and ordered them to stop. My companion said to me, "Now you see martial law!". This official yelled at them because they were performing without a license. It was an unpleasant experience. China Airlines ought to have given these people free flights for entertaining their disgruntled passengers. I was interested to see the Taiwanese in the audience get to their feet and abuse the official who had spoilt the fun.

During this and subsequent visits to Hong Kong, I would find myself wandering the length of Canton Road in the Mongkok district of Kowloon. The Chinese have a custom of grouping together all shops selling similar products, so you would have a goldsmiths' street, a street selling funeral paraphernalia, or, as in the case of Canton Road, a street of hardware shops. This was very convenient when looking for a piece of hardware—in this case, a bronze hand pump for emptying oil from the engine sump. In another street I found a shop making custom lampshades—quite unheard of in Taiwan.

Anton and I had voted ourselves a monthly salary of $1,200. I was the one who put money into the company and Anton did not have any, so he actually received the money while I got an IOU from the company each month stating that it owed me that amount. I received no salary at all for 14 months, although I continued to pay alimony to my ex-wife because I knew she had nothing else to live on. I had also been paying a monthly allowance to my two daughters, now aged 20 and 21, but they wrote to me to say that they felt I had done enough and they would take care of paying their own way from now on. This made me feel very good—not so much because of the money, but because they had taken this attitude.

During that first trip to Hong Kong, I bought myself a small portable CD player and a handful of CDs to relieve some of the austerity in my life. In Kaohsiung at that time there were three Chinese TV stations and one English-language radio station, ICRT, that broadcast news and music not to my taste. Their newsreaders were not too well informed—one of them pronounced the Champs-Elysées as "Champs" (as in "you are real champs") followed by "day leeze"!

I wrote and told Anton about my trip to Hong Kong and the fact that I had bought myself a CD player. He wrote me back a blistering, three-page diatribe, accusing me of wasting money. I was absolutely furious! Here he was, living in his comfortable apartment in Newport Beach, while I was working my butt off, sweating buckets in filthy conditions in my hardship posting, and paying his salary out of my own pocket! I could tell that he had been slurping martinis while writing his letter because he had worked himself into ever more extreme and ridiculous statements as the letter progressed. Anton was a real Jekyll and Hyde character. Most of the time he was very charismatic and the life and soul of the party, and it was his influence which had set us on our present path, but he had a dark side. As those who knew him well will attest, the closer you got to him, the more likely he was to turn on you and abuse you without warning. He had a tongue like a sword, which left wounds hard to heal.

Taiwan is essentially a beautiful place. In fact, its Portuguese name, *Liha Formosa,* means "beautiful Island". But mankind had imposed on its beauty extreme ugliness which, over time, depressed the spirit. The buildings were ugly, the cars were ugly, and everything was drab. One day, after I had been in Taiwan for three months, I walked out of one of the buildings at the yard and was astonished to see high mountains that I had never even suspected existed. They were beautiful and about 12 miles distant. That evening after work I drove towards them, feeling my spirits lift. I passed through the small town of Santimen and started to climb in my oversize Cleopatra's Barge. I soon came to a barrier across the road. I found out that all of Taiwan's mountain areas were closed off to the general population and you needed a permit to enter. The areas were reserved for Taiwan's aboriginal people, who are the island's original inhabitants and who came from the south—not from China. In fact, Taiwan has 165 mountains over 3,000 metres (9,800 feet). It has the largest number and density of high mountains in the world. I also discovered Kenting, at the southern tip of the island, which was another pleasant area to get away from the dense industrial development.

We had a bunch of middle-aged clean-up ladies working in the yard. They wore pointy Chinese hats with a scarf tied over the top, and were well covered with gloves and arm protectors. They were a jolly lot, cackling like hens. I could tell from their body language that they were making a lot of ribald comments about me, but I could not understand what they were saying and no one would translate. One day in the yard, I saw them struggling to move a wheeled set of steps across the concrete. One of the wheels was stuck against a small water hose. I leaned over and lifted it over the hose. It was not heavy and I thought no more about it, but I must have pulled a muscle in some obscure way because the pain in my back grew to be intense over the next few days. One night, lying in bed, I wanted to take a pee and my back was giving me hell. Ever so slowly, I inched toward the edge of the bed. I was almost there when my back went into some kind of spasm so powerful that it threw me back into the centre of the bed. It was several minutes before I could summon the courage to start the process of moving again.

During this time, old Mr. Ling passed away from complications with diabetes. It was he who had brought us into the company, and he was a very nice gentleman. I was very sad at his passing. If he had died the previous year, we would certainly not be at Tung Hwa. I flew up with other key personnel from the yard to attend his funeral. I dosed myself up with handfuls of aspirin to control my back pain during the long ceremony.

After I returned to the yard, somebody recommended that I make an infusion of tea from a special plant which, he said, grew well behind the lumber shed. I found the plant growing in rich profusion and took some home to make a brew. The brew had a strange, bitter taste, but I drank it down. It was only later I discovered it grew so well in the preferred spot for the men to take a pee. Maybe that was why the plant grew so luxuriantly. My back did not seem to improve but, although it took a while, whatever had been causing the problem cured itself.

There were no health and safety rules in Taiwan, and I was always trying to instil some rudimentary safety practices into the workers. Ironically, it was me who seemed to have the accidents. On one occasion I was using a big grinder to cut off some excess screw lengths inside the boat. I was wearing regular glasses and a chip of a screw flew off and embedded itself in one eye. They took me to an eye doctor in the nearby town of Ping Tung. He could not use a magnet to extract the fragment because it was stainless steel, but he managed to get it out. On another occasion, sparks from overhead welding on the new building were showering down on the unprotected boat deck non-skid. I went galumphing back to protect the roof and, not looking where I was going, plummeted down through the aft hatch to the cockpit. I escaped unscathed except for a few bumps and bruises, but I reckon that every one of the early boats included a small sample of my blood.

Slowly the tooling progressed, and after about six months we had our first hull and deck. It is hard to believe but, by the time you add in all the minor moulds, the total exceeded 50, and many of these were still being made while work started on construction of the first boat. Chuck had managed to sell the first boat to Mr. and Mrs. Fusco from Santa Barbara in California. This was a significant risk on their part, and it only happened because the Fuscos trusted Chuck and because Chuck trusted me, based on my years building Grand Banks. Mrs. Fusco paid a visit to the yard to see their boat under construction.

Other overseas visitors were manufacturers' representatives. One of these was from a company selling engines and generators from Seattle. Most builders were turning to sleek Euro designs, and when he saw from the shape of our boat that we were bucking the trend, he asked whether I thought we were doing the right thing. I said that I really did not know and only time would tell, but I felt there was no point in following the herd. This was the kind of boat I believed in and which I knew how to build. We were not trying to set the world on fire; I was sure there must be others who felt the same way that I did about what a boat should look like.

We also had a visit from a group from the Caterpillar Engine Company, under the leadership of their Customer Service Manager, Gene Wineland. They wanted to show me their recommended fuel system, and I was able to show them that we had already installed it.

On March 10th, 1986 the door of my office cell opened and Fred Hong introduced himself. He said that he had been hired to be my assistant. I asked whether he had any experience with boats, and he said that he had not. He had been working first with a company making boilers and more recently with a company making golf clubs. I asked him whether he was going to be on the technical or the sales side of the company. He said, "Sales, I think."

479

I have never had any problem sharing my knowledge with others, but I don't relish doing it to people if they are not going to make use of it, because it is then just a waste of effort. However, I could certainly do with the help, especially when it came to passing on instructions through someone other than John Sun, whom I did not trust to do so accurately. Fred had been hired by Mr. Ling's son, Steven, after old Mr. Ling had passed away. John had no time for Steven and, effectively, Fred was Steven's spy in the yard, which obviously did not go down well with John. Fred was of enormous help to me, and without him it would have been very difficult, if not impossible, to have made the Fleming as successful as it turned out to be.

Thanks to Chuck, we managed to sell two boats on the west coast and, with the help of Tom Wright, who had put me up for the failed coup at American Marine, we managed to get an order from Florida. This last became problematic because the proprietor of the marina that ordered the boat sold out to some dodgy Greeks who were very difficult to deal with, but in the nick of time, we had met the terms of the contract. Anton was always on my case about why it was taking so long. Slowly but surely, the boat came together, and hull no. 1 was complete and ready to ship in November 1986—13 months after I had arrived in Taiwan. In retrospect, I think that was pretty good going. I had to start in a brand new country, knowing nobody, and create the tooling, the detail design, and the boat itself from scratch. Of course there is a lot more to a boat than simply the structure. There are also all the electrical, mechanical, and plumbing systems, every one of which I designed myself, along with selecting each and every component. In any project of this sort you find yourself having to solve significant problems at the rate of about six per hour.

Boats built in the Orient tend to be heavier than the naval architect's estimate, so I raised the bootstripe 2 inches higher than shown on the drawing. For those unfamiliar with the term, the bootstripe is that line which runs around the hull just above the water. As this boat was not going to touch the water until it arrived in the U.S., I added an additional fudge factor by raising it an additional 2 inches at the bow, compared to the stern, in case the boat trimmed down by the bow. A boat which is bow down is unacceptable, but down a little by the stern looks OK.

John Sun continued to be obstructive right up to the end, and I did not realize until much later how much grief he was giving Fred, who never mentioned it. One of the last bones of contention was the painting of the fibreglass exhaust pipes in the engine room. These were very prominent and needed to be painted. I kept chasing for this to be done but nothing happened. Even when the boat was loaded onto its trailer, ready to leave the yard, they remained unpainted. It finally got to the stage that I stood in front of the tractor, already hitched to the trailer and ready to leave, and said that I was not getting out of the way until someone painted the effing exhaust pipes.

This did the trick, and the trailer headed for the main gate towed by a very undersized tractor. Despite the firecrackers let off as it passed through the gate, the trailer got hung up on the camber of the road. But eventually, with much smoke from spinning tyres, it was pulled clear, and the first Fleming 50 set of on the initial leg of its long trip to California.

The yard was 12 miles from the harbour and the road trip was not easy, as the boat had to pass through a few small towns along the way. One problem was low, overhanging cables. These were dealt with by people on the flying bridge pushing them up with wooden poles with a cross bar at the top.

At that time there was a toll bridge across a wide river. As the boat was too high to pass under the toll booth, it had to be diverted to one side, which meant large concrete blocks having to be removed and replaced by labourers with bamboo poles slung over their shoulders. A pedestrian bridge at a school was the last height hazard, which we cleared with just a few inches to spare. The air draft of the boat was reduced by having it sit bow down in its shipping cradle. This meant that the drains on the boat deck did not function as they would when the boat was sitting level, so special measures had to be taken during shipping, which did not always work as intended. We tried to get the shipping crews to block up the front of the cradles, but we had no control over them and they frequently ignored our requests. Once the boat arrived at the docks, it had to wait a few days before being loaded aboard the ship. I gave instructions to make sure that the batteries were disconnected before the boat was loaded and left for California. It was around this time that Gil Hensen, the Dutch guy I had employed in Singapore, showed up again in Taiwan. I employed him a second time to keep an eye on things while I was away from the yard.

It might be wondered why the boat did not undergo sea trials in Taiwan before shipping. Martial law was still in effect, making it extremely difficult to organize sea trials. You had to obtain permits for everyone on board from military authorities, and you had to take along a half-dozen soldiers with clunky boots and serious weapons. There were no launching facilities, so a mobile crane had to be hired at enormous expense. With money in short supply, we decided to take the risk of shipping without a sea trial.

About three weeks later, our baby arrived in Long Beach. Included in the welcoming committee on the dock were Larry Drake—the naval architect; Mr. and Mrs. Fusco—the intrepid buyers; Chuck Hovey—our dealer, who had risked his reputation on the boat; Anton—my partner; and myself. They were all there to judge my work on the first of this totally new design built by an unknown yard in a country with a dodgy reputation. It was our future—along with the boat—that hung in the balance as the first Fleming motoryacht dangled from the slings above the waters of Long Beach harbour.

As she settled in the water, she floated evenly along her bootstripe. My fudging had worked! We clambered 20 feet down the vertical steel ladders to get on board. We checked below. No leaks! So far so good! I checked the batteries and found them still connected. When we tried to start the engines—nothing! The batteries were completely flat. They would not even power an indicator light. Even the generator battery was flat.

We borrowed a couple of jumper cables and used the battery from a dockside crane to get the generator started so we could charge the main engine batteries. However, after six hours they still lacked sufficient power to do any more than produce a click from the starter solenoid. We went off to purchase a new, fully charged, 8D battery and used ropes to lower it down to the boat.

These are heavy batteries, and the boat was being bounced around in the wake from passing tugs. Eventually we manoeuvred it into place and got the engines running. The next thing we needed was fuel. It was now after 6:30 p.m., and two of the harbour's three fuel docks were already closed. At the last one, the attendant was just leaving and we yelled at him as he was walking up the dock. He agreed to give us fuel, but said it would have to be cash only. We all emptied our pockets and pooled what we had. It should be just sufficient to get us to Newport Beach. Having had nothing to eat all day, we were all starving, so we left the boat at the dock and went to find something to eat. It was after 9:30 when we finally headed out into Pacific Ocean for the 40 miles to Newport Beach. The open ocean in the dark is not the ideal venue in which to run an entirely new, untried boat!

Once at sea we started getting alarm signals, which were very scary, especially as we could not identify the cause. It turned out that Larry, who was at the helm, was pushing down on the instrument panel so that the back of one of the instruments was coming into contact with a fitting on top of the hydraulic steering pump. The trip took four anxious hours, and it was with great relief that we turned into Newport Beach harbour and tied up at the dock outside Chuck Hovey Yachts at 1:30 in the morning. We had reached an important milestone now that the first boat had left the nest.

Chapter 3

November 1986 to April 1988

Taiwan

I explain the reasons for starting a new project in Mexico. My daughter Jackie comes to Newport Beach. Anton has a heart attack and I break my leg. I relate the problems we encounter in Mexico, leading us to abandon the project.

After having been born in Hong Kong and brought up in Hong Kong and Singapore, my daughter Jackie found England claustrophobic and decided to come to California. She arrived while I was away in Taiwan and moved aboard *Lion's Den*, which was parked outside Chuck Hovey's office. Her first job was cleaning boats, then she moved on to working in various restaurants.

After the first boat shipped, I left Gil Hensen to keep an eye on things, and went first to Hong Kong for Christmas shopping and continued on to LA. Nicky had by this time also come to California, so I enjoyed a wonderful Christmas with both my daughters and with Anton and Leslie. I went back to Taiwan for a couple of weeks before returning to LA at the end of January. Anton had always been very keen on flying, and I also had an interest, but not as passionate as his. Pushed by Anton, we decided to share a half-share in a Beech Sundowner aircraft. This was not as extravagant as it sounds. The Sundowner is a low wing, 4-seater monoplane and this one cost around $20,000. Anton and I had a quarter-share each, which amounted to only $5,000. The monthly cost of renting a hangar was only about $30, so the plane was very much cheaper to own and operate than even a small boat.

I made another trip to Taiwan in March and returned two months later in time for the arrival of the second boat. Our original plan was that I would design and supervise the construction of the first boat and then live in California while the yard continued to build boats to meet our orders. After the shipping of the first boat, we believed that the toughest and most difficult part of setting up our business was behind us. How wrong we were! 1987 turned out to be a year full of challenges. It is often said that it is just as well we cannot see into the future. If we knew what lay ahead, many of us might never have initiated a course of action that ultimately turned out to be successful. We began to suspect that our plans might not smoothly follow the course we had in mind when we hosed off the second boat and water cascaded in a waterfall down the salon aft bulkhead and over the microwave in the galley. That was just the start of a host of problems.

On the subsequent boat, John Sun had substituted a cheaper type of timber for the beams supporting the salon floor so that, before long, it began to sag and had to be propped up from below. We had tried a new type of packless stuffing box on the early boats. For the uninitiated, this is the gland that prevents water from entering the hole through which the rotating propeller shaft penetrates the hull. It transpired that this type of seal did not work well with the Swedish-made Aquadrive drive systems we were using to keep the boats quiet and free of vibration. Anton and I flew up to Sacramento in the Sundowner to retrofit a conventional stuffing box on the third boat. There is a saying that there are old pilots and bold pilots but no old, bold pilots. Anton tended towards the bold and this was not a flight without its hazards. We were forced lower and lower by rain and poor visibility in the Central Valley and had to keep putting down at a succession of small airstrips.

To save time, money and hassle, I had decided to swap out the stuffing boxes while the boat was in the water. To do this I had to disconnect the shafts from the Aquadrives, loosen off the existing stuffing boxes, then dive under the boat and, by grabbing the propellers, pull the shafts back, while Anton, inside the boat, slid the existing stuffing boxes over the inner end of the shafts and replaced them with the new ones. The tricky part was the moment of changeover, when there was no stuffing box in place on each shaft and water gushed into the boat at a prodigious rate. Sliding the shafts aft was no problem because, being at an angle, we had gravity working with us, but pushing them back uphill was going to be much more difficult. I achieved this by putting my feet on the propeller blades, locking my hands around the forward edge of the rudder, and pushing with my legs. All this had to be done in murky water, while holding my breath. We had no scuba gear—or indeed the knowledge how to use it—but all those years of experience of working underwater on the houseboat held me in good stead!

With the exchange rate continuing to slide, coupled with our growing lack of trust in the yard, we decided it would be prudent to organize a second string to our company bow. The obvious place was in Mexico which, superficially, had much to recommend it. There were large numbers of Mexicans working in California whom most employers found to be very reliable and hardworking. Mexico was right next to California instead of thousands of miles away across the other side of the Pacific Ocean and the labour costs in Mexico were appreciably less than those in Taiwan.

Early in 1987 we were introduced to the Cabrales family, who owned and operated a shipyard that built and repaired steel shrimp boats in Puerto Penasco, located at the head of the Gulf of California—also known as the Sea of Cortez. We met them in California and then flew down to visit their yard. We reached an arrangement whereby they would provide the facilities and build the tooling under our supervision, while we would provide the design and oversight and sell the boats. We worked with Larry Drake on the design of a Fleming 48.

Anton arranged for Larry Drake to move to Penasco to get the project started. Larry had previously spent time in Central America working on a boat project for John Newton after he had left American Marine, but he was now quite a few years older and he found Penasco very hard going. Progress was very slow, and

486

Anton and I used to fly down to Penasco and land at the airstrip outside the town. Anton would give poor Larry a hard time in an officer-to-lower-rank type of way. Eventually I moved to Penasco and we hired another guy from California called Chuck Guy, who was experienced in tooling. Through the Cabrales family, I rented a small apartment close to the beach while Chuck lived in his own camper.

Anton and I flew down a few times in the Sundowner, passing the Superstition Mountains in southern Arizona and stopping at Mexicali for the border crossing. On one occasion I was at the controls flying towards Penasco from Mexicali when I spotted a tiny object in the sky ahead of us. I just had time to ask Anton what he thought it was when the Aero Mexico passenger jet swept over us, descending on a reciprocal course into Mexicali as we climbed out of it.

Most of the time, I drove the 500 miles from Newport Beach to Penasco. It was a long drive, first to San Diego and then east along Interstate 8, which climbed to over 4,000 feet before dropping to below sea level at El Centro. A turn off at Gila (pronounced "Heela") Bend led through the Arizona desert to the town of Ajo (pronounced "Ah-ho"), followed by a placed named Why (good question), before reaching the Mexican border at Lukeville. In Arizona, the road passed through the Organ Pipe Cactus National Monument, where the landscape was dotted with multi-armed saguaro cactus of the type which featured in cartoons and Western movies.

The U.S. customs and immigration office in Lukeville was smart, business-like, and flying the Stars and Stripes. On the other side, the border was marked by a Mexican flag hanging from a pole over a kiosk in the middle of the road. It was manned by a lethargic guy with his legs propped on the window sill, who waved you on with a languid arm. In an instant you passed into the Third World, with the road potholed and lined with shacks. The first town was Sonoita, where a road branched off to Puerto Penasco on the Gulf. For one section the road did not deviate one single degree from a dead straight line for 36 miles!

Penasco was a small and rather ramshackle town with only

two paved streets. It was a popular beach destination for people coming from Phoenix, Arizona, but it was not fancy and certainly no resort, although there were a number of beach houses owned by Americans. The harbour was home to a fleet of battered and rusting shrimp boats, but the catch was all trucked out and very little of its value remained to benefit the town.

On my first night in Penasco I was dazzled by the sight of the night sky. Crammed with millions upon millions of stars, the Milky Way blazed a shining path right across it. I had not seen skies like this since I left Africa, a quarter of a century earlier. After so many years living in cities with atmospheric and light pollution, I had forgotten what the sky at night really looks like. Using binoculars, I was able to see four of the moons of Jupiter, as well as several galaxies.

There was a small naval base and every morning we heard the bugle for the morning parade. The small contingent of sailors would stand to attention as the flag was raised, while a guy with a broom swept the parade ground around their feet.

One evening, while sitting on our balcony looking at the Gulf, Anton and myself noticed a glow over the horizon followed by the big flare of what looked like an explosion. We debated whether we should do anything and decided that we should report it to the naval base. With the language barrier we had some difficulty getting past the main gate, but eventually we were taken to an officer who spoke English. The net result of this was that they did nothing. Maybe they did not have any boats or maybe the situation was already under control, as there were a number of fishing boats in the area. We went down to the harbour and waited with a group of townspeople. After a couple of hours, a fishing boat arrived. There had been a fire and explosion on one of the boats, which had sunk. One man had died of a heart attack.

I tried to learn some Spanish. It was certainly much easier than Chinese, not only because the letters were the same as English, but also because if you knew some Latin and French besides English, you could usually make a guess at the meaning of a Spanish word. One day I asked old man Cabrales the identity of the man whose face was on a Mexican coin. *"Bandido"* he said.

"Chief *Bandido*."

About this time, I heard from Taiwan that John Sun had resigned once too often and he was being let go, which I think was a good thing. I wanted Fred Hong to take over, but he had told Steven that he was not ready for that responsibility, so the job of managing the yard was given to a guy called Roger Lee. Shortly afterward, I made a trip to Taiwan where I met Roger, who did not give me a good impression. He invited me out to dinner one night, during which he proceeded to run down and criticize everyone in the company, including Fred. He then went on to try to promote boats built by his previous company. There was no point in arguing with him and I could not wait for the evening to end. I told Steven and Fred about their manager's disloyalty. Fred took over as manager one year later, at the end of April 1988. In the meantime, we had to deal with Roger, who was useless.

In June 1987 I had a phone call from Anton's wife, Leslie. She told me that Anton was in intensive care having suffered a heart attack. Anton later told me that he awakened in the middle of the night not feeling well, and Leslie had driven him to Hoag Hospital which, fortunately, was only about 10 minutes away. He was able to walk into the emergency department and when the admitting nurse asked him what was the matter, he said, "I'm fucking dying," and dropped dead on the floor. This was the literal truth. His heart had in fact stopped beating, but they resuscitated him and brought him back. Anton then started on a lengthy recovery period, which put him out of action for several weeks. He was a person with a demanding ego which, he admitted, took a beating when he was overtaken by elderly ladies on his daily exercise around his apartment complex.

With Anton out of action, I was busier than ever. Boatbuilding continued in Taiwan so, in addition to spending time in Penasco and California, I was making regular trips to Tung Hwa. In fact, my passport shows that I passed through Hong Kong 18 times between January 1987 and January 1990.

Boat no. 3 arrived in Florida in October 1987, and I flew to Miami to assist with the offload and delivery up the coast to the marina at a place called Eau Gallie, near Melbourne. I still did not have any reportable income so, in those more rational days, I did not qualify for a credit card, which made travel very tiresome. I stayed the night in the hotel at Miami airport and they treated me like a potential thief. Not surprisingly, I had to pay cash up front, but they even refused to connect the room phone. When I wanted to rent a car I had to pay a $300 deposit, and even then they were extremely reluctant to rent me a vehicle. I don't recall the actual offload but I do remember the dolphins playing in the wake on the 150-mile trip up the Florida coast to Eau Gallie.

The marina was run down and had recently been taken over by a Greek family, with no boating knowledge, as a business venture. The father was a traditionalist from the old country who spoke little English. When the boat was visited later, it had sooty crosses in the headliner above each door where he had made the sign of the cross using a candle. I noticed a manatee drifting in the water around the boat. Also known as sea cows, these mammals graze on aquatic plants in shallow water. They are protected in Florida, where they are vulnerable to being struck by boat propellers.

Being closer to Taiwan than the U.S. East Coast, boat number no. 5 arrived in California shortly after no. 4. This boat belonged to a guy who worked with Hollywood, and he used the boat as his office. He covered the bulkheads with faux snakeskin executed in mauve vinyl. Yuk! He made a trip in the boat down to Mexico, and when he arrived back in Newport Beach he said that about 900 gallons from the main forward fuel tanks had "disappeared". I asked what he meant by this, and he said that he had not used the fuel but it was no longer in the tanks. There was no sign of any leaks, and I said that if the fuel had leaked into the bilge and been pumped overboard by the automatic bilge pump, he would have smelled the fuel and it would have left a shimmering trail on the water all the way to the horizon. I was convinced that the fuel was still in the tanks, even though the sight glass registered zero and no fuel came out when the valves were open. The only way to check for sure was to undo the fitting at the base of the tank. These things are never very easy to get to, and when I undid the fitting— as proof that the tank was indeed full—fuel came spurting out with the force of a 3-foot head behind it. I put my thumb over the end of the pipe and it had the same effect as putting your thumb over the end of a garden hose! I was absolutely drenched in stinking diesel by the time I was able to reconnect the fitting. The problem was caused by the fuel line at the base of the tank executing a U-shaped bend where it connected to the fuel standpipe. Heavy welding grit from inside the tank had settled into the base of the U and blocked the line. The sight gauge, being on the standpipe, also registered zero.

The boat owner also reported that the fuel tanks leaked when they were brim full. This turned out to be because the tank makers had continued to drill 1/4-inch holes in the top of every tank for fuel gauge fittings after we had issued instructions to the yard to stop installing them because of their unreliability. The fix was to install screws into the tapped holes, but the problem was to access them. On one tank, hydraulic steering lines had first to be removed, which meant being soaked in hydraulic oil as well as diesel while jammed into a tight space and reaching at arm's length over the top of the tank. I put my clothes through the washer four times but they still stank of diesel and I had to throw them away.

Boat no. 6 arrived at Chuck Hovey Yachts in January 1988. The customer was a large man and very demanding. Even though he had seen a boat before he placed his order, he told Chuck that the toilets were too small for his large bum and he wanted them changed. This was impossible to do without major changes to the heads (toilet rooms) but Chuck did not want to tell him this and did nothing. The customer then went ahead and made changes to the tune of $10,000 and sent the bill to Chuck, who did not pay it. This led to threatened lawsuits. One evening I was relaxing on *Lion's Den* after work when Chuck called me and said that this customer had called him and demanded that he go down to the boat and take care of a vibration problem. Chuck did not want to face the man and asked that I go in his place. I was equally reluctant but felt I had no choice.

When I arrived at the boat, I asked the customer about the condition of the propellers and he told me that a diver had been down in the last couple of days to check everything out. I then spent the next two hours in the engine room, taking the Aquadrives apart and checking everything. I could find nothing wrong so I went back on deck and asked again about the props. I received the same answer but decided that to be sure I had to go down and check them for myself. I stripped down to my underpants and went under the boat. As I suspected, the props were covered in marine growth. I came back on deck and told the owner that the props were the source of his problem. When I left, he was threatening to murder the diver!

Not long after this it was my turn to have a spell in the hospital—this time in Mexico. I was back in Penasco, working on the deck plug of the Fleming 48, when I jumped down from the roof over the salon to the cabin trunk on the foredeck. It was only three feet but I caught my heel on the edge of the roof, and I landed on my side rather than on my feet. When I tried to move I felt a sharp pain in my upper thigh, so acute that it took me nearly one hour to work my way off the plug, onto the workshop floor, and into the office. Old man Cabrales took me first to a local chiropractor, who wisely decreed I should go to the local clinic. There they took an X-ray and determined I needed to go to the small hospital in San Luis, about 200 miles away. They loaded me onto a mattress in the back of a Datsun pickup and drove me over the rough roads to the hospital. It was not a journey I would care to repeat. It took around four hours and for much of the way it was dark. I was comforted by being able to see the familiar constellation of Orion swooping back and forth from the back of the truck as the road twisted and turned.

When we reached the hospital, they admitted me and operated on me the next morning. The neck of my femur was cracked just below the hip joint. The surgeon cut open my thigh and screwed a stainless steel reinforcing pin in place. After the anaesthetic, they were concerned that my lungs be exercised properly. They didn't have one of those things you blow into that pushed a ball up a tube, so, with some embarrassment, they improvised a water-filled bottle with two tubes so that you had to breathe out by blowing air though the water. Five days later I went back to Penasco, and within 10 days of the accident I was back at work and driving a car.

Although plenty more challenges lay ahead, this was

492

undoubtedly the low point in the story of Fleming Yachts. Anton was still recovering from his heart attack, and I was on crutches following my accident. We were facing frustrations in Mexico and quality problems in Taiwan. We were dropping behind in orders to the extent that we were at serious risk of Taiwan legitimately taking over the Fleming project.

It was also at this time that I received a letter from Tim Ellis demanding the return of his $10,000 investment. I wrote to him and said that we were still facing a number of difficulties and only just scraping by so there was no spare cash to allow returning investors' money. He then wrote me a really snotty—almost threatening—letter which made me mad. If he had been reasonable I would have done everything I could to get him his money, but because he took the line he did, I told him that if he demanded the money immediately I could only send him $5,000. If he was prepared to wait a few months, he could have the whole amount. He demanded the $5,000, so that is what I sent him. His rude letter cost him $5,000!

The car I was using to get around and make the drive back and forth to Newport Beach was an elderly Oldsmobile. It was extremely hot in Mexico, with the temperatures frequently over 100 degrees. The car could not be driven over 50 mph without it overheating, and there was no possibility of using the air-conditioning for the same reason. This meant that the entire journey of over 500 miles had to be driven below 50 mph with the windows open and with air blowing in at furnace heat. The elevation varied from below sea level to over 4,000 feet where it crossed the Cuyamaca Mountains east of San Diego. Driving back to California about six weeks following my accident, I had a puncture in the desert miles from anywhere. I changed the wheel but, as no one had checked it for years, the spare was almost as flat as the tyre I had removed. I turned the vehicle around and drove at 25 mph back to Ajo. I had just enough money to buy a used tyre. When I crossed the border at Lukeville, the officer had asked where I was headed. When I told him California, he told me to be careful. "They are all crazy there" he said! When I passed through El Centro, the radio announcer said that temperatures were normal for the time of year—112 degrees! I couldn't wait to reach the mountains and relief from the blistering heat.

As a change from the Oldsmobile, Chuck Guy offered me an elderly VW Beetle that he very kindly said I could use. The road license had expired, and before it could be renewed in California it needed a smog test. Unfortunately, it was not in good enough condition to pass the test, so the car had no current road license which meant that it also had no insurance. I had a Singapore driving license which was not valid in California, so I also lacked a driving license. Having the car in Mexico, none of these deficiencies were of much significance, but were potentially serious omissions if I drove the car in California. I discovered that the small town of Ajo in Arizona had a Department of Motor Vehicles (DMV) office which opened once per month. Arizona did not require a smog test and this gave me the opening I needed to rectify the situation.

On the appropriate day I drove from Penasco to Ajo and went to the DMV office. I said that I wanted to re-register the car in Arizona and, after a battle with rusty bolts, we removed the California plates. Then the official asked me for proof of insurance. I had to admit that I didn't have any, so he said that without insurance he could not let me have the plates—not even the ones he had removed! I asked where I could get insurance and he told me at the other side of town. So I drove off to look for an insurance office, now being even more illegal and broadcasting the fact by having no license plates!

Ajo had depended for its existence on a large copper mine. After the mine closed, it became a retirement town with a police force that had little to do other than lie in wait to catch errant motorists speeding through on their way to the Mexican border. They lurked up side streets and hid behind bushes but, by good fortune, I escaped their attention and reached an office offering insurance. I still had no credit card and only had sufficient cash to pay for one month. I filled in the paperwork and then they asked me for my driving license! I said that I didn't have one of those and they told me that without a driving license they could not issue me insurance!

In the DMV I had noticed that they were issuing driving

licenses, so I went to get into the car to return to DMV. The doors of the VW were locked and I saw the keys dangling from the ignition switch! Good Grief! Could the situation get any worse? I borrowed a wire coat hanger from the insurance office, broke into the VW and drove, still minus plates, back to the DMV and said that I wanted to apply for a driving license. There was a pile of booklets on the counter which were the equivalent of the British Highway Code, setting out all the rules of the road. I feverishly skimmed through one before accepting the multiple choice form from the clerk. I had barely got started on filling it in when she went left the room, leaving me entirely alone with my booklet and my form! I looked up the answers to questions I was not sure about and included a couple of deliberate mistakes. When she returned I gave her the form, and a few minutes later, for the sum of $7.50, I was issued with an Arizona driving permit. For the third time I ran the gauntlet of the police traps and was rewarded with insurance, then back to the DMV, where Arizona plates were fixed to the vehicle. I was now a legal but nervous wreck!

While Anton was recovering from his heart attack, I moved *Lion's Den* from Newport Beach to San Diego, where not only were the slip rents cheaper, but it was also closer to Mexico. On one occasion there was a tsunami alert from an earthquake in faraway Japan. I thought it was unlikely to affect San Diego harbour, but I thought I would be an awful fool if I lost my only asset because I couldn't be bothered to head offshore for a while. But I dithered about making a decision because it was quite a trek to the harbour mouth. In the end I just made sure I had adequate fuel and water and was well provisioned. I doubled up the mooring lines and hoped for the best which, in this case, worked out OK.

Anton slowly recovered from his heart attack and had been working with Chuck Hovey to sell the Fleming 48. Even though the tooling was still in its early stages, they had succeeded in obtaining orders for four boats, with deposits on three of them. A couple who were one of the first buyers were of German origin. They made a visit to Penasco, and, over lunch and in not very veiled terms, they made it clear they thought Hitler had made a mistake in not completing the job of eliminating the Jews, and that his actions were perfectly correct and justified. I kept my mouth shut but had a hard time eating my lunch!

During the building process, construction of the tool has to be meticulously accurate but is basically very simple. In the early stages it requires just wood, nails and lots of putty and sandpaper. Nothing was available in Penasco, so all the materials had to come from Phoenix. We told Salvador Cabrales that we would need more sandpaper in about six weeks, and he said that would be no problem and his truck would pick it up on one of its regular runs to Phoenix. As the end of the six-week deadline drew near, there was no sign of the sandpaper and we kept reminding Salvador. Finally, when it got down to the last few days and materials were running short, he told us that the truck was on its way. Later he told us that it had been delayed at the border. It ultimately turned out that there was no truck; they did not even have a truck to send! By this time work on the project had stopped because the workers had no sandpaper. Anton and I flew to San Diego, bought sandpaper and flew it back to Penasco, which made it the most expensive sandpaper in the world!

On another occasion Salvador invited Anton and myself to his house for dinner at 8 p.m. We arrived at the due time to find the house in total darkness. We knocked on the door a few times and eventually it was opened by a servant woman who spoke no English. She was able to convey to us that no one was home. We went away and returned about one hour later, thinking that, because everything in Mexico was late, maybe we had made a mistake by turning up on time. Still no Salvador, so we went to a local restaurant for dinner. The following morning, Salvador came into the office demanding to know why we had not shown up the previous evening. We told him that we had been there twice and he told us that he was there all the time, which was an obvious lie which he compounded by saying that, when we did not appear, he went round the local hotels looking for us. This was completely ridiculous because he was the one who had found us the apartment in which we were living.

For recreation, Chuck and myself explored the local mountains, especially El Pinacate which was made up of black, cinder-like volcanic rocks and was extremely rugged. From 1965 to 1970, NASA sent its astronauts there to train for lunar excursions, given the similarity of the terrain to the lunar surface. Chuck also had his own small plane, and one day we flew across the Sea of Cortez to the small town of San Felipe. As we looked down on the Sea of Cortez, currents from the remnants of the Colorado River traced intricate, tree-like patterns through the aqua waters of the Gulf.

Working in Mexico was certainly different from both the U.S. and Taiwan. I recall one American visitor telling me that while it is possible to learn to work with the Mexican culture, don't ever try to change it. That, he said, was the road to insanity! While you are in the moment, so to speak, it is sometimes hard to see the forest for the trees, and it was not until I was on a flight to Taiwan early in October 1988 that the reality of our situation became clear to me. If we could not count on reliable supplies of a few simple things like putty and sandpaper, how could we rely on obtaining the multitude of items needed to construct a boat? The shortage of a single component would be enough to prevent completion of the boat, and our customers would quite justifiably not be sympathetic to our supply problems. Once you start making commitments to others, the situation becomes much more serious, as your reputation and integrity are at stake. The warning signals could not be clearer if they had been blazoned across the sky in letters of fire. It would be madness to continue the project in Mexico.

On my return from Taiwan I conveyed my feelings to Anton about the inadvisability of continuing in Mexico. He agreed and we slowly began to remove our belongings and equipment, until one day we flew out a planeload of stuff and I drove away with a loaded vehicle. We were a little worried in case we would get stopped at the border because the Cabrales family had some pull in the area, but we had no problem. The tooling had reached the stage where the hull mould had been removed from the plug, and the deck and flying bridge plugs were almost finished. We just walked away from the work, effectively leaving $80,000 on the table.

Through advertising and magazine articles people began to

hear about the Fleming 50, and sales began to pick up. In October 1988 we built a boat for an Austrian living in Italy named Herb Denk. He wanted to take delivery of the boat in California and drive it through the Panama Canal and across the Atlantic to Spain! To do this, he needed to carry more fuel capacity, so we adjusted the mould and built the boat at 53 feet. After a short sea trial out to Catalina Island, 20 miles off the coast of California, Herb proclaimed, "OK! We Go!" and a couple of days before Christmas 1988, off he went, with a couple of companions. He had to carry extra fuel on deck, but he made it safely, arriving in Barcelona on May 22nd, 1989, after a voyage of 9,300 miles. Herb had a custom of rewarding himself after a task successfully accomplished—such as a long hike completed, a meal well prepared, decks washed or countless other excuses—with a draft of liquor suitable for the time of day. According to the severity of the task, these were graded as a "little schluk", a "pre-manoverschluk", or for something really deserving, a full blown "Grand Manoverschluk!"

Along the way, Herb called at La Guaira, the port for Caracas, in Venezuela. Here his boat caught the eye of Carlos Kuntze, who had been the Grand Banks dealer in Venezuela and who was the person put into quarantine by the medical authorities in Singapore for arriving without a yellow fever inoculation. When he enquired of Herb who had built the boat, Carlos was surprised to hear that it was Anton and myself both of whom he knew. He contacted Anton, and this chance encounter ultimately led to the sale of three boats in Venezuela!

After we abandoned Mexico, I returned full time to Taiwan and we began the slow climb out of crisis mode. With Fred as manager of Tung Hwa, we could at last concentrate on building boats without being side-tracked by ridiculous side issues. Martial law had ended in Taiwan in 1987, and life there had become more pleasant. Anton had mostly recovered from his heart attack. The doctor told him that it had been caused by his smoking, and if he continued to light up it was only a matter of time before he had another attack, which would most probably kill him. Anton went to a hypnotist to help him kick the habit, which he did—for a while.

By this time, with a bit more money in the kitty, I was actually receiving a salary and all the back pay the company owed me. We voted ourselves a pay increase to $1,500 per month, and Anton had decreed that we would each receive a bonus of $10,000 with the shipment of each boat. As we could be located anywhere, we looked into the possibility of moving up to the Seattle area. We looked around the area and were quite taken with Bainbridge Island, across Puget Sound from Seattle. Ultimately we decided to stay in Southern California, but I later bought a small plot of land overlooking Eagle Harbour on Bainbridge Island as a deposit for the future. While involved in that transaction, I stayed in a B & B called Mary's Farm. Mary was a singing teacher and she prevailed on me to sing. I told her that I could not sing in tune, and she said not to worry as she ran classes she called, "Singing for people who can't sing". She eventually bullied me into singing with her, accompanying me on the piano, and I found that under her tutelage I could in fact still sing quite well. It's amazing what you can do with the right teacher!

Chapter 4

Taiwan

April 1988 to July 1992

I meet Louisa. The U.S. luxury tax demolishes boat sales. I take a Trans-Siberian Railway trip with my daughter Nicky. I visit my great-grandfather's croft on the island of Jura, in the Hebrides, and join a Norwegian customer on his Fleming yacht to Norway via Holland through rough seas.

Back in Taiwan, work was less intense and it was possible to consider some social life away from the yard. I continued to buy pirated books at the shop run by a lady called Shirley, who spoke some limited English. She was always on at me to meet the lady school teacher who taught her daughters English. I had continued to resist this because I had to remain single minded and focused on my work, and I really had no time to devote to anything outside that.

When, on New Year's Day 1989, Shirley brought up the subject again, I cautiously agreed to meet the teacher she had in mind. Shirley immediately picked up the phone, talked to the lady in Chinese, then handed the phone to me. It was quite an awkward moment and I really did not know what to say. The lady's name was Louisa and we had some conversation, agreed to meet in a few days, and then hung up.

Shirley wanted to know what Louisa had said and I told her that we had agreed to meet in a few days. With a sigh of exasperation, Shirley immediately picked up the phone again and, in Chinese, told Louisa what I understood to be the English equivalent of "Get your arse down here right away!". Shirley told me that Louisa—whom she described as "short and fat"—would arrive shortly. In my experience the Chinese are never very shy in stating their opinions!

That is how I came to meet Louisa, who remains my close friend 25 years later. Through her, I visited her school and spoke to the kids in English. I also helped her—rather ineffectually it must be said—with some minor drama she was teaching the kids. Over the next few days and during the upcoming Chinese New Year, I accompanied her on outings with her extended family, which numbered as many as 23 persons when we all sat down for dinner.

My leg had been giving me some minor trouble, so I consulted a doctor. An X-ray showed that the screws holding the pin in place had passed right through the bone and out the other side, so that they were tearing into the muscle every time I moved. He also advised me that so long as the reinforcement remained in place, the bone would never reach its full strength, so the pin should be removed. I was admitted into a six-person ward in the Kaohsiung Medical Centre, where there were three men and three women. All the patients except me were there as a result of traffic accidents.

Nursing in Taiwan is rather different from what we are used to in the West. While the medical care of the patient is handled by the nurses, all other aspects of patient care are expected to be done by family members, and there is a roll-out bed beneath the hospital bed for the use of the care-giver. Of course I did not have a family member to take care of me. None of the other patients spoke any English and they were very curious about my situation.

This was not long after I had met Louisa, and when she showed up the other patients plied her with questions. Louisa had recently introduced me to a young Taiwanese student called Jennifer for one-on-one lessons in English conversation, and when Jennifer came to visit my fellow patients were even more curious. One of the ladies in the ward was one of those cheerful, gossipy types you find in any culture. She was the one with the most questions, and when someone had to sign a form accepting the responsibility for my operation, she immediately volunteered to sign it!

The following morning my bed was wheeled out of the ward to some side ward where they started putting tubes in me and gave me drugs to calm my nerves. Then I was wheeled into the elevator with lots of other people and taken down to the second floor. There my bed was pushed up against an opening in the wall and I was transferred through it to a gurney on the other side, which was the sterile operating suite. I was then wheeled into the operating theatre and placed on the operating table.

I chatted a bit with the staff and then someone snuck up behind me, put a mask over my face, and I was out. I awoke seemingly a few minutes later to find it was all over. Later they gave me the pin removed from my leg and thought it was quite amusing as they hadn't used pins of that size and type for quite a number of years.

I was still traveling back and forth between Taiwan and California and was keen to start putting down some sort of roots. For many years, real estate had proved to be a secure investment in California. I could not afford to buy anything near the coast so, in November 1989, I put down a deposit on a home in Lake Arrowhead as a place to retreat to on my trips back from Taiwan. Lake Arrowhead is a community 5,000 feet up in the San Bernardino Mountains, about 80 miles inland from Newport Beach. The mountains are cloaked in pine trees and the area is very different from the coastal region. In a typical example of the way I always seem to buy property, I drove up to Arrowhead on a Monday to meet a real estate agent, and I had settled on a house and agreed a price by Thursday.

Just after Christmas, I was staying in my new house with daughter Jackie when we went to one of the local supermarkets to get supplies. It was very busy and I remarked on this to the clerk at the checkout counter. She said it was always busy before a major storm. Storm? I looked at Jackie. This was the first we had heard of any storm, so we went back into the store and bought more stuff. That night it began to snow, and by morning our car

502

was just a hump with the snow at least two feet deep. The roads up there are a network of lanes and it was five days before the snow ploughs were able to reach us and we were able to get out. At the base of the mountain, 5,000 feet below, it was just the usual sunny California, with no hint of the conditions on the mountain.

Nicky worked at the Biarritz restaurant in Newport Beach for four months during the winter of 1986-87, then went traveling, Lonely Planet style, in Hawaii, Australia, New Zealand and on to Japan. She called me from Japan to tell me that she had pretty well run out of money. I told her to get to Hong Kong and see the person who handled our business affairs there. From there she made her way to England and, eventually, back to California.

Nicky had to keep leaving California for immigration reasons and flew out to Taiwan to meet me in January 1990. She met a guy called Tom on the plane and offered him a lift and they— together with Louisa and myself—rented a car and went on a tour of Taiwan. Hiring a car was not easy in those days. You had to pretty well sign your life away to get one, and the vehicles were pretty ropey. We drove all over Taiwan with worrying clunking noises coming from beneath the floor. We followed the amazing road through scenic Taroko Gorge and stayed for the night at some place high in the mountains, where it was very cold. The desk clerk who checked us in looked like he had just come from Mongolia, muffled up in a padded jacket and wearing a hat with ear flaps! Beds in Taiwan are as hard as concrete, and it isn't so long since they gave up using a wood or porcelain block for a pillow.

The following month Nicky and myself went to Thailand and visited Chiang Mai and Chiang Rai. We took a trip on one of the rivers in a longtail boat, which was quite hilarious. In the upper reaches of the river, the boat kept running aground on sand banks and everyone had to get off and push. The Fleming family have always tended to travel like refugees, and Nicky and I had our gear in large brown paper bags like those you get at a supermarket checkout. These are not very ideal for traveling in a small open boat with water in the bilge. When we picked up the bags the bottom dropped out and dumped all the contents into the bilges.

We travelled back to Bangkok on the train, sitting opposite a chain-smoking Buddhist monk.

Actually Thailand is a delightful country, often called the "Land of Smiles"—the exceptions to this being some of the foreign visitors. By this time, we were used to California, where total strangers greet each other as a matter of course. At one hotel we said good morning to a German gentleman and he glared at us as if we had murdered his mother. Strange people! I returned to Taiwan and Nicky continued on to England.

The business was now beginning to run more smoothly, so of course some idiots had to step in and upset the apple cart. In this case it was the U.S. Congress, who decided over a weekend in September 1990—when no one was looking—to impose a luxury tax on certain items, including yachts costing more than $100,000. The intention was to soak people perceived as rich, but they overlooked the fact that the targeted group could—and did—exercise their right not to buy. Boat sales in the U.S. instantly collapsed, resulting in the immediate loss of at least 7,600 boatbuilding jobs. Eventually this figure grew to more than 30,000, for whom the government had to cover the cost of unemployment benefits in addition to the revenue they lost from the companies who had been building boats. The tax losses exceeded the amount of the new tax revenue. It was a classic example of the law of unintended consequences. This ill-advised law was not scrapped for three years, but the arguments about repealing it started the day it was imposed so of course no potential boat buyer wanted to be the muggins who paid a non-refundable tax that was about to be scrapped. People who can afford to buy boats do not generally arrive at that position by being stupid.

By a strange twist of fate, this misguided decision ultimately led to our advantage. Chuck Hovey had ordered two boats, no. 25 and no. 26, but after the tax was imposed, he told us that he could not take the second boat, which was already under construction. In the meantime, a Norwegian called Egil Paulsen who lived in Singapore had been visiting the London Boat Show. We were not exhibiting in the show but our dealer, Alan Taylor, had placed a small advertisement in the catalogue. Egil had already settled on buying a Norwegian-built boat when he spotted the advertisement, and, on a Sunday in January—just hours before catching his flight back to Singapore—he drove down to Hamble, near Southampton, to visit Alan Taylor.

Egil was impressed with the boat and, as Singapore was in the same region of the world as Taiwan, I was delegated to work with him. I cannot say that I was overjoyed because I was already carrying a pretty big workload. To cut a long story short, Egil flew to Taiwan from Singapore. I showed him around the yard and told him about Hovey's second boat—hull no. 26. Up to this point, Egil had owned only sailboats, and he was looking to buy a Fleming 55 with naturally aspirated engines the following year. No. 26 was a Fleming 53 with turbocharged engines, due to be completed within a few months. While enjoying a Chinese meal, washed down with copious quantities of beer, Egil asked me if it would help if he bought no. 26. I replied that of course it would. He said, "Make me a deal." I said that I made boats—not deals—and I would have to refer it to Alan Taylor and Anton. This I did. A deal was struck, and Egil became the very welcome buyer for no. 26.

Egil was a ship owner and quite a demanding client. He still maintains that he did not request many changes, but the file shows that he made over 90! He named the boat *Ozmaiden* and wanted her delivered to England in time for him to use during the approaching summer of 1991. We worked hard to complete the boat with all its changes in time, and after considerable difficulty finding a ship, we managed to get the boat delivered to Southampton to meet his schedule. For various reasons Egil did not in the end take the boat to Norway in 1991, but I was able to accompany him on the journey the following year, which I will describe in due course.

After Egil's boat was finally aboard the ship taking her to Europe, Nicky arrived in Taiwan on one of her periodic rough travels around the world. I had long had an ambition to travel on the Trans-Siberian Railway. All the time I had lived in Hong Kong it had intrigued me that it was physically possible to board a train in Kowloon railway station—then located at the Star Ferry—

and travel by rail all the way to London. Politically, it was almost impossible, because at that time both China and the Soviet Union were rabidly communist countries.

By June 1991, however, times had changed, and we made arrangements to go on this rail journey of about 6,000 miles over seven time zones. We spent a couple of days in Hong Kong before flying to Beijing, where we stayed in a very nice Holiday Inn. Every day we visited such well-known sights as Tiananmen Square, the Forbidden City, the Summer Palace, the Temple of Heaven and the Great Wall. Nicky—like myself, in younger days—was used to returning to some cheap hovel at the end of an exhausting day of sightseeing. It was a big step up to be able to return, dirty and sweaty, to a nice room, enjoy a shower, eat a good meal and then retire to a comfortable bed. This is definitely a better way to see the world!

I had been under the impression that we were just a pair of travellers taking the train, but after we received a message to rendezvous under the clock at Beijing Railway station, we discovered we were the only Westerners in a group of about 20 Hong Kong Chinese. Nothing wrong with that, but it was unexpected. A train for Moscow left every day. On alternating days, it was either the Russian train, which went via Manchuria, or the Chinese train, which went via Outer Mongolia. We happened to be on a Russian train. The food on the Chinese was reputed to be much better and I can well believe that! When we arrived at the train there was an English guy remonstrating with a Russian official who was saying over and over "No problem! No Problem!"

"But I *do* have a problem!" came the plaintive response.

It was a fascinating journey which, in common with all such extended journeys in some form of transportation, was really two journeys rolled into one. On one hand there was life aboard the train and all the characters and personalities with whom you interact during the time you are together. On the other, you are riding a magic carpet from which you are a detached observer viewing the tapestry of events unrolling past the window.

There is no space here to describe the journey in detail, but there were certain vignettes which stay in my mind. Early one morning we halted briefly in a marshalling yard which was full of panting steam locomotives. It was quite cold and steam hung in the air as figures dressed in blue overalls and Mao caps, armed with oil cans and rags, ministered to their powerful machines.

We stopped at Shenyang and Harbin, both places freezing in winter, and reached the Chinese/Russian border, delineated by watch towers and a barbed wire fence that stretched to the horizon. Actually the train stopped twice—first to be inspected by Chinese officials as we left China, then by the Russians as we arrived in their country. Russian railways were constructed with a different gauge from those of neighbouring countries. Supposedly this was to discourage foreign forces from using them to invade the country—which was indeed a factor during the German invasion in WWII. However, at other times, this caused great inconvenience. At Zabaylalsk, on the Russian border, the whole train had to be jacked up and all the bogies rolled out and replaced by others—a process taking several hours.

Work on building the Trans-Siberian railroad started in 1891 and was brutally hard. Temperatures dropped below 50 °F during the winter, and summer was plagued by mosquitos. Much of the line was built over permafrost and, even today, the poles carrying lines beside the railway lean drunkenly as the ground beneath them melts and refreezes. Horses and even timber had to be imported. Much of the work was done by convicts and slave labour, using wooden shovels! The total distance from Moscow to Vladivostok is 5,753 miles, covering seven time zones. There is one train every day in each direction. The journey takes seven days so there are fourteen trains running the route at any one time.

In our case we joined the main line from Vladivostok at Irkutsk, situated on Lake Baikal, which is said to hold one-fifth of the world's fresh water. Construction of the section of the line around the lake had been extremely difficult, and for seven years, starting in 1897, trains were loaded onto ferries to bridge the gap between the western and eastern sections of the line. Amazingly, the ferries were built in Newcastle, England, before being dismantled and re-assembled in Irkutsk. We broke our journey here and our little group were met by two local tour guides and, in another surprise, by a young woman who had flown here from Moscow and who accompanied us for the rest of our journey. Her name was Masha Guitina, and this was her first trip to Siberia. We spent two days in Irkutsk before continuing our journey.

Nicky and I shared a compartment with Masha and a Russian guy. The upper bunks folded down during the day to form back rests for the lower seats. Each car had an attendant known as a provodsnitsa who kept the samovar stoked, which provided hot water for tea. There was a dining car that served basic food such as rye bread, sliced cucumbers, and some kind of milk that was deliberately soured. The Cantonese Chinese from Hong Kong were all regular working folk such as book keepers or, in one case, a taxi driver. They had saved their money and were using this rail trip simply as a cheap way to get to Europe for a holiday. Our tickets were priced in rubles and, with the current exchange rate, cost us just over the equivalent of $100 for the six-day trip, including food! For a Russian, the cost was the equivalent of only $6! The Russians with whom we were able to communicate all wanted to know what the other passengers earned. Even our fellow passengers from Hong Kong felt obliged to lie so as not to make the Russians feel bad. At that time a doctor in Russia only earned the equivalent of about $600, which was less than the Hong Kong taxi driver!

The train stopped briefly at such places as Krasnoyarsk, Ekaterinburg—where Tsar Nicolas and his family had been executed in 1918—and Yaroslavl before arriving in Moscow. At every stop, an army of sturdy women went along the train, checking for cracked wheels by striking each one with a hammer. They also checked and changed any worn-out brake shoes. We crossed huge rivers like the Yenesay and the Ob. Both these rivers flowed north, which meant that their upper reaches thawed first, releasing huge blocks of ice from upstream to batter the bridges each spring.

We spent a few days in Moscow touring Red Square, the Kremlin and other well-known spots. We visited a couple of Russian Orthodox churches. I am not a religious person, but of all the various churches, mosques, temples and synagogues I have entered during my travels, the Russian churches have been imbued with the most powerful atmosphere. They have been by far the most richly decorated, and the priest, in his robes, tall headgear and impressive beard is an imposing figure as he swings his censer back and forth, filling the air with the pungent fumes of incense. In one tiny church the atmosphere was made more intense by the presence of a huge acolyte, dressed all in black, with enormous boots and hands the size of dinner plates, who must have suffered from some kind of gigantism.

We visited Moscow University, where I was surprised to see posters for Amnesty International and photos critical of Russian police beating up demonstrators in the Baltic States. It has to be remembered that this was in the early days of the breakup of the Soviet Union and the political situation was still fluid.

From Moscow we took the train to Leningrad, whose name had yet to revert to its original name of St. Petersburg. This beautiful city was founded by Tsar Peter the Great in 1703. At the time of our visit it looked very tired and our guide told us that it was unlikely to improve until property was put back into private hands after being publicly shared—as was so vividly portrayed in the film *Dr. Zhivago*. On our tour we passed Lenin University where, our guide announced, Lenin once studied law before "becoming a criminal himself!"

Leningrad had suffered terribly when it was bombarded and held under siege for 872 days by the Germans during World War II, resulting in the deaths of 1,500,000 people—many due to starvation. We visited the Grand Palace which had been rebuilt after its near total destruction by German troops. The famous fountains were being reconstructed and our guide, after pointing out that the people carrying out the work were actually working, explained to us that this was because they were from Poland!

After a few days we returned to Moscow. Nicky continued by train to Germany, where she visited the Dachau concentration camp before continuing on to the UK, while I took an Aeroflot flight to Bangkok en route for Taiwan. Service was pretty basic compared to what we are used to. I sat next to a black guy from

509

Mali who, in broken French, asked me for help filling out his immigration form for Thailand. Once I had done this, I received similar requests from all his traveling companions, of whom there were six or seven. I did wonder why this group of young guys from the Southern Sahara was traveling from Moscow to Bangkok on Aeroflot!

Arriving in the vivacity and tropical colour of Thailand was a breath of fresh air after the austerity of Russia. The shops in Bangkok airport were vibrant with orchids and piles of fresh fruit. I treated myself to a bunch of scarlet, juicy rambutans while awaiting my connection to Kaohsiung.

I was only back in Taiwan for a couple of months before I flew to UK with Louisa. We went for a driving tour around the country, staying in a different bed and breakfast place each night. We visited Wales and the Lake District before arriving on the west coast of Scotland. My great grandfather had been born and brought up on the island of Jura, in the Inner Hebrides, and I took this opportunity to visit the place—but it was not easy.

There was no longer a direct ferry from the Scottish mainland to the island, and we had first to go to the adjacent island of Islay (pronounced "Eye-lah"). We crossed the width of that island to Port Asksaig, to catch the Feolin Ferry across the narrow sound between the two islands. I had been told there was a bus you could catch on the Jura side that would take you the 7 miles up the single track road to Craighouse, the island's only village. This turned out not to be true. All there was on the Jura side was a simple shelter with a notice pinned to the door saying: "Please keep door shut to keep sheep out!"

Jura had a human population of around 200, who shared the island with about 5,000 red deer. I decided that this was as far as we would get on this first visit. It was raining and rather cold, and we returned to Port Askaig on the next ferry. I have a photo of Louisa muffled up complete with scarf and looking very cold on the ferry on this August afternoon. From here we made our way back to the mainland, continued our tour, and returned to Taiwan.

In July of 1991 Burr Yacht Sales was appointed our U.S East

Coast dealer. Art Burr had been a very successful Bertram dealer for many years, and his young staff thought he had lost his mind when he added our much slower and more conservative boat to his portfolio. However, the Fleming gradually won them over, and they became our most prolific and enthusiastic supporters over the years.

Early in 1992 we sold our first boat in Japan. This was hull no. 36, and the buyer, who was from Osaka, sent his representative to Taiwan for several months while the boat was under construction. I picked him up at his hotel every morning on my way to work and dropped him off in the evening. The boat had to be built to Japanese regulations and I was informed that the forepeak—which divided the anchor locker from the forward cabin—had to be watertight with no openings. But, I protested, how are we going to access the chain locker? The response was simply a smile accompanied by the slight hiss of an intake of breath and upturned hands with a hint of a bow from the waist.

I had originally wanted the forward cabin to be as long as possible, but I had been forced to move the bed aft from the bulkhead to provide sufficient width for the headboard. This resulted in a shelf at the forward end of the bed. I realized that if we moved the bulkhead aft by the width of this shelf, there would just be sufficient room to access the forepeak through a hatch on the foredeck. Although moving the bulkhead aft reduced the fore and aft length, it actually made the cabin appear larger because the width of the bulkhead greatly increased due to the flare of the bow. It also provided better access to the foredeck while allowing it to be sealed off from the rest of the boat by a watertight collision bulkhead. This was one of those cases in which an apparent snag metamorphosed into a winning situation.

A few months following the completion of this boat, I was finally able to accompany Egil on his trip to Norway. I was keen to go because my cruising experience up to that time had been almost non-existent, and I wanted to correct that deficiency and learn the functioning of modern electronics. Other crew members on the trip were: Ben, a young, British, qualified boat captain; Alex, a British engineering type whom Egil dubbed Chief

Engineer; Angus, an Aussie, the cook; and Sven, a Norwegian friend of Egil's with little boating experience. When the time came to leave Southampton, on a nasty day in July, Egil was showing signs of anxiety. Although he was an experienced yachtsman, he was nervous about the complexity of this twin-screw powerboat. He said that whether we left or not had to be a 100 per cent decision on the part of the crew. We all said we were ready to leave, and I added that the boat was designed for just such a trip, even if the weather was a bit snotty. Egil then said he had to go to the local chandlery to buy some last-minute gear. We viewed this as another delaying tactic so while he was away, Alex and myself started the engines, untied the spring lines, and were on the dock ready to release the bow and stern lines by the time Egil returned.

Once under way, I came to realize that the combined on-board knowledge in the use of the electronic charting system did not extend much beyond switching it on. The sea conditions were unpleasantly rough and Egil, who was prone to sea sickness, soon retired to his bunk in the forward cabin. As night descended, we navigated from headland to headland along the English coast, guided by a succession of lighthouses each with its unique pattern of flashing lights. Ben also began to feel ill, and in a case of unfortunate timing, I went below to take a pee in the guest head just moments before he came down to throw up. Finding the door locked he went into Egil's cabin to use the toilet in his quarters but failed to make it in time and tossed his cookies all over the owner's bed!

This left just Alex and me to drive and navigate the boat. Fortunately, Alex had experience while I, although familiar with the systems and construction of the boat, had virtually none! I was hoping that conditions would improve once we got out of the English Channel and into the broader expanse of the North Sea. Actually they became worse.

The winds had been blowing from the north for about one week. The southern portion of the North Sea is relatively shallow, so the waves had built up and were short and steep. It was like being inside a washing machine as the boat pitched up and down and sheets of spray were dumped over the boat. Although I had been on my feet for 36 hours and still felt surprisingly alert, I knew it was only a matter of time before I was hit by fatigue and the same applied to Alex. I realized that this was one of those situations in which even a minor problem could precipitate a major crisis.

We were down to 6 knots, due to the conditions, and Alex estimated we had at least another 38 hours to go before we could expect any relief. He studied the chart and reckoned that if we turned in toward the Dutch coast right away, we could seek shelter in the port of Vlissingen. He went below to put this suggestion to Egil, who agreed. Actually, Egil told me later that he felt so ill that he was past caring that his boat was in the hands of inexperienced crew and that death would have been a happy release. That was certainly true for Ben who was stretched out on the settee in the salon with only the occasional groan to indicate that he had not already died!

With dawn breaking, we turned the bow toward land. The wind and waves now came from aft, and what had been a white knuckle ordeal turned into an exhilarating ride as *Ozmaiden* picked up her skirts and fled before the mountains of grey water rising behind the transom. As we surfed down the fronts of the waves, the log registered speeds as high as 18 knots and spray exploded to either side of the boat in hissing sheets of foam. Almost imperceptibly, a grey sliver of land rose above the tossing horizon, and in less than four hours, we were alongside Vlissingen lock in blissfully calm water. It really brought home to me the meaning of the word "haven" or *havn*, which is the European word for harbour.

After taking a few hours to recover, Egil and Alex went off to visit the local weather station and returned with the news that the northerly winds were predicted to continue for several more days. Alex proposed that we continue the journey through the Dutch canals. We spent the next week cruising in flat, calm water through some of the 4,600 miles of canals that lace the Netherlands. In the 10th century town of Haarlem, where the narrow canal twists and turns though picturesque streets, a cheerful operator waved as we passed through the first of many bridges which had to be raised to let us pass. At the next bridge, the face at the controls looked familiar, and by the third there was no doubt— it was either the same man or his twin brother. We watched as the bridge closed behind us and saw him jump on his bike and start pedalling furiously to his next rendezvous. The canal was only open in one direction at a time, and he would work his way back and forth with each convoy of boats.

We exited the canal system at the German border and briefly re-entered the North Sea before turning into the estuary of the River Elbe at Cuxhaven. From here we passed through the Kiel Canal into the Baltic and thence to Frederikstad, near Oslo.

This trip, in July 1992, was the first of many passages in a Fleming 55. I went on to accompany Egil on other cruises in *Ozmaiden* that will be briefly described in upcoming pages. Each one of these trips became the subject of magazine articles which were used in marketing the boats. It was on one of those cruises that I first met Duncan Cowie, who was later to be an important member of the Fleming team. Egil himself later moved from Singapore to Australia, where he was appointed our agent. Another of his captains, David Miles, became our dealer in the UK; and Adi Shard, who later took over my responsibilities in Taiwan, also cruised with Egil on *Ozmaiden*. By triggering the sale of hull no. 26 to Norway rather than California, the ill-conceived luxury tax became the catalyst for the genesis of a web of personal relationships that spans the globe and defines Fleming Yachts as it is today.

Chapter 5

July 1992 to October 1994

Taiwan

I revisit Jura and make a second boat trip to Norway via Scotland, during which I learn of Anton's death. I start Fleming Yachts in California, and Nicky joins the company. I make another boat trip, this time to Sweden and the Göta Canal. Boat orders return with the repeal of the U.S. luxury tax. Mary dies, and I fly to England.

After the trip to Norway with Egil, I returned to England to visit my sister in Devon and from there, in August 1992, I made another trip to Jura. This time I took a car to allow me some freedom of movement on the island. I stayed in the hotel in Craighouse for a couple of nights and was able to meet Gordon Wright, who had written the booklet about Jura I had picked up in a small tea shop at Port Askaig the previous year.

Gordon was extremely helpful and produced the census records going back to the early 1800s, which gave me immediate records for my great grandfather. At his suggestion I visited the vestry attached to the church where there were many historic photos, and I took photos of the photographs pinned to the wall. I also visited the graveyard and saw the gravestones for many of the ancestors mentioned in the census records along with one recent grave covered in flowers. The hotel was fully booked over the weekend so I spent two nights at a cottage offering bed and breakfast. It turned out that the couple who ran it had just lost their only son in a solo motorcycle accident on the island and it was his grave that I had seen. The father was the sole part-time policeman on the island, and he also acted as a gillie who accompanied hunters who came to the island to bag a deer. He told me that most of the hunters were from Belgium or Germany. He said that the deer were very wary and you had to stalk them from downwind, often from 3 miles away, crawling on your belly through swamp and heather until you were within 100 yards of your quarry. If the animal was only wounded, you had to go after it to finish it off. He said a deer wounded in the leg could "go for miles" and it could easily take three days to run it down. The deer, of which there were over 5,000 on the island, all belonged to the laird, and the hunter was not entitled to keep the meat.

I visited the "Laird", who lived in the big house at Ardlussa. He turned out to be quite young and had just returned from back-packing in Thailand. The estate extended over 26,000 acres on the island, but he said the land was very unproductive in the sense of being able to wrest a living from it. I noticed a target set up on the property. He said it was to make sure that the "punters", as he called them, could shoot straight before they were let loose on the moors. Not all of them could, and it was sometimes the gillie who actually pulled the trigger, although the so-called hunter took the credit for the kill.

I had brought with me a few black-and-white snaps taken by my aunts when they had visited Jura in the 1940s. By lining up various islets, mountains and other landmarks I was able to position myself in the exact spots from which the photos had been taken. I found out that the house where my great-grandfather lived was right across the other side of the island and required a 7-mile hike over the mountains through bracken higher than my head to reach it. I had already reached the end of the only road on the island. I was not equipped to make such a hike so I decided to leave that for another time. In any case, it was time for me to return to Taiwan and get back to work.

When I returned to the Scottish mainland, I looked up a distant relative who had lived at the bothy until he was 13. He lived in a place called Furnace, and he gave me the name of a lady who lived in Inverary. I went to see her and she took me to visit a feisty old man named Angus. Angus lived in a small cottage in town and had a fire burning in the grate and was wearing bedroom slippers in July. He wasn't remotely interested in family history. When we came to leave, the lady I was with said, "Well, see you around town Angus". To which he replied "Not if I see ye coming furst, ye won't!"

Since the introduction of the stupid luxury tax, we had received no orders. We were being kept going by the orders we already had in the pipeline, which were coming to an end. It did not seem to me that we could continue to pay ourselves with no income and I raised the subject with Anton, who was supposed to be handling the business side of the company. I told him that I didn't have any problem cutting back, but I didn't want to be told one day that there was no salary because there was no money in the bank. In the event that is exactly what happened—one day he said that there was no pay, so we had to go back to the IOU situation.

Anton had taken up smoking again. He tried to conceal it from me, but I wasn't fooled—a non-smoker can smell smoke 100 yards away. This led to his having a second heart attack, although it was not as serious as the first. Anton's main interest was in flying and he spent most of his time, and all of his money, building a three-quarter scale plywood replica of a Spitfire with a Jaguar engine. He became absolutely besotted with finishing this project, which I quite understood because I had felt much the same when I was an apprentice and was constructing my BMW special.

Anton's behaviour was becoming increasingly bizarre and hard to deal with. He would fly into violent rages for no apparent reason—quite often publicly, which was embarrassing. At other times he would be funny and charming, and people who did not know his dark side could not believe that he had one. His second wife, Leslie, left him and I had reached the point where I did not need to put up with the abuse any longer, and I decided to leave Fleming Yachts and look for something else.

Just before Christmas 1992, I told Steven and Fred about my decision to leave, but they prevailed upon me to stay. They said that they could not work with Anton. I was not surprised by that statement, because when I was recovering from my operation in Mexico, Anton had come to Taiwan to "negotiate" with the Taiwanese. He did this by issuing an ultimatum and then remaining in his hotel room waiting for them to capitulate and come to him. Of course this did not happen, so he sat in his hotel for three days with nothing happening. Anton was very disparaging about the Taiwanese. I will not repeat the language he used to describe them, but it made me mad because he was talking about the people who were building our boats and making it possible for us to earn our living. Even if you do not make overt comments about the way you feel, people pick up the vibes and act accordingly. I decided to hold off leaving for a while but to keep looking for other opportunities.

After cruising in Norway the previous summer, Egil and Alex had taken the boat back to Southampton. They had encountered rough seas, and Egil told me that the outboard berth in the port cabin had come loose, and they were looking for a way to isolate it with rubber from the hull. I told him that, because the space under that berth was very limited, I was using the structure of the berth to reinforce the hull and what he needed to do was to make sure that the berth was securely glassed to the hull—not to isolate it. He did not let on at the time, but later told me, that the damage had occurred when he had gone to sea under very rough conditions and the boat had fallen into a deep hole in the sea, and the resulting impact smashed a lot of wine bottles he had stowed below the forward berth! Be that as it may, the port berth should not have broken loose, and we beefed up the berth attachment lamination schedule on all the boats and never experienced another failure.

While I was in California, Anton raised the question of what should happen to the shares in Fleming Yachts should one of us die. I had never given this eventuality a moment's thought and naively assumed that if one of us should die, the other would assume control of the company. Anton said that we should have something in writing and that we should put a figure of $20,000 on the value of the deceased person's shares. After Anton had had his second heart attack, I saw the sense in what he was saying. When I next arrived in Taiwan, there was some disagreement at Kaohsiung airport between the taxi dispatcher and the driver, who decided to get his revenge by trying to frighten me. So he drove appallingly, even by the standards of a Taiwan taxi driver, including running almost every red light. I reacted by taking a magazine out of my bag, which I pretended to read. Using this incident as a pretext, I wrote a letter to Anton enclosing a signed memorandum along the lines he had suggested with other copies for him to sign and return to me.

When we had moved our operation to Mexico I had given up my apartment in Taiwan, and since that time, I had rented a series of single rooms. I was now staying in a modest hotel called the Utopia (hardly), not far from where Louisa lived. I was sitting in my hotel room early in the new year listening to the BBC World Service who were reporting on a tanker, named the *Braer*, in trouble off the Shetland Islands. The story progressed with each hourly broadcast until eventually the ship ran aground and broke up in tempestuous weather at the extreme southern tip of Shetland.

Egil had invited me to join him on another cruise to Norway during the following summer, and he had contacted me about the *Braer* incident because Shetland was on our proposed route. A few months later, not long before I was due to leave Kaohsiung prior to our trip, I had a phone call from Egil, who was still in Singapore. He told me that the skipper he had hired and who had assisted in moving *Ozmaiden* from Southampton to Kip Marina, in the Clyde in Scotland, had dropped dead of a heart attack. This tragedy did not alter our immediate plans but Egil felt he had to tell someone.

A few days later, in the summer of 1993, I met up in London with Egil, Angus from Australia and Alex. We drove up from London to Kip Marina, just outside Glasgow, where *Ozmaiden* was moored. Egil's wife was insistent that he always be accompanied by a professional captain, and to replace the unfortunate man who had died, Egil had taken on a Danish guy named Torkild, who normally skippered a square-rigged sailing vessel crewed by a succession of troubled kids. Torkild was an interesting fellow and many years later I heard a funny story about him. He was the speaker at a dinner at which he was supposed to give a talk about

519

dealing with fire aboard a vessel. Torkild had enjoyed the drinks rather too much and when it came time for him to speak, he just stood up and said, "Shout 'out' "! and sat down again.

The day we got underway the weather was grey and dreary—described as "dreach" by a local. We passed the Isle of Arran about which they say that if you can see it, it's about to rain, and if you can't, it's already raining. We entered Loch Fyne and were soon grappling with the first of the 19 hand-operated, do-it-yourself locks on the Crinan Canal, which allows boats to avoid passage around the often-rough Mull of Kintyre. Our flabby bodies, unaccustomed to the rigours of manual labour, protested as we struggled with the cranky cranks and heaved on the long beams to close the massive timber gates. Alex and Angus made some messy and hilarious attempts at making bread, while Egil went ashore to use one of those traditional red phone boxes to call the captain on his ship, which was awaiting orders off Kaohsiung. Egil said he could not fathom why some ship owners employed the cheapest captains and paid them as little as possible. "Pay peanuts, get monkeys" he said.

The canal terminated in the small village of Crinan, just across from Jura. Egil baulked at taking *Ozmaiden* through the Gulf of Corryvreckan, which was described in hair-raising terms in the almanac. We will hear more about this body of water later in these pages, but navigating such places is quite safe if you time it right. We made our way to Oban and thence up the Sound of Mull to Tobermory. The next morning a bridal veil of mist masked the town. So perfect was the stillness that we hardly dared to breathe. Using radar, we moved cautiously into the Sound of Mull until a fresh breeze tore the mist to tatters and swept it out into the grey Atlantic. We provisioned and fuelled at Fort William before entering the Caledonian Canal at Corpach, where we had to negotiate a flight of eight locks called Neptune's Staircase. We shared the locks with a sailboat which had taken part in the small ships evacuation of British troops from Dunkirk in 1940.

Over the next couple of days, we traversed the width of Scotland along the Great Glen. We negotiated 29 locks and crossed four lochs (lakes), including Loch Ness of monster fame.

We saw no monster but passed beneath the walls of Urquhart Castle, fought over by Robert the Bruce in the 13th century. The next day, we passed out through the sea lock at Inverness into the Moray Firth. From here our route took us north across the turbulent Pentland Firth to the Orkney Islands.

It was past midnight when we headed up Shapinsay Sound to Kirkwall. Despite the late hour, a couple of policemen sauntered by. "Just being nosy," one said. "Yon's a fine wee boat. Lucky ye didna' come last week. We had fog as thick as porridge movin' sideways a' forrty miles per hour." What I had taken to be a hairy fender lifted his leg to pee on a bollard as his master appeared from the shadows.

Later that morning we marvelled at the remains of the 5,000-year-old settlement of Skara Brae, Northern Europe's best preserved Neolithic settlement. It had been lost and forgotten until a severe storm in 1850 tore away some of the top cover and revealed the well-preserved underground dwellings. We also visited the well in Stromness where Sir John Franklin's vessels *Erebus* and *Terror* filled their water barrels early in their ill-fated voyage to search for the Northwest Passage. Captain Cook's ships *Resolution* and *Discovery* also watered here in 1780 on their return home from their failed search for the same route, during which Captain Cook was killed in Kealakekua Bay, Hawaii.

We gazed out over Scapa Flow, where the captured German fleet was scuttled by their crews after WW1 and where, in October 1939, an enterprising German U-Boat captain sneaked in and out past the defences to sink the British Battleship *Royal Oak*.

We continued north, moving easily over diminished swells under a sky overcast with pillowy squall lines. Occasional shafts of sunlight pierced the clouds, turning the sea to silver. Ahead of us the lone outpost of Fair Isle climbed slowly out of the sea, gradually revealing the houses of its 69 inhabitants, while towering cliffs dwarfed a few hardy fishermen riding the swells in their open cockleshell boats. The scarcity of people contrasted with the abundance of wildlife as the air around us was suddenly filled with birds that wheeled and swooped over the waves—fulmars, guillemots, arctic terns, gulls, puffins and huge gannets with dazzling-white, six-foot wings. Curious seals popped their heads out to watch. It was here that I received a call from Anton on the radio telephone. We exchanged news and he sounded very jovial. Little did I know that this was the last conversation we would ever have.

The only place for us to tie up when we arrived at Lerwick, in Shetland, was against the sea wall. We were awakened in the morning by the boat being slammed against it by the bow wave pushed ahead of the ferry from Bressay. It was a rude awakening but fortunately the damage to *Ozmaiden* was minor.

Having followed the fate of the tanker *Braer* with great interest, we were anxious to see the spot where it had run ashore. We hired a taxi and the driver told us that he had been out on the roads on the night of the accident. He told us that the wind was so strong, it was tearing the heather out by the roots and blowing it across the road. To reach the now-placid spot where the ship had foundered, we walked across a field carpeted with sea pinks. Only *Braer*'s bows were still visible above the surface where she had ridden the huge Atlantic rollers to her destruction on the jagged rocks. The starboard anchor was still snugged up to the hawse pipe. According to later reports, the ship lost power when spare pipes carried on deck broke loose in the heavy weather and snapped off the goose-necks from the bunker tank air vents. This allowed seawater to contaminate the diesel fuel, which put first the generator and then the main engine out of action. The ship drifted helplessly before winds as high as 100 mph and waves of 70 feet. In an incredible feat of flying under appalling conditions, the crew were taken off by helicopter before the ship struck the rocks. The winds remained at hurricane force for nine days.

We also visited Sullom Voe, the terminal for North Sea oil, and were pleasantly surprised by how inconspicuous it was.

The North Sea has a notorious reputation, so when a weather window opened, we took advantage of it and got underway at about 7 p.m. From Lerwick we headed out into the North Sea toward the coast of Norway some 200 hundred miles away. As darkness fell, the pilothouse became a world of its own in the green glow from the plotter and radar screens. The sound from the engines was no more than a reassuring heartbeat, quieter even than the rush of water past the hull. We skirted the edge of a group of oil platforms looking like aliens from *War of the Worlds* and had to alter course to avoid the only ship we met on the crossing.

I was on watch at dawn as we approached the Norwegian coast. It was misty with limited visibility, but the radar showed not only the coast but also a couple of other hidden vessels out there. Everything was nicely under control when Egil appeared, armed with a Good Morning towel. These were small Singapore-made towels with "Good Morning" embroidered on them. Egil had these in bulk and they were used for such tasks as keeping the boat free of dust. In a fit of early morning enthusiasm, Egil energetically ran his towel all over the control console, muttering remarks that started with "If" and ended with "do it yourself". He dusted all the instruments including the radar—spinning all the control knobs so that we instantly lost the image on the screen. The water off the Norwegian Coast is very deep and the depth sounder was flashing indicating that the bottom was beyond its reach. Egil said that it just needed resetting and turned off the circuit breaker. Unfortunately, this same breaker also controlled the autopilot and the GPS, so we lost them, as well. A conscientious navigator is supposed to know what course he is steering, but these days it is usually left to the autopilot, which automatically offsets deviations to allow for tide, etc. So in a matter of moments, we were blind and had lost our sense of direction. When I protested, Egil said it was good practice. Maybe—but off an unfamiliar rugged coast in fog with traffic? We slowed our speed and within a few minutes had everything back on track.

Our landfall was at Holmengraa, which means "grey rock". The deeper we penetrated into Sognafjord, which extends more than 100 miles inland, the higher and more brooding the mountains became. The water beneath our keel was an incredible 4,225 feet deep, with mountain peaks almost that high rising skyward from the surface. Egil had mentioned the possibility of tying alongside the cliffs but changed his mind when chunks of rock the size of Volkswagens broke free and plummeted into the depths.

Tiny towns huddled for shelter beneath towering mountains,

while diminutive farms, with pocket-sized hay meadows, clung to any precarious corner sufficiently level to permit cultivation. Everywhere waterfalls cascaded down precipitous crags, fed by the melting snow. Donning sweaters and heavy jackets, we stood on the flying bridge marvelling at the grandeur all around us, with the music of Grieg thundering from the speakers. We branched off into Aurlands Fjord and followed it to its very end, passing the Seven Sisters waterfall along the way. We found a berth in the small town of Flam, at the head of the fjord, and switched off the engines after 27 hours underway. This, I thought, is the very essence of cruising. Here we are surrounded by magnificent mountains and fjords in a country with different culture, food and language, yet we still sleep in the same berths and live in familiar surroundings. There is no other form of travel that provides the same experience. The following morning, we took a ride on a most amazing railway which, over a distance of 20 kilometres (12½ miles), climbed 863.6m (about a half-mile) from sea level, passing through 20 tunnels along the way.

Over the next few days we explored many of the other spectacular fjords that branch off from the Sognafjord. Wonder piled upon wonder until we ran out of superlatives to describe the breath-taking scenery. One evening we headed west toward a range of jagged, snow-capped peaks lit by the rays of the setting sun. A fierce wind with gusts as high as 38 knots kicked up, so we turned into Ese Fjord and anchored in the sheltering lee of the mountains, where the only sounds were of waterfalls tumbling down the sheer slopes. The next morning, I scrambled up a steep wild-flower-studded meadow, from which *Ozmaiden*, far below, looked like a toy boat.

In Fjaerlands Fjord, at the base of the Jistedalsbreen glacier, we reached our maximum northerly point of 61 degrees, 25 minutes—about the same latitude as Anchorage, Alaska. Though the sun sank briefly below the horizon each night, it stayed light enough to read a newspaper in the cockpit until well after midnight.

Our fjord tour complete, we headed south toward Bergen, where we moored alongside the wharf in the city centre. It was here that Alex and Angus had to return home, leaving just Egil and myself on board to take the boat back to Egil's residence near Fredrickstad, many miles to the south. I had received a message from Fred at Tung Hwa saying that Anton had overpaid around $80,000 for the last boat. This was completely out of character for Anton, with his negative attitude to the Taiwanese. I tried several times to reach him on the phone but got only his answering machine. I was tempted to call Chuck Hovey Yachts but hesitated to do so because, if Anton had been away working on his plane and I had called the dealer, he would have gone ballistic and I would never have heard the end of it.

When we reached Tananger, near Stavanger, I told Egil about my concerns and said that, if I did not hear from Anton that evening, I would call Chuck Hovey Yachts the following day. Egil persuaded me to call right away. I did and spoke to Maxine, the secretary and receptionist. Poor Maxine had to tell me that she had some bad news. In fact, she had some very bad news, and she went on to say that Anton had died some seven hours previously. Somehow I was expecting it, and it was not such a shock as you might think. The immediate question was where to go from here? I needed to get back to California as soon as possible, but I could not leave Egil in the lurch with no one to help him take his boat home, so we embarked on the marine equivalent of a series of forced marches to get back as soon as possible.

I had a phone call with Leslie, who needed money to handle Anton's funeral. She thought I had access to the company bank account in California and was surprised when I told her that I did not. I had personal money in the bank in Hong Kong, but they would not accept faxed instructions. Egil, whose bank allowed him to issue instructions by fax, very kindly offered to send the funds, which I repaid as soon as I could issue instructions to my bank. It was a rushed finale to a memorable trip, and I had much awaiting me on my return to California.

When I arrived I learnt that Anton had not suffered another heart attack, as I had assumed, but had died from acute leukaemia. He had complained of a small sore on his hand that had not healed. The doctor gave him some antibiotics, but over a period of three days he had collapsed and died. A memorial service was held in Newport Beach, a very tasteful affair at which myself and a number of Anton's friends spoke. When I looked into the company's business affairs, they were a mess. Anton had not filed taxes for two years, and even though we had not made a profit and no taxes were due, you are still obliged to file. There was a bunch of receipts all mixed up in a large brown paper envelope. Fortunately, because of my immigration status I had not been permitted to work in the U.S, and so I had not been officially involved in the California company. When Falmouth Yachts received a letter from the IRS, I wrote them to say that the sole proprietor was deceased and sent them a copy of the death certificate.

The letter I had sent to Anton setting out what should happen to the shares should one of us die was found, unsigned, among his papers. Fortunately, it was sufficient to prove intent. I paid Anton's two sons the $20,000 mentioned in the letter, plus I told them that Fleming Yachts owed Anton and myself $20,000 each. This was not recorded anywhere, but I told them that his share was, in all fairness, due to them. Anton did not have any money because he had spent it all on his plane, plus a couple of vintage Jaguar cars, so I paid his funeral expenses. The company itself was still struggling because, due to the stupid luxury tax, we had not received an order for 11 months.

I now had to decide where to go from here. It seemed to be generally believed by most people that I lacked business acumen and would probably screw up. I had a few offers from well-meaning people—who, no doubt, also had an eye on their own futures—to come into the company and run it. However, I always believed that most things are simply a matter of common sense, and I knew that I would not have made the mistakes that Anton had made, so I was quite confident that I could manage. At first I wasn't sure that we even needed a company in California. Fleming Yachts was now effectively just myself, and I dealt personally with a handful of dealers who all knew where I was and how to contact me at any given time. After giving it much thought, however, I decided that we needed to have a U.S. entity. I allowed Falmouth Yachts to die and started a new company with the name of Fleming

Yachts, Inc.—a California Corporation. One of my first actions was to organize a bookkeeper to keep the accounts and a company to look after the taxes.

Jackie and Nicky were both in England at the time because Mary was being treated for what appeared to be curable cancer. I wrote to Jackie, suggesting that, when she was available, she might join Fleming Yachts and run the California office while I was in Taiwan. She turned me down because, when she eventually returned to the U.S., she wanted to go to New Mexico and try to pursue her long-held dream of a western (in the cowboy sense) lifestyle. I decided not to press the point because there was no immediate rush and I thought she might change her mind. I was reluctant to ask Nicky and risk being turned down a second time! Also, she had the opportunity for a viable career in hotel management and catering. Then Jackie wrote to say that she thought Nicky was interested and might be hurt if I didn't ask. So I did ask, and she accepted, and that is how, in August 1993, she became a valuable member of Fleming Yachts.

Before Nicky started work, Louisa came over for a visit and we went on a road trip to the national parks of Sequoia and Yosemite, as well as to Mono Lake and the ghost town of Bodie. It was anything but a relaxed trip. At every opportunity, I had to use pay phones to access the answer machine in the Fleming Yachts office and deal with any messages left on it. How much easier it would have been in the age of cell phones and email!

Having decimated the boating industry in the U.S., the absurd luxury tax was finally abandoned during 1993. We badly needed to get new orders. I went to see Chuck and asked for his help. I said that I could give him a discount of $10,000 on any order he could give me. (Actually this would have been Anton's bonus, so it was not too painful!) As always, Chuck was very supportive and gave me an order for one boat. I then called Art Burr with the same discount and he offered to buy two boats—provided he could have the hull number I had already agreed to allocate to Chuck! I went back to Chuck, rather embarrassed, and told him what Art had said. He laughed and said, "What can I say?" So, within one week, I had three orders—the first for 11 months, and we never looked back after that until the wheels came off for everybody in 2008.

Now the sole owner of Fleming Yachts, and leaving Nicky in charge of the California office, I went to Taiwan in September 1993 for a few weeks before returning to the U.S. in October to attend the Annapolis Boat Show. Burr Yacht Sales had a Fleming 55 on display and there was always a queue of people waiting to view the boat. My clearest memory of the show was the evening it closed. In the middle of an exodus of muscle boats with booming megaphone exhausts, the Fleming 55 glided silently out of the harbour, looking every inch a lady in the evening light.

Nicky was back in California from her travels, living in Pasadena and working at a catering company. I spent the Christmas of 1993 in California with my daughters. We had a party of friends on board *Lion's Den*. Orders were now beginning to flow in, and the next few months were devoted to building up production and improving the boats. I had a policy of always introducing refinements on the next available boat. Some of these were a result of feedback from dealers or clients, some were due to new or improved equipment, and some stemmed from ideas that came to me—often in the middle of the night. I can state, quite honestly, that I never expected many of these refinements to be noticed by most people. I really only put them in to satisfy my own desires as a detail freak and because I thought they should be there. It has never ceased to amaze me how many people comment on the attention to detail and tell me that after owning a boat for several years they are still finding out why certain things were done the way they were. Looking back through the files, I see that we were averaging 10—15 refinements per boat, and that continues to this day.

The next major event, in the summer of 1994, was another trip with Egil in *Ozmaiden,* this time to Sweden. David Miles—who later became our dealer for the UK and most of Europe—was the captain on this trip. We collected the boat from her winter quarters at Malmon's Marina in southern Sweden, just south of the Norwegian border. The staff had laid on a bottle of chilled wine and a huge bowl of shrimp freshly boiled in sea water aboard the boat that had caught them. A beautiful arrangement of colourful freesias decorated the salon table. I have never forgotten the positive impression these thoughtful steps made to the start of a great trip. From there we made our way past Gothenburg to Copenhagen—capital of Denmark and one of the world's great maritime cities. Construction of a mammoth bridge linking Copenhagen with Malmo, in Sweden, started the following year. We headed north up the Baltic Sea to the Danish island of Bornholm, where we were joined by Alex. We continued overnight up the Gulf of Bothnia to Stockholm. Sweden's capital is built on a series of islands in waters which are fresh to the west and salt to the east. The medieval city of Gamla Stan stands on an island separating the two. Baltic traders, schooners, square-riggers, steamers and historic boats of every size and shape lined the wharves. On our first evening we took a dinner cruise on the steamer *Storskar*, celebrating her 125th year of service among the 24,000 islands of the Stockholm archipelago. Alex, an enthusiastic steam buff, immediately organized a visit to the engine room where, amid a symphony of whirling shafts, con-rods, levers, cams and ratchets, we travelled back to an age when steam was king.

Stockholm is a very interesting city which was spared the destruction inflicted on so many European cities during WWII. Of especial interest was a ship named *Vasa,* which capsized in the harbour on her maiden outing in August 1628. Despite initial attempts at recovery, she had remained in the mud on the bottom of the harbour for 333 years until she was salvaged and her timbers appeared once more above the surface in 1961. Although conservation is still ongoing, this historic vessel has been restored and is on display and open to visitors.

We stayed at a marina in Stockholm where the proprietor told us that he avoided frigid Swedish winters by escaping to Arizona. His dress code certainly reflected the Wild West more than what you might expect to see in Sweden, and the laundry room carried notices like: "Please remove ammunition before placing clothes in washer." He and Egil exchanged good-natured insults. Norway had been in a union with Sweden until 1905, so there is always rivalry between Swedes and Norwegians. This was the middle of June and they were still launching boats for the summer season. I later corresponded with him in August to send him some photos, and he told me that they had already started lifting boats for winter storage. Despite this short season and the incredibly high cost of living, Sweden has the highest boat ownership per capita of any country, although the boats tend to be smaller in size.

From Stockholm we returned to Gothenburg by way of the Göta Canal, on which work started in 1810. Parts of it were engineered by Thomas Telford, who was also responsible for the Caledonian Canal across Scotland. Sixty thousand men laboured for 22 years to build the Göta, using little more than wheelbarrows, gunpowder and wooden shovels. This was a very different kind of boating, moving placidly though calm water, the air redolent with the scent of apple blossom and wild flowers. The canal links the large inland lakes of Vattern and Vanern before dropping 105 feet into the Göta River through a series of large locks which bypass the Trollhattan Falls.

Tragically, Mary's cancer had returned and both Jackie and Nicky had returned to England to take care of her. I called in to see them on my return from Sweden. Mary's prognosis was not good and, although I had done what I could to support her in various ways, I was not very optimistic about the outcome. I returned first to Taiwan, then to California. Unfortunately, it was as I had feared, and on September 9th, 1994, Nicky called me in California to tell me that Mary had died. I immediately jumped on a plane and 24 hours later was with my daughters. Her funeral was arranged and people we had not seen for years came from far and wide to attend. I don't know why it so often takes a funeral to bring together friends and acquaintances we haven't seen for years. The funeral was memorable because it was held in a building with a large picture window overlooking the beautiful English countryside. A huge storm was brewing, and at a key moment in the ceremony there was a flash of lighting accompanied by a loud thunderclap. A low-flying military transport plane flew across the scene while the strains of "Amazing Grace" filled the chapel.

In October 1994 Jackie and Nicky returned to California, and shortly thereafter Nicky and I pitched in and bought Jackie a used Ford truck for her to take to New Mexico to start her life there. Of course I had known that she was interested in horses as a child, but I had not been aware that she had secretly nursed an ambition to live in the Wild West since an early age. I returned to Taiwan and there followed a number of years of reasonable stability, during which I ran the company with Nicky's invaluable assistance.

Chapter 6

Early 1995 to July 1998

Taiwan

I buy a house in Newport Beach and make a cruise to British Columbia with another Fleming customer. I start using digital video and become a U.S. citizen. I make another Norwegian cruise to Aalesund. I break my ankle in Taiwan and reconnect with Carole. I make my first trip to Antarctica. My nephew, Adi, joins Fleming Yachts. We design and start work on a larger boat.

When my income eventually reached the point where it exceeded my modest expenditure on a reliable basis, I had to think what to do with the surplus. Interest rates in the 1980s were well into the double digits, and the Hong Kong Bank were paying compound interest, accrued daily, on savings accounts. This was very satisfactory, and I should have left things as they were for as long as this situation existed. However, I somehow got talked into having an investment "portfolio". I should have known better! The previous time I had gone this route, in Singapore, it had been a disaster and so it proved this time—although, years later, it inadvertently led to a very positive outcome.

The investment company sent me monthly computer printouts showing how my "basket" of investments was doing. Early in 1995, the printout showed that my investments had, in one month, dropped in value by an amount more than double the annual salary I was paying myself for working like a dog. I was absolutely outraged. All these people in their natty suits had to do was to manage investments like mine while I was sweating blood earning real money. It made me realize that the money earned as a result of all my hard work had been reduced to figures on a computer printout, with no tangible evidence of anything real. The figures could just change from month to month and there was no explanation—or even "Sorry, old chap" —if, as in this case, the figures shrank to such a degree that it would take me more than two years of hard work to cover the paper losses. I thought then—and still do—that this was a game that had no rules and over which I had no control, and I didn't want to play any longer. So I told them to sell every share and turn them into cash. Of course they tried to talk me out of it, but I was disgusted and adamant.

I was still living on my Grand Banks and paying $700 per month for the slip. I figured that, if I could buy a house on the waterfront with a slip in front of it where I could keep my boat, the $700 could go toward paying the mortgage. At least it would be a tangible asset, and if the price went up or down it would still exist and I could see it, touch it and live in it when I was in the U.S. This epiphany came to me while flying back to California, and the following day I went to visit Chuck Hovey in his office and I told him my thoughts. He advised me that the best place to look was on the Balboa Peninsula. The next day was a Saturday and I decided to drive around the area. I saw one property that had a sign outside saying "Open House", meaning that it was available to walk into to take a look. I was too shy to do so and I continued looking in different neighbourhoods around the harbour. In the end I told myself not to be a fool and go back to look at the open house because that was the reason for it being open!

I was my usual scruffy self but, surprisingly, the real estate agent took my interest seriously and, to cut to the chase, I concluded a deal to buy the house by the following Thursday—less than one week after I had formulated my tentative plan! It was frighteningly expensive and it took all the money I had to put down the 25-percent deposit, but that property quadrupled in value over the next 12 years and proved to be the best possible investment I could have had.

In August of 1995, I had been invited to go on a different

cruise in a Fleming 55, this time to the waters off British Columbia, in Western Canada. In 1792, Captain Vancouver bestowed the highly inappropriate name of Desolation Sound on this beautiful area, having noted in his log that "there was not a single prospect that was pleasing to the eye"! What can he have been thinking? Today the area is sparsely inhabited and looks much like it did to Captain Vancouver, aside from the bald scars of clear cuts in the mantle of evergreen trees which cloak the soaring mountains.

My guide and host, Dick Clayton, had cruised these waters for many years and thought nothing of heading out by himself in search of salmon in his Fleming 53, *Divona Sea*. With its bears, eagles and natural beauty, this is undoubtedly one of the prime cruising grounds in the world. Due to tidal anomalies, sea levels in places only a mile or two apart can differ by as much as three feet; and the battle to correct this imbalance gives rise to maelstroms of rips, eddies and whirlpools. In narrow channels, currents reach speeds as high as 16 knots with every change in the tide, as water races back and forth to fill and empty long arms of the sea. The passes, as these are called, act as psychological filters, separating boaters who have neither the time nor the confidence to navigate them from more adventurous souls who view them as a challenge. Fortunately for me, Dick was one of the latter group. In fact, the passes do not pose any threat to a well-built boat provided they are navigated at slack water—which can, in some cases, last only a few minutes.

Squadrons of float planes use the channels as flyways, bringing fishermen and tourists to and from the lodges where they fish for coho and steelhead. They also act as convenient taxis, taking people to and from a boat in response to a GPS location. Each cruise aboard a Fleming was not only a wonderful experience for myself but provided grist for further magazine articles and reprints. More importantly it widened my cruising experience, enabling me to incorporate more useful and practical features into the production boats.

We had to produce brochures, which was quite a burden when there was so much else to do, but now people were starting to ask for videos as well. I learned that it would cost at least $50,000 to have a video made professionally, which made it completely out of the question, but I was sure I had the technical skills to make videos myself. I had the advantage of spending extended time in the yard, as well as on board completed boats, which would allow me to produce more interesting and informative videos.

Video at that time was VHS of very inferior quality, which degraded with each generation in the editing process. I still had all my 16mm film equipment but did not know how effectively this would transfer to video. I decided to have one of my existing films transferred to find out. I took it to a place in Santa Ana and discussed my options with the guy who ran the business. He told me that my timing was perfect, as we were on the brink of a revolution in digital video and editing. The first digital camera was the VX1000 made by Sony, and the problem was that they were in such short supply they were almost impossible to obtain. I was told that only three cameras had been allocated for the 40 Sony dealers in the whole of Southern California! I mentioned this to Art Burr, our dealer on the East Coast, and he managed to get hold of a camera for me from a dealer in central Florida in October 1995. It was with this camera that I got back into the business of making moving pictures.

My first project was to make a promotional video for the 55. I started off by shooting construction scenes at the yard. Having captured video on tape, the next step was to edit the footage. I made an expedition to NAB, the huge computer show in Las Vegas, to select a suitable programme. The show extended over several exhibition halls and was so crowded it was hard even to walk the aisles. The only recourse was to list which exhibits to visit and concentrate on those. I purchased a desktop PC loaded with the Speed Razor editing programme. This was early days in non-linear editing and it was a nightmare. The computer kept crashing or jumbling up the edited clips, destroying hours of work. After struggling with these frustrations for days, it then proved impossible to export the finished video. The only way to save the situation was to physically remove the hard drive from my computer and load it into another. It was not an encouraging start!

535

Chuck Hovey had long been pestering me about building a larger boat as a move up for his existing Fleming customers. I was not keen on the idea because I thought the 55 was quite large enough and, having no ambitions for empire building, I was reluctant to make the investment in time, effort and money such a project would involve. My bottom line was simply whether I was making enough money to support a reasonably modest lifestyle and whether I had enough time to enjoy it.

One day one of our 55 owners came to my office and asked whether, if I really did not intend to build a larger boat, I would have any objection if he went to Larry Drake and ask him to design him a larger boat to look exactly like a Fleming? Hmmm! Now that made me think! I realized that if I agreed with his proposal and then later wanted to build a bigger boat, I would be screwed. After mulling it over, I commissioned Larry to design a larger Fleming. I consulted with Chuck, and by the time we had incorporated all the features he wanted, the boat had grown to 73 feet. The design fees came to $10,000 and the guy whose request had sparked the work did not follow through, so I shelved the project.

During the summer of 1996 I accompanied Egil on another trip to Norway in *Ozmaiden*. This time we went from Sweden across the Skagerrack and around the southern tip of Norway up the west coast. It was hard to envisage navigation through these waters before the advent of modern charts. Imagine yourself surrounded on every hand by a labyrinth of rocks, islands, inlets and channels, all appearing almost identical. The obvious opening proves to be a dead end, while the correct route lies through a narrow, rock-strewn creek that starts improbably by heading in quite the wrong direction. Once lost, you could spend a lifetime trying to find your way out of this bewildering maze. GPS provides a huge advantage because, should you lose track, it tells you right away where you are, rather than you having to try to figure it out from what your eyes tell you. And it is very important to know your exact position because, everywhere, unmarked rocks lie in wait for the unwary.

We passed the entrance of the Sognefjord, which had been our landfall in 1993, and stopped at the beautiful little town of

Hardbakke, nestled at the foot of a mountain of bare rock. The streets of the town wound between boulders the size of houses and, apart from a short length of road linking it to an adjacent island, it was accessible only by water. The following morning it was the school boat—rather than the school bus—that disgorged its cargo of kids, colourfully attired in woolly hats and anoraks, on their way to their lessons.

The approaches to the town lay along natural channels bordered by high bluffs of absolutely barren rock. Large boulders, abandoned by retreating glaciers, perched precariously on the slopes and summits. We spotted a distant sign and wondered what it said. Alex, with his impish sense of humour, looked at it through binoculars and said, "It says 'do not throw stones at this sign.' ". The buds of ash trees were only now starting to reveal hints of life, and primroses still peered shyly out from the grassy banks.

From Hardbakke, we ventured out to a collection of small islands and skerries known as Bulandet. Remote and exposed, Bulandet is Norway's most westerly settlement and the first to encounter the onslaught of the North Sea gales. Farther north and still on the fringes of Norwegian settlement, we skirted the island of Kinn and its prominent landmark Kinnaklova, a huge, cloven rock from which the island gets its name. Nestled at the rock's foot is a 900-year-old church, still in use, and believed to have been founded by Celts fleeing religious persecution.

Weather is always a factor when cruising these waters and never more so than when planning to round the Statt Peninsula, which juts into the Norwegian Sea like a clenched fist at the end of a defiant forearm. Known locally as the Cape Horn of Norway, it acts like a magnet for winds that can whip placid seas into a fury in a matter of minutes. It is so notorious that serious consideration had been given to boring a huge tunnel at its landward end large enough to accommodate ferries and small freighters.

We used the faster speeds of which *Ozmaiden* was capable to sneak through a narrow weather window between two of the low pressure systems marching across the North Sea. We stopped for a couple of days in the town of Aalesund and from there penetrated the mountains and cruised the fjords leading to Geiranger. Along the way we passed Tafjord, where, in 1934, a rock of titanic proportions had broken loose, creating a tidal wave 200 feet high that had swept along the fjord, killing 41 people. As we penetrated deeper into the heart of this dramatic landscape, it was easy to understand how earlier generations isolated from each other during the long, dark nights of winter could have believed that malevolent trolls lived in these brooding mountains.

The big event for me was that on May 31st, 1996, I became a U.S. citizen. This had been a very long and tortuous process extending over 11 years. It had started when I applied for a Green Card in 1985 on the basis of my working with Falmouth Yachts.

The immigration department required that Anton advertise for my position in a number of publications of their choice and then interview those who applied for the job to prove that there was no American citizen who was qualified. The job called for experience in building boats in the Far East and marketing them to clients in the U.S. This was unique and specialized experience so, other than taking months, it was not too difficult to prove that I was the best-qualified candidate for the job. My application was approved in general, but I then had to face a series of additional hurdles.

Because I was living and working in Taiwan—which, following Nixon's visit to mainland China, was not recognized by America as being a legitimate country—the closest U.S. embassy through which I could formally apply was in Hong Kong. One of the initial requirements was a Certificate of Non-Criminal Activity from every country in which I had spent more than six months during my lifetime! In my case, this included a long list of countries which had once been British colonies but which were now independent, with their own governments and police forces. I thought that this was a hopeless task, but I applied to each and every one of them, including such places as Zimbabwe. Much to my surprise, they all eventually responded, and I sent the certificates to my immigration lawyer in Los Angeles. To obtain these certificates I had first to be fingerprinted by an officially recognized authority. For this I chose the Hong Kong Police Force, which meant, of course, that I had to travel to Hong Kong.

My waste-of-space lawyer then mislaid the certificates which I had gone to so much trouble to obtain. I wrote to all the various countries again to obtain duplicates, but every one of them replied to say that these were not available. So I had to start from scratch and reapply all over again, including flying to HK to be re-fingerprinted.

Once past this hurdle, the next step was a personal interview at the U.S. embassy in Hong Kong. I went there at the appointed time and was left standing outside on the sidewalk in the hot sun along with many others, as only a few people were allowed in at one time. Finally, I was permitted to enter and was interviewed by an American. He looked through my application and said that if I had really done all the things I claimed to have done, then I should have evidence to prove it and I should go away and return with the proof!

Fortunately for me I am a pack rat and I had kept copies of newspaper clippings and magazine articles documenting my involvement with American Marine. The problem was that all this stuff was stored in boxes and folders scattered between Taiwan, California, and England. It took me several months to collect and collate all this material, after which I returned to Hong Kong and the U.S. embassy with it all in a large binder.

I gave it to the clerk, who handed it to the American, who returned it to me together with a pack of Post-it notes with instructions to put one on every page showing where my name was mentioned. It took about an hour to do this, and I handed it back. I saw the American in the back of the office flip through it for maybe half a minute. He smiled (not at me); I doubt whether anyone had ever been able to produce so much evidence, and it was only luck and my packrat tendencies that had made it possible. I was now approved for a Green Card but had to wait for months before it was actually issued. When it did finally arrive, this precious, expensive, and hard-won document came through the regular mail in a plain brown envelope and was almost discarded with the junk mail. You would think that it would be sent registered or recorded mail.

Once you have had a Green Card for five years you can apply for citizenship with the very reasonable proviso that you must have spent a minimum of 50 per cent of that time in the U.S. In my case, I did not qualify because I spent most of my time working in Taiwan. In fact, the immigration officials at airports—most especially Seattle—often gave me a hard time whenever I returned to the U.S. I remember one official of Filipino origin pointing to the words on my Green Card which read "Permanent Resident" and asking whether I could see that. I said "I see it", told him that my work took me outside the country for extended periods, and asked him what were the rules governing the length of such absences. He just pointed again at the Permanent Resident words on my Green Card and asked again if I could see it. I guess he had reached the limits of his command of the English language.

I had to wait six years before I met the 50-per cent rule and, even then, by just 10 days. In fact, my interviewer in California insisted on checking with a higher authority to make sure that I still qualified. I was tested on American history and had to write a sentence in English without making a single grammatical or spelling error. I think that would be a challenge to many born in the country.

Finally, it was time for the mass ceremony in LA, which was very well executed. We had our precious Green Cards confiscated and were issued with a Certificate of Citizenship. We were issued with diminutive American flags and collectively chanted the Oath of Allegiance. We were encouraged to register to vote on the spot and I was bemused to see that I was required to register as a Republican, Democrat, or unwilling to declare. I thought this was truly bizarre. Which party I voted for would depend not only on their policies at the time of voting but also the quality of their candidates. It was my first intimation that democracy in the United States differed significantly from anything I had experienced in the past.

I had to leave the U.S. shortly after this to return to Taiwan. I was able to use my British passport when I arrived in Taiwan but I had a problem when I returned to the U.S. I no longer had my Green Card and I had not yet had time to acquire a U.S. passport, so I showed them my Certificate of Citizenship. This earned me a trip to what they call "secondary" and it took about an hour before they would allow me back into the country of which I was now a bona fide citizen.

On one of my many flights on Cathay Pacific I had read an article in their in-flight magazine about visiting Antarctica. I had long nursed ambitions to travel to this alien part of the world and had contacted Adventure Associates in Sydney and requested a brochure. By this time, Egil had retired and moved to Sydney, and I asked them to add his name to their mailing list. During 1996, Egil wrote to me to ask whether I would be interested in joining him and his sister on a voyage from Hobart to the Ross Sea. We had to book several months in advance, and it was hard to know for sure what I would be doing that far ahead, but I took a chance on it and we made the reservations. This was of course a very special trip, and I was sorry that I did not have more leisure to anticipate and savour the upcoming journey. Instead, it was more a matter of suddenly realizing that I was off to Antarctica the following week and it was yet another thing that had to be organized.

I flew to Sydney and stayed with Egil for a couple of days before flying on to Hobart, in Tasmania. Our ship, the *Bremen*, came into harbour early on the morning of January 7th, 1997. We boarded at four in the afternoon and were serenaded by a pipe band marching up and down the dock. *Bremen* was a purpose-built, expedition ship constructed in just nine months by Mitsubishi and staffed by German officers with Filipino crew. For this voyage the ship had been chartered by an Australian company, so most of the passengers were Australian.

The latitude of Hobart is just shy of 43 degrees South, so it is already well into the Roaring Forties. We encountered large swells as soon as we left the shelter of the Derwent River, and there were plenty of empty chairs in the dining room for the first few days of the trip. Voyaging to Antarctica is akin to visiting another planet. *Bremen* became our space ship and the outside world was irrelevant. It took one week to reach the Antarctic continent, with one stop along the way at sub-Antarctic Macquarie Island. All around us was the endlessly undulating sea, over which wandering albatrosses swooped effortlessly without a beat from their 10-feet wings. The ship's bridge was open 24 hours per day and only closed during moments of intense activity, such as docking.

We attended a series of voluntary lectures by every kind of -ologist you have ever heard of—ornithologist, zoologist, geologist, glaciologist, biologist, meteorologist—plus a historian. I was completely ignorant before going on the trip and, as usual, had done minimum research. I had no previous knowledge of the exploration of Antarctica other than the deaths of Scott's party on their way back from the South Pole. There were lectures on what is called the heroic era in the exploration of the continent. I learnt about Shackleton and other explorers who had endured unbelievable hardships in the early 20th century. There had been better maps of the moon than of Antarctica until as recently as the late 1950s.

Macquarie Island appeared over the horizon on the morning of the third day. The island was administered by Australia and had a permanently manned ranger station. A colourful character by the name of Ferret came on board and gave a talk.

The routine for landings was for the scout boat to go ashore first and select a suitable landing site. A succession of Zodiac rubber boats was launched from the ship, using a crane, and brought alongside the boarding platform at the side of the ship. The black Zodiaks were driven by members of the ship's crew, from officers to the women who doubled as waitresses. All passengers had previously been allocated a group. The order in which the groups were loaded —from first to last—was rotated with each successive landing. Everyone had to pass through an area called the mud room, where you donned or removed your boots. All boots had to be washed off after each landing to reduce the chance of carrying some kind of bug from one island or landing spot to another. There was a board on which there was a numbered tag for every passenger. When leaving the ship, we had to turn over our tag, then reverse it back again on returning aboard. The ship could not depart until the board had been checked and every passenger accounted for. The chance of survival for any passenger left behind and marooned in Antarctica was not too good.

The amount of wildlife came as a complete surprise to me.

542

The beaches were populated with hundreds of thousands of penguins of numerous species—including kings, rock-hoppers and royals—that only exhibited mild curiosity at our appearance. Lying all over the beaches were large numbers of elephant seals that entirely ignored our presence. In fact, you had to look where you were going to avoid tripping over them. Elephant seals are mammals which can dive to more than 2,000 feet and stay underwater for as long as two hours, slowing their heart rate to one beat per minute.

The following day we continued our journey south and crossed the convergence where freezing water from Antarctica meets relatively warmer water. Shortly thereafter, we spotted our first iceberg and entered the fringes of the pack ice. All the while, the period of darkness decreased until it disappeared altogether and we were bathed in continual daylight, with the ship's shadow stretching to the horizon. There is no room in this account to do more than touch on the highlights, but a visit to Antarctica is truly like visiting an alien planet. It is a jewellery box of wonders in which the only colours are blue, white and black. There is no vegetation and the only hint of green is from occasional algae growing on the surface of the ice. The ice itself can be the most intense electric blue. The inhabitants of this land were penguins, seals, whales and birds; and almost all ignored your presence unless you strayed too close to a skua's nest. The constant daylight confuses your biological clock and you are afraid to go to sleep in case you miss something.

We visited the hut from which Scott left on his ill-fated expedition to the pole. Although 80 years had passed, it was almost as if he and his men had departed the day before and were expected to return at any moment. There were leftover provisions on the shelves and clothes hanging on hooks. Scott's hut was later used by Shackleton's southern party when their ship, *Aurora*, was swept out to sea by a blizzard. The anchors lie still buried in the sand with the lines leading into the sea, and there remains the skeleton of a dog still chained to a peg with a collar around the bones of its neck. We also visited Shackleton's hut at Cape Evans, where a party from New Zealand were engaged in arresting the further decay of the many artefacts.

We cruised a short distance along the face of the Ross Ice Shelf—a body of ice about the size of France. Its seaward face, extending for about 375 miles, was about 100 feet high with a further 800 feet hidden beneath the surface.

We revisited Cape Adair on our return journey. The weather was very different this time and it was deemed too rough for a landing. One of our lecturers told us of a landing made by geologists using a helicopter. Before they had time to erect their tent they were hit by winds of over 100 mph, which lasted for 12 hours while they hunkered down among the rocks. The helicopter made it back to the ship but was damaged by the wind. One seaman was blown over the ship's side. He landed on an ice flow and broke his leg, so in that sense he was lucky. We later heard that on the trip after ours, the ship had had to steam at full speed for three days to hold her course against the wind, all the while dodging icebergs. Eventually they had to abandon the trip and return to Hobart.

North from here we encountered winds of Beaufort force 12 and wave heights of 50 feet, but most passengers had their sea legs by this time. Meals continued to be served in the dining room, with chairs tethered to the deck and loose furniture roped together. It was bizarre to look out over the tumultuous seas, watching albatross cruising serenely past the windows into the ferocious wind. We saw more icebergs and stopped at the Auckland Islands, where we went ashore to observe, close up, albatross sitting on their nests. We took on board a group of ornithologists who told us that the albatross allowed them to remove their eggs to weigh them and then replace them while remaining on the nest.

Three weeks after our departure we arrived back in Hobart, to be welcomed by a choir of schoolgirls. A couple of days later I was back in Taiwan, scarcely able to believe that I had just returned from the bottom of the earth. This was my first real journey since owning my digital video camera and I had captured several hours of raw video, but it was several years before I had the right equipment—and the time—to create a video of this amazing trip.

When we returned to Sydney and caught up with the news, we

learned that while we had been in Antarctica the Southern Ocean had been the scene of a major drama. Several yachts taking part in the Vendee Globe round-the-world race had come to grief in the rough conditions. The most publicized of these was Tony Bullimore, who was rescued on January 5th by the Australian navy after spending three days without food in an air pocket in his upturned boat. The whole event was captured on camera, and I was amazed, after I returned to the U.S., to find that no one had even heard of the incident. It is alarming how insular the U.S. media can be about incidents that occur overseas.

We also learned that on January 6th, Egil's erstwhile *Ozmaiden* crew member Alex Ritchie had been credited with saving Richard Branson's life in a balloon incident over Algeria. This had occurred less than 24 hours after the balloon "Virgin Global Challenger" carrying Branson, Alex and Per Lindstrand, had taken off from Morocco and set off east across the Sahara Desert. The balloon had crossed into Algeria at an altitude of 30,000 feet when it began losing height precipitously, hurtling towards the ground at 40 feet per second. I later watched a Nova documentary about the incident. In response to Branson's agitated "What shall we do?" Alex had laconically responded with the single word "Panic!" He had then donned a parachute and climbed out onto the exterior roof of the capsule, where he jettisoned a fuel tank and other equipment, slowing the balloon's descent and enabling it to make a safe landing.

Tragically, almost exactly one year later, again in Morocco, Alex was involved in a sky-diving accident which ultimately claimed his life. While training for another balloon bid for the round-the-world record, he fell some 13,000 feet onto a concrete car park when his Moroccan-packed parachute failed to open properly. Amazingly, he survived the fall and was taken back to Britain, where he underwent numerous operations, but he developed a form of blood poisoning and died three months later. It was very sad and his death seemed so unnecessary.

In September 1997, Chuck Hovey Yachts organized the very first Fleming owners' rendezvous. This was dubbed the Fleming Fling and was held at the new marina in the small town of Sidney, on Vancouver Island. Chuck wanted me to take the drawings of the Fleming 75 with me, but I firmly told him that I had no plans to build the boat and that the larger boat was not on the table for discussion.

The event was held over two days, on the 7th to 9th of September, and one of items on the agenda was a question and answer session with myself. One of the participants was a rather pushy individual who owned an older 55, which he was trying to bring up to date in line with newer models. He stood up from the back of the room and asked me about the Fleming 75. I answered by saying that a boat had been designed but had been shelved. More recently, the project had been moved from the shelf to the back burner, but there were no immediate plans to take it any further.

Within 10 minutes of the session's end, three people came up to me wanting to give me a deposit for the 75! I did not give them an outright "no" and told them I would think about it. I now realized that I was the only person standing in the way of building the boat. Tung Hwa had already told me that they wanted to do it. Nicky told me that she wanted the company to continue after I had, as she put it, "popped off". The dealers—and now the customers—wanted it. I felt as if I were standing alone holding up my hand in front of a wall of vehicles revving their engines. But I was also very aware that if I were to utter that single word "yes", it would be akin to lighting the fuse on a rocket and would set off an irrevocable chain of events from which there was no going back. A few days later, I did eventually say the magic word, thereby committing myself to three years of work to design, develop and deliver the first 75.

Also in September 1997, I attended the Southampton International Boat Show in England. We had a 55 on display and it was the first Southampton show we had been in for several years. While I was on the side of the boat away from the dock, I heard a voice I vaguely recognized asking whether this boat had anything to do with Tony Fleming. I walked around the cockpit and found myself face to face with a grey-haired man. We looked at each other for a couple of moments, and then I realized that he

546

was Jerry Phillips, with whom I had used to sail in Hong Kong 36 years ago!

We started chatting and he told me that there was a group of the same sailing crowd up in the beer tent. I went to meet them and so became re-acquainted with a group I had last seen when we were all in our 20s. They regularly meet at every Southampton Boat Show.

I exchanged contact details with Jerry and a few months later received a fax from him to which he had attached a photocopy of a page from the HK Police Gazette, stating that Carole was searching for me. Jerry asked me whether I wanted to be found. I told him "Yes", and he sent the details to the Gazette, which passed them on to Carole. She knew I had at some point been associated with the police and she knew I had been in Hong Kong. She mistakenly thought that the two events were connected, and in her search, which had started in March 1977, had contacted the HK Police Gazette in July of that same year. Carole got the news that I had been located on January 31 1998. We have since met and have been in regular contact by email ever since.

Life is full of strange coincidences. The fact that the boat bearing my name had been at the show and Jerry had the curiosity to ask had led to me meeting my old sailing buddies and being reunited with Carole, whom I had not seen since her wedding in 1960.

The Utopia Hotel in Kaohsiung, which had been my home for quite a while, was being demolished, so I moved to a slightly better hotel in the same area. There was a car park in the basement but only one elevator led to it, so I usually took the back stairs down from the lobby. One morning in the spring of 1998, being in my usual, heedless hurry, I caught my heel on one of the steps and fell backwards onto my leg, which folded beneath me. When I tried to stand, my left foot wobbled around at the end of my leg, which I knew was not good. These stairs were not really for the use of guests and were little used. I hopped on my good leg down to the next level, where I could catch the elevator. Once there, I had the choice of going up to the lobby and hopping across it, looking like a real idiot with my computer bag over my shoulder, or I could go up to the 12th floor and hop along to my room, where I could phone reception for assistance. I decided on the latter, and they sent a manager up to my room who called for an ambulance. I then phoned Louisa, who called Fred, who had just left his apartment to go to work. His wife took the call and yelled to him out of the window as he was getting into his car. The ambulance arrived and carted me off to hospital with its siren going (as they say in Taiwan) *"Oar—Eee! Oar- Eee!"* through the streets of Kaohsiung.

At the hospital they X-Rayed my ankle and told me it was fractured in four places. Good job! They admitted me, iced my ankle and scheduled me for surgery the following morning. Fred arrived and nervously impressed on the hospital that they really needed to fix me up, as we were at the start of a major project. No one is really indispensable (the cemeteries are full of indispensable people), but there was no denying that I was playing a key role at that time. Louisa showed up and kept me company.

The following morning, they prepped me for surgery. They did not want to give me a general anaesthetic because I had no close relatives in Taiwan. I asked what difference that made, and the surgeon told me that anaesthesia involved the heart and lungs and therefore more risk. I endured a spinal block administered with a scary needle and lay awake during the course of the operation, which lasted four hours. I could hear the noise of all the drills, etc., and the crew chatted away, although I couldn't understand what they were saying. They asked me whether I was happy with the background music.

I was in hospital for several days, during which I was visited by large numbers of people from the yard and from subcontractors and suppliers. A couple of guys from Caterpillar even flew from Hong Kong to visit me, and my room was full of flowers. I think that the nursing staff and doctors were most impressed! I know that I was!

The 75 had reached the stage where the planking lines had been marked on the hull plug, and Fred wanted me to review them before they went ahead and cut them. They came and got me out of hospital and drove me to the yard to take a look before returning me back to my bed. It was an extremely hot day and it was not a comfortable excursion. I was quite exhausted by the time I got back to my hospital bed!

After I was discharged, with a cast on my leg, I was given a bunch of pain killers and antibiotics. I immediately came out in a terrible rash caused by an allergic reaction to the antibiotic. I think my body had simply decided that it had had enough of that particular drug and rejected it. The reaction made me feel worse than at any other time since the accident, but it cleared up once they changed the meds, and I was only off work for about 10 days. Fortunately, as in Mexico, it was my left leg, so it did not affect my ability to drive a car with automatic transmission.

One of the first things awaiting me when I returned to work was a climb up on top of the boat deck, atop the deck plug, to figure out the next step of the design details. This was about 10 feet up in the air and I had to negotiate a set of wheeled steps on crutches. When I got up there, I realized that it was impossible to see the bow from the proposed helm position. I kept piling up wood blocks to raise my height, but had to clump my way to the forward end of the pilothouse roof before I could see the bow. I came to the reluctant conclusion that the boat would need to be constructed with a flying bridge on top of the pilothouse.

The breakfast served in the hotel was buffet style, and it had never previously occurred to me how difficult it was to serve yourself from a buffet display while on crutches. One of the waitresses accompanied me, putting my choices onto a plate as I pointed them out to her. It did make me realize—again—that if you plan on breaking a limb, don't break more than one at a time. Two legs—or even one arm and a leg—entirely change the rehabilitation scenario. For some reason the hotel kept the temperature in the dining room very cold. One day a small girl said something that made everyone laugh, and I asked for a translation. She had said it was so cold that her goosebumps had goosebumps!

Living in a place like Taiwan exposed me to a number of unusual experiences which are worth recounting if only to make you pause to realize how lucky we are. On a bus excursion to

Kenting, organized by a pub called the Dewdrop Inn, I found myself sitting next to a German who was one of a number of foreign advisors to Taiwan's large steel-making operation, China Steel. He told me that he was originally from East Germany, where his grandparents had been driven from their land when the Russians had chased the retreating Germans back west. Not surprisingly, the Russians were enraged and thirsting for revenge. They contaminated German farmland with oil to make it impossible to grow crops on it, leaving his grandparents on the verge of starvation. My acquaintance told me that, as a teenager, he managed to get permission to visit West Germany to attend a family wedding, after which he did not return to East Germany. He found lowly work in the steel industry and eventually worked his way up to his present position.

At the yard we had a janitor, I will call him Chang, who had an interesting story. As a young man during the 1940s he was married with a couple of kids, living with his wife in a rural village in Yunnan Province, in southwest China. Chiang Kai Shek's soldiers were approaching the area, seizing what they wanted from the local people and impressing young men into the Nationalist army. Chang decided he would be better off if he volunteered for what he expected to be a few months' service. In fact, Chiang Kai Shek was defeated by the communists under Mao Tse Tung, and the group of which Chang was part were driven into the jungles of Burma. Here they remained for several years until they were repatriated to Nationalist Taiwan. Many years passed, with no contact permitted between Taiwan and the communist mainland. Finally, mail was permitted to pass between the two territories, and Chang sent a letter to his old village address, not really expecting a reply. Instead he discovered that he was the patriarch of a large brood. His wife was still alive; his children had grown up and married and now had children of their own. There was a belief in those days amongst people on the mainland that people in Taiwan were immensely wealthy. There was also some resentment because those on the mainland who had relatives in Taiwan were treated with suspicion by the communist authorities and given a bad time because of it. This created a feeling that somehow the people in Taiwan "owed" those on the mainland. When restrictions further eased and Taiwanese were permitted to travel to the mainland—by way of Hong Kong or Macau—Chang visited his family, loaded with gifts. He found that they did not want to see him but what he had brought. He awoke one night to find his grandson rifling his pockets, looking for cash. He returned to Taiwan and received letters asking him to replace the family buffalo—even a letter from the headmaster of the local school, asking for funds to support the school! Because he was from Taiwan, they all assumed he was a rich businessman rather than just the janitor.

One evening after work, Fred and I were chatting outside the office before leaving for home. Fred exchanged a few words with one of the workers who was about to leave on his motorcycle. The following morning Fred told me that the guy on the motorcycle had been killed in a solo accident on his way home. A few days later I heard some excited chatter in the general office and went to see what was going on. Two security guards had just learned that the guy had been killed several days before, but the two of them said they had individually seen the guy in the yard on the evening after the date of his death. One of them had even spoken to him and said, "Working late tonight?" but the guy had not replied.

The painter foreman, whom we called Small Lin, was in the office while this was going on, and he said that the previous weekend he had been in his local temple when an immensely fat guy had been telling the priest that he had tried everything but did not know what to do about his weight. The priest had then asked the man whether he recalled knocking a guy off his bike with his car 13 years ago. He said that the man had died, and the supplicant had started driving to work by a different route and had subsequently sold his car. He said that the man he had killed was now right there and did he want to speak with him? The rest of the story is not recorded but it's food for thought!

I had watched my sister's son, Adi, grow up ever since he had been a baby. He was a keen surfer, and when he was a teenager I had invited him to stay with me in California to enjoy the surfing scene. During this visit, and again at his mother's house in Devon, he made me aware that he had some interest in working with me

551

on the boats. At that time, I still felt that Nicky and I could manage on our own and there was really no need, or indeed any room, for anyone else in the company. But, after my accident, I realized how much other people depended on me for their livelihood and that this was not a good thing. Also, I was now 63 years old and I really should be giving some thought to who was going to take over from me now that I had made the decision to build another boat. By this time, Adi had left school and was attending an engineering college in Bristol. I wrote to him and said that, if he was still interested in joining the company, Nicky and I would be delighted to have him. He wrote back to say that he was "over the moon" after receiving my letter!

When Adi had finished his studies, I arranged with Egil for Adi to join him for his upcoming cruise with the idea that, before joining me in the trenches, he could start off with an interesting experience that would provide a practical demonstration of how our boats are used. Egil's captain on that cruise was Duncan Cowie and, as we shall see later, this proved be yet another example of the uncanny convergence of events that seem to feature in the story of Fleming Yachts. With the cruise over, Adi flew to California, and in June 1998 we went from there to Taiwan.

Our first task after arriving in Taiwan was the inspection of two 55s which were completed and ready for shipment. Both boats had been sitting out in the blazing sun, which was dead overhead at this time of year. It was like walking into a couple of ovens while we went through the tedious 26-page check lists, which soon became soggy with sweat. This was hardly an ideal introduction and I half expected that Adi would chuck it in after the first day.

Actually, the timing for Adi to come aboard was ideal because with the 75 being in the early stages of its development, he could learn the boatbuilding process from beginning to end, including the engineering of all the myriad systems which go into a modern boat. For myself, having a new hand was initially more time consuming because everything had to be explained, instead of me just being able to get on with it myself. But learning to delegate is an absolutely necessary step unless you intend to keep doing everything yourself until you expire! I insisted that Adi learn

Chinese and not be a dummy like me when it came to communicating directly with the people who did the work.

Now that I had been joined by another person, I had decided to move to a small apartment and, with Louisa's help, I found one next to my old hotel, which had been demolished. The new building was called Shangri La, so I had moved from Utopia to Shangri La! Adi and I shared the apartment for quite a while, so the poor lad not only had to work for his uncle during the day but share an apartment with him the rest of the time! He survived the ordeal remarkably well!

Chapter 7

July 1998 to January 2002

Taiwan, Nicky's Operation

I make my second trip to Antarctica and cruise to the Norwegian Lofoten Islands, north of the Arctic Circle. We complete the first Fleming 72 and move the California office to above my garage. Duncan joins Fleming Yachts. My daughter Nicky is diagnosed with cancer. I meet up with Carole on a visit to England.

The next major event for me was another voyage to Antarctica—this time to the Antarctic Peninsula, leaving from the tip of South America. On December 30th, 1998, we left Ushuaia, billed as the most southerly city in the world, aboard the Russian ship *Akademik Sergei Vavilov,* a survey ship converted to carrying passengers. We undocked in a stiff breeze at six in the evening and departed down the Beagle Channel, headed for the Drake Passage and the Antarctic Peninsula. When I arose the following morning it seemed to me that the sun was in the wrong position, and a visit to the bridge confirmed that, instead of heading south for Drake Passage, we were headed northeast for the Falkland Islands. The decision had been made to do the trip in reverse because a violent weather system was now encompassing the notorious Drake Passage.

At sea on the evening of December 31st the dining room was festooned with streamers and we celebrated the arrival of 1999 in unusual surroundings. On New Year's Day we had our first landing on New Island—one of the Falklands group. We went ashore in Zodiacs and visited a mixed colony of albatross, rock-hopper penguins and king shags with piercing blue eyes.

In the afternoon we moved to another island called Steeple Jason, which was home to huge numbers of nesting, black-browed albatross. The weather was not good, with a fine drizzle and gusting winds. The ship did not anchor but held station offshore while passengers were landed on the rocky shoreline. If the ship sounded five blasts on its siren, we were instructed to return at once to the landing site. I had gone off by myself and found a wonderful spot surrounded by hundreds of magnificent albatross nesting only a few feet away or hanging on the stiff wind just a few feet above my head. To shelter from the wind and light rain I had tucked myself in the lee of a clump of tussock grass. I had no sooner got settled and started filming than the ship blew its siren. Disappointed, I returned immediately to the landing site to await my turn to make the journey in the Zodiac back to the ship.

It was a wild and exhilarating ride, with the boat pitching up and down in the steep waves and spray flying everywhere. Overhead, the air was full of albatross sweeping past on their huge wings. It did occur to me that this was a hazardous situation with the potential to end badly, but the sheer drama of the situation overrode any apprehension. It was an amazing moment that will forever remain vivid in my mind. When we reached the ship, the Zodiac was tossed up and down in the waves and hurled against the boarding platform, where crew members, knee deep in water, tried to secure it. Unlike *Bremen*, which had a door in its side, *Vavilov* was equipped with one of those long ladders suspended diagonally down the side of ship all the way from the deck to a small platform just above the waterline. Somehow, one by one, we managed to scramble onto the platform and up the ladder. When on deck, I took video of other Zodiacs battling the conditions. After all the passengers were safely aboard, one of the Zodiacs capsized—tossing its crew of two into the frigid water. Fortunately, it was the last boat but one, and the crew from the remaining Zodiac was able to recover their colleagues and their boat from the water.

From here we moved on to Port Stanley, the capital of the Falklands, where we went ashore the following day. Eight years had passed since Argentina had invaded the Falklands, which they refer to as the Malvinas, and events were still fresh in the minds of the population which numbered around 3,000. We were given a talk, accompanied by sound recordings, by one of the residents who had lived through the occupation. One of the few reasons for being allowed out on the streets of Stanley was if you had a baby, so the few available babies were shared around and used as a kind of passport to allow residents to get out of the house.

Back in the days of sail this was a thriving place, in part because of the California gold rush from 1848 to 1859. In 1847 alone, no less than 777 ships called at Port Stanley either to prepare for rounding Cape Horn or to come in for repairs after having done so. Rounding Cape Horn could be a gruelling affair for both man and vessel. In the winter of 1914 a ship called the *Edward Sewall* took 87 days to battle its way around the notorious cape. In Stanley cemetery, I came across a headstone on which was engraved the following moving lines:

> *Do'ye mind the day*
> *When we squared away*
> *An' ran her East by south*
> *When she trampled down the big Horn seas*
> *With a roaring bone in her mouth*
> *When the best hands twirled her bucking wheel*
> *An' dared not look behind*
> *At the growling greyback in her wake*
> *D'ye mind old pal, d'ye mind?*

This refers of course to rounding the Horn in a square-rigger and the word "mind" in this context is the Scottish word for "remember."

But times were a'changing. Brunel's steam-powered ship, *SS Great Britain*, was launched in 1843. With a steel hull 322 feet long, she had a 1000hp engine driving the first ever screw-type propeller in place of paddle wheels. She was abandoned, and actually scuttled, in the Falklands in 1886, having made 32 trips from Britain to Australia. In 1970 she was rescued from her watery grave, loaded onto a barge, and transported back to the very same dock in Bristol, England, where she had been built. I went to see her early in her restoration when she was still quite a mess. Today she is fully restored and open to the public.

The opening of the Panama Canal in 1914 eliminated the need for most shipping to make the lengthy and perilous voyage around the Horn, and the remote Falkland Islands settled back into obscurity.

From the Falklands we crossed 800 miles of the tempestuous Southern Ocean to the island of South Georgia. The taxi driver who had taken us to see the wreck of the *Braer* in Shetland had told us that he used to go to South Georgia to work at one of the whaling stations, but I had no real idea of where it was. I knew the Falklands conflict had been triggered when a group of scrap metal merchants had arrived, uninvited, on the island, which I had imagined to be a flattish piece of rock with the occasional wreck. As it turned out, the island was 106 miles long and between a little over a mile and 25 miles in width. Huge glaciers and snow fields covered 75 percent of its surface, and it boasted 11 peaks higher than 6,500 feet. When we made landfall, after two days and three nights at sea, all this magnificence was hidden from our view behind a veil of mist.

South Georgia once played host to several whaling stations, the last of which was closed in 1964. When the whaling companies left, they simply walked away and abandoned all their debris and wreckage to litter this otherwise pristine environment. There are two schools of thought about this. One is that it is typical of mankind to foul his nest and then, when it is no longer profitable, to walk away and leave someone else to clean up the mess—and that mess should be cleared up. The other view is that the stations are a part of history and provide a time capsule into a past way of life.

In Grytviken we saw canteens where tattered curtains still hung in the windows and tea urns sat abandoned on the counters. There were machine shops and store-rooms stocked with steel bars and sheets of metal. There were stacks of nested bathtubs, coils of rope and wicked, barbed harpoon heads scattered over the ground. Elephant seals snorted and grumbled among the buildings while elegant king penguins picked their way disdainfully through the debris. Southern fur seals had been completely eliminated from the island by the early 1900s but, over recent years, had re-established themselves now numbering some two million and making up 95 percent of the world's population. They were extremely aggressive and even the youngsters were inclined to charge you, although much of their aggression was bluff.

At least 175,000 whales were butchered here with at least some of their oil being used to create the munitions that fuelled the slaughter of the First World War. On the shore in front of Grytviken were a couple of catcher boats grounded and semi-sunk, with their harpoon guns pointing skyward. One of the buildings had been turned into a museum created and run by Tim and Pauline Carr, who had sailed here from England in their engineless sailboat, *Curlew,* built in 1905.

It was not just whales that left their bones in this place. There are a couple of graveyards containing the remains of people who came here and never made it back home. The most famous is Earnest Shackleton, who is buried in the Whaler's Cemetery, having suffered a heart attack aboard his ship *Quest* on January 5th, 1922 when he was only 48 years old. It was the 78th anniversary of his death when we were there, and I was asked to read some verses over his grave. The verses were the same as those he had read over the graves of three of his men at Cape Evans, five years before his own death.

We spent four very full days cruising the northern shore of South Georgia before taking our leave at Cape Disappointment—named in 1775 by Captain Cook, who, upon reaching it, was greatly disappointed to find out that South Georgia was an island and not the great white continent he was seeking.

This part of the Southern Ocean is littered with icebergs broken loose from the Larsen Ice Shelf in the Weddell Sea. Despite the story of the *Titanic,* it is not really the big bergs which are the main hazard but rather the smaller bergy bits, which are hard to spot and yet, with nearly 90 percent of their bulk beneath the water, can still be the size of a house. For example, only 21 inches of a bergy bit 16 feet thick will show above the water, and if it were to be 50 feet long by 25 feet wide, it could easily weigh 600 tons. Not something you would want to hit at 14 knots. Icebergs show up well on radar, and the screen looked like it had a case of measles. The ship's route ran right through the centre of the pack.

We arrived first at the South Orkney Islands and then the South Shetlands. These included Deception Island, so named because concealed in its centre is a flooded caldera large enough to accommodate large ships. It is accessible through an opening in the rim called Neptune's Bellows, which is 750 feet wide but obstructed in its centre by Raven Rock lurking eight feet below the surface. The island is volcanically active, and steam rising from the black sand beach heated the water. Those so inclined took a hot bath in the icy surroundings. The shore was littered with the remains of whaling activities, the bones of their victims, and of scientific stations destroyed in the eruptions of 1967 and 1969. Glaciers covered in thick layers of black cinder provided stark evidence of titanic struggles between fire and ice.

We continued on to the Antarctic Peninsula, being the first ship to navigate the Lemaire Channel during the current season. As the *Vavilov* pushed ice floes aside, the sea was trying to freeze. We had a memorable barbecue on the aft deck of the ship, with large flakes of snow fluttering down over the revellers, who by this time had got to know each other pretty well. Among them, gyrating in a slow dance, were an elderly man with one and a half legs who originated from the old Soviet Union and a lady in her 80th year. The people you meet on the cruises tend not to be your usual cruise ship passengers. Two weeks after leaving Ushuaia we crossed Drake Passage for Cape Horn. The weather was not exactly calm but very reasonable considering that waves over 100 feet high have been recorded in this area. Numerous albatross swooped around the ship as if in a living manifestation of the memorial on Horn Island which reads:

"I am the albatross that awaits you at the end of the earth. I am the forgotten soul of the dead sailors who crossed Cape Horn from all the seas of the world. They did not die in the furious

waves. Today they fly on my wings to eternity at the edge of the Antarctic winds."

We entered the Beagle Channel, named after the vessel in which Charles Darwin travelled to Galapagos and developed his theory on the origin of the species. As we approached Ushuaia, a series of rainbows arced over the port and surrounding mountains, marking a fitting conclusion to our amazing trip.

The first year of the 21st century was occupied in continuing work on the first 75 in the brand-new building which Tung Hwa had constructed especially for the project. They had built new buildings to accommodate the 55s, and now they had erected this huge building complete with large-capacity gantry cranes. This was a major commitment, based entirely on their belief in my capabilities which I found quite humbling.

During all of this, we continued to build Fleming 55s, and I had to attend selected boat shows, so I was pretty busy. On one occasion I had granted myself a couple of days off to visit friends in Florida following the Miami Boat Show. It always seemed that on the rare occasions I did this, a problem would arise with one or more of the boats, which made me feel like the boats themselves were maliciously demanding every second of my time. The first event to upset my plans was a phone call from our dealer from Caracas, who had taken delivery of a boat in Miami, to tell me that whenever it rained, water poured into the galley over the microwave. I felt I had no choice but abandon my plans and drive down there to solve the problem. It took two full days of investigation to find the leak and 10 minutes to fix. All the while, his wife was berating me for building leaky boats.

We had another boat headed to a buyer in California aboard a ship which collided with the dock in Seattle. The port authorities detained the ship for several months. During the course of their enquiries, no cargo, including our boat, could be unloaded. The retail buyer sued our dealer because of the delay, even though it could not possibly have been his fault, and insisted that, after it eventually arrived, the boat be commissioned in the yard of his choosing in San Diego. While the boat was in this yard, it developed strange blisters in the topsides which, to this day, have never been explained, as the boat was fine when it arrived from Seattle. Without any authority, the yard chosen by the buyer started sanding the topsides and, in so doing, wrecked the planking grooves. I had a phone call from the yard, while I was in Florida visiting some friends, telling me that they would not warranty their work. I flew back to California and gave instructions for the boat to be launched and removed from the yard forthwith and taken to an adjacent yard I knew I could trust. They later told me that the bulk of their work was correcting the damage done by the first yard. I was very angry about the whole affair and when, several months later, Chuck Hovey wanted me to go to the boat and meet with the owner, I said that the only reason I would go would be to piss in his shoes and I was relying on Chuck to identify which were the right pair of shoes to piss in!

In June I made another trip with Egil—this time to the Lofoten Islands, which lie well north of the Arctic Circle. *Ozmaiden* had been brought north to the town of Aalesund, on Norway's west coast, by Egil's captain, Duncan Cowie. Egil had long sung Duncan's praises, and when we met for the first time I was surprised to find out that he had acquired so much experience by his relatively young age of 27. A force 11 gale kept us in port for an extra day, but the following morning, under marginally improved conditions, we headed north into storm-tossed seas and sought the shelter of the labyrinthine waterways characteristic of the Norwegian coast. The wind was still sufficiently strong to drive water vertically upwards from a so-called waterfall.

The Arctic Circle was marked by a metal sculpture on the tiny island of Vikingen, and our GPS confirmed the latitude of 66 degrees 33 minutes North. We were just three days short of the summer solstice, and for the remainder of our trip, the sun never sank below the horizon. We were already farther north than Iceland and at the same latitude as Greenland, Baffin Island and Northern Alaska. But the moderating effects of the remnants of the Gulf Stream kept major ports—even well north of our location—ice-free throughout the endless nights of the Arctic winter.

At Bodo we refuelled at an unmanned fuel dock, which would

561

only dispense limited amounts of fuel at a time, forcing Egil to keep running his credit card to get sufficient fuel to fill *Ozmaiden*'s tanks. From here we made the six-hour crossing to the Lofoten Islands. Just south of Moskenes Island we passed the Maelstrom, a ferocious tide rip so infamous that its name has become part of the English language. As with Corryvreckan in Scotland, we kept our distance. The closest settlement to the Maelstrom is the abandoned village of Hell. We moored in the village of Reine, which has the reputation of being the most beautiful place in the whole of Norway—which, given the competition, is quite an achievement. We cruised the Kirke Fjord behind the village and I went ashore in the tender to photograph *Ozmaiden* against the background of stupendous mountains.

On the day of the summer solstice we moved to the western side of the islands to view the midnight sun on the longest day. We were lucky with the weather, and we watched the sun sink slowly from a cloudless sky towards the Norwegian Sea. When just a handbreadth above the horizon it changed its mind and started to rise again.

In Stokmarkness we visited a museum dedicated to the Hurtigruten (Coastal Express)—a ferry service running between Bergen and the Russian border at Kirkness, which has been the lifeline of this coast for more than 100 years. Later we went aboard the venerable *Harald Jarl*, due to be retired in two years' time. Built in 1959, she was dressed in celebration of her 40th year of service—having run 2,728,000 miles since her launching, still with her original Burmeister and Wain engine.

On June 25th we reached our maximum northerly position of 68 degrees, 37.039 minutes and reluctantly turned our bows south. Having come so far, it seemed a pity not to continue to North Cape, or even to Spitzbergen. But it was time for us all to return to more mundane responsibilities, and Duncan was left to get *Ozmaiden* the 1,000 miles back to Egil's home.

Back in Taiwan, the new 75 was approaching completion. Larry Drake, the naval architect who had designed the hull, had made some offhand comments that maybe the boat might have a tendency to float slightly down by the bow. I thought it would be a good idea to check this out before taking the boat to the harbour—but how to do it? Tung Hwa had a large pond on their property which had originally been built many years earlier when the factory had been used for manufacturing furniture. The pond had been used to soak logs to prevent them from splitting. The problem was that the pond was now almost inaccessible behind the new building that had been erected to build the boat.

Fred contacted the local crane company and they came out and said, "No problem". A couple of days later they came back with a 500-ton capacity mobile crane, lifted the boat over the top of a small building and a couple of trees, then lowered it into the pond. I noted where she floated and she was placed back into her cradle. It was evident that she was pretty heavy and down by the bow, so we raised the bootstripe with an additional increase at the bow.

The water tanks in this boat had been placed under the bed in the owner's cabin. The tanks had been made of polyethylene in California, which meant that they could not have baffles inside them. They were quite long and skinny, and I figured I could keep them constrained within a robust structure inside the bed. Seeking reassurance about this, I had been pressing the plumber to fill the tanks with water from the deck fills, which were about 8 feet above the tops of the tanks. This was eventually done one evening a couple of weeks before the boat was due to leave the yard. I came to work the following morning to check that everything was well, to discover that the tanks had inflated under the 8-foot pressure head and had erupted from the bed completely destroying it in the process!

Oops! What to do? I hastily designed some aluminium tanks and the order was sent out within hours to have them made by a local specialist company. We had them back in three days, and the next problem was to get them down the spiral staircase into the owner's cabin. The teak veneer surface around the staircase was tricky to do and we did our best to protect it with thin plywood before leaving the plumber and his crew to wrestle the four new tanks down the stairs during the evening. The following morning, the two smaller tanks were in place but two slightly larger ones could not quite make it, and the precious veneer had been damaged during the attempt.

To get the tanks down the stairs it was necessary to substitute a bevel for a sharp corner for the full length of the oversize tanks. They were returned to the manufacturer, to be returned two days later with just the corner instead of the full length being cut off. Back they went for further modification as the clock ticked on.

Finally, in the nick of time, the tanks were installed and the collateral damage repaired; and in October 2000, the boat made ready to leave the yard. The first step in transporting her the 12 miles to Kaohsiung harbour was to lift her onto a road trailer, using a huge mobile crane. This German-built machine had a capacity of 500 tons and arrived at the yard accompanied by a fleet of trucks carrying its counterweights. The control cab looked like the flight deck of a Boeing 747. It was operated by a most professional crew who communicated with one another using radio headsets. With the boat loaded, she was ready for the first leg of the long journey that would take her to California from the place of her birth. This was a saga in itself.

The road to Kaohsiung was obstructed by overhead power lines and cables carrying TV, telephone, and traffic lights, all of which had to be taken down and re-installed after the boat had passed. I counted an army of more than 100 people and 34 vehicles involved in the exercise. The police only permitted the boat to move between 10 p.m. and 6 a.m., so the journey took three nights and cost more than transporting the boat the remaining 6,000 miles from Kaohsiung to California.

Under one bridge we had only a few inches of clearance, and as the convoy approached the city, there were high-voltage power lines we could have passed under but which we avoided. A previous boat from another company had suffered a flash down in which the high voltage had bridged the two-foot gap and incinerated all the electrical equipment in the boat.

When we reached the Kaohsiung fishing port, the giant crane lowered the boat into the water, hemmed in by battle-scarred trawlers. The first challenge, after starting the engines and checking the systems, was to run the boat through the harbour and head for the Customs and Immigration dock, which was highly congested with all types of commercial vessels jockeying for position, while just a few yards away, ocean-going ships swept through the narrow channel. I was the only person with any experience of driving a boat and that was very limited. To add to the fun, this was a brand-new boat with unfamiliar handling characteristics and much larger than anything I had ever driven before. Every one of the 37 people on board had to present their ID cards—or, in my case, passport—at the Customs and Immigration dock on the way out of the harbour and on the way back. Following trials, we took our new baby to another part of the large harbour, where she was lifted out by the same mobile crane at a cost of $10,000 per day!

A few days later, the boat was loaded aboard the special ship that was to carry her across the Pacific Ocean. I was present for the offload in Long Beach harbour, where she was lifted off the ship by Herman the German—a huge floating crane seized by the allies from Germany after WWII. As with the 55, 14 years earlier, the reception committee included Chuck Hovey and the buyer of the boat.

In terms of size—best measured in terms of displacement— the 75 was 2½ times larger than the 55 and required a whole new way of thinking in almost every area. For this boat I had a special exhaust system designed and fabricated by a company in Florida. This was not a success, the problem being that the exhaust system got way too hot under continuous load. The only response forthcoming from the manufacturer was the same as you get from computer experts, i.e., "That's weird—it should have worked."

A solution was needed urgently because the owner wanted to take the boat several thousand miles to the East Coast, and it had to be out of California within 90 days or be liable for a 7½ percent sales tax. She was in a boatyard in San Diego, and with less than one week to go before the deadline, I took a room in a motel and worked with the yard until we had a workable solution. When the boat eventually reached Florida, I had another company rework the whole exhaust system from scratch at enormous expense.

2001 was a very busy year for us. Demand for the boats was

up and during the year we managed to ship fifteen 55s—more than one per month—plus four of the new 75s. The second 75 was purchased by a buyer in California who paid a $200,000 deposit and then said he wanted to convert the pilothouse into a "country kitchen" and turn the flying bridge into the only control station on the boat. This meant in effect eliminating the pilothouse from our pilothouse motoryacht. I said that we did not do country kitchens, but I prepared sketches for a modified design which went some way toward what the buyer had requested. His response was that if he could not have the full country kitchen then he did not want the boat—so I returned his deposit.

The 75s were much more complicated boats than the 55s, and it soon became evident that it was not enough simply to turn on a piece of equipment to see whether it worked and then turn it off again. Systems like air-conditioning had to be run for several days to check them out thoroughly. To aid in this, Tung Hwa built a test tank large enough to accommodate the 75, and every boat spent at least one month afloat in the tank before leaving the yard. From here they made the road journey to Kaohsiung—now only taking a few hours after Tung Hwa had paid a fortune to have all the cables permanently raised to permit passage of the boat.

In California, all the houses in my street, except mine, had some sort of accommodation built over the garage, so I decided it would make sense to follow suit and use the space over my garage for our office. The planning and construction was done over a period of several months, and the result worked very well because, while there was access from the street, there was just one door which connected it with the rest of the house. The office had its own fax and phones so I had no problem just closing the door at the end of the day and forgetting all about work. I had long ago realized that I was a morning person and it was a waste of time and energy trying to achieve anything of any significance much after 5 p.m. I found that I could achieve a much better result the following morning in half the time. While I was not actually running my business from my garage, I was now only a couple of sheets of plywood away from following that tradition!

In June 2001 I made a trip to England primarily to visit our dealer in Southampton, but I also used the opportunity to visit Carole and her husband, John, in St. Albans. So, on the afternoons of June 28th and 29th we were able to renew our acquaintance in person after 44 years! Unfortunately, at the time of my visit, Carole was going through a bad patch with her lungs and was temporarily confined to her bed, so I had to keep my visits short so as not to tire her.

Egil Paulsen, now firmly established in Australia, had a "picnic" boat designed and built for him by a company in Brisbane. A second, larger, boat was built by the same company for Egil's cousin in Sweden, and Egil asked Duncan Cowie to come to Australia to supervise its construction. Egil had a keen interest in our 75 and dearly wanted to come to California to take a look at it, but he was unable to get away from Sydney. As Duncan was passing through California on his way to Florida, where he was involved in taking a large sailboat across the Atlantic to England, Egil asked him to visit us and send him lots of photos of the 75.

Fortunately, I was in California at the time, and I wanted to make Duncan's visit interesting. We had a 75 in San Diego that needed to be brought the 80 miles up the coast to Chuck Hovey's office, so I arranged for Duncan to go down to San Diego and come back on the 75. After he got back, he told me that they had not been taking very good care of the boat and he began to enumerate all the defects he had spotted. It was while he was doing this that a light bulb suddenly went off in my head! By this time, we had well over 100 boats in service in various parts of the world, with more being added every month. These had created increasing demands on my time, which took me away from running the company and designing new features, so I had been on the lookout for someone to whom I could delegate these increasingly burdensome responsibilities. I realized that here was the guy I had been looking for. Like myself he had an aeronautical engineering background; he had been Egil's skipper for three years so knew the 55 intimately; and he had a much more extensive cruising background than I did. He had also just demonstrated that he had the necessary pernickety approach to quality.

After thinking about it for a couple of days I told Duncan that I had been looking for someone to add to our team and I would be pleased to offer him a job if he were interested. We both realized that he would lose the flexibility he currently enjoyed under his present lifestyle, but he would trade that for as much stability as you are likely to get in the marine industry. Duncan was interested and said he would think about it as he sailed across the Atlantic. As it happened, Egil was subsequently able to come to California. He spent three days poking through and photographing the 75 from every conceivable angle, but I did not dare tell him that I was thinking of poaching Duncan. About a month later, Duncan told me that he would like to join Fleming Yachts but he had prior commitments until October. And so it was that I met him at Baltimore airport on October 10, 2001, and he went with me to visit Burr Yacht Sales in Annapolis before we flew to California.

The following month I took Louisa to Hong Kong for a few days. On the day after we arrived we went down to breakfast and my cell phone rang. It was a tearful Nicky calling to tell me that she had just been diagnosed with colon cancer. I was shocked and stunned. She was just 35. Naturally the devastating news put a damper on the rest of the visit to Hong Kong. I was due to fly back to California in two weeks and I managed to bring the date forward by one week.

It was vital for Nicky to have her operation as soon as possible. The options were to have it in the extremely good local hospital, where it would be covered by insurance, or by a specialist in LA who did 40 such operations every week and who had operated on such people as Ronald Reagan and King Hussein of Jordan. That operation would not be covered by insurance and would cost $37,000. We asked the insurance company whether we could use the latter option with them paying what it would cost for the local hospital and me picking up the rest. They said that they could not go along with this suggested compromise. Obviously, anyone would pay whatever it cost to get the best outcome provided they had it in their power to do so—and luckily we did, so we went with the surgeon in LA.

Nicky had the operation just before Christmas 2001 and came

back to work shortly thereafter. Fortunately, she had help at home and she said it was more restful being at work than staying at home taking care of two young children! She still had to endure weeks of chemo and radiation treatment, and it turned out to be a huge serendipitous advantage to have the office attached to the house, where she could lie down and take a rest whenever felt exhausted. She was a real trooper.

Chapter 8

January 2002 to May 2005

Taiwan

I visit Yellowknife in Canada's Northern Territories to view the Aurora Borealis. Nicky undergoes treatment and runs the Paris Marathon. We build the Fleming 65, and I decide to retain the first boat and name her *Venture*. I make my third trip to Antarctica.

My main concern at the start of 2002 was of course Nicky's health. I felt very concerned about returning to Taiwan and leaving her without my personal support, but she was coping amazingly well and actually preferred to do it on her own. Although I now had the invaluable assistance of Adi and Duncan, this was not a year for going on extended trips. I did, however, make a long planned three-day trip to Yellowknife, in Canada's Northern Territories, to view the Northern Lights. After a very ho-hum international flight on Air Canada to Edmonton, I took a one-hour flight to Yellowknife on a First Nations aircraft. It was like being back flying on an oriental airline, with first class service and the choice of a nice hot meal.

We landed in Yellowknife where the temperature was a frigid -45 °F, which literally causes you to catch your breath. When people went to supermarket they left their car engines running in the car park, and you soon realized that something as simple as

570

dropping your glove could be a serious event and not just a minor inconvenience. When I bought my ticket I thought that I was doing something a bit out of the ordinary, but I found that I was only one of hundreds of people with the same idea, and I was the only non-Japanese among them! There is apparently a belief among the Japanese that if a baby is conceived under the Northern Lights it will bring good fortune to the child. I did see the lights, but not an especially dramatic show.

During that year we shipped thirteen 55s and three 75s, but it had become obvious that the difference in size and cost between the two models was far too much for 55 owners who wanted to move up to a larger boat. So I began to give some thought to building an intermediate boat to fill the gap. This started off at 60 feet but grew to 65. Sadly, Larry Drake had passed away, and I had to find a new naval architect. I selected Doug Sharp, whom I had known for a number of years. He had his office in San Diego and had previous experience of building boats in Taiwan.

Starting in April 2002, I worked with Doug on the design for the new boat, and over the next few months exchanged sketches and photos of the 55 to refine the lines and get all the angles just right. This time we were aided by a computer program called Rhino that made it possible to view the design in three dimensions. This revealed that we had a similar visibility problem from the flying bridge as we had on the 75. But the magic of computer design included a virtual "camera" which showed where your eyes needed to be in order to provide the required visibility. I was determined to avoid having a flying bridge on the top of the pilothouse roof, and the new tools allowed us to come up with a compromise which worked well. This involved some tricky sleight of hand with roof lines which were really only solved during construction of the actual plugs, on which we started work late in 2002.

We were greatly assisted in this by the constructive attitude of the carpenter who did the work. Adi and I would stand on the catwalk above the deck plug and walk back and forth viewing the roof over the pilothouse. We would see a flat spot and point it out to the carpenter, who would pick up instantly what we were talking

571

about. I should mention here that not everyone has the "eye". It seems you are born with it or not. I can spot an unfair line a mile away and so, fortunately, can Adi. On the other hand, I have encountered many people who are totally unable to spot a line which is miles out of true. The carpenter in this case also had it, and he would rush off and come back with a large bucket of putty and within two hours call us back to take another look. Very often if you fixed one place, it would affect another. We had three levels of roof to contend with, and the cambers of each had to blend together at their edges in a way that harmonized with the general lines of the deck. Because of the positive attitude of the carpenter we were able to persevere until we had it just right. Had he been grumpy and given to heavy sighs before going off with bad grace each time we asked, we would probably have settled for a result that was less than perfect.

The eye is the final arbiter when it comes to design, and it is necessary to move around and not make judgments from just one spot. A two-dimensional drawing puts your eye exactly opposite every point on the boat at exactly the same time, which is of course impossible, especially for something 65 feet long. Perspective comes into play and alters as you move your viewpoint. For example, if you are looking at the boat from the side, the bow will be farther away from your eye than the centre. Due to perspective, if you do not raise the top edge of the bootstripe at the bow it will appear to droop but its lower edge, being parallel with the water, needs to remain level.

By the end of 2003 we had built 144 55s, were still building the very complex 75s, and were now heavily engaged in creating the tooling for the 65. Tung Hwa extended the large 75 building to accommodate the new boat.

I have mentioned that one of the problems when designing and building the first boats of a new model is meeting the wishes of the early adopters before you have a chance to build and test the boat yourself. It had never been possible before but, with the 65, I made the decision not to sell the first boat but to hold it back so I could build it exactly the way I wanted and retain it for testing and photography. Also, we could use it as a test bed to try our concepts and equipment we could not risk using in a client's boat. I decided to call the boat *Venture* because it was a simple name and was appropriate for what I had in mind. Owning our own boat was a new venture for us and it was going to allow us to venture forth in the sense of "nothing ventured nothing gained".

With this in mind, I was now free to try ideas we could not previously have contemplated. I had read a magazine article about someone who had retrofitted a diesel electric system in his boat using motor-generators made by Siemens that were designed for use in buses. I contacted the company in Texas who had done the work and decided I would build 65-001 with this system. I designed the system and how it would be laid out in the boat, and I ordered the equipment. The engines were to be installed at the aft end of the engine room. There would be one large fuel tank across the forward end of the engine room which would be invisible because it would appear to be the bulkhead.

In September 2003, we had another Fleming Owners' Rendezvous—or Fleming Fling, as they are called on the U.S. West Coast. This one was in Elliott Bay, in Seattle. During the Q and A session, I announced to the assembly that I had decided to keep back the first 65 from sale and that I had decided to install a diesel/electric system in place of conventional drive.

Unfortunately, this turned out to be a premature announcement. We had the custom fuel tank made and ready to install in the boat when Siemens stepped in and said that they would handle this installation directly and that they wanted $360,000 to develop the software. I responded that I was putting my personal reputation on the line to build a boat at my expense with my name on it. We were installing a radical new system for which we had no assurance that it would even work and, even if it did, whether we could sell it at the same price or less than a conventional installation. There was no way I was going to pay a gigantic company like Siemens huge sums of money for them to develop software to use their equipment. It would be like me charging the buyer of a new model Fleming the entire cost of making the mould to build the boat. In my view Siemens should be supporting me to be the pioneer in developing a new idea from which they could benefit. They did not agree, so that was a deal breaker. I immediately switched the design to a conventional installation. It was just in time. In another six weeks it would have been too late. They later contacted me to reconsider, but I said that there had been the one opportunity and it was now too late. As subsequent events showed, I had made the right decision. Someone else with much more money and know-how than myself tried it and told me that I "had dodged a bullet!"

In August 2003 I made a visit to Scotland to dig a bit further into my roots. I knew that my family on my father's side had lived at a place called Carmuir's Farm, just outside Falkirk. I discovered on the Internet that this not only still existed but was now a Bed and Breakfast! I made my way there and, from all the evidence I had at my disposal, I concluded that the room in which I slept was the very room in which my father had been born! From the window I saw a strange-looking structure a couple of miles away across the fields. When I investigated, I found it was the Falkirk Wheel—a cunning device to lift and lower boats, floating in giant bathtubs, 80 feet between the Union and the Firth and Clyde Canals. My hosts at Carmuirs suggested I visit Falkirk library to look at the census records. I examined them on microfilm and found the names of my family—including my father, who was one month old at the time—in the 1901 census.

Some weeks prior to my visit I had researched, and booked on line, for a guy to take me by boat out to the west Coast of Jura from the small town of Crinan—which was at the western end of the Crinan Canal we passed through in *Ozmaiden* in 1992. Mike Murray took me to Glengarrisdale Bay in his catamaran *Gemini*. On the way we passed through the notorious Gulf of Corryvreckan, which Egil had stayed well away from. Mike regaled me with tales of the whirlpool called the Hag, and we spun around in some of the eddies. Upwellings, called "boils", would suddenly erupt beside the boat and we spun around in the vortices they created. After playing in these for a while, Mike dropped me off on a rock which served as a landing spot at Glengarrisdale. I arranged with him to collect me in three days' time and, as I watched the boat leave, I hoped that he would not forget! This was a very isolated spot, 7 miles across the mountains to the nearest vehicle track and no cell phone coverage. The bothy was the only structure still standing among a group of roofless buildings. It was painted white with a bright red roof, so it stood out from the rich green of the surrounding land.

I scrambled over the rocks and made my way through the long grass to the bothy. The door was not locked and I went inside. I had brought camping gear and a few provisions but the interior was pretty bare. There was of course no electricity or running water, and for toilet facilities there was a spade which you had to use well away from the bothy. Water had to be collected from a stream—locally referred to as a "burrn". It was the colour of whisky because of the peaty soil. The whole area was overgrown with bracken, a kind of coarse fern which dies off in September and grows afresh in the spring. This being August, it was higher than my head and very treacherous to walk through, as it concealed tussock grass and boggy holes. After pitching headlong a couple of times, I decided that I had better curtail my activities. Mike was not due back for three days and there was no chance he would be able to find me if I were laid out horizontally in a sea of bracken. However, I cut a bunch of it and spread it on the floor to make a rough bed and spread my sleeping bag on top.

The biggest plague in Scotland during the summer are "midgies", which dance in a cloud above your head and get into your eyes and nostrils. They are at their worst when the air is still and the humidity high. Fortunately, they were not too troublesome during my visit. I sat outside the bothy and contemplated the landscape, realizing that it had not changed since it was the home of my great grandfather and, in fact, for hundreds of years prior to that. It was a thought-provoking moment.

The following day, I was joined in the evening by a family with two kids, aged around nine and ten, who had walked here over the mountains. Despite the long hike, the kids still had the energy to leap around playing games. The ten-year-old boy had insisted bringing the most recently published Harry Potter book, which must have weighed about five pounds! We were later joined by a guy from New Zealand who had hiked the north/south length of the island along the tops of the mountains. He had been able to speak to his family in New Zealand from the high ground. How times have changed—but not to our immediate surroundings.

When the family left to return over the mountains the following day, I went with them as far as the ruins of the even more remote settlement of Achabrad. There was nothing remaining here except some tumbledown stone walls protruding from the ever-present bracken, with occasional foxgloves to provide a dash of colour. It was here, in fact, where my great grandfather, Donald McKechnie, had been born, before the family moved down the hill to marginally more hospitable Glengarrisdale. The next significant piece of land across the Atlantic to the west— where the winds came from—was Nova Scotia, so the air could certainly be described as fresh. They grew their own potatoes and vegetables and caught rabbits and fish. You could only travel on foot and the terrain was all up and down, so they had plenty of exercise. They all lived to a ripe old age on Jura.

Mike showed up on time the next day and we returned to the mainland through Corryvreckan. I drove back south to Southampton and attended the boat show, where we had a 55 on display. While I was there I ran into Colin Ayres, who had worked with me in Singapore in the 1970s. He told me about an idea he had for stabilizing a boat using gyros instead of external fins. I was all for trying new ideas in the new 65, so I committed to installing a pair in the boat.

Amazingly, the *James Caird*, the tiny boat that Shackleton had taken from Elephant Island to South Georgia, had survived and made it back to Dulwich College in London, where Shackleton had gone to school. I had long wanted to see the boat but it was often away on display in other countries so, as yet, it had not been available on my visits to England. This time I was in luck and I drove to the school. I pulled into a car park and asked a passer-by if he knew where the *James Caird* could be found. He indicated a nearby building. I went inside, expecting it to be locked away in some inaccessible spot, but found it in a hallway sitting on some grey, rounded pebbles and surrounded by a railing with a few notice boards explaining its history. The window sills in the building were stacked with kids' satchels and books. There was no

576

one around except myself. It was all delightfully casual, and I expect the kids never gave a second thought to this old boat; but here was the real thing, the actual boat which had made that remarkable trip. I could reach out and touch it.

I wasn't yet finished with Corryvreckan, which I still wanted to see living up to its reputation. It was the time of the equinoctial tides, so I arranged to fly over the Corryvreckan and the adjacent channel called Grey Dog at the time of full flood tide. The helicopter left from Edinburgh, so I drove up north again and visited my old prep school at Cargilfield, not far from Edinburgh Airport, which had been developed from Turnhouse, where my father had been stationed during the early years of WWII. I had an interesting flight, seeing a lot of the sights including Stirling Castle and Carmuirs Farm, where I had stayed. We then crossed the width of Scotland to Grey Dog and Corryvreckan, which did not appear much more turbulent than when I had passed through it with Mike. You really need a good westerly gale combined with a large flood tide to get it going.

We then flew over Glengarrisdale, the bothy and Achabrad before flying south to Loch Tarbert, which divides Jura nearly in two. Here we could see and photograph the raised beaches and the tortuous channels which led to the inner reaches of the loch. We returned to Edinburgh airport at 5.30, just as it was getting dark, and I drove through the night to a motel outside Heathrow for my flight the following morning. Due to roadworks on the M1 motorway, I was diverted as far east as Cambridge, which I did not appreciate!

During all these months Nicky had been undergoing, and recovering from, her treatment for cancer. When she had been diagnosed, she had been training to take part in the Los Angeles Marathon. This, of course, had to be abandoned due to the cancer, but in her mind, it remained an unfulfilled ambition. In the meantime, she had developed a fancy for everything French, so she decided to correct this omission by running the Paris Marathon. I went along with Louisa from Taiwan and some other friends to support Nicky, and she successfully completed the event, which was a tremendous achievement. We had a celebratory dinner at a restaurant and I stayed to settle the bill after everyone else in the party had left. The restaurant did not accept credit cards and would not accept any currency other than euros, of which I did not have quite enough. I told them that all I could suggest was that I promised to return the following day with the balance. They agreed to this and the following day I made it a top priority to return to the restaurant to settle the outstanding amount. When I introduced myself, they told me that it was they who had made a mistake in the billing and, in fact, I had overpaid. They had the balance sitting on a plate behind the bar, awaiting my return!

After our visit to Paris, Nicky and I flew direct to Southampton. Our 40-minute flight was delayed five hours. While we were waiting in the departure lounge, a young Filipino woman came over to us—presumably because she spotted Louisa as a fellow Asian. She was worried she might not be met at Southampton because of the long delay and would be stranded in a foreign town. We assured her that should she not be met, we would take care of her overnight and get her to where she had to go the following day. She had flown all the way from Manila, via Paris, to take up a job as a croupier aboard a cross-channel ferry. I was amazed by the courage and enterprise this took on her part and at another example of the lengths Filipinos go to in order to send money back to their relatives. A ferry representative was at Southampton to meet her, so she did not need our help.

Back in Taiwan, the day finally arrived to move *Venture* out of the building. This is always an exciting moment because it is not until a boat is clear of the building that you can really see what it looks like. Even then, it is sitting in a cradle on wheels, and you are on the ground looking up at it. The giant crane returned to the yard and gently lifted the boat into the test tank built for the 75. Now, with her floating in her element, we could get a better look at our creation, and we were pleased by what we saw. But there was still much to do. It is one thing to construct something that has the appearance of a boat, but it is quite another to breathe life into it. These days a boat of this size and sophistication contains all those amenities you expect to find in a modern home, and they must all continue to function under conditions equal to an earthquake of grade 8 on the Richter scale. In addition, she has to be self-contained for months at a time—supplying her own energy needs and water supplies. She contains literally miles of electrical cable and pipes and hoses carrying fresh and salt water, fuel and hydraulic fluids.

One important factor, frequently ignored, is scale. This is especially important in the case of a boat in which a single piece of furniture—or even a piece of wood—not scaled correctly will throw a whole area out of balance. Very few people are aware of this, but when they enter a correctly scaled environment, they immediately feel comfortable.

One day I went into the salon on the 65 and the carpenter had installed teak trims all around the large windows. For some reason he had used teak 1/2-inch-thick instead of our standard 3/8-inch. I agonized about it because, to my eye, it appeared really clunky. However, I was very reluctant to ask him to rip it all out and replace it, and I justified it in my mind that, with the exception of the piece under the window, all the others would eventually be hidden by drapes or curtains. On our boats, we offered teak louvre blinds for the windows, but to my mind these made the boat too "teaky" when they were down, and yet something was needed for privacy at the dock and also to cover the windows at night, when they became a series of black holes that sucked all the light out of the interior. After seeing them in a restaurant in Kaohsiung, I decided to use Roman Shades. The guy who made them assured me that they would fit into the same depth of slots we allowed for the teak blinds, but when we came to install them the depth was insufficient and the blinds would not work properly.

This was a blow and I asked the carpenter to rout out the 1/2-inch-thick fascia pieces to open up the slot. I remember it was a Saturday with heavy rain and he was squatting on top of the TV cabinet trying to do what I had asked of him. He was sighing deeply and shaking his head. I left to go to the office and when I returned a few minutes later I was taken aback to find him whaling away with a hammer and chisel, busting up the fascia pieces. Actually I was secretly pleased because now they could be replaced with the correct thickness, but I was still concerned about the width of the slot for the shades. I asked the carpenter when he would be fashioning the replacement parts. He told me Monday, so that gave me one day to consider the best solution and I asked him to check with me before making anything. I came up with a zigzag section, which not only slimmed down the appearance of the moulding but provided more clearance for the blind and added a cosmetic detail on the inboard side. The carpenter had the modified fascias made and installed on all the windows by late Monday.

I have described this in detail because it is typical of the many hundreds of problems that inevitably arise and require solutions on a daily basis when developing a new product. When making every decision, many factors have to be considered such as appearance, cost, function, availability of materials and whether it lies within the skill set of the people who will make it. It is much better to have a simple design made well than a more intricate design poorly executed. A balance has to be struck between all these factors, and sometimes it is not until after the part is made that you can see that the balance was in the wrong place. You are then forced to decide whether you can accept it or whether it needs to be done over again.

After having to make décor decisions on my own boat, such as which granite to use, I had more sympathy with the owners who I had often (privately) criticized for dithering. Choosing upholstery and curtains is not an irrevocable situation if you make a mistake, but granite countertops are hard to change.

We had installed two large gyros supplied by Colin from Australia. They weighed almost half a ton apiece and were physically very large. They were designed to spin at around 5,000 rpm, and it was imperative they be securely mounted because if one were to come loose it would destroy the boat. It took several minutes to run them up to speed and we found that they rumbled and grumbled. Colin came up from Perth and we rigged poles out from the side of the boat so we could get it rocking to determine its natural roll rate. When we started just one gyro—and well before it reached its operating rpm—it became impossible to move the boat. It was as if it was set in concrete—just like magic.

Finally, at midnight on November 20th, 2004, *Venture* left the yard and made the now-familiar journey to the harbour.

Venture was lowered into the congested fishing harbour and prepared for trials. We had gone to even more trouble than usual to make this boat extra quiet, but when we ran the boat in the South China Sea the noise on the aft deck was deafening. People had their fingers in their ears and we measured over 100 decibels in the cockpit. In addition, the boat tended to squat, threw up a tremendous wake, and did not respond well to the steering. Not a very successful sea trial!

The first step in reducing the noise levels was to design, fabricate and install mufflers for the exhaust. Because the engine room had been laid out to suit the gyros, the mufflers had to be installed in the lazarette under the cockpit, where space was very tight. I had the design done by the morning following the sea trial, and it took only a couple of days for the guys at the yard to make the moulds, the parts and finally, the mufflers and have them installed in the boat. It was a truly heroic effort. The subsequent sea trial showed the boat to be much quieter, but there had not been enough space to isolate the mufflers from the hull, and the resulting vibration in the cockpit produced pins and needles in your feet! Not exactly the perfect solution!

We ran up the gyros again but they were noisy. I was concerned about how much it would cost to remove the gyros in the U.S., so I asked that they be taken out. This produced some very long faces but, using wood blocks, pieces of pipe for rollers, and a manual chain hoist, the crew had both gyros out of the boat in the course of a morning. The gyros would now need to be replaced with conventional fin stabilizers, with the work being done when the boat was in the harbour. This was not really permitted in the docks, but the boat was too high to leave by road from her location, and we had holes in the hull so she could not go back in the water. We were granted permission to work on the boat for one week. We had security on the boat over the weekend but not during weekdays, as we had people on the boat every day.

Fate threw us another curved ball when the first tropical cyclone to strike Taiwan in 108 years arrived on Friday December 3rd. The workers were off for the day and there was no one around to protect the boat. When the crew returned on Monday, they found that someone had stolen a stabilizer actuator out of the cockpit. In doing so, the thief had damaged the wide, teak cockpit coaming, which had to be replaced. This was a disaster. The boat was due to ship in a few days and there was no replacement actuator immediately available. Delivery from the factory in the U.S. was six weeks, plus shipping. Fred sent people scouring the local scrap metal dealers to see if they could locate the missing part. Eventually he was able to borrow an actuator from a competitor's yard and had a replacement later flown out to them from the U.S. at great expense. For every person working hard and doing a responsible job there is always a miserable little weasel waiting in the wings to cause mayhem to further his own selfish interests.

Despite all the last-minute setbacks, *Venture* made it back in the water and was loaded aboard a special-purpose ship, the *BBC Russia*, on Christmas Eve 2004. We all went down to the docks early in the morning to watch her being loaded, Louisa included, and following the loading we went for lunch. That evening I caught a flight back to California and, due to the time difference of 16 hours, was able to attend a Christmas Eve party that same evening. It was a Christmas Eve to remember!

I had hired Richard Oates as captain for *Venture* and on January 14th, we went down to San Diego to watch her being offloaded from the ship. Offloading was supposed to be at 0900 but, as these things always seem to go, the sun was setting when we finally got underway, requiring a night passage up the coast. Although not ideal, it was much less fraught than the delivery trip on the first 55 because *Venture* had at least been run a few times in Taiwan. We arrived at 0130. *Venture* was the first of a new model and many people were anxious to see her. This included Chuck Hovey and also Art Burr and his staff from the East Coast. We also had a visit by a 90-year-old Frenchman who had flown all the way from France. Among the numerous visitors were clients who had ordered boats already in the production line. I was a bit nervous about this because there remained many adjustments before *Venture* was ready for prime time. However, the testing of hull no. 1 allowed us to correct all the important problems before hull no. 2 left the yard.

At the end of January 2005 I departed on another long-planned trip to Antarctica. This was aboard a new, purpose-built ship, *Orion,* constructed in Germany. We were originally supposed to join her in Punta Arenas, but for some reason this was changed at the last minute to Stanley in the Falklands. This meant flying first to Santiago in Chile. This was the second trip of her first season. She was U.S. Coast Guard approved, which meant that there were ominous rumours about access to the bridge being restricted and not open to passengers. As usual, 9/11 was given as the excuse, as it was for practically everything, including lousy service on airlines. Fortunately, the bridge restriction was not enforced on this trip. As far as I am concerned, having an open bridge is a major attraction for going on these trips and as soon as that facility goes away—so do I!

The ship was certainly very nice and more akin to a superyacht than an expedition ship, although in a perverse way I think I preferred the rough and ready approach of previous expeditions. We arrived at the new, military-run airbase in the Falklands, 36 miles from Stanley. The chatty bus driver who took us to the dock told us that, although the islands have half a million sheep, the islanders are not allowed to eat any because, being administered by Britain and therefore part of the European Common Market, there is no CE-approved slaughterhouse in the territory. If they want to eat lamb it has to be flown 10,000 miles from Britain! I saw my old friend the *Bremen* in the harbour. Sadly, she had been painted all white and looked a shadow of her previous self when she had a blue hull, white superstructure and orange trim.

We set sail at 7 p.m. that evening, January 31, for the 611 miles through the Drake Passage for Elephant Island. As a reminder, Drake Passage is the piece of water south of Cape Horn with a notorious reputation. We arrived off Elephant Island early on the morning of February 3, 2005. I was fascinated to see the spot where Shackleton and his men had landed and where they had been marooned for four months. I would dearly have loved to go ashore but, alas, it was too rough to permit a landing. From here

583

we made our way to the Antarctic Peninsula and visited many of the sites I had visited previously. The last time I had visited Paradise Bay it had been foggy and we had cruised in Zodiacs among the ghostly shapes of icebergs in freezing weather. This time we had bright sun and spectacular scenery.

We made a stop at the American-run Palmer Station and learned that the staff, who were on site for months, were very restricted in their movements. Stunning Lemaire Channel was only 20 miles distant, but they were forbidden to visit it because of the risks involved. It must have been frustrating for them to see us tourists board our luxurious ship and go directly there while it remained off limits for them. We went to Deception Island and, on this occasion, there was more steam rising from the black sand than during my previous visit but I was disappointed that the *Orion* did not penetrate as far into the caldera as had the *Vavelov*. This was a short trip, lasting only 10 days, so it was soon time for us to make our way across the Drake Passage to Cape Horn and thence to Ushuaia. I had not realized there were a group of islands called Islas San Diego in the middle of Drake Passage. They must have been a significant obstacle in the days of sail. Cape Horn was again not unduly rough and we arrived in Ushuaia in the early hours of February 10.

Back in California work continued on the commissioning of *Venture*. On the morning of April 4th, Richard and myself took the boat the 130 miles to Ensenada, in Mexico, arriving at Cruise Port Marina at 4:30 p.m. Here she stayed until Wednesday, April 27th, when she was loaded aboard a Dockwise ship. The open, centre section of these unique vessels can be flooded and has a door at the stern which opens to allow yachts to float into what is essentially a seagoing dry dock. When all the yachts are inside, the stern door is closed and the water pumped out so the yachts are now high and dry. At the other end of her journey, the procedure is reversed, and the yachts can be driven out of the ship under their own power with no cranes involved.

Nicky had driven down from California and, after loading *Venture* into the ship, we returned with her to Newport Beach for the weekend. On Monday, May 3rd, Richard and myself flew to

Vancouver and the following day, there was the ship, with her cargo of 27 yachts, sitting at the dock. By 10 a.m., Richard had driven *Venture* out of the ship's belly and a couple of miles to the dock of our dealer, Grand Yachts, at nearby Coal Harbour in the heart of downtown Vancouver. What a contrast in less than one week! The mountains across the harbour still wore a mantle of snow and the city parks were bright with colourful rhododendrons.

Although I did not realize it at the time, this was the start of a whole new way of life for me.

Chapter 9

May 2005 to the End of 2007

Taiwan

Venture is shipped to Canada and I make my first cruise in her. I visit the North Pole in a Russian nuclear-powered icebreaker. Nicky and I attend a ceremony in Cannes to accept the award for the best boat of the year, for the Fleming 65. Venture takes part in the FUBAR Rally to Mexico. My sister dies.

Our first few days in Vancouver were occupied in showing off the boat. This included a formal boat parade in front of the Royal Vancouver Yacht Club for which we had to dress up and masquerade as ladies and gentlemen. This event marked the official start of the 2005 cruising season on May 14th. We later attended another function at the yacht club itself where there were Mounties in scarlet uniforms, flags raised and lowered, and a canon fired. They evidently celebrated the start of every season very formally in this part of the world.

One of the many advantages of keeping back hull no. 1 of the new model was to allow us to decorate the interior to our taste and arrange professional photo shoots at the time and place of our choosing. In June we took pictures from a helicopter of *Venture* cruising beautiful Howe Sound, just north of Vancouver city, with a background of snow-capped mountains. We also took her into Indian Arm—an unexpectedly beautiful arm of the sea hidden from view beyond the commercial docks and a railway bridge.

With this phase over, it was time to take *Venture* to Delta Marine Services, on Vancouver Island, for work on correcting the remaining problems. We removed the exhaust system in the lazarette and reworked it to isolate it from the hull. This significantly reduced the vibration, which was improved still further by swapping out the engine mounts for those of a different specification. We fixed the imprecise steering by replacing the expensive, axe-blade rudders with those with our usual aero foil shape, sent over from Taiwan. It is very normal for every new design to require some tweaking, but I was glad that *Venture* was my boat and I could attempt radical solutions without being worried about an understandably anxious customer.

Venture was still at Delta when I left for three weeks at the end of June for a pre-arranged trip to the North Pole aboard the Russian nuclear-powered icebreaker *Yamal*. I flew first to Helsinki, Finland, where I visited with a Fleming 55 owner and took a look at his boat. I travelled with other participants on a charter flight to Murmansk where we endured a lengthy immigration process before being taken by bus to the docks to join our ship.

Due to the last gasp of the Gulf Stream—now called the North Atlantic Drift—Murmansk is an ice-free port despite its latitude of almost 69 degrees. The city was the destination for the Arctic convoys bringing supplies to Russia from the Allies during WWII. It was flattened by the Germans and many people lost their lives. In their memory, an immense statue of a soldier wearing a cape stands overlooking the harbour. Even Ernest Shackleton was here at the end of an earlier conflict against the Bolsheviks, just after WW1. This was after he returned from his epic boat journey in Antarctica during which he had barely escaped with his life.

Yamal was a truly amazing vessel and one of a fleet of nuclear-powered icebreakers. She had two nuclear reactors heating water to generate steam to drive six steam turbines which together generated 75,000 horsepower. The electrical energy was fed to three 19-foot-diameter propellers each capable of delivering 25,000 horsepower. She had a top speed of 22 knots in open water and could maintain three knots through ice 10 feet thick. She had

587

an estimated range of four years!

The undocking of any vessel is always a moment of drama—akin to the raising of the curtain at the start of a theatrical production. This is especially true for an expedition ship departing for remote regions where no one is entirely sure what lies ahead. Given that our intended destination was to be the North Pole, the feeling was heightened still further by the playing of stirring patriotic music through the PA system. Tugs eased us away from the dock and we moved slowly down the Kola River.

I had brought two video cameras with me. My good one had just returned from service and I had a small back up. Imagine my dismay when, as we left the dock at the start of this unique journey, my main camera refused to function! I rushed down to my cabin to grab the backup to video our departure. The main camera refused to function because it falsely claimed there was moisture inside the camera. I fooled it into working by shooting the cabin hair dryer into it. The problem occurred at the start of every tape but included a "gotcha" element which made it impossible to run the tape on past the lead in.

We dropped off the pilot near the mouth of the river and were soon embraced in a light fog. Despite all the modern navigation gear, an unfortunate seaman was delegated to stand a chilly lookout on the bow in accordance with regulations. We underwent the mandatory lifeboat drill. No lifejackets were issued, but survival suits were held in lockers adjacent to the lifeboats. We attended a lecture which demonstrated just how hard it was to struggle into a suit even for crew members who had done it before.

The ship had 105 passengers and 120 crew. During winter months the *Yamal* was used to break ice for sensible reasons, but during the off-season she was pressed into service to take people like me to the Pole. On these occasions, the regular crew were doubled up in cabins deep down in the hull and their usual cabins given over to tourists. The ship was restricted to the northern hemisphere because her cooling system was not designed to cope with tropical waters.

On the second day out, we began to see small ice floes. These gradually grew in number until we were pushing our way through an endless vista of ice with occasional leads called polynyas. We saw female polar bears with their cubs on several occasions, and the ship was halted to allow us to take photos. I had not realized until now that these magnificent animals strayed so very far from land. Our expedition leader, who had himself trekked from Russia to Canada in 91 days by way of the Pole, told us that they had seen polar bear tracks within a few miles of the Pole.

There was a big party arranged on the Fourth of July to celebrate American Independence Day. I found it hard to believe that, so soon after the end of the decades long Cold War, we were here celebrating the most American of events on a Russian nuclear-powered icebreaker en route to the North Pole. How bizarre is that and what a commentary on the idiocy of two groups of otherwise perfectly normal people being whipped up by their respective leaders to view each other as some kind of devil incarnate.

We had a couple of other on-deck BBQs along the way, plus a special ceremony when the ship formally asked King Neptune for official permission to enter his realm. When Neptune banged the shaft of his trident on the deck the head flew off, which was quite entertaining.

The ship exhibited its immense power, shouldering aside blocks of ice the size of buses and splitting the ice ahead of us with an explosive crack. It seemed quite unnatural to be aboard a ship ploughing through a static white landscape which lacked the movement you would normally expect. All the while, our progress through the ice was accompanied by non-stop rumbling and thumping and a fair amount of vibration, which was more noticeable low down in the ship. The bridge was open to visit 24 hours per day, plus tours were arranged for us to visit the engine room, the control room, and even to peer down at the reactors. There were over 80 radiation sensors around the ship. We observed the massive rams thrusting the single rudder back and forth.

We encountered pressure ridges as thick as 30 feet, which required *Yamal* to back up and ram as many as 19 times before breaking through. For a while it began to look as though we might have to turn back before reaching our goal—not because the ship could not reach it, but because she had to meet her schedule of being back in Murmansk by July 15th. The helicopter was launched to scout the way ahead, and we reached 90 degrees north on schedule on July 7th.

The plotter in the lobby displayed an erratic course, but this was because the lines of longitude became ever closer together as we approached the Pole. In fact, at the Pole itself, they converge at a single point from which every direction is south. As you approach the Pole you will be traveling north, but the moment you reach it you will be traveling south—even though you continue in a straight line! Everything around you looks the same and the only way you know you have arrived is when the GPS reads 90 degrees. That reading is so precise that it will be accurate only at one location on the ship. As the ice is continually on the move at 4 to 5 mph, we moved about 25 miles during the few hours we were stationary and, from every other indication, had remained at the Pole.

As soon as the captain found a solid block of ice, he beached the ship and we were able to disembark onto the ice for a BBQ, while three crew members armed with rifles kept a lookout for polar bears that might want to join the party. The sense of smell of one of these animals is so acute that they can scent a seal under the ice more than one kilometre distant. When stalking, they have been seen holding a paw or even a piece of ice in front of their face, to hide their distinctive black nose and eyes.

While on the ice, we were able to walk up to the bow of the ship, which had large teeth painted on it. The surface paint had been abraded by the ice but, amazingly, the undercoat was still intact. A post had been stuck in the snow that represented the Pole. We had a lady on board who was celebrating her 90th birthday on the day of our visit. She circled the pole—and therefore the world—three times in less than one minute to make sure she was there on her birthday! I called Nicky from the satellite phone at the very reasonable rate of $3 per minute to speak to her from this remarkable location. For those crazy enough to do it, open water had been found close to the ship where you could take the plunge. The water here is 13,000 feet deep and anyone who went in was tethered with a line around his waist. I was afraid that my heart would stop, so I preferred to stay warm and dry and shoot video.

After a few hours we started our return journey south, following the path of shattered ice we had created on the way north. The plotter in the lobby displayed both our northbound and southbound courses. It was interesting to see that they were parallel to one another but displaced by the amount the ice that had moved over the surface of the globe due to transpolar drift. Eventually most of the polar ice is spat out between Iceland and the east coast of Greenland.

On our way south we were able to take helicopter flights over the ship and watch it, looking very insignificant, smashing its way through the endless ocean of ice. We called at Franz Josef Land, an archipelago comprising 191 islands, located around 81 degrees north latitude. We landed by helicopter on Hooker Island, which had been a Russian meteorological station from 1929 to 1963. Despite its remote location, it was visited by the *Graf Zeppelin* airship in July of 1931. The station's staff was marooned here for four years during WWII, when communications were severed by German activity. It was a bleak and lonely place during our visit on July 12th in high summer. Being stuck there for four uninterrupted years with no end in sight must have been a miserable experience.

The day before we arrived in Murmansk was Bastille Day and, with a large French contingent on board, the dining room was set out with French flags and food. We arrived back in Murmansk early in the morning and were off the ship by 0800. *Yamal* was leaving the same afternoon for a return trip to the Pole. After a brief tour of the rather down-at-the-heels city and a visit to the huge monument, we boarded our charter flight to Helsinki. At the airport, I met an American who had just enjoyed two weeks of fly fishing in Siberian rivers. On the flight I spent time talking to the 90-year-old lady who had celebrated her birthday at the Pole. She told me that her husband had died when she was 77. For several

591

months she had sat at home moping before telling herself that she needed to stop that and get going. She had cracked her wrist on this trip, but within three weeks of returning home to Seattle she was off to Prince Edward Island, in Eastern Canada. Shortly after that she went to California to appear on a TV programme, and they sent her off to the Solomon Islands! She told me that her family thought she was nuts!

This was my last commercial cruise, as every subsequent journey was aboard my own boat.

I flew back to Canada and, during August, cruised with Richard and Louisa to the exquisite Princess Louisa Inlet, on the Canadian Coast north of Vancouver. From here we continued north to Desolation Sound before returning south to Coal Harbour, in the heart of Vancouver, to celebrate my 70th birthday. Nicky and her daughters also came to Vancouver, as did Jacky.

This event was followed by another Fleming Fling held in Elliott Bay, Seattle, from September 9th to 11th. From here we took *Venture* directly to the Seattle boat show in Lake Union, also in Seattle, which ran from September 15th to 18th. Here we had *Venture* on display to the public for the first time. Among the visitors were Singaporean staff from American Marine in Singapore, whom I had not seen since I left there in 1985.

With the season advancing, we were anxious to get going to take *Venture* south to California for the winter. Richard, myself, and another crew member left Seattle on September 19th and headed out through the Straits of Juan de Fuca. Evening was approaching when we approached Cape Flattery, and the timing was unfortunate. I had been cooking pork chops and we hit the open ocean when dinner was almost ready.

The weather was not ideal, but we were able to continue non-stop down the coast except for a few hours wait in Crescent City, which had been devastated by a tsunami in 1964. This was my first real experience of being on watch at night by myself. Everything in the pilothouse has to be darkened down to an amazing degree to allow you to be able to see anything outside the boat. The boat appears to be hurtling along much faster and you are relying utterly on your instruments. You just have to hope there are no whales or submerged containers to hit. You carry a great responsibility for the safety of the vessel and your sleeping crew members. At the end of a three-hour watch in the wee hours it is easy to find yourself beginning to nod off. If I found this happening, I would get out of the helm seat and stand. On the expedition ships, there was no seat—in one case, just a bum rest, to keep the helmsman alert.

We arrived at one o'clock on the morning of September 24th, 2005. Three days later we were off to Catalina Island for a photo shoot, involving a helicopter, for *Yachting* magazine. This event took us on a complete circumnavigation of Catalina Island.

Over the winter, we did some local cruising, including a visit to Long Beach to see the new *Queen Mary* next to the old *Queen Mary*.

I wanted to have another season in the Pacific Northwest, but we were unable to find a ship to take the boat north from Ensenada. The only alternative appeared to be from La Paz, which was in Mexico, at the southern end of the long, skinny peninsula of Baja California. About one month before we were due to leave, Richard resigned as captain. David Miles, who had been Egil's captain many years before and who had since given up that line of work to work as sales manager at our dealership in Southampton, had an interest in joining Fleming Yachts. The only position we had open at that time was to take charge of *Venture,* so he agreed to fill the post on a temporary basis.

We thought the 1,200-mile trip on *Venture* from Newport Beach to La Paz would be an ideal opportunity for us all to get together on one of our boats and provide Adi with some practical cruising experience. So it was planned for Adi to fly over from Taiwan and for us all to leave for La Paz on May 2nd, 2006.

All this changed when I received a phone call from Nicky at 6:30 on the morning of May 2nd. She told me that my sister, Adi's mother, had just died. I couldn't believe it. It was so sudden. I knew that she was being treated for diabetes, but I always felt that that was an inconvenience and not something which could suddenly kill you! The full details emerged later, but the immediate news was that the police had been called to her house when holiday renters arriving to stay in her cottage had called on the neighbours when they could not contact her. The only person the police knew how to get in touch with was my sister's adopted son, who had been in some trouble during his adolescence. He did not know that Adi had just arrived in California and gave them his telephone number in Taiwan. The British police called that number, which was answered by Adi's Taiwanese wife who, on hearing who was calling, jumped to the conclusion that something terrible had happened to her husband. She was soon reassured and she called Nicky in California, who then called Duncan, with whom Adi was staying after his long flight from Taiwan. This left Duncan with the unenviable task of telling Adi that his mother had died.

Obviously our plans to take the boat to La Paz had to be cancelled immediately, and it was very fortunate that we had not already been on our way when the tragic news came through. Within 24 hours, Adi and myself were at my sister's rural cottage, Hollands, in the heart of the Devon countryside, rather than being on a boat off the coast of Mexico. From the evidence that we found after we arrived, it was clear that my sister had been part way through cleaning the cottage for the renters when she had gone to lie down on the bed for a rest from which she never woke up. The cause of death was insulin deficiency.

The really sad part was that her son, Tom, had twice suggested coming down that weekend to celebrate his mother's birthday, which was on Tuesday May 2nd. She had turned him down because she said she had a mild stomach upset and she was busy getting the cottage ready for her guests. Had Tom been there, she would almost certainly not have died and could well have gone on to live for many years.

We were joined in Hollands by other family members, and we all stayed together in the cottage for several days before the funeral. It was actually a very cathartic process. I don't believe that we had ever previously been closeted together for any similar period. We all took turns in preparing meals for the whole group.

The police had done a very responsible job after they arrived. They arranged with a local farmer to milk the cows and keep an eye on the animals, and the dog and cats were placed in an animal shelter until alternative arrangements could be made by family members. What disgusted me was that the government confiscated a very large amount of my sister's net worth in death duties and then, when the skinny remainder was shared out amongst her children, taxed each of them on what they received.

A funeral was held in the local church in the small village of Littleham, and my sister was buried a few feet away from the urn containing her husband's ashes. It was a lovely but sad spot.

Back in the U.S., *Venture* left Newport Beach on May 4th and was taken down to La Paz by David, Duncan, and his father, who had flown over from England. David remained with the boat in La Paz until she was shipped up to Nanaimo, on Vancouver Island, at the end of May.

With David as captain, we cruised up the Inside Passage all the way to Juneau, in Alaska. It was a memorable journey, but I won't go into too much detail here as the trip has been covered elsewhere in articles and video. The Inside Passage runs all the way from Seattle up to Skagway and is in reasonably protected waters for the whole distance except for Queen Charlotte Sound, just north of Vancouver Island, and Dickson Entrance, just south of Ketchikan. At these two spots the route is open to the Pacific Ocean, and you may have to wait as much as several days for the right weather.

The whole region is mountainous and covered with trees. The scenery is magnificent and uncrowded. It is less populated today than it was a hundred years ago due to over-harvesting of trees and salmon. The towns are few and far between, and most are not connected by road to the outside world because of the huge mountains at their back. The water is mostly very deep, so it is hard to find anchoring spots—anything less than 70feet is suitable! It is very unwise to cruise at night because of floating logs.

When we pulled into Juneau harbour on our farthest point north, we noticed that the bilge pump was running. On further investigation, we saw that water was running from the starboard exhaust system into the boat when the engine was running. This turned out to be the latest manifestation of the same exhaust problems which we had been fighting since the start—specifically, trying to pack an exhaust system in the lazarette where there was really not room for it. Starting with hull no. 2, the muffler was installed in the engine-room where it should be, but our flirtation with gyros precluded that on *Venture*. After mulling it over, I decided not to spoil our trip by pulling everything apart in Juneau and figured that we really did not need the second engine for the type of cruising we were doing, so we did the remainder of the trip—including the 900 miles back to Vancouver Island—on the port engine, only starting the starboard engine to facilitate manoeuvring in tight quarters.

During the three weeks we were in Juneau, it rained every day but two, and both of those were accurately forecast ahead of time. On the first we took a helicopter ride onto the nearby glaciers, and on the second we flew in a light plane to Skagway, from where we took a train up White Pass (a.k.a. Dead Horse Pass), which was one of those used by miners during the gold rush to the Yukon in 1897. On our way south, we entered a fjord called Tracy Arm, where we pushed ice floes aside. Nicky and her kids joined us for this part of the trip.

In August we received an email from the staff at *Boat International* saying that the Fleming 65 was one of three nominees in her class for the International Boat of the Year Award to be held in Cannes, in September. The email finished with the words "YOU MUST ATTEND" in capital letters, which we felt must have some significance. Nicky, myself and David flew to Cannes, where we attended a party of some 800 people on a platform overlooking the Mediterranean along the Promenade des Anglais. The event was in a similar format to the Oscars, in that three nominees for each class were read out and then an envelope opened which contained the name of the winner. The Fleming 65 was declared the winner for 2006 and Nicky and myself went up to the podium to be presented with the trophy, which I accepted on behalf of everyone involved in the boat's design and construction, including the builders in Taiwan. I knew that the 65 would likely be the last boat in which I would be intimately involved and this was a fitting climax to that part of my career.

Venture was now back at Delta, and I had been toying with the idea of swapping the Cummins engines for MAN engines, built in Germany. This may seem rather an extreme idea if you are not a boat-builder, but I have always maintained that to be a successful builder you need to have a chainsaw mentality! There was nothing essentially wrong with the Cummins, which have an excellent reputation, but this particular model was extremely noisy—both mechanically and especially from the exhaust. Also, they were the first generation of electronic engines, in that they had the vulnerability of electronic controls but none of the advantages of the common-rail features, which provided smooth, quiet and economical operation. Now that the exhaust system had reared its ugly head, if ever there was a time to swap the engines this was it! Another reason for the change was that our customers on the U.S. East Coast had been demanding more power, and to meet this demand, we had been installing higher horsepower Caterpillar engines in the 65s. These engines were physically much larger, which restricted access around and over the top of them. Accessibility had always been an important part of our design philosophy, and we were not happy with how this had been compromised by the installation of the larger engines. The MANs would allow us to install higher horsepower in a smaller package.

In November 2006, Duncan, Adi and myself paid a visit to the MAN engine factory in Nuremberg, where they build 150,000 engines per year. They were all hand assembled, with parts being delivered to each station by small robotic trucks. Every engine was run on a dynamometer before leaving the factory.

Over the winter months of 2006-2007, the Cummins engines were removed and a pair of MAN engines installed at Delta Marine. I made a couple of trips to the yard from Newport Beach, including one when the snow was thick on the ground. I made measurements and sketches to engineer the changeover, but the real work was done by the yard, which made an excellent job of the installation. Being quieter, the MAN engines did not require such a large muffler, and we were finally able to fix the exhaust system once and for all.

David had returned to England and I took on Chris Conklin as *Venture*'s captain. We first met at Victoria Airport, on Vancouver Island and, although we did not realize it at the time, it was the start of a long collaboration. Work on *Venture* was not wrapped up until well into the summer months, and we only had time for some limited cruising around Desolation Sound and the Broughton Islands, which are attached to mainland Canada to the north and east of Vancouver Island. This area is barely inhabited and then, almost without exception, only during the summer months, when the very few marinas are open. One of the exceptions is Pierre's, where Pierre is in residence all year. During the summer, he has a pig roast every Saturday for which you have to make reservations because it is so popular. We went there for my 72nd birthday, when both Louisa and Jackie were present. From there we went to a deserted Indian village called Mamalilaculla and along the way saw pods of orcas which are resident in the area.

On the chart we noticed a place marked as Roaring Rapids. Any place with a name like that has to be visited! It turned out to be a narrow channel through which the water rushed in and out at every turn of the tide as it filled and emptied a long inlet of the sea. We went through it in the tender both at slack and also when it was running.

I had been invited to bring *Venture* south to act as one of the escort vessels for a rally to be known as the FUBAR being organized by retired film director Bruce Kessler. I am sure that everyone knows the real meaning of the term, but in this case it was interpreted to mean "Fleet Underway to Baja Rally!" So on September 2nd, 2007, Chris, myself, and two other crew members left Vancouver Island to take *Venture* down the coast to California to position her to take part in the FUBAR. There are few ports of refuge along this exposed coast, and these are often closed by the Coast Guard because the bars at the entrance are dangerous as soon as the weather kicks up. The weather on this trip was not very good and we had to run at 16 knots for five hours to get into the port of Eureka ahead of the weather, and before it got dark and we were faced with a tide-against-wind situation. Once inside, we

598

were trapped for five days, during which we hired a car and did some local sightseeing including visiting the magnificent coastal redwoods. Walking through them was like walking through a gigantic natural cathedral. The sad thing is that only three percent remains of what was here when the white man arrived, and even these are under threat.

We arrived in Newport Beach on September 11th and moved to San Diego on November 2nd. The idea of FUBAR was to encourage boaters who had never left the United States—or, in some cases, never been out of sight of land or been out overnight—to venture forth, with experienced boaters providing a security blanket.

The fleet of 50 boats left San Diego on November 7th after some preliminary events and seminars. The first stop was only 80 miles away in Ensenada. *Venture* did not have much to do as an escort vessel, but we did play host to Bruce Kessler, who had organized the event, and so we were, in effect, the command vessel. On our way to La Paz we stopped at places which ranged from small isolated villages to the grandest of resorts. At every stop, the local people were marvellously hospitable to this invasion.

We arrived in La Paz on November 19th, 2007 and, leaving *Venture* in the care of the modern Costa Baja Marina, returned home to California. The next question was where to go from here, and it was the answer to this question which gave rise to the greatest adventure of all.

Book 8

2007 – 2015

Retirement

I retire from actively running the company and summarize the many cruises undertaken in *Venture,* which include the voyage from Mexico to Nova Scotia via the Galapagos Islands and the Panama Canal. We face the economic crisis and build *Venture II,* taking her to Northern Europe and Iceland. I rediscover my old BMW in Concours condition in Germany. Fleming Yachts celebrates its 25th anniversary in Fort Lauderdale, Florida. I reconnect with Collyn and Rex and cruise to Prince William Sound in Alaska. I publish these memoirs.

For some time, I had been thinking about moving from my house on the waterfront to somewhere further away from the water. We had already moved the office from above my garage to an industrial unit in the nearby town of Costa Mesa. We needed more space and the new office had a small warehouse attached where we could store brochures, parts, etc.

I could not envisage ever keeping my boat in front of my house because Southern California was not a place I wanted to cruise; and property taxes, due each and every year for merely owning a boat in the state, were extremely high. My house was on a peninsula just three blocks wide—bordered by the Pacific Ocean on one side and the harbour on the other. I had become aware that the floor of my sitting room was just two feet above water level at high spring tide. This did not allow much leeway for global warming, earthquakes or tsunamis. In the summer, the local streets were jammed with traffic as people tried to access the beach, and with property values being what they were, people were buying houses and then tearing them down to rebuild. This had happened to the houses on both sides of me. I had been living in a construction site for nearly seven years, with all the noise and dirt that entailed and the street cluttered with construction vehicles. On the other hand, the value of the property had quadrupled during the 12 years I had owned it, and it seemed to be the right time to "git while the gittin' was good".

Nicky always likes to look at real estate and so, with her encouragement, we spent time on-line and driving around before settling on a very nice house in a quiet neighbourhood well above sea level but with impressive views over the ocean and the offshore islands of Catalina and San Clemente.

I had no problem selling my house and came close to getting my asking price. My new abode was cheaper so I did not need a mortgage. It was so nicely furnished that I bought the house with all the furnishings because I knew that my own stuff would not look nearly so attractive.

The one outstanding problem I had to deal with was my 30-year-old Grand Banks, *Lion's Den,* which was still tied up at the dock outside my house. All this was going on early in 2008 and I was planning to start our long cruise in March, so there was no time to waste. I decided to ship *Lion's Den* up to Delta, on Vancouver Island, and use her as a place to stay and also, being a boat I could easily handle on my own, I could use her for some limited cruising in the area. I booked space on a Yacht Path ship to take the boat from Ensenada to Victoria for $12,000, which I thought was reasonable. I asked Chris to take the boat the 80 miles south to Ensenada. As the boat had not been run for some time, it was necessary to test her out to make sure she could make the trip safely. Chris and I ran her through the harbour and, after some trouble with dirty fuel filters, took her out to sea and ran her up to speed. I did this the first time but not for long, as the engine was elderly and there was no need to overstress it. Chris then wanted to run it, and he again ran it up to full throttle and held her there. I was a bit nervous, but it was Chris who was taking the boat the 80 miles to Ensenada and he needed to have confidence in her reliability. I was just about to ask him to pull back the throttle when there was a loud and very expensive-sounding death rattle from the engine. We switched it off, which left us bobbing around out on the ocean. This now created a serious dilemma. The engine was a vintage British Gardner that few people had ever heard of in California. The boat could not now get to Ensenada to make the ship. And I was about to leave for an extensive cruise in a couple of weeks and, with my house sold, *Lion's Den* had to vacate her slip almost immediately!

The first thing was to get the boat back to her slip. We called Vessel Alert, which is the marine equivalent of AAA. Fortunately, I was a long-standing member, so there was no towing fee. While at the end of the tow rope, I called Brian at Delta to ask whether he knew if it was possible to take a GB 42 motoryacht to Vancouver by road transport. He told me that he would check, and a few minutes later he called me back in the affirmative and gave me a number to call in Seattle. I called the number to find out that they actually had a tow rig waiting in Southern California due to a last-minute cancellation. So I had an alternative course of action planned before we had even reached the dock!

As soon as we arrived, I went straight to the local shipyard, where I had a certificate for one free haul out which had been given to all participants of the FUBAR rally. At first the manager baulked at honouring it because no work would be done by the yard after the haul out, but I pointed out the enormous volume of work that Fleming Yachts had brought them over the years and, finally, he reluctantly agreed. The following day *Lion's Den* was towed to the yard, lifted out by the Travelift and placed on the transporter. What a relief!

Then the driver went around with his measuring stick and said that the boat was 3 inches over the 17-foot height limit, and he couldn't take the boat. He said it would have to be offloaded and returned to the water! Dismay! It was lunchtime and I went off to consider my options. I quickly realized that, of all the lousy alternatives, the least bad was to cut off the part of the boat structure that was too high. I returned to the yard with this decision to find out that they had reached the same conclusion. Within an hour, a guy wielding an edge grinder had cut 6 inches off the top portion of the flying bridge and the latest crisis was averted!

The transporter left a few minutes later and started on its long journey north. I packed up all the junk accumulated in my house and the residue of the office, promising myself that I would not unpack it at my new house without going through every file and piece of paper to chuck out unwanted items and organize what was left so I could find what I needed. The bulk of the packing I left to the moving company as, being responsible for breakage, they insisted on doing the packing. The problem was that my new house would not be available until after I left for the trip, so Nicky was stuck with the burden of the actual move.

I also decided early in 2008 that I should take myself off the company payroll and turn the running of the company over to Adi and Duncan. They had been handling the day-to-day work ever since the summer of 2005, and it was time for me to get out of the way. For the first few months I had asked that they copy me on every email, but I now restricted that request to only those which were relevant to myself. I continued to supply feedback from what I was learning from using the boat, and the new pattern for my life emerged in my becoming ambassador-at-large—making videos, publishing blogs, writing magazine articles, and being a guest speaker at yacht clubs and other events. I am not going into too much detail on each individual journey as they are extensively covered in blogs, articles, and videos—links to which can be found at the end of this chapter.

In March 2008 I flew down to La Paz and joined *Venture,* which was looking spick and span with new varnish, having been well looked after at Costa Baja Marina since she had arrived at the end of the FUBAR Rally. We cruised the Sea of Cortez before continuing down the Mexican coast to Los Suenos, in Costa Rica. From here we headed directly offshore into the Pacific Ocean, calling at the isolated Cocos Island on our way to the Galapagos Islands, where we crossed the equator. We spent eight days cruising among this amazing archipelago before heading the 900 miles back across the open ocean to the Panama Canal and up the East Coast of the U.S. In Florida our shadow fell across the lawns of houses lining the narrow canals, and on the 4th of July we were in New York within sight of the Statue of Liberty. We cruised the Hudson River and the Erie and Oswega Canals to reach Lake Ontario and the St. Lawrence Seaway. We followed the mighty St.

605

Lawrence River to Quebec and the Canadian Maritime provinces and we completed our cruise in September 2008 at Burr Yacht Sales, close to Annapolis, Maryland. Within one week of our arrival, *Venture* was on display at the Trawler Fest event in Solomons.

The next question was where to go from here? I had considered taking *Venture* across the Atlantic by way of Newfoundland, Greenland, and Iceland; but my research in Nova Scotia showed that this route was better suited east to west. We lacked the range to run directly from Nova Scotia to Iceland, and early in the season the waters off Cape Farewell in Greenland were subject to a dangerous mix of fog, ice and gales!

We all know what befell the economy in the fall of 2008. Naturally, this had a negative effect on boat sales. The yard in Taiwan needed an order for another 65, so I decided to put *Venture* up for sale at Burr Yacht Sales and use the money to pay for a new boat built to European specifications and shipped to England.

The best laid plans of mice and men often go awry. After her immense journey, *Venture* languished, unsold, for many months while the new boat, christened *Venture II*, was completed and shipped to Southampton, arriving July 4, 2009. After commissioning, we took a shakedown cruise along the south coast of England before tackling the North Sea and sailing up the river Elbe to Hamburg for a boat show. With the wind from the north, the weather was horrible, and we were stopped and checked en route by both French and Dutch patrol boats. From Hamburg we ventured back into North Sea, where the winds had now reversed direction and battered us from the south until we entered the European canal system at Harlingen, in the Netherlands. Here we followed the Ijssel and Rhine Rivers to Dusseldorf for another boat show.

I returned to California and, during the winter of 2009-2010 made videos about our recent trips in *Venture II*. I also made a DVD of our truck journey across Africa, using the colour slides which had languished in a box for the 50 years that had passed since our trip. This turned out to be very successful and I sent copies to Rex, who lived on a farm in Herefordshire, in England,

and to Collyn who lived in Sydney, Australia.

In the meantime, *Venture* was moved from Annapolis down to Florida with the idea of chartering her to clients interested in purchasing a new boat. This was not very successful and, with the approach of the hurricane season in June 2010, she had to move out of Florida. I saw little point in moving her back north and decided to ship her to Western Canada, where I had confidence she would be well cared for and she would be under my control.

Chris and I returned to England in April 2010 to take *Venture II* from Southampton to Iceland. At the time, ash from Iceland's volcano with the unpronounceable name was disrupting air travel, and most people considered us crazy. We called at the Scilly Isles, Eire, the Isle of Man, and Northern Ireland before arriving in Scotland, where our landfall was the Isle of Jura and the hamlet of Glengarrisdale, where my great-grandfather had lived as a child. There was something that appealed to me about his great-grandson bringing a boat for which he was responsible, built in faraway Taiwan, to the spot where his ancestor had spent his childhood all those years ago. I had long harboured an ambition to anchor *Venture* in Glengarrisdale Bay, but unfortunately this was not possible, as the small bay was exposed and the bottom too rocky for the anchor to grip. But I went ashore in the tender while Chris, aboard *Venture*, held station in the bay.

We spent a total of six weeks cruising the Inner and Outer Hebrides and were even able to visit the remote islands of St. Kilda, 40 miles out in the Atlantic, before continuing on to the Faroe Islands and from there to Iceland. Between the Faroes and Iceland, we were hit with the roughest conditions we had ever encountered. *Venture* handled them without any damage but we were all very relieved when we pulled into the harbour of Westmanjaer Island, south of Iceland.

I had originally intended only to visit Reykjavik, but I also wanted to visit the remote and uninhabited fjords in the northwest of the country, so I changed my plans to circumnavigate the whole country. We crossed the Arctic Circle and came within a few hours sailing of the east coast of Greenland. It was great temptation to transit the Denmark Strait but, alas, we had a deadline to be in the Southampton International Boat Show in September, so we could not take the time.

Within a week of our return to Southampton, *Venture II* was once again on display, looking none the worse for wear after her long journey. While in Southampton, I arranged to meet Rex, whom I had not seen since Singapore days. He looked very dapper and his riotous orange beard was now a neatly trimmed, grey Van Dyke. Rex came aboard *Venture II* in Southampton, and we reminisced and caught up on our lives since we had last met many years ago. Rex brought with him many of the original African colour slides, which were in much better condition than the copies in my possession. I had them digitized in England and then remade the DVD of our African trip when I returned to California. During the following winter I also made DVDs of our journey to Scotland, the Faroes, and Iceland. This journey also generated 25 magazine articles, so I was kept busy with my new career.

When we stopped in Dartmouth at the start of this trip, I met Nigel, who had been a De Havilland apprentice at the same time as myself. He told me that, while sitting in the waiting room on a recent visit to the doctor, he had seen an advertisement for my old BMW. I couldn't believe that it would have survived for all these years, but on my return from Iceland—during the winter of 2010-2011—I set out to try to track it down. I eventually succeeded with the help of an assistant editor of *Motor Sport* magazine, which had carried the advert. They put me in touch with the Historic BMW Club who were able to send me the history and photos of the car after it left my hands, as well as correspondence containing much speculation about its early history. Of course I was able to supply the missing information, along with additional photos. They sent me recent photos of the car, which was now in Germany and in immaculate, Concours d'Elegance condition.

Obviously, it was quite ridiculous to own two Fleming 65s (in addition to my elderly GB), so I decided to keep the original *Venture* and offer *Venture II* for sale. I felt that, being a newer boat, *Venture II* would be more saleable, plus I had more emotional ties to *Venture,* as she was the last boat in my career that I had personally designed and built. Also, she was now situated in my favourite cruising area and readily accessible from where I lived by flying or even driving.

During the following summer of 2011 we chartered *Venture* a few times and made a trip to the Queen Charlotte Islands off Canada's West Coast—now renamed Haida Gwaii. These islands are remote, and almost the entire southern island of Moresby is a nature reserve where no one is permitted to live. On our way north though British Columbia, we visited Dent Island resort, where the manager ran a jet boat to take visitors through three major rapids at full flow. Normally these passes should be avoided at all costs, so it was very exciting to be in the midst of the whirlpools, boils, and huge standing waves. It was hard to believe that, within three hours, the ferocious waters would be calm and still. Slack could be as little as 10 minutes before the waters reversed to become equally wild in the opposite direction. Timing was critical for safe passage in a conventional boat.

I had finally convinced myself of the absurdity of hanging on to *Lion's Den* so, after spending a ridiculous amount rebuilding her engine and bringing her back to mint condition, I listed her for sale. She was finally sold in August to a really appreciative buyer. She deserved a good owner who would use her and take care of her, and that is what she got. So now I had two of my major design and construction projects from the past—the BMW and *Lion's Den*—still very much alive and in mint condition. Also the record of the Trans Africa Expedition had been resurrected and converted into modern form from boxes of deteriorating slides.

The next major event was the 25th anniversary of the arrival of the first Fleming. This was held in Fort Lauderdale in October 2011, at the time of the International Boat Show. Two hundred and forty people attended the event, which was voted a great success. There were no speeches and the only entertainment was a roving magician who performed impossible feats before our very eyes. I was on my feet, talking non-stop, for five hours!

In the spring of 2012 I made a short trip to Taiwan and Tung Hwa, accompanied by Nicky and her two daughters. It was a very moving experience to see all the people I had worked with for so many years, and I had quite a lump in my throat when it was time to leave. *Venture II* remained unsold and was moved to Sweden where it was thought she might attract more buyers. Our dealer there suggested taking her to Stavanger, in western Norway, for a boat show. I agreed with his proposal but said I wanted to go along for the ride from Maarstrand, in Sweden, to Stavanger. Nicky and James also came along for the ride. We travelled in company with a Norwegian-owned Fleming 55, and it was great trip made even better when he became our guide after our arrival in Stavanger. We cruised the adjacent Fjords and picturesque towns on offshore islands. He even arranged for a friend of his to fly us over the fjords in his helicopter.

After my return from Norway, we took *Venture* to Glacier Bay, Alaska, visiting many scenic spots along the way—such as Tracy Arm, the glacier face at the head of Endicott and the marvellous Ford's Terror.

On the return journey we were joined by Fred Hong and his wife, who had flown to British Columbia from Taiwan. Fred was the manager of the yard in Taiwan, and after 27 years building our boats, this was his first opportunity to cruise one. We spent the next week visiting small, seasonal marinas around Desolation Sound.

In August I flew to Sydney for a boat show and owner's dinner. This visit gave me the opportunity to meet up again with Collyn. I stayed with him and his wife for several days and they kindly took me to visit the beautiful Blue Mountains. Naturally Collyn and myself had plenty of catching up to do after 40 years. Even though our physical appearance had greatly changed since we had last met, we were still essentially the same people.

During the winter of 2012-2013, I created new videos,

completed the first draft of these memoirs, and wrote more magazine articles, thus cementing the new pattern of my life. While working on my memoirs, I came across the names of the two Americans we had met while crossing the Sahara Desert northbound. One of them had a very unusual name so, not expecting any result, I typed it into the Internet search box and found someone of that name living in Pasadena about an hour's drive from where I lived. I called the phone number and asked the person who answered whether he was by any chance the person who drove a Jeep across the Sahara in 1959. Remarkably, it turned out that he was! He invited Nicky and myself to meet him for lunch at the Athenaeum in Pasadena; and, just before Christmas 2013, he invited me and my family to join him in viewing the Tournament of Roses Parade from his apartment along the parade route. Who would have thought that a chance meeting in the Sahara Desert in 1960 would have led to us watching the Rose Parade together in 2014—54 years later!

Venture II was finally sold in March 2013 to an English couple who had chartered *Venture* the previous August, while I had been in Australia. So, in that particular case, it turned out that chartering had been beneficial after all.

In April 2013 we took *Venture* all the way up to Prince William Sound in Alaska. On our way north, in the wilds of British Columbia, we were leaving a remote anchorage at the exact moment when *Lion's Den* was passing the entrance. It was an amazing coincidence, and we met *Lion's Den*'s owners for dinner that night in Prince Rupert. We saw them again in Ketchikan and Juneau, where they left for Sitka while we continued north, leaving the protection of the Inside Passage, and headed out into the hostile waters of the Gulf of Alaska.

Fortunately, the weather was uncharacteristically good and the waters were calm, which permitted us to visit Lituya Bay. This bay became notorious in 1958 when a massive landslide, triggered by an earthquake, created a huge local tsunami which reached the record height of 1,720 feet. A companion wave, 200 feet high, then ripped down the length of the bay, stripping the shoreline down to bare rock. Of the three boats anchored in the bay, only one survived—after being carried over the tops of the trees! Subsequent research showed that similar waves had been a regular event in the history of this bay. The bar at the narrow entrance was another hazard. It had accounted for the recorded loss of more than 100 lives. We spent two days anchored in this beautiful but treacherous bay without incident before continuing north to Prince William Sound, which hit the headlines in 1989 with the *Exxon Valdez* disaster. Exactly 25 years before this event, the Sound had been the epicentre of the 9.2 earthquake that devastated the area. We spent one month cruising the Sound and its many glaciers.

On our return journey south, back in the waters of British Columbia, we encountered Fleming 50-001, the very first boat I had struggled with in 1986. She had changed hands twice since she was new and looked in good condition. By chance we were heading for the same destination that evening, and I was able to meet up with her present owners and take a photo with the first 50 and the first 65.

A few months later, Chris brought *Venture* south back to Newport Beach. Shortly thereafter, 72-001 moved into an adjacent slip. Within the period of a few months, *Venture* (65-001) had been alongside *Lion's Den* (50-001) and 72-001!

Venture had not been in Newport Beach since 2007. In early December, we made a short trip to the Channel Islands, just off the coast of Los Angeles. Despite being so close to a major metropolitan area, these islands are nature reserves and could be as remote as any we have visited. They also have a reputation for rough weather, which was borne out when we encountered Santa Ana winds as high as 60 knots—the highest we had ever experienced!

One of the reasons I had brought *Venture* south was to visit the Sea of Cortez, in Mexico. However, an illogical and bizarre decision on the part of the Mexican government to seize over 300 visiting yachts at gunpoint caused me to change my plans. It is a shame because Mexico has the best marinas in North America, staffed by excellent people and clearly built to attract boaters from North America and Canada.

The story of my life is still being written and I hope that many cruises still lie ahead before I sling my hook! I have had the great good fortune to have been born lucky. I have enjoyed good health, which is probably the most important issue, and I have experienced a life that must surely be above average in variety and interest (which is the reason I was encouraged to write my memoirs). I was born into a comfortable environment at the right time in history to avoid being co-opted into the various conflicts of the 20th century. It may also turn out to be the optimum time to have been able to enjoy the comforts and inventions of human development before our civilizations are destroyed by them.

I have always believed that everyone is born with their own unique talent, and I explored many avenues in the search to identify mine. In the end I concluded that it was being moderately good at many things rather than being especially good at any one thing. Over time this grew into having the ability to navigate the divide between concept and reality—whether this was to imagine a car or boat and turn them into reality, or to design a stage set, oversee its construction and become stage manager, or to conceive and embark on a long journey and develop the necessary technical and artistic skills to make a film about it.

I have been fortunate to be born with a subconscious mind able to supply solutions to problems—provided I spend time thinking about them—like a terrier with a bone. I can always rely on getting an answer but cannot tell when or where it might appear. It comes in the form of "of course, that's what we need to do." Rather like the light bulb cliché. The analogy is the computer which, provided you supply adequate input, will spit out the answer. In this case the brain is the computer and it churns through a lifetime of experience (both conscious and subconscious and whether obviously relevant or not) and comes up with an answer. We generally refer to this as instinct or gut feeling, and I have come to rely on it.

It is important to identify and seize each and every opportunity that comes your way. I have never forgotten that I failed to sign up for a trip to Spitzbergen when I was at school and I resolved that I would never let that happen again. Sometimes this has meant opting for things about which I felt reluctant—for example, standing up and addressing a crowd of people—because I thought it would be a new experience. When opportunity knocks, open the door wide and greet it!

I am not normally one to quote Shakespeare but he expressed this idea very well:

"There is a tide in the affairs of men which, taken at the flood, leads on to fortune; omitted, all the voyage of their life is bound in shallows and in miseries."

Although our modern system tends to demand it, we worry too much about whether we are "qualified" to do something. The only qualification that really matters is whether or not we can do it. We can almost always achieve more than we imagine. The clichés abound. For example— "Nothing venture, nothing win" —which leads us neatly to the name of the boat! The dictionary definition of the word "venture" is "a course of action attended by risk". To achieve anything worthwhile, we must be prepared for risk. We cannot cross the street without it, and we can always think of a thousand reasons not to do something. My advice? Just do it!

In my opinion, the most important ingredients for success are determination and tenacity—the ability to stick with the program in the face of adversity. Conjuring up something new from thin air is always fraught with frustration—involving overcoming a seemingly endless succession of obstacles. As with many other experiences, only people who have been through the baptism of fire can appreciate what is involved. The creative process always follows the same path. The lessons learnt all those years ago from building my BMW, along with those learned with the GB, contributed to the creation of the Fleming. Even the videos are another manifestation of the same principles.

Aim high, stay focused and never give up!

Memoir Cruising Addendum

December 8th 2015

When I originally compiled these memoirs, I included an account of each of the cruises I had undertaken in Venture and Venture II. This made an already lengthy histoire even longer so I decided to eliminate that section. Because my hobbies include writing, photography and film-making, all these trips are covered in detail elsewhere so there is little point in including them in this book. Also, as I am continuing to cruise, that section of the memoir is always likely to be out of date. I have therefore decided to add this addendum to list the various cruises I have enjoyed over the years. I have marked those for which there are videos. These videos - and those still to come after publication of the hard cover of this memoir - can be viewed by going to:

www.Flemingyachts.com/Venture.html
and then clicking on the You Tube and other links on My Page.

Cruising Summary

My first, and very limited cruising was in day trips around Hong Kong in various GB's in the 1960's. This was followed by trips lasting up to one week on various GB's in the waters off Singapore, including the Straits of Malacca and the Tioman islands in the South China Sea off the east coast of Malaysia. Then came many wonderful trips to Norway and Sweden in Ozmaiden – a Fleming 55, and a cruise through British Columbia in another Fleming 55. These trips are summarized below.

Some are subjects of magazine articles (available through links on the Fleming Yachts website) but only two are covered in video.

1974. Cruise to Tioman Islands in the South China Sea. GB42
1977. Christmas cruise - Straits of Malacca. GB42
1978. Mediterranean cruise with Jean Jacques. GB42
1978. Virgin Islands with Carleton Mitchell. Hatteras 48 LRC
1980. Nassau to Georgetown, Bahamas. GB 49
1981. Canal du Midi. France. Canal boat.
1982. Hawkesbury River & Broken Bay north of Sydney, Australia. GB36
1983. GB 42 Lion's Den to the Tioman Islands. GB42

Trips with Egil Paulsen in Fleming 55 Ozmaiden.

1992. To Norway from Southampton via Holland and Kiel canal.
1993. To Norway via Scotland and Sognafjord.
1994. Sweden via Jota Canal.
1995. Desolation Sound, British Columbia, Canada with Dick Clayton.
     F55 Divona Sea
1996. Sweden to Aalesund.
VIDEO: Ozmaiden Norwegian Cruise.
2000. Lofoten Islands. Norway.
VIDEO: Ozmaiden visits Lofoten.

Cruising aboard my own boat started with Fleming 65-001, Venture, and then developed over the years into an ongoing series of journeys to increasingly remote destinations aboard Venture and Venture II. These are listed below together with the videos that document the trips.

Venture. Fleming 65-001
2005. Desolation Sound in British Columbia, Canada.
VIDEO: Venture Story.
2006. Vancouver Island to Juneau, Alaska.
VIDEO: Inside Passage.
2007. Broughton Islands, British Columbia, Canada.
VIDEO: Venture Summer.
2007. Fubar Rally, San Diego to La Paz, Baja California, Mexico.
VIDEO: Fubar Rally.
2008. Sea of Cortez to Galapagos and US east coast to Canada and Nova Scotia.
MANY VIDEOS: Alaska to Nova Scotia plus Venture to Galapagos and many others covering each segment in detail.

Venture II. Fleming 65-024
2009. UK south coast then Hamburg and Dusseldorf.
VIDEOS: Venture down the English Channel and European Excursion
2010. Circumnavigation of Iceland by way of Scotland and the Faroe Islands.
'IDEOS: Southampton to Scotland; Venture in Scotland; Faroes
    'and; Venture in Iceland; Venture comes home.
        'anger. Norway.
        'ure to Norway.

Venture. Fleming 65-001

2011. Vancouver to Haida Gwaii (Queen Charlotte Islands). Canada.
VIDEO: Venture to Haida Gwaii.
2012. Glacier Bay, Alaska.
VIDEOS: Venture to Alaska - Parts 1 through 3
2013. Prince William Sound, Alaska.
VIDEOS: Venture to Lituya Bay; Venture to Prince William Sound –
Parts 1 through 3
2014. Channel Islands, California.
VIDEO: Venture to the Channel Islands.
2014. West Coast of Vancouver Island. Canada.
VIDEO: Venture around Vancouver Island
2015. Aleutians Islands to Unalaska (Dutch Harbor). Alaska.
VIDEOS: Venture to the Aleutians - Parts 1 through 4

Copies of these videos are available on DVD from the Fleming Yachts website, Our Store, or can be viewed on line by going to www.flemingyachts.com/Venture.html and clicking on the You Tube link.

As mentioned in the Memoir, I have been fortunate to undertake journeys to many other areas – some of them mysterious and remote. Many of these are documented on Vimeo. Personal highlights include riding the trans-Siberian train from Beijing to St. Petersburg, crossing the Sahara Desert by truck, climbing Mt. Kenya and visiting Antarctica and the North Pole. Videos of these trips can be viewed by going to:
www.vimeo.com/tonyfleming or www.flemingyachts.com/Venture.html and clicking on the Vimeo link.

To take advantage of the mass of still photos and video accumulated during the course of my life, I am working on a video version of this memoir. At the time of publication of this book (December 2015), only three episodes have been completed and posted on Vimeo. Additional episodes will follow as time permits. They can be viewed by clicking on the Vimeo links mentioned above. The same website also provides links to blogs and magazine articles describing the trips and also to my website: www.mywanderingstar.com where there are collections of many photos.

Made in United States
North Haven, CT
24 February 2022

16416262R00339